Labor Relations in the Public Sector

In the last decade, public sector unions have encountered threats in the form of privatization of public services and the retrenchment of collective bargaining rights, as well as opportunities in increasing labor union popularity and activity. Retaining the structure that made the previous editions so popular, *Labor Relations in the Public Sector, Sixth Edition* has been completely revised to explore the most recent trends in membership figures, new legislation, court decisions, executive orders, and new politics as they influence bargaining rights. Updates include:

- Thorough examination and analysis of contemporary public sector labor relations and collective bargaining
- Careful exploration of important recent changes in the public labor relations and unionization landscape
- Complete analysis of financial and human resource outcomes of recent collective bargaining in the public sector
- Detailed investigation of collective bargaining institutions and processes in government.

In keeping with prior editions, the sixth edition addresses collective bargaining and labor relations at all levels of government, with comparisons to the private and nonprofit sectors. Designed to be classroom-friendly, this text includes discussions of the most recent literature and case studies, as well as end-of-chapter assignments. *Labor Relations in the Public Sector* speaks to multiple audiences including academics, students, and practitioners, and practical tips and advice are offered for those engaged in collective bargaining and labor relations. It is vital reading for undergraduate and graduate students in fields including public administration, public policy, political science, and labor studies. This book is also relevant to scholars of comparative policy, politics, and labor.

Patrice M. Mareschal is a professor and chair of the Department of Public Policy and Administration, Rutgers University, USA. Her areas of research and teaching include public and nonprofit management, human resources, labor relations, and public policy with a focus on teachers, police, and other public and nonprofit sector employees. She has partnered with various organizations to conduct publicly engaged scholarship, including: FMCS, SEIU, NJ AFL-CIO, and *In the Public Interest*. Prior to beginning her academic career, Dr. Mareschal worked in labor employment relations with Ford Motor Company and the National Labor Relations Board.

Richard C. Kearney is a retired professor and former director of the School of Public and International Affairs, North Carolina State University, USA. He previously held teaching and administrative positions at East Carolina University, the University of Connecticut, and the University of South Carolina. He has published widely in the areas of labor relations, human resource management, and state and local government. He is a retired member of AFSCME.

PUBLIC ADMINISTRATION AND PUBLIC POLICY
A Comprehensive Publication Program

EDITOR-IN-CHIEF
DAVID H. ROSENBLOOM
Distinguished Professor of Public Administration
American University, Washington, DC

RECENTLY PUBLISHED BOOKS

Public Management Reform in the Gulf Cooperation Council and Beyond
Mhamed Biygautane

The Politics of Collaborative Public Management
A Primer
Robert Agranoff and Aleksey Kolpakov

Deliberative Democracy, Public Policy, and Local Government
Joanna Podgórska-Rykała

Social Equity in a Post-Roe America
Gender, Race, and the Rule of Law
Lorenda A. Naylor and Heather Wyatt-Nichol

Policy Responses to the COVID-19 Pandemic
An International Comparative Approach
Edited by M. Jae Moon and Dong-Young Kim

Rulemaking
The Creation of Law and Policy by Government Agencies, 6th Edition
Cornelius M. Kerwin and Scott R. Furlong

Labor Relations in the Public Sector, Sixth Edition
Patrice M. Mareschal and Richard C. Kearney

For more information about this series please visit: https://www.routledge.com/Public-Administration-and-Public-Policy/book-series/AUEPUBADMPUP

Labor Relations in the Public Sector

Sixth Edition

Patrice M. Mareschal and
Richard C. Kearney

Routledge
Taylor & Francis Group
NEW YORK AND LONDON

Designed cover image: Getty Images

Sixth edition published 2026
by Routledge
605 Third Avenue, New York, NY 10158

and by Routledge
4 Park Square, Milton Park, Abingdon, Oxon OX14 4RN

Routledge is an imprint of the Taylor & Francis Group, an informa business

First edition published by Marcel Dekker 1984
Fifth edition published by Routledge 2014

ISBN: 978-1-032-51709-4 (hbk)
ISBN: 978-1-032-51713-1 (pbk)
ISBN: 978-1-003-40359-3 (ebk)

DOI: 10.4324/9781003403593

Typeset in Perpetua
by Apex CoVantage, LLC

Contents

List of Figures xiii
List of Tables xiv
List of Case Studies xv
Preface xvi

1 History and Development 1
- I. Introduction *1*
- II. Early American Unionism *2*
  - A. Ideological Battles in United States Unionism *4*
  - B. Business Unionism *5*
- III. Factors Contributing to Private Sector Union Decline *10*
  - A. Structural Elements *10*
  - B. Government Substitution *11*
  - C. Unfavorable Legal and Policy Environment *11*
  - D. Management Opposition *12*
  - E. Strategic Factors *13*
- IV. Unions in Government *15*
  - A. Early Years *15*
  - B. Why Government Employees Did (and Did Not) Unionize *18*
  - C. Rise of Public Employee Unions *19*
    - 1. Growth of Government *19*
    - 2. Private Sector Spillover *21*
    - 3. Changes in the Legal Environment *22*
    - 4. Era of Social Change and Turmoil *23*
- V. Why Government Workers Join Unions—The Individual Perspective *23*

References *26*

2 Unions Today **31**
I. Introduction *31*
II. The Federal Government *31*
III. Nonprofit Organizations *36*
IV. State and Local Government *37*
A. Determinants of State and Local Unionization *38*
B. Employee Organizations in State and Local Government *44*
1. General-purpose Unions *46*
2. Functionally Specific Organizations *48*
V. Prospects *56*
References *58*

3 Legal Environment of Public Sector Labor Relations **63**
I. Introduction *63*
II. Right to Form and Join Unions *63*
III. Labor Relations in Federal Employment: The Legal Basis *67*
A. Executive Orders *68*
B. Civil Service Reform Act of 1978 *71*
C. Exceptions from Civil Service Reform Act Coverage *72*
D. Federal Labor Relations Authority *75*
IV. Legal Basis of Labor Relations in State and Local Governments *77*
A. The Quest for Federal Legislation for State and Local Governments *78*
B. State and Local Government Policies *81*
C. States that Prohibit Collective Bargaining and/or Lack Collective Bargaining Policies *85*
D. States with Noncomprehensive Policies *90*
E. States with Comprehensive Collective Bargaining *93*
1. Employee Rights *95*
2. Employer Rights *95*
3. Administrative Agency *95*
4. Unit Determination *96*
5. Recognition Procedures *96*
6. Scope of Bargaining *97*
7. Impasse Resolution Procedures *97*
8. Union Security *97*
9. Unfair Labor Practices *102*
F. Initiative and Referendum *103*
G. Labor Relations in Nonprofit Organizations *104*
V. Summary *105*
References *107*

4 Fundamentals of the Bargaining Process 113
I. Introduction *113*
II. Public–Private Sector Differences *113*
A. The Environment *114*
1. Financial Setting and Incentives *114*
2. Nature of Work *115*
3. Role of Politics *115*
B. The Parties *116*
C. The Process *118*
III. Electing a Union and Getting a Contract: The Elements of Collective Bargaining *118*
A. Bargaining Unit Determination *118*
1. Community of Interest *120*
2. Desires of Employees *120*
3. Bargaining History *121*
4. Efficiency of Agency Operations *121*
5. Fragmentation of Bargaining Units *121*
6. Exclusion of Supervisory and Confidential Employees *122*
B. Representation Election or Show of Majority Support *124*
C. Certification of the Bargaining Representative *126*
D. Negotiating the Contract *127*
1. The Participants *128*
2. Role of the Public *140*
IV. Summary and Conclusions *142*
References *147*

5 Process and Politics of Public Sector Collective Bargaining 152
I. Introduction *152*
II. Internal Process and Politics *152*
A. Identifying Proposals *152*
B. Preparation for Bargaining *154*
C. Duty to Bargain *156*
D. Script *156*
E. Concession Bargaining *159*
III. External Politics *163*
A. Lobbying *164*
B. Electoral Activities *165*
C. Public Opinion *168*
D. Restrictions on Public Employee Political Activity *170*

IV. Internal Bargaining Processes: From Traditional to Interest-based Bargaining *171*
A. Traditional Negotiations *172*
B. Interest-based Bargaining *175*
V. Ratification of the Contract *181*
VI. Interest-based Bargaining's Potential *182*
VII. Summary and Conclusions *183*
References *186*

6 Financial Impacts of Unions and Collective Bargaining **191**
I. Introduction *191*
II. Budget Making and Unions *192*
A. Budgetary Process *193*
B. Budgetary Outcomes *195*
III. Unions, Wages, and Benefits *197*
A. Socioeconomic Factors *197*
B. Political Factors *199*
C. Politics and Decision Rules in the Compensation Decision Process *200*
D. Monetary Impacts of Unions: Approaching the Research Question *206*
IV. Are Public Sector Workers Paid More than Private Sector Workers? *207*
V. Comparing the Relative Effects of Unions in the Public and Private Sectors *211*
VI. Effects of Public Employee Unions on Compensation: Methodological Problems *212*
VII. Effects of Public Employee Unions on Compensation: A Review of the Findings *214*
A. Salary and Wages *214*
B. Benefits *218*
C. Evaluating the Union Effect on Wages and Benefits *220*
VIII. Responding to Public Sector Compensation Cost Increases *221*
IX. Productivity Bargaining (Gainsharing) *223*
X. Monetary Impacts of Federal Employee Unions *225*
A. Federal Wage System *226*
B. Classified Civil Service *228*
C. Collective Bargaining System *229*
XI. Conclusion *231*
References *232*

7 Union Impacts: Personnel Processes and Policies 241

I. Introduction *241*

II. Merit Systems *242*

A. Interface Between Collective Bargaining and the Merit System *246*

B. Accommodating Collective Bargaining and the Merit System *246*

C. Unions and Threats to the Merit Principle *249*

1. Union Security *249*
2. Seniority *250*
3. Affirmative Action and Diversity *251*
4. New Public Management *255*

III. Specific Impacts of Unions on Personnel Functions and Policies *257*

A. Management Rights *257*

1. Management Rights (Scope of Bargaining) *257*

B. Management Structure *260*

C. Personnel Processes *261*

1. Recruitment, Testing, and Selection *261*
2. Promotions *263*
3. Training and Development *263*
4. Position Classification and Staffing *265*
5. Workload and Scheduling *266*
6. Grievances *269*
7. Employee Discipline *269*
8. Dismissals and Layoffs *270*
9. Reductions in Force *271*
10. Other Human Resource Management Policies *272*

IV. Conclusion *284*

References *287*

8 Strike! 295

I. Introduction *295*

II. A Strike by Any Other Name *298*

III. Public Sector Strike Activity *299*

IV. The Right to Strike in Public Employment *302*

A. The Sovereignty Argument *302*

B. Distortion of the Political Process *303*

C. Lack of Market Constraints *303*

D. Essential Services *304*

E. The Postal Strike of 1970 *306*

V. Legislation Pertaining to Strikes *307*
VI. Public Policy and the Incidence of Strikes *310*
VII. Why Public Employees Strike *311*
A. Macro-level Factors *311*
B. Micro-level Factors *312*
1. Demographic and Attitudinal Factors *312*
2. Bargaining Power and Disagreement Costs *313*
3. Faulty Negotiations *314*
VIII. Strike Tactics *316*
A. The Union *316*
B. Management *319*
C. Contingency Planning for the Strike *319*
D. The Injunction *320*
E. Strike Penalties *322*
IX. Conclusions and a Look Ahead *327*
References *328*

9 Resolving Impasses: Alternatives to the Strike **334**
I. Introduction *334*
II. Private Sector Experience *335*
III. Impasse Resolution in Federal Employment *336*
IV. State and Local Government Impasse Procedures *337*
A. Mediation *340*
1. Traits of an Effective Mediator *343*
2. Advantages and Disadvantages of Mediation as a Technique for Resolving Impasses *344*
B. Fact-finding *346*
1. The Fact-finding Process *346*
2. Advantages and Disadvantages of Fact-finding *348*
C. Arbitration *350*
1. The Arbitration Process *351*
2. Advantages and Disadvantages of Arbitration *355*
D. Final Offer Arbitration *361*
E. Other Impasse Resolution Procedures *364*
1. Med-arb *364*
2. Arb-med *365*
3. Labor–management Committees *365*
4. Letting the Taxpayers Decide *366*
5. Unfair Labor Practice *367*
V. Search for Flexibility *368*
VI. Uncertainty: Benefit or Bane? *370*
VII. Conclusion: The Benefits of Impasse Procedures *371*
References *375*

10 Living with the Contract 382

I. Introduction 382
II. Collective Bargaining Agreement 383
A. Contents of the Agreement 383
B. Disseminating the Agreement 387
C. Administering the Agreement 388
III. Grievance Procedures 390
A. Causes of Grievances 392
B. The Grievance Process 394
C. Representation of the Grievant 397
1. The Steward 397
2. Union Duty of Fair Representation 398
IV. Grievance Arbitration 400
A. Arbitrability 401
B. Court Review of Arbitrators' Decisions 401
C. Selection of the Arbitrator 403
D. Problems in Grievance Arbitration 404
1. Monetary Costs and Delays 404
2. Repercussions for the Parties Involved in Arbitration 406
3. Lack of Diversity and Barriers to Entry to the Profession 407
4. Perceptions of Social Justice in Cases Involving Police Discipline 407
E. Standards for Arbitrator Decision Making 408
1. Past Practice 409
2. Prior Bargaining Record 409
3. Previous Arbitration Awards 410
4. Other Considerations 410
V. Grievance Procedures in Federal Employment 411
VI. New Directions in Grievance Handling 413
A. Expedited Arbitration 413
B. Alternative Dispute Resolution 414
C. Grievance Mediation 415
VII. Conclusion 417
References 421

11 Public Employee Unions in the Future 426

I. Introduction 426
II. Decline of Private Sector Unions 426
III. Challenges for Public Employee Unions 431
A. Fiscal Squeeze 431

B. Structural Challenges *433*
C. Public Policy Challenges *435*
D. Strategic Challenges *437*
IV. Opportunities *439*
V. Labor–management Cooperation and Participative Decision Making *443*
A. Advantages of Cooperation *443*
B. Conditions Necessary for Successful Labor–management Cooperation *446*
C. Future of Labor–management Cooperation *448*
VI. Public Employee Unions in the 2020s: Conclusion *449*
A. Obstacles *450*
B. Prospects *451*
References *453*

Index *461*

Figures

1.1	Public employment, by level of government, 1955–2022	20
1.2	Union membership, by public and private sectors, 1973–2023	24
2.1	A comprehensive model of state and local government unionization	41
3.1	Collective bargaining policy in the states, 2023	86
3.2	Right-to-work states, 2023	99
4.1	The collective bargaining process	119
4.2	Steps for determining the bargaining unit	120
5.1	Gallup poll: Do you approve or disapprove of labor unions?	169
5.2	Gallup poll: Approval level of labor unions, by political party	170
10.1	Grievance process	395

Tables

1.1	Membership in the Largest Private Sector Unions, 2023	8
1.2	Union Density for All Wage and Salary Workers, Public and Private, 2023	8
2.1	Major Postal Employee Unions, 2023	35
2.2	Bargaining Status, Political Ideology, and Union Density, 2022	39
2.3	Membership of Largest State and Local Employee Organizations, 2023	45
3.1	Major Federal Laws Affecting Public Sector Labor Relations	80
3.2	State Bargaining Status, 2023	82
4.1	Union Survey	144
5.1	Standards for Bargaining in Good Faith	157
5.2	Twenty Bargaining Homilies	160
5.3	Negotiating Your First Contract: Tips and Tricks for Management	161
5.4	Comparison of Traditional and IBB Principles	176
5.5	Contrasting Bargaining Approaches	180
7.1	Federal Management Rights Under Section 7106 of the CSRA	258
7.2	Nonmonetary Subjects Typically Included in Contracts	262
8.1	Permissive Strike States, 2023	308
9.1	State Legislation on Dispute Resolution Procedures for State and Local Employees, 2023	338
10.1	Types of Contract Provisions	384

Case Studies

2.1	Portrait of a Union Leader: Randi Weingarten, American Federation of Teachers	57
4.1	Whose Union Is It?	143
5.1	Sanitation Workers and the City of Belview, Minnesota—Contract Negotiation	183
6.1	The Merit Pay Dilemma	231
7.1	A Blooming Labor Dispute	285
7.2	A Chocolate High?	286
8.1	The Boston Police Strike of 1919	296
8.2	Faulty Negotiations in Chicago	315
8.3	The PATCO Strike	324
9.1	Tough Times in Garden Junction	373
10.1	Chain of Custody	418
10.2	The Arbitration Case of Keyshaun King	419

Preface

The field of labor management relations has undergone substantial changes and developments since the publication of the fifth edition of this book. To begin with, there was considerable turbulence in the legal environment. At the state and local levels, numerous laws were introduced to restrict public sector collective bargaining rights.

The rise of nongovernmental organizations such as the American Legislative Exchange Council (ALEC), Americans for Prosperity (AFP), and State Policy Network (SPN) as policy actors at the state and local government levels played a key role in both the privatization of public services and the retrenchment of collective bargaining rights. Legislative plagiarism and copy and paste lawmaking spurred the diffusion of restrictive public sector labor policies and efforts to shrink the size of government.

At the federal level, U.S. Supreme Court decisions *Harris v. Quinn* (2014) and *Janus v. AFSCME* (2018) substantially weakened collective bargaining rights for publicly funded home care workers and public employees in general. Policies for federal employees have been impacted by Executive Orders, appointments, and staffing shortages at the MSPB and FLRA.

The COVID-19 pandemic (March 2020–May 2023) had a major impact on public sector working conditions and collective bargaining. Public employees engaged in negotiations over working conditions and workplace protections, including proper ventilation and personal protective equipment. In addition, public employees faced opposition to mask and vaccine mandates in public spaces, such as public transit, public schools, and universities.

Despite these setbacks, union activity is on the rise. In 2018–2019 a wave of teachers strikes spread across the U.S. Several strikes occurred in more conservative states with limited collective bargaining rights, such as West Virginia, Oklahoma, and New Mexico. In 2021, discontent over inequality, working conditions, and low wages led to labor protests known as "Striketober." In the private sector, 10,000 John Deere workers and 1,400 Kellogg's workers went on strike.

The momentum continued with the UAW stand up strike against the big three automakers in 2023 and the seven-week strike by factory workers at Boeing in 2024. In the nonprofit sector, unions representing 75,000 Kaiser Permanente employees engaged in rolling strikes in 2023. There has also been a surge in union organizing in private sector businesses such as Amazon and Starbucks, as well nonprofit organizations such as colleges and universities, museums, social service organizations, and policy think tanks. For the past several years, union favorability ratings have hovered between 67% and 71%, among the highest levels of approval since the 1960s.

This sixth edition of Labor Relations in the Public Sector has been completely updated in terms of the scholarly and professional literature and relevant events. As in previous editions, collective bargaining and labor relations are addressed at all levels of government, with comparisons to the private and nonprofit sectors. Interest-based (win–win) negotiations and participative decision making (PDM) are prominent themes in discussions of the bargaining process, contract administration, and future prospects. The sixth edition features case studies that are intended to provide students with experiential learning opportunities. The fundamental organization of the book remains the same.

The sixth edition is designed to be classroom friendly. As before, the book is intended for use in graduate and undergraduate courses in labor relations, collective bargaining, human resource management, and problems in public administration.

We appreciate the comments and suggestions of professors and students who have used earlier editions of this book. Thanks also go to Charles J. Fleck and Kathy Fitzsimmons-Lopez at Rutgers University, who helped gather information and materials, prepare tables and figures, and update the references for the sixth edition. Patrice Mareschal is grateful to her children, Jacob and Alex, for inspiration and support. Richard Kearney is indebted to Kathy, Joel, Laura, Andrew, and Nicole for their love and support.

Patrice M. Mareschal
Rutgers University

Richard C. Kearney
North Carolina State University

Chapter 1

History and Development

I. INTRODUCTION

As the Industrial Revolution dawned in England in the mid-eighteenth century, the employer's authority was absolute and completely free from laws or government regulations. Employers unilaterally determined wages and the terms and conditions of employment for their workers. As a practical matter, all but the most skilled workers had to take jobs as they came, with little or no opportunity to influence compensation levels or the nature of work. Conditions in the factories were deplorable: poorly lighted and ventilated, noisy, dangerous, and dirty working spaces; 12- to 14-hour days, 7 days a week; and children as young as 6 years toiling on the factory floor. Early efforts to form trade unions were violently suppressed by laws forbidding organization as a criminal conspiracy that interfered with commerce.

It was a long, hard struggle for employees in England and Europe to gain the rights to organize and bargain collectively, and it took nearly 200 years in the United States. The transition from autocratic corporate authority to organized labor and collective bargaining was long, arduous, and sometimes bloody. Early union organizers and their supporters often met with brutal repression by police and hired thugs (see, e.g., Salmond, 2004; Green, 2006). Today, labor rights are held in nearly all nations. Labor, in this sense, is triumphant. But unions in the United States today face new sets of problems and challenges, the outcomes of which could well determine their very existence in the next few decades.

This chapter discusses the history and development of unionization and collective bargaining in the private sector and in government. The roots of government unions are traced through a historical examination of the American trade union movement. The development of public sector unionization is examined, including key factors that contributed to the growth of unions in government.

DOI:10.4324/9781003403593-1

II. EARLY AMERICAN UNIONISM

Labor organizations have existed in the United States since the earliest days of the Republic. The environment within which they have been created and grown, however, has not always been friendly or even tolerant.

The earliest domestic roots of American unionism may be traced to the self-help organizations formed by workers in the crafts and skilled trades prior to the Revolutionary War. These organizations were, in a sense, close cousins of the European guilds, whose own genealogy may be traced back to professional trade associations in the Middle Ages. The guilds regulated wages, working hours, product quality, and other concerns in trades such as bookbinding, weaving, and pottery making. The first guild to develop in the United States was probably the cordwainers (shoemakers) in 1648 in Boston, Massachusetts (Commons, 1980). This guild eventually evolved into what some historians believe to be the first American trade union—the Society of Master Cordwainers. The guilds were not true "unions" in that there was no separation of labor between worker and owner. Nonetheless, workers were united in a common cause of self-protection.

The early American labor organizations were based on handicraft technologies such as shoemaking, stonecutting, carpentry, hat finishing, and printing. Their membership was composed of skilled laborers organized along the lines of individual crafts. Today, such organizations are known as craft unions. It is not surprising that organized labor began with highly skilled, strategically situated workers, because they were the first to enjoy what is referred to today as bargaining power.

Public policy toward early labor organizations was, to put it kindly, suppressive. Unions had no legal basis for existence and were considered "criminal conspiracies in restraint of trade" under common law. This criminal conspiracy doctrine emerged from a court case involving cordwainers, in which a judge ruled it illegal for Philadelphia, Pennsylvania, shoemakers to act collectively in efforts to raise their wages. Several of the early craft unions were prosecuted for criminal conspiracy, but the doctrine was brought to an end by the Massachusetts court decision of *Commonwealth v. Hunt* (1842), which held that such organized labor activities were lawful.

Some local labor organizations entered the political arena during the 1820s and 1830s through affiliating with "workingmen's parties." These organizations sought to elevate the social and economic status of craft and skilled laborers. They pressed Congress and state legislatures for job-related concessions, such as the 10-hour day, and also for broader reforms, such as free universal education, an end to the military draft, abolition of debtors' prisons, and expansion of suffrage. Many of these organizations, which were strongest in large cities such as New York and Philadelphia, even took a short-lived step toward national organization in 1834 by forming the National Trades Union to coordinate the activities of the locals.

For the most part, early labor organizations paid scant attention to female laborers and their working conditions. This began to change when women working in textile mills in Pawtucket Rhode Island organized a strike in 1824. The strike took place in response to management's decision to extend the workday for all workers, while simultaneously cutting wages for women (Foner, 1984). The Lowell Female Labor Reform Association (LFLRA) was founded in 1845 and focused on political agitation and organizing women working in mills in New England. The LFLRA advocated for a greater role for women in the public sphere and partnered with the New England Workingmen' Association (NEWA) to petition the Massachusetts Legislature for a ten-hour day. The legislature rejected their petitions. However, the LFLRA did successfully unseat the state representative from Lowell who opposed their demands (Mattina, 2009).

It was during this same time period (1820s–1830s) that labor organizations began to penetrate public employment, as public workers in skilled occupations sought the ten-hour day and won in some cities by their private counterparts. Most of this activity was concentrated in federal naval shipyards in Philadelphia, Boston, and New York. Later, when agitation for the eight-hour workday began, the first employer to grant it was the federal government, at the Charleston Navy Yard, South Carolina, in 1842. According to Spero (1948, p. 87), the drive for the eight-hour day "led to the crystallization of the principle of the state as a model employer maintaining the highest possible working standards in its services as an example for others to follow."

During this early period of growth and development, unions' organizational health was highly dependent on national economic conditions; unions suffered during hard times and revived during more prosperous times. For example, there was a tremendous increase in union membership during the Civil War and immediately afterward as a consequence of industrial growth related to the war effort. The Depression of 1873, however, was accompanied by a startling decline in national union membership, from 300,000 to 50,600 within 5 years. By 1885, improved economic conditions pushed membership growth back to the 300,000 mark. The direct relationship between economic tailspins and union membership declines reversed early in the twentieth century. Unions declined during the prosperous 1920s and made their most spectacular gains during the Great Depression era of the 1930s.

Nonetheless, economic conditions continue to influence union fortunes. For instance, when unemployment is low and consumer demand for products is high employers tend to accommodate employee demands, perhaps even the demand for unions. Concurrently, risk-taking union advocates and organizers find it relatively easy to locate new jobs if they are fired. Thus, unionism is likely to flourish during favorable economic conditions but flag during periods of high unemployment and a weak economy (Reder, 1988, pp. 92–93).

Of course, many other factors also influence union fortunes. During the past seven decades, private sector unions have struggled with membership losses during good and bad economic times. The Great Recession of 2008–2011 was accompanied by the most severe attack on unions—particularly in government—since the 1930s. There was a reawakening of public sector unionism in 2018–2019 as a wave of teachers strikes spread across the U.S. in response to austerity conditions. Then in 2020 the spread of COVID-19 transformed public sector working conditions and collective bargaining.

A. Ideological Battles in United States Unionism

Even though labor organizations could no longer be legally prosecuted for criminal conspiracy in restraint of trade after the 1842 Commonwealth decision, this did not by any means signal a new era of tolerance and encouragement of unionism. Bitter union–management battles erupted during the 1870s. Employer "union-busting" tactics such as lockouts; espionage; blacklisting of union organizers; summary firings of "agitators"; and, to break strikes, club-swinging "goon squads" forced some unions to go underground and operate as secret societies. One of these societies—the Molly Maguires, formed by coal miners—met employer violence with violence of its own, perpetrating acts of arson and murder in the Pennsylvania coal mines.

Many opposing union philosophies competed for the allegiance of the American working class during the late 1800s and early 1900s. Some groups sought victories through the political process, whereas others advocated collective bargaining. Most organizations wanted to operate and pursue their goals within the boundaries of the capitalist system, but others spoke out in favor of the emerging European philosophies of socialism and communism.

Perhaps the strongest of the leftist groups was the Industrial Workers of the World (IWW), which rejected capitalism outright and strove to organize the global working class, take control of the state, and overturn the capitalist system.

Founded in 1905 by radical socialists and syndicalists, whose penchant for a good fight took precedence over "planning, negotiating, and politiking [sic]" (Stegner, 1990, p. 13), the "Wobblies" enjoyed their greatest strength among mining, lumbering, and agricultural workers in the western states of Idaho, Colorado, and Utah. (Their nickname reportedly was taken from a Chinese cook's pronunciation of IWW as "I wobble wobble.") The Wobblies committed numerous acts of industrial sabotage and were successful in leading several large strikes in the United States and other countries during World War I. Many martyrs were produced along the way, including the legendary Joe Hill, who just before his very public execution in 1915 cried to his fellow Wobblies, "Don't waste time mourning—organize!" However, severe repression by the federal government—including the incarceration and lynching of union leaders such as Joe Hill—and the lack of broad appeal of IWW philosophies to the American working class led to the organization's demise shortly after the war (see Rosemont, 2002; Buhle & Schulman, 2005). The Wobblies' utopian vision of "one big union" for the workers of the world remains a historical curiosity to all except a handful of diehards who have recently sought to revive the IWW through leftist movements (For current information on the Wobblies, see the IWW website: www.IWW.org.).

Other labor organizations on the ideological far left have enjoyed some support in the United States, including the Farm Equipment Workers, Tobacco and Allied Workers, United Office and Professional Workers, and Fisherman's Union. Two communist unions even managed to survive the McCarthy-era repression of the 1950s: the International Longshore and Warehouse Union (ILWU) and the United Electrical, Radio, and Machine Workers. But a number of factors have conspired to mitigate socialist- and communist-oriented labor organizations in the United States. The rigid class structures of Europe have never developed in the United States to set boundaries for class conflict, largely because of a relatively high standard of living for working people, a fairly steady economic growth with the opportunity for individual advancement and upward mobility, the diverse ethnic and religious characteristics of American immigrants, and a strong ethos of individualism in the American public. From a political perspective, organized labor has been hemmed in by the absence of a labor-based political party and by actions of federal and state courts that have constricted the boundaries of union political and organizing activities (Galenson, 1980, pp. 73–79; Forbath, 1991; Archer, 2010).

B. Business Unionism

The real battles within the labor movement in the United States have been fought not over questions of political ideology but over issues of which types of workers should be organized and by whom. The ethos of business unionism, as originally professed by Samuel Gompers, has dominated the American labor movement. Economic gains and improvements in working conditions have served as the primary objectives of trade unionism, not social and political change. Theories of the labor movement in the United States reflect the early ascendancy of business unionism, asserting that American workers have joined unions out of concern for job security (Tannenbaum, 1921; Perlman, 1928), as a means for democratizing the workplace (Webb & Webb, 1897), as a result of expansion of the job market from increased industrialization (Commons et al., 1936), from a crystallization of group interests arising from workers' social and economic situations (Hoxie, 1928), and in response to various pay and fringe benefit incentives (Olson, 1965). The Marxist (and IWW) philosophy that unions should form the locus of a working class consciousness and serve as the basis for restricting competition over jobs has never been widely accepted in the United States.

As already noted, the earliest organizing efforts were among the craft unions. Heavy industrialization, which began during the mid-1800s, provided a new and rapidly growing industrial labor force of unskilled and semiskilled workers who were not trade or craft oriented. Organization of this new pool of workers would have to be along "shop" lines, based on the place of work rather than the type of work. The Knights of Labor launched the first significant effort to capture this industrial segment of the workforce.

Originally formed in 1869 as a craft union for custom tailors in Philadelphia, the Knights gradually began to include other crafts under its organizational umbrella. Within ten years, it had evolved into the first national labor union in the United States. The Knights dropped its status as a secret society and, under the leadership of an affable Irishman named Terence V. Powderly, began to seek both craft and industrial affiliates throughout the country. By the time of its successful 1886 strike against financier Jay Gould and the Wabash Railroad, the Knights claimed a membership of 700,000. However, the Knights' membership was somewhat unstable and divisive, and a subsequent series of ill-conceived and violent strikes led to one defeat after another for the union (Phelan, 2000). By the turn of the twentieth century, the Knights of Labor was nearly extinct. Further organization of unskilled workers awaited the development of the Congress of Industrial Organizations (CIO) in the 1930s.

The remaining craft union pieces of the complex Knights of Labor organizational mosaic were quickly gathered by the American Federation of Labor (AFL), which was originally established in 1881 in Pittsburgh, Pennsylvania, as a federation for skilled craft workers. The 25 national craft union affiliates elected Samuel Gompers, head of the Cigar Makers Union, as their first president. The ultimate pragmatist, Gompers soon made the AFL a major actor in the American economic system. Gompers was, in essence, a free marketeer who rejected philosophical, political, and social issues in favor of advancing and protecting members' economic interests. Under his leadership, the AFL grew steadily, surviving both the Depression of 1893–1896 and a violent strike that broke the back of an AFL local at the Carnegie Steel Company in Homestead, Pennsylvania. The AFL also proved strong enough to withstand the scientific management movement of Frederick W. Taylor, court injunctions against strikes and other union actions, and years of stifling "yellow-dog contracts" (a contract in which a worker promised not to join a union while under the hire of an employer). There were, however, some dark times, particularly following World War I and during the early years of the Great Depression.

The AFL's resurgence after the Great Depression was, in the words of Sloane and Witney (1981, pp. 75–76), "in spite of itself," as the union "almost snatched defeat from the jaws of victory." A leadership gap was part of the problem (Gompers had died), but more to blame was the union's continuing reactionary posture against mass production workers whom the Knights of Labor had first tried to organize. The AFL's unrelenting refusal to allow unskilled industrial workers into the organization eventually prompted a secessionist movement steered by John L. Lewis of the United Mine Workers. After Lewis' efforts to gain affiliation for industrial workers failed at the 1935 AFL convention in Atlantic City, New Jersey, he did not exit meekly. According to Sloane and Witney (1981, p. 77), "Lewis, never one to camouflage his emotions for the sake of good fellowship with his AFL colleagues, left Atlantic City only after landing a severe uppercut to the jaw of Carpenter Union president William L. Hutcheson." Lewis then formed his own industrial union, which came to be known as the CIO. There followed another, later attempt to affiliate under the AFL banner, but it culminated in expulsion of CIO leaders and the more than 30 national unions that had joined forces with the CIO.

Lewis's independent CIO was highly successful in organizing industrial workers, such as those in the automobile and steel industries, so much so that the AFL finally recognized the error of its ways and began competing for unskilled workers. Not to be outdone, the CIO responded in kind by organizing craft workers. In 1955, after years of fierce interunion conflict and competition, the AFL merged permanently with the CIO, becoming "the united house of labor."

The labor battles had been fought not over political ideology or competing grand visions of American society but over organizing workers and the mundane bread-and-butter issues that remain paramount to this day: wages, benefits, working conditions, and job security. To George Meany, as well as to other mainstream labor leaders, ideology was "baloney" (Sloane & Witney, 1981, p. 94). Unions did become active in the political arena during the 1960s and remain so today, pressing a broad national agenda for social betterment and economic reform with varying degrees of success. However, no coherent ideology is apparent, and a capitalist mentality pervades the U.S. economy and polity (Godard, 2009). Ironically, the year following the AFL–CIO merger marked the beginning of a long and continuous decline in union organization in private employment.

In 1956, the first year in which the total number of U.S. white-collar employees exceeded the number of blue-collar workers, one-third of the nation's nonagricultural workers were unionized. By 2022, fewer than one in nine was a member, just 10.1% of the total workforce, the lowest level since 1916, and only 6.0% of private sector workers. The absolute number of private sector union members continued to rise until 1970, but it has since dramatically declined to 7.03 million (U.S. Bureau of Labor Statistics, 2023a).

In 2022 the total number of workers belonging to unions increased to 14.3 million. At the same time, the workforce grew by 5.8 million employees. The combination of factors led to an overall decrease in union membership rates (U.S. Bureau of Labor Statistics, 2023a). Table 1.1 provides membership figures for the largest private sector unions today. Table 1.2 shows union membership for all workers—public and private sectors—by state.

Table 1.1 Membership in the Largest Private Sector Unions, 2023

Membership Count	*Union*
1,400,000[a]	International Brotherhood of Teamsters
1,300,000	United Food and Commercial Workers International Union
1,100,000[b]	SEIU
850,000	United Steelworkers of America
720,000	International Association of Machinists and Aerospace Workers
700,000[a]	Communications Workers of America
675,000	International Brotherhood of Electrical Workers
500,000	Laborers' International Union of North America
500,000	United Brotherhood of Carpenters and Joiners of America
400,000	International Union of Operating Engineers
400,000	International Union, United Automobile, Aerospace, and Agricultural Implement Workers of America
370,000	United Association of Journeymen and Apprentices of the Plumbing and Pipe-Fitting Industry of the United States and Canada (UA)
300,000	Union of Needletrades, Industrial, and Textile Employees (UNITE HERE)

Note: Table contains self-reported figures from each organization's website.

[a] Denotes public and private sector membership.

[b] Denotes private sector membership only.

Table 1.2 Union Density for All Wage and Salary Workers, Public and Private, 2023

	Union Members		*Represented by Unions*	
State	*Total (K)*	*Percentage*	*Total (K)*	*Percentage*
Hawaii	125	21.9	134	23.4
New York	1,679	20.7	1,795	22.1
Washington	615	18	653	19.1
California	2,617	16.1	2,856	17.6
Rhode Island	81	16.1	89	17.7
Alaska	48	16	52	17.3
Oregon	281	15.5	305	16.9
New Jersey	619	14.9	666	16
Connecticut	236	14.2	256	15.4

(*Continued*)

Table 1.2 (Continued)

	Union Members		*Represented by Unions*	
State	*Total (K)*	*Percentage*	*Total (K)*	*Percentage*
Minnesota	382	14.2	411	15.2
Michigan	589	14	644	15.3
Illinois	735	13.1	789	14.1
Ohio	641	12.8	699	14
Massachusetts	413	12.7	447	13.8
Pennsylvania	715	12.7	767	13.6
Vermont	34	12.1	38	13.4
Maryland	327	11.6	372	13.2
Nevada	146	11.3	164	12.8
Montana	52	11.2	57	12.3
New Hampshire	70	10.1	77	11.2
Kansas	129	9.8	160	12.1
Missouri	257	9.6	284	10.6
Maine	48	9.2	61	11.5
West Virginia	64	9.2	69	10
District of Columbia	30	9.1	34	10.4
New Mexico	71	8.8	86	10.6
Delaware	38	8.5	42	9.4
Kentucky	141	7.9	185	10.3
Indiana	223	7.4	260	8.6
Alabama	149	7.2	173	8.4
Wisconsin	187	7.1	212	8
Iowa	105	7	132	8.7
Colorado	178	6.7	201	7.5
Nebraska	60	6.5	74	8.1
North Dakota	23	6.4	28	7.6
Mississippi	62	5.6	79	7.2
Wyoming	14	5.6	18	7.3
Arizona	169	5.5	189	6.2
Oklahoma	88	5.5	113	7.1
Tennessee	163	5.5	184	6.3

(*Continued*)

Table 1.2 (Continued)

State	Union Members		Represented by Unions	
	Total (K)	*Percentage*	*Total (K)*	*Percentage*
Arkansas	59	4.9	68	5.7
Idaho	39	4.7	49	5.9
Florida	414	4.5	511	5.6
Georgia	200	4.4	244	5.4
Louisiana	76	4.2	94	5.2
Texas	518	4.1	643	5.1
Utah	60	3.9	133	8.7
Virginia	146	3.7	175	4.5
South Dakota	13	3.1	17	4.2
North Carolina	125	2.8	173	3.9
South Carolina	35	1.7	40	2
U.S. Average	280	9.4	313	10.7

Source: U.S. Bureau of Labor Statistics. (2023a). *Economic news release: Union members summary*. https://www.bls.gov/news.release/union2.htm#union_a05.f.1

III. FACTORS CONTRIBUTING TO PRIVATE SECTOR UNION DECLINE

The fading fortunes of unions in the private sector have spawned a great amount of discussion and debate. Four major factors have contributed to union decline, although their relative importance is subject to dispute (e.g., Freeman & Medoff, 1984; Bennett & Kaufman, 2002).

A. Structural Elements

Structural elements refer to the broad social and economic changes that have affected the composition of the workforce, general nature of employment, shift of jobs from the heavily organized Northeast and Midwest to the predominantly nonunion South and Southwest, and demographic characteristics of the workforce. More specifically, the labor force has become increasingly female, minority, contingent, and part time, with correspondingly different needs from the mostly white male workers of the past. It is also increasingly white collar, as employment has shifted from union-dense manufacturing, mining, construction, and transportation jobs to white-collar and pink-collar services such as banking and finance, health care, insurance, telecommunications, and information technology. Historically, white-collar workers have been difficult to organize because of the prestige and professionalism associated with their jobs, special interests and needs that have not been attended to by unions, and the generally poor image of organized labor among this group (Sloane & Witney, 1981, pp. 10–13). Forces of globalization have pushed and pulled some traditionally union jobs to other countries (Farber & Western, 2001). In a sense, unions have also inadvertently contributed to their own decline. Union-ratcheted salaries and wages placed firms in Pennsylvania, Illinois, Michigan, and New York at a competitive disadvantage, encouraging many of them to move to low-wage nonunion states such as Texas, Tennessee, and North Carolina and, increasingly, to China, India, and other low-wage countries. The structural explanation seems compelling on the surface, but empirical investigations have determined that it does not tell the whole story of the factors underlying union decline.

B. Government Substitution

Union-advocated public policies have, over time, reduced the benefits of organizing and joining unions for individual workers. In addition to elevating wages, unions have aligned with other organizations to advocate for policy reforms that have effectively substituted for union-negotiated collective bargaining benefits. Workers' compensation, federal labor standards, child labor laws, social security, unemployment compensation, and an assortment of other such programs have improved the lot of potential union members. Legislation and court decisions help shield workers from unjust or arbitrary discharges (Neumann & Rissman, 1984; Coombs, 2008). Efforts to assess the government substitution effect, however, have found little empirical support for the argument (Coombs, 2008).

C. Unfavorable Legal and Policy Environment

It can be argued that the decline of unions is to some extent attributable to restrictions on labor organizing and other activities by Taft–Hartley, Landrum–Griffin, and other federal legislation. For example, Taft–Hartley significantly weakened the Wagner Act by prohibiting a requirement of union membership as a condition of employment (the "closed shop," which makes union membership mandatory "before" employment) and permitting "right-to-work" laws (which also bar the "union shop," which requires union membership "at the time of" employment). Taft–Hartley also restricts job slowdowns, sit-down strikes, and wildcat strikes. Moreover, the National Labor Relations Board (NLRB), which administers federal labor law and investigates and decides on allegations of unfair labor practices against employers and unions, has delivered a high proportion of unfavorable decisions to unions (Forbath, 1991; Gross, 1995).

The federal courts have been criticized for their antiunion decisions as well For example, the so-called MacKay Doctrine, promulgated by the U.S. Supreme Court in 1938 but not widely applied until President Ronald Reagan emboldened business by sacking 11,000 federal air traffic controllers in 1981, allows firms to hire permanent replacements for striking workers. These concerns have led union supporters to call for congressional actions to level a labor–management playing field that appears to be tilted against the unions. Yet Congress is heavily influenced by business interests who have frequently succeeded in rallying Republicans and conservative Democrats to defeat labor-friendly legislation. For instance, bills to ban permanent replacement of striking employees are regularly introduced in Congress but just as regularly defeated by business interests.

D. Management Opposition

Employer resistance to unions has progressed from "blackjacks to briefcases" (Smith, 2003). Toting those briefcases are employees of hundreds of management consulting firms specializing in union busting (Gagala, 1983, ch. 3; Bernstein, 1985; Bronfenbrenner & Warren, 2011). Various tactics bolster employer resistance to unions. Some are framed as "positive employee relations," which ostensibly means establishing a compensation system and working conditions that are as good as or better than those found in unionized workplaces. Other resistance techniques involve legal or illegal negative tactics to suppress unionization. These include hiring consultants to help contest union elections through tough, well-financed campaigns to keep unions out; stirring worker doubts about the potential benefits of unions; delaying certification elections until a majority of employees have lost interest in joining a union; and refusing to bargain collectively or negotiate and sign a contract even if a union is established. Often, union-busting strategies are implemented after employees initially express an interest in organizing.

Some firms also engage in blatantly illegal activities to fight unions, calculating that it is cheaper to pay a small fine to the NLRB now than to meet the demands of the unions later (Kleiner, 2001, pp. 528–532). Workers are threatened or intimidated, union organizers are fired, and lies and distortions are disseminated. Such employer opposition is asserted by some scholars to be the leading "cause of the slow strangulation of private sector unionism" (Freeman & Medoff, 1984, p. 239; see also Goldfield, 1987). The reasons for management intransigence are not difficult to fathom. Keeping unions out means higher profits for the firm and fewer headaches for management. It also means that certain managers keep their jobs; those perceived to be responsible for losing a union election may find themselves quickly on the street (Freeman & Kleiner, 1990, p. 363).

E. Strategic Factors

The strategic choices made—and not made—by union leaders have contributed to union decline. Some critical choices made decades ago, including the rejection of ideological approaches to labor's relationship to government and the failure to mount a labor party to compete for a legitimate voice in government, have debilitated labor's political power and influence today. Labor's long-term reliance on the Democratic Party for political clout continues to this day (Dark, 1999; Francia, 2006). To many Democrats, however, labor is just another interest group.

From the 1970s to 1998, unions spent less money on organizing new members and participated in fewer NLRB certification elections than in earlier years (the trend was reversed in 1998 with AFL–CIO President John Sweeney's organizing initiatives). What is more, managements won far more union elections than they lost. Merely to survive, unions must continually recruit new members. Organized labor has not told a compelling story of why today's workers should want to join a union, and neither has it manufactured the positive public image and support necessary to nurture a receptive audience of unorganized workers or a receptive general public.

Ultimately, the responsibility for strategic errors made by unions must be laid at the feet of unimaginative, reactive and—all too often—self-interested and corrupt union leaders. Private sector unions, like other failed or flagging organizations, have failed to adapt to a changing environment (Kearney, 2003). Labor has too often poisoned its own well by betraying its members through fraud and corruption and by forming indefensible alliances with organized crime (Fraser, 1998).

Can private sector union decline be reversed, or is it an inevitable part of a postindustrial society? Where is the bottom? The hemorrhaging has been going on for some 50 years and shows no signs of arrest. Unions had suffered earlier periods of decline (Rachlett, 1999). For instance, unions lost almost 40% of their membership from 1920 to 1933 and then recovered strongly. Another such reversal is plausible, but it presupposes more astute union leadership, more effective organizing strategies, effective coalition-building strategies with other powerful interest groups, a "mobilization of bias" in employer and public opinion in favor of unions (Schattschneider, 1988), and a more facilitative legal environment, among other factors (see Tillman & Cummings, 1999).

Some cause for optimism arose in 1995, when former Service Employees International Union (SEIU) president John J. Sweeney was elected president of the 13-million-member AFL–CIO (Dark, 1999, pp. 178–184). Sweeney, whose SEIU membership had doubled even as most other AFL–CIO affiliates' ranks thinned, worked hard to reverse labor's declining fortunes and provoked a far-reaching reexamination of labor's role in the twenty-first century. Sweeney took steps to include more women and minorities in union leadership positions, dedicated millions of new dollars to organizing drives, and greatly elevated labor's profile during the presidential election of 1996 and the congressional elections of 1998.

Sweeney's actions were not sufficient to stimulate a rebirth of labor in the U.S. private sector. For every action taken to rejuvenate the unions, business interests and their Republican allies countered with efforts to rewrite labor laws and other strategies designed to disadvantage unions, such as restrictions on using members' dues for political and lobbying expenses.

And it seems that each time the resuscitation of the sickly patient is being widely heralded, labor once again suffers an untimely relapse. Self-destructive leadership actions and decisions, including the almost predictable Teamster scandal, reinfect the union movement and send it back to its deathbed. Sweeney's desire to reinvent, reinvigorate, and reposition organized labor was effectively countered by congressional Republicans and business interests.

Then, in 2005, following a year of internal labor turmoil, rising dissatisfaction with Sweeney's leadership, and continuing decline in the private sector, four dissident unions seceded from the AFL–CIO. The new group, called the Change to Win Coalition (CTW), consisted of the United Food and Commercial Workers, UNITE HERE, the Teamsters, and SEIU; three other unions joined subsequently. Together, the seven unions make up less than half of total AFL–CIO membership. The rift was reminiscent of the old CIO split from the AFL in the 1930s. Several years later, amidst allegations of corruption in the SEIU, two unions, UNITE HERE and the Laborers' International Union of North America, left CTW and rejoined the AFL-CIO. Sweeney stepped down from his position in 2009 and Richard L. Trumka was elected president of the AFL-CIO.

Trumka steered the organization toward supporting immigrant workers and low wage workers in the restaurant industry (Greenhouse, 2014). In 2017, Trumka resigned from then U.S. President Donald Trump's Manufacturing Council in response to Trump's statements regarding violence at the Unite the Right rallies in Charlottesville, Virginia. Trumka issued a statement denouncing bigotry and domestic terrorism. Under his leadership, in 2019 the AFL-CIO formed a commission to study the future of work and a develop a plan to strengthen workers' bargaining power, demand workers' fair share of benefits derived from technology advancements, and promote continuous labor movement reforms (AFL-CIO, 2019).

Upon Richard L. Trumka's death in August 2021, Liz Shuler became the acting president of the AFL-CIO and shortly thereafter was elected to the position. Shuler is the first woman to hold the office in the history of the organization. Fred Redmond was elected secretary-treasurer at the same time and is the first African American to hold the office. Shuler called on the federation to "organize, innovate and reshape the labor movement," in the wake of the COVID-19 pandemic (AFL-CIO, 2022).

It is not clear whether the AFL-CIO's recent efforts to revitalize the labor movement as a forum for workers' voice will be enough to reverse the decades long decline in union density. Recent successes in union organizing in private sector businesses such as Amazon and Starbucks, as well nonprofit organizations such as museums and policy think tanks, offer a glimmer of hope for the labor movement. These gains have been facilitated by a tight labor market (Naidu, 2022).

However, these advances have been offset by employers' resistance to bargain, and allegations of employers' retaliation against union organizers. With deep pockets, and access to a multi-billion dollar industry of law firms and consultants in what is known as a union avoidance industry, employers are able to take advantage weak labor laws and a lengthy litigation process that fails to deter anti-union activity (Logan, 2019).

IV. UNIONS IN GOVERNMENT

A. Early Years

As noted earlier, public employee organizations first became active during the early 1800s, particularly in federal shipyards. However, until 1836, even in the shipyards they experienced limited success because their military bosses tended to be rather insensitive to the opinions of their workers. In that year, a Washington, D.C. naval shipyard strike and a mass demonstration prompted intervention by President Andrew Jackson, who personally granted the federal employees the ten-hour day they sought. Thus, a tradition of direct presidential involvement in federal labor problems was established, and it continues to this day.

The New York Letter Carriers formed the first federal employee organization of national significance in 1863. In 1886, the Knights of Labor chartered locals in Chicago, Illinois; Omaha, Nebraska; and other cities. Postal clerks were organized in 1888 in New York, and the National Association of Letter Carriers was established in 1890. Rural carriers formed their own national organization in 1903.

The rise of postal workers under the banners of their various organizations was not met with equanimity by the federal government. In 1895, Postmaster General William L. Wilson issued a departmental order prohibiting any postal employee from visiting Washington for lobbying purposes, at the risk of being fired. When intensive lobbying by postal workers and their organizations continued, much to the annoyance of the executive branch and some members of Congress, President Theodore Roosevelt retaliated in 1902 with his infamous gag rule forbidding all federal employees from seeking congressional legislation on their own behalf, directly or indirectly, individually or through their organizations (Spero, 1948 pp. 117–127). Postal employee militancy was also met with union-busting tactics that included the use of paid informers; disciplining and/or discharge of organizational leaders; and, ironically, opening of their personal mail (Nesbitt, 1976, p. 8).

Ever tenacious, the postal workers responded with an anti-gag rule campaign, spearheaded by a magazine, the *Harpoon*, which was edited by a railway clerk named Urban A. Walter. Finally, the postal workers, led by the AFL and the National Federation of Post Office Clerks, garnered sufficient congressional support to win the passage of the Lloyd–LaFollette Act of 1912, guaranteeing federal employees the First Amendment right to organize and petition Congress for a redress of grievances. Although the Lloyd–LaFollette Act had only a small effect on federal union-busting activities (which continued), it did denote a positive direction in the development of postal and other federal labor organizations as they increasingly began to seek the full labor rights granted to private sector workers in the National Labor Relations Act (Spero, 1948, p. 143).

Early organizational efforts outside the defense establishment and post office included "almost every civil occupation from charwoman to zoologist, from astronomer to stonecutter" (Nesbitt, 1976, p. 56). These efforts were rebuffed by the U.S. Civil Service Commission. In 1912, however, customs inspectors successfully organized on a national scale, and in 1917 the National Federation of Federal Employees was formed as an umbrella organization intended to cover all federal civilian employees except postal employees and those workers permitted to join AFL affiliates (Nesbitt, 1976). Two other significant general-purpose federal organizations followed: the American Federation of Government Employees (AFGE) in 1932 and the National Association of Government Employees soon thereafter. As will become evident later in our discussion, however, substantial growth in these and other federal organizations awaited the implementation of President Kennedy's Executive Order 10988 of 1962.

Organizational progress in the state and local government sectors was also uneven before the 1960s. A crafts orientation was clearly prevalent during the formative years, especially in local government, as teachers, firefighters, and police organized separately. The National Teachers Association (NTA) was formed in 1857. The National Education Association (NEA) was created in 1870 through a merger of the NTA and two other teacher associations. These early teacher associations were set up and directed by administrators and other school authorities to advance the interests of the teaching occupation and to provide mutual aid programs, but a steady accumulation of grievances eventually drove the teachers into a more aggressive posture. State laws and local ordinances forbade teachers from smoking, placed restrictions on their dress, imposed curfews, and even sought to regulate their leisure time.

In Westchester County, New York, for example, teachers were ordered to bed by 10:00 p.m. One North Carolina town admonished its teachers "to sleep at least 8 hours a night, to eat carefully, and to take every precaution to keep in the best of health and spirits" (Spero, 1948, pp. 298–300). In 1900, the Chicago and San Antonio, Texas, teachers' federations responded to such intrusive rules by affiliating with the AFL. Joined by other teacher organizations in 1916, they formed the American Federation of Teachers (AFT).

Firefighters and police began organizing during the late 1800s and the early years of the twentieth century, primarily as mutual benefit societies to provide pension and insurance programs and to fulfill the social needs of their members. In 1918, the AFL chartered the International Association of Fire Fighters, which remains the second oldest nationally affiliated state or local union (after the NEA). Police officers first applied for an AFL charter in 1897 in Cleveland, Ohio. By 1919, 37 police organizations had received certification in various municipalities. Growing militancy by police and firefighters, particularly in the larger cities, led to a relatively large number of strikes in the public safety services during 1918–1919.

One of these strikes—by police officers in Boston—took on serious national proportions after several days of unrestrained looting and mob rule and eventual intervention by Governor Calvin Coolidge and the Massachusetts National Guard. Negative public reaction to the 1919 Boston police strike set back public safety unionization by some 40 years (see Chapter 8). Local police benefit associations continued to exist, but little union activity took place again in the public safety services until the 1960s.

The largest state and local union today, the American Federation of State, County, and Municipal Employees (AFSCME), was born in 1932 as the Wisconsin State Employees Association. Efforts to expand its scope of organization to other states and to extend membership to local employees were made through a 1935 affiliation with the AFGE. However, the AFGE affiliation was unworkable and the AFSCME successfully won independent status the very next year (see Kramer, 1962). As in the case of public safety organizations in local government, AFSCME's progress was uneven. By 1950, it had reached a membership total of about 68,000, but in most jurisdictions the organization was "harassed, coerced, dismissed—or entirely ignored" (Spero & Capozzola, 1973, p. 18). Although the founder of AFSCME, Arnold Zander, eventually supported collective bargaining and the use of strike when deemed necessary, the formal goals of the organization were rather conservative, being "to stimulate the growth and extension of civil service and to improve existing merit systems" (Kramer, 1962, p. 31).

A leadership change at the 1960 national convention produced a new president, Jerry Wurf, with a more aggressive style, a more militant posture by the national union and its locals across the United States, and subsequent membership gains. Under Wurf's leadership, AFSCME also became aligned with the civil rights movement. In 1960, AFSCME added a bill of rights to its constitution that included protections for "race, creed, color, national origin, ethnicity, sex, age, sexual orientation, gender identity or expression, disability, immigration status, or political belief" (Washington Federation of State Employees, n.d.). Although Wurf was initially opposed to the AFSCME Local 1733's decision to call the Memphis sanitation workers' strike, he provided substantial resources to the strike once it was active. Wurf was a close associate of Martin Luther King and brought him into the sanitation workers' cause. Shortly after King's assassination he helped negotiate a contract settlement with the city (Dreier, 2019).

As the 1960s progressed, it became clear that government employers could no longer bank on a docile, passive worker who was content with a secure job and a modest salary and pension. Federal, state, and local government workers in many jurisdictions were on the cusp of launching a new venture that few had imagined.

The following section explores the reasons for the rise of public employee union in the United States after first considering the converse question that is begged, that is, why public sector organization lagged behind the private sector for some 30 years.

B. Why Government Employees Did (and Did Not) Unionize

In retrospect, there seem to be three principal factors that inhibited public employee unionism and collective bargaining prior to the 1960s: the sovereignty argument, the nature of government employment, and an unfavorable legal environment. Each of them is examined here.

Ideology for its own sake has never been widely embraced in the United States. For many government employers determined to resist unions, however, the doctrine of sovereignty assumed the aura of ideology, although the aura was somewhat dimmed by its self-serving usage by those opposed to unions. Briefly, the sovereignty argument contends that in a representative democracy the people are sovereign and their will is served by their elected representatives. If government, through these representatives' appointees or civil servants, bargains over terms and conditions of employment with a union, then sovereignty is violated through the illegal delegation of the people's sovereign power (Slater, 2004).

The argument would perhaps stand if the various American governments could demonstrate their delegative purity. However, representatives of the national, state, and local governments have for more than two centuries negotiated contracts and arrangements with private sector entities without the expressed permission of the electorate. (Examples include contracting weapons systems to private manufacturers or garbage collection to firms.) As a consequence of the daily violation of sovereignty throughout the country, invoking the doctrine in opposition to unions appears to be at best self-serving and at worst hypocritical. Stieber (1973, p. 17) sums up the counterargument well: "the doctrine of sovereignty as applied to employment has been substantially dismembered by legal and academic critics, joined by government lawmakers and rule makers. Governments, however supreme, make deals." They also make and sign legal contracts. Nonetheless, the sovereignty argument has been used with various degrees of success to stifle government unionization, and it continues to be a credo propounded by many political conservatives.

The nature of government employment also had a strong bearing on slow public sector union growth and development. A number of factors are salient here. Government work is predominantly white collar in nature, and government workforces frequently include disproportionate numbers of women and minorities. In the past, all three categories of employees were traditionally difficult to organize. Moreover, government employment, particularly at the federal level, has been characterized by strong job security, generous pensions, and merit system protections against partisan political pressure and other forms of management abuse. Merit systems offered an alternative to collective bargaining for determining wages, benefits, and working conditions and for providing formal grievance procedures for unhappy workers wishing to file complaints.

Finally, the legal environment for public sector unionism was highly unfavorable prior to the far-reaching labor law changes instituted at all levels of government during the 1960s. Many public employees were forbidden to strike or take other job actions and, most important, statutory provisions for recognizing public employee organizations and implementing collective bargaining were very rare. When unions asserted their rights to be recognized and to bargain with employers in courts, they were usually spurned by a hostile judiciary.

C. Rise of Public Employee Unions

As mentioned earlier, circumstances changed dramatically during the 1960s, as public employee unions and collective bargaining spread rapidly across jurisdictions at all levels throughout that decade and the next. Several important developments moved the unions to the forefront of government employment. Although the causal variables facilitating government union growth are complex, multiple, and interrelated, it is possible to identify several factors that significantly contributed to unionization: (1) the growth of government, (2) the private sector experience, (3) changes in the public sector legal environment, and (4) the social change and turmoil that characterized the 1960s and early 1970s (Shaw & Clark, 1972, pp. 901–904).

1. Growth of Government

During the 1960s and 1970s, the number of civilian government jobs approximately doubled, with most of the growth occurring in the state and local sectors. This greatly expanded workforce presented an attractive target for union organizers. By 1980, almost one of every six working people in the United States was employed at some level of government. From a base year of 1951, employment in the federal government rose by 24% to 2,866,000 workers in 1980, whereas state and local employment increased by about 227% to 13,383,000. The nation's total employment over this time period registered a gain of 89%.

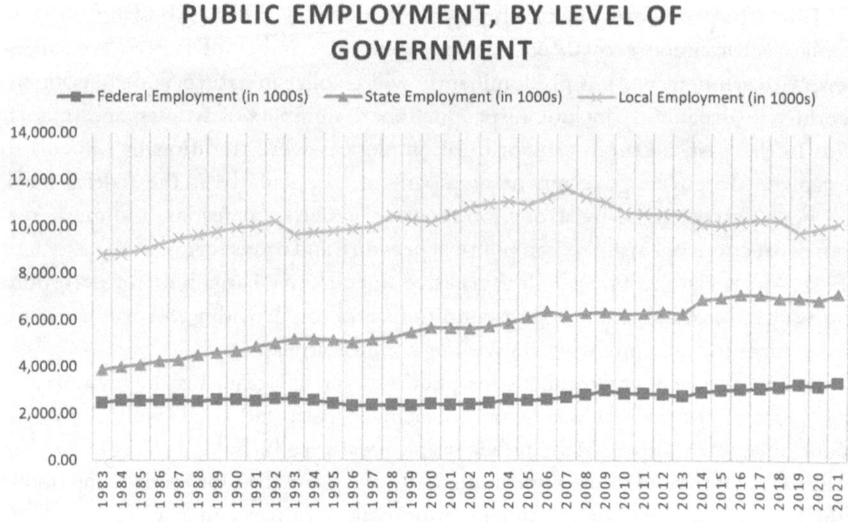

Figure 1.1 **Public employment, by level of government, 1955–2022: The Union Membership and Coverage Database can be found at https://www.unionstats.com/. For the years 1973–1981, data were collected from the May Current Population Survey (CPS). For the years 1983–2011, data were collected from the CPS Outgoing Rotation Group Earnings Files. There were no union questions in the 1982 CPS.**

Source: from U.S. Bureau of Labor Statistics. (2023a). *Economic news release: Union members summary*. https://www.bls.gov/news.release/union2.nr0.htm.

After 1980, the number of federal civilian employees actually declined, dropping from about 2.9 million in 1980 to 1.85 million in 1998, primarily as a result of massive downsizing during the Clinton–Gore administration. Federal jobs then rose in the early 2000s with the wars in Afghanistan and Iraq and federalization of airport security under the Transportation Security Agency (see Figure 1.1). The exit of military and civilian employees from Iraq and the withdrawal from Afghanistan, along with efforts to downsize the federal civilian government to help lessen an enormous budget deficit, resulted in a new wave of job cutbacks, further depressing federal employment levels in the early 2010s. The total number of federal civilian employees declined slightly in subsequent years from 2.9 million in 2010 to 2.87 million in 2022.

Several factors help explain the rapid gains in state and local government employment that commenced in the 1950s and continued until the Great Recession hit in 2008: first, national population growth necessitated additional government workers to service the expanding number of programs intended to address people's health, education, social service, and other needs. Second, the age distribution of the population shifted. Larger proportions of the population were situated in the "less than 25" and "65 years and over" ranges, the two groups that claim the bulk of government services. Finally, federal mandates for state and locally administered programs (including social services, transportation, and environmental protection programs) contributed to the surge in state and local jobs. In the period following the Great Recession, state and local government employment fluctuated somewhat between 19.6 million in 2010 to 19.23 million in 2022. Although there was a slight uptick over this period, those gains were wiped out from 2020 to 2022, most likely as a result of the COVID-19 pandemic.

Not surprisingly, government employment figures also depict a steady shift from blue-collar to white-collar jobs as well as gains in the proportion of women and minorities in government employment. More than half of public employees are women. African Americans, Latinos, and Asian Americans make up more than one-third of total public employment.

Along with the growth of government came increasing bureaucratization and depersonalization of the public service, twin forces that tended to isolate and alienate the individual employee (Shaw & Clark, 1972, p. 902; Shutt, 1986). No longer was most government employment characterized by a small "family" of people who know and relate to one another in a neighborly fashion from the top of the hierarchy to the bottom. Dissatisfaction with personalism, arbitrary management actions, and clogged communication channels within an increasingly complex organizational structure convinced many government workers of the need for intermediary organizations like unions to represent them collectively in their relationships with management.

Ballooning government employment rolls presented a very attractive organizing target for private sector unions, which were suffering from a precipitous decline in the number of blue-collar jobs in industry. Unions that heretofore had concentrated their membership drives on the private sector began courting public employees, often through their existing professional organizations. A natural community of interest among public workers such as teachers, firefighters, and police officers had found expression through professional associations and had preconditioned them to the values of organizational membership (Moskow et al., 1970, p. 287). Unions helped convince the members of these associations that they could enjoy the same benefits of unionization as union members in the private sector.

2. Private Sector Spillover

Unions in the private sector successfully won wage and benefit increases and improved working conditions for their members. This did not go unnoticed by public employees, who were becoming increasingly dissatisfied with government wages and conditions of employment. Even the traditional security of a government job became problematic in some jurisdictions.

The ponderous civil service systems entrenched in most large government jurisdictions were unable or unwilling to satisfactorily respond to public employee demands. For instance, wage and benefit adjustments typically required legislative—not collective bargaining—action. In light of these circumstances, public workers became more receptive to the notion of collective voice through unionization and began demanding compensation and labor rights equal to those in the private sector.

As private sector unions moved aggressively into the relatively unplowed and fertile fields of public employment, preexisting professional organizations rightfully felt threatened. Strong organizing efforts by emergent unions such as the AFT, for example, spurred the NEA to reconsider its own future role in public education and eventually to embrace the full panoply of union and collective bargaining activities. In many jurisdictions, predominantly private sector unions such as the SEIU and the International Brotherhood of Teamsters began to compete directly with the professional associations. In some cases, professional and fraternal organizations had to adopt an overt union strategy to survive. The rivalries between these various types of organizations led to increased militancy and intensified organizing drives, which, on the whole, further enhanced government unionization (Stieber, 1973, p. 830).

3. Changes in the Legal Environment

However widespread they are within a government jurisdiction, unions may be functionally impotent in the absence of a legal framework requiring public employers to recognize and bargain with them. Two events during the early 1960s indirectly contributed to the creation of a more favorable legal environment for enactment of public sector labor laws: first, the U.S. Supreme Court ordered reapportionment of Congress and the 50 state legislatures (*Baker v. Carr* [1962]; *Reynolds v. Simms* [1964]) on the basis of one person, one vote. These decisions ended or at least eased the domination of many state legislatures by rural, predominantly antiunion interests. Unions, which have always found their strongest support among people in metropolitan areas, soon discovered more sympathetic ears in the reapportioned legislative bodies of the states.

The second development encouraging bargaining legislation was President John F. Kennedy's Executive Order 10988 of 1962, which guaranteed unionization and bargaining rights for federal employees. This order might have been the turning point in state and local unionization. Although it is impossible to ascertain a direct cause-and-effect relationship between Executive Order 10988 and the subsequent enactment of labor relations legislation in numerous jurisdictions, it did have a substantial spillover effect in legitimizing public employee unionization and collective bargaining practices.

4. Era of Social Change and Turmoil

There was a massive infusion of young people and racial minorities into the public workforce during the 1960s. Both groups tended to be distrustful of authority and the existing management structure. Furthermore, both groups, on the whole, were favorably disposed to unions (Barrett, 1973). Meanwhile, public life in general was riddled with conflicts over the unpopular war in Vietnam, the civil rights movement, and rising pressure for social change.

Police officers, for instance, became "sick and tired of being harassed, cursed, spit on, and shot at" (Juris & Feuille, 1973, p. 18). Especially in large urban areas, police found themselves working in an extremely hostile environment inhabited by militant Black people and students whose ire was often directed specifically at law enforcement personnel. Supreme Court decisions that restricted police discretion, such as *Miranda v. Arizona* (1966), and community demands for civilian review boards to assess alleged police misconduct were seen as threats to the officers' professional and personal well-being. At the same time, public officials lodged increasingly adamant demands for "law and order" and improved police protection for the community. To many police officers, these intense and often conflicting external pressures, when examined in conjunction with perceptions of low pay and antiquated personnel practices, became unbearable. The options, as Hirschman (1970) has pointed out, were exit (resign), voice (protest), or loyalty (suck it up). Some, indeed, decided to look for other, less demanding lines of work; others chose to suffer through the experience while awaiting retirement. Many, however, elected to give voice to their complaints through unions.

Figure 1.2 displays the rise in public employee unionization in relation to unionization in the private sector.

V. WHY GOVERNMENT WORKERS JOIN UNIONS—THE INDIVIDUAL PERSPECTIVE

Identifying the broad societal forces that precipitated and accompanied the growth in public sector unionization during the 1960s and 1970s provides only a partial explanation of the union phenomenon. To gain a more complete understanding of collective action within government employment, one must also consider the problem from a micro-perspective—or individual perspective. What persuades the individual government worker to join a union?

Extensive research clearly shows that American workers join unions because they are dissatisfied. They want higher wages and better benefits, job security participation in decision making, and protection of their rights as workers. Job-related conditions especially conducive to unionization include hazardous, physically demanding, or repetitive tasks; little input into job-related decisions; and

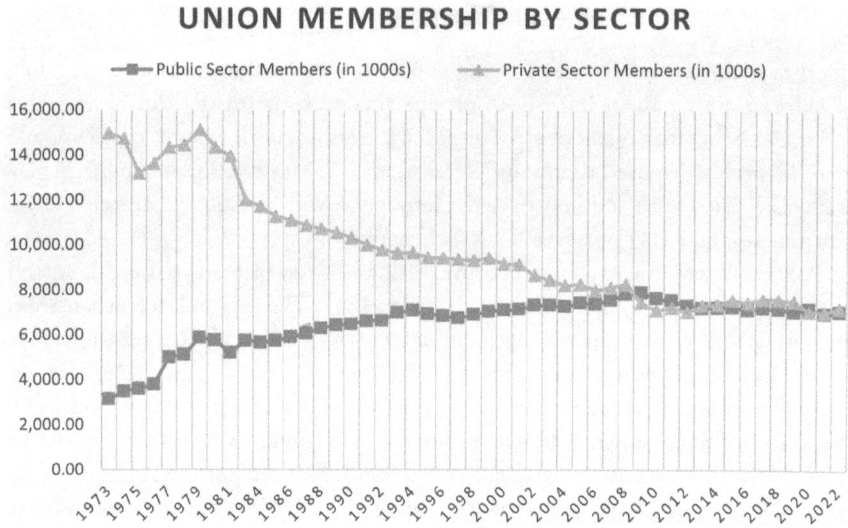

Figure 1.2 **Union membership, by public and private sectors, 1973–2023: the Union Membership and Coverage Database can be found at https://www.unionstats.com/. For the years 1973–1981, data were collected from the May Current Population Survey (CPS). For the years 1983–2012, data were collected from the CPS Outgoing Rotation Group Earnings Files. There were no union questions in the 1982 CPS.**

Source: From Hirsch, B. T., Macpherson, D. A, & Even, W. E. *The union membership and coverage database 2023*. https://www.unionstats.com/.

perceptions of arbitrary and unfair management actions and decisions (Hills, 1985; Sherer, 1987; Hundley, 1988; Premack & Hunter, 1988).

Seldom have political or ideological appeals persuaded U.S. workers to organize. Rather, the principal motive has been to improve conditions of employment through collective voice and action (Friedman et al., 2006). For blue-collar workers bread-and-butter economic issues are usually paramount. For white-collar workers, psychological reasons such as job security and the desire for a stronger voice in decision making are of somewhat greater significance (Kochan, 1980, p. 26). For almost all employees, job dissatisfaction "must be quite severe before a majority will support unionization as an option for improving these conditions" (Kochan, 1980, p. 26). Recent examples include janitors, nurses and other health-care providers, meat cutting and meatpacking plant workers, and agricultural laborers.

But dissatisfaction alone is not sufficient. Workers must also believe that union representation will be instrumental in securing the desired benefits and that the value of these benefits will exceed the costs associated with unionization. Race, gender, age, and life experiences also play a part in the propensity to join a union. Research indicates that women, African Americans, Latinos, the less educated, the young, and individuals who have been previously exposed to unions are more likely to join them, for example, than highly educated white males born of parents who are professionals (Leigh & Hills, 1987; Hundley, 1988; DeFreitas, 1993; Freeman et al., 2007; Martinez & Fiorito, 2009; Booth et al., 2010). No doubt these factors are related. For instance, historically women, African Americans, Latinos, and the less educated have had fewer opportunities for career advancement and thus may tend to see unions as a vehicle for gaining status and pay. Individuals with these union-friendly characteristics are also more likely to have union parents.

Union membership is still higher among men (10.5%) than women (9.6%), but the gap is closing. In 2022, African Americans (11.6%) had higher rates of union membership than Whites (10.0%), Latinos/Hispanics (9.0%), and Asians (8.3) (U.S. Bureau of Labor Statistics, 2023a, 2023b). Historically, women and minorities were systematically discriminated against by unions in both the public and private sectors. In the 1960s and early 1970s, however, the civil rights movement and the women's movement forged links with organized labor. The current pattern in which women, Latinos, and African Americans are joining unions reversed a long-term pattern in which these groups were least likely to join. Today, low-paid women and minority employees often have the most to gain from unions, and many public employee organizations in particular have recognized the potential for membership gains represented by unorganized minority groups, including recent immigrants.

The case of Latinos is complex and remains a work in progress for researchers. The Latino labor force has rapidly expanded in the United States, largely because of high immigration rates from the Caribbean, Central America, and Mexico. However, the growth rate of Latino union membership, although it now exceeds that of whites, has not kept pace with the increasing penetration of the labor force. Among the factors that may be depressing unionization among Latinos are immigration status, short duration of residence in the United States, and deficient English-language skills (DeFreitas, 1993, p. 285; Milkman, 2000; Briggs, 2001).

As this segment of the population continues to surge and unions fully recognize their organizing potential and reach out to Latinos, higher unionization rates are possible. The success of the "justice for janitors" campaign in organizing large numbers of Hispanic custodial workers in Los Angeles and San Diego, California, and many other cities is one indication of the potential for low-skilled, low-paid immigrants to join unions (Johnston, 1994; Devinatz, 2008). Heroic struggles by immigrant workers in New York City to overcome their "illegal" status, employer opposition, and the challenges of a new social and economic environment have been chronicled (Ness, 2005).

Overall, labor unions contribute to higher wages and better access to benefits for Latino workers. For example, in 2022, nonunion Latino workers' weekly earnings were 73% of those of union members ($804 versus $1087) (U.S. Bureau of Labor Statistics, 2023b). During the course of the pandemic, Latinos in labor unions experienced greater employment stability. This may be due in part to the types of jobs unionized Latinos held, management and professional, compared to non-unionized Latinos in service occupations. In addition, pandemic-related job losses were generally less severe in the public sector than in the private sector (Gonzalez & Galdemez, 2021). (Future prospects for public employee unions are addressed in Chapter 11.)

REFERENCES

AFL-CIO. (2019). *Report of the AFL-CIO commission on the future of work and unions*. https://aflcio.org/sites/default/files/2019-09/Report%20of%20the%20AFL-CIO%20Commission%20on%20the%20Future%20of%20Work%20and%20Unions_FINAL.pdf

AFL-CIO. (2022, June 12). *Liz Shuler elected AFL-CIO president at 2022 convention alongside secretary-treasurer Fred Redmond* [Press release]. https://aflcio.org/press/releases/liz-shuler-elected-afl-cio-president-22-convention-alongside-secretary-treasurer#:~:text=In%20her%20acceptance%20speech%2C%20Shuler%20delivered%20a%20call,moonshot%20to%20organize%20and%20activate%201%20million%20workers

Archer, R. (2010). *Why is there no labor party in the United States?*. Princeton University Press.

Baker v. Carr. (1962). 369 U.S. 186.

Barrett, T. (1973). Prospects for growth and bargaining in the public sector. *Government Employee Relations Report*, *534*, F1–F4.

Bennett, J. T., & Kaufman, B. E. (2002). *Future of private sector unionism in US*. M.E. Sharpe, Inc.

Bernstein, J. (1985, May). The evolution of the use of management consultants in labor relations: A labor perspective. *Labor Law Journal*, 292–299.

Booth, J. E., Budd, J. W., & Munday, K. M. (2010). First-timers and late-bloomers: Youth—adult unionization differences in a cohort of the US Labor Force. *ILR Review*, *64*(1), 53–73.

Briggs, V. M. (2001). *Immigration and American unionism*. Cornell University Press.

Bronfenbrenner, K., & Warren, D. (2011). The empirical case for streamlining the NLRB certification process: The role of date of unfair labor practice occurrence. ISERP Working Paper Series 2011.01. Institute for Social and Economic Research and Policy. Columbia University.

Buhle, P., & Schulman, N. (2005). *Wobblies! A graphic history of the industrial workers of the world*. Verso.

Commons, J. R. (1980). American shoemakers, 1648–1895. In R. L. Rowan (Ed.), *Readings in labor economics and labor relations* (4th ed., pp. 57–69). Irwin.

Commons, J. R., & Associates. (1936). *History of labor in the United States*. Macmillan.

Commonwealth v. Hunt (1842). 45 Mass. Ill, 38 Am. Dec. 346.

Coombs, C. K. (2008). The decline in American trade union membership and the "government substitution" hypothesis: A review of the econometric literature. *Journal of Labor Research*, *29*, 99–113.

Dark, T. E. (1999). *The unions and the democrats: An enduring alliance*. Cornell University Press.

DeFreitas, G. (1993). Unionization among ethnic and racial minorities. *Industrial and Labor Relations Review*, *46*(2), 284–301.

Devinatz, V. G. (2008). Social-movement unionism and US labor. *Journal of Collective Negotiations*, *32*(3).

Dreier, P. (2019, May 17). The man who put public-employee unions on the map. *The American Prospect*. https://prospect.org/labor/man-put-public-employee-unions-map/

Farber, H. S., & Western, B. (2001). Accounting for the decline of unions in the private sector: 1973–1998. *Journal of Labor Research*, *22*(3), 459–485.

Foner, P. S. (1984). *First facts of American labor*. Holmes and Meier.

Forbath, W. E. (1991). *Law and the shaping of the American labor movement*. Harvard University Press.

Francia, P. L. (2006). *The future of organized labor in American politics*. Columbia University Press.

Fraser, S. (1998, Summer). Is democracy good for unions? *Dissent, 45*, 33–39.

Freeman, R. B., Boxall, P. F., & Haynes, P. (Eds.). (2007). *What workers say: Employee voice in the Anglo-American workplace*. Cornell University Press.

Freeman, R. B., & Kleiner, M. M. (1990, April). Employee behavior in the face of union organizing drives. *Industrial and Labor Relations Review, 43*, 351–365.

Freeman, R. B., & Medoff, J. L. (1984). *What do unions do?* Basic.

Friedman, B. A., Abraham, S. E., & Thomas, R. K. (2006). Factors related to employees' desire to join and leave unions. *Industrial Relations*, *45*(1), 102–110.

Gagala, K. (1983). *Union organizing and staying organized*. Reston Publishing.

Galenson, W. (1980). Why the American labor movement is not socialist. In R. L. Rowan (Ed.), *Readings in labor economics and labor relations* (4th ed., pp. 70–80). Irwin.

Godard, J. (2009). The exceptional decline of the American labor movement. *ILR Review*, *63*(1), 82–108.

Goldfield, M. (1987). *The decline of organized labor in the United States*. University of Chicago Press.

Gonzalez, N., & Galdemez, M. (2021). *More than solidarity: How labor unions preserved Latino jobs*. UCLA Latino Politics Institute. https://latino.ucla.edu/wp-content/uploads/2021/09/More-than-Solidarity-How-Labor-Unions-Preserved-Latino-Jobs-1.pdf

Green, J. (2006). *Death in the haymarket: A story of Chicago, the first labor movement and the bombing that divided guilded age America*. Pantheon Books.

Greenhouse, S. (2014). Advocates for workers raise the ire of business. *The New York Times*, B1. https://www.nytimes.com/2014/01/17/business/as-worker-advocacy-groups-gain-momentum-businesses-fight-back.html

Gross, J. A. (1995). *Broken promise: The subversion of U.S. labor policy 1947–1994*. Temple University Press.

Hills, S. M. (1985, January). The attitudes of union and nonunion male workers toward union representation. *Industrial and Labor Relations Review, 38*, 179–194.

Hirsch, B., MacPherson, D., & Even, W. (2023). *Union membership and coverage database*. http://www.unionstats.com/

Hirschman, A. (1970). *Exit, voice, and loyalty*. Harvard University Press.

Hoxie, R. F. (1928). *Trade unionism in the United States*. Appleton.

Hundley, G. (1988, Fall). Who joins unions in the public sector? The effects of individual characteristics and the law. *Journal of Labor Research*, *9*, 301–323.

Johnston, P. (1994). *Success while others fail: Social movement unionism and the public workplace*. Cornell University Press.

Juris, H., & Feuille, P. (1973). *Police unionism*. Heath.

Kearney, R. C. (2003). Patterns of union decline and growth: An organizational ecology perspective. *Journal of Labor Research*, *24*(4), 561–578.

Kleiner, M. M. (2001, Summer). Intensity of management resistance: Understanding the decline of unionization in the private sector. *Journal of Labor Research*, *22*(3) 528–532.

Kochan, T. A. (1980). *Collective bargaining and industrial relations*. Irwin.

Kramer, L. (1962). *Labor's paradox*. Wiley.

Leigh, D. E., & Hills, S. M. (1987, Spring). Male-female differences in the potential for union growth outside traditionally unionized industries. *Journal of Labor Research, 8*, 131–142.

Logan, J. (2019). The new union avoidance internationalism. *Work Organisation, Labour & Globalisation*, *13*(2), 57–77.

Martinez, A. D., & Fiorito, J. (2009). General feelings toward unions and employers as predictors of union voting intent. *Journal of Labor Research*, *30*, 120–134.

Mattina, A. F. (2009). Lowell female labor reform association. In I. Ness (Ed.), *The international encyclopedia of revolution and protest*. https://doi.org/10.1002/9781405198073.wbierp0926

Milkman, R. (2000). *Organizing immigrants: The challenge for unions in contemporary California*. ILR Press.

Miranda v. Arizona. (1966). 384 U.S. 436.

Moskow, M. H., Loewenberg, J. J., & Koziara, E. C. (1970). *Collective bargaining in public employment*. Random House.

Naidu, S. (2022). Is there any future for a US labor movement? *Journal of Economic Perspectives*, *36*(4), 3–28.

Nesbitt, M. B. (1976). *Labor relations in the federal government service*. The Bureau of National Affairs.

Ness, I. (2005). *Immigrants, unions, and the new U.S. labor market*. Temple University Press.

Neumann, G. R., & Rissman, E. R. (1984). Where have all the union members gone?. *Journal of Labor Economics*, *2*(2), 175–192.

Olson, M. (1965). *The logic of collective action*. Harvard University Press.

Perlman, S. (1928). *Theory of the labor movement*. Macmillan.

Phelan, C. (2000). *Grand master workman: Terence powderly and the knights of labor*. Greenwood Press.

Premack, S. L., & Hunter, J. E. (1988). Individual unionization decisions. *Psychological Bulletin*, *103*(2), 223–234.

Rachlett, P. (1999). *Learning from the past to build for the future* (pp. 87–96, R. M. Tillman & M. S. Cummings, Eds.). Lynne Rienner.

Reder, M. W. (1988, Spring). The rise and fall of unions: The public sector and the private. *Journal of Economic Perspectives*, *2*, 89–110.

Reynolds v. Simms. (1964). 84 S. Ct. 1362.

Rosemont, F. (2002). *Joe Hill, the IWW and the making of a revolutionary workingclass counterculture*. Charles H. Kerr Publishing Company.

Salmond, J. A. (2004). *Southern struggles: The southern labor movement and the civil rights struggle*. University of Florida Press.

Schattschneider, E. E. (1988). *The Semisovereign people. A realist's view of democracy in America*. Harcourt Brace Jovanovich College Publishers.

Shaw, L. C., & Clark, T., Jr. (1972, August). Collective bargaining and politics in public employment. *UCLA Law Review*, *19*, 887–1051.

Sherer, P. D. (1987). The workplace dissatisfaction model of unionism: What are its implications for organizing blacks and women? In *IRRA 40th annual proceedings* (pp. 135–141). Industrial Relations Research Association.

Shutt, R. K. (1986). *Organizations in a changing environment*. State University of New York Press.

Slater, J. E. (2004). *Public workers: Government employees unions. The law, and the state, 1900–1962*. Cornell University Press.

Sloane, A. A., & Witney, F. (1981). *Labor relations* (4th ed.). Prentice-Hall.

Smith, R. M. (2003). *From blackjacks to briefcases: A history of commercialized strikebreaking and unionbusting in the United States*. Ohio University Press.

Spero, S. D. (1948). *Government as employer*. Southern Illinois University Press.

Spero, S. D., & Capozzola, J. M. (1973). *The urban community and its unionized bureaucracies*. Dunellen.

Stegner, W. (1990). *Joe Hill: A biographical novel*. Penguin Books.

Stieber, J. (1973). *Public employee unionism*. The Brookings Institution.

Tannenbaum, F. (1921). *The labor movement, its conservative functions and social consequences*. Putnam.

Tillman, R. M., & Cummings, M. S. (1999). *The transformation of U.S. unions: Voices, visions and strategies from the grassroots*. Lynne Rienner.

U.S. Bureau of Labor Statistics. (2023a). *Economic news release: Union members summary*. https://www.bls.gov/news.release/union2.htm#union_a05.f.1

U.S. Bureau of Labor Statistics. (2023b). *Labor force statistics from the current population survey*. https://www.bls.gov/cps/cpsaat22.htm

Washington Federation of State Employees. (n.d.). *WFSE civil rights*. https://www.wfse.org/wfse-civil-rights

Webb, S., & Webb, B. (1897). *Industrial democracy*. Longmans.

Chapter 2

Unions Today

I. INTRODUCTION

This chapter surveys the organizational landscape of public employee unions including the factors that are correlated with unionization. The key term is diversity. For virtually every generalization about public employee unions, there are noteworthy exceptions. Public sector unions vary along many dimensions and across levels of government and the nonprofit sector. They are different in terms of affiliation. Some are federated with national organizations such as the AFL–CIO. Others are local independent organizations with no national affiliation. Some unions representing government workers also organize and bargain for workers in the private and nonprofit sectors (e.g., Service Employees International Union [SEIU]). Others (e.g., the Fraternal Order of Police [FOP]) essentially restrict their boundaries to public employees. There are unions with membership rolls numbering more than 1 million, and there are unions whose ranks are counted in double digits. The occupations of union members are also highly diverse. Clerical personnel, firefighters, nurses, social workers, welders, physicians, architects, and university professors all work under union banners. Wherever workers experience high levels of job dissatisfaction, unionization is a possibility.

II. THE FEDERAL GOVERNMENT

Despite the early recognition in a presidential executive order of federal employees' right to organize, federal unions operate within a legal framework much less favorable than that which governs private sector labor relations. The scope of bargaining in federal labor relations is quite restricted; federal employees represented by bargaining units do not have to join the union, and there is a strong no-strike policy. Federal employee unions represented 28.2% of the 3.99 million civilian workforce (including postal workers) in 2023 (U.S. Bureau of Labor Statistics [BLS], 2024).

DOI:10.4324/9781003403593-2

Between 1964 (the first year for which such data were collected) and 1968 federal employee union membership figures climbed rapidly to about half of the total federal civilian workforce. The high watermark was 1987, when 59% of federal employees were covered by collective bargaining agreements. But dramatic reductions in the size of federal employment, particularly through outsourcing of union-dense blue-collar and technical jobs, have driven down the number and percentage of employees represented by unions.

Federal labor relations policy, as embedded today in the Civil Service Reform Act of 1978 and subsequent agency-specific legislation and presidential executive orders (see Chapter 3), severely constrains the potential influence of federal unions on wages, benefits, and working conditions. It is important to note that federal law prohibits membership-enhancing union security provisions such as the Fair Share, which requires individuals whom the union represents in collective bargaining to either join the union or pay their "fair share" of union dues for representational expenses. This provides an ideal situation for encouraging free riders, who enjoy the benefits of union representation in collective bargaining and grievance procedures, but who are not required to contribute out of their own paychecks for union services. Free riders pose a serious problem for federal unions, which are mandated by law to represent, equally and fairly, all members of their bargaining units, whether they belong to the union or not. Financial resources are the primary measure of a union's strength and ability to finance representational and political activities, and members' dues make up a substantial proportion of such financial assets.

Many federal employees are, indeed, free riders. For example, the largest federal union, the American Federation of Government Employees (AFGE), represented approximately 750,000 bargaining unit members in 2023, but less than half of them were dues-paying members (AFGE, 2023a, 2023b). All told, out of the approximately 3.9 million full-time wage and salary workers in the federal government only about one-quarter actually belong to a union and pay dues (BLS, 2024).

The most notable exception to this pattern of free riding is the U.S. Postal Service. As noted in Chapter 1, postal workers were instrumental in early federal employee unionization efforts. They are the most highly organized of all federal workers today. They enjoy their own statutory framework, which was won in the aftermath of a 1970 postal strike. As a consequence, postal unions have full private sector collective bargaining rights, with the exception of union security provisions and the right to strike. Postal union membership figures are almost equal to the proportion under contract, about 90%. The near absence of a free-rider problem for postal unions is attributable to these superior bargaining rights and, in turn, to the union's greater success in winning improvements in wages, benefits, and working conditions from management.

Federal employee unions represent workers in nearly every agency, from the U.S. Department of Agriculture to the U.S. Information Agency. The largest number of represented employees are civilian workers for the Department of Defense and the departments of Homeland Security, Veterans' Affairs, and Treasury. Some 100 unions represent employees in at least one federal bargaining unit; the National Treasury Employees Union (NTEU) alone represents about 87,250 federal workers in 35 different agencies and departments (Bur, 2021; NTEU, 2023).

It is useful to review briefly the principal federal unions and some of their distinctive characteristics. The largest federal union, AFGE, represents 750,000 federal and District of Columbia government employees. AFGE was created by the AFL–CIO in 1932 when a preexisting organization, the National Federation of Federal Employees (NFFE), withdrew from the AFL–CIO over jurisdictional and policy conflicts.

AFGE membership today is heaviest in the District of Columbia area and, somewhat surprisingly, in the Southeast, where large numbers of civilians are employed in military facilities. AFGE has substantial minority and female representation both in the rank and file and in leadership positions. Its current national president, Everett Kelley, and National Secretary Treasurer, Eric Bunn, are African American. Jeremy Lannan, the national vice president for women and fair practices, is the first openly gay person elected to a top leadership position with AFGE.

Employees represented by the AFGE include approximately 32,000 National Guard dual-status technicians across the country. In 2016 the Ohio National Guard unilaterally ended the collective bargaining relationship with its local upon contract expiration. After a lengthy battle, the Supreme Court ruled in 2023 that the technicians have collective bargaining rights under Federal Labor Relations Authority (FLRA) (AFGE, 2023c).

In 2022 the AFGE won an election to represent professional and nonprofessional employees at the Defense Health Agency (DHA). Established in 2013 as a relatively small agency, the DHA provides support for joint operating forces and combat. In recent years the DHA has grown dramatically as part of the largest reorganization in the Department of Defense (DOD) since 1947. The AFGE is seeking to represent all health care workers among the 45,000 civilian employees who have been transferred to DHA. To date, AFGE has won FLRA decisions to represent workers in DHA headquarters and 17 markets. In 2023 the AFGE created a new local that aims to represent over 10,000 federal employees working for U.S. DOD and other government agencies in Europe (AFGE, 2023d).

Former AFGE president Kenneth Blaylock helped convince convention delegates in 1976 to approve a resolution supporting extension of the union's jurisdiction to military personnel. Although a vote of the total membership soundly defeated the resolution, merely raising the issue was enough to generate severe consternation and apprehension in the defense establishment and, subsequently, in Congress.

Ostensibly, the American military would appear to offer a ripe environment for union organizers. Pay is low in relation to comparable work for private defense contractors, and many civilian jobs (although benefits are competitive or even superior) and working conditions certainly do not rank among the finest, or for that matter, the safest. In addition, a highly defined and rigorously enforced division exists between military "management" and "labor," represented by distinctions in uniformed dress, privileges, and other factors, creating a natural and sometimes intense adversarial relationship between officers and enlisted personnel. Not of least importance to the unions is the huge number of potential members in the active military (more than 1.3 million in 2023).

Organization of the armed forces in several Western European nations (e.g., Germany, Holland, Sweden, and Belgium) shows that military unionization is feasible. However, some rather serious objections may be lodged. The strike issue is of obvious importance, as is the matter of maintaining military discipline. Other troubling questions involve allocation of less desirable job assignments, effective representation of diverse military occupations by a single large union, and the potential scope of bargaining. Joining a labor union or organizing military personnel by any union is prohibited by federal law and a Department of Defense directive. Civilian workers in defense establishments may belong to unions, but uniformed personnel may not.

As AFGE's major competitor, NFFE has historically assumed a lower profile in its organizing and political tactics. NFFE began in 1917 as an affiliate of the AFL but withdrew in 1931 largely because of opposition to the strike and other aspects of collective bargaining as practiced by AFL affiliates in the private sector. NFFE even opposed the conservative provisions of Executive Order 10988 for some time. The timid posture of the organization led to steady declines in its membership until 1967, when new leadership was elected. NFFE, like AFGE, then purged a no-strike pledge from its constitution and assumed a more active political posture. NFFE, currently affiliated with the International Association of Machinists and Aerospace Workers (110,000 employees covered by collective bargaining agreements in 39 agencies and departments), is much smaller than AFGE and suffers even more from the free-rider problem.

The third largest federal organization, with 87,250 employees covered under bargaining agreements in 35 federal entities, is NTEU. NTEU is a nonaffiliated union that began in the Internal Revenue Service in 1938 (as the National Association of Collectors of Internal Revenue) and has since expanded throughout the Department of the Treasury and other federal agencies. Its aggressive organizing drives made NTEU one of the fastest growing federal unions, and it enjoys a higher percentage of dues-paying members than most other federal unions.

The National Air Traffic Controllers Association (about 20,000 air traffic controllers, engineers, and safety-related professionals) rose from the ashes of the Professional Air Traffic Controllers Organization, which was effectively destroyed by the actions of President Ronald Reagan. Two major associations (the Senior Executives Association and the Federal Managers Association) represent upper-level federal employees in lobbying the president and the Congress for improvements in compensation and working conditions and greater respect for the public service, but under federal law they cannot engage in collective bargaining. The Federal Managers Association claims to represent the interests of 200,000 federal supervisors, managers, and executives.

Postal employees, who officially work for a quasi-government corporation, are represented by several major organizations. The oldest, the National Association of Letter Carriers (206,000 active-duty letter carriers), was founded in 1889 and later became an affiliate of the AFL–CIO. The other, larger postal organization is the American Postal Workers Union (295,000 members), formed in 1971 through an amalgamation of five smaller organizations that represented clerks, carriers, and crafts workers. Other postal organizations of significance today are the National Rural Letter Carriers Association (97,000 members) and the National Postal Mail Handlers Union (47,000 members) (see Table 2.1).

Prospects for membership growth in postal unions are rather dismal. With membership figures already around 90%, postal unions can gain little or no benefit from attempting to enlist the remaining represented (but nonunion) workers. Continuing technological changes, and competition from private firms such as Amazon, United Parcel Service, DHL, and Federal Express, along with years of rising operating deficits that have exhausted the patience of Congress, have resulted in large job cuts in the postal service.

Recurring threats to privatize the U.S. Postal Service present additional challenges. In 2013 Postmaster General Patrick R. Donahoe attempted to end the Saturday delivery of mail and launched an effort to install mini post offices in Staples stores (Ecker, 2018). A presidential task force convened in 2018 to assess the on the U.S. Postal System concluded that it was on an untenable path and proposed full or partial privatization (Martin & Titolo, 2020). In 2020, Postmaster General Louis DeJoy banned employee overtime, limited truck trips from mail processing centers, and removed mail collection boxes in urban and rural areas, reduced postal retail hours, and ordered 671 mail-sorting machines to be dismantled (Rubio, 2021). The Postal Reform Act of 2022, signed into law in April 2022,

Table 2.1 Major Postal Employee Unions, 2023

Organization	*Membership*
American Postal Workers Union	222,000
National Association of Letter Carriers	295,000
National Rural Letter Carriers Association	97,000
National Postal Mail Handlers Union	47,000

Source: Data from union websites (http://www.apwu.org, http://www.nalc.org, http://www.nrlca.org, http://www.npmhu.org).

provides some stability to the future of postal service but the prospects of bipartisan efforts in the future remain uncertain

Prospects seem equally doubtful for the other federal unions, most of which remain unable to bargain over the important issues of wages and benefits and continue to lack union security provisions that would allow them to increase their dues paying membership. Far-reaching reductions in force, since 1992, have reduced the absolute number of civilian jobs, translating directly into membership losses and a concomitant weakening of federal union strength and influence. Although small gains were made in organizing federal employees and enforcing workplace rights, the fortunes of federal employees shift with presidential elections, that is the president of the United States can shape federal employees' workplace rights and working conditions through executive orders and appointments of agency directors.

III. NONPROFIT ORGANIZATIONS

Churches, some schools, charities, hospitals, clubs and fraternal organizations, credit unions, lobbying organizations, museums, and even labor unions themselves are nonprofit organizations. Although there are various legal distinctions based on state and federal law, as organizations with 501(c) tax-exempt status under the Internal Revenue Code, all nonprofit organizations exist for purposes other than generating profits. They rest uneasily in a vast and expanding gray area of organizational society: neither government nor business but typically partnering or otherwise interacting with both. They range in size from a one-woman day care center to a massive hospital complex.

The nonprofit or "third sector" is an attractive organizational arena for unions. The nonprofit sector encompasses many of the nations' fastest growing occupations and organizing in the nonprofit sector has gathered speed in recent years. For example, health care occupations are projected to have 1.8 million openings per year over the period of 2023–2032 (BLS, 2023a). Hospitals and other health-care organizations account for the largest portion of the nonprofit sector's resources, making them particularly tempting targets for union organizing. Other targeted organizations social service providers, museums, policy think tanks, and advocacy organizations.

Employee characteristics also play a role in the upsurge. Nonprofit employees tend to be younger, progressive, and altruistic (Rendon, 2023). Women typically outnumber men in nonprofit organizations. In 2022, roughly two-thirds of those employed in the nonprofit sector were women (BLS, 2023b). Caregiving tasks and emotional labor that are typical in social service agencies are often undervalued. Both groups of workers have traditionally been expected to donate labor in service of the organizational mission. Many nonprofit employees have turned to unions as a way to improve their standard of living and working conditions and to preserve professional autonomy (Pynes, 2017).

Labor statistics resources do not permit identification of the extent of union membership and representation in the sector. Existing data are sketchy, although it is known that a significant portion of the membership of SEIU, AFSCME, National Nurses United, Office and Professional Employees International Union (OPEIU), and other unions with significant presence in the third sector is composed of nonprofit workers. Moreover, the Nonprofit Professional Employees Union (NPEU-IFPTE) is focused specifically on representing the nonprofit sector. Since 2018, NPEIU expanded from representing 300 workers across 12 employers to representing 1,500 workers in 50 organizations (Rendon, 2023). Similarly, Nonprofit Employees United (a division of OPEIU) represents nonprofit union members who work in advocacy and social service organizations across the country. From 2019 to 2023, NPU added 68 nonprofits to its roster of organized workplaces (Rendon, 2023). As will be discussed in Chapter 3, nonprofit workers are incorporated within the provisions of the National Labor Relations Act, which governs employer–employee relations in the private sector.

IV. STATE AND LOCAL GOVERNMENT

Opposition to public sector bargaining intensified after the financial crisis of 2008 and converged in Northern industrial states such as Wisconsin, Michigan, Ohio, and New Jersey. This trend was driven in part by the American Legislative Exchange Council (ALEC), an advocacy organization that endorses limited government, free markets, and federalism and designs "model policies" for state and local governments. ALEC's model legislation served as the basis for many of the efforts to rescind public sector collective bargaining rights at the state and local levels.

Beyond the legislatures, three U.S. Supreme Court cases focused on overturning the precedent set in *Abood v. Detroit Board of Education* (1977) for an agency fee requirement. That is, public employees who chose not to join a union that had been democratically elected were required to pay an "agency" or "fair share" fee to cover the costs of non-political activities that the union incurs for collective bargaining. In the first of these cases, *Harris v. Quinn* (2014), the U.S. Supreme Court ruled that the collection of agency fees from home care workers who do not wish to join or support the union was unconstitutional. In the second case, *Friedrichs v. California Teachers Association* (2015), the court deadlocked in June 2016. In the third case *Janus v. American Federation of State, County, and Municipal Employees, Council 31* (2018) the court overturned *Abood* on the grounds that it interfered with public employees' free speech rights. Since unions have a legal duty to represent all workers in the bargaining unit, the ruling on this case poses an enormous free-rider problem for public sector unions.

In 2023, according to the U.S. Bureau of Labor Statistics, 30% of state government employees and 39% of local government employees belonged to labor organizations. When occupation is considered, the most heavily organized are protective service occupations, followed by education, training, and library occupations (BLS, 2024).

A. Determinants of State and Local Unionization

Econometric models have been reasonably successful in explaining private sector unionization, assisted, from a practical perspective, by a national legal setting that places all private workers and employers on an equal footing under the National Labor Relations Act and its amendments. These econometric models indicate that levels of unionization are influenced by wage and benefit levels, the rate of unemployment, urbanization, region, "right-to-work" laws, and various worker- and job-related characteristics. What they largely miss, due to a lack of data, is the contribution of worker dissatisfaction to unionization.

Determining the correlates of state and local unionization is more problematic because of the complex legal environment (one set of laws for federal workers and 50 sets for the states, plus numerous executive orders, local ordinances, legal rulings, provisions, and practices). It is well accepted that organizational membership is closely related to the presence and scope of state bargaining legislation. Those states with the most permissive legal environment report the highest levels of union membership. Table 2.2 provides information about organized state and local employees for all 50 states, the presence or absence of collective bargaining laws, and a measure of state political ideology.

The relationship between public employee labor relations policy and unionization, however, recalls the chicken and egg dilemma. This intriguing question of which comes first receives further discussion in Chapter 3; for now, let it suffice to note that the relationship is reciprocal: political pressure from unions helps foster favorable policy outcomes from the state and local legislative processes, and, at the same time, union organizing drives have been aided greatly by laws encouraging or mandating collective bargaining.

Economic models are not particularly helpful for understanding or explaining public sector unionization. A more useful approach is to treat unionization in government as a socioeconomic, political, and policy phenomenon. Figure 2.1 displays a suggestive comprehensive model that identifies the direct and indirect effects of the state's socioeconomic environment, the political culture, the state political system, and labor relations policy.

As shown in Table 2.2, unionization is lowest in the Sunbelt states, such as Arizona, Arkansas, Mississippi, North Carolina, South Carolina, Texas, and Virginia. Clearly, collective bargaining laws make a difference in levels of unionization. Even within a single state, the salience of law can be seen. State labor relations policy

Table 2.2 Bargaining Status, Political Ideology, and Union Density, 2022

State	*State Collective Bargaining Law*[a]	*Local Bargaining*	*Citizen Political Ideology Score (2016)*[b]	*State Union Density (2022)*[c]
Alabama		Local Government	38.24081802	8.4
Alaska	X	All	50.63251114	17.3
Arizona		None	44.4156189	6.2
Arkansas		None	41.90975189	5.7
California	X	All	64.17390442	17.6
Colorado	X[d]	None	52.40300751	7.5
Connecticut	X	All	97.00153351	15.4
Delaware	X	All	70.44623566	9.4
Florida	X	All	52.07305145	5.6
Georgia		All	47.78772354	5.4
Hawaii	X	All	77.92569733	23.4
Idaho		Firefighters/ teachers	24.30561829	5.9
Illinois	X	All	62.8222847	14.1
Indiana		Teachers	41.66567993	8.6
Iowa		All	54.41446686	8.7
Kansas	Y	All	40.06189728	12.1
Kentucky		Police/Firefighters	45.85549545	10.3
Louisiana		None	45.0276413	5.2
Maine	X	All	63.92627716	11.5
Maryland	X	Education/Park/ Police/Local Government	62.58415222	13.2
Massachusetts	X	All	79.93876648	13.8
Michigan	X	All	58.04266357	15.3
Minnesota	X	All	56.31476212	15.2
Mississippi		None	45.52982712	7.2
Missouri	X[e]	All	47.35276794	10.6
Montana	X	All	43.05156326	12.3
Nebraska	X	All	30.71600723	8.1
Nevada		All	57.18942261	12.8

(*Continued*)

Table 2.2 (Continued)

State	*State Collective Bargaining Law*[a]	*Local Bargaining*	*Citizen Political Ideology Score (2016)*[b]	*State Union Density (2022)*[c]
New Hampshire	X	All	58.11856079	11.2
New Jersey	X	All	66.74701691	16
New Mexico	X	All	60.1779213	10.6
New York	X	All	74.57221985	22.1
North Carolina		None	52.38257217	3.9
North Dakota	Y	Teachers/All Local Government	26.52579308	7.6
Ohio	X	All	50.38021088	14
Oklahoma		None	23.98082542	7.1
Oregon	X	All	63.08698273	16.9
Pennsylvania	X	All	53.0580864	13.6
Rhode Island	X	All	81.67412567	17.7
South Carolina		None	46.05901337	2
South Dakota	X	All	38.08566284	4.2
Tennessee		None	42.01704788	6.3
Texas		Police/Firefighters	44.41168976	5.1
Utah		Teachers	28.80175591	8.7
Vermont	X	All	85.57233429	13.4
Virginia		Limited[f]	50.68711472	4.5
Washington	X	All	59.90585709	19.1
West Virginia	Y	All	32.55799484	10
Wisconsin		None	53.82595062	8
Wyoming		Firefighters	28.2977047	7.3

[a] "X" denotes collective bargaining. "Y" denotes meet and confer.

[b] Citizen political ideology scores were calculated by Berry et al. (2007). Lower scores denote political conservatism; higher scores denote political liberalism. Data are current as of 2016. https://rcfording.wordpress.com/state-ideology-data/

[c] Union density refers to the percentage of employees represented by unions (union coverage) in each state. Data are current as of 2022. https://www.bls.gov/news.release/union2.t05.htm.

[d] Collective bargaining granted through executive order.

[e] Collective bargaining granted through court decision.

[f] State law allows bargaining at the local government level if the county, city, or town grants the authority through a local ordinance or resolution.

may be the single most critical element that determines the fortunes of unions in state and local government.

In 2011–2012, collective bargaining laws fell under a determined Republican-led assault in several states, including Wisconsin (where bargaining rights were eliminated for all but police and firefighters), Ohio, Tennessee (teachers), Oklahoma (local government), Idaho (teachers), and other states. In these and other states, a significant shift in the political climate has resulted in shocking membership losses. In Wisconsin, union membership dropped from 50% to 37% in a single year (Gilbert, 2013).

Following the *Janus* decision, a few states have enacted laws to safeguard and promote public sector unionization. For their part, unions have devised new tactics to organize workers in the current legal environment. There has also been an increase in worker activism, although this may be due in part to the pandemic and social unrest related to high profile racial incidents and social inequities (Hodges, 2021). Although public sector unions lost fee payers, they have not suffered a drastic loss of members. In some cases, unions have experienced a slight uptick in membership (DiSalvo, 2019).

The socioeconomic environment portrayed in Figure 2.1 may be operationalized through variables such as wealth (personal or family income), level of education, unemployment rate, urbanization, and manufacturing. Wealth and high levels of urbanization and manufacturing activity were conventionally conducive to unionization in industry, which in turn became correlated with government unionization. Historically, bad economic times and government fiscal crises, such as the 2008 Great Recession, were accompanied by retrenchment and reductions in force, which slowed unionization. High unemployment inhibits unionization because employees are concerned about layoffs and hesitate to jeopardize their jobs by joining a union.

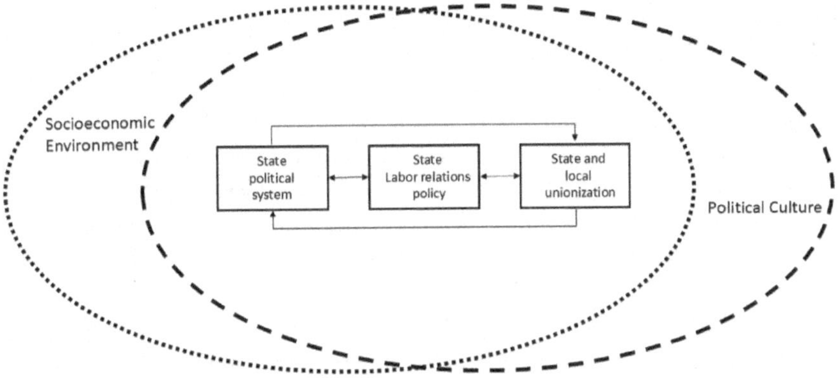

Figure 2.1 A comprehensive model of state and local government unionization.

Traditionally, education levels tended to be inversely related to unionization because a highly educated workforce earns good pay, has more individualized bargaining power, has better working conditions, and generally perceives less need for unionization. However, this changed with the COVID-19 pandemic. Perhaps due to the collective trauma, burnout, and the always on call nature of remote work, more highly educated workers are forming and joining unions, from Starbucks baristas to pharmacists and doctors.

Political culture shapes unionization through historical and demographic forces. As originally formulated by Elazar (1966), a traditionalistic culture, with its elitist and paternalistic elements, should be hostile to unions, as certainly has been the case in the South. A moralistic political culture is more conducive to unions, with its emphasis on equity, collective choice, and "doing good." The individualistic political culture views politics as a marketplace, with the primary purpose of government and politics being the furtherance of individual and business interests. Thus, unions face greater obstacles in states with such a culture than in moralistic states, but through effective political action they can win bargaining rights.

Political culture is related to ideology. States characterized by political liberalism (typically Democratic "Blue States") are more favorable toward unions than are politically conservative states. Political ideology also helps determine public policy in the states. As shown by Berry et al. (2007), changes in citizens' "policy mood" can lead to policy change by influencing the actions of state and local officials. The expectation is that collective bargaining finds a friendlier policy environment in politically liberal states than in conservative states. Evidence for this expectation is shown in Table 2.2.

Obviously, political culture, socioeconomic environment, and political ideology have a strong regional bias. A brief look at unionization in the Sunbelt states demonstrates that conclusion. Generally speaking, the Sunbelt states (those below the Mason–Dixon Line and extending to the West Coast) do not have the characteristics that have been associated with unionization in other regions. Although Sunbelt growth has been generally accompanied by gains in urbanization, industrialization, and economic diversity; a healthy business climate; and massive in-migration of people from other regions and countries, unions in neither government nor industry have done an effective job of attracting members and winning bargaining rights. Two special factors seem to be operating in the Sunbelt to discourage unionization: the political culture and ideology, on the one hand, and determined union resistance tactics by employers on the other. The latter is at least partly a product of the former.

To preserve the values comprising traditional political culture, employers in the Sunbelt have become highly sophisticated in applying union resistance tactics. Some, such as the meat packing and processing company Smithfield Foods, have regularly employed extralegal means to fight off the unions. In 2021, Amazon fought off an organizing campaign in Bessemer Alabama using a variety of tactics including distributing inaccurate lists of employees, describing other ways to spend money than paying union dues, and telling workers they don't have to pay dues in Alabama. Amazon spent $4.3 million on anti-union consultants in 2021. It also fired the lead organizer in the campaign. Amazon eventually reinstated the organizer after she filed a complaint with the NLRB.

Most firms and many governments, however, have practiced the more gentle union suppression tactics of "positive human resource management," which involves offering competitive wages and benefits, good working conditions, and participative decision-making programs. Whatever rubric management assigns to the activity, unions tend to perceive it as at best union-averse behavior and at worst "union-busting." Often, specialized law firms and management consulting firms are retained to direct the employer's antiunion strategies and train employers in "union-avoidance" tactics. Although these strategies and a predominantly antiunion climate are also in evidence in other portions of the United States, they are strongest in the Sunbelt.

Large gains in public sector union membership and influence do not seem likely in the Sunbelt, unless permissive legislation is enacted or union-friendly governors issue executive orders extending collective bargaining rights. These possibilities, in turn, presume a shift in public mood in favor of bargaining (Berry et al., 2007). In most of the Sunbelt, a vicious cycle seems to be present in which the traditionalistic, conservative political culture, conservative political ideology, Republican legislative and executive branch majorities, and the absence of union strength diminish the chances of new collective bargaining legislation, and in the absence of a favorable legal environment, union membership gains remain arduous.

Nonetheless, there is some basis for not writing off all prospects for union growth in the region. The area continues to prosper economically and to develop characteristics similar to geographic areas with more highly unionized states Surveys have reported a strong reservoir of potential support for unions in the region, particularly among Latinos and African Americans. Moreover, population shifts and socioeconomic change have influenced political ideology, tending to make it less conservative. The problems, however, remain substantial. Unions have not yet discovered a means to break through the barriers of politically conservative influences and adapt to the abiding conditions and norms of the region.

Looking again at Figure 2.1, it can be seen that the state political system is linked to the socioeconomic environment and to political culture and ideology. The state political system encompasses factors such as executive–legislative relations, legislative professionalism, interparty competition, and the political and economic strength of private sector unions. For example, competitive two-party states should be more conducive to unionization because union interests are more likely to receive legislative representation. Similarly, a strong Democratic Party presence in the three branches of state government should facilitate unionization in government; traditionally (and to this day), Democrats have been more "pro-labor" than the "pro-business" Republicans.

Why, today, are government workers organized in much larger proportions (about 5:1) than workers in private sector employment? There are several major reasons. One reason is the legal environment, which, with the exception of the nonbargaining states, is more amenable to signing up members and keeping them on the rolls than the private sector legal environment under the National Labor Relations Act. Second, most public employees are protected by a blanket of civil service rules and regulations that prevent management from firing them for engaging in union activities. Third, a prime objective of unions is greater worker participation in decision making, and there is evidence that managers in government organizations are generally more willing to share authority and decision making than their counterparts in business (Morse, 2008; Morse et al., 2007). Part of this willingness is no doubt associated with the prevalence of highly educated professional and white-collar employees in many government organizations and the sense that both management and labor are working "for the people." Finally, government managers have much less to gain from actively opposing unions than do business managers.

B. Employee Organizations in State and Local Government

Public employee organizations may be categorized according to several characteristics. The first important distinction is between associations and unions. State and local government employee associations were organized in the first half of the twentieth century as mutual benefit and service-providing organizations (Stieber, 1973, p. 8). These early organizations provided credit unions, group benefit plans for health and life insurance, and other member services; some even handled grievances. Although most associations were concerned with serving their members and, in some cases, enhancing the status of various government-related professions, they also engaged in legislative and executive branch lobbying activities in efforts to win favorable treatment for their members. However, these early employee associations did not seek collective bargaining as the fundamental means for winning improved wages, benefits, and working conditions from government employers.

A second type of categorization involves the nature of the employer. Some of the public employee unions are primarily public, such as the FOP, whereas others are mixed membership unions claiming membership in government and industry and, increasingly, in the nonprofit sector as well. Examples of mixed membership unions are SEIU, the International Brotherhood of Teamsters (IBT), and, increasingly, AFSCME. Third, unions may be distinguished by the functional coverage of their organizing activities. Some, like AFSCME, are general-purpose organizations, which seek out members at all levels of government and in almost any

Table 2.3 Membership of Largest State and Local Employee Organizations, 2023

Organization	*Membership*
National Education Association	3,000,000
AFSCME	1,600,000
AFT	1,720,000
SEIU	1,000,000[a]
American Federation of Government Employees	750,000
Fraternal Order of Police	367,000
International Association of Firefighters	341,000
International Brotherhood of Teamsters	200,000[a]

Source: data from union websites (https://www.nea.org/, https://www.afscme.org/, https://www.aft.org/, https://www.seiu.org/, https://www.afge.org/, https://fop.net/, https://www.iaff.org/, https://teamster.org/).

[a] Denotes public membership only.

occupation. Others, such as the International Association of Firefighters (IAFF), are functionally specific, concentrating membership in a single government job category. Table 2.3 displays the largest state and local employee organizations and their memberships.

Most professional associations in state and local government initially opposed collective bargaining and the other trappings of unions; some still do. However, once a collective bargaining law was adopted, associations adapted to it by seeking certification as bargaining representatives, then participating in collective bargaining, and negotiating written agreements. By the early 1970s, there was a marked convergence in goals, strategies, and tactics among many of the associations and the unions. Some of the state and local associations have maintained their independence while functioning as unions. Other associations have merged with unions. For instance, the Illinois State Employees Association merged with SEIU, as did the California State Employees Association, and the State Employees Association of North Carolina. The Massachusetts State Employees Association joined with the National Association of Government Employees and the New York, Ohio, Arizona, and Mississippi civil service employees' associations affiliated with AFSCME.

Nevertheless, many associations remain predominantly service-oriented lobbying organizations that do not engage in collective bargaining. Examples include the South Carolina and Virginia state employees' associations. In 2020 Virginia passed a law that allows public sector unions to engage in collective bargaining at the local level (county, city, town) provided that the local government adopts an authorizing ordinance or resolution. However, the law excluded state-level employees, higher education workers, and state-paid contractors. State employees' associations, such as Virginia Governmental Employees Association (VGEA), are advocating for expansion of collective bargaining rights.

Although there has been some debate on the relative effectiveness of independent unions versus unions affiliated with national labor organizations, it is difficult to sort out key empirical dimensions of organizational influence and power. However, the consensus seems to be that independent organizations can be as effective as or even more successful than affiliated organizations, depending on factors such as leadership, group cohesiveness, financial and human resources, community acceptance, and the general labor environment.

Competition over members and collective bargaining recognition led to some rather severe interunion conflicts during the late 1960s and early 1970s (Spero & Capozzola, 1973, pp. 32–37; Stieber, 1973, pp. 89–100). A stable and comprehensive legal environment in the majority of states, embodied by formal nonaggression pacts between some of the larger unions, has helped alleviate some overt conflict. However, internecine union warfare occasionally breaks out, as it did in 2005 when SEIU, the Teamsters, and five other unions split off from the AFL–CIO to form a new federation called Change to Win.

A major battlefield is the nonprofit sector's health-care providers and workers in child care and nursing home establishments. The fight between SEIU and AFSCME over child-care providers in Iowa was likened by the state's human services director to "the Bloods versus the Crips" (Walters, 2006, p. 29). Other AFSCME–SEIU clashes have erupted in the health-care sector in California and in the Midwest. In 2016, AFSCME and SEIU signed a resolution to collaborate on growing the labor movement and organizing workers and communities to the fight against growing inequality. The pact recognizes the differences in culture and structure between the organizations and past struggles. At the same time, it calls on both organizations to build on their common purpose.

Public employee unions may be characterized by their membership and organizing targets as general purpose or functionally specific.

1. General-purpose Unions

The paramount general-purpose organization in government is AFSCME. Membership estimates were about 1.6 million in 2023 (see Table 2.3). It is the largest AFL–CIO affiliate. AFSCME's greatest membership gains were registered during 1962–1978. The union lost about 10% of its membership from 2009 to 2012 (Hananel, 2012a).

AFSCME has 19 organizational occupation units. These are: Attorneys and Judiciary Employees, Behavioral Health (50,000), Corrections (62,000 corrections officers and 23,000 corrections employees), Early Childhood Education, Emergency Services, Environmental Stewardship, Health Care Workers, Higher

Education, Home Care, Housing, Human Services, K-12 Schools, Law Enforcement, Library Workers (over 25,000), Museums and Cultural Institutions, Nurses (over 60,000), Probation and Parole, Public Administration, Public Works, and Transportation (AFSCME, n.d.-a).

Internally, AFSCME is organized through an "international" office and its executive committee, 58 regional councils, and some 3,400 locals that report to the councils. The current president, Lee Saunders, was elected in 2012 following a 31-year reign by Gerald McEntee. Saunders is the first African American to serve as AFSCME's president (AFSCME, n.d.-b). The president appoints his or her own staff, which performs executive and judicial functions for the organization. The highest policy-making body is the International Convention. The convention is held annually; delegates decide basic policy questions. The locals elect their own delegates and operate under their own constitutions, with the number of delegates determined by total membership. Between conventions, policy is developed and implemented by the executive committee. Dues are apportioned among the national, local, and council (regional) organizations. Dues increases are tied to average earnings increases of full-time state and local government employees.

As an organization, AFSCME is an indefatigable political activist closely aligned with the Democratic Party. It has not hesitated to take positions on salient questions of domestic and foreign policy or to enter the electoral arena with large campaign contributions to friendly candidates and massive get-out-the-vote drives. Its principal political action committee, PEOPLE (Public Employees Organized to Promote Legislative Equality), typically ranks as one of the top campaign fundraisers in national elections. AFSCME's primary purpose in much of its political activity has been to legitimize and expand the bargaining rights of public employees, principally through electing Democratic members of Congress and state legislatures. Within its own ranks, AFSCME usually has taken care to ensure proper representation of women and people of color, who hold a number of important national offices and a majority of the national membership.

Three other strong, general-purpose organizations operate in government, all of them mixed unions with a major presence in the private and nonprofit sectors. SEIU counts more than 1 million of its members in government employment, but the union is also strong in the nonprofit services and health-care sectors, as well as in education. SEIU's major organizing campaigns recently have focused on health-care workers, day-care providers, and long-term care workers, using the themes of quality care and consumer protection within the rapidly growing health-care industries to attract new members. The union reports more than 1.1 million members in health care, including nurses, home-care workers, nursing-home workers, and lab technicians. SEIU has also rung up victories and attained a significant presence among janitors and security guards (SEIU, n.d.-a).

SEIU is governed by a 68-member executive board, which makes policy decisions at its national meetings. SEIU counts more than 150 local affiliates organized into 15 state councils SEIU (n.d.-b). SEIU President Mary Kay Henry replaced long-time president Andy Stern in 2010. She served for 14 years and passed the torch to April Verrett in 2024 (SEIU, 2024).

The IBT has been a strong competitor of SEIU and AFSCME in some local government jurisdictions. The IBT has organized approximately 200,000 public employees (out of a total membership of 1.3 million). The IBT public membership includes employees in public schools and universities; law enforcement, firefighters, and other emergency services workers; workers who support the military or maintain roads; and health-care and hospital workers. President Sean M. O'Brien leads the union with a 26-member executive board elected at-large and by geographic area. Local delegates meet once every 5 years. (IBT, n.d.)

2. Functionally Specific Organizations

A substantial amount of unionization in government has occurred along professional lines, similar in some respects to craft organization in the private sector. The major organizations in education, police and fire protection, health care, and miscellaneous government professions are examined next.

a. Education: Primary and Secondary

Public education is the largest public employer by far in state and local government—more than 10.9 million individuals work in public education (including elementary and secondary, higher, and other education). Of those employed in public education, 8.2 million work at the local level, almost entirely in elementary and secondary education. In 2022, state and local governments' employee payroll costs totaled at $94.4 billion. Of this amount, $36.1 billion was spent on education payroll (U.S. Census Bureau, 2023a, 2023b).

Nonetheless, schools across the U.S. continue to face staffing shortages as result of the lingering effects of the COVID-19 pandemic. According to a brief issued by the National Center on Educational Statistics (2022) 18% of public schools reported one teaching vacancy in October 2022 and 26% reported multiple teaching vacancies. In addition to teachers, public schools also struggled to fill non-teaching vacancies. Across public schools, 6% of non-teaching staff positions were vacant.

Two organizations have dominated the union movement in education: the independent National Education Association (NEA) and the AFL–CIO-affiliated American Federation of Teachers (AFT). The NEA, the largest labor union in the United States, claims a national membership of about 3 million active and retired members. The NEA operates with 14,000 local affiliates with its primary strength in mid-sized cities and suburbs. Its largest state affiliate is the California Teachers Association, with a whopping 310,000 members. Eighty percent of its members are classroom teachers.

The AFT, with a membership roll of about 1.72 million, is concentrated in large cities such as New York, Boston, Chicago, Minneapolis, and Denver. The AFT has presented itself as an aggressive union seeking collective bargaining rights for teachers since its inception in 1919. In contrast, the NEA was born in 1857 as a professional organization open to both teachers and supervisory personnel. Even though many NEA locals function as unions today, and the national organization is officially labeled a "union" by the Bureau of Labor Statistics and the Internal Revenue Service, a large portion of the members are found in locals that do not engage in collective bargaining relationships.

Early in its history, the NEA proclaimed that discussions on teachers' salaries with the local school board or superintendent were "unprofessional." The national organization's attitude changed, however, with the 1961 election of New York City's United Federation of Teachers (an AFT affiliate) as teacher bargaining agent for the city—a painful loss for the NEA. Soon thereafter, the NEA leadership made a number of policy changes, including support for "professional negotiations" and "professional sanctions" against arbitrary or unethical school management practices. The NEA also began sponsoring state legislation for teacher bargaining. Today the NEA has a Collective Bargaining and Member Advocacy (CBMA) Department. The primary purpose of the CBMA is to promote members' collective bargaining rights over such issues as salaries, pensions, health benefits, and legal services. It also encourages members to engage in the public policy process at the federal, state, and local levels.

Although there is little doubt that the NEA and the AFT have become more alike in their strategies and activities, there remain important differences that have stifled recurring attempts to merge. Beginning in 1969, formal merger discussions were held and some NEA and AFT locals did join ranks (e.g., in Flint, Michigan). The national leadership of the NEA eventually backed out for three major reasons: AFL–CIO affiliation (the NEA did not desire it); the composition of bargaining units (the NEA wanted to retain supervisory personnel in some locals); and, in general, more conservative NEA policy positions on a number of issues (Stern, 1979, pp. 63–64).

The organizations officially decided to go their separate ways, with the NEA continuing to limit its membership to professional education personnel and the AFT electing to pursue the organization of teachers' aides, paraprofessionals, library workers, cafeteria workers, bus drivers, and noneducation employees in civil service and health care (Stern, 1979, pp. 66–67). Drawing the two organizations even farther apart was the rancorous conflict over President Carter's proposed Department of Education in 1979. The NEA supported the new department (which was subsequently created), whereas the AFT, led by the late President Albert Shanker and encouraged by the AFL–CIO, fought it adamantly.

During the 1980s, the two organizations continued to compete for new members and to raid the others' jurisdictions for representation rights (see Cooper,

1988). Nonetheless, on several occasions in the 1990s, efforts were undertaken to bring the two organizations together but to no avail. Periodically, merger discussions resume (most recently in 2012), but significant differences have so far kept the two unions at arm's length. Today, a "partnership" between the NEA and the AFT helps advance common goals through a joint council, although the two organizations remain fiercely independent.

Perhaps the differences between them are best illustrated by their leadership. AFT President Al Shanker, who died in February 1997, was a charismatic figure whose persuasive and respected voice influenced education policy debates from the White House to the schoolhouse. His arguments for higher national education standards and other reforms received much attention during the 1990s. Shanker was an aggressive New Yorker with a sharp voice and wit as well as undisguised policy ideas.

Replacing Shanker as AFT president was Sandra Feldman. Feldman also rose from the ranks of New York City teachers, progressing through the organizational hierarchy to the presidency in 1998. She was a Shanker disciple who, in many ways, served out his legacy as a strong voice for teachers and education policy issues. Feldman resigned in 2004 due to illness. She was followed briefly (and innocuously) by Edward J. McElroy (2005–2008), then by Randi Weingarten, a tough NYC union negotiator who, like Feldman, rose through the union ranks to the presidency. Weingarten is a complex and highly controversial leader who has served as a lightning rod for criticism of teachers and their unions. Case Study 2.1 provides a deeper examination of Weingarten.

In comparison to the AFT, the NEA has been headed up by relatively lower profile individuals. The successive presidencies of Mary Hatwood Futrell, Keith Geiger, Bob Chase, Reg Weaver, and Dennis Van Roekel faced the challenge of holding together a highly diverse constituency with 14,000 chapters in both bargaining and non-bargaining settings. Delegates at the representative assembly in 2014 set a historical precedent by electing women and persons of color to the top three NEA leadership positions. These were Lily Eskelsen García (President), Becky Pringle (Vice President), and Princess Moss (Secretary-Treasurer). As of 2024, the leaders are still in place with the exception that Noel Candelaria succeeded Princess Moss in the Secretary-Treasurer position.

Although NEA leadership is aligned with the Democratic Party, its positions on social welfare issues have generally been more moderate than those of the AFT. But the NEA, until very recently, was less likely than the AFT to make accommodations to education reform issues such as teacher evaluation and merit pay. Under the new leadership team, the NEA has taken more progressive stances on social issues. For example, in 2015 delegates to representative assembly adopted a resolution acknowledging the existence of institutional racism in the United States and outlining strategies to eliminate its patterns and practices. Similarly in 2018 the representative assembly passed a resolution identifying the existence of White supremacy culture as a main cause of institutional and structural racism (NEA, 2021).

b. Higher Education

Collective bargaining by public college and university faculty in the United States was initiated in 1967 by the AFT at the U.S. Merchant Marine Academy. Approximately 525,000 professors, professional staff, and graduate students are represented by faculty unions today. Two-year colleges report the highest level of organization followed by four-year colleges and research universities. Among the larger universities with organized faculty are the California State University system, the State University of New York system, Rutgers University, and the University of Connecticut.

The major faculty unions are the NEA, the AFT, and the American Association of University Professors (AAUP). The NEA first dabbled in organizing college faculty in 1870 with the creation of a higher education unit, which was dissolved during the 1920s but re-created in 1943. After an early emphasis on teachers' colleges and community colleges, the NEA moved strongly into more comprehensive higher education institutions in the early 1970s (Ladd & Lipset, 1973, pp. 6–7). The AFT first focused its energies on organizing the nation's two-year campuses but, following the path of the NEA, has since gained the right to represent faculty at four-year institutions.

The AAUP, like the NEA in elementary and secondary education, existed for many years as a professional association not interested in collective bargaining or other union-like activities. The AAUP was founded in 1915 to help protect academic freedom and tenure rights and to advance faculty salaries through information gathering and other modest lobbying activities. Campus organizing successes by competing groups (the AFT and, ironically, the NEA) forced the AAUP to the table. After the collective bargaining strategy was officially adopted in 1972, however, the AAUP suffered losses in membership, primarily due to more effective organization and representation by its rivals, dropouts among faculty at noncollective bargaining institutions, and the negative fallout of the U.S. Supreme Court's Yeshiva decision (discussed in Chapter 4).

Many AAUP chapters continued to eschew collective bargaining. Nonetheless, the AAUP demonstrated moderate success by organizing faculty at 80 colleges and universities. The collective bargaining chapters include the University of Alaska, University of Connecticut, University of Rhode Island, Portland State University, Rutgers, the University of Illinois, the State University of New York campuses, and the University of New Hampshire (AAUP, 2020). In 2022, the AFT and AAUP officially merged to address shared challenges that higher education was facing. Together they represent more than 300,000 faculty (AFT, 2022).

A large majority of the organized institutions are publicly supported colleges and universities. The predominance of faculty organization in public institutions results from the Yeshiva decision of the U.S. Supreme Court in 1980. The Court ruled that faculty at private colleges are "managers" under the National Labor Relations Act and therefore are not protected for collective bargaining purposes (National Labor Relations Board [NLRB] v. Yeshiva [1980]). Yeshiva has directly resulted in the denial of bargaining rights at more than 80 institutions (Metchick & Singh, 2004, p. 54). Management responsibility, according to the Court, is found in the faculty's "absolute authority over such matters as grading, teaching methods, graduation requirements . . . student discipline . . . academic calendars, and course schedules." The Yeshiva decision has not damaged unionization in state and locally supported institutions, and the ruling does not require a private academic institution to forgo faculty bargaining if it determines on its own that faculty, adjunct professors, and teaching assistants are not "managers" (Metchick & Singh, 2004).

A number of theorists have attempted to explain the reasons for the rather shocking reversal of scholars' historical aversion to unionism. Faculty in American higher education long valued a tradition of high social status and acute professional independence, two norms in deep conflict with the egalitarian and collective values associated with those occupations most given to unionization (Ladd & Lipset, 1973, pp. 2–4). However, conditions changed rapidly in academe during the late 1960s and early 1970s. Low salaries became less acceptable, and threats to the sacrosanct tradition of academic tenure arose through reductions in force at some financially hard-pressed institutions.

In addition, many higher education institutions underwent a metamorphosis in size and mission that stimulated faculty organization. For example, former teachers' colleges were upgraded to major state universities, with a concomitant change in the administration's research-related expectations for faculty. Other institutions had grown so large, so fast, that seemingly vast and unresponsive administrative bureaucracies had arisen. Such a strong degree of administrative centralization led many faculty members to seek a unified and collective voice of their own, particularly in the context of the social turmoil of the 1960s, much of which was concentrated on or around campuses (Ladd & Lipset, 1973, p. 4). Finally, it should be noted that almost all organized college and university faculties are in states that are characterized by a legislative environment conducive to faculty unionization and collective bargaining. Rarely do faculty organize into unions in the absence of permissive legislation.

Interest remains in faculty unionization as state legislatures cut higher education funding and push colleges and universities toward a business model of operations run by administrators acting like corporate CEOs (Schmidt, 2012). Traditionally, union organizing campaigns have been more successful in larger public colleges and universities (Julius & DiGiovanni, 2019). Over the past decade gains in higher education unionization have occurred on a large scale, especially following the great recession.

Over the period of 2013 to 2019, 118 newly created faculty collective bargaining units were certified and added 36, 264 members. The new bargaining units covered 20,160 faculty and professionals at public colleges and universities, 15,898 at private nonprofit institutions, and 206 at private for-profit institutions (Herbert et al., 2020). Some of the most rapid growth in unionization occurred with the organization of part-time faculty and graduate assistants, who engage in part-time teaching and research but are paid far less than regular faculty and who enjoy few, if any, benefits (Herbert et al., 2023).

The campaigns for part-time or adjunct faculty have focused on the degradation of working conditions, akin to the gig economy (Angulo, 2018). As Rhoades (2017) notes, the adjunct faculty are bargaining not only for equitable pay but also for dignity and respect on campus and improved quality of learning conditions for students. Given the lack of participation contingent faculty have in shared governance and their precarious employment status, it is difficult for University and College administrators to prevail on the argument that they are managerial employees under the Yeshiva doctrine (Herbert et al., 2020).

Similarly, graduate teaching assistants (TAs) and research assistants (RAs) shoulder heavy loads in teaching classes (relieving the declining ranks of tenure-track professors) and conducting research while working on their dissertations. TAs and RAs usually receive tuition reimbursement and a modest stipend for their efforts, but many believe this is small recompense for what amounts to full-time work as well as full-time study for a PhD (Maynard, 2012). TAs and RAs certainly feel like "employees" and as such should be eligible for collective bargaining.

The first graduate student association to win recognition was at the University of Wisconsin (Madison) in 1969. Since then, graduate assistants have successfully organized at other public campuses in California, Illinois, Indiana, Michigan, Minnesota, New Jersey, New York, and other states. From 2013 to 2019, an additional 16 graduate employee collective bargaining units were recognized, with a total of 19,627 members. Of these units, 12 represented solely graduate student employees and four covered both graduate and undergraduate employees (Herbert et al., 2020).

The upsurge continued in 2022–2023 with nearly 35,700 students gaining union representation across 30 new collective bargaining units. In a break with historic trends, the 2022–2023 wave of student employee organizing spread beyond public institutions. Specifically, three-quarters of the new graduate assistant units and all the undergraduate bargaining units were at private colleges and universities. The successful drives included prominent institutions such as Yale University, the University of Chicago, and Johns Hopkins University (Herbert et al., 2023).

The growth in union organizing has been accompanied by increased strike activity. From 2022 to 2023, higher education employees engaged in 20 strikes (Herbert et al., 2023). Graduate workers struck at multiple institutions including the University of California system, University of Michigan, Temple University, and several universities in Illinois. The strike at Rutgers University included three unions that represent full-time faculty members, adjunct faculty members, graduate workers, postdoctoral associates and counselors, and faculty who teach at the university's medical and public health facilities.

c. *Protective Services*

Firefighters are among the most highly organized of municipal employees. A large majority belong to the IAFF, although AFSCME represents a small number and various independent organizations speak for firefighters in some jurisdictions. With its roots in early social and benefits societies for firefighters, the IAFF was founded as an AFL affiliate in 1918. It has a highly decentralized structure with a small national headquarters and staff in Washington, D.C., which functions mainly to distribute information on salary, benefits, and other job-related topics to the locals, provide technical assistance for collective bargaining, and actively lobby Congress and state and local legislative bodies for greater firefighter compensation and favorable treatment with other issues. The 3500 IAFF locals have a high degree of autonomy in their activities and in their bargaining relationships with local governments. About 341,000 members were reported by the IAFF in 2023, including a growing number of emergency medical personnel (U.S. Department of Labor, 2023).

Police officers are represented by several national organizations. Some locals are affiliated with general-purpose unions: AFSCME (whose first police affiliate was chartered in 1937 in Portsmouth, Virginia), SEIU, and the Teamsters (although their latest membership figures are relatively low). The International Union of Police Associations (IUPA), which is in essence an "association of associations," is affiliated with the AFL–CIO. The IUPA serves as a coordinating body for local, independent police associations and conducts police wage and benefit surveys, among other activities. Its membership is heaviest in the southern states, Massachusetts, and New York. The IUPA also reports local corrections officer affiliates (IUPA, n.d.).

The FOP is the oldest and largest police organization, founded in 1915. The national FOP provides collective bargaining assistance to locals, actively lobbies governments at all levels, and offers a wide variety of professional services. Its 373,000 members and 2200 "lodges" are concentrated in the north-central and southern states (FOP, n.d.). Other national police organizations include the International Brotherhood of Police Officers, created in 1964, which also represents correctional officers, EMTs, and paramedics, and the National Association of Police Organizations (NAPO), which is a coalition of police unions and associations that advances members' interests through political and legal advocacy and education. Founded in 1978, NAPO reported representing 1000 unions and associations and more than 241,000 sworn officers in 2023 (NAPO, n.d.).

d. Health Care

The nation's burgeoning health-care industry presents an enticing organizing target for the unions. Nurses, technical employees, maintenance workers, clerical workers, and employees in nursing homes, assisted living facilities, clinics, and other health-care facilities face uncertainties (e.g., facility mergers and privatization) and experience dissatisfaction (e.g., low wages and tough working conditions) that make unions look attractive. "Professional" health-care employees in proprietary and nonprofit institutions were excluded from collective bargaining coverage until an amendment to the National Labor Relations Act in 1974 unleashed intense organizing activity by the American Nurses Association, AFT, UNA (an affiliate of AFSCME), SEIU, and other unions. The SEIU health-care division represents approximately 1 million health-care employees across the following occupations: doctors, nurses, home care and nursing home workers, lab techs, environmental service workers, and dietary aides (SEIU, n.d.-c).

The health-care sector represents a ripe fruit ready for union picking as the nation's population continues to age, with a growing number of people entering nursing homes, long-term care facilities, and other health-care institutions. Even physicians, looking for an antidote to the perceived intrusions of HMOs, managed care organizations, and insurance companies into doctors' pay and autonomy with patients, have been actively exploring union representation. In 1999, the American Medical Association voted to form a labor union on behalf of profoundly discontented practicing physicians.

In the wake of the pandemic, doctors are facing exhaustion. The primary contributors are excessive workloads, onerous electronic health records reporting systems, loss of autonomy, and administrative overload (Hubbell, 2022). The SEIU conducted one of the largest recent organizing campaigns at Allina Health Systems in Minnesota and Wisconsin. The new bargaining unit covers 400 primary and urgent-care physicians along with 150 nurse practitioners and physician assistants (Scheiber, 2023).

Other recent campaigns have focused on physicians in training. To illustrate, physician training centers representing nearly 4,000 house staff have unionized at the University of Massachusetts, the University of California (Riverside), the University of California (San Francisco), the University of Illinois (Chicago), the Greater Lawrence Family Health Center, the University of Vermont, Stanford University, and the University of Southern California (Lin et al., 2022).

A key issue, however, is the status of private and nonprofit sector physicians under the National Labor Relations Act. Are they "employees" of HMOs, for instance, and therefore employees who may engage in collective bargaining? Or, like professors in private colleges and universities, are they "supervisors," who are excluded from National Labor Relations Act coverage (as a 2006 ruling of the National Labor Relations Board determined in the case of registered nurses)? Eventually, this question may have to be resolved by the federal courts.

V. PROSPECTS

When union strength is measured by the proportion of potential public and private sector members who actually belong to a union, the United States trails all other industrialized or "developed" countries. Union strength in the United States has declined significantly in the private sector since its 1954 peak and has dropped slightly in government since its peak in the mid-1980s. Union membership has also declined in most other industrialized countries, but labor remains politically strong, particularly in Germany, the Netherlands, and the Scandinavian countries. The membership losses appear to be the result of various forces, including reductions in the size of heavily organized public sectors, the shift to services and information-related employment in the private sector, and the expansion of the temporary and part-time ("contingent") work forces.

Despite these setbacks, union activity is on the rise. In 2018–2019 a wave of teachers strikes spread across the U.S. Several strikes occurred in more conservative states with limited collective bargaining rights, such as West Virginia, Oklahoma, and New Mexico. The COVID-19 pandemic highlighted the importance of providing workers with collective voice in the workplace. It fueled worker unrest and led many workers to engage in collective action.

In 2021, discontent over inequality, working conditions, and low wages led to labor protests known as "Striketober." In the private sector, 10,000 John Deere workers and 1,400 Kellogg's workers went on strike. In the nonprofit sector, more than 30,000 Kaiser Permanente threatened to walk out. There was also an uptick in union activity at nonprofit organizations such as museums and policy think tanks. As of 2021, Americans' union approval rating was 68%, the highest Gallup has measured since 1965.

Finally, the spread of COVID-19 transformed public sector working conditions and collective bargaining. Front line workers in both the public and nonprofit sectors were exposed to work-related illness and psychological stress. This included workers in health care, mass transit workers, trash collectors, postal employees, and law enforcement/public safety/first responders. Many of these employees faced opposition to mask and vaccine mandates in public spaces. Collective negotiations over working conditions expanded to include workplace protections, such as proper ventilation and personal protective equipment.

It is unclear whether recent developments will lead to a reversal of declining fortunes of unions worldwide. Indeed, many of the same negative patterns for organized labor that have been observed in the United States appear to be present across the globe. Chapter 11 addresses the future of public employee unions in detail.

CASE STUDY 2.1 PORTRAIT OF A UNION LEADER: RANDI WEINGARTEN, AMERICAN FEDERATION OF TEACHERS

Perhaps the toughest job in public sector labor relations is that of Randi Weingarten, president of the AFT. Quickly rising through the organizational ranks, Weingarten is, to friends and foes alike, the face of teacher unionism. She is a prominent player in national education policy and a tireless defender of those who earn their living in the classroom.

With a majority of her membership opposing virtually every proposed education reform—charter schools, merit pay, teacher evaluation, and ending tenure—Weingarten shoulders heavy organizational challenges. She must "humanize" America's teachers by representing them favorably to the public and policy makers, while countering undesirable education reform initiatives and influencing national, state, and local policy makers to view the AFT agenda favorably. To succeed, Weingarten must navigate the perilous waters between education policy reformers and rank-and-file union membership. If she sails too close to the reformers' positions, she risks forfeiting her membership's support, and even her job. But if her advocacy for more teachers pay, benefits, and privileges is too strident and unyielding, she places her national education policy voice in jeopardy. The stakes are high: education quality, children's futures, and the survival of collective bargaining for teachers.

So far, Weingarten has been a successful union leader. She uses her distinctive voice to bring others to her point of view. Yet she has proven to be adaptable to concerns of others when necessary, while recognizing and seizing opportunities. Weingarten, like all union leaders, has suffered setbacks. But she has been resilient, showing the capacity to learn from them. Weingarten has been effective at playing both offense (proposing and advocating new education quality initiatives to develop teachers and improve their classroom performance) and defense (fending off attacks on teachers and their unions).

Vicious political attacks on the AFT and Weingarten have taken a toll on public sentiment toward teachers and their unions. The popular 2010 documentary *Waiting for Superman* portrayed teacher unions and Weingarten in particular as education reform villains. More recently, Mike Pompeo has referred to her as "the most dangerous person in the world" and went on to say that teachers' unions were trying to destroy the country. Much of the recent criticism stems from school closures during the pandemic. Early in the pandemic, teachers were viewed in a positive light for continuing to teach children remotely with few resources. However, the mood shifted during the summer of 2022 as evidence emerged on learning loss due to remote instruction.

Following George Floyd's murder, the AFT took up the mantle of racial equity. A counter movement arose with the formation of Moms for Liberty (M4L). M4L advocated for a return to in-person, maskless instruction; limits on the teaching of race-related subjects and promotion of gender; promotion of vouchers and school choice; and expanded rights for parents at all levels of government.

Through it all, Weingarten continues to advocate for strengthening public education. She recently laid out a four-pronged strategy that includes: expanding community schools, promoting experiential learning, addressing staff shortages, and deepening the partnership between families and educators. Although in the past it could be said that many of Weingarten's opponents recognize her basic integrity and the validity of the role she plays in the education policy arena, in the current polarized environment that may no longer be true.

Sources: Gabriel (2010), Kearney (2011), Mahler (2023), Medina (2008), Weingarten (2023).

REFERENCES

AAUP. (2020). *Collective bargaining*. https://www.aaup.org/programs/collective-bargaining

Abood v. Detroit Board of Education. (1977). 430 U.S. 209, 975 Ct. 1782.

AFGE. (2023a). *AFGE at a glance*. https://www.afge.org/about-us/afge-at-a-glance/AmMerica

AFGE. (2023b, January 9). *AFGE ends December with highest membership in 2022*. https://www.afge.org/article/afge-ends-december-with-highest-membership-in-2022/

AFGE. (2023c). *AFGE scores victory at supreme court in case involving dual-status national guard technicians*. https://www.afge.org/article/afge-scores-victory-at-supreme-court-in-case-involving-dualstatus-national-guard-technicians

AFGE. (2023d). *AFGE launches new local to serve unrepresented employees in Europe*. https://www.afge.org/article/afge-launches-new-local-to-serve-unrepresented-employees-in-europe/

AFSCME. (n.d.-a). *About AFSCME: Jobs we do*. https://www.afscme.org/about/jobs-we-do

AFSCME. (n.d.-b). *About AFSCME: Leadership*. https://www.afscme.org/about/leadership/lee-saunders

AFT. (2022). *2020–2022 State of the union report.* https://www.aft.org/about/sotu

Angulo, A. J. (2018). From the golden era to the gig economy: Changing contexts for academic labor in America. In K. Tolley (Ed.), *Professors in the gig economy: Unionizing adjunct faculty in America* (pp. 3–26). Johns Hopkins University Press.

Berry, W. D., Ringquist, E. J., Fording, R. C., & Hanson, R. L. (2007). The measurement and stability of state citizen ideology. *State Politics and Policy Quarterly, 7*(2), 111–132.

Bur, J. (2021). Answers to federal workers' questions about government labor unions. *Federal Times.* https://www.federaltimes.com/management/hr/2021/09/01/answers-to-federal-workers-questions-about-government-labor-unions/

Cooper, B. S. (1988). National union competition and the school reform movement: Will the NEA and AFT merge? In *41st proceedings of the IRRA.* IRRA.

DiSalvo, D. (2019). *Public-sector unions after janus: An update.* Manhattan Institute. https://manhattan.institute/article/public-sector-unions-after-janus-an-update

Ecker, M. (2018). Efforts to privatize the United States postal service: Labor's response. *Labor Studies Journal, 43*(3), 173–188.

Elazar, D. J. (1966). *American federalism: A view from the states.* Crowell.

FOP. (n.d.). *About the FOP.* https://fop.net/about-the-fop/

Friedrichs v. California Teachers Association. (2016). 578 U.S. ____.

Gabriel, T. (2010, October 15). Despite image, union leader backs school change. *New York Times.* https://www.nytimes.com/2010/10/16/education/16teacher.html

Gilbert, C. (2013, February 9). The politics of Wisconsin's declining union membership. *The Journal Sentinel.* www.jsonline.com

Hananel, S. (2012a, June 8). Rift over political spending divides huge union. *AP: The Big Story.* http://bigstory.ap.org/article/rift-over-political-spending-divides-huge-union

Harris v. Quinn. (2014). 573 U.S. 616.

Herbert, W. A., Apkarian, J., & van der Naald, J. (2020). *2020 supplementary directory of new bargaining agents and contracts in institutions of higher education, 2013–2019.* https://www.hunter.cuny.edu/ncscbhep/assets/files/SupplementalDirectory-2020-FINAL.pdf

Herbert, W. A., Apkarian, J., & van deer Naald, J. (2023). Union organizing and strikes in higher education: The 2022–2023 upsurge in historical context. In R. Milkman and J. Naald (Eds.), *The State of the Unions 2023: A Profile of Organized Labor in New York City, New York State, and the United States* (pp. 6–32). City University of New York.

Hodges, A. C. (2021). The US labor relations system after Janus v. AFSCME: An early assessment. *Employee Responsibilities and Rights Journal, 33*, 49–60.

Hubbell, G. P. (2022). Physician unions and work-life balance. *Missouri Medicine, 119*(5), 406–407.

IBT. (n.d.). *Teamsters structure*. https://teamster.org/about/teamsters-structure/

IUPA. (n.d.). *Home*. https://iupa.org/our-legacy/

Janus v. American Federation of State, County, and Municipal Employees, Council 31. (2018). 585 U.S. ___.

Julius, D. J., & DiGiovanni, Jr., N. (2019). Academic collective bargaining: Status, process, and prospects. *Academic Labor: Research and Artistry*, *3*(1), 11.

Kearney, R. C. (2010). Randi Weingarten, the American federation of teachers, and the challenges of policy leadership in a hostile environment. *Public Administration Review*, *71*(5), 772–781.

Ladd, E. C., Jr., & Lipset, S. M. (1973). *Professors, unions, and American higher education*. American Enterprise Institute for Public Policy Research.

Lin, G. L., Ge, T. J., & Pal, R. (2022). Resident and fellow unions: Collective activism to promote well-being for physicians in training. *JAMA*, *328*(7), 619–620. https://doi.org/10.1001/jama.2022.12838

Mahler, J. (2023, April 28). The most dangerous person in the world is Randi Weingarten. *The New York Times Magazine*. https://www.nytimes.com/2023/04/28/magazine/randi-weingarten-teachers-unions.html

Martin, J., & Titolo, M. (2020). The United States postal service-the one word that makes all the difference. *Texas Law Review Online*, *99*, 72.

Maynard, M. (2012, February 29). Graduate students campaign to unionize. *Stateline*. http://www.pewstates.org/projects/stateline/graduate-students-campaign-to-unionize-85899375396

Medina, J. (2008, April 3). A schools veteran girds for a broader battlefield. *New York Times*. https://www.nytimes.com/2008/04/03/education/03weingarten.html

Metchick, R. H., & Singh, P. (2004). Yeshiva and faculty unionization in higher education. *Labor Studies Journal*, *28*(4), 45–65.

Morse, R. S. (2008). Developing public leaders in an age of collaborative governance. In R. S. Morse & T. F. Buss (Eds.), *Innovation in public leadership development* (pp. 79–100). M. E. Sharp Inc.

Morse, R. S., Buss, T. F., & Kinghorn, C. M. (2007). *Transforming public leadership for the 21st century*. M. E. Sharp Inc.

NAPO. (n.d.). *About*. https://www.napo.org/about/overview/

National Center on Educational Statistics. (2022). *U.S. schools report increased teacher vacancies due to covid-19 pandemic, new NCES data show*. https://nces.ed.gov/whatsnew/press_releases/3_3_2022.asp

National Labor Relations Board v. Yeshiva University. (1980). 444 U.S. 672.

NEA. (2021). *NEA and racial justice in education*. https://www.nea.org/resource-library/nea-and-racial-justice-education

NTEU. (2023). *Who we are, what we do.* https://www.nteu.org/who-we-are/what-we-do

Pynes, J. E. (2017). Labor relations in nonprofit organizations. *The nonprofit human resource management handbook: From theory to practice* (pp. 166–184). https://www.philanthropy.com/article/here-come-the-nonprofit-unions

Rendon, J. (2023, January 10). Here come the nonprofit unions. *The Chronicle of Philanthropy.* https://www.philanthropy.com/article/here-come-the-nonprofit-unions

Rhoades, G. (2017). Bread and roses, and quality too? A new faculty majority negotiating the new academy. *The Journal of Higher Education*, *88*(5), 645–671.

Rubio, P. F. (2021). Unintended consequences: The US postal service conundrum of service, business, labor, and politics. *Employee Responsibilities and Rights Journal*, *33*, 125–141.

Scheiber, N. (2023, December 3). Why doctors and pharmacists are in revolt. *New York Times.* https://www.nytimes.com/2023/12/03/business/economy/doctors-pharmacists-labor-unions.html

Schmidt, P. (2012, April 2). Study finds continued growth of unions for faculty members and graduate students. *The Chronicle of Higher Education.* http://chronicle.com

SEIU. (2024). *Mary Kay Henry, Visionary SEIU leader who championed fight for $15 movement, challenged status quo, will not seek re-election.* https://www.seiu.org/2024/02/marykaytopasstorch

SEIU. (n.d.-a). *These fast facts will tell you how we're organized and what we do.* https://www.seiu.org/cards/these-fast-facts-will-tell-you-how-were-organized/#:~:text=We%20are%20the%20second%20largest%20union%20of%20public,including%2080%2C000%20early%20learning%20and%20child%20care%20professionals

SEIU. (n.d.-b). *These fast facts will tell you how we're organized and what we do.* https://www.seiu.org/cards/these-fast-facts-will-tell-you-how-were-organized/how-are-we-structured/p3

SEIU. (n.d.-c). *Everything you need to know about seiu healthcare.* https://www.seiu.org/cards/everything-you-need-to-know-about-seiu-healthcare

Spero, S. D., & Capozzola, J. M. (1973). *The urban community and its unionized bureaucracies.* Dunellen.

Stern, J. L. (1979). Unionism in the public sector. In B. Aaron, J. R. Grodin, & J. L. Stern (Eds.), *Public sector bargaining* (pp. 44–79). Bureau of National Affairs.

Stieber, J. (1973). *Public employee unionism.* The Brookings Institution.

U.S. Bureau of Labor Statistics. (2023a). https://www.bls.gov/ooh/healthcare/home.htm

U.S. Bureau of Labor Statistics. (2023b). https://www.bls.gov/spotlight/2023/for-profit-nonprofit-and-government-sector-jobs-in-2022/home.htm#:~:text=Women%20were%20strongly%20represented%20in%20private%20nonprofit

%20organizations,among%20those%20working%20in%20government%2C%20at%2056.6%20percent

U.S. Bureau of Labor Statistics. (2024). *Economic news release: Union membership (annual) news release*. https://www.bls.gov/news.release/archives/union2_01232024.htm

U.S. Census Bureau. (2023a). *Census of governments, survey of public employment & payroll summary report: 2022*. https://www.census.gov/content/dam/Census/library/publications/2023/econ/2022_summary_brief.pdf

U.S. Census Bureau. (2023b). *2022 Census of governments, survey of public employment & payroll datasets & tables*. https://www.census.gov/programs-surveys/apes/data/datasetstables/2022.html

U.S. Department of Labor. (2023). *Office of labor-management standards, file number: 000-317 (LM-2) 09/30/2023*. https://olmsapps.dol.gov/query/orgReport.do?rptId=876217&rptForm=LM2Form

Walters, J. (2006). Solidarity forgotten. *Governing*. www.governing.com

Weingarten, R. (2023). Defending public education: Reclaiming our schools' promise and purpose. *American Educator, 47*(2), 3–9.

Chapter 3

Legal Environment of Public Sector Labor Relations

I. INTRODUCTION

The legal basis for government labor relations and collective bargaining is a hodgepodge of statutes, ordinances, attorney general opinions, executive orders, and court decisions. The federal government does not have a single policy governing labor–management relations for all of its workers, and to say that state and local government labor policies vary widely is a gross understatement. Some states continue to prohibit collective bargaining in government at all levels, whereas in others virtually all public employees are in a bargaining unit. Most states forbid public employees to strike, but some permit strikes under certain conditions. Such extreme labor relations diversity is in stark contrast to other industrialized nations, wherein a single national collective bargaining law prevails for all public workers.

This chapter describes the legal environment of public sector labor relations in federal, state, local, and nonprofit sectors and introduces the major institutions and political actors that establish the legal context, including the president, Congress, federal and state courts, state and local legislative bodies, governors, attorneys general, and the public. After a brief examination of the right to form and join unions (a right that is shared by virtually all public employees in the United States), the federal context of labor relations is described, including the 1978 Civil Service Reform Act (CSRA). The remainder of the chapter focuses on the state and local legal environments, the basic provisions of comprehensive bargaining laws, and authorization for unionization and collective bargaining.

II. RIGHT TO FORM AND JOIN UNIONS

Before 1967, public employee assertions of the right to form and join unions were frequently met by words similar to those of Justice Holmes in the case of *McAuliffe v.*

DOI:10.4324/9781003403593-3

City of New Bedford (1892). Holmes allowed that whereas the petitioner in the case, a former policeman who had been fired for engaging in electoral activities,

> may have a constitutional right to talk politics . . . he has no constitutional right to be a policeman. . . . There are few employments for hire in which the servant does not agree to suspend his constitutional right of free speech. . . . The servant cannot complain as he takes the employment on the terms which are offered him.

Although *McAuliffe* did not directly address the issue of freedom of association, the case was influential because it invited

> judges to analyze governmental restrictions on public employees' First Amendment rights in a curious way; that is, as if public employees were different from everyone else; as if, with respect to public employees, government is especially empowered to restrict the political and civil rights the rest of us enjoy.
>
> (Wellington & Winter, 1971, p. 70)

In other words, government could condition employment on forfeiture of the employees' right to organize, thereby restricting application of the First Amendment right of association solely to workers in private employment. Holmes' line of reasoning was cited as late as 1963 by the Supreme Court of Michigan in the case of *AFSCME Local 201 v. City of Muskegon* (1963), upholding the constitutionality of a regulation issued by Muskegon's chief of police that prohibited labor unions.

Denial of the right of government workers to form and join unions was buttressed by the sovereignty doctrine. A sovereign government, the argument goes, has the power to fix through law the terms and conditions of government work. This power is unilateral, and it cannot be given away or shared through negotiations with a public employee organization. But the counterpoint to the sovereignty argument is a strong one. As noted by Wellington and Winter (1971, pp. 71–73), the right of Americans to freely join together in what constitutional framer James Madison called "factions" has long been recognized as characterizing a free society and constituting a necessary safeguard against a tyranny of the majority:

> Organizations based on mutual economic interests, such as trade associations or labor unions, are paradigms of associations, factions, or as they are usually called today—interest groups. Such groups are absolutely necessary to the survival of political democracy in the United States. They are the means by which individuals make claims upon government; thus they are important to the structure of our federal system. . . . [T]he point is that unless individuals can freely band together to advocate whatever they please, we shall not have democracy.

These arguments are interesting in their own right, but what is important is how they have been applied by the federal arbiters of constitutional disputes—courts. Since 1967, the federal courts have held that the First Amendment's freedom of association clause outweighs government sovereignty claims. The first in a long line of cases was *Keyeshian v. Board of Regents* (1967), in which the U.S. Supreme Court ruled that public employment could not be predicated on workers relinquishing the right of free association. Other important decisions include *Atkins v. City of Charlotte* (1969), in which a U.S. district court invalidated a North Carolina state law that prohibited law enforcement personnel and firefighters from joining or being members of labor organizations because it violated the right of association and the Fourteenth Amendment's equal protection clause, and *Letter Carriers v. Blount* (1969), a case in which a federal district court found that a federal statute and oath intended to prevent postal workers from asserting the right to strike, and from joining any organization claiming the right to strike, violated the First Amendment.

The landmark case supporting the right of public employees to organize and join unions, however, is *McLaughlin v. Tilendis* (1967). In this case, one Cook County, Illinois teacher was dismissed and another one's contract was not renewed because of their alleged association with the local chapter of the American Federation of Teachers (AFT). The Seventh Circuit of the U.S. Court of Appeals held that these actions violated the employees' right of free association and that they unjustly interfered with the employees' right to due process under the Fourteenth Amendment. The court concluded that "unless there is some illegal intent, an individual's right to form and join a union is protected by the First Amendment." He or she cannot be disciplined or dismissed for joining a union or advocating that others join.

Today, then, the constitutional right of public employees to organize and join unions is protected by the courts. The sovereignty-based "doctrine of privilege," which granted public employees few rights vis-à-vis their employer, has been discarded by the courts. It is now accepted that public employees also have the rights (1) to engage in protected political activities and (2) to receive due process through a written statement of reasons for dismissal and/or a formal hearing (*Cleveland Board of Education v. Loudermill*, 1985).

In public employee–employer relations, the U.S. Supreme Court's reasoning in *Pickering v. Board of Education* (1968) established a foundation for public employees' freedom of expression and organizational dissent. Here the court determined that public employees' unique position inside of government allows them to contribute to the discourse on matters of public concern (Roberts, 2023; Rosenbloom & Chanin, 2016). If the employee is found to be voicing a matter of public concern, then the state's interest in restricting public employees' First and Fourteenth Amendment rights must be weighed against the employer's need for an efficient workplace that is free of disruptions. These protections were later extended to public employee's workplace speech in *Givhan v. Western Line Consolidated School District* (1979; Roberts, 2023).

Following these decisions, public employees enjoyed greater constitutional protection than private sector workers. However, in the early 2000s, the pendulum swung back toward management rights. Specifically, public employees' rights to free speech were circumscribed by the Court's ruling in *Garcetti v. Ceballos* (2006). In this case, the Court determined that public employees' First Amendment rights do not protect speech that is made as part of their professional responsibilities. This type of speech is commonly referred to as *work product* (Roberts, 2023; Rosenbloom & Chanin, 2016).

Eight years later, the U.S. Supreme Court revisited the issue of public employees' free speech rights. In *Lane v. Franks* (2014) the Court attempted to distinguish between work product speech and speech on matters of public concern that employees learned about while on the job (Rosenbloom & Chanin, 2016). In this case, the employee was compelled to testify in a series of public corruption trials. The Court ruled that the public employer (a college) violated Lane's First Amendment rights by firing him after he provided truthful court testimony pursuant to a subpoena. The balance between public managers' goals of an efficient and effective workplace free of organizational dissent and public sector employees' goal of exercising voice in the workplace is not static. It will continue to shift with changes in the legal and political environment.

Although public workers enjoy the right to form and join unions, they do not have a constitutional right to collective bargaining with their employer. Permissive legislation or other authorizing actions are normally required (*Smith v. Arkansas State Highway Commission Employees Local 1315*, 1979). In *Indianapolis Education Association v. Lewallen* (1969), the Seventh Circuit Court ruled shortly after *McLaughlin* that "there is no constitutional duty to bargain collectively with an exclusive bargaining agent. Such duty when imposed is imposed by statute." However, nothing prevents a public employer from voluntarily engaging in collective bargaining in the absence of enabling legislation.

Private sector labor relations and collective bargaining are governed by (1) the Railway Labor Act (RLA) of 1926 and (2) the National Labor Relations Act (NLRA) of 1935 (also known as the Wagner Act), as amended by the Labor Management Relations Act of 1947 (the Taft–Hartley Act) and the Labor Management Reporting and Disclosure Act of 1959 (the Landrum–Griffin Act). In the RLA, Congress sought to establish labor–management peace in the railroad industry by requiring firms to negotiate with bargaining representatives selected by railroad employees. The RLA was extended to the airline industry in 1936.

Under the NLRA, which provides coverage to all other private sector workers, labor policy is administered by the National Labor Relations Board, which investigates and adjudicates allegations of unfair labor practices (ULPs) and administers matters concerning composition of the employee bargaining unit and selection of the union to represent the bargaining unit. Passage of the NLRA encouraged private sector workers to form and join unions and engage in collective bargaining with their employers. Taft–Hartley balances the NLRA by imposing certain restrictions on union procedures and conduct, such as prohibiting compulsory union membership. Landrum–Griffin requires unions to meet various internal operating standards, such as guaranteeing their members rights of free association and speech, maintaining certain financial records, and accounting for expenditures.

With the precipitous decline of private sector union membership, unions and their allies claim that terms of the NLRA and restrictive decisions by the National Labor Relations Board have tilted the playing field to the advantage of employers. In 2009, unions orchestrated a drive to rebalance the field through the Employee Free Choice Act (EFCA). This proposed legislation requires employers to accept a "card check" as demonstration of majority support for the union instead of a lengthy, secret ballot election ripe with possibilities for the employers' antiunion propaganda and discrimination to "reeducate" workers as to the dangers of union representation (Drummonds, 2009). Following a hopeful campaign in which passage seemed to be within reach, union hopes were dashed as the EFCA was greeted by presidential indifference and stout business and Republican resistance. The bill languished in committee and then died.

The NLRA specifically exempts public employees. Section 2(2) of the Taft-Hartley amendment to the NLRA states that "the term 'employee' includes any person acting as an agent of an employer, directly or indirectly, but *shall not include* [emphasis added] any state or political subdivision thereof." It also excludes agricultural workers, independent contractors, supervisors, managerial employees, small businesses employees, and domestic workers.

III. LABOR RELATIONS IN FEDERAL EMPLOYMENT: THE LEGAL BASIS

Although employee organizations have existed in federal employment since the 1830s, it was 1960 before any union was formally recognized by a federal employer (with the exceptions of the Tennessee Valley Authority, the Bonneville Power Administration, and a handful of other quasi-governmental organizations). Furthermore, no statutory basis existed for federal employee collective bargaining before the passage of the CSRA of 1978.

The Pendleton Act of 1883 established the federal merit system and gave Congress the authority to regulate the wages, hours, and working conditions of federal workers. It did not grant a collective voice for employees. As workers began to organize extensively anyway, two presidents (Theodore Roosevelt in 1902 and William Howard Taft in 1906) felt obliged to issue executive orders to preclude employee organizations from collectively lobbying Congress for improved wages, working conditions, or other matters, upon threat of dismissal. These "gag rules" stifled federal union activity until 1912, when passage of the Lloyd–LaFollette Act guaranteed federal workers the right to petition Congress and to join labor organizations, as long as those organizations prohibited strikes against the federal government. As a result, federal employees were permitted to lobby members of Congress for pay increases and improved benefits and working conditions. Employer–employee relationships, however, continued to be determined unilaterally by management.

As private sector unions received statutory permission for collective bargaining under the 1935 NLRA (Wagner Act) and the RLA, public employee organizations continued to be ignored. The only mention of public unions in the 1947 Taft–Hartley Act was Section 305's prohibition of federal employee strike activity. Thereafter, federal employees attempted to gain statutory recognition for their organizations through support of the Rhodes–Johnson bill, which failed repeatedly in Congress from 1949 to 1961. This proposed legislation would have required federal agencies to meet and confer with employee representatives and establish an arbitration board to resolve federal labor disputes. Finally, recognition was won indirectly in the administration of President John F. Kennedy. Kennedy, who was strongly supported by organized labor throughout his campaign, appointed a presidential task force headed by Secretary of Labor Arthur Goldberg to recommend a labor–management relations program for the federal service. The task force's recommendations were embodied in President Kennedy's Executive Order 10988 (E.O. 10988) of 1962, which became the foundation of federal employee labor relations and collective bargaining.

A. Executive Orders

E.O. 10988 established for the first time the principle that federal workers have the right to form and join unions and bargain collectively. It proved to be tremendously important in public sector labor relations, stimulating employee organization and collective bargaining at all levels of government. Within 2 years, 730,000 employees were covered by collective bargaining agreements (Blum & Helburn, 1997). Although many of the provisions of E.O. 10988 were supplanted by subsequent executive orders and provisions of the CSRA of 1978, it is useful to consider the labor relations framework the order established.

The order covered almost all federal workers with the exception of uniformed military, the Federal Bureau of Investigation (FBI), the Central Intelligence Agency (CIA), and others whose work involved security needs. Three forms of recognition for labor organizations were provided: informal recognition was granted to any organization that could demonstrate it represented a minimum number of employees; formal recognition was gained when the organization could claim at least 10% of the workers in a proposed bargaining unit as members; and exclusive recognition, the only form of recognition allowed under present federal policy, was awarded to an organization that gained the support of the majority of a unit's employees. Exclusive recognition meant that the designated union had the right to meet and confer with agency management over personnel policies and practices and working conditions affecting all members of the bargaining unit represented by the union. Determination of the bargaining unit was based on the NLRA model of an identifiable "community of interest" among employees. Further corresponding to the NLRA, managers and supervisors were excluded from exclusive bargaining units.

E.O. 10988 established a code of fair labor practices to regulate the interactions between unions and management. The code, essentially consistent with provisions in the NLRA, stipulated various ULPs by both unions and federal agencies and listed procedures for hearing complaints. (Examples of ULPs are coercion of employees, discrimination, and "bad faith bargaining.") Certain management rights enumerated in E.O. 10988 remain important to this day and continue to be in effect in most federal collective bargaining contracts:

To direct employees of the agency
To hire, promote, transfer, assign, and retain employees in positions within the agency, and to suspend, demote, discharge, or take disciplinary action
To relieve employees from duties because of lack of work or other legitimate reasons
To maintain the efficiency of government operations entrusted to them
To determine the methods, means, and personnel by which such operations are to be conducted
To take whatever actions may be necessary to carry out the mission of the agency in situations of emergency

E.O. 10988 served as the basic legal framework for federal labor relations for about seven years, but dissatisfaction arose from a variety of sources, particularly unions. From their perspective, the executive order did not go far enough. The scope of bargaining was severely restricted by the management rights clause and by prohibitions against bargaining over wages, benefits, and union security provisions. Furthermore, although striking was forbidden no substitute for striking had been provided, and final authority for the implementation and administration of the executive order, including the arbitration of grievances, remained with the respective federal department and agency heads. The scales were clearly tilted in favor of management.

President Richard Nixon's Executive Order 11491 (E.O. 11491) of October 1969 was intended to alleviate these and other deficiencies. The deficiencies had been officially identified by two presidential committees: one appointed by Nixon's predecessor, President Lyndon Johnson (whose recommendations were not acted upon by a president awash in more pressing issues, including the war in Vietnam), and the other by a Nixon-appointed review committee headed by Secretary of Labor George P. Schultz. The Schultz Committee advised six major policy changes (Fox & Shelton, 1972, p. 118), most of which were adopted in E.O. 11491 of 1969. A Federal Labor Relations Council (FLRC) composed of the chairman of the Civil Service Commission, the secretary of labor, and one or more presidential designees was named to administer and interpret the new executive order, decode major labor policy issues, and hear appeals resulting from decisions rendered by the new assistant secretary for labor–management relations (ASLMR). The ASLMR's duties included resolving unit determination and representation disputes, supervising and certifying elections, and hearing ULP allegations and other alleged violations of labor relations procedures and standards.

E.O. 11491 abolished the unwieldy formal and informal types of recognition, retaining only exclusive recognition. The non-bargaining status of supervisors remained unchanged, but the scope of bargaining, contrary to union aspirations, was restricted even further. In addition, financial disclosure and reporting requirements similar to those set forth for private unions under the Landrum–Griffin Act were imposed on federal unions.

Major changes were made in procedures for resolving bargaining impasses and grievance disputes. Binding grievance arbitration was authorized as negotiable for the first time. To resolve impasses, two new entities were created: the Federal Mediation and Conciliation Service (FMCS) to mediate labor disputes and the Federal Service Impasses Panel (FSIP) to settle impasses or recommend impasse resolution procedures to the parties involved. Thus, a neutral third party could now overrule agency heads and resolve impasses over contract negotiations and grievances.

Nixon amended E.O. 11491 with Executive Order 11616 of 1971, which among several relatively minor changes made mandatory the use of the negotiated grievance procedure for settling contract disputes. Further amendments to E.O. 11491 were issued in 1975 by President Gerald Ford. This final document in this chain of presidential directives, Executive Order 11838, marginally broadened the scope of bargaining, encouraged the consolidation of small bargaining units, defined "supervisor" more specifically, and implemented minor procedural changes.

Thus, the early legal basis of federal labor–management relations was determined incrementally through a series of executive orders, rather than through statutes. Even though executive orders have the effect of law, their provisions are much easier to modify or abolish than provisions written into statute. Any subsequent president, or Congress, may take action to rescind or alter an executive order, whereas legislation can be modified or abolished only through formal congressional action. Not surprisingly, legally insecure federal employees continued to lobby for a statutory guarantee for collective bargaining. Their demands were embodied, at least in part, in the Civil Service Reform Act (CSRA) of 1978.

B. Civil Service Reform Act of 1978

Passage of the CSRA was one of the few significant legislative victories for the administration of President Jimmy Carter, although today, many scholars and practitioners regard it as a well-meaning failure at best. There is no doubt that the CSRA was the most important piece of legislation regarding federal employment since the Pendleton Act nearly 100 years earlier.

The Reform Act proceeded quickly and relatively unhindered through the congressional process. Its rapid progress may be attributed to a number of factors, the most important being the strong support of the president, the influential leadership of Civil Service Commission Chairman Allan (Scotty) Campbell, widespread support among career civil servants, and the reform-mindedness of a post-Watergate Congress. Furthermore, Title VII of the CSRA, the chapter on federal labor–management relations, was endorsed, with some reservations, by the American Federation of Labor–Congress of Industrial Organizations (AFL–CIO) and the largest federal employee union, the American Federation of Government Employees (AFGE). Although the National Treasury Employees Union (NTEU) and the National Federation of Federal Employees opposed the measure, mainly because they felt the scope of bargaining continued to be too narrow, their resistance did not stop the passage of the legislation.

Federal employee labor rights were placed into statute by Title VII of the CSRA, the Federal Service Labor–Management Relations Statute. The act also created the Federal Labor Relations Authority (FLRA) to administer the labor relations program and established the Office of Labor–Management Relations within the U.S. Office of Personnel Management (OPM). The Office of Labor–Management Relations provides technical advice to federal agencies on labor policies, leadership, and contract administration.

Under the CSRA, most General Schedule (GS) and wage grade employees enjoy "the right to form, join or assist any labor organization, or to refrain from any such activity, freely and without fear of reprisal, and each employee shall be protected in the exercise of such rights," including the right to present a labor organization's views to agency heads and other officials in the executive branch, and the right to "engage in collective bargaining with respect to conditions of employment." Conditions of employment are defined as "personnel policies, practices, and matters, whether established by rule, regulation, or otherwise, affecting working conditions." Excluded from the scope of negotiable issues are wages and benefits, prohibited political activities, union security arrangements (e.g., union shop and fair share), and position classification. Thus, the scope of bargaining for federal employees, in essence, remained unchanged.

The severely circumscribed scope of bargaining continues to be a topic of controversy and profound union discontent. President Clinton's Executive Order 12871 of 1993 expanded the mandatory federal scope of bargaining to embrace previously permissible topics, including the numbers, types, and grades of employees and positions as well as the technology, methods, and means of performing work. Clinton's executive order was revoked by President George W. Bush in 2001.

An important provision of Title VII expanded the scope of grievance activities. Under Title VII, all federal labor agreements must include negotiated grievance procedures, with binding arbitration as the final step. Previously, grievance arbitration was optional. Other sections of Title VII recognize the right of federal workers to engage in informational picketing, authorize official or "union" time for union representation, and allow checkoff of dues at no cost to the employee or the union.

CSRA's Title VII covers most federal employees except for supervisory personnel; members of the armed forces; foreign service employees; and workers in the Government Accounting Office (GAO), FBI, CIA, National Security Agency (NSA), Tennessee Valley Authority (TVA), U.S. Postal Service, and certain other exemptions, as described in the following section. Employees of the TVA, a government corporation, bargain collectively under the 1935 "Employment Relationship Policy," created as part of the New Deal legislation of Franklin D. Roosevelt. Postal workers, as a result of a settlement with the Nixon administration following a 1970 postal strike involving 200,000 employees, gained bargaining rights through the Postal Reorganization Act of 1970, which removed them from the authority of executive orders and granted full NLRA collective bargaining rights with the exception of the right to strike and union security provisions. Armed forces personnel are prohibited from collective bargaining and engaging in other union activities such as strikes and picketing by a secretary of defense directive of October 5, 1977. GAO, FBI, CIA, and NSA personnel have no legal authority for collective bargaining.

C. Exceptions from Civil Service Reform Act Coverage

As noted, President Clinton's Executive Order 12871 modestly expanded the scope of bargaining under Title VII. Most importantly, it directed federal agencies to develop "partnerships" with unions representing their workers. Through collaboration and cooperation, labor–management partnerships resulted in improvements in customer services, technology, quality of work life, and overall quality of labor–management relations over the span of about seven years. President Clinton's directives sent a clear message that unions played a legitimate role in helping governmental agencies achieve their missions (Masters et al., 2020).

Upon assuming office in January 2001, the decidedly antiunion President Bush immediately rescinded Clinton's executive order and dissolved existing partnerships. He also set about revoking the bargaining rights of certain employees in the Department of Justice and elsewhere. Following the terrorist attacks of

September 11, 2001, the Bush administration sought and won congressional approval of a new department, the Department of Homeland Security (DHS). Twenty-two existing security-related agencies with some 175,000 employees including the Federal Emergency Management Agency, Coast Guard, Immigration and Customs Enforcement, Border and Transportation Security, and other entities, were consolidated in the behemoth department.

After a vicious battle with unions and congressional Democrats, President Bush won the authority to waive collective bargaining rights for designated DHS employees on the grounds of national security (Masters & Albright, 2003). Transportation Security Administration baggage screeners were the first to be exempt from Title VII. For other DHS employees, the scope of bargaining was narrowed and management authority was expanded. DHS managerial discretion over pay, discipline, position classification, and other personnel matters was enlarged. Collective bargaining disputes would no longer be addressed by the FLRA, but instead by a new DHS labor relations board. The new DHS human resource management (HRM) system also restricted the review authority of the Merit Systems Protection Board (MSPB) for adverse actions against employees and created a new pay banding system to replace the long-standing GS pay system.

Federal unions led by NTEU and AFGE filed suit against the new rules on grounds that the Bush administration had exceeded the authority granted to it by congressional legislation establishing DHS. A federal district court ruled in favor of the unions in 2005 (*NTEU v. Michael Chertoff*, 2005). The district court decision was basically upheld by the U.S. Court of Appeals for the D.C. Circuit in 2006, but many important questions remained unanswered, and the rules were permitted to go forward. Finally, in October 2007 collaboration between the OPM and MSPB led to implementation of the new rules for nonunion personnel in the DHS. Decisions concerning the 50,000 DHS employees covered by collective bargaining agreements came with the next round of bargaining (Barr, 2007).

Similarly, a new HRM system for the Department of Defense (DoD), called the National Security Personnel System (NSPS), was approved and final regulations were issued in 2005. Like the contested DHS changes, the DoD HRM system reduced the scope of bargaining, established a new agency-specific labor relations board, expedited disciplinary and dismissal processing, and implemented a pay banding scheme (Thompson, 2007, p. 111). Upon appeal by the unions, a federal district court enjoined the implementation of the DoD rules in 2006 (*AFGE, et al. v. Donald H. Rumsfeld*). On appeal, a divided three-judge panel overturned the district court decision. Turning to Congress, the unions won a prohibition on NSPS rules implementation through the National Defense Authorization Act of 2008. In the reauthorization of this act in 2010, Congress abolished the NSPS altogether (Kellough et al., 2010, p. 417).

President Bush's "failed effort to impose radical personnel reforms" on DHS and DoD workers was the product of mixed motivations (Kellough et al., 2010).

At its heart was the antiunion ideology of the president and his supporters. Other more legitimate concerns included a perceived need for improvement in HRM techniques, such as position classification, examination, and performance appraisal. There was also a manifest desire to exercise greater executive control over the federal bureaucracy so that the administration's policy preferences would receive sympathetic attention (Kellough et al., 2010). That the federal unions would fight the new personnel rules so fiercely in courts and in Congress was no surprise.

With President Obama, the pendulum moved slightly toward supporting unions. President Obama issued E.O. 13522—Creating Labor Management Forums to Improve the Delivery of Government Services (2009). This order encouraged the creation of forums and created a National Council on Federal Labor Management Relations to assess the performance of the forums. The parties to the forums were limited to discussing permissive bargaining subjects. Also, during the Obama administration, TSA Administrator John Pistole granted limited collective bargaining rights to airport screeners. Specifically, collective bargaining was restricted to the performance management process, awards and recognition process, attendance management guidelines process, and shift bids. The memorandum also specified that the TSA leadership would remain neutral during union organizing campaigns (Pistole, 2011).

President Trump took a more adversarial approach to labor management relations. With E.O. 13812, (2017), President Trump revoked Obama's order creating labor management forums. The language in this E.O. took the additional step of preventing federal agencies from using public funds for labor management cooperation in the future (Masters et al., 2020).

On May 25, 2018, President Trump issued three more executive orders that weakened labor rights and tilted the balance in favor of management rights. E.O. 13836 (2018), expedited the timeframe allowed to complete bargaining and directed agencies to avoid bargaining over topics deemed to exceed the statutory scope of bargaining. E.O. 13837 (2018) restricted the use of official time for collective bargaining activities. Official time refers to the time that federal employees spend representing bargaining unit members. The activities include engaging with management in discussions of grievances, dispute resolution, labor relations training, labor-management relations, and department initiatives. E.O. 13839 (2018) weakened due process protections for federal workers subject to discipline.

President Biden took a markedly pro-labor stance toward federal employees. In E.O. 14003 (2021), Biden declared that federal employees were "the backbone of the Federal workforce, providing the expertise and experience," required to ensure the government functions effectively. E.O. 14003 revoked the three E.O.'s issued by President Trump on May 25, 2018 and directed heads of agencies to "suspend, revise or rescind" actions taken under these orders. The order also restored the right to bargain over permissive subjects, such as the numbers, types and grades of employees assigned and methods, means, and technology used to perform the work. Finally, E.O. 14003 tasked the director of OPM with conducting a study to develop recommendations for raising the minimum wage for Federal employees to $15.00 per hour.

In April 2021, President Biden issued Executive Order 14025 Worker Organizing and Empowerment (2021). Although not aimed entirely at federal employees, this E.O. took a whole-of-government approach to protecting workers' rights. It established a task force composed of over 20 agency heads and Cabinet leaders to review existing policies and make recommendations to support workers' rights to engage in collective action.

The task force report issued in 2022 positioned the federal government as a model employer. It outlined over 70 recommendations, aimed at reducing impediments to organizing, improving enforcement of existing laws, and creating resources for workers on unions and collective bargaining. Several recommendations specifically targeted the federal workforce, such as reinstituting labor management forums, expanding collective bargaining rights for the TSA's screening workforce, and standardizing guidelines for union organizer access to military bases and installations (Harris & Walsh, 2022). Moreover, the task force is publicly tracking federal agencies' progress toward its goals (Task Force on Worker Organizing and Empowerment Progress, 2023).

D. Federal Labor Relations Authority

The FLRA is a three-member, presidentially appointed bipartisan entity charged with integrating all labor relations administrative functions previously divided among the FLRC, the ASLMR, the FSIP, the FMCS, and executive agencies. The terms run for five years, staggered by two-year intervals.

The FLRA is intended to serve as the final authority in federal labor relations matters, but judicial review of most authority rulings by the U.S. Court of Appeals is permitted. Specific functions of the FLRA are very similar to those of the private sector National Labor Relations Board (NLRB). They include (1) determining bargaining units, (2) supervising and conducting union elections, (3) resolving allegations of ULPs (this constitutes the bulk of its activities), (4) resolving exceptions to arbitrators' awards, and (5) deciding issues concerning what is negotiable between labor and management. The FLRA is served by a general counsel—appointed by the president to investigate ULP allegations and to serve as prosecutor in such cases—and a number of administrative law judges. The FSIP remains an ongoing organization within the FLRA, continuing its original executive order function of resolving federal impasses. The FMCS, an independent agency, has broadened its mission to include preventive mediation and alternative dispute resolution.

In its primary role as the principal adjudicatory body for federal labor-management relations, the poorly regarded FLRA has come under heavy criticism from the courts, unions, and management. It has frustrated all parties for its sluggish pace in making even pro forma decisions and decisions that tend to drive unions and agencies to seek judicial resolution. Some of this frustration in recent years is due to understaffing. For example, President Trump left the FLRA's Office of the General Council (OGC) vacant from 2017 until he left office in 2021. Although Trump did nominate a candidate to fill the position in 2019, the Republican controlled senate failed to approve the nomination. This meant the FLRA could not adjudicate cases of unfair labor practices that came before it (Kellough, 2023).

President Biden's attempted unsuccessfully to fill the OGC position. In March 2021 Charlotte Dye was assigned to serve as Acting General Counsel. In August 2021, President Biden nominated Kurt Rumsfeld to serve as General Counsel. The Senate failed to approve the nomination. President Biden nominated Mr. Rumsfeld again in January 2022 and the Senate returned the nomination (without approval) in January 2023. Charlotte Dye continued to serve as acting General Counsel. However, in February 2023, the Government Accountability Office (GAO) determined that Ms. Dye's ongoing service as Acting General Counsel was in violation of the Vacancies Act's time limitations (U.S. GAO, 2023). The General Counsel position remained vacant as of March 2024.

The FLRA provides four alternative dispute resolution paths, creating needless confusion and redundancy and often ultimately resulting in court review. The length of dispute resolution is measured in years rather than months, not exactly a morale booster for either employees or managements. For example, a recent FLRA accountability and performance report indicates that the average of arbitration case appeals decided/resolved by the FLRA was 395 days in 2021, 405 days in 2022, and 299 days in 2023. Overall, the FLRA made progress in reducing pending cases in the fiscal year (FY) 2023 closing out the year with 98 pending cases, as compared to 100 pending cases in FY 2022 and 153 pending cases in FY 2021. However, this progress is unlikely to continue in FY 2024 due to vacancies in key Presidential positions. Of particular concern is the lack of a third member on the authority to break ties when the other two members disagree. Moreover, the many of backlogged cases are entail complex issues that will require a substantial amount of time to resolve when the authority is fully staffed (U.S. Federal Labor Relations Authority, 2023).

The CSRA did not represent radical change in the basic federal labor relations framework, essentially placing into code what had originally been created through executive orders. Now long of tooth, the CSRA has been subjected to serious criticism from many different quarters. Significant problems beset the CSRA. Among the most pressing are the obsolescence of the GS classification and pay system, and the "balkanization" of the federal personnel system with "multiple sets of personnel rules that have created governance concerns" across the federal bureaucracy (Thompson, 2010, p. 41). A more recent report by the National Commission on Military, National, and Public Service (2020) described the GS system as rigid.

Similarly, a report prepared for the National Academy of Public Administration (Kettl et al., 2017) portrayed the federal government's human capital system as broken and called for a new approach that treats workers as assets instead of liabilities.

Title VII has received special opprobrium from the unions. To all interested parties, parts of the legislation are ambiguous. According to the union perspective, the FLRA is biased and ponderously slow. Union security restrictions depress membership, and free-rider problems abound. The narrow scope of non-postal bargaining, particularly the exclusion of wages and benefits from negotiations, leaves little for the unions to bring to the bargaining table. Left with filing grievances as one of the few tactics available to them, unions are pressured by dissatisfied and frustrated members of the bargaining unit.

Taken together, the weaknesses of Title VII have promoted "fierce disagreement and hostile litigation" (Tobias, 1998, p. 263) and marginalized human resource managers. To illustrate, President Trump's attempts to exempt adverse personnel actions from grievance procedures along with a ruling that unions must seek remedies from the FLRA raised concerns among leaders and members of AFGE and NTEU (Katz, 2019). Similarly, an attempt by the FLRA to revisit the standards by which arbitrators' fees are awarded in cases where the federal agency is determined to be at fault reaffirmed unions' perspectives of bias and elevated anxieties that the agency was becoming politicized (Wagner, 2019).

From the management side, President Trump attempted to dismantle OPM by placing the policymaking authority of OPM under the control of the Executive Office of the President. Trump's plan also called for placing the remaining personnel services provided by OPM under the General Services Agency (GSA). Although Trump's plan eventually failed, there was substantial turnover among the agency leadership as OPM cycled through five directors during his term (Kellough, 2023). Likewise, the MSPB was understaffed during President Trump's term. As of January 2021, the MSPB lacked a quorum to resolve disputes. The board had no members between March 2019 and January 2021 as the Senate failed to confirm Trump's nominees (Ogrysko, 2021). The lack of a quorum hampered the MSPB's ability to issue decisions on petitions for review (PFRs) and other cases and resulted in a backlog of 3071 cases in 2021. The MSPB was also prevented from issuing reports of merit systems studies, promulgating regulations, and providing whistleblower protections during Office of Special Counsel investigations (U.S. Merits Systems Protection Board, 2021).

IV. LEGAL BASIS OF LABOR RELATIONS IN STATE AND LOCAL GOVERNMENTS

The legal framework for federal employee unionization and collective bargaining is somewhat fragmented, but the majority of workers are covered under two statutes: the CSRA and the Postal Reorganization Act. But compared to that of the private sector and the federal government, the legal basis for state and local government labor relations is a Byzantine web of myriad statutes, ordinances, court decisions, executive orders, attorney general opinions, and other policy articulations. If ever the state and local governments have served as political laboratories, it is in public sector labor relations. The advantages of diversity are many. But there are also important disadvantages of policy fragmentation for governments and their workers.

Since the mid-1970s, there has been recurring public debate on national labor legislation for state and local government employees, which would force a substantial amount of standardization in the legal environment of labor relations. On several occasions (most recently 2021), it appeared that national legislation stood a reasonably good chance of passage. After briefly considering the pros and cons of a national law for state and local collective bargaining and the possibilities for adoption of the idea in the future, we examine in detail the diffusion and the general characteristics of state and local collective bargaining policies today.

A. The Quest for Federal Legislation for State and Local Governments

A number of bills have been introduced in Congress with the intent of federally regulating state and local government labor relations. Three basic approaches have been represented in the proposed legislation. One seeks to amend the NLRA to cover some—or all—state and local government employees. The reasoning behind this approach is that public employees should have labor rights identical to those enjoyed by private sector workers. Accordingly, the jurisdiction of the NLRB would be extended to cover nonfederal public employee collective bargaining, thereby preempting existing state and local government policies.

A second approach to federal legislation would create a new federal labor authority to cover state and local government bargaining: in other words, an NLRB or FLRA for state and local employees. The act would be administered by a National Public Employment Relations Commission, much like the NLRB. This proposal receives strong union support and would supersede all existing state and local bargaining laws and any other inconsistent statutes.

The third approach to a federal statute envisions a state–federal partnership, with the federal government setting minimum standards for labor relations and collective bargaining and ensuring conformity through the federal power of the purse, much as federal highway safety requirements and the mandatory 21-year legal drinking age were implemented. This "minimum standards" or "partial preemption" approach avoids complete federal takeover of labor relations while permitting a measure of continued state and local experimentation. States already conforming to the federal standards would have authority to administer their own programs without federal interference.

Proponents of various bills have argued that federal legislation would decrease the incidence of strikes by (1) making union recognition mandatory, thereby eliminating the need for recognition strikes and (2) stipulating impasse procedures designed to preclude strikes. Proponents further contend that federal legislation would provide equal treatment for all state and local government employees in the United States. Labor relations uniformity would, as an added benefit, enable a common national approach to training all labor relations participants, thereby enhancing the overall quality of labor–management relations.

Opponents of the proposals fail to see the purported advantages of uniformity. "In the case of public employee unionism," argued Wellington and Winter (1971, pp. 53–54), "uniformity is most undesirable and diversity in rules and structure virtually a necessity." Regulation by the states "provides a more flexible approach than national legislation." State officials are likely to be more sensitive to problems of local government than federal officials, and legislation that proves to be inappropriate can be modified more easily at the state level than at the national level. Other critics contend that any form of federal regulation or mandate would violate the autonomy of state and local governments and, furthermore, that there is no "one best way" to regulate public employee unionization and collective bargaining.

A bill titled "HR 980: Public Safety Employer–Employee Cooperation Act of 2007" was introduced in the U.S. House of Representatives. It passed by a healthy majority (314 to 97), and chances for its passage in the Senate were looking reasonably good when the bill's champion, Massachusetts Senator Edward Kennedy, was hospitalized and diagnosed with a brain tumor. The bill languished in the Senate while Congress fixated on the national financial crisis and then adjourned for the holidays and to await installation of the Barack Obama administration.

HR 980 was designed to provide collective bargaining rights for state and local "public safety officers," defined as law enforcement officers, firefighters, and emergency medical personnel. The scope of bargaining included hours, wages, and working conditions. Strikes and lockouts were prohibited. The existing FLRA would have been charged with issuing regulations for union recognition and collective bargaining in the states without existing provisions. The FLRA would also have taken responsibility conduct and supervise elections of bargaining representatives, ensure good faith bargaining, and hear allegations of ULPs. Nonbargaining jurisdictions lobbied hard to stop the passage of HR 980, calling it an unfunded mandate and an unconstitutional intrusion into state and local affairs. Ultimately the bill died in Congress in August 2009.

More recently, "HR 5727: Public Service Freedom to Negotiate Act of 2021" was introduced in the U.S. House of Representatives. The bill would have provided collective bargaining rights for a broader group of public service employees than HR 980. Similar to HR 980, it banned strikes by selected public safety employees and charged the FLRA with administering the Act. It was introduced in the House and referred to the House Committee on Education and Labor on

October 26, 2021. The bill appeared to have broad support, with 202 co-sponsors across 39 states. However, only four of the sponsors were Republicans. No further action has been taken on the bill.

Would either bill have withstood a court challenge? The bills would have offered a test similar to that decided by the U.S. Supreme Court in *Garcia v. San Antonio Metropolitan Transit Authority* (1985) on the applicability of the federal Fair Labor Standards Act to state and local governments. The court's view on congressional authority over state and local governments has vacillated during the nearly three decades since *Garcia*, so it remains possible that congressional preemption of state labor relations policy could be declared unconstitutional on Eleventh or Fourteenth Amendment grounds (Clark & Powers, 2003). Because public employees

Table 3.1 **Major Federal Laws Affecting Public Sector Labor Relations**

Legislation	*Subject Matter*
Civil Rights Act of 1964	Prohibited employer discrimination on the basis of race, color, gender, religion, or national origin
Equal Employment Opportunity Act of 1972	Extended Civil Rights Act of 1964 requirements to public employers and extended the enforcement powers of Equal Employment Opportunity Commission
Age Discrimination in Employment Act (1967)	Prohibited discrimination by the employer against employees aged 40–70 years
Occupational Safety and Health Act (1970)	Prescribed health- and safety-related working conditions
Employee Retirement Income Security Act (1974)	Addressed pensions, health care, disability, and accident plans
Urban Mass Transportation Act (1964)	Required that interests of employees, including collective bargaining rights, be protected when ownership of the transit system changes
Social Security Act of 1935	Stipulated personnel policies for state and local workers paid in whole or in part with federal grant dollars
Fair Labor Standards Act (as amended)	Applied federal wage and hour laws to state and local governments
Americans with Disabilities Act (1990)	Caused changes in personnel policies for mentally and physically disabled workers
Civil Rights Act of 1991	Reversed and altered 12 U.S. Supreme Court decisions that had narrowed civil rights protections
Family and Medical Leave Act (1993)	Ensured that leave is available to employees for authorized medical reasons and for compelling family reasons

do not hold a constitutional right to engage in collective bargaining, employers are not required to grant such a right unless specified by state law or local ordinance.

Although national bargaining legislation remains high on the wish list of unions and may be reincarnated in the future, congressional action is uncertain. Organized labor's political influence in Congress is weak; a presidential veto of such a bill might squelch it, and the record now shows that the decentralized approach to state and local labor relations has functioned reasonably well. Other national laws may be enacted that influence labor relations at the margins (see Table 3.1), but an all-embracing policy change stands a dim chance at present.

B. State and Local Government Policies

Today, representing a celebration of policy diversity, more than 100 separate statutes govern state and local labor relations, augmented by numerous local ordinances, court decisions, attorney general opinions, and executive orders. State legislation, for instance, ranges from a single comprehensive statute providing coverage for all public employees in Iowa to coverage of only firefighters in Wyoming and total prohibition of collective bargaining in North Carolina. Public employees in some states bargain under the authority of an attorney general's opinion (North Dakota), executive order (Colorado), or civil service regulations (Michigan state employees).

The earliest legislation regulating state and local government employer–employee relationships aimed to abolish strikes by public workers. Shortly after World War II, eight states enacted no-strike laws with stiff penalties for violators. In other states, beginning in 1951, laws were passed that established the right of public workers to join employee organizations and provided a limited degree of support for developing some form of bilateral relations between government jurisdictions and their workers. Several local governments passed ordinances or issued executive orders regulating collective bargaining. As Schneider (1988, p. 197) observed, "The stand that any form of bargaining in the public sector was impossible was crumbling in the face of experience and political expediency." Finally, in 1959 Wisconsin broke out of the state legislative limbo with a law establishing collective bargaining rights for local government employees. Today, legislation or other policies imposing a duty to bargain or meet and confer with at least one group of public workers are in effect in 46 states.

Most of the bargaining laws were enacted over a period of about ten years, from the mid-1960s through the mid-1970s. A variety of important issues had to be faced by the state lawmakers, including (1) whether each jurisdiction within a state should be permitted to establish its own labor relations policy or all jurisdictions should conform to a single policy applied uniformly, (2) whether one comprehensive law should apply to both levels of government and all occupational functions or separate policies should be established for state and local governments and for each functional category, (3) who or what entity should administer the policy, and (4) what labor relations and collective bargaining principles and procedures should be adopted. Legislative outcomes were hammered out in fierce battles fought between public employee unions, public employers, and numerous interest groups.

Since the mid-1970s, most legislative activity has focused on refining existing policy rather than enacting new legislation. Only four states have passed major collective bargaining laws since the 1970s—Ohio, Illinois, New Mexico, and Washington—although others have implemented collective bargaining through executive orders, court decisions, and local ordinances. Oklahoma passed a duty-to-bargain law for municipal employees in 2004, however, this law was overturned in 2011.

Table 3.2 shows the legal framework for collective bargaining in 2023. If there is a trend today, it appears to be in the direction of revoking or weakening collective bargaining rights, as recently seen in Indiana, Idaho, Ohio, Oklahoma, Tennessee, Wisconsin, and other states. As Anzia and Moe (2016) note, the Republican party has become more homogeneously conservative and anti-union than it was in the 1970s and 1980s. A more unified political ideology was evident in a number of collective bargaining rollbacks that have occurred since 2011.

Table 3.2 State Bargaining Status, 2023

State	*State*	*Local*	*Police*	*Firefighters*	*K–12 Teachers*
Alabama	N	Y	N	Y	Y
Alaska	X	X	X	X	X
Arizona	N	Y	N	X[1]	N
Arkansas	P	P	X	X	P
California	X	Y	X	X	X
Colorado	X	X	X	X	N
Connecticut	X	X	X	X	X
Delaware	X	X	X	X	X
Florida	X[2]	X[2]	X	X	X[1]
Georgia	P	P	P	X	P
Hawaii	X	Y	X	X	X
Idaho	X	X	N	X	X
Illinois	X	X	X	X	X
Indiana	P	P	N	X[1]	X
Iowa	X	X	X	X	X

(*Continued*)

Table 3.2 (Continued)

State	*State*	*Local*	*Police*	*Firefighters*	*K–12 Teachers*
Kansas	X	X[3]	X	X	X
Kentucky	P	X	N	X	N
Louisiana	X	X	N	X[1]	N
Maine	X	X	X	X	X
Maryland	X	X	X	X	X
Massachusetts	X	X	X	X	X
Michigan	X	X	X	X	X
Minnesota	X	X	X	X	X
Mississippi	N	N	N	X[1]	P
Missouri	X	Y	N	X	X
Montana	X	X	X	X	X
Nebraska	X	X	X	X	X
Nevada	X	X	X	X	X
New Hampshire	X	X	X	X	X
New Jersey	X	X	X	X	X
New Mexico	X	X	N	X	X
New York	X	X	X	X	X
North Carolina	P	P	P	P	P
North Dakota	X	X	N	X	X
Ohio	X	X	X	X	X
Oklahoma	P	P	X	X	X
Oregon	X	X	X	X	X
Pennsylvania	X	X	X	X	X
Rhode Island	X	X	X	X	X
South Carolina	P	P	P	X[1]	P
South Dakota	X	X	N	X	X
Tennessee	P	Y[4]	P	X[5]	X[6]
Texas	P	Y	P	X	P
Utah	N	N	N	X	N
Vermont	X	X	X	X	X
Virginia	P	X[3]	X[1]	X[1]	X[1]
Washington	X	X	X	X	X
Washington, DC	X	X	N	X	X

(Continued)

Table 3.2 (Continued)

State	*State*	*Local*	*Police*	*Firefighters*	*K–12 Teachers*
West Virginia	N	N	N	X[1]	N
Wisconsin	X	X	X	X	X
Wyoming	N	N	N	X	N

Source: data from state websites, state legislative summaries, National Conference of State Legislatures, and various newspaper articles.

Notes:

X Collective bargaiOning provisions
Y Meet and confer provisions
P Collective bargaining prohibited
N No provisions or law
1 Local
2 As of 2023, a public sector union must have 60% of covered employees paying dues to stay active
3 Opt-in required
4 For transit workers only
5 Non-enforceable
6 Collaborative conferencing

Most state labor relations policies reflect a realization of the value of developing a formal framework to direct bilateral relationships between public workers and their employers. Clearly, many variations in policies exist, but the pattern has been to extend comprehensive coverage to all state and local government workers. Thirty-one states and the District of Columbia currently provide bargaining coverage by statute for most major employee groups, with either a single comprehensive public employee relations policy or separate policies for different functions. The remaining states have a mix of policies that regulate employer–employee negotiations. Some states specifically prohibit collective bargaining for some or all public employees. Others do not have public policies permitting collective bargaining but allow some categories of employees to meet and confer rights (see Table 3.2).

As noted in Chapter 2, bargaining laws are both a product of public employee unionization and a stimulant of unionization. This reciprocal relationship has been both observed and validated in the scholarly literature (Waters et al., 1994; Farber, 1987). Specifically, politically influential public sector unions have spurred the enactment of bargaining legislation in the states, and newly passed collective bargaining laws have been associated with a growth in union membership. In Washington, some 65,000 new union members were registered after a state bargaining law was enacted.

When bargaining rights are revoked, membership plummets. Union membership in Indiana declined by about two-thirds from 2005 to 2010 after Governor

Mitch Daniels rescinded an executive order issued by his predecessor that permitted collective bargaining for state workers. Similarly, public sector union membership in Wisconsin declined precipitously after the passage of Act 10 in 2011. From 2011 to 2021 public sector unions in Wisconsin have lost roughly 11,500 members per year (Wisconsin Policy Forum, 2022).

Bargaining laws are the single most important factor in determining the nature and temperament of public employer–employee relationships in state and local governments. The states with comprehensive bargaining laws tend to share certain traits and experiences. Generally, they are industrialized, urbanized, and relatively affluent states of the Frostbelt. Many of them have traditionally been policy innovators.

Strong private sector unionization (indicating pro-union sentiment) is associated with comprehensive public sector bargaining policy at the time it is adopted and so is the alignment of the political stars—most of the comprehensive statutes were enacted by liberal Democratic majorities in state legislatures and signed by a Democratic governor (see Hundley, 1988, pp. 302–303; Saltzman, 1985). In Ohio, comprehensive bargaining bills were passed in the legislature in two consecutive sessions, only to be vetoed by Republican Governor James Rhodes. The third time was the charm, when newly elected Democratic Governor Richard Celeste signed the bill in 1983. It took 14 years of legislative struggle and a new Democratic governor for Washington state employees to win full collective bargaining rights in 2002.

Aside from comprehensive laws, in the decades from the 1960s through the 1980s, most collected bargaining laws were enacted under divided government. In some cases, collective bargaining provisions were adopted under unified Republican government. For example, Iowa, New Hampshire, South Dakota, and Vermont granted collective bargaining rights to state employees under these circumstances (Anzia & Moe, 2016).

C. States that Prohibit Collective Bargaining and/or Lack Collective Bargaining Policies

The following states prohibit collective bargaining for some or all public employees: Arkansas, Georgia, Indiana, Kentucky, Mississippi, North Carolina, Oklahoma, South Carolina, Tennessee, Texas, and Virginia. North Carolina and Virginia are formally on the legislative record as being hostile to collective bargaining—both have passed laws that prohibit it. Despite the prohibition, "informal bargaining" occurs regularly in some North Carolina school districts and local governments (Rhodes & Brown, 1992), and strikes have occurred in Virginia.

In the case of *Virginia v. Arlington County Board of Education* (1977), the Virginia Supreme Court unanimously ruled that public employers in that state had no authority to recognize a union or negotiate and enter into a binding agreement without express statutory authority. (At the time of the decision, about 30,000 local government workers were under collective bargaining contracts, which immediately became void.) The Virginia legislature forcefully and unequivocally reified the court ruling with a 1993 statute:

> No state, county, municipal, or like governmental officer, agent, or governing body is vested with or possesses any authority to recognize any labor union or other employee association as a bargaining agent of any public officers or employees, or to collectively bargain or enter into any collective bargaining contract with any such union or association or its agents with respect to any matter relating to them or their employment or service.
>
> (VA Code 40.1–57.2)

However, as noted in Chapter 2, Virginia enacted a law in 2020 that allows public sector unions to engage in collective bargaining at the local level (county, city, town) provided that the local government adopts an authorizing ordinance or resolution. The law does not provide collective bargaining rights for state-level employees, higher education workers, and state-paid contractors. State employees' associations, such as Virginia Governmental Employees Association (VGEA), are advocating for expansion of collective bargaining rights.

Several states lack formal policies for some categories of workers and allow it for others. For example, Utah and Wyoming lack formal policies for all workers except firefighters. Similarly, West Virginia lacks formal policies for all workers but allows local governments to bargain with firefighters. Arizona allows local governments to bargain with firefighters and meet and confer rights for local government employees. Arizona has exhibited a schizophrenic posture on state employees. In December 2008, then-governor Janet Napolitano granted them meet-and-confer rights, which were swiftly revoked by her successor (see Figure 3.1).

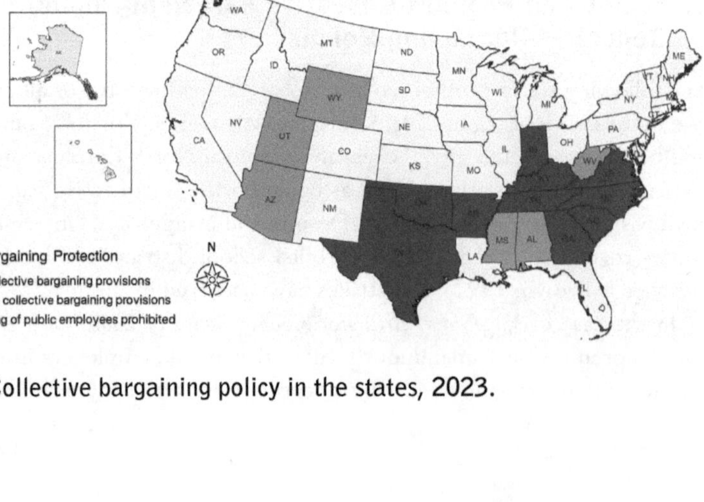

Figure 3.1 Collective bargaining policy in the states, 2023.

It is difficult to categorize Wisconsin, which passed a law in 2011 that prohibits public worker unions from bargaining over benefits and working conditions and limits what they can bargain in wages to the rise in the Consumer Price Index. And to bargain over wages, locals must first "recertify" (a majority of bargaining unit members must vote that they want the local). Since 2011, 983 public sector unions in Wisconsin held recertification votes. Of the public sector unions going through recertification, only 381 were successful as of 2021. The remaining unions either failed to achieve a majority vote or chose to stop replying for recertification by the end of 2021, which means they are no longer bargaining. These figures do not include unions representing police and firefighters because workers in these professions were exempted from Act 10 (Wisconsin Policy Forum, 2022).

History and political culture have predisposed the southern states against unions. Slave-based plantation economies gave way to antiunion corporate owners and industries such as textiles that continued the traditions of intimidating and controlling workers. In the 1950s, beatings and physical tactics were replaced by psychological techniques, including appointment of antiunion preachers and teachers in "company town" churches and schools. Both southern culture and political conservatism, which emphasize individualism and self-reliance over communitarianism and are rooted in a system of stratification and rigid social barriers, continue to drive anti-union sentiments today (Hogler et al., 2015).

As mentioned at the beginning of this chapter, public employees in states that do not specifically prohibit collective bargaining enjoy the right to form and join unions. They also have the right to petition their employers as individuals or through an organization, but there is no concomitant obligation on the part of the government employer to meet with the organization, engage in collective bargaining, or even withhold organizational dues from paychecks. However, if the public employer voluntarily elects to conduct negotiations with a union in the absence of enabling legislation, the courts have generally upheld the bargaining relationship, with at least one exception.

When a service changes from private ownership to public ownership, an interesting problem arises in those states that deny negotiating rights for public employees. Just such a situation developed in several instances involving local government takeovers of private transit systems. Prior to the transfer of ownership, of course, collective bargaining agreements are administered under the authority of the NLRA. Upon change in ownership, however, private sector policies no longer apply. The new transit authority must retain the existing contractual arrangements with the union under Article 13(c) of the Urban Mass Transportation Act of 1964, which states that "workers and unions will lose no rights as the result of public takeovers financed by federal funds." (Most urban transportation services are partly subsidized with federal dollars.) The implications for the new public owner are quite clear, but possibly disturbing.

Without a preexisting legal framework to guide labor relations, the city, county, or special-purpose government may find itself in the midst of a dilemma. One rather imaginative solution is the "Memphis formula," which was developed in that city prior to the passage of Tennessee's 1971 bargaining law for transit employees. Under the Memphis formula, government owners of a transit system contract out transit activities to a management services firm, which bargains collectively with the union. The management firm thus serves as the bargaining agent for the local government under the authority of the NLRA (Oestreich & Whaley, 2001).

Of course, ownership can change in the opposite direction as well, with functions formerly operated by government being contracted out to a private or nonprofit organization. In this event, private sector law (the NLRA) normally applies. However, there is a certain irony with respect to transit systems. As stated earlier in this section, the Urban Mass Transportation Act of 1964 requires, among other things, that existing labor rights be preserved when transit operations change ownership. Early on, most ownership changes involved public takeovers of private systems. Today, the trend is to privatize transit through contracting out.

Local governments and transit managers argue that the requirement to protect labor rights, including collective bargaining, impedes contracting out because union contracts, which exist in 95% of transit systems, are not acceptable to potential private transit contractors (Luger & Goldstein, 1989). Iseki et al. (2005) note that contracting out public transit services is more complex than a simple make or buy decision. Although transit directors and managers are concerned with cost efficiency, they also take labor relations and the political climate into account and in some cases attempt to mitigate negative impacts on workers.

One key consideration is that the workers operating and maintaining the equipment are generally the same whether the transit system is publicly or privately owned. Unionized labor does not simply vanish when the systems are outsourced to private companies. However, operators at multinational firms are better equipped to bargain with the unions and provide a layer of separation between labor unions and the transit authority tasked with planning and budgeting for the system. This distance limits public sector unions' political power and allows private firms to reduce costs (Jerch et al., 2017). Nonetheless, the legalities surrounding transit ownership and labor rights remain far from settled, as do those associated with changing ownership of other state and local services, such as sanitation and utilities.

In most of the states that do not permit negotiations with government workers, antipathy toward unions, unionization, and collective bargaining remain strong. For many policy makers in these states, the sovereignty argument still holds water. In upholding a 1959 ban on public sector bargaining in North Carolina, for example, a U.S. district court reasoned as follows:

> To the extent that public employees gain power through recognition and collective bargaining, other interest groups with a right to a voice in the running of the government may be left out of vital political decisions. . . . All citizens have the right to associate in groups to advocate their special interests to the government. It is something entirely different to grant any one interest group special status and access to the decision-making process.
>
> (*Atkins v. City of Charlotte*, 1969)

Pressure occasionally builds in North Carolina to invalidate the 1959 state law that prohibits public workers from collective bargaining. (The law was enacted in response to the efforts of Jimmy Hoffa's Teamsters seeking to organize the Charlotte police department). In 2006, Local 150 of the United Electrical, Radio, and Machine Workers of America filed a complaint with the International Labor Organization (ILO) contending that the state's prohibition of collective bargaining violates international labor law's basic principles of freedom of association. The complaint was upheld by the ILO and filed with the federal government and the state of North Carolina (to no effect).

Unrest among municipal sanitation workers in Raleigh led to meetings with the mayor, and their tales of low pay, tough working conditions, and arbitrary management actions gained them widespread sympathy in the capital city. Aggressive lobbying by the State Employees Association of North Carolina (SEANC) nearly won a vote on a bargaining bill in the state House of Representatives in 2007, and in 2008 SEANC formally affiliated with the Service Employees International Union (SEIU). Nonetheless, North Carolina remains a decidedly nonunion state with suppressive public policy against collective bargaining in government.

Other states, such as South Carolina, have had to confront few real "problems" with organized public employees. Any sort of legal basis for unionization or collective bargaining is unlikely to be established in the absence of strong organized pressure by public employees, a Democratic governor, and Democratic majorities in the legislature. Like its neighbor to the north, South Carolina has exhibited a long-standing aversion toward unions in the private as well as the public sector. Unions are still associated in some minds with communism, socialism, and other "foreign doctrines."

Many in the South still hold a basic suspicion of the purposes of unions and a fear that they exist in the public sector only to extort money from the public through winning unwarranted wage and benefit increases. In the case of some southern states, racial prejudice has also played a role in fostering antiunion feelings. A high percentage of minorities are found in many public services, especially sanitation, health care, and custodial functions. Though largely forgotten today, the Memphis sanitation strike of 1968 and the 1969 Charleston, South Carolina hospital workers' strike convinced some people that public unions were serving as vehicles for increasing black militancy.

Today, in the group of states that do not formally permit negotiations with public workers, the policy of no labor relations appears to be a calculated choice of state decision makers interested in providing a "good business climate" by holding down public employee compensation. In some non-bargaining states, however, a considerable amount of bargaining or meet and confer does transpire but without the statutory regulation provided by a labor relations law. Labor relations policies in these states may be established by local ordinances or on an ad hoc basis by mayors, city managers, department heads, and school boards.

Indeed, it is safe to assume that some form of bilateral decision making between public employers and workers takes place somewhere within each of the non-bargaining states discussed in this section. In Louisiana, for instance, teachers bargain with school boards in several districts, even though such activities are not protected by state legislation. The Louisiana courts have ruled that collective bargaining in public education is not inconsistent with law or public policy and is therefore permitted (Dilts et al., 1993).

Even in a few South Carolina school districts, representatives of the National Education Association (NEA)-affiliated South Carolina Education Association assemble at the same table with school board representatives and the district superintendent to "sit and talk" about teachers' wages, benefits, and working conditions. In these and other non-bargaining jurisdictions, bilateral discussions and decision making make more sense than other alternatives for resolving disagreements with public employees. Public employee unions and associations can play an important representational role even in the absence of collective bargaining. They can lobby the legislature or city council, represent members in grievance proceedings, file equal opportunity complaints, and attempt to influence policies and procedures through campaigns and elections.

D. States with Noncomprehensive Policies

Historically, within the states that have policies permitting some form of bilateral relations for one or more employee groups, firefighters and teachers are the most common beneficiaries. Police, municipal employees, and state workers have operated less frequently under a labor relations policy. This is not surprising when one considers the history of teacher and firefighter organizational activity and the strength of their national labor organizations. What is somewhat unexpected is the relatively low incidence of collective bargaining policies for police officers. Perhaps this is a legacy of the persistent ill will that followed the infamous 1919 Boston police strike (see Chapter 8) and a function of the comparatively weak and divided national police organizations.

However, the tide may be turning in favor of police unions. Wade (2018) finds that, following the Great Recession, state legislative attempts to restrict collected bargaining rights have targeted teachers, while shielding police and firefighters.

Various studies have connected these trends to state and local politics. Specifically, teachers' unions tend to lend most of their support to the Democratic Party (Wade, 2018). Police unions, on the other hand, tend to be more bipartisan. Although they favor Republicans, police unions also allocate some donations and support to Democrats (DiSalvo, 2022). In 2022, law enforcement officers had the right to engage in collective bargaining in at least 42 states and the District of Columbia. The rights are granted either under state statutes or by local jurisdictions (National Conference of State Legislatures, 2022).

Most of the policies in this category were enacted through statute, and a large majority of policies require collective bargaining rather than meet-and-confer activities. In principle, the two approaches are quite distinct. "Meet and confer" is an activity peculiar to the public sector. It implicitly rejects the legitimacy of transferring private sector bargaining rights to public employees in that it formally denies bilateral (equal) decision-making responsibility for the unions. Under meet-and-confer policies, an employer retains final decision-making authority—there is no obligation to negotiate and sign a written agreement. Furthermore, meet-and-confer laws typically are less comprehensive in their treatment of labor relations issues, such as determining and representing bargaining units, establishing an administrative framework, and settling disputes and ULPs.

Although a meet-and-confer approach is sometimes favored by management, unions argue that the arrangement more closely approximates "collective begging" than collective bargaining. Actually, true meet-and-confer activities rarely take place. In reality, employers adopt a modified approach to bilateral relations that more closely approximates collective bargaining than meet and confer and that results in a signed agreement. Often, it is not an easy matter to distinguish between the two.

Nearly half of the comprehensive bargaining states achieved across-the-board coverage in an incremental fashion, authorizing negotiations first for one or two occupational categories and then later for others. California is such a case, as are Maine and Washington. It is plausible that other states presently offering non-comprehensive coverage will eventually enact legislation for additional occupational categories. However, the struggle is likely to be a difficult one for unions, as illustrated by setbacks suffered by public workers in Indiana, Kentucky, and most recently Florida.

In 1980, Indiana's original comprehensive state and local government bargaining law was declared unconstitutional on the basis of a technicality (Klingner & Smith, 1981). Efforts to enact a new statute in the late 1980s foundered because of gubernatorial vetoes. The election of prolabor Democrat Governor Evan Bayh stirred hopes for passage of a bargaining bill in 1992, but the bill did not pass the Senate. Governor Bayh did issue an executive order that lasted for 16 years granting state workers the right to collective bargaining. But on his second day in office in 2005, Governor Mitch Daniels rescinded it.

In a case study of Kentucky, Wanamaker (1977) offered some perspective on the Herculean tasks involved in winning bargaining legislation. Police and firefighters lobbied strongly for four years before the Kentucky General Assembly authorized collective bargaining statutes for the two groups, and even then the legislation was restricted in scope to counties with a population of more than 300,000. Only one county fit that description: Jefferson County (which contains Louisville) (Lexington's population has since also exceeded 300,000). In 2010, Kentucky granted police, firefighters, and corrections officers in urban-county government the right to engage in collective bargaining (KY Rev Stat § 67A.6902, 2022).

Teachers' hopes for a bargaining statute that same year (1972) were dashed when the governor vetoed a bill that had passed both houses of the legislature. The next year, Kentucky teachers decided that their best strategy was to join a coalition of several other public employee unions to seek the passage of a comprehensive bill permitting bargaining for all Kentucky public employees. The coalition was composed of virtually every important employee organization in the state: American Federation of State, County, and Municipal Employees (AFSCME); AFL–CIO; Associated Professional Firefighters of Kentucky; Fraternal Order of Police; Kentucky Nurses Association; and local chapters of the American Association of University Professors, NEA, and AFT. However, groups opposing bargaining legislation carried more clout in the General Assembly. Business interests, school administrators, the Chamber of Commerce, the Farm Bureau, and the Municipal League managed to kill the bill in legislative committee.

Frustrated by their notable lack of success with the legislature, the teachers next tried the executive branch, asking the new Democratic governor to extend them bargaining rights through an executive order. The strategy was declared illegal by the attorney general. As of 2010, teachers were negotiating with school boards in nine Kentucky school districts (Office of Education Accountability, 2010), even though they lacked a statutory right to bargain.

While it is difficult to get an accurate update on how many districts currently negotiate with labor organizations, the Kentucky Educators Association (n.d.) represents about 44,000 working educators and classified education support professionals across the state. In 2023 the Kentucky legislature passed a law (SB 7) that prohibited the collection of union dues through payroll deduction for teachers and other state and local government employees. Police and firefighters were exempted from the law. Again, the teachers pursued this issue in court. A circuit court judge overturned the law, ruling that it made an unconstitutional distinction between categories of public employees (Clark, 2023).

As one might suspect, the circumstances surrounding the Florida case are unique. The judicial role in public sector labor relations in the South has typically consisted of responding to requests from government employers for injunctions to halt job actions. And, as discussed previously, early court decisions regarding the legality or constitutionality of collective bargaining frequently were anathema to negotiating rights for public employees. In Florida, however, the state supreme court in effect initiated and implemented a comprehensive bargaining policy (Miller & Canak, 1991).

In the case of *Dade County Classroom Teachers Association v. Ryan* (1968), the Florida Supreme Court enforced a provision in the 1968 revised constitution that afforded the state's government workers the same right to engage in collective bargaining as Florida's private sector employees. The court held that, except for the right to strike, it was incumbent on the state legislature to enact appropriate legislation to set regulations and standards implementing this constitutional provision. Nonetheless, collective bargaining legislation failed to pass during the 1969–1971 legislative sessions.

In the following year, the chief justice of the Florida Supreme Court notified the legislature that failure to implement the constitutional requirement for bargaining legislation for public employees would force the court to issue its own guidelines in lieu of legislation. When legislation still was not forthcoming, the court appointed a seven-person commission that issued guidelines for court-mandated collective bargaining. Shortly thereafter, with a legal gun held to its collective head, the legislature enacted the Public Employee Relations Act of 1974.

For many years, Florida met the conditions generally considered necessary to provide comprehensive collective bargaining rights. However, in 2023 the Florida legislature passed a bill (SB 256) restricting public sector collective bargaining rights and the Governor Ron DeSantis signed it into law. Specifically, the law prohibits public employers from allowing automatic deduction of union dues from payroll. In addition, the law requires that unions ensure that 60% of covered employees pay union dues. If the union membership rates fall below 60%, unions must conduct recertification elections. Police, firefighters, and correctional officers are exempt from the law. Tens of thousands of workers in other categories have lost union representation. Some of the hardest hit groups of workers include teachers, non-instructional university employees, and municipal workers. AFSCME alone lost over 42,000 state employees across four bargaining units (Pinos, 2024).

E. States with Comprehensive Collective Bargaining

Of the states that provide for collective bargaining for all major groups of state and local government workers, only two are in the Sunbelt: California and Hawaii. In most states with comprehensive labor relations policies, a more conventional approach was employed. Staudohar (1973) provided an interesting description of the events preceding the passage of the Hawaii Public Employee Relations Act of 1970, one of the nation's most comprehensive state collective bargaining statutes. Hawaii has had a history of strong organized labor since World War II. As early as 1950, public workers were granted the right to organize and present proposals and grievances to their employers.

Even in this labor-friendly environment, however, public employees had to work hard for the passage of collective bargaining legislation. A bill that would have granted limited bargaining rights failed in 1965. But in 1967 a meet-and-confer statute requiring discussion on working conditions, personnel policies, and other matters was enacted, and the new 1968 state constitution mandated a public employee collective bargaining law. The struggle then turned to questions of how bargaining was to be structured.

A total of eight bargaining bills were considered during the next two years, each bill substantially differing in major provisions, and each supported by separate interest groups and employee organizations. Major points of contention were as follows: (1) bargaining over wages as opposed to using a prevailing wage rate tied to private sector pay, (2) union security provisions, (3) appropriate bargaining units, and (4) the right to strike. The issue of appropriate bargaining units was especially salient in Hawaii. It is a small state that has only four counties. The county governments provide many traditional municipal government services, such as police and fire protection, public works, and sanitation, whereas the state handles typical county functions such as welfare services and property taxation. In the 1970 act, it was decided to establish statewide bargaining units to provide uniformity in personnel practices.

The right to strike also presented a sensitive issue in a four-county state where education, for example, is governed by a single jurisdiction and a teachers' strike can cripple the education system of the entire state. After concluding that prohibitions of strike in other states had been ineffective—and at times even dysfunctional—the legislature granted a limited right to strike. Before striking, Hawaii unions must first exhaust mandatory dispute settlement procedures, wait through a cooling-off period, and give a ten-day notice of the intent to strike to the employer and the public employee relations board (PERB). In addition, no strike may threaten public health or safety, which effectively prohibits police and firefighter strikes. Ironically a strike was called to spur desired legislative action on the very day the legislature was scheduled to vote on the collective bargaining bill.

The first states to enact comprehensive bargaining legislation tended to be strong two-party states with active and powerful organized labor groups and a large manufacturing sector. These early innovators, such as Michigan, Rhode Island, New York, Massachusetts, Delaware, and Connecticut, patterned their legislation on the NLRA. Most of the subsequent public sector labor relations statutes also were guided by NLRA principles on employee labor rights, scope of bargaining, unit determination and recognition, ULPs, and other bargaining topics.

In Missouri collective bargaining came in through the courthouse door, although the case was less dramatic than Florida's. In May 2007, the state supreme court overturned 60 years of a policy prohibiting collective bargaining by public employees. In response to litigation from the Missouri NEA, the court interpreted language from the 1935 Missouri Constitution that granted collective bargaining rights to "employees" in the state. According to the court, "'employees' plainly means employees. There is no adjective; there are no words that limit 'employees' to private sector employees" (Lieb, 2007, p. 2).

The major elements of typical comprehensive labor–management relations legislation are briefly examined in the following subsections. (Each of these concepts is further discussed in Chapters 4–10.)

1. Employee Rights

Generally, the NLRA (Section 7) rights apply to public workers:

> Employees shall have the right to self-organization, to form, join, or assist labor organizations, to bargain collectively through representatives of their own choosing, and to engage in other concerted activities for the purpose of collective bargaining or mutual aid and protection, and shall also have the right to refrain from any or all of such activities.

In the comprehensive bargaining states, all nonsupervisory workers are typically guaranteed recognition and bargaining rights on request. Some bargaining states incorporate a clause stating that employees also have the right to refrain from joining a union, engaging in other union-related activities, or paying union dues.

2. Employer Rights

The great majority of state statutes provide a management rights clause excluding certain matters from the scope of negotiations. Typical management rights include the right to determine the nature of work to be performed and how it is to be performed; the tools and equipment necessary to do the work; retention of traditional personnel management functions, including recruitment, hiring, promotion, and dismissal; and the right to determine the mission of the agency and maintain the efficiency and effectiveness of government operations. Some states (e.g., New Hampshire) stipulate that existing merit system provisions are excluded from collective bargaining, whereas others (e.g., Washington) provide that negotiated agreements supersede all existing policies or regulations.

3. Administrative Agency

All comprehensive statutes designate some form of administrative machinery to administer public sector labor relations. The administrative agency may be an existing entity such as the state department of labor or the Civil Service Commission or, as is the norm, a PERB or something with a similar name. Regardless of which strategy is employed, it is important to establish an administrative agency to resolve recognition claims by employee organizations, certify bargaining representatives, provide training in rules and techniques of collective bargaining, conduct research and disseminate information, hear complaints of ULPs, resolve disputes between the parties, and otherwise provide authoritative interpretations of existing policies. A major advantage of the PERB is its neutral posture, which is necessary if the agency is to develop the confidence and respect of both parties that is required for its effective functioning. PERBs are normally composed of three to five members appointed by the governor for staggered terms of office.

4. Unit Determination

A PERB or some other administrative agency determines the appropriate bargaining unit of employees. A bargaining unit consists of one or more workers represented by a single union under one contract. These workers select a bargaining agent (union) to represent them as a unit. The most commonly used criteria for unit determinations are "community of interest" among the employees; duties, skills, and working conditions of the employees; desires of the employer; the history of employee representation; effects on the efficiency of agency operations; the exclusion of supervisory employees; and the avoidance of unnecessary fragmentation of units. The number of recognized bargaining units varies widely from state to state. New York, for example, has hundreds of local government bargaining units, whereas Hawaii has only a handful. In practice, unions often determine the bargaining unit's boundaries by way of their organizing activities and the initial "showing of interest" through petition signatures.

5. Recognition Procedures

Once the parameters of a bargaining unit are determined, employee organizations compete over the right to represent that unit's members in collective negotiations. All comprehensive statutes, such as the NLRA, provide for exclusive recognition, wherein a single union has the authority to speak on behalf of all employees in the bargaining unit. A union's exclusive recognition is usually obtained through an expression of support by a majority of workers via a secret ballot. An election is conducted in cases in which two or more unions compete to represent the bargaining unit. The PERB administers the election and certifies the results. The winning union must receive a majority of the votes cast. A runoff election is held when no organization receives a majority vote. After exclusive recognition is authorized by the administrative agency, management must deal only with that labor organization in bargaining matters, and the union must effectively and fairly represent all individuals in the unit, whether they are dues-paying members or not. Most statutes also establish procedures for decertifying a previously recognized organization.

In almost all other countries, recognition is achieved through signatures of a prescribed percentage of employees. In the U.S. several states have passed laws mandating that public sector unions be certified if they can demonstrate that a majority of employees support the union. This method is commonly referred to as "card check" and typically requires unions to submit signed authorization cards. The following states have strong provisions for card check recognition: California, Illinois, Massachusetts, Maine, New Jersey, New Mexico, New York, Oregon, and Washington (Lewis, 2020).

6. Scope of Bargaining

Collective bargaining items may be mandatory, permissive, or prohibited depending on provisions of the bargaining policy. In the absence of specific language, administrative agencies or the courts resolve ambiguities in the scope of bargaining.

Although scope of bargaining provisions varies greatly, most comprehensive policies follow the NLRA in mandating a broad scope of negotiations over wages, hours, and other terms and conditions of employment. As noted earlier, most states exclude certain management rights or civil service provisions from negotiations, including the right to supervise or manage employees, determine agency mission, and make most HRM decisions. The norm is to treat all topics as negotiable unless specifically excluded by statute or administratively interpreted to fall within the realm of agency "mission." As a general rule, management prefers a narrow scope of bargaining, whereas unions seek a broad scope. Because the vital interests of both parties are at stake, battles over the scope of bargaining tend to break out frequently.

7. Impasse Resolution Procedures

In the private sector, impasses may ultimately (and legally) be resolved by a strike. In public employment, however, strikes are either prohibited or subject to restrictive conditions. Thus, the need for other procedures to resolve impasses is quite clear. With only one or two exceptions, state labor–management relations policies address the need to resolve impasses resulting from grievances and contract negotiations. Each state with a comprehensive labor relations statute provides for one or more forms of dispute resolution that are either invoked by the administrative agency or left for the parties to adopt voluntarily. The three primary dispute settlement devices are mediation, fact-finding, and arbitration. Most states that permit strikes make them subject to compliance with prestrike impasse procedures.

8. Union Security

This provision addresses the topics of membership, payment of dues or fees, and arrangements for sustaining a functional employee organization. Prior to 2018, there were five possibilities for securing the institutional viability of a union as the exclusive representative of a bargaining unit as discussed later. However, the union shop and agency shop/fair share mechanisms are no longer viable options as a result of the U.S. Supreme Court's decision in *Janus v. American Federation of State, County, and Municipal Employees, Council 31 et al.* (2018), as discussed later in this section.

Closed shop: under this arrangement, the prospective employee must become a union member prior to beginning the job and maintain membership as a condition of continuing employment. The closed shop approach is illegal in both public and private sectors under the Taft–Hartley amendments but continues to exist de facto in a few settings, principally through "hiring halls" that vet job applicants.

Union shop: here, all continuing and new employees must, as a condition of employment, join the union within a specified time period (usually 30 days) and maintain their membership through the duration of the contract. Unlike the closed shop approach, there is no preemployment membership requirement. This arrangement is provided for in only a few states, and it applies to a limited number of employee functions.

Agency shop/fair share: under this provision, employees are not required to join a union, but they must still pay the employee organization a sum of money equivalent to union dues (agency shop) or a portion of union dues to defray the union expenses incurred during contract negotiations and administration of an agreement (fair share).

Dues checkoff: most public employee relations laws permit an arrangement in which the employer automatically deducts union dues or agency fees from paychecks of employees and remits the funds to the employee organization. The dues checkoff is normally found in conjunction with one of the other union security provisions.

Maintenance of membership: this arrangement requires all union members to maintain their organizational affiliation as a condition of employment. Nonmembers need not join. Few states explicitly provide for this arrangement, although in practice it is prevalent in contract language throughout the comprehensive bargaining states.

Union security policies are desirable for unions because they help increase or maintain membership and ensure a high rate of dues payments. A financially sound union is a more secure union and a more powerful organization politically. Furthermore, union security provisions obviate the problem of "free riders," who enjoy the benefits of exclusive union representation in contract negotiations, grievance procedures, and other activities without paying organizational dues. It is also argued that union security is beneficial for the public employer, who gains labor peace from a stable union with a steady membership and income.

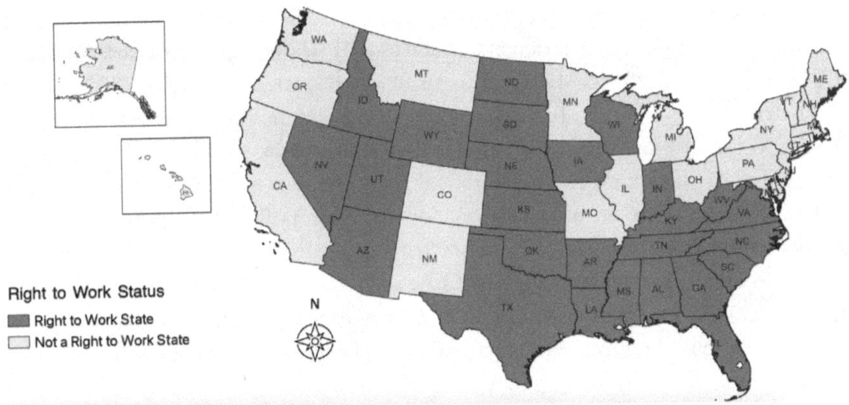

Figure 3.2 Right-to-work states, 2023.

A powerful argument against the union shop and closed shop approaches is that they violate an individual employee's right to freedom of association and speech under the First Amendment by compelling the individual to join or financially support a union. These arguments prevailed in the *Janus v. AFSCME* case. Currently, 26 "right-to-work" states prohibit union security arrangements requiring union membership or financial contributions as conditions of employment (i.e., union and agency shops). Eleven right-to-work states are in the old Confederacy; the remainder are scattered about the United States mostly to the west of the Mississippi River (see Figure 3.2). Among the right-to-work states, only three that passed legislation following the great recession, Indiana (2012), Michigan (2012), and Wisconsin (2015), have a history of strong organized labor or are traditional industrialized states. Unions are adamantly opposed to right-to-work laws and have fought to have the authorizing provision removed from Section 14(b) of the Taft–Hartley amendments since its adoption in 1947. Michigan subsequently repealed right-to-work legislation in 2023. Although right-to-work laws do not directly apply to public sector unions following the *Janus v. AFSCME* decision, they provide a good indicator of the state political culture with respect to unions.

The empirical evidence is not clear on whether right-to-work laws hinder union growth and effectiveness through depressing the number of dues-paying members. Preexisting antiunion sentiment may inspire the adoption of right-to-work laws and lower workers' interest in unions. Alternatively, right-to-work policies may independently depress future unionization by constricting union financial resources with which to recruit new members and effectively represent the bargaining unit. One review of scholarly research indicated that right-to-work laws do depress union membership by 3%–8% in the long run and boost free riding by 6%–10% (Moore, 1998). Another review estimates that right-to-work laws depress union density by 8.8% (Hogler et al., 2004). More recent scholarship shows that declines in union density in states that passed right-to-work laws after 2012 range from 7.8% in Michigan to 15.9% in Kentucky (Murphy, 2023).

The reasoning behind a ban on union security arrangements is that unions are private voluntary organizations in which membership should be by conscious free choice of the worker. An individual made to join a union or pay dues may be forced to support an organization, ideology, or political program that he or she does not condone. Thus, union security provisions may appear to violate an employee's First Amendment rights of free speech and association. It is also argued that union security measures conflict with the merit principle because all public employees should be hired and retained on the basis of their job qualifications and performance, not membership in an organization.

The federal courts have upheld the right of individual states to bar union security provisions through right-to-work laws (*Davenport v. Washington Education Association*, 2007). The federal courts have also addressed the First Amendment rights of free speech and association that are raised when a union uses dues for purposes not related to collective bargaining, such as campaign support for a political candidate or legislative lobbying. If an employee objects to financially supporting these activities, does this not constitute a violation of free speech? Concerned about this question, the federal courts have determined the procedural safeguards that a union must establish for nonunion members to receive a rebate of nonchargeable fees.

In a trilogy of cases, the U.S. Supreme Court upheld and protected private sector employees' First Amendment rights under the RLA (Mitchell, 1978). In *Railway Employee Department, IAM v. Hanson* (1956), the court found that a union security agreement was constitutional as long as dues collection did not serve as a "cover for forcing ideological conformity . . . in contravention of the First Amendment." In *International Association of Machinists v. Street* (1961), the court held that unions cannot utilize dues to support political causes if an employee objects. And in *Brotherhood of Railway Clerks v. Allen* (1963), the Supreme Court suggested that unions adopt a voluntary plan to enable dissenters to avoid having a portion of their dues used for political expenditures. The principles developed in these three cases were applied to the public sector in *Abood v. Detroit Board of Education* (1977) and *Communications Workers of America v. Beck* (1998).

It is not a simple matter to draw a bright line distinguishing between acceptable and unacceptable uses of service fees. This problem was first addressed in the private sector case of *Ellis v. Railway Clerks* (1984), in which the court decided that "the test must be whether the challenged expenditures are necessarily or reasonably incurred for the purpose of performing the duties of an exclusive representative of the employees in dealing with the employer on labor–management issues." The court specifically approved national union conventions, social activities, and publications as "necessarily or reasonably incurred" while prohibiting a portion of the service fee for activities not directly related to contract negotiation, administration, or grievance handling. In *Ellis*, the court also found "inadequate" the union's scheme for rebating the portion of the service fee not spent on allowable items. By collecting an amount equal to full dues and then refunding a portion later, the union was in effect borrowing from nonmembers and not providing them with a viable mechanism for challenging the size or proportion of the rebate (Darko & Knapp, 1985).

In *Chicago Teachers Union v. Hudson* (1986), the Supreme Court specified a procedure for drawing a line between acceptable and unacceptable uses of a service fee. The Chicago Teachers Union had negotiated a contract with the Board of Education, requiring nonmembers to pay a service fee of 95% of members' dues. The court ruled that the union was required to give nonmembers "an adequate explanation of the basis for the fee, a reasonably prompt opportunity to challenge the amount of the fee before an impartial decision maker, and an escrow for the amounts reasonably in dispute while challenges are pending." The nonunion employee was "entitled to have his objection addressed in an expeditious, fair, and objective manner" (this is now known as a "Hudson notice"). In the case of *Lehnert v. Ferris Faculty Association* (1991), the Supreme Court provided further instruction by devising a three-part test to determine the share of dues that may be deducted for a nonmember's agency fee.

Under *Lehnert*, expenses are chargeable to nonmembers if they are (1) germane to collective bargaining activities, (2) justified by the government interest in labor peace and avoiding free riders, and (3) not significantly burdensome to free speech. Permissible expenditures include national and state union convention expenses and strike preparation costs. Lobbying, electoral, and other political activity costs are disallowed. The Supreme Court dived deeper into the agency fee issue in a 2012 ruling, *Knox v. SEIU Local 1000*, requiring that unions provide a notice to nonmembers in the bargaining unit specifying the use of fees and permit the employees to opt out of paying them. Moreover, the court held that when a union issues a supplemental fee assessment it must provide a second notice with the opportunity for nonmembers to object.

The *Ellis* and *Chicago Teachers Union* decisions cast doubt on the constitutionality of agency fee practices in a number of state and local jurisdictions. At least two states, Minnesota and New Jersey, have acted to keep the service fee issue out of the federal courts by statutorily providing for a maximum service fee percentage of 85% of full union dues (Volz & Costa, 1989). Although this approach held promise for balancing the unions' free-rider problem against the First Amendment rights of nonmember workers, more litigation has followed in the state courts. Generally, the *Lehnert* principles have been applied by state courts, but there are inconsistencies, with expenses found to be chargeable to union dues in one state, for example, and not chargeable in another (Lund & Maranto, 1996, pp. 35–45). The facts of the individual situation determine which union expenses are payable with nonmembers' dues. Several states have explicitly identified chargeable expenses (e.g., California and New Jersey).

As noted earlier and in Chapter 2, three U.S. Supreme Court cases gradually eroded the precedent set in *Abood* for an agency fee requirement. In the first of these cases, *Harris v. Quinn* (2014), the U.S. Supreme Court ruled that the collection of agency fees from home care workers who do not wish to join or support the union was unconstitutional. In the second case, *Friedrichs v. California Teachers Association* (2016), the court deadlocked in June 2016. In the third case, *Janus v. AFSCME* (2018), the court overturned *Abood* on the grounds that it interfered with public employees' free speech rights. Since unions have a legal duty to represent all workers in the bargaining unit, the ruling on this case poses an enormous free-rider problem for public sector unions.

9. Unfair Labor Practices

Following the model of the NLRA, bargaining statutes specify ULPs that must not be committed by public employers or unions. These ULPs are intended to protect the rights of the parties under law.

Prohibited practices by public employers include the following:

- Interfering with, restraining, or coercing public employees in the exercise of their rights granted under statute
- Dominating, interfering with, or assisting in the formation or administration of an employee organization
- Encouraging or discouraging membership in any labor organization through discrimination in hiring, tenure, or other terms or conditions of employment
- Questioning employees about their union sentiments
- Discharging or discriminating against an employee because he or she has filed charges or given testimony under the labor relations statute or because he or she has formed or joined an employee organization
- Refusing to meet and bargain in good faith with the recognized employee organization
- Denying rights of exclusive representation to the duly designated bargaining agent
- Refusing or avoiding statutory impasse procedures
- Instituting a lockout
- Dealing directly with employees rather than with their bargaining representatives on matters within the scope of bargaining
- Violating the terms of a collective bargaining contract

ULPs by an employee organization may include the following:

- Interfering with, restraining, or coercing public employees in the exercise of their rights granted under statute
- Interfering with, restraining, or coercing a public employer with respect to protecting the exercise of employee rights under statute or selecting a bargaining representative
- Refusing to meet and bargain collectively with a public employer in good faith
- Refusing or avoiding statutory impasse procedures
- Engaging in or instigating an illegal strike
- Hindering or interfering with an employee's work performance or productivity

Upon written notice from an employer or a union plaintiff, the administrative agency determines whether a ULP has occurred. The accused party has a certain period of time in which to respond (normally seven days). If the alleged ULP is found to have taken place, the administrative agency generally has the authority to issue a cease-and-desist order against the accused and to reinstate any unjustly dismissed employees—with back pay—or issue other remedial orders.

F. Initiative and Referendum

As discussed at the beginning of this chapter, state legislation is not the sole means of regulating labor relations in the public sector. Court decisions, attorney general opinions, and executive orders have played significant roles in establishing labor relations policies in a number of states. And in some states, most notably California, an additional vehicle for public policy making has been utilized to govern labor relations: the public referendum.

Eighteen states permit citizen initiatives to amend the state constitution and adopt statutory law, and 23 states have initiative provisions in place to change statutory law. Most states also allow local initiatives and referenda. Under California's version of home rule, a local government can amend its city charter through action by the legislative body (council), a charter commission, or a citizen initiative petition. Normally, charter amendments or ordinances are enacted by the council. However, the initiative petition plays an important part in California local governance. The local initiative was used by police and firefighters to set wages, establish retirement systems, and enact rules governing working hours as early as 1907 (Crouch, 1978, p. 191). A state initiative created the civil service system for California local government workers, and the process also has been utilized to establish prevailing wage principles and parity formulas.

California's state initiative procedure requires supporters to obtain the valid signatures of at least 8% of the total votes cast for all gubernatorial candidates in the last general election for a statewide initiative and 5% of the votes cast for a statutory initiative. Proposition 13, which severely limited state taxation and expenditures, is perhaps the most famous, or infamous (depending on one's perspective), statewide measure ever passed. A number of local initiatives are decided each year throughout the state.

That California's use of the initiative has been so popular is a function of the state's political system. California has long been known for its weak political parties. Because interest aggregation and articulation must occur if democracy is to be a reality, other entities, namely, interest groups, have assumed direction and a significant degree of control over politics of the state. California politics is interest-group politics, and nowhere else have interest groups enjoyed more successful application of the initiative procedure as a means of influencing and determining public policy as in California. Needless to say, organized labor is one of the most powerful interest groups.

The California State Employees Association and California Teachers Association have used the state initiative process to achieve goals denied them at the bargaining table. However, rising voter discontent with large salary gains by police and firefighters culminated in a rebellion of sorts in San Francisco in 1975, when the city government refused to honor the wage and parity amendments. Police and firefighters went on strike, but voters used the initiative procedure against them by approving strong antiunion charter amendments. Since then, antiunion initiatives have also been passed in Oakland, Santa Barbara, San Diego, and other California cities. California witnessed its fair share of antiunion initiatives as part of the fallout from the Great Recession, as did several other initiative states. Most failed at the ballot box. In Ohio, voters overturned a legislatively adopted law weakening collective bargaining in 2011.

Through the initiative process, state employee organizations have suffered both dramatic defeats and stunning victories. Union victories include defeating "paycheck protection" initiatives that would have required unions to obtain permission from their members each year before spending their dues for political purposes were defeated in California (1998, 2005, and 2010), Oregon (1998, 2000, 2008), and Colorado (2007, 2008),

The tremendous expense of conducting initiative campaigns has dampened the interest of public employees in this method of policy change. (In California, it costs more than $1 million just to place an initiative on the ballot.) However, employee organizations participate aggressively when their interests appear to be threatened.

G. Labor Relations in Nonprofit Organizations

As a general rule, nonprofit organizations occupy an uncertain legal terrain (see Chapter 2). The NLRA is the governing law for nonprofit organizations, but in some cases state law prevails. As observed in Chapter 2, the rapid growth of the nonprofit sector along with a friendly environment for labor and its causes have heightened union interest in organizing nonprofit agencies and workers.

AFSCME, SEIU, and the Office and Professional Employees Association have enjoyed some recent success in organizing workers in nonprofit foundations, cultural organizations, day care centers, schools, and churches. They are aggressively pursuing health-care workers in hospitals, home care, nursing homes, and other institutions paid wholly or in part under contracts with state and local governments (Kearney, 2010; Mareschal, 2006). In several states, including California, Oregon, and Washington, the SEIU used the ballot initiative process to win policy changes that create public authorities as home care aides' employers of record and then won collective bargaining rights to represent them under state law (Delp & Quan, 2002; Mareschal, 2006). An executive order by Governor Eliot Spitzer in 2007 granted home-based childcare providers collective bargaining rights in New York (Greenhouse, 2007).

Nonprofit management tends to be at a disadvantage when unionization occurs. The board of directors and chief executive officer may find themselves in unfamiliar territory and with little or no knowledge of the NLRA or state labor provisions. Even if they are inclined to fight unionization, they rarely have sufficient funds to hire a union-busting firm.

From a practical perspective, nonprofits differ fundamentally from firms and public government organizations in their missions, assumptions, and operating procedures. For example, a nonprofit that operates a number of assisted-care homes for the aged and disabled under a state contract may find itself in a dispute with one or more unions demanding a substantial wage increase. If the nonprofit cannot or refuses to pay, the assisted-care workers may legally walk out the door, abandoning their patients. What is the role of the state government in such a situation? Legally, it probably has insufficient authority to intervene unless, as in California, the workers are employed by and paid through an agency of the state government. Morally and politically, it must act to protect the lives and well-being of citizens who do not have the resources to take care of themselves. Such crises have induced governors to take direct action to hike employee pay by unilaterally amending the operating contract with the nonprofit.

V. SUMMARY

This chapter describes the legal basis of labor relations in federal, state, and local governments in the United States, including the right to form and join unions, and the various statutes, ordinances, executive orders, attorney general and court decisions, and public referenda that have established labor relations policies for public employees.

The "political laboratory" of labor relations policies in the states was examined by classifying state policies into three groups: those with no statutory bargaining rights, those with partial coverage, and those with comprehensive policies mandating bargaining. Major provisions of typical collective bargaining legislation were outlined, including employee and employer rights, administrative agencies, unit determination, recognition, scope of bargaining, impasse resolution procedures, union security, and ULPs.

Unlike in the private sector, there is no single, coherent legal framework for public sector labor relations. In the federal sector, the CSRA regulates labor-management relations through an increasingly inadequate framework that has not withstood the test of time. Federal unions struggle to justify their existence in the absence of union security arrangements and of a broad scope of negotiable topics. The prohibition of bargaining over wages and benefits is particularly burdensome to the federal unions. The Reform Act itself is in dire need of reform.

It has been only a little more than four decades that public employees in the United States have enjoyed the legally protected right to form and join employee organizations. Many state and local government employees still do not have statutory collective bargaining rights, and prospects do not look good for substantial change. Regional variations in labor relations policies and union membership persist, with Sunbelt states likely to continue denying bargaining rights to public workers.

With a few possible exceptions, the legal environment will probably be altered only at the margins, although the recent cases of Wisconsin, Ohio, and Florida demonstrate the power of antiunion forces to retract collective bargaining rights. Barring the emergence of a new prolabor majority coalition in the respective state legislative bodies or a profound change of course by Congress and the president, any policy changes are likely to suppress—rather than facilitate—unionization and collective bargaining.

Since 2011, numerous bills aimed at dismantling labor standards and reducing public services were introduced in statehouses across the country. The main focus was on collective bargaining rights, dues deduction, payroll deductions for political action, and right-to-work legislation (Lafer, 2017). The American Legislative Exchange Council (ALEC) was a key driver of the legislation. ALEC is a conservative policy organization funded primarily by corporations, corporate trade groups, and corporate foundations.

Many of the bills introduced over this time period map closely to the language in ALEC's model legislation, in what is referred to as legislative plagiarism (Peck, 2016). For example, in 2023 alone four states passed paycheck protection acts preventing public employers from withholding dues from public employees. Florida's law covered all public employees except police, firefighters, and correctional officers. Arkansas, Kentucky, and Tennessee passed similar legislation targeting teachers.

In the post-Janus era, ALEC continues to push model legislation aimed at prohibiting paid release time for union activities, affirming workers' Janus rights, and requiring periodic re-certification of unions (Slabinski, 2019). ALEC's stated goal for the model legislation is to reduce the political power of public sector unions and their members. Given the current environment of intense political partisanship and polarization, the attempts to weaken public sector collective bargaining rights are likely to continue.

The legal environment for public sector labor relations is important and deserves careful attention. It is strongly associated with the levels of unionization, extent and nature of collective bargaining, and general character of employer–employee relations. The legal environment of public sector labor relations underlies and shapes everything that follows in this book, and it largely determines who wins or loses on the labor–management playing field.

REFERENCES

Abood v. Detroit Board of Education. (1977). 430 U.S. 209, 975 Ct. 1782.

AFSCME Local 201 v. City of Muskegon. (1963). 369 Mich. 384, 120 N.W. 2d. 197.

Anzia, S. F., & Moe, T. M. (2016). Do politicians use policy to make politics? The case of public-sector labor laws. *American Political Science Review, 110*(4), 763–777.

Atkins v. City of Charlotte. (1969). U.S. Dist. Ct. 296, F. Supp.

Barr, S. (2007, December 10). Compromise on Pentagon pay system, union rights. *Washington Post.* www.washingtonpost.com

Blum, A. A., & Helburn, I. B. (1997). Federal labor management relations: The beginning. *Journal of Collective Negotiations, 26*, 256–277.

Brotherhood of Railway Clerks v. Allen. (1963). 83 S. Ct. 1158.

Chicago Teachers Union v. Hudson. (1986). 475 U.S. 292.

Clark, J. (2023, September 9). Ky. judge strikes down law targeting teachers union dues. *Louisville Public Media.* https://www.lpm.org/news/2023-09-12/ky-judge-strikes-down-law-targeting-teachers-union-dues

Clark, T., Jr., & Powers, J. J. (2003). Constitutional and practical pitfalls of a federally-mandated public sector collective bargaining system. *Journal of Labor Research, 24*(4), 621–641.

Cleveland Board of Education v. Loudermill. (1985). 470 U.S. 532, 118.

Communications Workers of America v. Beck. (1998). 487 U.S. 735, 1088 S. Ct. 2641, 101 L. Ed. 2d 634.

Crouch, W. W. (1978). *Organized civil servants: Public employer–employee relations in California.* University of California Press.

Dade County Classroom Teachers Association v. Ryan. (1968). 225 So. 2d 903.

Darko, R. J., & Knapp, J. C. (1985). A guide to the changing court rulings in union security in the public sector: A union perspective. *Journal of Law and Education, 14*(1), 57–69.

Davenport v. Washington State Education Association. (2007). 127 S. Ct. 2372, 551 U.S. 177, 168 L. Ed. 2d71.

Delp, L., & Quan, K. (2002). Homecare worker organizing in California: An analysis of a successful strategy. *Labor Studies Journal*, *27*(1), 1–23.

Dilts, D. A., Boyda, S. W., & Sherr, M. A. (1993). Collective bargaining in the absence of protective legislation: The case of Louisiana. *Journal of Collective Negotiations*, *22*(3), 259–265.

DiSalvo, D. (2022). Interest groups, local politics, and police unions. *Interest Groups & Advocacy*, *11*(2), 263–277.

Drummonds, H. H. (2009). Beyond the employee free choice act: Unleashing the states in labor-management relations policy. *Cornell Journal of Law & Public Policy*, *19*, 83.

Ellis v. Railway Clerks. (1984). 466 U.S. 435.

Farber, H. S. (1987, November 13). The recent decline of unionization in the United States. *Science*, *238*, 915–920.

Fox, M. J., Jr., & Shelton, H. E., Jr. (1972, May). The impact of executive order 11491 on the federal labor management relations program. *Journal of Collective Negotiations*, 113–124.

Friedrichs v. California Teachers Association. (2016). 578 U.S. ____.

Garcetti v. Ceballos. (2006). 547 U.S. 410.

Garcia v. San Antonio Metropolitan Transit Authority. (1985). 469 U.S. 528.

Givhan v. Western Line Consolidated School District. (1979). 439 U.S. 410.

Greenhouse, S. (2007, May 12). Child care workers get right to unionize. *New York Times*. https://www.nytimes.com/2007/05/12/nyregion/12childcare.html

Harris, K. D., & Walsh, M. J. (2022). *Whitehouse task force on worker organizing and empowerment report to the president*. https://www.whitehouse.gov/wp-content/uploads/2022/02/White-House-Task-Force-on-Worker-Organizing-and-Empowerment-Report.pdf

Harris v. Quinn. (2014). 573 U.S. 616.

Hogler, R. L., Hunt, H. G., & Weiler, S. (2015). Killing unions with culture: Institutions, inequality, and the effects of labor's decline in the United States. *Employee Responsibilities and Rights Journal*, *27*, 63–79.

Hogler, R. L., Shulman, S., & Weiler, S. (2004). Right-to-work legislation, social capital, and variations in state union density. *Review of Regional Studies*, *34*(1), 95–111.

Hundley, G. (1988, Fall). Who joins unions in the public sector? The effects of individual characteristics and the law. *Journal of Labor Research*, *9*, 301–323.

Indianapolis Education Association v. Lewallen. (1969). 72 L.R. Rm. 2071 (7th Cir.).

International Association of Machinists v. Street. (1961). 367 U.S. 740.

Iseki, H., Ford, A., & Factor, R. J. (2005). Contracting practice in fixed-route transit service: Case studies in California. *Transportation Research Record*, *1927*(1), 82–91.

Janus v. American Federation of State, County, and Municipal Employees, Council 31. (2018). 585 U.S. ___.

Jerch, R., Kahn, M. E., & Li, S. (2017). The efficiency of local government: The role of privatization and public sector unions. *Journal of Public Economics, 154*, 95–121.

Katz, E. (2019, October 7). With go ahead from OPM, agencies press forward with efforts to cripple federal unions. *Government Executive*. https://www.govexec.com/pay-benefits/2019/10/go-ahead-opm-agencies-press-forward-efforts-cripple-federal-unions/160429/

Kearney, R. C. (2010). Public sector labor—Management relations: Change or status quo?. *Review of Public Personnel Administration, 30*(1), 89–111.

Kellough, J. E. (2023). *The fragility of merit: Erosion of the foundation of public service under trump*. Review of Public Personnel Administration. https://doi.org/10.1177/0734371X231214973

Kellough, J. E., Nigro, L. G., & Brewer, G. A. (2010). Civil service reform under George W. Bush: Ideology, politics, and public personnel administration. *Review of Public Personnel Administration, 30*(4), 404–422.

Kentucky Educators Association. (n.d.). *About KEA*. https://www.kea.org/about/

Kettl, D., Hausser, D., Raadschelders, J., Sanders, R., & Soloway, S. (2017). No time to wait: Building a public service for the 21st century. *National Academy of Public Administration*.

Keyeshian v. Board of Regents. (1967). 385 U.S. 589.

Klingner, D. E., & Smith, D. B. (1981). What happens when a state's collective bargaining law is declared unconstitutional? The case of Indiana. *Journal of Collective Negotiations, 10*(1), 85–94.

Lafer, G. (2017). *The one percent solution: How corporations are remaking America one state at a time*. Cornell University Press.

Lane v. Franks. (2014). 573 U.S. 228.

Lehnert v. Ferris Faculty Association. (1991). 500 U.S. 507.

Letter Carriers v. Blount. (1969). 305 F. Supp. 546 (D.D.C.).

Lewis, C. M. (2020, December 22). The stunning workers' victory in New Mexico that you haven't heard about. *In These Times*. https://inthesetimes.com/article/new-mexico-workers-rights-victory-publicsector-union

Lieb, D. A. (2007, May 30). *Mo.: Bargaining rights for public employees*. Retrieved June 14, 2007, from http://www.Forbes.com

Luger, M. I., & Goldstein, H. A. (1989). Federal labor protections and the privatization of public transit. *Journal of Policy Analysis and Management, 8*(2), 229–250.

Lund, J., & Maranto, C. L. (1996). Public sector laws: An update. In D. Belman, M. Gunderson, & D. Hyatt (Eds.), *Public sector employment in a time of transition* (pp. 21–58). IRRA.

Mareschal, P. M. (2006). Innovation and adaptation: Contrasting efforts to organize home care workers in four states. *Labor Studies Journal*, *31*(1), 25–49.

Masters, M. F., & Albright, R. (2003). Federal labor-management partnerships: Perspectives, performance, and possibilities. In J. Brock & D. Lipsky (Eds.), *Going public: The rule of labor-management relations in delivering quality government services* (pp. 171–210). Industrial Relations Research Association.

Masters, M. F., Albright, R., & Gibney, R. F. (2020). The ebb and flow of federal sector labor-management relations policies under four successive presidents. *Employee Responsibilities and Rights Journal*, *32*, 139–166.

McAuliffe v. City of New Bedford. (1892). 155 Mass. 216, 29 N.E. 517.

McLaughlin v. Tilendis. (1967). 398 F. 2d. 287.

Miller, B., & Canak, W. (1991, January). From "porkchoppers" to "lambchoppers": The passage of Florida's public employee relations act. *Industrial and Labor Relations Review*, *44*, 349–366.

Mitchell, M. S. (1978, November). Public sector union security: The impact of Abood. *Labor Law Journal*, 697–711.

Moore, W. J. (1998). The detriments and effects of right to work laws: A review of the recent literature. *Journal of Labor Research*, *XIX*(3), 445–469.

Murphy, K. J. (2023). What are the consequences of right-to-work for union membership? *ILR Review*, *76*(2), 412–433.

National Commission on Military, National, and Public Service. (2020). *Inspired to serve: The final report of the National Commission on Military, National, and Public Service.* www.inspire2serve.gov

National Conference of State Legislatures. (2022). *Statutory summary. Civil and criminal justice: Collective bargaining database.* https://www.ncsl.org/civil-and-criminal-justice/collective-bargaining-database

NTEU v. Chertoff. (2005). 385 F. Supp. 2d 1 (D.D.C. 2005). http://cbpunion.org/DHS Regulations/CollyerDecision.pdf

Oestreich, H. H., & Whaley, G. L. (2001). *Transit labor relations guide.* Mineta Transportation Institute.

Ogrysko, N. (2021, January 13). Historic absences at MSPB hit 4-year mark, creating potentially costly backlog. *Federal News Network.* https://federalnewsnetwork.com/workforce-rightsgovernance/2021/01/historic-absences-at-mspb-hit-4-year-mark-creating-potentially-costly-backlog/

Peck, J. (2016). The right to work, and the right at work. *Economic Geography*, *92*(1), 4–30.

Pickering v. Board of Education. (1968). 391 U.S. 563, 88 S. Ct. 1751.

Pinos, G. (2024, February 19). Here's the state of Florida's public employee unions. *WLRN.* https://www.wlrn.org/government-politics/2024-02-19/florida-public-employee-unions-bargaining-rights

Pistole, J. S. (2011). 100-administrator's determination regarding collective bargaining. *Op. TSA Administrator*. https://www.govexec.com/pdfs/02041112.pdf

Railway Employee Department, IAM v. Hanson. (1956). 351 U.S. 255.

Rhodes, T. L., & Brown, R. G. (1992). Divided we fall—employee perceptions of a legal prohibition on collective bargaining: A closer look. *Journal of Collective Negotiations*, *21*(1), 1–14.

Roberts, R. (2023). Democracy at risk: The public employee freedom of speech crisis. *Administration & Society*, *55*(3), 613–631.

Rosenbloom, D. H., & Chanin, J. (2016). What every public sector human resource manager should know about the constitution. In *Public human resource management: Problems and prospects* (pp. 16–31). CQ Press.

Saltzman, G. B. (1985, April). Bargaining law as a cause and consequence of the growth of teacher unions. *Industrial and Labor Relations Review*, *38*, 335–351.

Schneider, B. V. H. (1988). Public sector labor legislation—an evolutionary analysis. In B. J. Aaron, J. R. Grodin, & J. L. Stern (Eds.), *Public sector bargaining* (pp. 191–223). Bureau of National Affairs.

Slabinski, M. (2019, March 29). A current glimpse of public sector union policy in the states. *ALEC*. https://www.alec.org/article/a-current-glimpse-of-public-sector-union-policy-in-the-states/

Smith v. Arkansas State Highway Commission Employees Local 1315. (1979). 441 U.S. 463, 101 L.R.R.M. 2091.

Staudohar, P. D. (1973, October). The emergence of Hawaii's public employment law. *Industrial Relations*, *12*, 338–351.

Task Force on Worker Organizing and Empowerment Progress to Date as of March 20, 2023. https://www.whitehouse.gov/wp-content/uploads/2023/03/WH-Task-Force-on-Worker-Organizing-and-Empowerment_3.17-Implementation-Update_Final.pdf

Thompson, J. R. (2007). Federal labor-management relations reforms under Bush: Enlightened management or quest for control? *Review of Public Personnel Administration*, *27*(2), 105–124.

Thompson, J. R. (2010). Toward "flexible uniformity"? Civil service reform, "big government conservatism," and the promise of the intelligence community model. *Review of Public Personnel Administration*, *30*(4), 423–444.

Tobias, R. (1998). Federal employee unions and the human resource management functions. In S. E. Condrey (Ed.), *Handbook of human resources management in government* (pp. 258–274). Jossey-Bass.

U.S. Federal Labor Relations Authority. (2023). *Performance and accountability report 2023*. https://www.flra.gov/system/files/webfm/FLRA%20Agency-wide/Public%20Affairs/PAR/FLRA%20FY2022%20PAR.pdf

U.S. Government Accountability Office. (2023). *Violation of the time limit imposed by the federal vacancies reform act of 1998: General counsel, federal labor relations authority, B-334563.* https://www.gao.gov/products/b-334563

U.S. Merit Systems Protection Board. (2021). *Annual report for FY 2020.* https://www.mspb.gov/about/annual_reports/MSPB_FY_2020_Annual_Report_1800131.pdf

Virginia v. Arlington County Board of Education. (1977). 232 S.E. 2d. 30, 94 L.R.R.M. 229 1.

Volz, W. H., & Costa, D. (1989, March). A public employee's "fair share" union dues. *Labor Law Journal*, 131–137.

Wade, M. M. (2018). Targeting teachers while shielding cops? The politics of punishing enemies and rewarding friends in American state collective bargaining reform agendas. *Journal of Labor and Society*, *21*(2), 137–157.

Wagner, E. (2019, March 4). FLRA plan to review arbitration standards alarms unions. *Government Executive.* https://www.govexec.com/management/2019/03/flra-plan-review-arbitration-standards-alarms-unions/155293/

Wanamaker, D. K. (1977, September). Kentucky: From organizing the street sweepers to bargaining in the sunshine. *Southern Review of Public Administration*, 175–191.

Waters, M. S., Hill, R. C., Moore, W. J., & Newman, R. J. (1994). A simultaneous-equations relationship between public sector bargaining legislation and unionization. *Journal of Labor Research*, *XV*(4), 355–372.

Wellington, H. H., & Winter, R. K., Jr. (1971). *The unions and the cities.* Brookings.

Wisconsin Policy Forum. (2022). *State drop in unions among nation's largest.* https://wispolicyforum.org/wp-content/uploads/2022/02/Focus_22_04_Unions.pdf

Chapter 4

Fundamentals of the Bargaining Process

I. INTRODUCTION

Collective bargaining and other forms of management–union relations in government are replete with formal and informal procedures, official and unofficial participants, and—perhaps above all else—politics. This chapter examines the multidimensional bargaining process in the public sector and attempts to shed some light on the mysteries of labor–management negotiations. At the outset, it is important to understand the ways in which collective bargaining differs between government and the private sector. Next, the basic elements of the bargaining process are considered in some detail. The chapter concludes with a look at the internal and external politics of public sector collective bargaining.

II. PUBLIC–PRIVATE SECTOR DIFFERENCES

Perhaps because of the sovereignty doctrine or, in some cases, the shock of early union successes in government, the differences in collective bargaining between the public and private sectors are often overstated. Upon close inspection, one sees that the same sort of people and occupations are involved in government and corporate jobs and not uncommonly the work is identical. The day-to-day activities of the welder, the classroom teacher, the vehicle operator, the maintenance person, the medical technician, the scientist, and the information technology specialist are indistinguishable regardless of public or private ownership of their place of employment. Most would dispute the claim that the duties of the county hospital nurse are somehow less "essential" than those same duties performed in private hospitals. Moreover, the principles and processes of collective bargaining exhibit many more sectoral similarities than differences.

Nonetheless, important distinctions can be drawn between government and business concerning the environment, actors, and procedures of collective bargaining.

DOI:10.4324/9781003403593-4

A. The Environment

Chapter 3 established that the environment of collective bargaining in government differs from that of business in the legal framework, particularly with regard to statutory and regulatory policy. Three additional environmental factors distinguish collective bargaining in the two sectors: (1) financial setting and incentives, (2) the nature of work, and (3) the role of politics.

1. Financial Setting and Incentives

Corporate financial policy and decision making are driven by the profit motive. A business entity cannot remain a going concern unless assets and net income exceed liabilities and net expenses over the long haul. In simple terms, a corporation that falters must fold its tent and move its operations to a more favorable location (most recently to Asia), declare Chapter 13 bankruptcy, or negotiate a takeover by a more successful firm. Private sector organizations adjust financial policy in response to the demands of the marketplace. For example, increased labor costs may be passed on to consumers through boosting product prices; they may be offset through introducing productivity improvements; or they may be absorbed internally through lower profits. Alternative strategies include moving production offshore to countries such as China, India, Mexico, or Brazil. In recent years, many corporations have simply have simply contracted out jobs and functions locally to smaller businesses that compete against each other in what Weil (2014) has labeled the fissurization of employment.

As the mortgage debt crisis and the ensuing Great Recession (2008–2012) showed, general-purpose governments sometimes confront serious fiscal crises and revenue–expenditure imbalances, but they cannot "go out of business." Municipalities may file bankruptcy under Chapter 9 of the federal code, but they cannot lock their doors, lay off all employees, and cease the provision of public services. The Great Recession spawned a number of municipal, county and special district bankruptcies, including those in Vallejo and San Bernardino, California; Jefferson County, Alabama; and Harrisburg, Pennsylvania. The uninterrupted provision of law enforcement, fire protection, potable water, sewer services, and trash collection is critical to the health and well-being of the citizenry. These jurisdictions may have defaulted on their debt instruments and current accounts payable, laid off employees, turned hat-in-hand to their state governments for bailouts, and taken other steps to get a financial grip, but they could not retreat from their legal and moral obligation to provide essential services to their residents.

There is no profit motive in government. Higher service provision costs must be passed on to consumers through a fee or tax increase or ameliorated through productivity gains. Government's fiscal choices are constrained because there are no "profits" to reduce, and a balanced budget is mandated by law.

2. Nature of Work

In addition to financing, the type and scope of government services differ from services provided by the private sector. In general, government services are labor intensive. They also tend to be monopolistic. Typically, there is no convenient alternative supplier of police and fire protection, water, sewage, or garbage pickup. This is not to say that no alternatives exist. For example, in rural areas, one may sink one's own well, install a septic tank, and take the trash to the nearest sanitary landfill in the trunk of the family vehicle. Volunteer fire departments are responsible for protecting the great preponderance of property in the United States. Private schools educate some 6 million students in grades K–12. Similarly, private security firms can perform the police and military functions, to some extent, as demonstrated by the U.S. Department of Defense contractors in Iraq and Afghanistan, who outnumbered uniformed troops.

Indeed, one is hard pressed to imagine a single government function that could not, in theory (if not in practice), be performed by a nongovernmental entity. However, the point is that alternative services are not immediately available in most cases. The implications of an employee strike in services essential to the health and safety of a community are obvious and not to be taken lightly.

3. Role of Politics

Public sector labor relations are deeply and inherently suffused in politics at many different levels. The activities of all labor unions (organizing workers, lobbying elected and appointed officials, influencing public opinion, and representing workers in collective bargaining and grievance procedures) are political in nature. However, the level of politicization is much higher in the public sector.

The primary distinction between the politics of public and private sector unions and collective bargaining rests in the basic contexts of the two systems: the public arena (and public policy) versus the marketplace (and corporate policy). Private sector firms are responsive to the citizenry primarily through adjusting to and influencing consumer demand for their products. In the public sector, government service providers must be responsive not only to their immediate "customers," or service recipients, but also to elected officials, civil servants, the voting public, other levels of government, and certain private and nonprofit organizations.

Collective bargaining assumes a multiparticipant character, with its outcomes highly dependent on the political interplay among unions, elected officials, interest groups and taxpayers. In addition, the access points of labor organizations to the government employer are much more numerous than those of private sector unions. For example, in government, public employees may help elect their own employers through voting and campaign support. As explained by Stieber (1973, p. 20), "In both public and private sectors, organized employees use power to affect the distribution of resources and the management of men [sic] and materials. In the private sector they do this primarily as employees. In the public sector they exert influence as employees, as pressure groups, and as voting citizens." Similarly, Anzia and Moe (2015) contend that public employees influence how state and local governments operate and are closely connected to politics and policymaking.

The principal reason that government employees are involved at a high level in politics is that legislative bodies have the authority to appropriate funds; enact laws that permit, regulate, or prohibit collective bargaining; and even supersede agreements between labor and management. Public employees generally have high levels of participation in voting and politics (Rosenfeld, 2014). Therefore, both labor and management engage not only with one another but also with whatever political entities and individuals can help them realize their objectives. This is not to say that private sector bargaining is apolitical and that private meetings with public officials do not occur or that broader constituencies are completely insignificant. But engaging in external politics away from the table is generally considered bad faith bargaining in the private sphere.

B. The Parties

The principal players in private sector labor relations have well-defined roles. The union team entails the union leadership, bargaining representatives, and rank and file members. The management team includes designated labor relations specialists and negotiators. Both parties are likely to have legal counsel at the table or readily available. Team membership may vary on occasion as specialists are brought in to address special topics, such as the future costs of pension or health-care benefits.

Management authority is securely situated at the top of the organizational hierarchy. Major corporations delegate responsibility for contract negotiations to specified individuals within various facilities or geographic locations. Management is rewarded according to that division's contributions to corporate profits; profits depend in large measure on minimizing labor costs.

Typically, facility executives are assisted in collective bargaining and contract administration by a human resource director or industrial relations specialist, whose future with the company depends on his or her success in negotiating and administering the contract. Labor lawyers are often consulted or contracted with to prepare for and conduct negotiations. There are strong career and financial incentives to "deliver" for corporate executives. Of course, union negotiators who do not deliver for their membership face the same grim possibility as does management's negotiator: losing the job.

Management's labor relations roles in public sector collective bargaining are less clearly defined. Separate staff functions for labor relations are found predominantly in the largest local governments and in states with comprehensive bargaining laws and many years of bargaining experience. In other jurisdictions, the responsibility for labor relations is not clearly fixed. This is unsatisfactory for at least two reasons: (1) no individuals are held directly accountable for promoting and protecting management's interests and (2) when labor relations is not treated as a distinct function or specialization, it is likely to be a secondary duty of the management negotiators and not receive the careful attention it deserves. Faced with a well-prepared opponent, a disorganized or indifferent participant may pay high costs.

Blurred management responsibility for labor relations fosters motivation problems. Motivation suffers when a poorly trained, part-time negotiator fails to see how this temporary job assignment will further his or her career because top management has not helped him see the connections. Unclear management responsibility also invites the union to exploit any fragmentation or inconsistency in management's position. Although projecting team solidarity on both sides of the table is a time-honored tradition, certain differences usually exist, and ostensible team solidarity is sometimes an illusion. A good negotiator can detect fragmentation/breaches in solidarity and can capitalize on it.

Negotiations are not a war game or an exercise in animal cunning. No amount of style or glibness can substitute for preparation and teamwork. It is imperative to come to the table focused, organized, and prepared to work hard to reach a settlement. It is one thing to fail to successfully negotiate an acceptable contract because of intractable issues or the other party's determination not to make concessions. It is quite another for negotiations to break down because of a lack of clear lines of authority, carelessness, or failure to prepare.

The diffuse nature of management authority in government is compounded by weak or unfocused labor relations responsibility. Even those with only passing familiarity with federal and state constitutions seem to believe intuitively in the separation of powers and checks and balances among institutions of government. Power is divided both between levels of government (federal/state/local) and within individual governments (executive/legislative/judicial), and all relationships are characterized by elaborate provisions for checks and balances. What happens at one point of the federalism matrix may be influenced by what happens at other points. For example, state legislatures sometimes reject collective bargaining settlements agreed to by the parties and the executive branch.

In this context, labor relations responsibility is ambiguous. With respect to municipal government labor relations, for example, the federal government regulates some working conditions, the state legislature may establish benefits packages, and the city council may set salaries. A coherent chain of command may be lacking and can be further muddied by the election cycle. Such diffusion of management authority poses serious problems especially during the early stages of a collective bargaining relationship, and it encourages unions to circumvent formally designated management representatives through "end runs" to more sympathetic individuals. At the very least, the process becomes highly political.

A final nettlesome problem in government concerns the merit system provisions. Collective bargaining processes and agreements may mesh or clash with merit system policies. For this reason, central personnel office staff should participate in or closely observe the negotiation process to discern how any agreement might relate to provisions of the merit system.

C. The Process

Finally, public and private sector labor relations differences exist in the process of collective bargaining. Some of them are obvious. For example, the diffusion of management authority results in multiple decision points in government labor relations. As noted earlier, the bargaining process is highly politicized in government and subject to influence by citizens and interest groups. Additionally, some of the formal elements and steps in collective bargaining differ, such as the legal absence of the strike option in most government jurisdictions and the subsequent reliance on other impasse resolution procedures. Section III discusses the elements of the collective bargaining process in government in more detail and highlights the distinctions between the public and private sectors where appropriate.

III. ELECTING A UNION AND GETTING A CONTRACT: THE ELEMENTS OF COLLECTIVE BARGAINING

Informal meet-and-confer arrangements in which negotiations are not sanctioned are not uncommon in government, but such interactions do not constitute collective bargaining. This section restricts discussion to conventional collective bargaining relationships. "Collective bargaining" refers to the continuous process in which representatives of the employer (government) and employees (the union) meet jointly to establish the terms and conditions of employment for workers in a bargaining unit. The discussion proceeds sequentially from bargaining unit determination to contract ratification (see Figure 4.1). Strikes, impasse resolution procedures, and contract administration receive extensive treatment in subsequent chapters.

A. Bargaining Unit Determination

A specific group of employees must be identified for the purposes of collective bargaining; this group of employees is the bargaining unit. The appropriate bargaining unit may be (1) specified by a state public employee relations board (PERB) or other administrative agency, in accordance with statute; (2) arrived at through adjudication on a case-by-case basis; or (3) accepted as defined by a union

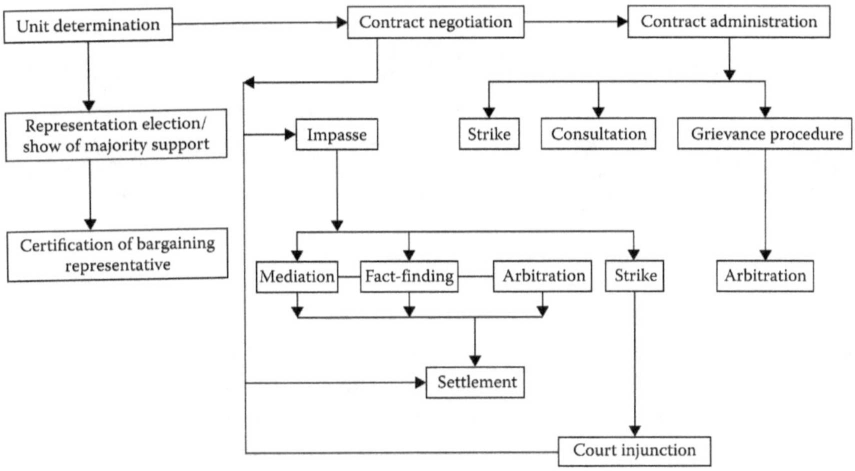

Figure 4.1 The collective bargaining process.

seeking recognition as the bargaining agent with a show of majority support from members of the intended bargaining unit. Support for the union is documented by a majority of eligible employees signing cards or petitions for union recognition as bargaining agent.

In the private sector and nonprofit sectors, unit determination depends on the type of firm or nonprofit organization and its functions. The National Labor Relations Board (NLRB) certifies bargaining units in the nonpublic sector. In instances in which a union and management disagree on unit composition, the NLRB is the final arbiter of what constitutes an "appropriate unit." In federal employment, unit determination is the responsibility of the Federal Labor Relations Authority (FLRA).

During the early (pre-statutory) years of collective bargaining in state and local governments, the makeup of the bargaining unit was frequently decided by the union's preferences. Management simply concurred out of weakness or indifference. In most cases today, however, the process is set forth in statute or in the administrative procedures of a state public employee labor relations board.

Unit determination and certification usually require multiple steps: petition for a certification election, proper showing of employee interest in the election, a hearing to establish the petition's validity, determination of the unit boundaries by an administrative entity, and final certification (see Figure 4.2). A proper showing of interest typically requires signed cards or a petition demonstrating that at least 30% of the workers in the proposed unit desire collective bargaining representation. The hearing is used to gather information on the validity of the show of

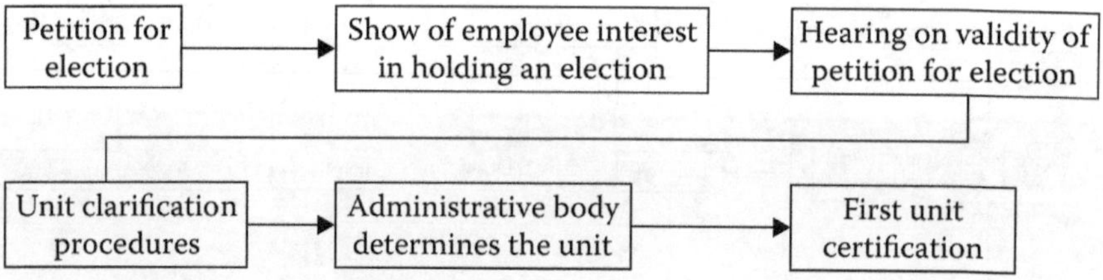

Figure 4.2 **Steps for determining the bargaining unit.**

interest and the timeliness of the petition. A petition is timely only if (1) there has not been a representation election within the past 12 months, (2) an existing certification is not in effect, and (3) a valid collective bargaining contract is not in effect (Rubin, 1979, p. 123).

Statutory and administrative agency criteria for unit determination decisions vary greatly but usually take into account these factors: (1) community of interest, (2) desires of the employees, (3) bargaining history, (4) efficiency of agency operations, (5) avoidance of bargaining unit fragmentation, and (6) exclusion of supervisory and confidential employees. The parameters of the unit may depend in part on the union's membership structure. The American Federation of State, County, and Municipal Employees (AFSCME), for example, may desire a citywide non-uniformed bargaining unit, whereas the International Association of Firefighters is likely to want uniformed firefighters only. The union's bottom line is that it wants a unit that will support it in the representation election and that will be sufficiently strong and united to negotiate a favorable contract. A certain degree of workforce solidarity is needed (Martinez et al., 2011).

1. Community of Interest

Usually, the most salient criterion in determining the bargaining unit, "community of interest," refers to duties, skills, and abilities held in common among employees. These employees are engaged in similar work or are treated in a like fashion by management.

2. Desires of Employees

Normally, employees sort themselves into appropriate bargaining units based on community of interest and union petitions. In some cases, workers are polled by the relevant labor relations board. Workers with clear conflicts of interest are not usually placed within the same unit (e.g., teachers and principals).

3. Bargaining History

"Bargaining history" refers to previous relationships between labor and management within the jurisdiction, including patterns of negotiation and recognition that may reflect traditions, past practice, or appropriateness of how units were first developed.

4. Efficiency of Agency Operations

The efficiency of agency operations becomes a factor if a proposed unit would disrupt standard human resource management policy and practice to the detriment of agency performance, work routines, or other factors.

5. Fragmentation of Bargaining Units

Fragmentation of bargaining units, which is most often found in the absence of legislative guidelines or administrative regulations, is related to unit size and the occupational characteristics of unit members. The conventional wisdom is that a large number of small bargaining units create serious administrative problems for management. Such problems include multiple, time-consuming negotiations; constant problems in administering the labor agreements; end runs to elected officials or other third-party "friends"; leapfrogging (where each union fights to position its wage increase and other bargaining gains at a level higher than any other union); and disruptive jurisdictional battles and rivalries between competing organizations (Spero & Capozzola, 1973, pp. 142–145).

Additional disadvantages of a large number of small bargaining units are the difficulty of maintaining uniformity and equity in wages, benefits, and working conditions for all workers in the jurisdiction; a greater potential for conflicts and job actions; and problems estimating future wage and benefit costs in the jurisdiction's budget. In a nutshell, fragmentation means inefficiency and complexity. In a state government with 50 bargaining units, management might have to go to the table half a hundred times with assorted unions. Significant administrative support is required on behalf of both parties. Administering numerous contracts with multiple unions can be a nightmare for management and a headache for union leaders (who find that what they have negotiated is compared by their members with the performance of every other bargaining agent).

The bargaining unit is, in effect, the election district in which employees vote for a union (or for no union) to represent them. Objective criteria for unit determination notwithstanding, unions have a pragmatic interest in organizing units for which they can win elections against both competing unions and the employer. An analogy is found in activities to reconfigure—or redistrict—congressional and state legislative districts following each decennial census. Although the principles of good government and fair representation may be espoused to justify a change in boundaries, gerrymandering districts to favor one candidate or party over another is common practice.

Due to these widely recognized problems with bargaining unit proliferation, there is a tendency to consolidate existing units. In New York City, for example, 400 units were collapsed into fewer than 100 over a 10-year period; in the federal government, the Civil Service Reform Act encouraged a 32% drop in the number of bargaining units from 1975 to 1981. At the state level, problems with unit fragmentation have led to a trend toward statewide units.

The boundaries of bargaining units are not etched in stone. They may be amended through unit clarification procedures such as accretion—which permits assimilation of employees filling newly created positions—and consolidation, which combines two or more existing units into a single entity. A consolidation might involve combining police and firefighters into a single unit within a public safety department. However, strong professional identification by members of each group often leads to vigorous opposition to consolidation. Many police and firefighters' unions have negotiated a ban on consolidation into the contract.

Despite arguments in favor of large units, numerous small bargaining units do offer certain advantages. In general, it is simpler to identify the bargaining interests of a small unit. There is evidence that in some cases, small, occupationally based units reflect the needs and objectives of their members better than units organized along departmental or agency lines (Perry & Angle, 1981).

On the other hand, diverse membership interests within a broad unit can create negotiating problems and internecine tensions that the union may find difficult to manage. The union may have trouble placating each faction in the bargaining unit. In addition, a small group of craft or other specialized workers might have its interests ignored within a larger unit and thus can make a case for separate recognition. This is closely related to the community-of-interest principle, which posits that employees with similar work and job interests should be located within the same unit. Finally, from the perspective of the public employer, small bargaining units can be dealt with effectively in some cases through a strategy of divide and conquer. Small units tend to be weak in political power and thus easier for the employer to dominate.

6. Exclusion of Supervisory and Confidential Employees

The sixth criterion usually taken into account in unit determination decisions is the exclusion of supervisory and confidential employees. In the private sector, Taft–Hartley excludes supervisors from membership in a bargaining unit. Although it once was simple to distinguish private sector supervisors from nonsupervisory employees, more recently, greater decision-making responsibility for workers in manufacturing, the service sector, and health care has complicated the situation. Some rulings by the NLRB have expanded the definition of "supervisor," thereby reducing the number of private sector workers eligible for union representation. Others, however, have narrowed the supervisory distinction. In several cases, the U.S. Supreme Court has become involved in either upholding or overturning NLRB decisions (e.g., *NLRB v. Kentucky River Community Care* [2001]; *Oakwood Healthcare, Inc.* [2006]).

Supervisors in the federal government are likewise prohibited from being represented in a bargaining unit. Several states, like the federal government and the National Labor Relations Act (NLRA), deny all bargaining rights to supervisors. Some states exclude only certain classes of "bona fide" supervisors. Others permit supervisory bargaining by creating separate units for supervisors. For example, the American Federation of School Administrators (AFSA) provides representation for over 20,000 primary and secondary school Principals, Vice Principals, Administrators, and Supervisors (Department for Professional Employees, n.d.). The most prevalent approach, used by some 22 states, is to provide for mixed units of supervisors and rank-and-file employees. Forces such as downsizing, decentralization of authority, and rampant politicization have pushed local government supervisors in the direction of collective bargaining to protect their jobs and to secure pay raises commensurate with those won by their unionized subordinates.

The conventional operating assumption is that supervisors are part of management and therefore should not be permitted to bargain in league with their subordinates. Moreover, supervisors included in subordinates' bargaining units face significant role conflicts, may become loyal to management, or may be less effective in dealing with disciplinary problems and grievances. However, evidence concerning these assumptions is mixed, and the question of supervisors' bargaining rights remains very much unresolved in the public sector.

In government, the laws, job titles, and other position characteristics are highly variable, and "sprawling bureaucracies make empty shells of many impressive titles" (Spero & Capozzola, 1973, p. 145). Furthermore, public sector managers frequently hold close working relationships with and perform many of the same duties as the rank and file, particularly in functions such as police and fire protection, nursing, and teaching. As team approaches to work have expanded, role ambivalence among public sector supervisors has grown.

The principle that legitimate, bona fide supervisors should not be placed with their subordinates in bargaining units is seldom disputed. The bona fide supervisor is the primary management agent in contract administration. To promote the efficiency, effectiveness, and purposes of the organization, he or she should be committed to the management point of view. The key determination that must be made is who is a bona fide supervisor and who is a supervisor only in title.

Some collective bargaining statutes and administrative procedures spell out what constitutes a bona fide supervisor and exclude those individuals from bargaining units composed primarily of subordinates. Less-than-bona-fide supervisors are placed within units of rank-and-file employees. Several states have adopted this approach, including Connecticut, Nevada, and Oregon, which apply an NLRA-type operational test to the definition of supervisor and then exclude only bona fide supervisors from bargaining law coverage. Typically, bona fide supervisors have "independent judgment" as demonstrated in their authority to hire, fire, promote, and discipline or are involved in policy formulation, collective bargaining, or contract administration activities.

When managers join a union and win collective bargaining rights, they may encounter some interesting role conflicts. As managers, they tend to have a natural antipathy to unions, and they will fight tooth and nail to defend management rights. But as union members themselves, managers are aligned against their own appointed and elected bosses. In a sense, these "supervisors have discovered how to have it both ways: managerial authority with union benefits" (Piskulich, 1995, p. 281).

That supervisory identification is not always a cut-and-dried affair is illustrated by two examples. In complex higher education institutions, the management line is drawn at the level of the department head in some universities and at the dean's office in others. Department heads are true "middle managers," with responsibilities in the classroom as well as in hiring and evaluating faculty and staff; setting departmental goals and objectives; and making merit pay, tenure, and promotion determinations. There is a long-established tradition of "faculty governance" in higher education, but in large, bureaucratic institutions, this is more an ideal than reality. Recall from Chapter 2 that the U.S. Supreme Court ruled that faculty at Yeshiva University held certain managerial duties—including involvement with hiring and retention decisions—and therefore had to be excluded from faculty bargaining units (*National Labor Relations Board v. Yeshiva University,* 1980). This decision effectively disenfranchised private college and university faculty from collective bargaining rights under the NLRA.

A second example of role confusion among supervisors and employees is seen in nursing. Here, the question of "independent judgment" is salient. The occupational hierarchy in the field of nursing includes nurses, registered nurses, charge nurses, nurses' aides, and head nurses, some of whom do exercise independent judgment in patient care or as supervisors of other nurses (Huckell, 2008; Matthews, 2010; Fisk, 2012).

B. Representation Election or Show of Majority Support

When de facto bargaining arrangements exist within a legal vacuum, a union has already been selected to represent workers and no new election need be held if a collective bargaining statute is enacted. In most instances, however, there must be a formal determination of which union, if any, shall represent the unit in collective bargaining. This may be accomplished through a representation election or by the employer's voluntary recognition of a unit representative. The latter normally occurs only when a single employee organization seeks recognition and is able to demonstrate to the satisfaction of the employer that it enjoys the support of a majority of the employees in the unit.

If more than one union is involved or majority support has not been demonstrated to the employer's satisfaction, a representation election is normally held. The election may be requested by the employer or, under some state laws, by a union. If the union asks for an election, it usually must present evidence (a "showing of interest") indicating a show of support of at least 30% of the bargaining unit. This showing of interest or support is typically done by employees signing authorization cards designating a union to represent them or by signing a petition for the same purpose.

For years, private sector unions have made it a legislative priority in Congress to enact a "card check" bill amending the NLRA to grant bargaining rights upon presentation of signed authorization cards by a majority of the unit (most recently embodied in the Employee Free Choice Act). Unions believe that the current requirement for a secret ballot election disadvantages them. As noted in Chapter 3, nine states have enacted card check provisions for public employees seeking to unionize. In comprehensive bargaining states, the show of support is typically validated by the state labor relations agency.

Once it is decided that a representation election will be conducted, a number of procedural issues must be resolved, including who will pay for the election and who will administer it. Typically, the PERB or other state labor board will do both. Next, the agency must determine who is eligible to vote (typically, those employees working within the unit on election day), when the election is to be held (usually within 30 days), the type of election (public or secret ballot), and what vote percentage is required for certification (usually the majority of votes cast).

As a general rule, the secret ballot is preferred by certifying agencies. Use of the secret ballot, a longstanding tradition within the American democratic experience, helps protect voting employees from undue preelection pressures from management or the union and, after the election, from retributive measures taken by a sore loser. A union election for representation rights looks much like any election for public office. For example, there are voting booths, voter lists, and rules against campaigning near the polling sites.

Before voting day, the employer posts notices of the forthcoming election and takes other steps to ensure a large turnout of eligible voters. Each of the principal parties usually is permitted to post observers at the polls and at the site where election results are compiled. The ballot itself includes the names of all organization demonstrating a show of support along with a choice of "no representative." In the event that none of the choices receives majority approval, a runoff election is held between the top two. Voting matters, particularly when turnout is low. In Florida's first election for a statewide administrative clerical unit of nearly 30,000 employees, AFSCME gained certification of the unit with only about 5,000 votes.

For its part, the union will arrange and call a meeting, distribute information by print and electronic media, recruit and train volunteers, and persuade bargaining unit members to support it. The union's job is made easier if the workplace consists of employees and jobs characterized by low morale, high levels of stress, job insecurity, arbitrary management actions, and low levels of compensation (Godard, 2011).

During the period preceding the election, management sometimes attempts to influence the results through various tactics. Employer-induced election delays can help management's cause (Riddell, 2010). Public concern with future salary increases or costly benefits packages can also boost the employer's chances. Union suppression tactics may even continue after a union election victory, through procedural objections, court actions, and other activities. As noted in Chapter 1, employers in the private sector sometimes use illegal tactics such as threats and reprisals to suppress unions, and often they get away with it. Such behavior is less common in government, but not unknown. Because these are all considered unfair labor practices, charges can be filed by the injured party with the appropriate labor board for redress. If such a board does not exist, the aggrieved party may turn to the courts.

If an employee organization wins majority support and various challenges to the election are resolved short of a change in outcome, the union is certified as bargaining representative. Obviously, if "no representative" is victorious, the unit remains unrepresented and no collective bargaining will occur. If a union wins the vote, an "election bar" typically prohibits new elections for a specified period of time to give the union sufficient time to negotiate a contract and otherwise "prove itself."

C. Certification of the Bargaining Representative

Certification by the state or local labor relations agency (or FLRA in federal employment and NLRB in the private and nonprofit sectors) normally stands for at least one year from election day. The status of unit representation thereafter may be challenged by a rival organization or by dissidents within the certified union through petition for a decertification election. Election procedures similar to those outlined in the preceding discussion then come into effect to determine if the union will be decertified as bargaining representative—a fairly common outcome in the private sector since the early 1980s but rare in the public sector. The process works in the same way as certification, only in reverse, with a showing of interest of 30% to decertify the union and a subsequent vote.

Workers may decertify unions for various reasons, including non-responsiveness to member needs and demands; antiunion campaigns by the employer; the union's failure to win and maintain favorable wages, benefits, and working conditions; and raids by competing unions. For example, union givebacks in negotiations with the State of Connecticut in 2011 provided an opening for raids on bargaining units of correctional officers and other state employees (Walters, 2011b). If the union loses a challenge, it ceases to function as bargaining representative. A second election may then be held to select a new representative; otherwise, the collective bargaining status of the unit is dissolved. In Florida, public sectors unions may be required to hold a "re-certification" election if the number of dues paying members falls below 60% of the total employees in the bargaining unit (see Chapter 3 for more details).

The employer grants exclusive recognition to the successful employee organization. Exclusive recognition provides significant benefits to the employer, the employees, and the union. The employer is assured that the union, and only that union, will represent all employees in the bargaining unit whether they are members of the union or not. Management will have only one organization to deal with, simplifying administration, saving time, and eliminating costly interunion struggles.

The union is guaranteed that management will deal with it alone concerning any issue within the scope of bargaining, both at the bargaining table and during administration of the contract. Exclusive recognition also benefits employees because a negotiated contract applies to all members of the bargaining unit even if they are not dues-paying union members. The organization has a duty to fairly represent all employees without any form of discrimination or favoritism (*Vaca v. Sipes,* 1967). However, the duty of fair representation can be a double-edged sword for a union. If a union fails to adequately represent a member of the bargaining unit, it may be sued for lost earnings or other damages (*Bowen v. U.S. Postal Service*, 1983).

D. Negotiating the Contract

After union recognition, we move into the heart of labor relations—negotiation of the contract between union and management representatives. Bargaining is a way to change the terms and conditions of a relationship and to make decisions between competing workplace alternatives. What happens at the bargaining table determines the substance, tone, context, and commitments in labor relations during the next one to three years. The satisfaction of employees with their wages, benefits, and working conditions—not to mention the union and its leadership—is directly influenced by the outcome, as is the financial solvency of the jurisdiction. At issue as well is the nature of the relationship between the parties. Poor relations between some unions and employers have little to do with present-day issues but rather reflect bitter memories of unresolved prior conflicts. Resentments and vengeance can blur the primary objectives of the bargaining process, which are to provide both parties with an agreement they can live with, achieve good working relations with representatives of the other party, and protect the interests of the jurisdiction's citizens.

1. The Participants

a. The Union

Management and union representatives are the primary participants in contract negotiations. Unless an impasse necessitates the intervention of a third-party neutral or other individual(s), labor and management representatives, often assisted by professional negotiators, hammer out the terms of the labor agreement on their own. Later, of course, the contract must be ratified by the union rank and file and by elected public officials, but the contract wheeling and dealing is the responsibility of the individuals sitting across the table from one another. The primary union figure—not only during contract negotiations but throughout virtually the entire process of labor–management relations—is the union leader or president of the local. Although the union leader has many responsibilities, it is primarily what he or she delivers to the membership from the bargaining table that determines their tenure in the position.

The job of the union leader is a demanding one, requiring strong political, managerial, interpersonal, and oratorical skills. Union leaders have been found to exhibit high activity and energy levels, strong goal direction, idealism, and a desire to change things for the better (Sayles & Strauss, 1967, pp. 58–60). Successful union leaders must be sharp negotiators and effective public relations people as well. They are faced constantly with the need to prove themselves to their membership, who may include militant extremists, avowed dissidents, loyal supporters, and the apathetic. "The script," according to Spero and Capozzola (1973, p. 115), "calls for a mixture of reason, explosive talk, threats, fear, justice, optimism, and pessimism."

Union leaders must be careful not to appear too friendly with management or they risk dissension in the ranks that may produce a strong opposing faction and ultimately result in membership rejection of a negotiated contract. Obtaining ratification of agreements is probably the most difficult—and delicate—problem union leaders confront. The membership may spurn the proposed contract because of dislike or distrust of the leader, overblown expectations for a settlement, disenchantment because of more substantial gains won by other organizations, or for any number of other reasons. Thus, it is critical that union leaders keep their fingers on the pulse of the organization and be highly persuasive in communicating with the membership.

In instances of union coalition bargaining, such as between state employee unions and the state executive branch, the challenge of membership support is even greater. For example, in 2011, two Connecticut unions unexpectedly broke ranks and spurned a deal that had been painfully negotiated to avoid widespread layoffs in exchange for wage and benefit givebacks. In other examples, unions have worked in coalition with other bargaining units and with community groups to advance their interests. For example, the United University Professions (UUP) partnered with state and local labor organizations and community groups for contract campaigns and political mobilizing. At Rutgers University multiple academic bargaining units formed a coalition with community groups known as RutgersOne. These coalitions fought successfully for academic gains and to redress systemic racism and structural deficits in supporting higher education (Rhoades, 2021).

A time-tested means of "rallying the troops" for a leader whose status and position are challenged is to create a crisis and an "us versus them" situational perception—not a difficult task given a highly adversarial and emotional bargaining context. One of the great stories is that of the overt enmity between the late union leader Mike Quill, president of the Transport Workers Union (TWU), and his nemesis, Mayor John Lindsay, during the 1966 New York City transit strike. Quill took great delight in humiliating Lindsay, publicly calling him a "pip-squeak" and an "ungrateful sourpuss" (Horton, 1973, pp. 80–81). Quill carried his disdain for the mayor and other opponents to new theatrical heights. During the strike (Raskin, 1972, pp. 129–130),

> The TWU chief was near death from heart disease; he had to swallow great gobs of pills in his moments of privacy; but none of them dulled his appetite for melodrama. He went before the television camera to tear up no-strike injunctions like confetti. When a judge ordered him carted off to jail, he said, "Let the judge drop dead in his black robes."

Although such drama may help unite the rank and file behind the union leader and draw clear lines of battle with management, it can severely inhibit agreement making and compromise when carried too far. In such cases settlement may come only after a protracted and painful strike. As management–union relations have matured, such histrionics have yielded to cool professionalism and quiet political deal making. In many settings, bargaining responsibility is turned over to union staff, with the leader active only behind the curtain.

Perhaps more so than most organizations, unions are victimized by the "Iron Law of Oligarchy." As originally described by Michels (1949), the Iron Law of Oligarchy refers to control of an organization by a small, self-perpetuating, self-interested elite. The membership, except during times of extraordinary provocation, remains apathetic. Even when new leaders emerge, they soon revert to oligarchic tactics to thwart opposition and ensure their own survival. This pattern does indeed appear to be applicable to most large labor organizations where a leader emerges, consolidates power, and, along with a small but loyal staff, controls the organization's activities with an iron fist. Contract rejections by union membership may reflect dissatisfaction with this situation and the perception (sometimes accurate) that the leadership is cutting "backdoor deals" with management while maintaining an elaborate public charade.

More recent studies show that unions can disrupt the iron law of oligarchy when the following conditions are present: political crises, influence from outside activists, and centralized pressure from the international union (Voss & Sherman, 2000). One prominent example of overcoming the hierarchy and bureaucratic structures of the labor unions is the #RedForEd teachers' strikes of 2018 in West Virginia, Arizona, and Oklahoma (Tarlau, 2023). Collective bargaining rights are relatively weak in these states and teachers' unions have traditionally relied on other tactics, such as legislative lobbying and electoral politics. In all three cases, the use of digital technology, e.g., Facebook, facilitated diverse personal expression on a large scale. The union infrastructure provided the scaffolding for teachers to connect, legitimize their grievances, and coordinate strike activity. The union leaders only got on board with the massive collective action when networked teachers' movements insisted on using more forceful tactics (Tarlau, 2023). As part of the process, the unions built alliances with students, parents, and community groups to demand more equitable allocation of resources.

The roles and behavior of rank-and-file union members received some early scholarly attention. Child et al. (1973) suggested a four-celled typology of member attachment to the union, based on the congruence between union policies and member expectations. "Cardholders," the most typical members, are committed to the organization as long as they benefit from its policies. "Troublemakers" are highly involved in union affairs, but their notion of what union policies should be is not congruent with that of the ruling elite. The "stalwarts" also are very active in the organization, but they are loyal to the leadership and personally identify with union objectives. Finally, "alienated members" may be ideologically opposed to the notion of union or, in some cases, are defeated former troublemakers who have withdrawn from active union involvement.

Researchers have been interested in identifying the correlates of employee commitment to the union. The level of commitment is important because it helps determine union effectiveness in organizing, bargaining, retaining membership, and taking political action (Gallagher & Clark, 1989). Four dimensions of union commitment have been identified (Gordon et al., 1980): (1) union loyalty—member pride in the union; (2) responsibility to the union—the extent to which the member fulfills the obligations and duties of membership; (3) willingness to do work on behalf of the union; and (4) belief in the concept of unionism or a pro-union bias.

Interesting differences characterize male and female members. Women tend to believe there is more to be gained from union membership and express greater loyalty to the organization than men, but women appear to feel less responsibility to the union and are not as willing to work for it. This divergence is due in large part to what Rooks (2003, p. 33) refers to as the "cowboy mentality." Leadership positions often involve extensive travel, long hours, unpredictability, and emotional stress. Various studies have identified patterns of behavior in which male members promote their own interests by excluding female members. These include the use of unfamiliar jargon and procedures, informal male networks, male-dominated bargaining agendas, and scheduling meetings at night or in taverns (Cobble, 1990; Kirton & Healy, 1999).

In her study of Black and Latina labor leaders, Dickerson (2006) notes that structural changes are needed within labor unions to amplify the voices of women and people of color in the labor movement. Specifically, she highlights the importance of constituency groups and caucuses to develop minority leaders, promote minority concerns within the larger labor movement, and establish connections between minority communities and unions. Bryant-Anderson and Roby (2012) contend that members must first gain experience at lower levels of leadership, such as union stewards, before they can advance into upper levels of leadership. Here they find that white women and people of color face frequent resistance to establishing themselves as effective leaders and suggest that both racism and sexism may impede their ability to be successful in higher level leadership positions. Simply having a presence in leadership positions is not enough to create a hospitable environment. Beyond descriptive representation, women and people of color must have substantive roles in decision making and have a place at the bargaining table to get their issues on the agenda (Kirton, 2017).

Perhaps counterintuitively, union commitment is found to be positively related to commitment to the employer: the quality of one relationship apparently feeds the other (Gallagher & Clark, 1989, pp. 58–60). However, union commitment is bolstered by a poor relationship between the member and his or her immediate supervisor, particularly when the supervisor and/or the employer is believed to have broken their "psychological contract" with the worker by failing to maintain jobs or benefits, for example. Members also appreciate democratic processes (Jarley et al., 1990), an effective grievance procedure (Clark, 1989), a certain level of personal trust and confidence in the union leader (Hoell, 2004; Twigg et al., 2008), and, of course, a union that produces the bread and butter—good pay and benefits (Fiorito et al., 1988). The perceived positive impact of the union on compensation, benefits, working conditions, and other valued outcomes is known as "union instrumentality"; it is one of the strongest correlates of union commitment (Turnley et al., 2004), along with pro-union attitudes (Fiorito et al., 2010; Bamberger et al., 1999).

Are union members more satisfied with their jobs than nonmembers? Earlier research findings were somewhat contradictory in that despite unions' ability to raise wages, unionized workers were less satisfied with their jobs than nonunionized workers (Freeman, 1978; Kochan & Baderschneider, 1981). Later models suggested that by creating a formal grievance system, unions were able to solve workplace problems and reduce quit rates (Freeman & Medoff, 1984). Studies conducted in the 2010s cast doubt on unions' abilities to combat inequality (Milkman, 2013; Rosenfeld, 2014).

However, more recent research demonstrates that the relationship between union membership and job satisfaction has flipped since the Great Recession. That is, unionized workers are now more satisfied with their jobs than their nonunionized counterparts. The relationship holds for both younger and older workers (Artz et al., 2022). The key mechanisms identified for the turnabout are the stable hours of employment and the job security provided by collective bargaining agreements.

b. Management

The initial problem that must be resolved by a jurisdiction becoming involved in union–management relations is developing a satisfactory operational definition of "management." Public sector management tends to be diffused, subject to political pressures, and conflicted.

Diffused Authority—In government, there are myriad complications in identifying and designating management for the purposes of collective bargaining. Power and decision-making authority are divided among the three branches of government. For instance, human resource management authority is situated within the executive branch, whereas budget authority resides with the legislative body. Both are critical to negotiating outcomes, yet the two functions are seldom coordinated. In addition, budgetary and personnel authority are themselves fragmented among various agencies, departments, and individuals. Further management identification problems are created by overlapping functional responsibilities and jurisdictions among the approximately 89,000 governmental entities in the United States; state and county social service agencies provide one typical example.

Jurisdictional confusion in management authority is compounded by the intergovernmental nature of government revenues. It is highly unusual for a public jurisdiction to raise all its funds from its own sources. The vast majority of governmental entities draw revenues from a variety of sources, including other governments. The federal grant-in-aid is the prototypical example, in which billions of federal dollars are transferred to state and local governments for various functions. The transfer of dollars is almost always accompanied by "strings" on how those funds may be spent.

When the strings are attached to personnel-related expenditures, as they often are, management authority in a very real sense is one level of government removed from making certain personnel-related decisions, thereby obscuring who has human resource management decision-making authority at the bargaining table. Similarly, federal strings on grant spending can affect funding available for employee compensation. Diffused management authority to make decisions concerning labor–management relations frustrates government managers. It presents unions with opportunities for end runs and spawns management conflicts. But legislative or other authoritative specification of precisely "who" is to represent management for purposes of collective bargaining and contract administration helps surmount some to the inherent difficulties of diffused authority.

Multilateral Bargaining—The diffusion of public management authority has been the focus of a considerable body of research, much of it focused on a common outcome of diffusion—multilateral bargaining. Multilateral bargaining is characterized by a plethora of direct and indirect participants, official and unofficial, all of whom seek to influence the outcome of negotiations. According to Kochan (1973), multilateral bargaining develops from four factors: (1) goal diversity among management officials, (2) dispersion of management power, (3) open management conflicts, and (4) union political influence and access to management officials.

Based on an early analysis of negotiations in city governments, Kochan (1973) demonstrated the variety of professional goals and personal agendas brought by management officials into the bargaining process. Elected officials are most concerned about their constituencies and prospects for reelection, whereas department heads, city managers, budget directors, and human resource directors are driven by different considerations. Overt evidence of goal diversity is displayed, for example, when a city council refuses to ratify a proposed contract that has gained union and management bargaining team approval, as the Jacksonville (Florida) City Council did in rejecting five negotiated contracts in 2012. The financial problems faced by states during and after the Great Recession prompted the Minnesota legislature to reject state bargaining contracts, insisting that increased pay and benefit costs were unsustainable (Ragsdale, 2012). As a rule, a high degree of goal diversity translates into elevated levels of management conflict during negotiations, characterized by multilateral, multiparty bargaining.

Management Conflict—From a broad perspective, the dispersion of management power and authority results from the constitutional separation of powers in American government and the precept of checks and balances. Conflict between and within branches of government is an innate part of politics, as is conflict between federal, state, and local governments. The greater the dispersion of authority, and the more it is fueled by political and personal agendas, the greater the conflict within the ranks of management.

Open conflicts are especially inimical to effective management negotiations. Such conflicts often develop and fester when unresolved personal and professional frictions and controversies spill over into the collective bargaining process. Kochan (1973, p. 25) provides the following example from a dispute over police and firefighter salary parity (wage equalization):

> Clear and open disagreement among management officials existed on what the city's position should be on this issue. The city personnel director, who was acting as chief negotiator, vigorously opposed it. The mayor did not take a position at the outset of the dispute but ended up arguing in support of it. The city council was rather evenly divided on the issue. Finally, there were two civil service types of bodies involved in the dispute and one opposed parity and one supported it.

A predictable result of this open conflict was an impasse over the parity issue. Hearings were conducted by one civil service commission, the council passed various resolutions in response to the impasse, and the second civil service body sought court action. A three-day strike prompted a final settlement.

Kochan (1975) developed a model of management conflict and multilateral bargaining through an analysis of city government. According to the model, goal incompatibility among management officials and the extent to which decision-making authority is dispersed determine the level of internal management conflict, which in turn determines the extent of multilateral bargaining. Union negotiating and political tactics such as end runs can expand the scope of conflict and multilateral bargaining. The important policy question is how to resolve internal conflicts so that management effectiveness is not diminished.

Specification and Centralization of Management Bargaining Authority—The initial response of most jurisdictions to unionization and collective bargaining has been to superimpose the new bargaining responsibility over the existing organizational structure (Burton, 1972). Thus, management attempts to utilize existing expertise and personnel while maintaining prevailing authority relationships. However, the time-consuming nature of bargaining and the typical dearth of labor relations expertise among existing staff intensify the dispersion of management authority, heighten conflict, and create an altogether unstable and unfavorable situation for management.

It is usually effective to concentrate authority in the executive branch when coordinating and conducting collective negotiations. Typically, organization for collective bargaining is centralized within the executive branch (especially in those jurisdictions that are large and/or have comprehensive bargaining units) within a labor relations office or agency. Full-time specialists may be appointed as chief management negotiators.

The ideal situation, according to labor relations experts, is to specify clearly in statute or administrative regulations exactly where management responsibility for collective bargaining is located. Most comprehensive bargaining states have done this. Nonetheless, bargaining remains inescapably multilateral. Internal management cohesiveness may improve, but multiple external actors, such as legislative bodies and interest groups, remain actively engaged.

Management Bargaining Responsibility in the Three Levels of Government—There is no conventional model of management representation for collective bargaining in government. The actors and their roles vary greatly among jurisdictions and levels of government.

Federal government: in federal employment, collective bargaining is essentially an individual agency's responsibility subject to the provisions of the Civil Service Reform Act and the oversight of the FLRA. (Excepted agencies have their own arrangements, as discussed in Chapter 2.) The national negotiating team normally is composed of full-time labor relations specialists appointed by agency heads. In the Social Security Administration, a team of professionals from the Center for Negotiation and Dispute Resolution negotiates agreements with the American Federation of Government Employees. The Congress has no direct involvement in collective bargaining. Overall, the federal system is highly decentralized, with around 4,000 bargaining units and a wide variety of bargaining participants.

State government: during the early history of collective bargaining in state government, management negotiating responsibility was frequently added to the duties of existing bodies, such as the state civil service commission or department of labor. In some cases negotiating responsibility was handed over temporarily to designated individuals on a part-time basis. Such arrangements became untenable as bargaining activities expanded. Eventually, most states centralized negotiating responsibility within the executive branch under the ultimate authority of the governor.

Composition of the bargaining teams varies among states, but a general operating principle is to include a chief negotiator with direct responsibility to the governor, a budget or finance officer, a personnel officer, and representatives from the relevant state agencies. As a rule, it is important to include agency representation in negotiations. Agency management must live with the contract on a day-to-day basis and thus has a very high and direct stake in the bargaining outcomes. Agency management should be involved throughout the bargaining process, including in formulating management positions, and evaluating the potential impact of union demands on agency budget and personnel. Generally speaking, the larger the bargaining unit conducting negotiations, the greater the extent of agency head involvement.

The role of the state legislature in collective bargaining activities is usually quite limited. Nonetheless, the legislative body has the final legal and budgetary responsibility to ensure that negotiated agreements are in tune with the public interest and fiscal limitations. Unacceptable bargaining outcomes may lead to legislative override and renewed negotiations, as they did in 2012 in Minnesota. New Jersey legislators also acted unilaterally and outside the bargaining process to roll back negotiated pension and health-care benefits for some 750,000 state workers and retirees in 2011.

From the management perspective, bargaining proceeds best when the executive and legislative branches are unified on major negotiating issues and resistant to union efforts to win favorable settlements through the end run. Legislative–executive cooperation is attained through early, regular, and meaningful communications between legislative leaders and staff, the governor, and the bargaining team on key issues being negotiated, when and how they are resolved, and remaining sources of contention. If the legislative body feels blindsided with the terms of a negotiated contract, it may reject it outright, sending the whole process back to the table. Similarly, a governor may veto a bargaining settlement that the legislature supports.

Governors have taken an active role in state collective bargaining, often assuming personal responsibility for brokering deals with the unions. Connecticut Governor Dannel Malloy worked within the collective bargaining process, including participating in all-day discussions, to exact $1.6 billion in union concessions to help balance the troubled state budget in 2011. After an initial deal was spurned by rank-and-file union members, Malloy threatened, cajoled, and argued to convince the state's 15 unions to sign on to a deal that all parties could live with (Keating, 2011b). Governors Rick Snyder (Michigan), Chris Christie (New Jersey), Andrew Cuomo (New York), and Mark Dayton (Ohio) were also deeply involved in negotiations with state workers in 2011–2012.

In 2023, Governor Phil Murphy (New Jersey) became involved in contract negotiations between labor unions and Rutgers University. Murphy and his staff met with the union and management teams for several months prior to the unions going on strike in April 2023. When the strike began, Governor Murphy advised the management team not to seek a court-ordered injunction against the striking workers. The Governor then called the bargaining teams into his office for five days of intensive dialogue and negotiations. The strike ended when Governor Murphy announced that the parties had developed a framework for a tentative agreement.

Approximately 35 states have state labor relations agencies that act as quasi-judicial bodies with administrative and general oversight authority for labor relations. The agencies consist of three to seven members (usually three) appointed by the governor. There may be labor and management representatives and one or more "neutrals," or all may be neutral members. The Connecticut State Board of Labor Relations consists of three members and two alternates appointed by the governor for a four-year term; Ohio's three-member board is appointed by the governor for a term of six years. Because the state agency is charged with protecting the rights of both labor and management, it is critical that the appointees be acceptable, credible, and legitimate in the eyes of both parties.

In at least nine of the comprehensive bargaining states, the agencies were created solely for the purpose of administering and overseeing labor relations. Some states, however, have placed labor relations administrative responsibility within existing entities, such as the state department of labor, the state personnel office, or the civil service commission. Other states have lodged administrative responsibility in existing functional entities, such as the state board of education. The opinion of most labor relations professionals is that the optimum situation is centralization in an entity created expressly for public sector labor relations. This type of arrangement encourages professionalism, centralizes executive financial controls, promotes consistent compensation and human resource management policies statewide, and, in general, helps stabilize and rationalize union–management relations.

Although combining public and private sector labor relations functions within an existing agency also offers certain advantages, including reduced administrative costs and the use of existing experienced personnel, public–private sector differences in labor relations are substantial enough to require staff personnel with distinctive backgrounds and training. However, none of the possible organizational arrangements is inherently superior. As Helsby & Tener (1979, p. 34) explain, "the single most important ingredient appears to be the caliber of the persons selected for and employed by the agencies . . . the ideal is to combine good law with top quality appointments."

Local government: as might be expected, local government has the widest variety of management participants in collective bargaining. There are, of course, tens of thousands of municipal, county, town, school district, and other local governments within the United States, and each has its own set of labor relations policies and actors. Some of the actors have expertise in labor relations, but the majority, especially those employed in small to medium-sized governments, can hardly be considered labor relations professionals. Consequently, labor law firms are often retained to assist in preparing for and conducting contract negotiations.

Management representation in local government follows a similar centralizing path as that of state government. In some cases, aborted attempts by mayors or council members to negotiate for the city or county led to centralized management responsibility within the executive branch. However, the structure of municipal or county government influences union–management interactions and the locus of management authority. In "strong mayor–council" forms of government, the mayor is the center of gravity and the embodiment of management authority. In "weak mayor" cities, the council may play a significant or even dominant role in labor relations. In the council–manager form of government, primary executive branch authority for labor relations typically resides in the city manager's office.

Although it is difficult to pinpoint any specific union advantages or disadvantages related to city government structure, it would be logical to assume that the council–manager form results in reduced leverage for the unions, primarily because the council tends to remove itself from the bargaining process and the mayor is essentially a figurehead. Moreover, it may be argued that city managers view themselves as management representatives and therefore tend to oppose union demands and protect management authority. Furthermore, the city management profession tends to attract individuals who are politically and socially moderate to conservative, and not union advocates.

In some council–manager cities, the manager takes on the role of chief negotiator; in others, the assistant manager is appointed to that job. Often, both are team members. In large to medium-sized cities (>100,000 population), professional negotiators, consultants, city attorneys, and labor relations staff frequently act as management negotiators regardless of government form. In small cities (<100,000), a part-time bargaining team approach has yielded gradually to delegating bargaining responsibility to the city attorney or a labor relations professional. The most common approach appears to be city manager/assistant manager, city attorney, personnel director, and department head in council–manager cities. In mayor–council forms of government, a chief administrative officer or other representative of the municipal labor relations office (large city) or mayor's office (small to midsized city) typically is joined on the management team by an attorney, personnel director, department head, and, in some cases, the budget director (Chandler & Judge, 1993; Hebdon, 2000).

The logic behind the presence of the legal and human resource officers is obvious—they will have to administer the city payroll and benefits, position classification plans, personnel procedures, and the final labor contract, all of which are affected by the outcomes of negotiations. A legal officer or attorney may prove valuable in assessing important questions of law in the proposed contract. Labor lawyers and other labor relations professionals are increasingly serving as chief city negotiators and team members in mayor–council cities. They are particularly likely to sit on negotiating teams in cities with an extensive union presence and history of high levels of strikes and other job actions (Gely & Chandler, 1993; Hebdon, 2000).

The role of the department head is more nebulous. Department chiefs rarely are directly involved in negotiations, largely because they want to avoid a potentially adversarial relationship with department personnel. The department heads usually participate only insofar as they furnish information to the regular management team, make relevant recommendations, and, in general, serve as observers and advisors. The specialized knowledge and direct interest of department heads in bargaining outcomes argue strongly for some form of participation, even if they merely dispatch their personnel director or assistant to serve as liaison with the bargaining team.

Mayors and members of council rarely sit on the management bargaining team. A deadlock, however, may force their intervention as mediators. Eventually they will have to approve or disapprove the agreement that is submitted to them in their official capacity as elected officials. Where management conflict is at a high level and the local government is highly politicized, however, the mayor and/

or individual council members may fall victim either to the "hero syndrome"—by attempting to arrange a settlement personally—or to an end run by a union seeking to circumvent the bargaining team. Such direct involvement may have a political price in the next election. It can be a no-win situation for elected officials. If they take a hardline stance against the unions, they risk sacrificing union votes in the next election. If they side with the union, fiscally conservative voters will likely cast their votes for another candidate.

During and after the Great Recession, "strong" mayors in midsized to large cities were effectively forced into direct involvement in negotiations. Fiscal crises must be addressed by strong mayors, who must find a means to reduce expenditures to balance the budget. Because the largest proportion of municipal operating budgets are dedicated to wages and benefits, mayoral actions may encounter union opposition. In 2012, the nation's third largest city, Chicago, witnessed a showdown between Mayor Rahm Emanuel and city workers in which Emanuel ordered work rule changes, layoffs, and other actions unpopular with the unions. Mayoral–union tensions came to a head with a 9-day strike by 26,000 Chicago teachers and school workers. Throughout the crisis, Emanuel was deeply and personally involved in negotiations with leaders of the Chicago Teachers Union (CTU), asserting his responsibility to protect the city's taxpayers and to be their voice (Davey & Greenhouse, 2012; Davey, 2012).

The CTU went on strike again in 2022 over issues related to the Omicron surge in the COVID-19 pandemic. The issues in contention included COVID-19 testing, use/provision of masks, and remote learning. After acrimonious negotiations with the mayor, Lori Lightfoot, the parties reached a tentative agreement and ended the five-day strike. The settlement terms include remote learning options on a school-by-school basis and a requirement that the district provide KN95 masks to students and teachers (Perez & Kapos, 2022).

For conventional collective bargaining, both management and the unions must designate a chief negotiator. The duties of the chief negotiator are to present one side's views and, in general, to serve as chief spokesperson. The chief negotiator leads the discussion during caucuses and serves as the main link with other local government (or union) officials. The most valuable attributes of the chief negotiator are personal integrity, patience, stamina, intelligence, strong communication skills, and intimate familiarity with the issues, motives, and pressures in the negotiations. Practice and painstaking preparation are also demanded.

Administration of local government labor relations varies among and within states. For example, in public schools, the chief administrative agency may be the state board of education. Alternatively, labor administration may be provided by the superintendents of the individual school districts or where schools are established by municipal, town, or county governments, by their local government's central labor relations agency. In large cities, there is usually some form of central labor relations office, although often it is exclusively devoted to management interests. The most prominent example of an independent agency is New York City's Office of Collective Bargaining (OCB), which was created jointly by the city and municipal unions. It is composed of two management representatives appointed by the mayor, two labor representatives appointed by the unions, and three "impartial" members elected by unanimous vote of the city and labor representatives. OCB also includes a Board of Certification and a Board of Collective Bargaining. The former has the task of determining bargaining units and certifying unions. The latter determines the scope of bargaining determinations, issues advisory opinions on city bargaining law, handles grievance arbitration, and helps resolve disputes arising during negotiations.

Some state administrative agencies exercise administrative oversight over labor relations in local governments. Iowa's PERB, for instance, oversees allegations of prohibited practices, enforces the duty to bargain in good faith, aids in dispute settlement, and determines the appropriate bargaining unit. Although local administrative machinery may exist, those states that have established statewide agencies often exercise overall responsibility for local government labor relations.

2. Role of the Public

The role of the general citizenry in collective bargaining varies by jurisdiction. Public participation in the negotiation process can range from an active and formal role at the bargaining table to simple citizen access to the terms of the negotiated agreement. Public involvement represents, of course, a major point of departure from private sector collective bargaining, where there is no meaningful third-party role for the general public.

Public access to collective bargaining may be either direct or indirect. Direct access provides a formal and legal means of citizen involvement through, for example, comments on bargaining proposals, public hearings on negotiations, trilateral bargaining with citizens participating in bargaining sessions, citizen observation of open negotiating sessions, or voter referenda on contract settlements or other labor relations issues. Indirect access includes citizen or interest group participation in hearings on the budget, use of court injunctions, lobbying elected officials on behalf of one of the negotiating parties, and opening up informal lines of communication to legislators and other elected officials.

With the call for more accountability and transparency in government, the trend has been toward formal—or direct—access. Public disclosure and open meetings laws expose government policy making to some extent in all states and localities. However, most such laws exempt collective bargaining activities, thus permitting negotiations to be carried out behind closed doors. Also, tides of public distrust and resentment of government in general and "underworked and overpaid" public employees in particular have led to demands for increased citizen oversight of public sector collective bargaining. After all, the taxpayer must pay the final costs of the negotiated settlement. Where the perception exists that elected officials have not effectively represented the public's interest in negotiations, movements for direct citizen involvement may ensue.

Several states have institutionalized a public role in collective bargaining through "sunshine laws." Eighteen states require some sort of bargaining in the sunshine (i.e., in public). Florida's collective bargaining law is the strongest, mandating that all negotiations be held in public. Kansas law provides that teacher bargaining be open. California's statutes for state employees and public schools require initial bargaining proposals to be presented at a public hearing and new proposals to be made public within 48 hours. A reasonable period of time must be allowed for the public to become informed and express opinions on all proposals before a new round of negotiations begins. In Montana, Maine, Florida, and Oregon, students in higher education institutions have the right to attend negotiations. In Idaho, the state teachers' law mandates that minutes of negotiating sessions be made public and that contracts be ratified in open meetings. Sunshine bargaining is optional (both parties must agree to it) in Iowa, Massachusetts, New Jersey, and several other states.

Much debate has raged on the pros and cons of bargaining in the sunshine. Advocates of sunshine laws contend that public deliberation on important public policy issues promotes citizen understanding and confidence in government and makes government more responsive to voter concerns. It deters misappropriation of public funds and conflicts of interest and helps the public become a constructive partner in reaching hard decisions on difficult problems. It is also believed to help moderate union demands by subjecting them to formal public and media scrutiny.

Public management, union leaders, elected officials, and professional labor negotiators are all quick to point out the disadvantages of bargaining in the sunshine. Open negotiations are time consuming and may promote rancorous conflict and stalemates, thus destroying productive working relationships. The presence of the media may encourage "bargaining through the press" and grandstanding instead of constructive bargaining over the issues (Cassidy, 1979, p. 12). The process may "take on the aspects of a poorly produced drama where emotions upstage good judgment and egos, not issues, get the best lines" (Sherman, 1979, p. 274). Skeptics also assert that sunshine bargaining suffers from inexpert and uninformed reporting in the media and very little citizen interest.

Although the advantages and disadvantages of bargaining in the sunshine have not yet been systematically assessed across the states, it has become apparent particularly from the Florida experience (where substantial majorities of labor and management representatives have supported it) that many of the criticisms have been exaggerated (West & Feiock, 1989). For instance, despite delays caused by the presence of the media and other representatives of the public, the content of the vast majority of agreements has not been affected. Moreover, the stringent requirements of some of the sunshine laws may be circumvented through creative actions. In one state requiring that school board meetings be open, for example, mediators have avoided open meetings by carrying out delicate negotiations with a few of the board members at a time or by meeting with the board in executive session over "personnel issues."

It is clearly consistent with democratic processes for citizens to have a formal third-party role in public sector collective bargaining. Examined judiciously, collective bargaining as it is presently conducted in most jurisdictions may or may not be conducive to the best interests of the public. Appointed officials typically control the negotiations and final agreements are usually rubber-stamped by elected representatives. Public participation is sparse and indirect, coming perhaps only in the guise of after-the-fact judgments. Yet, citizens have a fundamental right to hold officials accountable for how their tax dollars are being spent.

There is no one best way to involve the public in collective bargaining. Given the high levels of citizen discontent and distrust in government that have generally prevailed for the past several decades, the benefit of the doubt might be given to inclusive, sunshine-style experiments. Exclusion of the public builds neither confidence nor trust, and it perpetuates voter ignorance.

IV. SUMMARY AND CONCLUSIONS

Collective bargaining shares common structures and processes in the public and private sectors. At the same time, bargaining in these venues also differs in many important respects. These include the environment of labor relations, the major actors and their motivations, and some aspects of the process itself.

Unit determination raises a number of important issues in public sector bargaining, including criteria with which to determine the unit and its size, fragmentation of bargaining units, and the inclusion or exclusion of supervisors. Once the unit is determined, a representation election is held to select the organization that will represent the unit in collective bargaining, or the employer may voluntarily recognize the union upon a showing of majority support. The victor is certified as exclusive representative of the bargaining unit.

The next step is negotiation of the contract. The union leader and designated management representatives play the starring roles. It is difficult, however, to identify "management" in the public sector because of the large number of interested parties who participate directly or indirectly in multilateral bargaining. This is reflected in the wide compositional variety of management bargaining teams within and among the three levels of government. Public concern with some of the more obscure aspects of bargaining has led to increased interest in sunshine bargaining and the institutionalization of a public voice in collective bargaining.

The collective bargaining process in government is highly politicized, with politics pervading behavior at the bargaining table and suffusing the labor relations environment. Collective bargaining has been compared to a Shakespearian play, complete with actors, roles, and scripts. The ending of the play, however, is not predetermined. It depends on the bargaining power of the parties, how they play the game, and whether the bargaining is primarily about "getting to yes" or just getting the best of the other side. Bargaining outcomes also depend on the effectiveness of public employee unions as interest groups engaged in lobbying, electoral activities, and public opinion making.

CASE STUDY 4.1 WHOSE UNION IS IT?*

Introduction

Simon looked down at the stack of petitions on his desk. Union members were reacting with their signatures to rumors they had heard regarding the layoff of 500 workers among five large bargaining units totaling 2,500 members. They were calling for the ouster of the current union president and all union stewards. A membership survey (see Table 4.1), conducted by union leaders to determine the preferred bargaining path for the union, had produced results that the union leadership did not concur with. Out of five possible scenarios, the largest majority of respondents had indicated that Scenario 4 was preferred, yet the union was negotiating for Scenario 5.

Simon, a union steward for Bargaining Unit #4 (500 members) in the state Department of Transportation (DOT) for 15 years, was not accustomed to feeling uneasy with the posture of the union he represented. But this one made him wonder.

Cleaning Up the State Budget Crisis

The latest budgetary crisis in state government had caused the governor once again to request concessions from all state employee unions. The concessions took the form of an increase in the length of the work week from 37.5 to 40 hours with a corresponding increase in pay. The increased work week was meant to calm state residents, who viewed state workers as underworked and overpaid and who wanted massive layoffs to reduce their personal state income taxes. Because the budget supporting the state workers' salaries was not to increase, the extension to 40 hours per week would result in layoffs in every union and bargaining unit, including an estimated 100 in Simon's.

Workers in the union who had been with the state for more than ten years had a nice pension built up, full medical benefits upon retirement,

Table 4.1 **Union Survey**

Please indicate which scenarios are acceptable or not acceptable to you regarding a 40-hour work week. The current work week is 37.5 hours. Please mark each scenario

Scenario 1–The contract provides for no general wage increase for five years, skips the payment of one annual increment, makes no guarantee to avoid layoffs, and institutes a 40-hour work week phased in with pay

- Acceptable - Not Acceptable

Scenario 2–The contract provides for three 2% general wage increases in January of the last 3 years of a 5-year period, skips the payment of one annual increment and delays the payment of the other annual increments for 5 months, makes no guarantee to avoid layoffs, and institutes a 40-hour work week phased in with pay

- Acceptable - Not Acceptable

Scenario 3–The contract provides for general wage increases that keep pace with inflation, pays annual increment on time, makes no guarantee to avoid layoffs, and does not institute a 40-hour work week

- Acceptable - Not Acceptable

Scenario 4–The contract provides for no general wage increases, pays annual increment and lump sum payments on time, makes a guarantee of no layoffs for general and special transportation fund employees, and institutes a 40-hour work week with pay

- Acceptable - Not Acceptable

Scenario 5–The contract provides for general wage increases that exceed inflation, pays annual increments on time, institutes a 40-hour work week with pay, and results in 500 P4 bargaining unit employees being laid off

- Acceptable - Not Acceptable

and job security. They were not eager to work an extra 2.5 hours a week, even with additional pay. Ernie Banks, with the DOT for 19 years, made it his business to know how his share of the pie would be affected. And he did not like what he saw.

"Simon, Ernie here, just wondering about the union's stand regarding the 40-hour work week proposal. We're not going to work longer hours, are we?"

"Well, Ernie, you know I'm always out to protect our interests. What do you think about it?"

"Don't like it. I'm getting ready to start thinking about retirement. The last thing I need to do is work longer hours. You keep on protecting our rights, okay, buddy?"

Simon swallowed hard as he hung up the phone. The "good" days in state government were over. Every year now, it was how much will you give up. Three years with no increases and now an addition of 2.5 hours per week. But the message was not getting to the older union members. They wanted to hold on to an era gone by, when unions got much of what they asked for.

Ernie knew the leaders in the union. He called the president, negotiators, and steward by their first names. And he let each of them know that he expected his union to protect his rights earned through 19 years of state service.

Union Represents Many Faces

Brenda McGuire worked as an entry-level engineer at DOT. She got the position right out of college, and although the wages were lower than those in the private sector, she opted for the job security of working for the state. After two years, she felt fairly comfortable performing her duties and understood how the state government functioned. She was happy to have a steady job.

Jason Steel, Brenda's coworker, stopped her on the way to a meeting.

"Did you hear about the layoffs?"

Brenda bristled, "No, what have you heard?"

"The older union members are selling us out. The union won't agree to reduce wage increases to compensate for the 40-hour work week, so the governor is going to order layoffs. Anyone with under 3 years of service has no seniority."

Brenda thought of her daughter who had just started private preschool. That would have to stop with no job. "Well, what can we do?"

"There's a meeting right after work to discuss the options for the younger members of our union. Seems there are a lot of us who don't believe the union represents us. We're pretty certain that we younger members represent the majority. There's talk that we may try to get rid of Evans and all of the union officials. Maybe you should attend."

[*DOT Commissioner's Office*]

"There's a message here from three of the field supervisors. They're wondering why the union has agreed to layoffs. Each of them has field staff with fewer than three years' experience with the department. They are concerned that they will not meet their deadlines or fulfill their other management responsibilities if they lose staff. All would like a return call from you."

Commissioner Smith was not certain how to proceed. He had major projects with funding that were going to suffer serious delays if the layoffs went through. That would reflect badly on his executive management objectives and he would lose the bonus he had been working toward. He also had people who had worked in the department for more than 20 years who had little sympathy for the "youngsters" who could lose their jobs. He needed their experience to make the projects go.

Smith called Simon, the union steward, to request a meeting.

[*Simon's Office—Phones Ringing*]

"That makes 420 against and 80 for. The callers are not appreciating the stance of the union on this one. Saying we don't care about young families, only the retirement-age workers. Is this really worth it? I heard rumors that they may call for your resignation," said Samantha Edwards, Simon's longtime assistant.

Simon sat down heavily. There did not seem to be a way out. Another phone rang.

"Commissioner's on the phone . . . wants to come over for a meeting to discuss the options."

"Oh, great."

[*After-Work Meeting of Bargaining Unit 4 Members*]

"I say we get rid of Simon. He is so out of touch with the majority of this bargaining unit. Who does he think he's representing?"

"I need my job. I don't really want to work more hours, but I need the job. We do what we have to do."

"Can we oust Simon? Will that help our cause? Do we have legal recourse if we see no hope of our views being represented?"

Simon knew the contract inside and out. He had special coverage under the contract that made him the last to go if layoffs ever went that deep in the agency. They called it superseniority. He also knew that "incompetence, inefficiency, neglect of duty, or misconduct" were grounds for dismissal.

The contract survey that the union members had filled out had shown that the majority of members opted for Scenario 4, which did not include layoffs. Although this information had not been publicly acknowledged, it had somehow found its way back to the membership. In fact, the union had decided to opt for Scenario 5 because they thought they would end up in a better bargaining position by asking for as much as possible and then, perhaps later, conceding on some points. The union's plan, however, had backfired. Now they faced a membership who sought retribution for not having their wishes followed.

[*Simon's Office*]

"Commissioner Smith is here."

Simon got up to present his plan.

Discussion Questions

1 What are the main issues in this case study?

2 If you were union steward Simon, how would you proceed?

3 Are layoffs preferable to givebacks in this situation?

4 Would the ouster of the union president and stewards help the younger union members?

5 What are the possible outcomes of this situation?

REFERENCES

Anzia, S. F., & Moe, T. M. (2015). Public sector unions and the costs of government. *The Journal of Politics*, 77(1), 114–127.

Artz, B., Blanchflower, D. G., & Bryson, A. (2022). Unions increase job satisfaction in the United States. *Journal of Economic Behavior & Organization*, *203*, 173–188.

Bamberger, P. A., Kluger, A. N., & Suchard, R. (1999). Research notes: The antecedents and consequences of union commitment: A meta-analysis. *Academy of Management Journal*, *42*(*3*), 304–318.

Bowen v. U.S. Postal Service. (1983). 103 S. Ct. 588.

Bryant-Anderson, R., & Roby, P. A. (2012). The experience of leadership: Women and men shop stewards' perspectives in ten trade unions. *Labor Studies Journal*, *37*(3), 271–292.

Burton, J. F. (1972, May). Local government bargaining and management structure. *Industrial Relations*, *11*, 123–140.

Cassidy, G. W. (1979). An analysis of pressure group activities in the context of open meeting and public employee relations laws. *Journal of Collective Negotiations*, *9*(*1*), 3–17.

Chandler, T. D., & Judge, T. (1993). Collective bargaining with police unions: Characteristics of negotiators and bargaining strategies. In *The municipal year book 1993*. International City Management Association.

Child, J., Loveridge, R., & Warner, M. (1973, January). Towards an organizational study of trade unions. *Sociology*, 7, 71–91.

Clark, P. F. (1989). Determinants of the quality of union-management relations: An exploratory study of union member perceptions. *Journal of Collective Negotiations in the Public Sector*, *18*(2), 103–115.

Cobble, D. S. (1990). Rethinking troubled relations between women and unions: Craft unionism and female activism. *Feminist Studies*, *16*, 519–548.

Davey, M. (2012, September 10). Teachers' strike in Chicago tests mayor and union. *New York Times*. www.nytimes.com

Davey, M., & Greenhouse, S. (2012, September 19). School days resume in Chicago as the lessons from a strike are assessed. *New York Times*. www.nytimes.com

Department for Professional Employees. (n.d.). *American federation of school administrators*. https://www.dpeaflcio.org/american-federation-of-school-administrators

Dickerson, N. T. (2006). "We are a force to be reckoned with": Black and Latina women's leadership in the contemporary US labor movement. *WorkingUSA*, *9*(3), 293–313.

Fiorito, J., Gall, G., & Martinez, A. D. (2010). Activism and willingness to help in union organizing: Who are the activists? *Journal of Labor Research*, *31*(*3*), 263–284.

Fiorito, J., Gallagher, D. G., & Fukami, C. V. (1988, January). Satisfaction with union representation. *Industrial and Labor Relations Review*, *41*, 294–307.

Fisk, C. L. (2012). Supervisors in a world of flat hierarchies. *Hastings Law Journal*, *64*, 1403.

Freeman, R. B. (1978). Should we organize? The effects of faculty unions on academic compensation. In *Working paper no. 301*. National Bureau of Economic Research.

Freeman, R. B., & Medoff, J. L. (1984). *What do unions do?* Basic Books.

Gallagher, D. G., & Clark, P. F. (1989, Spring). Research on union commitment: Implications for labor. *Labor Studies Journal*, *14*, 52–71.

Gely, R., & Chandler, T. D. (1993). Determinants of management's organizational structure in the public sector. *Journal of Labor Research, XIV*(4), 381–397.

Godard, J. (2011). Uncertainty and the correlates of union voting propensity: An organizing perspective. *Industrial Relations: A Journal of Economy and Society*, *50*(3), 472–496.

Gordon, M. E., Philpot, J. W., Bun, R. E., Thompson, C. A., & Spiller, W. E. (1980). Commitment to the union: Development of a measure and examination of its correlates. *Journal of Applied Psychology*, *65*(4), 479–499.

Hebdon, R. (2000). Labor-management relations in the United States, 1999. In *The municipal year book: 2000*. International City Management Association.

Helsby, R. D., & Tener, J. B. (1979). Structure and administration of public employment relations agencies. In M. K. Gibbons, R. D. Helsby, J. Lefkowitz, & B. Z. Teher (Eds.), *Portrait of a process—collective negotiations in public employment* (pp. 31–54). Labor Relations Press.

Hoell, R. C. (2004). The effect of interpersonal trust and participativeness on union member commitment. *Journal of Business and Psychology*, *19*(2), 161–177.

Horton, R. D. (1973). *Municipal labor relations in New York City*. Praeger.

Huckell, B. (2008). Who's the boss? Supervisors, professionals, independent judgment, and the NLRA: A post-Oakwood healthcare review. *Labor Law Journal*, *59*(3), 236–264.

Jarley, P., Kuruvilla, S., & Casteel, D. (1990). Member–union relations and union satisfaction. *Industrial Relations: A Journal of Economy and Society*, *29*(1), 128–134.

Keating, C. (2011b, August 20). Malloy hails union deal: Others skeptical. *Hartford Courant*. www.courant.com

Kirton, G. (2017). From "a woman's place is in her union" to "strong unions need women": Changing gender discourses, policies and realities in the union movement. *Labour & Industry: A Journal of the Social and Economic Relations of Work*, *27*(4), 270–283.

Kirton, G., & Healy, G. (1999). Transforming union women: The role of women trade union officials in union renewal. *Industrial Relations Journal*, *30*, 31–45.

Kochan, T. A. (1973). *Resolving internal management conflicts for labor negotiations (PERL no. #41)*. International City Management Association.

Kochan, T. A. (1975, February). City government: A path analysis. *Industrial Relations*, *14*, 90–101.

Kochan, T. A., & Baderschneider, J. (1981, October). Estimating the narcotic effect: Choosing techniques that fit the problem. *Industrial and Labor Relations Review*, *35*(*1*), 3–20.

Martinez, A. D., Fiorito, J., & Ferris, G. R. (2011). Solidarity revisited: Group-level effects on individual-level union voting. *Journal of Labor Research*, *32*(1), 61–74.

Matthews, J. (2010). When does delegating make you a supervisor?. *Online Journal of Issues in Nursing*, *15*(2).

Michels, R. (1949). *Political parties*. Free Press.

Milkman, R. (2013). Back to the future? US labour in the new gilded age. *British Journal of Industrial Relations*, *51*(4), 645–665.

National Labor Relations Board v. Yeshiva University. (1980). 444 U.S. 672, 103 LRRM 2526.

NLRB v. Kentucky River Community Care. (2001). http://www.law.cornell.edu/supct/html/99–1815.ZO.html

Oakwood Healthcare Inc. (2006). *Decision on review and order*. http://www.aha.org/content/00-10/Oakwood.pdf

Perez, J., & Kapos, S. (2022, January 10). Chicago schools, teachers reach tentative deal to end classroom shutdown. *Politico*. https://www.politico.com/news/2022/01/10/chicago-schools-teachers-deal-stalemate-526868

Perry, J. L., & Angle, H. L. (1981, Winter). Bargaining unit structure and organizational outcomes. *Industrial Relations*, *20*, 47–59.

Piskulich, J. P. (1995). Collective bargaining among local government executives: The standoff in Michigan. *Labor Law Journal*, *46*, 479–485.

Ragsdale, J. (2012, August 30). GOP legislators derail new state union deals. *Star Tribune*. www.startribune.com

Raskin, A. H. (1972). Politics up-ends the bargaining table. In S. Zagoria (Ed.), *Public workers and public unions* (pp. 122–146). Prentice Hall.

Rhoades, G. (2021). Working in coalition, and wall-to-wall: The new progressive normal. *Journal of Collective Bargaining in the Academy*, *12*(1), 4.

Riddell, C. (2010). The causal effect of election delay on union win rates: Instrumental variable estimates from two natural experiments. *Industrial Relations: A Journal of Economy and Society*, *49*(3), 371–386.

Rooks, D. (2003). The cowboy mentality: Organizers and occupational commitment in the new labor movement. *Labor Studies Journal*, *28*(3), 33–62.

Rosenfeld, J. (2014). *What unions no longer do*. Harvard University Press.

Rubin, R. S. (1979). Procedures in unit determination. In M. K. Gibbons, R. D. Helsby, J. Lefkowitz, & B. Z. Teher (Eds.), *Portrait of a process—collective negotiations in public employment* (pp. 122–134). Labor Relations Press.

Sayles, L. R., & Strauss, G. (1967). *The local union*. Harcourt, Brace & World.

Sherman, J. J. (1979). The role of the public in the bargaining process. In M. K. Gibbons, R. D. Helsby, J. Lefkowitz, & B. Z. Teher (Eds.), *Portrait of a process—collective negotiations in public employment* (pp. 269–277). Labor Relations Press.

Spero, S. D., & Capozzola, J. M. (1973). *The urban community and its unionized bureaucracies*. Dunellen.

Stieber, J. (1973). *Public employee unionism*. The Brookings Institution.

Tarlau, R. (2023). Networked movements and bureaucratic unions: The structure of the 2018# RedFored teachers' strikes. *ILR Review*, *76*(5), 833–863.

Turnley, W. H., Bolino, M. C., Lester, S. W., & Bloodgood, J. M. (2004). The effects of psychological contract breach on union commitment. *Journal of Occupational & Organizational Psychology*, *77*(3), 421–428.

Twigg, N. W., Fuller, J. B., & Hester, K. (2008). Transformational leadership in labor organizations: The effects on union citizenship behaviors. *Journal of Labor Research*, *29*(1), 27–41.

Vaca v. Sipes. (1967). 386 U.S. 171, 87 S. Ct. 903.

Voss, K., & Sherman, R. (2000). Breaking the iron law of oligarchy: Union revitalization in the American labor movement. *American Journal of Sociology*, *106*(2), 303–349.

Walters, J. (2011b, August 21). Cracks only growing in union solidarity: Attempted raid on membership highlights fractures among state employee unions. *Hartford (CT) Courant*. www.courant.com

Weil, D. (2014). The fissured workplace: Why work became so bad for so many and what can be done to improve it. In *The fissured workplace*. Harvard University Press.

West, J. P., & Feiock, R. C. (1989, Spring). Support for sunshine bargaining in Florida: A decade later. *Review of Public Personnel Administration*, 9, 28–50.

Chapter 5

Process and Politics of Public Sector Collective Bargaining

I. INTRODUCTION

Collective bargaining in the private sector is about profits, products, labor markets, and productivity—in short, economics. In government, politics, not profits or prices, is paramount, within an environment composed of a rich variety of interests with clashing views and values. The outputs of the bargaining process in government—decisions rendered concerning staffing levels, compensation, and the allocation of tax dollars—are produced in this often chaotic milieu. The direct participants are clearly political players, locked in a political contest with high stakes for both the players and the public.

II. INTERNAL PROCESS AND POLITICS

Collective bargaining is both a relationship and a process. It involves both formal and informal relationships that continue over time between labor and management with the purpose of jointly determining wages and other terms and conditions of employment. The process embraces activities that include identifying proposals, preparing for bargaining, negotiating an agreement specifying the terms and conditions of employment for a fixed period of time, and administering the agreement on a day-to-day basis. (Contract administration is discussed at length in Chapter 10.) The formal collective bargaining process prevailing in most jurisdictions is discussed in the following sections.

A. Identifying Proposals

Both sides in the bargaining process anxiously anticipate the receipt of proposals that either alter the existing agreement or identify new issues in the collective bargaining relationship. Initial agreements are particularly difficult because they represent the first attempt by the concerned parties to significantly change

DOI:10.4324/9781003403593-5

preexisting processes used to solve problems and determine the terms and conditions of employment. Today, most contract bargaining involves parties who have already negotiated one or more formal agreements.

As proposals are being readied on both sides, decisions must be made as to how to package them and sort out the more important from the less important. A "bargaining book" or spreadsheet can cross-reference contract clauses and provide the history and meaning of contract terminology and clauses. Negotiators bring their teams together to help them make these strategic determinations and to talk about readiness and strategy. There are a lot of "what if" scenarios to ponder. A division of labor is made in terms of contract sections and language. One or two team members may be assigned to watch the interpersonal dynamics, body language, and facial expressions on the other side of the table. The customary principle is to have a single spokesperson for each team.

How are subjects for negotiation identified? The union will have a standing list of issues, many of them arising from difficulties with the existing contract. Some issues may arise from a reexamination of compromises made during past negotiations that are no longer satisfactory because relevant facts have changed. Other union demands may resurrect objectives not realized in past contracts but that are still important to the labor organization. The union holds membership meetings in which its rank and file can raise new issues or provide guidance that limits the chief negotiator's discretion on key matters that might have to be brought back to the membership for discussion. Some unions do a special mailing or survey to solicit input from their members. Others use social media to disseminate and collect points of view.

Invariably, certain individual members will insist that a pet problem or concern become part of the bargaining proposals, usually to no avail. In successor agreements, there is typically a series of complaints emerging from grievances that the labor organization lost because present contract language did not support its position before an arbitrator. If the local union is affiliated with a national union, matters that were identified as priorities during the past national meeting may be advanced. The challenge is to pare down the membership's "wish list" into a package of realistic proposals.

Management brings proposals to the table, too. This may seem obvious, but for years in some jurisdictions the union was the only moving party at the table. Management's posture was to react to what the union wanted. This has changed. Management understands that there is more to negotiating an agreement than getting the state legislature or city council to pay the bill. Contracts cover nearly all human resource (HR) management functions, issues, and operational matters that deeply influence how an organization's work gets done every day. Managers have ideas too about how to change the organization to make it run better, but union cooperation may be required. Effective managers are not indifferent to how people feel about their work. Managers do their homework by examining grievance files, the scope and cost of benefits, wage surveys, and practices in other departments or agencies. When both management and union come to the table ready, the negotiations process proceeds more efficaciously than if they just stroll in from the golf course.

B. Preparation for Bargaining

Preparation is the most critical component of bargaining success. The best prepared party, the one that has done its homework, is usually the one that emerges from negotiations with the balance of its objectives secured. It is an axiom that "table time is showtime, but preparation time is dough time."

Preparation usually entails the following steps:

1 Establish a bargaining committee and a negotiating team, including a chief spokesperson
2 Analyze the experience under the previous contract (if any). This process often starts soon after the current agreement is signed. Department heads and supervisors are asked to determine problem areas from the management's perspective and offer advice on the next contract. Both parties study the grievance records under the old contract, including arbitration awards, and consider the motives, strategies, views, and likely demands of their counterparts on the opposite team. The union committee solicits and screens issues arising from the membership
3 Analyze wage and benefits data, particularly comparable information from similar jurisdictions and occupational groups. Conduct a wage and benefits survey if necessary. Respond to the other party's requests for data. The union reviews the employer's budget and other financial data
4 Analyze recent legal developments and relevant agreements in other jurisdictions for personnel, law, and policy changes
5 Prioritize demands and prepare justifications for them
6 Arrange joint pre-negotiation conferences to establish the rules of the game and determine schedules. Include preliminary discussions on acceptable data, facts, and definitions to be used during negotiations
7 Make formal presentations of written proposals and demands
8 Set the bargaining agenda, including which issues will be considered first. Attempt to resolve simple, noncontroversial matters first to create a cooperative atmosphere. Consider dividing controversial issues into those that are primarily economic in their implications and those that are not, and decide whether to take up issues as a package or break them down into smaller decision units
9 Arrange negotiating sessions. These should normally be held during regular working hours for short (one- to three-hour) periods of time. They should

be held at a "neutral" location at the workplace or elsewhere. Provide for separate, private caucus rooms. The minutes of each meeting should be maintained by a neutral secretary and kept by each party as well
10 Conduct negotiations. Convene caucuses to exchange reactions of members of the bargaining team, reconsider tactics and strategy, and check with superiors for guidance and direction
11 Draft and sign a written agreement
12 Ask union membership and the legislative branch to ratify the written agreement

The reality of the bargaining process is not nearly as orderly and straightforward as these steps imply. The process is highly dynamic. It changes in response to the role behavior and personalities of the participants, the actual and perceived bargaining power of the parties, and any number of other tangible and intangible factors that may impinge on negotiations.

Not surprisingly, unions and management increasingly rely on information-based technology. Such technology helps them to develop and respond to proposals, keep historical records and personnel data, analyze the costs of alternative wage and benefit proposals, and compare contracts and data across other jurisdictions. In the early part of the twenty-first century Shostak (2002) predicted that the availability of spreadsheets and database management software would lead to the advent of "cyberunions" which knit together information technology to redefine, reinvent, and reinvigorate themselves. Shortly thereafter, additional studies highlighted unions' use of websites and email (Stevens & Greer, 2005) and blogs, short videos, and audio clips (Pinnock, 2005) to communicate with members and potential members.

Over the past two decades technology has changed the world of work and union representation. In many ways, technology makes union organizing, collective bargaining, and engaging workers in collective action easier. To begin with, virtual meeting platforms facilitate communication and information sharing with bargaining unit members in diverse locations. Instant messaging applications allow unions to share updates, documents, and resources with workers in real time. Online forums help build a sense of community, encourage conversations about workplace issues, and get perspectives from others within the labor movement. For example, the #REDforEd strikes and bargaining that swept across the country in 2018–2019 were driven by a combination of networked activism and traditional union infrastructure. Facebook provided a forum for discussion and information sharing and the union infrastructure channeled the networked collective action (Tarlau, 2023).

The challenge for unions is to keep up with the rapidly changing digital technology. Even labor unions with well-staffed digital media departments are no match for the resources marshalled by government agencies (Bernards et al., 2024). It is now quite easy for employers to surveil workers both in the workplace and on social media (Rogers, 2023). Within the workplace, employers can legally monitor internal communications such as emails, phone and video calls, and internal communications applications. Outside of the workplace employers are increasingly monitoring social media channels and leveraging new sources of data to discourage union activity (Rogers, 2023). In some cases, employers blast-text their employees to inhibit union support (Bernards et al., 2024).

C. Duty to Bargain

All state bargaining laws include the duty of the parties to bargain or meet and confer "in good faith." In most of these states, the duty to bargain closely approximates that defined for the private sector by the National Labor Relations Act (NLRA). It applies only to mandatory subjects within the scope of bargaining. Permissive subjects may be discussed at the discretion of the parties. Prohibited topics, such as those listed in a management rights clause, may not be enforceable even if they find their way into a written agreement. The NLRA (Section 8) describes the duty to bargain as follows:

> The mutual obligation of the employer and the representative of the employees to meet at reasonable times and confer in good faith with respect to wages, hours, and other terms and conditions of employment . . . but such obligation does not compel either party to agree to a proposal or require the making of a concession.

In essence, the obligation to bargain in good faith, as interpreted by the courts, requires active participation in negotiations with a sincere effort to reach an agreement. It is a cooperative state of mind that is embodied in specific standards of behavior. In the public sector, the states that provide for collective bargaining (rather than meet and confer) have adopted statutory standards that closely approximate the NLRA's standards (see Table 5.1).

Once a term or condition is legally inserted in a signed and ratified contract neither party is obligated to reopen discussion on that term or condition during the life of that contract. Such discussions may ensue, however, if mutually agreed upon.

D. Script

In the traditional model of collective bargaining, the procedures and activities are sometimes compared to those of a poker game, complete with bluffs, deceptions, and the luck of the draw. The bargaining process is highly variable across jurisdictions, but certain common strategies and informal patterns of behavior are recognizable everywhere.

Table 5.1 Standards for Bargaining in Good Faith

1	Time limits for commencement of negotiations. Parties must furnish notice of the intent to modify or terminate an existing agreement, usually within at least 60 days of contract expiration
2	Obligation to provide information. The public employer is required to provide relevant information on any matter within the mandatory scope of bargaining that the employee organization formally requests
3	Prohibitions against bypassing the bargaining representatives. In an effort to avoid end runs, some jurisdictions prohibit communications between union representatives and any other official who is not a designated management bargaining representative
4	Requirement that the employer should make no unilateral changes in existing wages, hours, and working conditions while negotiations are underway (Unilateral implementation is usually permitted for nonmandatory bargaining subjects.)
5	Prohibition against work stoppages during negotiations
6	Formal procedures to resolve impasses
7	Duty to manifest the bargaining agreement in writing and to execute it
8	Prohibition against bad faith bargaining, which exists when one party or both parties simply go through the motions without any real intention of reaching an agreement. Indications of bad faith bargaining include dilatory tactics, failure to offer proposals or counterproposals, or refusal to make concessions on any issue. (The U.S. Congress presents a great example of bad faith bargaining.)
9	Requirement that both parties sign the written, negotiated agreement

For example, the chief negotiator is normally the only bargaining team member to speak at the table. He or she seeks to keep the other team members under control and restrained from speaking out of turn (unless it is part of the script). Team members strive to keep a "poker face," uttering a squeal of delight on hearing a generous counteroffer is not recommended. Disagreements among team members are carefully concealed to prevent the opposing team from driving a wedge between them and weakening their overall position. Usually, one person on each side acts as a recording secretary, keeping detailed notes of the proceedings. Recording devices are normally forbidden. They can cause problems later if, for example, heated words are exchanged, and individuals say things they later regret.

As noted earlier, one member of the team may be assigned the responsibility of observing members of the opposing team. This member scans faces for telling expressions, eye contact, or blinking. He or she also listens for voice tone and volume, involuntary sighs, laughs, or other nonverbal language, and observes body language for gestures or other indications of true feelings and reactions. All can convey important messages (Lincoln, 2000). Davis (2023) notes that the bargaining process involves a substantial amount of emotional labor and coping skills. If the process is not managed well, it can lead to exhaustion and burnout.

During the initial presentation of demands and proposals, there may be some grandstanding as each side tries to assess the resistance points of the other and the strength of feelings on separate issues. At this stage, union leaders in particular sometimes make demands "that exhibit a greater use of imagination than that shown by Fellini or Hitchcock" (Sloane & Witney, 1981, p. 190). For instance, a Long Island, New York, police association once demanded "85 concessions, including a gymnasium and swimming pool; 17 paid holidays, including Valentine's Day and Halloween; and free abortions." This strategy, sometimes called "blue-skying," is intended to (1) appease influential members of the union by formalizing their pet demands, (2) allow ample room for later concessions, and (3) raise new issues that may become important in future contract negotiations. As one would expect, management usually takes the full plate of demands with hoots of disbelief or at least with a grain of salt, rejecting some items outright and ignoring others. Serious demands must be justified with documentation, appropriate data, and compelling arguments.

A classic illustration of the "script" in the traditional bargaining model involved negotiations between the New York City Transit Authority and President Mike Quill of the Transport Workers Union (Spero & Capozzola, 1973, p. 108):

> Along about May or June every other year, Quill . . . would summon members of the press to announce the demands of the TWU for justice, the 30-hour week and various other possible—and impossible—goals to be enshrined in the forthcoming contract with the Transit Authority. "Or else,' Quill would thunder, "the trains won't run!" After the rejection of the union's demands by the Transit Authority and possibly the breaking off of a meeting or two, quiet would descend upon New York for the balance of the summer. In the fall, a series of meetings, usually stormy, would take place, building up to a peak in early December, when someone, usually the TWU leader, would break off negotiations. Quill would warn that there would be no transportation for Christmas shoppers unless talks became serious. The Transit Authority would announce that there was no money to meet the union's "exorbitant" demands. Just in the nick of time a third party would step in, at the request of the Mayor, to mediate the dispute. Shoppers would be saved, the negotiations would begin to build up to a New Year's climax. Both parties would be summoned to city hall; the mediators would move from the union to the Mayor to the union, building suspense as they went. Finally, a settlement would be announced—usually in time for late television and radio news broadcasts and the morning papers, and Quill would declare that the embattled transit workers had been victorious.

In less dramatic settings, after initial meetings have permitted each party to size up the other and estimate its "true" bargaining position, serious negotiations begin over the substantive issues. The negotiating atmosphere from that point on depends on a number of factors, including the past history of the bargaining relationship and outcomes, the basic attitude of the employer toward unions, macroeconomic factors, the employer's financial situation, the political environment, and the motivations of management and union representatives. As a general rule, the talks take on increasing intensity as the deadline approaches for completing. The expectations of the parties in "the game" are that if one side moves toward the other on one or more issues the second party will reciprocate.

Informal discussions away from the bargaining table, known as side bars, may be used to privately explore possible avenues toward compromise. All-night bargaining may become necessary. There is nothing like the tedium and discomfort of around-the-clock bargaining to separate the insignificant issues from the truly important ones. Negotiations continue until an agreement is attained or all movement toward a settlement stops and the two parties declare an impasse. In general, for a settlement to be reached both sides must avoid rigid or unrealistic positions and try to remain flexible, while keeping in mind the reciprocal nature of the bargaining relationship (see Tables 5.2 and 5.3).

E. Concession Bargaining

Flexibility is usually in short supply when government fiscal problems produce crisis or concession bargaining. Unions, which often have contributed significantly to fiscal problems through predictable activities designed to drive up wages, expand benefits, and maintain jobs, are asked to make givebacks to the employing jurisdiction.

Concession bargaining has always occurred in the private sector during the down cycles of capitalism. The first major experience with it in the public sector came in 1975, as a consequence of New York City's fiscal collapse (Maier, 1987). Concession bargaining is more commonplace during economic recessions, whenever state and local fiscal crises erupt and "doomsday budgets" threaten to shred services to the bare minimum. During and after the Great Recession, concession bargaining became the norm, as fiscally desperate state and local jurisdictions clawed for all available savings. Wells (2020) notes that public sector unions' ability to maintain better wages, benefits, and working conditions despite offering concessions at the bargaining table made them a target for politicians seeking retrenchment.

Cities, confronted with various budget gaps, have been known to turn off streetlights; lay off hundreds and thousands of employees; and close libraries, clinics, and even city zoos. Governors have instituted rolling one-day shutdowns of state governments, during which "nonessential" employees stay home without pay. For essential employees, unpaid workdays are ordered. Public employees in nearly all jurisdictions have begun copaying health-care insurance premiums

Table 5.2 **Twenty Bargaining Homilies**

1	Know the law and contract provisions
2	Be sure that you have set clear objectives on every bargaining item and that you understand on what grounds the objectives were established
3	Do not hurry; practice patience
4	When in doubt, caucus
5	Be well prepared with firm data to support clearly identified objectives
6	Always strive to keep some flexibility in your position—do not get yourself out on a limb
7	Do not concern yourself only with what the other party says and does—find out why. Remember that economic motivation is not the only explanation for the other party's conduct and actions
8	Respect the importance of face-saving for the other party
9	Constantly be alert to the true intentions of the other party, with respect to not only goals but also priorities
10	Be a good listener
11	Build a reputation for being fair but firm
12	Learn to control your emotions—do not panic. Use emotions as a tool, not an obstacle
13	Be sure as you make each bargaining move that you know its relationship to all other moves
14	Measure each move against your objectives
15	Pay close attention to the wording of every clause negotiated; words and phrases are often the source of grievances. In this situation, a lawyer can be your friend
16	Remember that collective bargaining is by its very nature part of a larger, more comprehensive process
17	There is no such thing as having all the pie
18	Learn to understand people and their personalities; it may pay off during negotiations
19	Consider the impact of present negotiations on future negotiations
20	Shake hands all around the room when the agreement is signed

Source: the author, with the contributions of federal management negotiator John Dodd (interviewed by the author).

for themselves and their families and increasing their deductions for prescription drugs and medical procedures. Deals in some jurisdictions will cost future employees pensions and paid health care altogether.

Concession bargaining implies changes in the script. Instead of asking for more, unions must fight to avoid giving back what they have already gotten. Management

Table 5.3 Negotiating Your First Contract: Tips and Tricks for Management

1	Do not forget your basic logistical requirements. You will need laptop computers, secure Internet access, thumb drives, a printer, memory sticks, an overhead projector, tape, paper, scissors, a copy machine, and maybe even a three-hole punch. Plan ahead
2	Remember bargaining discipline. Know who will speak for your side. Know and understand the rules for calling a caucus before sitting down at the table
3	Go for a small agreement early. Agree that the weather is nice, crummy, cloudy, cold, or whatever. The important thing is to obtain a mindset of agreement. This may sound trivial, but it is important because it works
4	Once you are bargaining, go for another small agreement early. Select something that neither side cares about. Your goal, once again, is to obtain a mindset toward agreement
5	Find out as much as you can about the union's agenda. Find out as much as possible about potential schisms in the union's bargaining team
6	Foster poor discipline on the union team by talking directly to members rather than to their principal spokesperson
7	Listen to what they say. Explore alternatives. They may want less than you think they do and less than you were willing to give. Go first with your initial proposals, but do not go first with your last best offer
8	Use interest-based techniques. The union does not care a fig about your position
9	Be respectful and courteous. Never talk down to the union
10	Be patient. Negotiating labor agreements is a frustrating endeavor. Often, it is the most patient team that gets the best contract
11	Do not believe everything that is said, but do not call anyone a liar
12	Movement is the most important thing. If the parties keep moving toward the goal (a contract), you will eventually get there. Do not allow yourself to get stuck on anything. This can lead to impasse and a general mindset of futility
13	Ask the union to explain their proposals. Sometimes they want something that you will be happy to give them, but they do not ask for it in the right way. Properly done, management can end up writing (for better or worse) almost all the language that ends up in the contract
14	Remember the old school crossing instructions: stop, look, and listen

Source: the author, with the contributions of federal management negotiator John Dodd (interviewed by the author).

takes the bargaining initiative, seeking wage and benefit givebacks and changes in work rules. If the union refuses to bend, layoffs are one likely alternative. Connecticut offers a helpful example of concession bargaining.

Facing a projected state budget deficit of \$3.2–\$3.5 billion, Democratic Governor Dannel P. Malloy sought to negotiate up to \$2 billion in union concessions over 2 years. This sum, plus record high tax hikes and substantial program reductions, would move the state budget into balance as required by the constitution. Failing a deal, Malloy threatened to lay off up to 5,000 workers across state government (Applebome, 2011).

Following 2 months of negotiations, union representatives for 45,000 state employees agreed to $1.6 billion in givebacks from wage freezes, a higher retirement age, and other concessions. The union won a guarantee for no layoffs for 4 years and other relatively minor provisions. Tense negotiations had been conducted with a cordial tone, exemplifying good faith bargaining.

But when union leaders took the agreement to their 34 bargaining units for ratification, they were shocked by resounding rejections. Malloy stepped back into the fray by threatening 7500 layoffs and drastic spending cuts by shuttering Department of Motor Vehicles offices, courthouses, ferries, and even jails. He then began sending out pink slips.

Union leaders called for new talks. Following tense, marathon bargaining sessions, a new agreement was drafted with clearer language but only modest changes and the same $1.6 billion in savings (Keating, 2011b). Meanwhile, the coalition of unions met and adopted a simplified voting process that made ratification easier. Once again, the membership voted. This time, only two bargaining units—the Connecticut State Police Union and a Service Employees International Union (SEIU) local representing prison guards—voted in the negative. The contract was adopted, and Malloy laid off 56 state troopers and 23 corrections officers (Phaneuf & Pazniokas, 2011).

Concession bargaining poses serious problems for unions. Members react to layoffs and other management concessionary threats with "insecurity, frustration, and strong suspicion" (Craft et al., 1985, p. 169). Frustration mounts as hard-fought gains from past contract negotiations come at risk. Union leaders tend to lose their credibility and control over the rank and file. Combined with low levels of public support, these patterns portend a loss of union power and influence. Future relations with management are more likely to be confrontational and adversarial. Frustrated unions, weakened at the bargaining table, are likely to seek to win objectives outside the bargaining process, through grievances, the courts, and the political arena.

Ironically, a financially weak government employer may flex its muscles and become stronger at the bargaining table. Retrenchment presumes reducing, or at least holding the line on, personnel expenditures, which means reductions in force, wage freezes, rollbacks on pensions and health-care benefits, and similar actions. If the unions are uncooperative, the public employer can act unilaterally in several important ways besides layoffs. For instance, most state bargaining laws provide that financial agreements in labor contracts depend on legislative appropriation of funds, which might not be forthcoming in a fiscal emergency. Also, the U.S. Supreme Court and lower courts have recognized that a state may break a bargaining contract in certain cases of financial emergency (Befort, 1985, pp. 1243–1251). In a worst-case scenario, local governments can seek bankruptcy protection under Chapter 9 of the Federal Bankruptcy Code and, presumably, break union contracts.

In general, fiscal crises tend to stiffen the backs of public employers, shift public blame to unions, and tip the balance of power in management's favor. Fortified by support from unhappy taxpayers, public management in fiscally stressed states and localities can successfully limit, and in some cases recover, previous union bargaining gains. In some instances, as shown recently in Tennessee, Wisconsin, and other states, unfriendly governors and legislatures may revoke bargaining rights completely.

To illustrate, Milkman and Luce (2017) show that following the Great Recession, political attacks on public sector unions spread across states and that public opinions about unions became more polarized according to political party. Beginning in 2011, many state legislatures passed laws either eliminating public sector unions or restricting their bargaining rights. Public employees' wages and pensions were cut and there were steep reductions in public services including public schools and libraries, local health departments, and public transit. The legislation and cutbacks were driven in large part by the American Legislative Exchange Council (ALEC) (Lafer, 2017).

III. EXTERNAL POLITICS

In public sector collective bargaining, the intensely political nature of the enterprise frequently spills over from the bargaining table to the broader environment of labor–management relations and vice versa. Public employee unions are influential and active interest groups whether contract negotiations are taking place or not. As interest groups, they participate in lobbying, campaigning, and other activities typical of organized interests seeking to mold public policy to the benefit of their members. Government unions differ in that they enjoy a special place in the public decision-making process in those jurisdictions where they have gained collective bargaining rights (Anzia & Moe, 2019; DiSalvo, 2015).

Public officials are legally required to recognize and bargain with unions in bargaining jurisdictions, an advantage rarely available to other interest groups. In addition, most labor–management decisions are made in private and beyond the immediate influence of other interest groups that also stake claim to a piece of the public pie. Although public employee unions do enjoy distinct access points not available to other groups, it must be recognized that government employees are vulnerable to counteracting political pressures.

They may, for instance, have their jobs taken away from them for participating in an illegal strike, the union may suffer the wrath of the voters in an antiunion referendum, or hostile elected officials may seek to curtail collective bargaining rights. Other interest groups cannot be slapped down so resoundingly when they offend the general public. To lessen their vulnerability and to manipulate levers of power and influence beyond the bargaining table, public employee organizations engage in a medley of political activities. This discussion on external politics considers the major political activities of public employees and their unions, specifically lobbying, electoral activities, and efforts to influence public opinion.

A. Lobbying

Union lobbying activities assume a variety of forms, including writing letters and e-mails to elected officials; producing blogs and wikis; introducing, preparing, or sponsoring bills; making presentations on proposed legislation at hearings and meetings; providing information to elected officials; and cultivating an ongoing atmosphere of trust and cooperation with elected officials. Lobbying activities may be specific (aimed at a specific objective such as legislative approval of a wage increase) or diffuse (promoting goodwill toward unions among legislators). For example, home care workers in Oregon represented by the SEIU engaged in extensive letter writing campaign, took part in one-on-one visits with legislators, and spoke out at public forums to influence public policies related to home care (Mareschal & Ciorici, 2021). Before collective bargaining was institutionalized in government, lobbying constituted the preeminent means of political influence for public employee organizations, and for non-bargaining employee associations it still does.

Lobbying efforts are usually directed at members of legislative bodies, because of the legislative role in structuring the legal environment and approving the financial provisions of any negotiated agreement. However, executive branch officials are also targets. Most lobbying activities are concentrated at the same level of government, that is, the teacher union focuses on members of the school board, the firefighters lobby the city council and the mayor, and state employees devote their attention to state representatives and the governor. Nonetheless, local government organizations often attempt to influence legislative decisions at the state level when state law controls local terms and conditions of employment or when a more general piece of legislation is of indirect interest to the union. An example of a specific state-controlled policy is a statewide health-care benefits package for teachers or, in the case of firefighters, statewide fire safety standards. General legislation of interest could involve tax increases or taxation and expenditure limitations.

Union interest and active involvement in the legislative process is appropriate and legitimate. Public employee organizations are registered to lobby in most states. Some unions retain full-time professional lobbyists in their state capital and in Washington, D.C. Others employ their own members, particularly when lobbying at the local level. A group of police officers, firefighters, or teachers visiting local representatives usually gets a hearing. After all, they are voters and people of some influence.

When lobbying takes on the look of an end run, certain activities are questioned. There are instances in which elected officials' concern for their personal political futures has compromised the process of collective bargaining. The end run occurs when employee representatives discuss demands with officials who are not part of the bargaining team. If successful, an end run can result in a union winning from the legislative body what it was denied at the bargaining table. The tactic is inimical and chilling to collective bargaining. It makes future negotiations more problematic and undercuts management authority. In several states, the end run is treated as an unfair labor practice.

As is the case with most interest groups, it is difficult to measure the direct effects of public employee union lobbying. Recent studies, however, have found that politically active teacher unions exert a significant influence on education reform policies (DiSalvo & Hartney, 2020; Flavin & Hartney, 2015) and that legislators consider them to be highly effective lobbyists (Moe, 2006; Hrebenar & Thomas, 2004). To illustrate, teachers unions exerted substantial influence on school districts' re-opening plans during the COVID-19 pandemic (Hartney & Finger, 2022).

At the national level, unions in neither government nor industry have been particularly effective over the past three decades. The limited impact of union lobbying activities may be due to a number of factors, including declining private union membership and leveling off of public union membership, hostility on the part of employers and the public, statutory restrictions on union political activities, anti-union bias in the media, ineffective and unimaginative leadership, and the decline of political liberalism. To these might be added the conflicting philosophies among union leaders and members, the divided partisan political loyalties of members, the myopia of narrow occupational interests, increased competition from other interest groups, and the growing dominance of antiunion corporate interests.

B. Electoral Activities

Electoral activities are designed to help elect candidates for public office who are believed to be sympathetic to a union. The relationship clearly is intended to be reciprocal: "we'll help you win the election if you will support the union." Union electoral activism is common; indeed, it is expected. Because federal law prohibits direct contributions of union dues to candidates for political office, political action committees (PACs) are used to raise and disburse "voluntary" contributions to candidates. As a consequence of the U.S. Supreme Court's *Citizens United v. FEC* decision in 2010, state and federal laws governing union and corporate spending on political activities and elections were effectively rendered invalid, unleashing a flood of PAC and "Super PAC" dollars in the 2010 and 2012 elections. Super PACs can spend money in support of or opposition to candidates, as long as they do so independently of any candidate's campaign. *Citizens United* also freed unions to use dues money to fund campaign activities to reach out to nonmembers (Greenhouse, 2011a).

In the 2021–2022 election cycle, public sector unions contributed $15,266,803 from their PACs to candidates. Among public sector unions, the two largest donors were the American Federation of Teachers (AFT) and the American Federation of State, County, and Municipal Employees (AFSCME). Respectively they gave $2,349,000 (AFT) and $2,345,000 (AFSCME) through PACs to "friendly" congressional candidates, nearly all of whom were Democrats (Open Secrets, n.d. a). Nonetheless, corporations have billions of dollars to draw upon in contests versus unions, whose own financial resources are much more constrained. For example, Super PACs raised $2,737,855,088 in 2022 and spent $1,365,474,321 in 2022 (Open Secrets, n.d. b).

Unions commonly endorse candidates for state, local, or national office. This of course implies that the candidate will be the recipient of the "union vote," which is usually understood to include each member's voting age family. If the candidate wins, the union presumably enjoys access and favorable consideration. If, however, the endorsee loses, the union "later finds itself dealing with the victor, who may have a long memory" (Spero & Capozzola, 1973, p. 91). Instead of officially putting the employee organization out on a limb, union officials will sometimes proffer an informal endorsement through public statements supporting the candidate's record.

The official or tacit endorsement of a candidate is accompanied by contributions of money, human resources, or both. This may represent the most effective labor tactic in American electoral politics because it is directly related to voter turnout for union-supported candidates. As a member of the firefighters' union in Hartford, Connecticut, said long ago, "councilmen are interested in two things, the vote and money. We supply both," (Gerhart, 1973, pp. 26–27). In 2024, AFSCME was ranked among the top five of all PACS based on the following combination of expenditures: contributions to candidates, total fundraising, total spent, and total spent in independent expenditures and communication costs (Open Secrets, n.d. c). When considering only public sector union PACS, the top five donors in 2024 were AFSCME, American Federation of Teachers (AFT), International Association of Firefighters (IAFF), National Association of Letter Carriers (NALC), and National Education Association (NEA) (Open Secrets, n.d. d).

Human resource contributions include door-to-door canvassing of prospective voters; distributing campaign literature; stuffing envelopes; operating telephone banks; driving union voters to the polls; and developing and maintaining e-mail lists, web posts, and blogs. Such direct aid in some instances produces very tangible returns in future wage and benefits packages and increased agency and departmental expenditures and favorable legislation (Gely & Chandler, 1993;

Hammer & Wazeter, 1993; O'Brien, 1996). These direct campaign activities are generally considered to be more effective than monetary contribution alone.

The American Federation of Labor–Congress of Industrial Organizations has taken candidate support to a new level in New Jersey, where the federation recruits, trains, and supports candidates for state, county, and municipal offices. Candidate training includes a two-day workshop at Rutgers University, in which they learn about fundraising, media relations, campaign finance reporting, issue framing, and other elements of an effective race (Pérez-Piña, 2010). Sojourner's (2013) analysis demonstrates that unions promote members' electoral office holding. Over the past ten years, the AFL-CIO has expanded the training program across states. In the 2018 midterms, 964 union members were elected to public office across the country at various levels of government. Elected union member candidates have successfully sponsored bills protecting workers' rights that were enacted into law in Connecticut, Illinois, Maine, Nevada, New Jersey, New Mexico, and Rhode Island (Union Candidates, n.d.)

Union electoral activities can help a favored candidate win office and perhaps ensure a sympathetic ear in the legislative body, and research shows that unions help mobilize general voter turnout (Leighley & Nagler, 2007). However, no union or any other interest group can guarantee the delivery of all or even most of the votes. This is especially true at the national level, where the political views of union leaders often differ markedly from those of the rank and file.

Some unions, such as the huge District Council 37 of AFSCME in New York, are potent political forces that can mobilize strong support for union-supported candidates or issues. But union leaders must work hard to politicize, educate, and activate the members. Most count on a dedicated core of union activists for campaign activities. District 37 sponsors "campaign courses" and other educational opportunities to entice members into politics and to hone their political skills. Of course, the union also aggressively encourages its members to register and vote on Election Day.

How successful are unions in organizing the vote? Empirical research indicates that union members are more likely to register and vote than nonmembers (Freeman & Medoff, 1984; Rosenfeld, 2014). Union households made up 16% of the national electorate in 2022 (Gallup, 2022). Do members vote in accordance with the wishes of their union? More often than not they do, but support varies by jurisdiction and by election. Unions must compete with larger socioeconomic, political, and "value" issues for the voting allegiance of their members. One study found that members who attend union political meetings, read the union newsletter, and otherwise actively participate in their organization are more likely to support the union-endorsed candidate than the less active rank and file (Juravich & Shergold, 1988).

Historically, the union vote has strongly favored liberal and Democratic candidates, although some erosion in this pattern was noted beginning with the

1968 presidential election (Masters & Delaney, 1987, p. 343). From the mid-1990s until today, the congressional strength of the Republican Party has encouraged legislative attacks on laws and policies that benefit unions and their members. The Democratic Party continues to be the only potentially friendly political port in a storm, despite regular assertions—occasionally followed up by action—by union leaders that Democratic candidates who are not in the camp of organized labor will not receive union campaign support or votes.

Unquestionably, relations between unions and the Democratic Party frayed during the Great Recession and even longtime union supporters in Congress and state legislatures questioned, or in some cases rejected, negotiated wage and benefit awards. Former allies also questioned teacher union resistance to proposed education reforms (Mehta, 2012; Rich, 2012). It is important to recognize that unions negotiate and play a game of give and take with individual candidates and officeholders more so than with the political party (Dark, 2003, p. 458). A union that is displeased with one candidate may quietly defect to another or strongly endorse a candidate from a different political party. A third-party movement is frequently a topic of discussion among frustrated unionists, but the political reality is that votes for third-party candidates increase the likelihood of Republican electoral victories (Delaney et al., 1999).

The most important question, of course, is whether the union vote makes any difference in public policy. In other words, does the union vote elect national, state, and local officials who support and help secure union political objectives? The answer depends on the time, place, issue, and union. Generally, the unions have fought a defensive battle for the past three decades. It also depends on whether the glass appears to be half empty or half full. Unions have counted precious few legislative victories (e.g., occasional hikes in the minimum wage, defeats of school choice, Obamacare), and labor rights have been seriously diluted in some states. Unions have been a major—although usually losing—force in issue advocacy for immigration reforms, trade agreements, and health-care reforms (Francia, 2006).

C. Public Opinion

Interest groups intend to influence public opinion as well as voting behavior. Some labor organizations directly undertake campaigns specifically designed to affect public opinion on various issues of immediate or long-range concern to the union. Information may be conveyed to the public through press releases, television and radio spots, websites, blogs, informational picketing, rallies and demonstrations, and other techniques. As unions rallied with public demonstrations and building occupations in Wisconsin, Ohio, Indiana, and elsewhere in attempts to stifle unfavorable legislation in 2011–2012, emotions—and noise levels—ran high.

AFSCME, for example, engages in a variety of efforts to shape public opinion. Operating through its umbrella organization, the Public Employees Organized to

Promote Legislative Equality, AFSCME coordinates its national political activities to influence public opinion on affordable health care, civil rights, social equity issues, collective bargaining rights, and unions themselves. Through these efforts AFSCME promotes programs as diverse as antipoverty programs, higher minimum wages, immigration reform, pay equity, and consumer and environmental protection. AFSCME, SEIU, and other unions concentrate some of their public opinion initiatives on national "image" advertisements designed to promote the organization and the union movement in general.

Public approval ratings of unions generally declined during the 1980s and 1990s but experienced modest gains during the early 2000s. Public approval of unions nose-dived to an all-time low of 48% in 2009 before changing course. This was due in large part to the Great Recession. During and immediately following the Great Recession labor critics advanced the narrative that unions were too demanding and stubborn and that their members enjoyed wage and benefit levels experienced by few of their private sector counterparts. Unions countered that public support has suffered due to a barrage of advertisements and other messages portraying them as being greedy and supplicative.

Once the economy recovered from the recession around 2017, approval ratings started trending upward. In the early 2020s, approval ratings moved above the standard long-term average of 62% (see Figure 5.1). This appears to be the

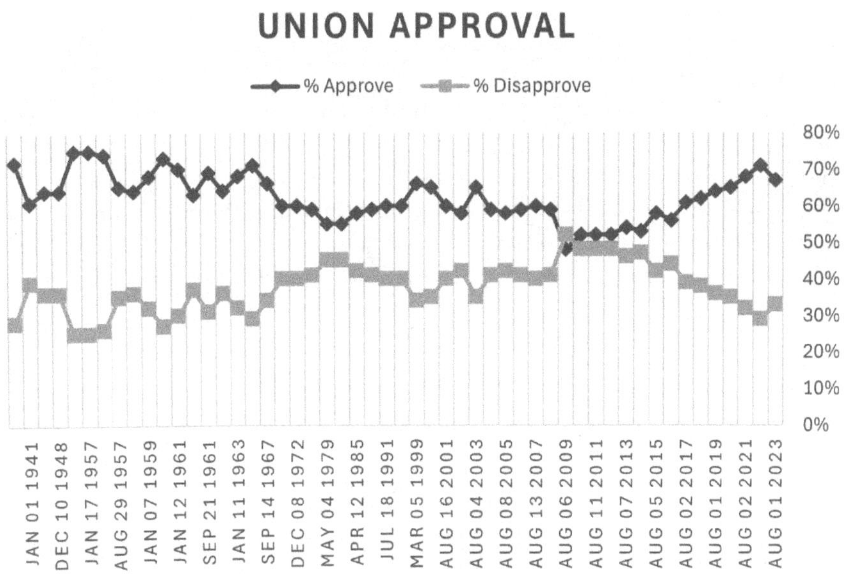

Figure 5.1 Gallup poll: Do you approve or disapprove of labor unions?

Source: Saad, L. (2023). More in U.S. see unions strengthening and want it that way. *Gallup.com*. https://news.gallup.com/poll/510281/unions-strengthening.aspx.

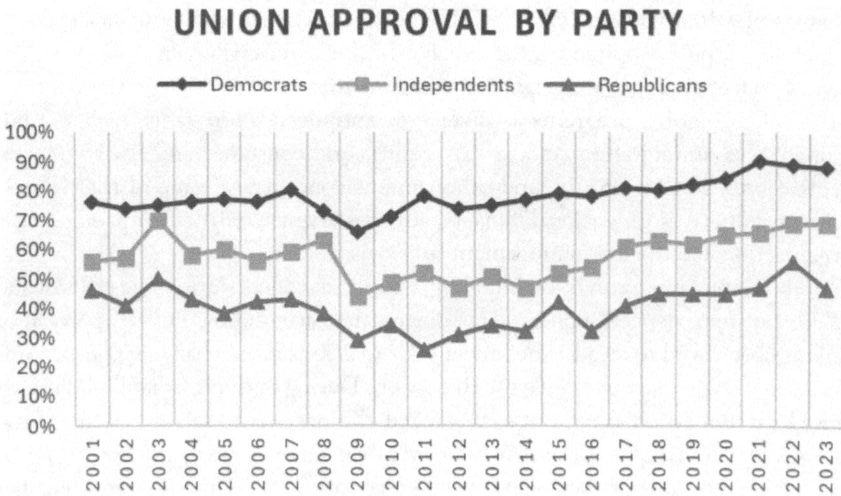

Figure 5.2 **Gallup poll: Approval level of labor unions, by political party.**

Source: Saad, L. (2023). More in U.S. see unions strengthening and want it that way. *Gallup.com*. https://news.gallup.com/poll/510281/unions-strengthening.aspx.

result of greater awareness of poor working conditions, the collective exhaustion and stress of the pandemic, and the social unrest around the murder of George Floyd and others. Unions held the promise for better jobs. As of 2023, the union approval rate was 67% (Saad, 2023).

Figure 5.2 shows how public opinion of unions is bifurcated between Democrats and Republicans. Overall, Democrats have more favorable opinions of unions, Republicans have less favorable opinions, and independents fall in between the major parties. Nonetheless, approval has been trending upward for all three groups since 2009. In 2023, 88% of Democratic voters and 69% of independents approved of unions. In contrast, only 47% of Republicans approved of unions (Saad, 2023).

D. Restrictions on Public Employee Political Activity

Civil servants have been involved in political activities of one sort or the other since the earliest days of the Republic. In a legal and constitutional system characterized by multiple levels of legislative, executive, and judicial decision-making authority at three levels of government, government workers and their unions will always have strong incentives to exploit various access points. Collective bargaining, legislative politics, and litigation are not mutually exclusive processes.

Given the pervasive presence of politics in government labor–management relations, a salient issue arises: should political activity by public employees be restricted? If so, how? As observed in Chapter 3, court interpretations of the First Amendment have narrowed union activities with regard to political expenses paid with dues from nonmembers who are in the bargaining unit; this weakens union speech. So does recent state legislation to prohibit automatic deduction of union dues from government paychecks.

Another limitation on political activity is through statute. The first national statutory limitations on union political activities were included in the Pendleton Act of 1883. In 1939, the Hatch Act further restricted federal employee activities. It was extended to state and local government workers paid with federal dollars in 1940. Thereafter, most states and many local governments enacted their own "little Hatch acts" to apply to non-federally funded employees. The laws taken together are highly diverse. Some prohibit all electoral activities except voting; others permit public employees to run for office. Most restrict partisan political activities, reflecting their origins in the reform struggle against the patronage and spoils systems. All constrain union members' political activities in one or more ways.

Hatch Act–like restrictions have been eased through legislative actions and court decisions. The constitutionality of the Hatch Act has been upheld by the U.S. Supreme Court (*United States Civil Service Commission v. Letter Carriers*, 1973). However, it is generally ignored, on the whole, by both public workers and their employers, with some exceptions.

Unions would like to abolish virtually all restraints on political activities by public employees. Federal employee unions lobbied successfully for Congress to pass and President Clinton to sign an overhaul of the federal Hatch Act in 1993. The amendment permits most federal employees to engage in political activities that were previously prohibited, including distributing partisan campaign literature, working for partisan candidates and campaigns, soliciting votes, and holding office in political parties. Pressure for similar laws at state and local levels continues, with varying degrees of success. At the same time, it is difficult to justify denying public workers the fundamental constitutional rights enjoyed by their counterparts in the private sector.

IV. INTERNAL BARGAINING PROCESSES: FROM TRADITIONAL TO INTEREST-BASED BARGAINING

When union and management representatives come to the table, they bring issues important to them with respect to the current contract and the agreement that is about to be negotiated. They aim to improve or eliminate old vocabulary and create new language for the future. Through this process, both the collective bargaining document and the relationship between the parties is reshaped.

The union usually submits and explains its proposals first. An opening statement sounds the theme for this round of negotiations and reminds management how dedicated, hardworking, and long-suffering these employees have been. Management follows the union by making its own statement, usually indicating the employer's deep concern for the agency it represents, pointing out its regard for its loyal and dedicated workers, but stressing its sacred duty to protect the interests of the general public. Management is clear about its willingness to find ways to help solve problems. It then customarily reminds the union of various limitations that make it difficult to accommodate all of the union's demands, particularly those of a financial nature. There are countless possible responses from the union to management's statement, but the most common may be that it is not a problem of ability to pay, but rather willingness to pay, for the union's demands.

The opening statements, and responses, are meant to convey to each party what the other wants or does not want. In a sense, during this initial session each party is reminding the other that it has equal standing in the process and that it must be treated with respect. Much of what is said is expected, but it is not unusual to hear things that are quite unanticipated. This introductory period also signals the tone the negotiations might take, and teams begin the bonding process as the real bargaining is about to begin. Both sides pledge to work in good faith.

This is all part of the opening dance ritualistically performed by the parties. Nonetheless, serious messages get delivered and sophisticated negotiators glean important information or suppositions about what to expect in future meetings. The parties watch nonverbal communication quite closely during this time, searching for clues to attitudes on the other side that may be predictive of what is to follow. The parties also try to identify individuals who may represent problems—or opportunities—in the bargaining process. When the initial exchange is completed, the parties are ready for serious negotiations.

A. Traditional Negotiations*

Traditional negotiations fit the stereotype that most people have about collective bargaining. This image represents what Fisher and Ury (1981) characterize as the "hard" approach to bargaining and what Walton and McKersie (1965) refer to as distributive (zero-sum) bargaining. It features (1) looking at participants as adversaries and wanting to win at all cost, (2) lacking trust of the other side, (3) trying to force the other party to make concessions through sheer use of power, (4) using threats, and (5) seeing issues in dualistic terms (e.g., "right or wrong" and "sensible or irrational"). In terms of collective negotiations, the hard bargaining approach frames the issues using two contested perspectives with only one possible outcome: win or lose.

* David G. Carnevale made important contributions to the following discussion in an earlier edition of the book. His assistance and insights are greatly appreciated.

"Positional" is the word often associated with traditional bargaining. Having a position means having a specific idea on how any differences or problems should be resolved. Many people believe that there is a "right" answer to any question or problem. At the bargaining table, the attachment to a single "correct" concept or solution makes reaching settlements very difficult. The dynamics are such that one side publicly digs into its position and rejects or denigrates the ideas of the other. As negotiators become more and more identified with a singular view of the world, they are less able to listen to contrary arguments. A mere difference of opinion can quickly turn into a personal matter. Threats or statements such as "under no circumstances will we ever" might be made. Obviously, such behavior does not help the parties to reach a settlement and it has a deleterious impact on the relationship between the parties. For example, a management team that refuses to negotiate in good faith and demands that the union accept its nonnegotiable positions on all issues (a tactic known as "Boulwarism") leaves the union few choices: concede or go to arbitration (or strike). A prisoner's dilemma is created (Leventoglu & Tarar, 2005). However, the parties have to work together once the contract is settled. A party can win the bargaining battle but lose the war.

Fisher and Ury (1981) also describe a "soft" approach to bargaining, which is the opposite of the traditional forceful method but also dysfunctional in the long run. In the soft strategy, negotiators—like the family dog—want to see people as friends or colleagues. They make concessions to show their good faith in wanting to reach an agreement and have a tendency to yield to pressure. They perceive conflict in general as an uncomfortable and unseemly sort of fighting that is to be avoided. Soft strategists do what they can to dodge trouble and are overly willing to make compromises and accommodations to demonstrate their willingness to be collaborative. They forget that they have representational responsibilities for one side or the other and that it takes two serious strategies to fashion an agreement that works for both parties.

Avoiding conflict can lead to more problems in the future than directly confronting it when it first needs to be engaged. Collective bargaining is a process that fully recognizes that conflicts in the workplace are natural and that the parties need to resolve their differences peacefully and productively. Soft bargaining undermines the process and does damage to the public, public institutions, and public employees. It does not advance either of the major objectives of collective bargaining: to achieve a workable contract and to maintain a productive relationship between the parties. In this regard, the soft approach is "lose–lose." Avoiding conflict may be wise on some occasions. However, as an overall philosophy of bargaining it courts disaster.

Traditional or distributive bargaining is adversarial and conflict oriented by nature. As in a game of poker, neither side reveals its hand to the other. It involves deception and bluffing and a number of other games that negotiators play. The desired image is to be tough and clever.

For example, during negotiations between the California State Employees Association and its own staff (union staffs are often unionized and bargain with the leaders of the union), the management team proposed installing time clocks and maintained an apparent seriousness about the issue throughout the negotiations. No manager actually wanted time clocks, but the issue was included in the package so that it could be conceded near the end of bargaining when things were most intense. This was a way of giving the union a win (no time clocks) in exchange for something that the management really wanted.

During the same negotiations, the management's chief negotiator would deliberately leave on the table at the end of the day some of the notes that were routinely passed between team members. The notes were full of false information. As expected, the union read the notes and spent time developing defenses against management strategies that were in fact nonexistent. It is no wonder that trust levels are low in negotiations in which one or both sides are intent on manipulating the other.

It is difficult under such circumstances to tell what is real and what is an illusion. Rumors are commonplace during negotiations, and they are often personal and negative in terms of individuals and organizations on both sides. It is also common for people to treat colleagues suspiciously if they are on the "wrong side" or appear to be insufficiently loyal to the side they are supposed to support. Information frequently gets distorted, sometimes intentionally. All of these gamesmanship dynamics make it difficult to come to mutual terms in solving problems. Fundamentally, traditional bargaining is adversarial, contentious, and emotionally draining. It does ultimately produce a settlement, but the costs may be destructive to the relationship.

The traditional approach to bargaining is about power, not collaborating for mutual gain. The behavioral characteristics associated with the traditional approach are competition (win–lose and zero-sum assumptions), aggression, resistance, hostility, and even bullying (Barrett, 1995). It is replete with contentious tactics, including gamesmanship, "guilt tripping," irrevocable comments (if–then messages), and threats (Rubin et al., 1993). The traditional approach attempts to wear down, seduce, manipulate, threaten, and dominate.

Personal attacks are not unusual, and sarcasm has a central place in the discourse. For example, during negotiations between the Police Benevolent Association and New York City's extraordinarily wealthy Mayor Michael Bloomberg, the union did not hold back from personal attacks. The chief negotiator spoke emotionally at a rally and on camera, yelling the following: "we are not asking to be rich like you, Mr. Mayor. All we are asking for is to make our lives better for our families" (Steinhauer, 2004). The New York City teachers' union claimed that the mayor did not want a settlement, just a scapegoat to blame for his failure to improve public education (Greenhouse, 2004). Bloomberg's predecessor, Rudy Giuliani, turned the tables on striking transit workers in 1997, accusing them of crippling the transportation system and delaying emergency services, thus placing the lives of citizens at risk. In Wisconsin, AFSCME Executive Director Marty Beil spewed personal insults on state legislators whose votes he did not like, calling the senate president a "whore" and the speaker of the house and his brother "lightweights," "crybabies," and "whiners" (Greenhouse, 2011b).

In a 2022 dispute between the Chicago's Teacher Union (CTU) and Mayor Lori Lightfoot, the president of CTU called Lightfoot "relentlessly stupid," (Esposito, 2022) and Lightfoot accused the CTU of bringing chaos to the Chicago's Public Schools system and making it "a laughingstock all across the country," (Kapos & Niedzwiadek, 2022). The underlying idea is that "I cannot get what I want unless you don't get what you want." This is zero-sum thinking. Every concession is seen as a loss. The problem with these tactics is that much of what is being done appears to be personal and threatening. It raises emotions, and any perceived attack generates reciprocal behavior. A spiral of conflict spins as sides form, positions harden even more, communication is impaired, hostility escalates, and threats become issues until the top of the spiral is reached where people want revenge more than a fair and workable contract.

The style and approach of traditional bargaining is rough on the problems and tough on the people (Fisher & Ury, 1981). Traditional talks gone awry damage the ongoing working relationship between the parties, disrupt teamwork, lower productivity, and spawn an "us versus them" work climate that is destructive to the creation of high-performance organizations. Everything tends to become personal. During efforts to settle the 2012 Chicago teachers' strike, Chicago Teachers Union President Karen Lewis and Mayor Rahm Emanuel clearly illustrated the problems of personalization. Lewis tagged Emanuel a "bully" and a "liar." Emanuel was less public with his own thoughts, but he played hardball politics (Davey & Yaccino, 2012). Both were described as "biting, pushy, witty, and unwavering" (Spielman, 2011).

Contemporary public administration theory and practice are marching in an entirely different direction from the assumptions, values, and practices of traditional bargaining. The principal leadership and management models in government and business today rely a great deal on collaboration and participative decision making at all levels of organizations (Kearney & Hays, 1994). Teamwork, reinvention, reengineering, quality, benchmarking, learning, and other innovations (and, unfortunately, fads) depend on trust and the use of genuine dialogue to improve performance. How organizations negotiate labor agreements, and their outcomes, both real and intangible, matter greatly in delivering high-quality public services.

B. Interest-based Bargaining

Interest-based bargaining (IBB) is also known as win–win bargaining, integrative bargaining, and principled negotiations. The IBB method is intended to change the operating assumptions of persons who have learned to negotiate in traditional ways using traditional tactics (comparison of the two approaches is presented in Table 5.4).

Table 5.4 Comparison of Traditional and IBB Principles

Traditional	*Interest Based*
Issues	Issues
Positions	Interests
Arguments	Options
Power and forced compromise	Standards and problem solving
Short-term gain	Long-term relationship
Win-lose outcome	Win-win outcome

It is worth pointing out that win–win may overstate what is possible in many negotiating settings. The term makes it sound as if differences can be resolved without costs, but "win–win" ought to be used with care because it is important to keep people's expectations realistic. The level of expectations in any form of bargaining is an important factor determining how the talks will go. Obviously, parties that expect to get a lot, or perhaps everything that they desire, are usually in for a comeuppance.

"Winning" in IBB means reaching an agreement that both parties can live with. Such an agreement satisfies the interests of both parties and encourages smooth administration once the pact is consummated. The idea that each side can go to the bargaining table and have all its desires met without making some concessions or having to engage in give and take is unrealistic and can make the negotiations extremely difficult. This is why mediators are cautious about the win–win phrase. Instead, what negotiators and mediators focus on is helping the parties to understand that the real spirit of the win–win philosophy means being assertive about one's needs and, at the same time, being willing to actively listen to what the other party wants. The idea is that agreements are produced more efficiently and equitably if the interests of both sides are taken into account. Another underlying aspect of the win–win philosophy is that there are many ways to solve problems if people agree to work together. Interest-based negotiation is not a soft approach, in which people have to like each other and bend over backward to make concessions. It is, instead, a method to get a tough job done in a way that settles the immediate problems and sets conditions for improved future working relationships. It is meant to be efficient and fair to both sides.

The principles of IBB are as follows:

1 Negotiate on the merits of a proposal; do not reject it out of hand because someone from the other side suggested it
2 Separate the people from the problem, which means "do not shoot the messenger" and do not blame someone from the other side for doing his or her job

3 Be hard on the problem and professional with the people; avoid assigning blame and recognize the value of face-saving
4 Determine the interests of the other side instead of just reacting to their positions; understanding the overall interests helps to open up more options for solving problems
5 Avoid fighting issue by issue, position by position, from an adversarial posture; when called for, consider using a facilitator to help generate dialogue and to mediate
6 Invent options for mutual gain; brainstorm to identify a range of possible options that reconcile differences and advance shared interests
7 Have someone chart the ideas that are brainstormed by the groups in the room, and then post the charts on the walls so that there is one set of data that is public and available to all; type up the charts each evening, and give them to the parties the next morning so that everyone is working from the same set of notes
8 Establish criteria upon which a proposal may be judged on the merits, and have the parties determine whether any idea satisfies the interests and criteria of both parties; these become likely candidates for inclusion in the contract (Fisher & Ury, 1981)
9 Develop a best alternative to a negotiated agreement (BATNA) that you can live with

An example would be helpful. In one state the parties knew from the outset that they would have a good deal of difficulty in getting a contract, so they asked for two labor facilitators (mediators) to help them with this new process called IBB. Before the mediators agreed to facilitate an entire agreement, they put the workers and management through IBB training. The parties were told to pick a real problem, one that was a problem in the relationship that would certainly find its way to the bargaining table and that they had not been able to resolve. They chose a problem involving welders.

After some very basic training in IBB, the parties were broken into groups and about 40 people went into brainstorming on how to fix the problem. This is a well-tested technique for inventing options for mutual gain. The groups came up with more than 60 ideas, which were written on a board. The criteria were then established: the solution had to be affordable, it should be legal, it should not lead to any layoffs, it should be ethical, and so on. About a dozen of the ideas fit the criteria. Two or three ideas were especially good and were used to settle the issue. In this particular case, an entire labor agreement was negotiated using the IBB method in slightly more than one week.*

* David Carnevale contributed to this discussion on IBB.

It would be nice to think that negotiators move smoothly and enthusiastically to IBB and away from the more pathological aspects of traditional bargaining, but it is not that easy. Individuals have different perceptions of the world. Some are open to changing their worldview, and others simply are not. Some negotiators begin the IBB process but revert to traditional tactics. The actual negotiations experience frequently involves some traditional methods and some IBB techniques. Compromise and give-and-take strategies tend to prevail in any negotiation. Things may proceed smoothly for a while, but eventually someone or something pushes the parties back to where they started—being suspicious, confrontational, and adversarial.

It is normal. Even the closest family, friendship, or marriage contains some conflict. People forced to address difficult issues do not behave consistently with models. They say and do what they feel is right at the time. It is a challenge for a facilitator to allow venting and regression while gently prodding folks back to the IBB method. Bargaining takes place in real time, and actions and reactions naturally occur. It does the facilitator no good to disallow a discussion because it fits the wrong model or is not timely. It is a sure way to get the facilitator replaced. The process has a way of working itself out in its own way and in its own time. Solid advice for facilitators and mediators is "try not to step on the conversation."

There are times and places where traditional bargaining is called for because of the comfort zone of the parties, nature of the issues in dispute, intense constituent pressures from the union's side, or the high level of strain being exerted downward from upper management in a public agency. Some traditionalists like the model they use because it is predictable and they know how to play the game. The idea of a new process like IBB is viewed as risky. Both union and management sides have many of the same fears. There are those who stereotype the other ("unions are destructive and unnecessary" or "managers do not care about employees and cannot be trusted").

Some negotiating situations are doomed from the start. You cannot bargain successfully with a two-year-old, a madman, an ideologue, or a fool. If one party is irrational, any agreement (other than to cease negotiations) is extremely unlikely. Perceived fairness and legitimacy of the bargaining process encourages the interpersonal trust that enables win–win solutions (Leach & Sabatier, 2005).

Another barrier to implementing IBB is intraorganizational conflict. Friction, disagreement, or just plain personal animosity may surface within the union team or among union members not part of the team. Similarly, elected and appointed officials may be working counterproductively behind the scenes. Interpersonal and professional conflicts may play a role as well. Many a negotiator has to keep one eye looking across the table and the other on the behavior of people ostensibly on their side. Bargaining teams from both sides rarely have the internal solidarity they seek to project.

Other confounding factors can interfere with getting a good agreement. Negotiation is a dispute resolution mechanism, which means that it is inherently about conflict. There are honest differences of opinion about issues. This helps to explain why some negotiations can be so contentious. There is rarely agreement among a group of people on what it is the organization should be doing or where it should be headed. This manifests itself in the bargaining strategy. People may come to terms with where they would like to go but have differences on how to get there. So, we have disputes on ends and means.

People have different values and ideologies and do not let go of them easily. There are personality conflicts. The same "facts" may be viewed in very different ways. People's perceptions in every aspect of life tend to be self-serving and distorted. We tend to attribute bad motives to people who disappoint us but are quick to blame situational factors beyond our control for our own failings. People do not communicate very effectively. Memories are short, and information gets confused. Perhaps it is accurate to say that people are better at being assertive about their own needs than listening to the other party express its needs.

Traditional bargaining and IBB should be appreciated as methods and techniques that are conducted in the thicket of human personalities and emotions that exist at every workplace. Some situations are favorable for IBB, and some are not. Healthy organizations are conducive to IBB; sick ones are usually not. Table 5.5 summarizes the differences in attitudes and behaviors among hard, soft, and principled bargaining.

If these factors are not enough, there are a few more that make any successful conclusion to bargaining problematic. First, there is the pressure of time. Bargaining may start slowly, but there is normally a legal or other deadline that has to be met if the contract is to be placed before the jurisdiction's legislative body for ratification. Late-night bargaining against the clock is not uncommon. Second, there is the problem of union ratification. Each member of the bargaining unit gets to vote on whether to accept an agreement or to send their negotiators back to the table. "Soft" negotiators may push their chairs back from the table with the assumption that bargaining is essentially a friendly process, but the deals they make will have trouble being ratified because of the perception that they are too weak or "sellouts." In other words, a dominator-dominated relationship confounds a win–win solution.

Another problem, "unresolved prior conflict," means there will be no new agreement until some past issue is resurrected, rectified, and reinterred. Experienced negotiators characterize this as "sin bagging." Issue after issue may come and go, and the parties may avoid dealing with them. Then, one day an incident breaks the dam and all of the past problems come flooding out at once. This is another example in which problem avoidance today may cause the price of peace to be higher tomorrow.

Table 5.5 **Contrasting Bargaining Approaches**

Soft Bargaining	*Hard Bargaining*	*Principled Negotiations*
Participants are friends.	Participants are adversaries.	Participants are problem solvers.
The goal is agreement.	The goal is victory.	The goal is a wise outcome reached efficiently and amicably.
Make concessions to cultivate the relationship.	Demand concessions as a condition of the relationship.	Separate the people from the problem.
Be soft on the people and on the problem.	Be hard on the people and on the problem.	Be soft on the people but hard on the problem.
Trust others.	Distrust others.	Trust, but verify.
Change your position easily.	Dig in to your position.	Focus on interests, not positions.
Make offers.	Make threats.	Explore interests.
Disclose your bottom line.	Mislead as to your bottom line.	Avoid having a bottom line; have a BATNA instead.
Accept one-sided losses to reach agreement.	Demand one-sided gains as the price of agreement.	Invent options for mutual gain.
Search for the single answer: the one they will accept.	Search for the single answer: the one you will accept.	Develop multiple options; decide on one later.
Insist on agreement.	Insist on your position.	Insist on using objective criteria.
Try to avoid a contest of will.	Try to win a contest of will.	Try to reach a result based on standards independent of will.
Yield to pressure.	Apply pressure.	Reason and be open to reason; yield to principle not pressure.

The prevalence of integrative (win–win) or distributive (traditional win–lose strategy depends to a great extent on the distance between the union's objectives and those of the employer. A cooperative approach tends to prevail if the two sides are not far apart to begin with. Coercive tactics tend to prevail when a large gap separates bargaining objectives. The gap between the positions of the parties is referred to as the "bargaining zone" (Walton & McKersie, 1965). The bargaining zone spans the distance between the resistance points of each party, that is, the point beyond which a strike or impasse will result. Each side tries to determine the resistance point of the other. A negative zone exists if there is a gap between the farthest point of compromise acceptable to each party. For instance, if the union will accept no less than a $2 per hour wage increase and management is unwilling to agree to a penny more than $1.50, a negative zone exists and impasse is likely. A positive zone is characterized by overlapping resistance points: the union wants no less than $1.75 and management has already decided to grant up to $2. Here, settlement is a foregone conclusion.

The resistance points of the respective parties depend to a large degree on their bargaining power. Power, as defined by Robert Dahl (1957, p. 203), is the extent to which A can get B to do (or not do) something that B otherwise would not (or would) do. In the words of Chamberlain and Kuhn (1965, pp. 162–190), power "is the ability to secure an agreement on one's terms." Power is a product of the resources available to each party with which to influence bargaining outcomes. The resources that may be used include money, votes, political party support, budgetary expertise, negotiating skills, information technology skills, access to the media and elected officials, and potential or actual job actions. In government, power resources are predominantly political. In the private sector, they are primarily economic.

Collective bargaining is about dealing with differences and constructing a relationship. If it is treated purely as a game or a contest of wills, IBB techniques will be inappropriate. Getting good settlements that the parties can live with is a formidable task given the nature of the processes used, mindsets of the parties, history and nature of the relationship, psychological nature of human beings, and complexity and difficulty of the issues.

After negotiations are finished and signatures made, certain post-negotiation rituals are performed. Handshakes and congratulations are exchanged around the room. Joint media releases are issued. Printed and electronic copies of the contract are distributed. Union leadership and top management publicly recognize the achievements of the bargaining teams. A deep sense of satisfaction (and relief) is experienced by all (Oestreich & Whaley, 2001: Appendix A1).

V. RATIFICATION OF THE CONTRACT

Two critical steps remain once a contract has been negotiated. First, bargaining unit membership must ratify the contract in a vote, which usually requires a supermajority, depending on the union's procedures. Ratification is typically not a problem, but occasionally a vocal faction may work hard to reject the contract or the terms might simply be unacceptable to a majority of the unit membership. Union leadership may have overpromised and underdelivered.

The second critical step is ratification by the state legislature or local council. At the state level, a legislative committee may first review the contract and make a recommendation to the entire body. This stage is typically not a problem, either. But legislative rejections have increased recently as budget problems and conservative politics intervene. Connecticut legislators shot down a negotiated pay increase for 27,700 state workers in 2012 out of unhappiness with how employees are paid and because of the costs of health care (Ragsdale, 2012). If the contract is rejected at this stage, or the legislature fails to act on it, the terms do not go into effect. Rarely does the legislative body have the legal authority to unilaterally modify the agreement. Instead, negotiations must resume and produce a contract both the union and the elected representatives find acceptable.

Sometimes, union and legislative contract ratification is not the end of the story. There is always the governor, who has the authority to veto legislative approval of contract terms, as Iowa Governor John Culver did in 2008. An aggrieved party can always turn to the courts for relief, although usually without satisfaction if the issues being litigated are a product of a negotiated and signed contract. The courts will likely be more sympathetic to hearing a union complaint that management or the legislature unilaterally changed the terms of an existing contract. For instance, the Florida legislature cut state employee pay by 3% without renegotiating contracts. A court held that the law doing so was an "unconstitutional taking of private property" that violated the terms and conditions of employment (Klas, 2012). However, in consideration of the financial problems of Richmond, California, the California Supreme Court ruled that local governments can lay off employees without union consultation or negotiations during conditions of financial exigency (Egelko, 2011).

VI. INTEREST-BASED BARGAINING'S POTENTIAL

Collective bargaining mostly follows the traditional model, although IBB is spreading to a growing number of jurisdictions. IBB promotes the kind of work climate that is consistent with teamwork. It has the potential to make collective bargaining a strategic asset in organizations because it pushes to the surface numerous problems that management may not know exist. In other words, the bargaining process gives management and employees at all levels an opportunity to talk constructively about mutual problems that can be rectified. Organizational learning and performance are enhanced. In a broad sense, IBB is part of the trend toward greater employee involvement and participation (Kearney & Hays, 1994). It is a type of empowerment and sharing of responsibility. IBB also comports with the growing presence of alternative dispute resolution, which is being used throughout government and the private sector to help resolve disputes involving family, labor relations, civil relations, commercial interactions, custody disputes, and many others. IBB is similar in process to many organizational development third-party peacemaking and team-building interventions. Further, as public and nonprofit administrators know, the handling of conflict through negotiations is an important part of the day-to-day operation of every public service organization. Negotiations expertise is an important skill at work and in life.

VII. SUMMARY AND CONCLUSIONS

The bargaining process commences with each party communicating its proposals to the other. Many political and psychological considerations are relevant in determining which proposals to make and how to portray them. As in the courtroom, preparation is a critical component of the process. Both parties are bound by law and practice to bargain in good faith.

Government fiscal constraints in many state and local jurisdictions have produced an emphasis on concession bargaining, in which unions are pressed to make financial or work rule givebacks to their employer. Although traditional, zero-sum bargaining remains the norm, a great deal of attention is being given to interest-based, win–win negotiations. The latter approach differs substantially from the former in its assumptions, processes, and potential outcomes. However, it involves significant changes in thought and behavior and naturally provokes resistance from parties who want to cling to a more conventional approach.

CASE STUDY 5.1 SANITATION WORKERS AND THE CITY OF BELVIEW, MINNESOTA—CONTRACT NEGOTIATION

Instructions

Two negotiating teams should be formed, each consisting of three to six individuals. The teams should be named before the day of the exercise and given sufficient time to organize and prepare themselves for the negotiations. A leader and a recorder should be elected by each team. The job of the recorder is to record proposals, counterproposals, agreements, and other useful information in a "negotiations ledger." A laptop computer may be useful.

The teams should negotiate an agreement, record their final settlement in writing, and calculate the financial costs of the settlement. The length of the negotiations should be one to three hours. If one or more items go to arbitration (see later), the instructor or a designated individual should serve as the arbitrator.

Background

The Belview Sanitation Department (BSD) has 75 employees. Seventy are members of the bargaining unit, which is represented by the Sanitation Workers of America. The BSD collects household and business trash and recyclables twice per week throughout the city limits. It utilizes

20 garbage trucks and 5 vehicles for collecting recycled aluminum cans, paper, glass, and plastics. Three employees work on each garbage truck and two on each recycle vehicle. The rolling stock is getting a bit old: the garbage trucks average about 8 years and the other vehicles around 5 years. The technology is somewhat outdated as well. Some nearby jurisdictions, for example, use one- or two-person garbage trucks that collect household trash in large, green "herbie curbies." This technology requires residents to push their herbie curbies out to the street once per week and then return them to the rear of the house.

During the past two decades, the BSD employees received competitive pay raises and their benefits package compared favorably with those of neighboring jurisdictions. There was an illegal strike to gain union recognition about 20 years ago, but until recently relations between the union and management were good. Then came the Great Recession. Moreover, because of a recent state supreme court ruling, strikes by public employees are now legal, although none has yet occurred. Deadlocked negotiations have gone, instead, to binding arbitration. The present 2-year contract expires in 3 days. Negotiations have gone nowhere during the past month, but now the parties are prepared to engage in a marathon bargaining session to settle the remaining issues.

Interests of the Parties

Wages: the union is asking for an increase of $1.25 per hour for the first year of a new contract and $1 for the second year. Management, preferring a 3-year contract, has countered with an offer to freeze wages for 2 years and provide a raise of 50¢ an hour for the third year. The average hourly rate for sanitation workers is $15 per hour, slightly below the regional average of $15.75.

Health-care benefits: the City of Belview currently pays the full cost of medical insurance for its sanitation workers, currently valued at $300 per month. Approximately 75% of the employees have dependents also covered under the city health insurance program. Under the existing contract, the city pays 50% of the total cost of $400 for dependent coverage, which is $200 per month. The union is asking for full (100%) coverage of dependents. Management has received notice from the preferred provider organizations that the cost of each policy will increase by $50 next year. Management wants employees to copay

25% of their personal health-care insurance and 100% of dependent coverage.

Sick leave: the present contract includes 7 paid sick days. The BSD workers claim that the nature of their work causes them to be ill and injured more frequently than other city employees, and they are asking for 10 paid sick days. Other city employees also have 7 days.

Assignment

1. Negotiate and record your agreement on pay and benefits. If no agreement has been reached on one or more issues when time expires, the disputes will have to be submitted to conventional arbitration. Each party must develop a written defense of its positions and perceived interests
2. Each party should calculate the costs of the economic items, including the wage increase (at 2,080 h/year), health insurance benefits, and sick leave
3. Reflect on the bargaining approach employed by each team

Management roles

1. **Sanitation director:** the sanitation director is very paternalistic. Although a strong advocate for the sanitation department, the director is rather antiunion (which is viewed as an indicator of disharmony and distrust). However, the director favors full funding of the family health-care option.
2. **City manager:** the city manager wants to keep his or her job (after all, this is a truly wonderful place to live). Pleasing the city council—encouraging economic development while avoiding tax increases—is paramount. Introducing herbie curbies (as long as the change does not cost too much) and controlling escalating health-care costs are of major importance.
3. **HR director:** the HR director is an advocate of progressive personnel practices. The HR director opposes changes in sick leave benefits due to cost. Similarly, the HR director is concerned about health-care costs.

Labor roles

1 **Union shop steward:** the union head is a truck driver with over 16 years of experience. He or she favors changes in the vacation system and opposes the proposed retirement changes.

2 **Chief sanitation worker (with 6–10 years of experience):** with four young children, he or she is a strong advocate for the family health-care package. The chief sanitation worker is the "spokes-person" for the younger workers and is considering a challenge to the shop steward at the next union election.

3 **Truck driver (with 11–15 years of experience):** as a "maxed out" employee, he or she favors the change in pay increases. He or she also does not like the retirement changes proposed by management.

4 **Sanitation worker (with 0–5 years of experience):** for this younger worker, pay increases in any form and family health care are important factors.

Should the approach be hard, soft, principled, or a blend?

REFERENCES

Anzia, S. F., & Moe, T. M. (2019). Interest groups on the inside: The governance of public pension funds. *Perspectives on Politics*, *17*(4), 1059–1078.

Applebome, P. (2011, May 13). Connecticut unions agree to $1.6 billion in givebacks. *New York Times*. www.nytimes.com

Barrett, J. T. (1995). *P.A.S.T. is the future: A model for collective bargaining that works!* (4th ed.). Jerome Barrett & Sons Publishing Co.

Befort, S. F. (1985). Public sector bargaining: Fiscal crisis and unilateral change. *Minnesota Law Review*, *69*, 1221–1275.

Bernards, N., Ford, M., Kahn, S., Rogers, B., Schömann, I., Shierholz, H., & Whatley, S. (2024, March 11). Technology and organized labor. *PS Quarterly*. https://www.project-syndicate.org/magazine/technology-ai-what-does-it-mean-for-organized-labor-unions-by-nicholas-bernards-et-al-2024-03

Chamberlain, N. W., & Kuhn, J. W. (1965). *Collective bargaining* (2nd ed.). McGraw-Hill.

Craft, J. A., Abboushi, S., & Labovitz, T. (1985, Spring). Concession bargaining and unions: Impacts and implications. *Journal of Labor Research*, *VI*, 167–180.

Dahl, R. (1957, July). The concept of power. *Behavioral Science*, *2*, 201–205.

Dark, T. E. (2003). To reward and punish: A classification of union political strategies. *Journal of Labor Research, 24(3)*, 457–472.

Davey, M., & Yaccino, S. (2012, September 11). Teachers' leader in Chicago strike shows her edge. *New York Times*. www.nytimes.com

Davis, R. S. (2023). Public sector unions: Demands, emotions, and behavior. In *Public personnel management* (pp. 148–162). Routledge.

Delaney, J. T., Fiorito, J., & Jarley, P. (1999, Summer). Evolutionary politics? Union difference and political activities in the 1990s. *Journal of Labor Research, 20*, 277–295.

DiSalvo, D. (2015). *Government against itself: Public union power and its consequences*. Oxford University Press.

DiSalvo, D., & Hartney, M. (2020). Teachers unions in the post-Janus world: Defying predictions, they still hold major clout. *Education Next, 20*(4), 46–55.

Egelko, B. (2011, January 25). California high court sides with Richmond on layoffs. *The San Francisco Chronicle*. www.sfgate.com

Esposito, S. (2022, January 10). CTU union head accuses mayor of being 'relentlessly stupid' in her position on reopening schools. *Chicago Sun Times*. https://chicago.suntimes.com/education/2022/1/10/22876191/chicago-public-schools-teachers-union-reopening-coronavirus-covid-testing-classes-canceled

Fisher, R., & Ury, W. (1981). *Getting to yes*. Penguin.

Flavin, P., & Hartney, M. T. (2015). When government subsidizes its own: Collective bargaining laws as agents of political mobilization. *American Journal of Political Science, 59*(4), 896–911.

Francia, P. L. (2006). *The future of organized labor in American politics*. Columbia University Press.

Freeman, R. B., & Medoff, J. L. (1984). *What do unions do?* Basic Books.

Gallup. (2022, September 1). What percentage of U.S. workers are union members? https://news.gallup.com/poll/265958/percentage-workers-union-members.aspx

Gely, R., & Chandler, T. D. (1993). Determinants of management's organizational structure in the public sector. *Journal of Labor Research, XIV*(4), 381–397.

Gerhart, P. F. (1973). *Political activity by public employee organizations at the local level: Threat or promise (PERL no. 44)*. IPMA.

Greenhouse, S. (2004, December 15). Deep distrust slows contract talks with teachers. *New York Times*. www.nytimes.com

Greenhouse, S. (2011a, September 25). A campaign finance ruling turned to labor's advantage. *New York Times*. www.nytimes.com

Greenhouse, S. (2011b, February 22). Union leader minces no words when labor issues are at stake. *New York Times*. www.nytimes.com

Hammer, T. H., & Wazeter, D. L. (1993). Dimensions of local union effectiveness. *Industrial and Labor Relations Review, 46*(2), 302–319.

Hartney, M. T., & Finger, L. K. (2022). Politics, markets, and pandemics: Public education's response to COVID-19. *Perspectives on Politics*, *20*(2), 457–473.

Hrebenar, R., & Thomas, C. (2004). Interest groups in the states. In *Politics in the American states: A comparative analysis*. CQ Press.

Juravich, T., & Shergold, P. R. (1988, April). The impact of unions on the voting behavior of their members. *Industrial and Labor Relations Review*, *41*, 374–385.

Kapos, S., & Niedzwiadek, N. (2022, January 5). Chicago mayor: Teachers union made us a "laughingstock". *Politico*. https://www.politico.com/news/2022/01/05/chicago-mayor-lightfood-teachers-union-laughingstock-526600

Kearney, R. C., & Hays, S. (1994). Labor management relations and participative decision making toward a new paradigm. *Public Administration Review*, *54*(1), 44–51.

Keating, C. (2011b, August 20). Malloy hails union deal: Others skeptical. *Hartford Courant*. www.courant.com

Klas, M. E. (2012, March 6). Judge rules against the state in pension case, creating potential budget gap. *Miami Herald*. www.miamiherald.com

Lafer, G. (2017). The one percent solution: How corporations are remaking America one state at a time. In *The one percent solution*. Cornell University Press.

Leach, W. D., & Sabatier, P. A. (2005). To trust an adversary: Integrating rational and psychological models of collaborative policymaking. *American Political Science Review*, *99*(4), 491–503.

Leighley, J. E., & Nagler, J. (2007). Unions, voter turnout, and class bias in the U.S. electorate, 1964–2004. *The Journal of Politics*, *69*(2), 430–441.

Leventoglu, B., & Tarar, A. (2005). Prenegotiation public commitment in domestic and international bargaining. *American Political Science Review*, *99*(3), 419–433.

Lincoln, M. G. (2000). Negotiation: The opposing sides of verbal and nonverbal communication. *Journal of Collective Negotiations*, *29*(4), 297–306.

Maier, M. H. (1987). *City unions: Managing discontent in New York City*. Rutgers University Press.

Mareschal, P. M., & Ciorici, P. (2021). Against all odds: Achieving collective action among home care workers in Oregon. *Labor History*, *62*(3), 334–352.

Masters, M. F., & Delaney, J. T. (1987, April). Union political activities: A review of the empirical literature. *Industrial and Labor Relations Review*, *40*, 336–353.

Mehta, S. (2012, September 3). Teachers unions' alliance with democratic party frays. *Los Angeles Times*. www.latimes.com

Milkman, R., & Luce, S. (2017). Labor unions and the great recession. *RSF: The Russell Sage Foundation Journal of the Social Sciences*, *3*(3), 145–165.

Moe, T. M. (2006). *Union power and the education of children*. Hoover Institution Press.

O'Brien, K. M. (1996). The effect of political activity by police unions on nonwage bargaining outcomes. *Journal of Collective Negotiations*, *25*(2), 99–116.

Oestreich, H. H., & Whaley, G. L. (2001). *Transit labor relations guide*. Mineta Transportation Institute.

Open Secrets. (n.d. a). *Public sector unions PACs contributions to candidates, 2021–2022*. https://www.opensecrets.org/political-action-committees-pacs/industry-detail/P04/2022

Open Secrets. (n.d. b). *2022 outside spending, by super PAC: 2022 financial activity for super PACs*. https://www.opensecrets.org/outside-spending/super_pacs

Open Secrets. (n.d. c). *Top PACs: Top 20 PACs to candidates, 2023–2024*. https://www.opensecrets.org/political-action-committees-pacs/top-pacs/2024

Open Secrets. (n.d. d). *Public sector unions PACs contributions to candidates, 2023–2024*. https://www.opensecrets.org/political-action-committees-pacs/industry-detail/P04/2024

Pérez-Piña, R. (2010, October 29). Program by New Jersey union grooms candidates. *New York Times*. www.nytimes.com

Phaneuf, K. M., & Pazniokas, M. (2011, August 23). Malloy lays off defiant state police, correction supervisors. *The Connecticut Mirror*. http://ctmirror.com

Pinnock, S. R. (2005). Organizing virtual environments: National union deployment of the blog and new cyberstrategies. *WorkingUSA*, *8*(4), 457–468.

Ragsdale, J. (2012, August 30). GOP legislators derail new state union deals. *Star Tribune*. www.startribune.com

Rich, M. (2012, September 24). Seeking allies, teachers' unions court GOP, too. *New York Times*. www.nytimes.com

Rogers, B. (2023). *Data and democracy at work: Advanced information technologies, labor law, and the new working class*. MIT Press.

Rosenfeld, J. (2014). *What unions no longer do*. Harvard University Press.

Rubin, J. Z., Pruitt, D. G., & Kim, S. H. (1993). *Social conflict: Escalation, stalemate and settlement* (2nd ed.). McGraw-Hill.

Saad, L. (2023). More in U.S. see unions strengthening and want it that way. *Gallup.com*. https://news.gallup.com/poll/510281/unions-strengthening.aspx

Shostak, A. B. (2002). Today's unions as tomorrow's cyberunions: Labor's newest hope. *Journal of Labor Research*, *23*(2), 237.

Sloane, A. A., & Witney, F. (1981). *Labor relations* (4th ed.). Prentice Hall.

Sojourner, A. J. (2013). Do unions promote members' electoral office holding? Evidence from correlates of state legislatures' occupational shares. *ILR Review*, *66*(2), 467–486.

Spero, S. D., & Capozzola, J. M. (1973). *The urban community and its unionized bureaucracies*. Dunellen.

Spielman, F. (2011, July 18). Rahm Emanuel sends layoff notices to city workers in union showdown. *Chicago Sun-Times*. www.suntimes.com

Steinhauer, J. (2004). Labor demands cast a rich mayor in a miserly light. *New York Times*. www.nytimes.com

Stevens, C. D., & Greer, C. R. (2005). E-voice, the internet, and life within unions: Riding the learning curve. *WorkingUSA*, *8*(4), 439–455.

Tarlau, R. (2023). Networked movements and bureaucratic unions: The structure of the 2018# RedForEd teachers' strikes. *ILR Review*, *76*(5), 833–863.

Union Candidates. (n.d.). https://unioncandidates.org

United States Civil Service Commission v. Letter Carriers. (1973). 413 U.S. 548. http://supreme.justia.com/cases/federal/us/413/548/case.html

Walton, R. E., & McKersie, R. B. (1965). *A behavioral theory of labor negotiations*. McGraw-Hill.

Wells, D. D. (2020). *From collective bargaining to collective begging: How public employees win and lose the right to bargain*. Temple University Press.

Chapter 6

Financial Impacts of Unions and Collective Bargaining

I. INTRODUCTION

Most state and local governments intermittently suffer the throes of fiscal crises. The fiscal problems that can assault governments are legion: inflation, recessions, increased service demands and costs, shifts in population and tax base, declining intergovernmental aid, expensive court orders or settlements, tax and expenditure limits, citizen resistance to tax increases, infrastructure deterioration, burdensome federal mandates, and so on. The list is almost endless. Severe fiscal stress ran rampant during the Great Recession and its aftermath as virtually all state and local governments, as well as the federal government, struggled to balance their budgets. Some failed; among them were Jefferson County, Alabama; Central Falls, Rhode Island; and San Bernardino, Stockton, and Mammoth Lakes, California. All filed for bankruptcy protection during 2010–2012. Financial adversity has become a chronic affliction for some state and local governments, particularly those that have been net losers in coping with the challenges of technology and global markets. The major social, economic, and political forces contributing to government fiscal stress show little sign of abatement.

Meanwhile, state and local government payroll costs have risen steadily in the past decade. State and local governments employ roughly 19.2 million workers. Of these 14.9 million are full-time equivalent workers, and 4.3 million are part-time workers. In 2022 total state and local payroll costs exceed $ $94.4 billion, an increase of 16.9% from the 2017 level of $80.8 billion (U.S. Census Bureau, 2023).

The conventional wisdom is that unions, through collective bargaining and various political activities, contribute to state and local fiscal difficulties by inflating payrolls and operating budgets. It is often asserted that the primary impact of public employee unions is to drive up the cost of wages and benefits. Because 40%–70% of the typical local government and school district operating budget is allocated to employee compensation, strong union influence in setting pay and benefits can, indeed, press financially troubled local jurisdictions up against the

DOI:10.4324/9781003403593-6

fiscal wall by achieving monetary gains that they cannot afford. State government payroll costs represent a smaller percentage of the operating budget, but they are also influenced by union pressures for wage and benefit increases. Government remains a highly labor-intensive enterprise. Therefore, if unions drive up pay and benefits, then they also establish an upward bias on state and local expenditures. In the private sector, a firm may recapture compensation increases through higher prices or improved productivity or absorb them through reduced profits. In government, a wage increase may result in a tax or fee hike or a service cutback. This restricts the options available to government, complicates decision making, and draws the attention of local residents.

This chapter assesses the financial impacts of public employee unions. There are two major types of impacts: impacts on the budgetary process and outcomes and impacts on employee wages and benefits. After a description and appraisal of union influences in budgeting, the empirical literature is examined to identify the dollars and cents wage and benefits effects of unionization. Various factors that influence wage and benefits outcomes are discussed, including parity arrangements, prevailing pay rules, seniority rules, and comparable worth criteria. The consequences of public sector wage and benefits decisions for government decision makers are considered, along with possible citizen reactions to these decisions. A brief description and analysis of gainsharing and productivity bargaining is followed by a look at the financial impacts of federal employee unions and collective bargaining.

The chapter provides no simple, quantitative answer to the question of what the specific financial impacts of unions and collective bargaining on government are. The nature, size, and significance of union effects on budgeting, pay, and benefits are variable, complex, and multifaceted. The major conclusions are that (1) whereas unions have exercised an upward influence on budgeting and compensation outcomes in most jurisdictions, the overall effects have been moderate and not as substantial as the monetary impacts of unions in the private sector and (2) the magnitude of the impact varies greatly over time, function, and jurisdiction.

II. BUDGET MAKING AND UNIONS

The annual (or in some states, biennial) operating budget determines who gets what monies for which purposes. To the extent that budgetary allocations go to public employee compensation, there is much less money for other expenditure items. For public employees, the operating budget determines the size of their raises, the scope and cost of health insurance, as well as retirement and other benefits. In tough economic times it also determines which of them will retain their jobs. Not surprisingly, unions are active participants in the budget-setting process through collective bargaining and political activities intended to influence the decisions of elected and appointed officials in the executive and legislative branches.

A. Budgetary Process

In the absence of unions, employee compensation is determined almost unilaterally by elected officials and public sector management. In the case of a council–manager form of government, where mayoral power is typically weak, department heads make expenditure recommendations to the city manager, who formulates a budget for consideration by the council. In this highly simplified model, compensation decisions are implemented after the council ratifies the budget.

Public employees have no formal role in determining wages and benefits under this non-bargaining model. Their chief collective influence over compensation levels is limited to statements at budget hearings and informal lobbying of the manager and council as one of a plethora of interest groups in the local political arena. Indirectly, public employees may exercise some collective impact on wages and benefits through electoral support of "friendly" candidates. Acting as individuals, workers may attempt to convince superiors to recommend them for higher pay. Once compensation decisions are rendered, however, public workers must usually accept their pay allocations without recourse.

The situation is not dissimilar for unrepresented state employees, who do exercise at least a modest collective voice through their state employees' associations. These associations often deliver testimony and introduce data before legislative budget committees. They also support legislative and executive branch allies through electoral activities. However, individual state employees are largely at the mercy of legislative and gubernatorial decisions, and the pay distributions of supervisors.

Public employees enjoy direct formal access to budget making as well as informal channels of influence such as lobbying and campaign and election activities. At the state level, unions negotiate their terms and conditions of employment with a management team representing the executive branch. The legislature typically honors the results by incorporating them into the budget.

The procedural implications of this bilateral (or, one might say, multilateral) arrangement for budgeting can substantially impact the budget timetable. Public employee unions can seriously constrict the ability of budget makers to rationalize, control, and manage the budget. In the absence of collective bargaining, allocations for wage and benefit increases are normally settled well ahead of legislative ratification, guided by department head and budget staff recommendations and anticipated revenues.

Under collective bargaining, however, wage and benefit allotments cannot be finalized until contracts are negotiated and signed between the jurisdiction and its various employee organizations. Uncertainty occurs when bargaining is extended near or past the legal deadline for having a budget in place. When this happens, the government may have to enact a continuation budget, seek new revenue sources, or take other measures to provide for an undetermined increase in compensation.

Unions have been known to take advantage of the situation by deliberately drawing out negotiations beyond the budget finalization date in an effort to maximize contract gains.

Most state and local government jurisdictions try to complete all collective bargaining contracts expeditiously. Yet, reconciling the budget and bargaining schedules is a regular problem. Some jurisdictions have attempted to resolve the problem of coordinating bargaining and budgeting through legislation. For example, collective bargaining must begin a specified period of time before budget making in New Hampshire and Massachusetts. Hawaii and Iowa tie the bargaining schedule to the fiscal year. Quite a few bargaining jurisdictions declare an impasse automatically if no agreement has been signed by a specified time and proceed to mediation or arbitration. Various formal and informal venues for legislative consultation and participation are also provided in some states, including Minnesota (legislative hearings), Connecticut (formal consultation), and California (legislators may attend and speak at bargaining sessions). Still, late contract settlements are not unusual even in those jurisdictions that attempt to eliminate them through statute.

When jurisdictions are in the early years of a multiyear contract, the budget schedule can become derailed because of fiscal shortfalls. This occurred in numerous jurisdictions during the Great Recession as unions were asked to give back negotiated wage and benefit increases to avoid layoffs or furloughs. In some instances, statewide contracts were reopened, with high-stakes budget negotiations being needed to produce new agreements in New York, Pennsylvania. New Jersey, California, and other states.

What kinds of problems do late settlements create? Clearly, there is a certain loss of efficiency. Continuation of bargaining past the final budget date makes the budget process less predictable and controllable for management. Financing late settlements may necessitate shifting of other allocations, enacting supplementary appropriations, or adopting new revenue measures. Layoffs, furloughs, or service cutbacks are also a possibility.

Budget makers anticipating a late settlement may decide to earmark or "hide" dollars in unrelated budget lines or contingency accounts to pay for delayed wage and benefit settlements or to keep in reserve for other financial emergencies. Such hiding behavior is rather common and generally considered to be part of the bargaining game by both parties. Although hiding tactics are successful to varying degrees as a means of coping with late settlements, their utility in holding down union compensation gains remains a matter of speculation. Unions are certainly not oblivious to the possibility that management has tucked away some resources. Moreover, in this age of transparency public sector managers should consider the possible repercussions of concealing funds in case unions, the media, or citizens discover their actions.

Unions play their own budget games. They may attempt to bring supervisors into their support group by implicitly tying together a pay hike for bargaining unit members with a salary increase for supervisors. Union spokespersons may seek out the relevant media, soliciting reports and anecdotes supporting the credibility and importance of government programs and how important new dollars are for service maintenance and improvements. Alliances with client groups help turn up the heat on the legislative body during budget deliberations.

Late contract settlements may or may not cause problems with respect to the financial situation of the government depending on the amount of compensation that is finally agreed on. In some instances, a settlement well beyond the contract expiration date can help make a moderate pay increase more acceptable to public employees by reducing rank-and-file expectations. As workers yearn more and more for their lump-sum retroactive checks and increases in weekly paychecks, they tend to become more "realistic" in their expectations. However, when late, unanticipated salary increases must be absorbed in an agency's own predetermined budget, and services may suffer.

Clearly, integration of bargaining and budgeting makes the budgeting process more convenient, more controllable, and less stressful for management. The quandary lies in finding an effective means to achieve coordination. Statutory requirements that bargaining be concluded prior to a budget completion date apparently have not had the intended outcome. Often the budget finalization date comes and goes while negotiations run on with no significant legal consequences. However, non-statutory steps can help link budgeting with collective bargaining. For instance, negotiations can begin early in the fiscal year. Certain benefits such as pensions can be provided uniformly, thereby simplifying bargaining. In general, revenue and expenditure data can be transmitted to management and labor negotiators and analysts in a timely fashion. The widespread infusion of information technology into budgeting has helped to speed up the flow of financial information to all parties, aiding budget preparation and analysis in numerous ways.

State and local bargaining and budget making are likely to remain askew where collective bargaining prevails, with mandatory budget adoption dates serving only as benchmarks. In such a context, budgeting can be frustrating for all concerned parties, including the interest and clientele groups seeking government largess for their special programs and concerns. State and local discretionary funds are already highly constricted because of tax and expenditure limitations, federal mandates, citizen opposition to taxing and spending, and many other factors. With more and more special interests fighting over a shrinking government budget pie, the level of conflict climbs. The additional uncertainty introduced by a tardy collective bargaining settlement elevates the intensity of the budget battle even more.

B. Budgetary Outcomes

Because personnel costs constitute a large proportion of the operating budget for state and local governments, an increase in wages and benefits will likely result in higher budget outlays. How will the growth in the compensation bill be funded? In the absence of sufficient new revenues from economic growth or state or federal grants-in-aid, the local jurisdiction must weigh various options, including hiking the property tax rate or user fees, reducing other expenditures, reducing or contracting out services, seeking productivity gains from ongoing operations, freezing vacant positions, or using reserve funds (Kearney, 2005, pp. 30–31). Of course, compensation costs rise whether unions are in the picture or not, with "catch-up" or cost-of-living adjustments and seniority and merit pay increases. Nonetheless, unions are typically blamed by public officials, political conservatives, and the media for creating financial difficulties. The vitriol often smears the government itself for being "bloated" with workers who receive excessive wages and generous benefits.

Empirical research indicates that unions are, indeed, associated with larger budget outlays in cities, although the impact appears to be moderate when other budget-expanding and budget-restricting factors are considered. Specifically, collective bargaining is linked to higher personnel expenditures (as a proportion of the operating budget), but the strength of the relationship varies by city size and the functional area examined. It is also tempered by declines in employment levels. The union effect apparently was once relatively lower in large cities (100,000+ population), suggesting that large cities may cope with union-driven compensation increases by cutting back on employment and service levels (Benecki, 1978; Kearney, 1979). Later studies (Zax, 1988; Lewis & Stein, 1989; Valletta, 1989; O'Brien, 1994) found that municipal unionization and collective bargaining are associated with higher expenditures, notwithstanding city size. The important point is that municipal unions influence the budgetary process to their members' advantage by driving up personnel outlays through collective bargaining and political activities.

However, in some cases there appears to be a tradeoff between pay and positions—an "employment effect." Collective bargaining clearly boosts compensation levels, as discussed in detail later in this chapter. Its effects on total city expenditures, however, are less certain (Valletta, 1989, pp. 438–439; O'Brien, 1994), probably because wage and benefit increases are sometimes accompanied by reduction in the number of jobs in bargaining units or in non-bargaining departments. In the words of union critics, collective bargaining has "greatly distorted state spending priorities" contrary to citizens' best interest (McGinnis & Schanzenbach, 2010).

Do unions protect pay levels at the expense of jobs? In some areas the answer is yes. Under union contracts, reductions in force are applied with reverse seniority—"last hired, first fired." Junior rank and file employees typically constitute a relatively noninfluential minority of total union membership. The more numerous senior members of the bargaining unit are not generally vulnerable to layoffs, and they may choose to protect their pocketbooks instead of other employees' positions (Freeman & Medoff, 1984).

The negative relationship identified between unionization and employment (Clark & Ferguson, 1983; Stein, 1990, p. 491; Trejo, 1991; O'Brien, 1994) also indicates that some union-related factor or set of factors is at work to hold down job levels. Perhaps unions prompt a cutback in the quality and quantity of services, enabling job cuts. Or management may be able to institute productivity and technological improvements to maintain service levels with a reduced number of workers.

Of course, there is always the possibility that bureaucratic fat is being sliced off instead of muscle. Indeed, unions may force city officials to become more efficiency minded. On the other hand, union political activities can push overall city employment levels higher (Freeman & Valletta, 1988; Valletta, 1989; Zax, 1989). For instance, union campaign contributions and endorsements of political candidates have been found to significantly affect the demand for services—and employment—of police officers and firefighters (Chandler & Gely, 1995).

In brief, research findings on the union impact on budget outcomes and employment levels are often in conflict. The disparate results may be attributed to the variable time periods and employee functions examined, quality of available data, and researcher's methodological approach. Most likely, other salient yet unmeasured factors remain unaccounted for in the empirical research, such as the average age of the bargaining unit, quality of union and management leadership, and sense of solidarity among union members.

III. UNIONS, WAGES, AND BENEFITS

A popular research topic for the community of labor relations scholars has been the impact of unions on wage and nonwage compensation. It is also one of the most important topics for research because it represents a fundamental measure of union power and organizational success or failure. A variety of factors influence government wage and benefit levels, including social, economic, and political forces and conditions; decision-making rules and processes; and circumstances peculiar to particular jurisdictions and settings. Before one can isolate the effects of unions and collective bargaining on compensation, these micro- and macroeconomic factors must be satisfactorily taken into account.

A. Socioeconomic Factors

The socioeconomic forces that establish boundaries within which public sector compensation determinations are made are many, diverse, and interrelated. Economists refer to them as labor market factors or, more specifically, labor supply and demand factors. These are outlined in the following list.

Five variables that help measure the supply—or availability—of labor are cost of living, labor concentration, labor force composition, opportunity wage, and employer demand for workers:

1 "Cost of living" represents how much one must spend to acquire the necessities and wants of life, as well as how rapidly prices are rising. A high and rising cost of living is associated with higher public employee wage and benefit levels, but, in some cases, it is also associated with a shrinking labor force, as workers move to jobs located in areas with lower costs of living. The cost of living also varies according to geography. In general, wages are higher in New England, the mid-Atlantic, and the Great Lakes and Pacific states; about average in most of the Midwest; and lowest in the South and Southwest. Within regions, the cost of living tends to be higher in metropolitan areas and lower in small and rural communities. Unions often base wage and benefit demands on measures of cost of living, such as those compiled by the U.S. Department of Commerce (e.g., the consumer price index)
2 "Labor concentration," or "labor density," refers to the number of potential workers within a labor market. Wages and benefits normally are greater in government jurisdictions with high levels of population and population density. Several explanations exist for this phenomenon. These include the availability of a well-trained and educated labor force in heavily populated areas, a stronger tax base from which to extract resources for employee compensation, a high urban cost of living, and the simple expectation that highly populated cities and states will remunerate their workers more generously than rural jurisdictions
3 The "composition of the labor force" is a third labor supply variable. These "human capital" variables account for differences in compensation that occur as the result of variations in education, experience, race and ethnicity, and gender of the workforce. Because of vestiges of racial, ethnic, and gender discrimination, as well as personal choices (e.g., a woman temporarily leaving the workforce to have children and raise a family), white males still enjoy pay advantages over their African American, Latino, and female counterparts that cannot be attributed to different backgrounds in education and job experience. Although equal opportunity and affirmative action laws and policies have assuaged these disparities, equal pay for equal work is not yet a reality across all U.S. governments
4 The "opportunity wage" is a fourth labor supply influence on wages and benefits. Briefly, the opportunity wage is that which would be available to the same individual for work in a similar occupation for another government, private, or nonprofit sector employer. Raiding nearby municipalities for highly qualified or otherwise desirable workers is a common phenomenon

in many metropolitan areas, and many state and local governments compete in the job market with private firms, nonprofits, other jurisdictions, and even the federal government. Thus, there are pressures on the employer to keep wages and benefits at levels high enough to discourage employee turnover for more generous economic rewards elsewhere and at the same time attract well-qualified job seekers in a competitive labor market.

5 Three factors related to employer demand for labor are "fiscal capacity," "monopsony," and "unemployment":

a) Fiscal capacity is positively associated with wage and benefit levels. Generally speaking, wealthier state and local governments with high tax bases and relatively low expenditures enjoy revenue advantages that may accrue to the benefit of public employees. Related factors are the amount of funds obtained through federal grants-in-aid and other intergovernmental transfers, as well as tax effort. For example, a relatively poor state may pay quite competitive wages and benefits if it receives large amounts of federal aid and taxes its citizens heavily

b) Monopsony is, in effect, a monopoly in the labor market that is exercised by a single employer. Thus, an employer demands a large enough quantity of a particular type of labor so that the wages within one or more occupations are pushed downward. For example, a geographically isolated municipality with a single school district exercises a monopsony over public school teachers who have no alternative education employment available to them (except, of course, in the private sector, where wages in most cases are lower for teachers). Teachers, like nurses and university professors, may be disadvantaged in the labor market when there is a scarcity of alternative places of employment within reasonable commuting distance (Merrifield, 1999). However, the relevance of the monopsony argument to the public sector appears to be rather limited when other occupations such as law enforcement and fire protection are considered

c) Finally, unemployment rates are inversely related to compensation. High levels of unemployment exert a downward pressure on wages, as the number of job seekers exceeds employment opportunities. Jurisdictions in areas with low levels of unemployment may be forced to pay a wage premium to attract qualified employees.

B. Political Factors

Political factors also have an impact on government compensation outcomes. Numerous political variables influence pay and benefits. Three key forces are highlighted here: the legal environment, the nature of government management, and government structure.

The legal environment of public sector labor relations affects compensation in a variety of ways. Bargaining laws reflect union power and influence in the political arena, which spills over into wage and benefit decisions. One would expect, for example, that public employees benefit from more favorable compensation outcomes in a state with a comprehensive bargaining law, such as Iowa, than in a state like South Carolina, which prohibits collective negotiations. Arbitration laws also may influence compensation outcomes. A study of police bargaining over a ten-year period found that the availability of interest arbitration is associated with higher police salaries (Feuille & Delaney, 1986; see also Chapter 9). Research also has identified a positive relationship between the availability of arbitration and the earnings of other local government workers, including teachers (Zigarelli, 1996). Many additional elements in the legal and policy environment can affect compensation levels, including a legal or de facto right to strike (Zigarelli, 1996), taxation and expenditure limitations, the threat or reality of outsourcing, and the setting of certain employee benefits statewide (teacher pensions, for instance).

How management organizes itself for wage and benefit decisions is relevant to compensation outcomes. As noted earlier, in nonunion settings such decisions may be rendered unilaterally—by a city manager or state legislature, for instance. In contrast, multilateral negotiations frequently take place where collective bargaining exists. One expects that unilateral compensation determination would tend to hold down wages and benefits, whereas the involvement of multiple actors, which often reflects internal management conflict and political forces, would play out to the represented employees' advantage.

The structure of government itself may affect public employee compensation outcomes. "Reformed" political institutions such as a council–manager government, nonpartisan elections, and at-large or mixed constituencies may tend to minimize the access of public workers to the decision-making arena. Public employees should have stronger influence on wage and benefit decisions where they find it relatively easy to apply political pressure on elected officials. Thus, mayor–council systems, partisan elections, and single-member electoral districts should be associated with more favorable compensation outcomes. However, empirical research on the structure of government variable reports mixed findings (Ehrenberg, 1972; Gerhart, 1976; Lewis & Stein, 1989; Chandler & Gely, 1995).

C. Politics and Decision Rules in the Compensation Decision Process

As noted in Chapter 3, in nonunion jurisdictions the role of the public worker in compensation decisions is normally limited to informal individual or group requests for a satisfactory increase in monetary awards. When public employee unions enter the scene by way of formal or informal bilateral negotiations, the compensation determination process assumes an important new political dimension. This process is discussed here.

The politics of compensation involve union activities in election campaigns including member support of and financial contributions to candidates and political action committees. Politicians may trade favorable pay and benefits for union political support (Hammer & Wazeter, 1993; O'Brien, 1994; Chandler & Gely, 1995). Union tactics include lobbying elected and appointed officials; collecting, analyzing, and disseminating pertinent information on pay and benefits; and influencing citizen opinion through public relations. Unions may apply raw political power through real or threatened job actions, warnings of electoral defeats, and other intimidating behavior.

Formal and informal decision rules also influence pay outcomes. Union and management each strive to win acceptance of decision rules that work to their perceived advantage. At the same time, several rules have been widely accepted by both parties: the across-the-board increase, the prevailing rate, pay parity, cost-of-living adjustments, comparable worth, and the ability to pay. Unions usually prefer to have increases awarded across the board or in equal percentages (e.g., a 5% hike for everybody). This limits management discretion and is perceived to be fair by most bargaining unit members.

The challenge is that an equity-based decision rule does nothing to encourage or reward special effort or outstanding performance, and this disturbs management. Merit pay or pay for performance ties remuneration to achievement and maximizes management discretion to reward high performance and productivity. It may take the form of incentive pay or group performance bonuses. In principle, it makes a great deal of sense, and it has been widely adopted in some form throughout the government at all levels. In practice, merit pay is plagued by a multitude of problems (Bowman, 2010; Kellough & Selden, 1997; Park & Berry, 2014), including a tenuous link to employee performance, a perception of supervisory favoritism, and relatively meaningless merit pay amounts (Perry et al., 2009; Bowman, 2010). Unions generally, often successfully, oppose it.

The "prevailing rate" for pay is important both symbolically and substantively. Symbolically, it represents a fair day's pay for a fair day's work. Substantively, it keeps workers reasonably satisfied and helps preclude attrition of the workforce to higher paying area employers. The prevailing rate is determined from secondary sources, such as the U.S. Bureau of Labor Statistics' Area Wage Surveys or data from national, state, business, or labor organizations, or calculated independently through salary and benefits surveys by individual jurisdictions. All states and the great majority of local governments with populations of 10,000 or more conduct such surveys either regularly or intermittently. Some are mandated by law; others are done informally.

Typically, data comparing a jurisdiction's salaries and benefits with those of neighboring public and private organizations are sought for "benchmark" jobs such as key entry-level positions. Through mail, telephone, or Internet surveys, wage data are obtained from other relevant employers. Benchmark positions must be closely comparable in job descriptions; knowledge, skills, and abilities required; and hours worked. Examples include beginning schoolteachers, administrative assistants, police sergeants, and social service caseworkers. It is also important to collect data on benefits. Variability in benefits sometimes makes meaningful comparison problematic, but the dollar value of major benefits such as pensions and health care should be considered.

At first blush, establishing the prevailing rate through surveys appears to be rather objective and straightforward. However, politics is inherently involved. For example, which employers should be surveyed? What should be the scope of the investigation? Survey outcomes are related to characteristics of responding employers, including population and geographic size, fiscal capacity and status, prevailing labor climate, and cost of living. Thus, how the sample is drawn helps to determine results. Moreover, interpretation of survey results is subject to dispute. Should data from extreme or "outlying" respondents be tossed out? Are benchmark positions truly comparable? Should respondents be classified by population size, geography, or some other characteristic? Should both union and nonunion employers be surveyed?

With so much judgment and discretion involved, employee organizations often seek to determine the prevailing rate independently. Specifically, they may conduct their own surveys or seek the help of national union staff in gathering wage data. Data collected by unions and public employers may be shared, but each tends to look suspiciously at the survey results produced by the other.

"Parity" is the third decision rule widely used by management and labor, particularly in many local government jurisdictions. The parity rule is an old one. As early as 1898, a parity provision for police and firefighters was in effect in New York City (the police were still fighting against it in 2013), about 65 years before collective bargaining began its great period of growth in urban areas. Parity may be set at 100%, where two occupational groups always receive the same levels of pay and benefits, or it may be set at a certain percentage of the pay of a key occupation. For example, police officers in Hawaii receive a 5% pay advantage over firefighters.

After one bargaining unit negotiates a raise, a comparable increase is automatically granted to the other unit. Parity provisions usually apply to the police and fire functions, with the police setting the pay standard. However, parity also may exist between other workers in the public sector and their private sector counterparts. For example, the New York City Council recently lent its support for a plan to bring wages for FDNY emergency medical technicians into parity police and firefighters (Rose, 2024).

Parity rules may be embodied in collective bargaining contracts, state or local legislation, or city charters, or they may be implemented informally. Sometimes, as in New York City, parity rules become the subject of intense rivalry between police and firefighters. Firefighters, who often seek to achieve or maintain parity with police, claim that they work longer hours and perform more dangerous work. They must spend more time away from home and family, and their job requires a substantial amount of technical training and expertise.

Police officers respond that their job is more dangerous, involves more intensive work, and requires greater use of interpersonal skills. Furthermore, police officers claim that they need higher entry-level pay to attract recruits into the demanding and hazardous field of law enforcement. Police unions sometimes attempt to break parity arrangements, and they have been struck down by the courts in several jurisdictions, including local governments in Maine, Connecticut, and New York, on the grounds that they effectively withdraw bargaining rights from a union that is not a party to the arrangement.

In recent years, parity clauses have been contentious. For example, the police union in St. Louis, Missouri sued the city over the police and firefighter parity clause that was embedded in the city charter. The union argued that the city had interpreted the clause to allow raises for firefighters without giving raises to the police, and that management opposed raises for police because of the parity (Labor Relations Information System, 2016). In Houston a battle between police, fire, and the city government over parity pay has been ongoing since 2018. The firefighters won parity pay through a ballot initiative in 2018, the city won a trial judge's ruling in 2019 that the proposition violated the Texas Constitution, the appellate court overturned the lower court ruling in 2021, and the Texas Supreme Court struck down the voter-approved initiative in 2023 (McGuinness, 2023).

Another decision rule is "cost of living," which, of course, usually is rising. Cost-of-living arguments tend to resonate with voters and public officials, who understand the pain of salaries that are stagnant in value. Unions want to incorporate inflation's effects in salaries so that members do not lose ground in purchasing power. During periods of price inflation, unions seek to negotiate escalator clauses so that future wage increases track cost-of-living increases. Slowdowns in inflation may provoke the elimination of public sector escalator clauses.

"Comparable worth" rose to prominence in the public sector in the 1980s largely because of public employee unions. As a compensation decision rule, it means equal pay for work of comparable value. Equal pay for equal work is a widely accepted legal principle, but comparable worth is a contentious issue that challenges conventional market-based wage-setting practices.

In the 1960s, the vast majority of working women were employed in only a handful of occupations. Few alternatives were available, beyond teaching, nursing, and clerical work. In these "female ghettos," women earned less than 60% of the median pay of males. Today, there are essentially no occupational barriers that large numbers of women have not broken down, yet as a group they still earn only about 78% of what men do. Frustration with this wage gap continues. Supporters of comparable worth argue that the wage differential is primarily caused by continuing (if voluntary) job segregation and wage discrimination. Comparable worth seeks to address these sources of gender-based pay inequities.

Opponents counter that comparable worth takes wages beyond the market law of labor supply and demand and would wreak devastating results on national, not to mention organizational, pay policies. They further contend that wage discrimination is a myth. Women are paid less because many of them are part-time and temporary workers, they tend to leave the labor force to give birth and raise children, and they choose to segregate themselves in lower paying jobs.

In the absence of congressional action, the arguments for and against comparable worth have been addressed in courtrooms and state and local legislative bodies across the country. The bell for the first round of the comparable worth fight was sounded in San Jose, California, in 1981. The American Federation of State County, and Municipal Employees (AFSCME) Loca 101 tried to force the city to implement comparable worth adjustments to close a pay gap identified by a salary study. An agreement between union leaders and city officials was quickly reached that hiked the pay of about 20% of the city's employees (Flammang, 1986).

Two important court cases also arose from the West Coast: *County of Washington v. Gunther* (1981) and *AFSCME v. State of Washington* (1983). In the first case, female jail "matrons" (guards) sued Washington County, Oregon, under Title VII of the Civil Rights Act of 1964 because they were paid 30% less than male guards for substantially equal work. A lower court ruled against the matrons, but a federal court of appeals reversed the decision and was later narrowly upheld by the U.S. Supreme Court. In the second case, AFSCME spearheaded a class action suit against the state of Washington for failing to act on several comparable worth studies that the state had commissioned. The studies had discovered a 20% gender-based wage gap for comparable positions. The union argument prevailed in the U.S. District Court but was later overturned on appeal. Nonetheless, the state of Washington settled with AFSCME and the 15,500 female workers it represented and fully implemented comparable worth within ten years.

AFSCME President Gerald McEntee recognized the potential benefits of the comparable worth issue for the union, observing that "the ruling in Tacoma (Washington) is going to reach into every one of the 50 state governments, every one of the 3041 counties, and each and all of the townships and cities and school districts. In fact, it is going to affect every one of the nearly 83,000 public jurisdictions in this land" (quoted in Legler, 1985, pp. 241–242). McEntee may have overstated his case, but other public employee unions joined AFSCME in latching onto comparable worth during the 1980s, recognizing it as an excellent tool for organizing the female labor force in government.

The basic comparable worth methodology is point factor analysis. Critical job factors, which typically include knowledge, skills, and abilities, are identified for male- and female-dominated positions and assigned numerical scores on the basis of their relative importance to the organization. The factor scores are summed for each position. Jobs with equal or nearly equal scores receive equal pay. For example, an administrative secretary's wages might be brought up to the level of a transportation department crew leader or a state grain inspector or the pay of a nurse might be raised to equal that of a truck repair foreman.

The comparable worth movement gained traction in the public sector in the 1980s and 1990s. However, it was never adopted by the private sector and has not been incorporated into federal law (Rubery, 2019). Instead, the Lily Ledbetter Fair Pay Act was passed by Congress in 2009, but it is weakly enforced. Not surprisingly, the gender pay gap for women has barely budged from 80 cents for every dollar earned by men in 2002 to 82 cents on the dollar in 2022 (Kochar, 2023). In addition, there are substantial challenges to using equal value or comparable worth to address the ways in which work is rewarded. In most cases there has been a shift toward assessing individualized competence, merit, and other performance-based compensation plans (Rubery, 2019).

Today, unions have shifted their efforts to pay transparency, pay equity, and living wage campaigns through legal actions, the collective bargaining process, and state and local legislation. From 2019 to 2022 pay equity laws were introduced in two-thirds of the states. Some of the key areas of progress include requiring employers to collect and report data, expanding equal pay protections beyond sex, and allowing fairer comparisons of work. For example, in 2021 Connecticut and Rhode Island amended their equal pay standards to equal pay for "comparable work," based on such indicators as skill, effort, and responsibility and performed under similar conditions. In 2019, Colorado, New York, and Illinois also broadened their equal pay provisions (National Women's Law Center, 2023).

When faced with employee demands for compensation increases, whether based on comparable worth or other factors, public employers often invoke the "principle of ability to pay." In a sense, it is more of a negotiating tactic than a decision rule, but its omnipresence certainly demands discussion. Usually, the ability to pay principle is argued in the negative. In making an "inability to pay" argument, the government is claiming that it is unable to grant its workers more than a certain amount in wages and benefits because of revenue shortfalls, expenditure demands, or other contingencies. Ostensibly, inability to pay is a valid argument. Nevertheless, public employee unions often translate inability to pay as unwillingness to pay. Certainly, the issue is subject to debate. For example, when is the government unable to pay? When it defaults on outstanding debts? When it fails to meet its payroll? Or before such crises arise?

Surely, if a state or local government is prohibited by law from running an operating deficit, then a union-proposed wage settlement that would force the budget into the red could be successfully countered by an inability-to-pay argument. However, government employers raise the inability-to-pay flag so frequently that unions no longer salute it and instead demand exquisite details on revenues, expenditures, and debts and assiduously search for money hidden in the budget. Management may seek to bolster its own case with figures on cash flow, debt and debt service levels, inadequately funded retiree pension and health-care benefits, pending or actual court decisions that present future liabilities, legally mandated budget expenditures, and various comparisons with wage and benefit levels and tax burdens in other jurisdictions.

Unions carefully examine management's data and financial projections and calculate their own. Often, assistance is available from national unions, which maintain budget analysis staff. Most have the capability to conduct econometric analyses. The National Education Association, for example, has a budget analysis software package for local school districts. In general, information technology and resources have greatly simplified such analyses. A thorough union review of data will also examine the proposed budget, including expenditure forecasts and economic assumptions, past budgets, external audit reports, budget reviews, and financial statements. The union review is also likely to include minutes of council or legislative meetings, news reports, bond prospectuses, promotional literature, independent fiscal data from citizens' groups, "inside" information from personnel in key offices, a search for contingency funds or other hidden monies, and human resource reports on unfilled positions (Leibig & Kahn, 1987, pp. 194–204; Toulmin, 1988, pp. 622–623).

D. Monetary Impacts of Unions: Approaching the Research Question

Unionization (the extent—or density—of employee organizational membership) and collective bargaining (formalized labor–management decision making within a collective framework) push salaries and wages upward. Even in the absence of collective bargaining, unions may influence compensation policies. Unions in one jurisdiction may affect compensation levels in neighboring, nonunion settings through a "threat effect," as employers seek to discourage employee organizing by paying competitive wages and benefits.

In the 1960s and 1970s, unions and collective bargaining in government were unknown quantities that aroused reactions running the gamut from blind, ideological devotion to fearful, virulent criticism. The most influential and thought-provoking attack on public sector unions and collective bargaining was set out in a controversial Brookings Institution study in 1971. According to *The Unions and the Cities*, union activity and collective bargaining distort the democratic political process:

> The distortion results from unions obtaining too much power, relative to other interest groups, in decisions affecting the level of taxes and the allocation of tax dollars. The distortion therefore may result in a redistribution of income

> by government whereby union members are subsidized at the expense of other interest groups.
>
> (Wellington & Winter, 1971, p. 167)

Wellington and Winter (1971, pp. 30–31) contend that public employee unions "leave competing groups in the political process at a permanent and substantial disadvantage." They offer several major reasons: (1) some government services are essential, so prolonged interruption resulting from a strike directly threatens public health and safety; (2) the demand for public services is relatively inelastic and insensitive to changes in price because government services lack close substitutes and competitive service providers rarely exist; and (3) the disruption of government services inconveniences voters who may punish political leaders in the next election. Implicitly, "rent-seeking" elected officials solicit and reward union political support. Thus, the authors argue that unions in government inherently have greater power than those in the private sector. A product of this power advantage, one would logically assume, is higher compensation for unionized government employees compared to their union counterparts in private employment or nonunionized colleagues in other governmental units.

Have public sector unions achieved wage and benefit gains that outstrip their union counterparts in the private sector and nonunion workers in other governmental jurisdictions? Wellington and Winter (1971) furnish no quantitative data to support their assertions. At the same time, these claims have been tested by other researchers.

IV. ARE PUBLIC SECTOR WORKERS PAID MORE THAN PRIVATE SECTOR WORKERS?

Until the rise of unions in government in the 1960s and 1970s, public employees were consistently underpaid relative to similar workers in the private sector. Since then, several studies have attempted to compare wage and benefit levels in public and private sector employment. It is generally agreed that public employees improved their pay position relative to private sector workers in most occupational categories from the late 1960s through the mid-1970s (Reder, 1975; Field & Keller, 1976; Orr, 1976).

Have public employees continued to close or even reverse the pay gap? Which sector pays the highest today? The findings are mixed on these questions. The answer depends on government function; the level and size of government; time period; methodology; and, apparently, the political values or ideology of the researcher.

The first study to directly address relative public–private sector pay (Smith, 1976) determined that federal workers made substantially more (10%–20%) than similar private sector workers, but state and local employees enjoyed only a very slight (1%–2%) advantage. Subsequent research has tended to support these findings (Linneman & Wachter, 1990), although state and local earnings growth lagged the private sector during the 1980s according to one researcher (Krueger, 1988). Two studies using 1991 data found that public sector employees earned a "significant wage premium" that exceeded private sector wages by 5.4% and total pay and benefits by 10.3% (Choudhury, 1994). The public sector compensation advantage rose to 25% when the shorter government workweek was taken into account, leading Cox and Brunelli (1992) to call for cutting state and local jobs, reducing payroll, and contracting out government services to save money. However, recent research on state and local governments indicates that the government wage premium no longer exists and in fact has been reversed to a wage deficit, as will be seen later.

Research results are mixed when federal employees are singled out. Perloff and Wachter (1984) and Krueger (1988) found that postal employees were much better paid than similar private sector workers. On the other hand, there are longstanding shortages in some federal position classifications due to inferior pay and benefits. Engineers, doctors, and other health-care personnel are three examples. U.S. Bureau of Labor Statistics' wage comparability studies consistently find that private sector workers are paid substantially more than most federal employees for similar work. Independent studies by the U.S. Governmental Accountability Office, the Merit Systems Protection Board, the Federal Pay Agent, and consulting firms have arrived at the same conclusion and point to a high turnover rate for federal workers leaving for higher pay and better opportunities elsewhere.

These studies, however, are suffused with methodological difficulties and swamped by the magnitude of the task. For example, the aggregate data used in many of the studies, including the aforementioned ones, do not account for important information, including occupational categories, position levels, units of government, geographic differences, or variances in individuals' education and experience. As observed by Miller (1996, p. 21), the comparability question should be framed as follows: "if two persons are doing the same job, at the same level of duties and responsibilities, with one person performing that job in state or local government service and the other in private industry, are they also paid alike?"

Several studies address some of the major methodological pitfalls in comparing public and private sector earnings. Belman and Heywood (1995) compared public and private sector earnings in seven states, statistically controlling for occupation and individual worker characteristics (e.g., age and experience). Results indicated that lower-level government employees earned more than their private sector counterparts, but mid-level to upper-level employees in government were paid less than those in the private sector. For the seven states examined, six underpaid local government employees and three underpaid state government workers compared to similar workers in the private sector.

Bender and Heywood (2010) extended the Belman and Heywood methodology to a large (50,000–60,000 households) national sample of workers and statistically controlled for age, education, and other demographic characteristics. They found that state and local government employees are, on average, comparably compensated or slightly undercompensated relative to their counterparts in the private sector. An important finding of this research is that state and local employment disproportionately consists of occupations that garner high earnings. Some of these relatively highly paid jobs are not directly comparable to jobs found in the private sector (e.g., firefighters and police officers). Moreover, government work demands a more highly educated workforce and a much greater proportion of managerial and professional employees than the private sector (Belman & Heywood, 1995, p. 196, 2004).

The aforementioned studies, along with the research conducted by a Bureau of Labor Statistics economist (Miller, 1996) identify interesting patterns in the data. State and local employers pay more than private industry at the low end of the pay scale and private firms pay better than state and local governments for higher-level jobs, particularly those involving administrative and professional responsibilities and more years of education. But highly paid, highly educated administrative and professional employees comprise 30% of the local and 40% of the state labor force, compared to only 10% of private employment. This distribution artificially pushes the average earnings of government employees above that of private sector employees unless occupation is taken into account. When education and other demographic factors are controlled for, state and local employees earn 11%–12% less than comparable private sector workers (Bender & Heywood, 2010). Moreover, this public sector earnings disparity has grown over the past four decades.

The related issue of pay compression is troubling for public employers. The relatively high-paid positions at lower levels of government organizations are typically easy to recruit for and staffed with qualified workers. On the other hand, the relatively low-paid positions at upper and upper-middle levels of agencies and departments do not compare favorably to positions with similar responsibilities in business. The result is difficulty in recruiting and retaining mid- to top-level government officials.

The paycheck represents only a portion of the total compensation picture. Benefits, which typically consume one-third of the total compensation package, are very important. The evidence with respect to the dollar value of benefits favors government workers but increasingly less so as a consequence of state and local policy changes driven by budget pressures from the Great Recession. In a study of both wages and benefits, i.e., total compensation, Keefe (2012) finds that state and local government employees earn 6.35% less than similarly situated private sector employees. When controlling for working hours, there is still a significant public-sector penalty of 3.7% for full-time state and local government employees compared to private sector employees.

With regard to specific benefits, state and local pension plans traditionally provide more generous payouts than the average private sector plan. State and local workers can also expect to retire with fewer years of service and to experience more growth in their monthly retirement check (from cost-of-living adjustments (COLAS)) than private employees. Even so, pension plans with COLAs are still subject to change. In a recent study of state and local government pension plans, Fitzpatrick and Goda (2020) found that every year between 2005–2018 over half of public sector workers were subject to changes in COLA formulas. In 2005 and 2006, the formula changes usually resulted in increases. In contrast, during the periods 2007–2010 and 2013–2016, the majority of plans adjusted the COLA formula downward. By 2017, COLA formula adjustments began ticking upwards again.

Moreover, the financial risk for funding future pension payments continues to be assumed by most government employers in "defined benefit plans," which promise retirees monthly pension checks with the specific amount based on years of service and salary levels. With defined benefits plans the government is on the hook as far as cost-of-living adjustments are concerned. Firms, on the other hand, typically pass along the risk to future retirees under "defined contribution plans," which determine the amount of retirement benefits based on investment choices made by the employee. Poor choices translate into low payments.

Public–private differences exist for other benefits as well. Health-care insurance for public employees, retirees, and their dependents is more widely available and often more generous than insurance provided (or not provided) by firms. Vision and dental care benefits are comparable. Public workers typically enjoy more annual sick and vacation leave than their private sector counterparts (Kearney, 2003). Taking the dollar value of benefits into account, the public–private compensation differential falls to an estimated 6.8%–7.4% in favor of private sector workers (Bender & Heywood, 2010).

Generous—but sometimes underfunded—pension and retiree health-care plans became a topic of great concern with the accounting standards adopted by the Governmental Accounting Standards Board, requiring public reporting of accrued, unfunded benefits. In the wake of the Great Recession, many state and local governments revealed startling levels of unfunded liabilities, and the total gap between promised pension and health-care benefits on the one hand and funds set aside to pay for them on the other was a shocking $1.38 trillion (Pew Center on the States, 2012). For example, in 2012 New Jersey had fallen $108 billion short in setting aside money to pay for pensions and retiree health care (Pew Center on the States, 2012). Although some fiscally responsible state and local governments were in relatively good shape, most were confronted with the need to step up retiree funding, reduce benefits, or do both.

Following the recession a substantial proportion of state and local governments reduced such benefits through legislative action or revised collective bargaining contracts. Jurisdictions including Colorado, Minnesota, and Vermont hiked copays for health care and pensions, dropped dependent health-care coverage, raised minimum retirement age and time-in-service requirements, and mandated that defined contribution plans replace defined benefit plans for new workers (Maynard, 2012). As a result, state and local employee benefit levels progressed toward closing the gap with private sector employees in both unionized and nonunionized settings.

As of 2021, states were making substantial enough contributions to their retirement systems to keep pension debt stable. Even the states that performed the worst in 2014—Kentucky, Michigan, New Jersey, and Rhode Island—were above the threshold for potential insolvency in 2021 (Pew, 2023). Although the COVID-19 pandemic led to some turmoil in the markets, by 2023 the funded status of state and local pensions was roughly 78%, an increase of 5 percentage points since 2019 (Aubry & Yin, 2023). In the fiscal year 2022, several states made contributions above actuarial requirements. These include Arizona, California, Connecticut, and Virginia. Connecticut is particularly interesting because state policy requires that surpluses in the state's budget reserves be contributed to the retirements systems (NASRA, 2024).

V. COMPARING THE RELATIVE EFFECTS OF UNIONS IN THE PUBLIC AND PRIVATE SECTORS

What is the compensation impact of unions in the public and private sectors? In which sector are unions most effective in driving up wages and benefits? The empirical evidence is fairly conclusive that private sector unions have been more successful than unions in the public sector. The most comprehensive examination of unions and wages in business is Lewis's *Union Relative Wage Effects: A Survey* (1986). According to Lewis, the wage effects of unions were 10%–15% from the late 1950s to the late 1970s. Later research indicates that this differential prevailed into the mid-1990s but has declined somewhat since (Hirsch & Schumacher, 2001). However, measurement error is more likely due to declining unionization in the private sector (Hirsch, 2004), so any specific comparison is subject to dispute. The relative wages of unionized workers in business tend to rise during periods of recession and fall during inflationary times and, in general, they vary greatly across time, occupation, and the state of the economy.

Direct comparisons with union wage effects in government indicate that private sector wage gains ran about 10% higher when controlling for occupation in the time period from 1960 to the late 1990s (Shapiro, 1978; Moore & Raisian, 1987; Ashraf, 1997; Blanchflower & Bryson, 2004). Bender and Heywood (2010) determined that private sector unions are associated with a wage premium of 22.7% versus a public sector wage premium of 11.2%, that is, a difference of 11.5%. Thus, it appears that, in general, private sector workers have gained more in terms of pay from unionization than their counterparts in public employment.

Unions in both sectors appear to change the distribution of earnings as well. As noted earlier, unions have been associated with salary compression, reflected in a reduction in the spread between the average pay of the lowest and highest ranking employees in an organization. To a union member, salary compression may be interpreted as less salary inequity between management and rank and file through collective bargaining—a good thing. Unions are also associated with a lessening of inequality in earnings between women and men (Card et al., 2020; Kerrissey & Meyers, 2022).

In principle, unions seek greater egalitarianism in pay structures throughout the economy. For those laboring in very-low-paying jobs, unions desire a "living wage." This typically takes the form of a push for a hike in the minimum wage to a level that is conducive to self-support. Unions have been influential in boosting state minimum wages above the national level and in convincing Congress in 2007 to pass a staggered minimum wage increase. Minimum and living wage campaigns have a desirable secondary effect for unions in government because increasing private sector pay reduces the impetus for privatization of public services.

VI. EFFECTS OF PUBLIC EMPLOYEE UNIONS ON COMPENSATION: METHODOLOGICAL PROBLEMS

Like all research conducted in the social sciences, where laboratory-like conditions cannot usually be approximated, research concerning union effects on public employee compensation suffers from certain methodological shortcomings. Seven specific problems have plagued researchers in this area of investigation:

Measurement error and unexplained variance: almost without exception, multiple regression analyses intended to isolate the relative influence of unionization on wages and benefits have been unable to account for much more than half of the total variation in compensation for the occupational group under consideration. Poor specification and measurement of independent variables appear to be the culprit. The result is that union impacts could be overstated.

Operationalization of "union": some studies have employed measures of unionization that are simply inadequate. For example, many ignore the potential role of nonaffiliated employee organizations or employee groups that do not call themselves unions even though they represent their members in wage and benefit negotiations. The most appropriate measures of unionization are (1) whether there is a contract and (2) the percentage of employees belonging to a union. These data are not easily available.

Unit of analysis: most pay studies routinely aggregate data across states and localities to make broad nationwide conclusions about union effects. State- and city-level results may be confounded by variability in union representation and legal environment. For example, some state or local agencies may engage in bargaining, whereas others may not, and some, as a matter of policy, may consistently pay higher salaries to their employees than what local firms pay their own (Belman & Heywood, 1995). Aggregation of data across governments obscures internal differences in bargaining outcomes. Generally, the study of individual functional areas (e.g., police, sanitation, and social welfare) is recommended, controlling for legal environment (Ichniowski et al., 1989).

Threat effects: employers may raise pay and benefits of nonunion workers to forestall threatened unionization or to prevent morale problems that could result in losing valued employees. Thus, in jurisdictions that experience high levels of union density and collective bargaining, bargaining tends to set market-wide pay and benefit levels, driving up payroll costs for all employers, making union–nonunion comparisons difficult.

Cross-sectional research designs: most compensation studies limit the scope of investigation to a narrow time range, usually a single year. Time-series research designs that attempt to capture the changing union influence over a longer period of time are preferred. This shortcoming primarily is a function of the lack of adequate longitudinal data on public employee unionization.

Neglect of benefits as a dependent variable: the dollar value of benefits should be included as part of a total compensation package if researchers are to depict the full financial impact of public employee unions. Although wages are the most visible aspect of bargaining settlements, benefits can be the most burdensome in the long term, as shown by the underfunded retiree benefits. Indeed, benefits may represent the most significant long-term union influence of all. There is evidence of a tradeoff between pay and benefits when unions participate in determining the compensation package.

Unions tend to favor increases in benefits (or fight harder to maintain existing benefit levels) over pay hikes for several reasons. First, unions reflect the desires of the "median member," who is older, typically more established in a life pattern, and concerned with health-care protection, a pension, and similar benefits (Freeman & Medoff, 1984). Second, there is a public choice argument for public employee benefits. From a political perspective, maximizing benefits over salaries makes sense. Pay hikes are highly visible to taxpayers and easy for them to oppose. Improvements in benefits, while perhaps even more expensive in the long run, provide union members with highly valued rewards that have lower taxpayer visibility (Belman & Heywood, 1991, pp. 112–113; Peng, 2004). Finally, most public workers, whether in a union or not, enjoy certain tax advantages from taking compensation increases in the form of employer-provided benefits. In summary, if benefits are not captured in the research design, union-associated impacts will likely be significantly understated.

The values and political ideology of researchers: economic and social science research should be objective and free of investigator bias, but unfortunately sometimes it is not. For instance, there are at least three possible values or perspectives that researchers may associate with the public employee pay issue. First is equity: should public and private sector employees be paid equally for equal work, whether unions are in the picture or not? The second value is efficiency: should the public sector pay no more than is necessary to attract and retain an adequate supply of workers and consider privatizing all possible activities? The third value is government as the model employer: should public organizations be the standard-bearers for how to remunerate and treat workers fully and fairly by paying high salaries and benefits and offering the best feasible working conditions? How a researcher personally feels about these values or perspectives may influence his or her assumptions, methodology, findings, and conclusions.

VII. EFFECTS OF PUBLIC EMPLOYEE UNIONS ON COMPENSATION: A REVIEW OF THE FINDINGS

Taken together, published scholarly studies on unions and public employee pay indicate that unions have exerted a slight to moderate influence on pay, depending on the methodology employed, state or local function examined, and time period observed. Although compensation impact studies have been relatively few in recent years, basic patterns may be discerned over time.

A. Salary and Wages

Most research on the effects of union activity on public employee salaries and benefits uses a traditional economic approach. Public sector labor supply and demand equations are specified to "solve" the wage and/or benefits rate of public workers while statistically controlling for various nonunion influences. Multiple regression analysis is the most common statistical technique. Through multiple regression procedures, input and decision process variables (such as socioeconomic characteristics of the labor market and government structure, respectively) are held constant, permitting the isolation of any specific union-related impacts on pay.

Teachers: most of the early studies on public employee union influence were concerned with the occupational category that continues to receive the bulk of scholarly attention—K–12 classroom teachers. It is understandable that public education has dominated scholarly interest in this field of research. About one half of all state and local government employees work in public education, and a majority of these workers are classroom teachers. Their sheer numbers, magnified by aggressive political and organizing activities, parental concern, and public visibility, ensure that teachers are frequently in the spotlight.

The results of union and teacher compensation studies have been inconsistent. Overall, teacher salaries barely kept pace with the cost of living in the 1990s and rose less than wages for other full-time employees. Generally speaking, researchers who have aggregated their data at the state level have not found a significant association between unionization and teachers' salaries. Those who have examined data at the school district level have uncovered statistically significant associations between unionization and teacher pay. The mean wage effect of teacher unions calculated by averaging available research findings was approximately 5% during the 1960s and 7% in the 1970s–1990s, indicating a union advantage varying from 1.0% to 28.8% of base pay (Delaney, 1988; Freeman & Valletta, 1988; Winters, 2011). Most of the research finds that the greatest salary advantage accrues to senior teachers, who presumably enjoy greater bargaining power than less experienced teachers.

Unfortunately, none of these earlier studies attempted to account for the non-salary aspects of teachers' earnings and their relationship to unionization. More recent work takes these other variables into account. For example, Frandsen (2016) finds that laws mandating collective bargaining increased unionization in the teaching occupation but had little effect on pay and benefits. A subsequent study by Brunner and Ju (2019) found that mandatory collective bargaining laws increased wages for state and local government employees by about five to eight percentage points, and for teachers alone the increase was ten percentage points.

McGee and Winters (2017) examine both salary and retirement compensation for teachers in Philadelphia and New York. The authors find that the traditional final-average-salary defined benefit pensions (FASDB) greatly increase the total compensation premium for more experienced teachers. Moreover, they contend that teachers receive the experience premiums in the absence of evidence of significant differences in quality of teaching between less and more experienced teachers.

Pay for teacher performance has become a highly controversial issue. Such merit pay approaches encompass individual bonuses or base pay increases, special pay for teachers in high-demand subjects such as math or biology, statewide teacher bonuses, and "combat pay" for teaching in less desirable schools (especially those in high-crime areas) (Goldhaber et al., 2010). Although pay for performance sounds like a sensible means for encouraging high performance and dedication on the part of teachers, controversy arises over exactly how to measure these qualities and who should be responsible for doing the assessment. What factors should be taken into account: student scores on standardized exams or overall school improvement? Should the principal be in charge of assessment and acting on the results, or a peer group of teachers? What pay increment represents a meaningful raise or bonus?

Research has cast doubt on the effectiveness of teacher pay for performance (Podgursky & Springer, 2007). Although teacher unions have been vehemently opposed to merit pay plans, public and political pressure to improve public education has forced the American Federation of Teachers and the National Education Association to assume a more cooperative stance. As a result, teacher pay experiments are under way in most states.

For example, one recent study focused on changes in teacher compensation in Wisconsin after the passage of Act 10, in June 2011 (Biasi, 2021). Specifically, Act 10 prohibited collective bargaining over teacher salary schedules. In response, many districts replaced seniority-based pay schedules with flexible pay schedules that allowed for variations among teachers with similar years of service and credentials. Biasi (2021) found that the flexible pay plans increased pay for teachers with fewer years of experience and without graduate degrees. The new pay system also raised the quality of teachers in flexible pay districts (due to the arrival of high-quality teachers from other districts). Pham et al. (2021) found that the effect of salary incentives, such as merit pay, vary across subjects and school levels. In addition, they concluded that not all pay for performance plans motivate teachers. In some instances, merit pay may improve recruitment and retention, but once the incentives end, teachers are likely to seek higher pay elsewhere.

College and university faculty: early faculty studies matched unionized institutions with nonunion institutions with similar characteristics and found relatively modest salary and benefits advantages for unions during the late 1960s to mid-1970s (Birnbaum, 1974; Morgan & Kearney, 1977). In percentage terms, the salary advantage for organized faculty ranged from 11% in 1970–1971 (Freeman, 1978) to only 2% in 1977 (Barbezat, 1989). Apparently, however, the union-related advantage for faculty leveled off in later years (Marshall, 1979; Guthrie-Morse et al., 1981), and unions may even have been a net detriment to faculty salaries since the 1980s in doctoral and research institutions (Hendrick et al., 2010; Hu & Leslie, 1982; Kesselring, 1991; Ashraf, 1997; Ashraf & Williams, 2008). However, collective bargaining appears to be more favorable for community college faculty, in a range of 2%–6% (Ashraf, 1998; Henson et al., 2012). A more recent review of the literature finds that few studies have been able to identify the long-term influence of collective bargaining on faculty compensation. The authors conclude that the impact of unionization on salaries remains unclear (Julius & DiGiovanni, 2019).

A post-pandemic analysis of higher education faculty salaries overall shows that salaries increased by an average of 4% from 2021 to 2023, but over the same period inflation was nearly 6%. The end result was a loss in purchasing power. Moreover, faculty teaching in community colleges earned roughly 75 cents on the dollar compared to faculty in research institutions. Similarly, for faculty in liberal arts and comprehensive institutions wages ranged from 78 to 81 cents on the dollar compared to the wages earned by faculty at research institutions (NEA, 2024).

Past research indicates that senior tenured faculty benefits more from unionization than junior faculty (mostly from across-the-board raises instead of merit-based pay raises) (Barbezat, 1989). Also, unionized faculty tends to enjoy superior benefits in comparison with their nonunion colleagues (Guthrie-Morse et al., 1981). More recent research finds that salary increases are often offset with reductions in employment. For example, a 10% raise in salary is associated with a 1.75% decline in employment for full time lecturers, a 2.6% decline for assistant professors, and a 1.4% decline for associate and full professors (Zhang et al., 2021). Furthermore, the researchers find that the part-time faculty unions advocate for expanding the ranks of part-time faculty members, thereby limiting the growth of full-time teaching faculty (Zhang et al., 2021). The precarious financial situation for colleges and universities has led to an increasing reliance on contingent workers. Taken together, these factors make it difficult to discern the impact of union status on college and university faculty.

Police officers: according to published research, organized police have experienced a salary advantage from 4% to 8%, which peaked around 1977 and has declined since (Ehrenberg & Goldstein, 1975; Hall & Vanderporten, 1977; Kearney & Morgan, 1980a, 1980b; Feuille & Delaney, 1986; Trejo, 1991; Chandler & Gely, 1995). One study suggests that police unions temporarily force up salaries, but the threat effect pulls pay to the same level in nonunion police departments functioning within the same state legal environment (Ichniowski et al., 1989).

More recent research shows that unions increase the average starting salary for officers, and that salary supplements improve with longer union presence (Doerner & Doerner, 2010). Frandsen (2016) demonstrates that collective bargaining increases police officers' hourly wages by 7%. It also significantly reduces the workweek. Brunner and Ju (2019) determine that collective bargaining increases the wages of police officers by 12%.

Unionized police do appear to hold an advantage with respect to benefits. A national study of cities of 25,000 and above for the 1981–1984 period found a "very large and strongly positive association" between police bargaining and retirement and insurance benefits (Feuille et al., 1985; Hunter & Rankin, 1988). Doerner and Doerner (2010) found that unionization results in better buy-back policies for unused leave. Presumably, the union advantage persists today.

Firefighters: early research on firefighter unionization identified a wage advantage of 2%–18%, averaging about 8% (Ashenfelter, 1971; Ehrenberg, 1972; Smith & Lyons, 1980; Trejo, 1991). In general, both police and firefighters have more generous defined benefit pensions and retiree health-care coverage. More recently, Frandsen (2016) found that collective bargaining for firefighters yields an hourly wage premium of 10%–15%. In a similar study. Brunner and Ju (2019), that collective bargaining yielded an 8% wage premium for firefighters.

Pension benefit generosity is roughly 25% greater for police and firefighters than it is for other government employees (Aubry & Wandrei, 2020a). The average costs of retiree health care benefits for police and firefighters are also substantially higher than they are for other public employees in part due to both the premium subsidy and the longer period of coverage prior to Medicare eligibility.

Public employees in both occupations are eligible to retire at younger ages and the benefits are paid for longer periods of time (Aubry & Wandrei, 2020a).

Other municipal employees: an assortment of research efforts has investigated the union compensation effects of other local government workers, including sanitation: 0%–17% (Karper & Meckstroth, 1976; Chandler,1995; Hoover & Peoples, 2003); hospital employees: 8%–12% (Feldman & Scheffler, 1982); and secretaries: 14% (Gomez-Mejia & Balkin, 1984). Inclusive studies of city and county workers across various functions find that bargaining increases monthly payroll by 8.5% (Zax, 1989) and hourly compensation by 5.6% (Zax, 1988). "Common function" employees such as blue-collar and clerical workers experience an average positive impact from unions of 8%–10% (Freund, 1974; Ehrenberg & Goldstein, 1975; Belman et al., 1997).

State employees: state government has received little attention from scholars, except for higher education. One study (Kearney & Morgan, 1980b) of various categories of state employees across the United States found that unions captured a combined salary and benefit gain of approximately 4% for their members. Research using 1991 data indicates that unionized state employees enjoy a wage premium of about 7% over nonunion workers (Belman et al., 1997; Kearney, 2003). Brunner and Ju (2019) find that wages for state and local employees are 5%–8% higher in states with mandatory collective bargaining laws. However, the authors focus solely on wages, not on total compensation.

In conclusion, unions are associated with higher wages and benefits in state and local governments, but the magnitude of the impact varies widely over time, function, and study methodology. The best estimate of an overall union effect is probably 5%–6%, which is well below the 10%–15% union compensation advantage associated with the private sector. However, the dearth of research on union wage effects in the 2000s means that one should exercise caution in assuming that the union-associated pay differential continues today.

B. Benefits

Benefits typically make up 20%–40% of the total compensation package in government, averaging 38% in 2023 (compared to an average of 29.6% of the total compensation package for private sector workers) (U.S. Bureau of Labor Statistics, 2024). The quantity and quality of benefits vary considerably across states, localities, and employee functions. The most costly are defined benefit pension systems and health-care insurance. Unfortunately, benefits information is very difficult to collect, standardize, and operationalize. In addition, research is complicated by the lag between the time when benefits increases are won and the time when their effects become measurable. The sheer variety of potential benefits also defies precise measurement and comparison (Kearney, 2003). They include the following:

1 Insurance (medical, mental health, dental, hearing, vision, disability, life, malpractice, workers' compensation, unemployment compensation, and spousal or partner insurance)
2 Leave (sick, vacation, holiday, education, military, jury duty, voting, family, maternity, paternity, union business, funeral, and personal)
3 Retirement (pensions, social security, and optional and supplemental retirement plans)
4 Survivor's benefits
5 Severance pay
6 Employee development (tuition reimbursement, book or software allowances, and time off for education and training)
7 Employee assistance programs and wellness programs
8 Dependent and elder care
9 Longevity pay
10 Premium pay (emergency overtime, call-in and callback pay, police court time, compensatory time, shift differentials, standby time, holidays, and hazardous duty)
11 Miscellaneous (meals, parking fees, professional travel expenses, moving expense, uniform allowance, automobile allowance, legal services, and retirement counseling)

As noted, retirement and health-care benefits are the most significant from a public employer's cost standpoint. This is particularly true for police officers and firefighters whose pensions typically commence after only 20 years on the job and who may experience extended job-related health-care problems. Research (Kearney, 2003) finds that state employee unionization pushes up the cost of retirement and retiree dependent health care to a statistically significant level. Frandsen and Webb (2020) note that public employee retirement benefits have increased substantially over the past five decades. Moreover, laws mandating collective bargaining in the public sector have had a sizeable impact on pension generosity. That is, roughly \$11.6 billion in annual state and local government pension payments to retirees (based on 2008 data) may be attributed to collective bargaining rights. Similarly, approximately \$9.4 billion in annual state and local government contributions to pension systems may be attributed to collective bargaining rights (Frandsen & Webb, 2020).

Retirement payments typically amount to 50%–100% of the employee's final salary figures, with annual adjustments for cost of living. The burden on government revenues can become substantial. As of 2022, state and local governments sponsored over 4,000 pension plans. Most (86%) of state and local government employees had access to a defined benefit (DB) pension plan in 2022, and most of those workers participated in the DB pension plans. In many cases these plans include COLAs (Urban Institute, n.d.).

At the same time, a growing number of states and localities are moving away from expensive DB plans (in which the government funds the full cost of pensions, which are based on years of work experience and age) to defined contribution (DC) plans (in which the pension recipient has a proportion of his or her salary deducted and invested in retirement plan choices along with a contribution by the employer) or to hybrid plans. The hybrid plans combine traditional DB plans with DC plans. However, with the hybrid plans the DB portion is less generous than it is with standalone DB plans. The key driver for the shift to alternative plans is cost savings. Employer contributions for the DC and hybrid plans are generally lower than they are for traditional DB plans. However, the cost savings are gradual because the alternative plans are typically offered to new employees. Staes and local governments face legal constraints in changing future benefits for existing workers (Aubry & Wandrei, 2020b).

Bargaining over public employee pension funds may include how the funds are invested. Traditionally, investment decisions concerning pension funds are handled by the employer and its investment advisors. But unions argue that the trillions of dollars in public employee pension fund assets represent deferred compensation and therefore should be controlled by public workers or their representatives, not by management. In addition, unions prefer investment policies that favor in-state firms and firms with pro-union policies. And, in some cases, they want pension fund assets to be invested to advance certain social and political objectives.

A benefit undergoing rapid reconfiguration today is employee and retiree health-care insurance. Spiraling health-care costs have damaged employers' budgets and employee pocketbooks. The average cost of state health-care plans has been growing annually in double digits. Health-care plans have become a major flash point in collective bargaining as employers, in cost-cutting moves, are adopting managed care plans and other arrangements that require larger financial contributions from employees but sometimes permit fewer health-care options.

C. Evaluating the Union Effect on Wages and Benefits

A review of the literature concludes that unions boost wages and benefits in government. The impact varies along dimensions of time, space, methodology, and function in response to numerous and highly variable social, economic, and political factors. The union compensation impact, which has averaged 5%–6% for salaries and perhaps even more for the dollar cost of benefits, is much less than the impact attributed to private sector unions. Nonetheless, the effects are strongly felt in states and localities, which are much more labor intensive than most private enterprises. Considering, for example, that if 50%–75% of a school district's revenues are dedicated to teacher pay, a 6% or 8% salary increase exacts a substantial toll on the school budget. Firms, especially large ones, can usually enhance efficiencies or pass along salary and benefit hikes to the consumers of their goods and services. Governments have fewer options for funding the price of a new labor agreement.

Clearly, public sector constraints do help limit union-inspired employee compensation gains. These constraints are powerful, even though they differ in nature from the private sector market constraints of competition, profits, and product prices. In government, political and economic forces help contain union demands. Budgets must be adopted, taxes levied, bonds issued, and user fees imposed within a context of participatory democracy.

Citizens' groups, particularly those with an antitax bent, pay attention to wage and benefit settlements, and look over the shoulders of responsible elected officials Citizen oversight behavior helps stiffen the backbone of public officials during contract negotiations and reduces the scope of union demands. A patently equitable compensation settlement may proceed relatively unmolested, with little media or public attention. Citizen review is tacit in such instances. When bargaining outcomes appear to be excessive, the media and general public may respond with outrage. A bond issue or tax proposal may go down to defeat at polling places, or an aroused electorate may defeat incumbent politicians running for reelection.

In the aftermath of the Great Recession, the vitriol of political conservatives directed toward governments and their workers, exacerbated by the resistance of fiscal conservatives to public spending, had turned the tables against generous wage and benefit settlements. As indicated earlier, benefits were a special target of state and local governments. Among state actions regarding public compensation were the following:

- Washington's 54,000 state employees suffered a 3% salary reduction over 2 years and a hike in health insurance contributions
- Ohio increased pension contribution rates and the minimum retirement age
- West Virginia eliminated health insurance premium funding for new workers
- New York raised the minimum retirement age from 55 to 62 years, increased employee pension contribution rates, and extended pension vesting to 10 years of service

VIII. RESPONDING TO PUBLIC SECTOR COMPENSATION COST INCREASES

Though wage and benefit increases have been attenuated since the onslaught of the Great Recession, they cannot be entirely contained, and funds must be set aside to pay the bills. Within a context of limited competition or substitutability for government services and general fiscal austerity, public managers have a variety of options available to them:

1 Raise taxes. Local property taxes can usually be increased without a referendum. State or local sales or income tax hikes must receive voter or legislative approval. Elected officials, of course, rarely favor the option of

a tax increase and usually exhaust all other remedies first. Some state laws preclude tax increases when statutory taxing or spending limits have been reached

2 Increase other revenues. User fees or charges may be raised to cover compensation awards within a particular government function. For example, water rates, trash collection fees, recreation charges, or sewer charges can be hiked. This option may be subject to state law or local ordinance, and, like a tax increase, it can be highly visible and subject to vehement citizen resistance
3 Borrow the necessary funds. Bonds or short-term notes may be issued and sold, with the proceeds diverted to worker payrolls. A second option is to borrow from employee pension funds. Restrictive legislation, however, may prohibit borrowing and, in principle, borrowing to pay operating costs is a bad idea
4 Cut back elsewhere in government spending. This may take the form of an across-the-board reduction in all departmental appropriations or more selective reductions
5 Divert capital expenditure allocations to personnel costs. Capital construction or purchasing projects may be postponed or eliminated so that wage and benefit settlements can be honored
6 Divert intergovernmental revenues. State and local jurisdictions may be able to channel grant-in-aid funds to meet some personnel costs
7 Mandate a hiring freeze. Unfilled positions may remain unfunded, with further savings realized through attrition. This is often the first step taken to address budget shortfalls
8 Impose layoffs. Reductions in force may be implemented across the board or by department, agency, or program. Camden, New Jersey, axed almost half of its police department employees and one-third of its firefighters in 2011
9 Offer a "golden handshake." Provide incentives for early retirement. Florida, Wisconsin, Ohio, New York, and other states did so in 2010–2012
10 Adopt a temporary attrition policy. Vacated positions will not be filled until the budget is in better shape
11 Furlough employees by placing them on temporary, unpaid leave
12 Reduce the quantity or quality of services. For instance, trash can be collected once per week rather than twice weekly (quantity), or leaf and yard trash pickup can be eliminated (quality)
13 Cut working hours and reduce wages proportionately. Compensatory time off may be substituted for overtime
14 Adopt labor-saving technology. Technology is available in functions such as trash collection (one-person trucks), human resource management functions (e.g., payroll processing), and other services

15 Contract out (outsource) services to other jurisdictions or to private firms. Water, engineering, fire protection, and sanitation are good candidates for this strategy
16 Consolidate existing functions. Some financially pressed local governments have consolidated police and fire functions into a public safety department. Other alternatives exist as well
17 Refuse to fund negotiated payroll or benefit increases, making the argument of inability to pay. Collective bargaining laws in at least 11 states offer this final option to public employers. For example, the Iowa law provides, "No collective bargaining agreement or arbitrator's decision shall be valid or enforceable if its implementation would be inconsistent with any statutory limitation on the public employer's funds, spending, or budget or would substantially impair or limit the performance of any statutory duty by the public employer." The efficacy of this strategy may be questioned, however, because courts generally have affirmed the obligation of public employers to implement agreed-on compensation increases
18 Reopen labor contracts and negotiate union givebacks
19 Declare bankruptcy. When a state or local government is insolvent, it can, in theory, file for protection under Chapter 9 of Title II of the Federal Bankruptcy Code. As noted earlier, several local governments took this option in the aftermath of the Great Recession
20 Engage in productivity bargaining and/or a gainsharing program to reap financial savings

IX. PRODUCTIVITY BARGAINING (GAINSHARING)

Productivity bargaining involves the "negotiation and implementation of formal collective bargaining agreements which stipulate changes in work rules and practices with the objective of achieving increased productivity and reciprocal worker gains" (Newland, 1972, p. 807). Thus, employee rewards are linked to increases in productivity through the bargaining process. Collective bargaining is not a prerequisite for collaborative productivity enhancements. Dollar savings may also be captured through productivity improvements or changes in work procedures agreed on by labor–management committees or partnerships.

In the United States, productivity bargaining has been attempted within a variety of industrial concerns, including meatpacking, steel, railroads, and longshoring. In government, the experience is still limited to a relatively small number of jurisdictions, primarily municipalities.

Some jurisdictions have had success with work rule "buyouts." These involve a payment of money (for bonuses) or other financial inducements by management to the bargaining unit in return for union acceptance of changes in work rules that hinder productivity. The parties' agreement is formalized in the collective bargaining contract. Work rules that might be changed include work scheduling, work processes, minimum number of employees on a crew, or any previous understandings or agreements that tend to obstruct the introduction of labor-saving technologies and approaches.

"Gainsharing" (essentially another name for productivity bargaining) refers to a financial incentive system in which a financial bonus is offered for measurable increases in productivity attributable to extra efforts by employees. Here, management and the union work together in identifying barriers to productivity and implementing changes that enhance productivity. Outcomes are measured and the monetary savings that ensue are shared.

Gainsharing has been adopted in various forms in state and local governments. Examples include the following:

Detroit, Michigan: a productivity bonus was granted to sanitation workers based on savings from attrition and reductions in overtime pay.

New York City: sanitation workers agreed to use one-person trucks and run longer collection routes in exchange for a 17% raise over 4.5 years.

New Rochelle, New York: a gainsharing program was implemented in which productivity gains were used to help fund wage increases. The sanitation department reduced crew size from four employees per truck to three through attrition.

Indianapolis, Indiana: in collaboration with AFSCME Council 62, gainsharing programs were implemented in the public works department.

Productivity or gainsharing savings may be paid out to workers on a one-time basis as a cash bonus, used to augment their salaries, or deferred into a shared savings plan for retirement. Most productivity provisions require a defined split of savings (e.g., 50%) between management and labor. Some of the productivity bargaining experiences have achieved a measure of success in cost savings and/or quality of service improvements. Most productivity or gainsharing experiments, however, have been relatively short lived, lasting through a single collective bargaining contract. And there have been several reports of embarrassing failure for productivity bargaining, especially from management's perspective, where the agreement had unintended negative consequences.

To succeed, productivity and gainsharing programs require strong employer and union leadership and consistent oversight, widespread employee involvement, accurate measurement of service outputs, mutual trust and respect, training in interest-based problem solving, and win–win expectations (Holzer, 1988; Matzer, 1988, pp. 185–186; Gill, 2009). Where such conditions do not exist, productivity improvement programs can collapse. In Detroit, for instance, problems arose in determining who was to receive productivity bonuses besides the sanitation workers on trucks. Dispatchers, clerical employees, and supervisors also wanted a piece of the action. In other jurisdictions, lack of commitment by key participants and difficulty in negotiating the terms of the productivity bargaining agreement and in sustaining the productivity efforts have led to a loss of interest. Additional problems include the natural resistance of management and union bureaucracies to change, difficulties in developing accurate and meaningful standards for measuring tradeoffs between service efficiency (quantity) and effectiveness (quality), failure to link productivity bargaining/gainsharing with overall program goals or agency mission, distrust between parties, and interference by elected officials.

Ironically, a serious obstacle to meaningful productivity gains is cost. It often takes money to save money. For example, substantial productivity gains may ensue from technology enhancements and improved data collection, both of which require additional expenditures. Adding, rather than reducing, staff may enhance productivity (e.g., purchasing a new crime-fighting technology such as COMPSTAT and hiring staff to operate it). Productivity, especially in government, becomes a popular buzzword when money is tight, and retrenchment is under way. Under these conditions, there is less money for productivity enhancements such as capital or human resource investments or financial incentives.

More recent research on productivity bargaining/gainsharing has been influenced by the spread of new public management (NPM), with its emphasis on performance, efficiency, and effectiveness. Kalleberg et al. (2006) hypothesized that incentive programs such as gainsharing and bonuses would have less appeal in the public sector where the focus is on mission, not on profits. Instead, the authors found that public sector organizations were more amenable to high performance work systems (HPWS) that involved teams, multiskilling, and participatory decision making and that provided opportunities to advance the organizations' mission. Similarly, Knies and Leisink (2018) contend that public organizations are more likely to implement practices that align public service motivation with the mission of the organization, while addressing the challenges of limited managerial discretion and bureaucratic red tape. The promise of HPWS in the public sector deserves further attention and experimentation. The popularity of interest-based negotiations can promote such initiatives. Almost everyone desires and benefits from improved government performance. Bargaining over HPWS offers a means of containing government costs by directly involving employees who are most knowledgeable about service provision problems, thereby permitting them to become a part of the solution.

X. MONETARY IMPACTS OF FEDERAL EMPLOYEE UNIONS

The environment surrounding unions and pay determination in federal employment is quite different from the situation prevalent in state and local governments. Most relationships between unions and federal agencies are well structured, and compensation determination is generally unilateral.

The federal government, in theory, could pursue one of several possible strategies in setting wages and benefits for its employees. As a conservative approach, it could seek to award its workers as little as possible, assuming that government employment is either a privilege or not difficult work and, above all, that the taxpayer should be protected from the unnecessary burden of high federal employee wages and benefits. A far different strategy would be to assume the role of a model employer, awarding above average salaries and benefits to its workers as a model for other employers. A middle-of-the-road approach, the one long accepted in federal employment, is to apply the principle of prevailing wage.

Unlike in state and local governments, the prevailing wage principle has a long formalized role in federal compensation determination. The principle was first established through statute by Congress for federal navy yard workers during the Civil War. It was extended to employees of the U.S. Government Printing Office in 1924 by the Kiess Act, to Tennessee Valley Authority (TVA) workers by the Tennessee Valley Authority Act of 1933, and to other federal employees by the Classification Acts of 1923 and 1949. However, the prevailing wage principle was not explicitly applied to nonindustrial (classified) employees until the passage of the Salary Reform Act of 1962, which established that civil service salaries should be comparable to those of similar workers in the private sector. The Federal Pay Comparability Act of 1970 reaffirmed this principle and delegated authority to the executive branch to make periodic adjustments to the pay of federal schedule, foreign service, and other federal employees to establish comparability with private sector workers. These acts were major steps in coordinating federal pay setting.

Procedures for determining the prevailing—or comparable—wage vary by agency and by type of employee. They are established through collective bargaining in TVA, by conference in the Government Printing Office, by the U.S. Bureau of Labor Statistics and the President's Pay Agent for white-collar (General Schedule [GS]) workers, and by wage boards for blue-collar employees. There are separate pay systems for blue-collar (wage board) workers, GS employees, the National Security Personnel System, the Foreign Service, the Veterans Health Administration, the Senior Executive Service, the Postal Service, administrative law judges, air traffic controllers, and senior-level scientific and professional positions. In general, positions are compared based on the similarity of functions performed; knowledge, skills, and abilities (KSAs); supervisory responsibility; and related factors.

The three largest categories of employees for purposes of pay are the federal wage system (FWS), classified civil service, and collective bargaining system.

A. Federal Wage System

Approximately 192,455 federal hourly blue-collar workers in federal civilian service are covered by the FWS as of 2023 (U.S. Government Accountability Office

(GAO), 2024). Specifically excluded are agencies exempt from the general classification and pay laws, including the TVA and the National Security Agency. Although the FWS retains final authority for pay determination, federal unions have substantial rights of participation. The FWS is administered by the Office of Personnel Management (OPM). The organizational structure consists of a National Wage Policy Committee of 11 members, equally divided between management of federal agencies and union representatives. The director of OPM serves as the odd member of the committee, receiving policy recommendations regarding the FWS.

The OPM coordinates wages regionally through designating a "lead agency" within local wage areas. This lead agency, typically the largest federal employer in the area, administers local wage surveys and sets pay schedules for all agencies within its geographic area, working with the Bureau of Labor Statistics when feasible. Based on the survey results, wages may be adjusted several times during the fiscal year. FWS wage rates and increases are based on position classification. There are 15 grades, each with five steps. Employees move up a step and receive a 4% increase as they meet time and performance standards. Three wage rate schedules apply: wage grade (nonsupervisory workers), wage leaders ("leader–employee"), and wage supervisor (supervisory employees).

Union participation is achieved in local wage areas through an agency wage committee consisting of two union members, two management members, and a chairperson appointed by the lead agency. The agency wage committee advises the lead agency on pay determination procedures. Further union participation occurs through local wage survey committees, which conduct pay scale surveys on private industrial job categories in more than 125 localities in the United States.

The right to participate in wage setting through the prevailing pay principle is an important one for federal unions that are precluded from formal bargaining over wages and benefits. Determination of the prevailing rate of pay for any particular occupation is a rather inexact undertaking that is greatly influenced by the research methodology, techniques used to gather and present wage data, characteristics of the firms selected for comparability purposes, and individuals collecting the data. Strong union participation can potentially serve as a powerful substitute for formal collective bargaining over wages.

However, blue-collar wage increases have been severely restricted by Congress during the past several decades. In January 2021, President Biden issued an E.O. 14003 directing OPM to implement a $15 minimum wage for FWS and GS employees stationed in the U.S. In January 2022, OPM issued specific guidelines for how agencies should adjust wage rates. The policy applies to all executive branch agencies except the U.S. Postal Service and the Postal Regulatory Commission. The changes are expected to impact roughly 67,000 employees (U.S. OPM, 2022). OPM and the Department of Defense have noted that the FWS wage schedule rates in 2023 do not align with prevailing wage rates in some areas. The wage schedule falls below market rates in some areas and rises above market rates in others. These variations are due in part to the $15 minimum wage (U.S. GAO, 2024).

B. Classified Civil Service

About 1.5 million classified federal employees are covered under the GS wage system, approximately half of total federal civilian employment (U.S. GAO, 2024). These white-collar workers are placed in a series of pay grades (GS-1 to GS-15), each with a salary range and 10 salary steps. Under the Federal Pay Comparability Act of 1970, the Federal (or President's) Pay Agent, consisting of the secretary of labor and the directors of the OPM and the Office of Management and Budget, made a GS pay increase recommendation to the president each year based on Bureau of Labor Statistics' surveys of comparable private sector wages. This recommendation took effect unless the president put forward an alternative and justified it "because of national emergency or economic conditions affecting the general welfare." Congress then had 30 days to overturn the presidential proposal by joint resolution; otherwise, it was implemented automatically.

However, not a single president accepted the pay agent's recommendation, and Congress overrode the president's pay alternative only twice—in 1984, changing the increase from Reagan's 3.5% to 4%, and in 1990, from George H. W. Bush's 3.5% to 4.1%—so that by 1990 the cumulative underpayment of GS workers had amounted to approximately 300% (President's Pay Agent, 1990). The pay disparity continues to be most pronounced for federal employees living in large metropolitan areas with high costs of living. For example, in 2023 it was 99.2% in the San Jose-San Francisco-Oakland area (President's Pay Agent, 2024).

Recruitment and retention problems associated with this sizeable pay inequity were extensively documented by the OPM, the Merit Systems Protection Board, and various federal agencies. Larger influential agencies began appealing to Congress for special pay systems for their employees, raising the distinct possibility of a return to a balkanized federal pay structure. Congress recognized and attempted to address this inequitable situation through the Federal Employees Pay Comparability Act (FEPCA) of 1990.

Under FEPCA GS employees were to receive pay increases matching the average annual salary gains in the private sector in each major geographic area beginning in 1992. Starting in 1994 and continuing for 9 years, extra pay increases were to be awarded to GS employees in high-cost-of-living metropolitan areas until their pay reached 95% of local wage levels. However, because federal wages everywhere continued to fall further behind wages in business, the President's Pay Agent divided the nation into 32 locality pay areas. The Bureau of Labor Statistics surveys employers on 25 occupations in each geographic area.

All of this activity has had a limited impact because the pay agent's recommendations have often been rejected. The locality pay allowed under FEPCA is substantial enough to reduce disparities, but no president since 1994 has approved the fully authorized amount (Friedman, 2024). Over the period of 2011 to 2015, private sector wages increased by an average of 1.9% per year. However, elected officials approved wage increases for federal employees that were, on average, less than half a percent per year during this period (Congressional Budget Office (CBO), 2024). Wage increases for federal employees continued to fall below wage growth in the private sector for most years between 20016 to 2022. Surprisingly, lawmakers fully implemented the wage increase specified by FEPCA in 2020 and 2022 (CBO, 2024). Nevertheless, the federal pay disparity with the private sector remains substantial, according to the President's Pay Agent. The full pay disparities for basic GS payroll averaged 54.23% in 2022. When locality pay is considered, the pay disparity in 2022 was 24.09% (President's Pay Agent, 2024).

Overall, federal workers tend to be older, have higher levels of education, and clustered in professional occupations. Using a human capital approach analyzing wages and total compensation, a slightly different picture emerges. When controlling for education levels, in 2022 federal employees with a high school education or less earned a 17% wage premium over their counterparts in the private sector. On average, federal workers with a bachelor's degree earned 10% less than their peers in the private sector. Climbing up the educational ladder, federal employees with a professional degree or a doctorate earned 29% less on average than similarly situated private sector employees (CBO, 2024).

When the cost of benefits is taken into account, the picture shifts further. The average cost of benefits for federal employees across all levels of education in 2022 was approximately 43% higher than it was for similarly situated private sector employees. When examining total compensation (wages and benefits) there are variations across education levels. Total compensation for federal employees with a high school education or less in 2022 was 40% higher on average than it was for their counterparts in the private sector. Total compensation for federal workers with a bachelor's degree was 5% higher than it was for private sector workers with the same level of education. The disparity was more substantial and in the opposite direction for highly educated federal employees. That is, total compensation costs for federal employees with a professional degree or a doctorate in 2022 were 22% lower than those for similar private sector employees (CBO, 2024).

C. Collective Bargaining System

Several groups of federal workers set their wages through collective bargaining patterned on the private sector National Labor Relations Act model. The largest groups are the Bonneville Power Administration, the TVA, and the Postal Service. These groups are discussed in the following paragraphs.

Collective bargaining in the TVA developed shortly after Congress established the authority in 1933. Due to flexible enabling legislation, the TVA operates virtually autonomously in the area of labor relations, subject only to merit and efficiency requirements for employee hiring and promotion and a ban on political considerations in personnel actions. As a consequence of a progressive management attitude toward labor and the presence of strong craft unions in the public utility industry, the prevailing rate principle was applied very early in setting wages. By 1940 a formal contract was signed between the TVA and a craft union.

Today, wages and benefits are the subject of bargaining for both blue- and white-collar TVA workers. As the result of generous calculation of the prevailing wage, compensation levels at TVA exceed those generally prevailing in the region. However, economic downturns and a redefinition of agency mission have recently prompted hard bargaining by management, resulting in union pay concessions and a significant reduction in force.

Collective bargaining arrived in the Postal Service with the passage of the Postal Reorganization Act of 1970, which abolished the 181-year-old Post Office Department and created the Postal Service as an independent entity within the executive branch. For the first time, postal unions were allowed to negotiate wages and benefits. The various postal unions have always been successful lobbyists, using strong organizations and nationwide memberships to encourage Congress to award high postal employee pay and benefits. The strongest evidence of success followed the postal strike of 1970. As a price for settling the strike, postal unions offered their support for the Postal Reorganization Act. They received substantial pay increases, full bargaining rights over future pay determinations, and a formal comparative wage policy.

Wage and benefit gains for Postal Service employees have been consistently higher under collective bargaining than under previous arrangements. As noted earlier, postal workers also appear to be paid substantially more than comparable private sector employees. Nevertheless, severe budget problems year after year have resulted in many postal workers taking early retirement. Total postal employment plummeted from 787,000 in 2000 to about 525,469 in 2023 (U.S. Postal Service, 2024).

Air traffic controllers have navigated a stormy sky. Several years after the morbid death of their union predecessor, the Professional Air Traffic Controllers Organization, air traffic controllers organized a new union called the National Air Traffic Controllers Association (NATCA). In August 1998, NATCA signed a contract with the Federal Aviation Administration (FAA) that won its 14,300 members $200 million in salary increases and a staffing reorganization that significantly reduced the ratio of supervisors to controllers (Walters, 1999). Air traffic controllers received the right to bargain over pay in an amendment to the FAA's 1996 appropriation bill that exempted the agency from Civil Service Reform Act restrictions on bargaining over wages and benefits.

Thus, union participation in federal wage setting varies from direct involvement for those engaging in wage and benefit bargaining, to modest involvement for wage system employees, to no direct role for GS employees. Indirect union influence is brought to bear through lobbying activities. Not surprisingly, pay for collective bargaining employees measures up to private sector wages. GS and FWS employees have fared less well. Federal employees and their unions have been looking hopefully toward the possibility of significant restructuring of the federal pay system, including greater agency discretion in setting pay and even a new performance-based pay system.

XI. CONCLUSION

The evidence is sufficiently clear to conclude that public employee unions, especially at the state and local levels, affect budgetary and compensation determination processes. They make budgeting and pay setting highly complex and politicized Unions have driven up total personnel costs in some jurisdictions and pushed up wages and benefits virtually everywhere. However, economic and political constraints help restrain union influence, increasingly so for the past two decades.

In many bargaining jurisdictions, the level of pay increases won in new contracts is somewhat anticlimactic. Silent understandings and cues about what the jurisdiction can afford to pay tend to give the outcome greater predictability. As a consequence, a substantial portion of negotiations today involve nonmonetary benefits and working conditions, which are topics explored in Chapter 7.

CASE STUDY 6.1 THE MERIT PAY DILEMMA

A newly ratified state collective bargaining contract provides for a 3% across-the-board raise for all state employees and a 2% merit increase. The means for distributing the merit raises were left to the discretion of agency heads. At the State Department of Corrections, agency managers met over a period of three weeks before deciding to allow unit heads to allocate the merit raise according to their own best judgments.

You are the chief warden at a medium-security prison just outside the state capital. The largest bargaining unit in your organization consists of corrections officers. All officers will receive the 3% across-the-board pay hike. But how should you distribute the merit increase? A number of alternatives occur to you.

Total payroll for your 60 corrections officers is $2.4 million (average salary is $40,000). The merit pool consists of $48,000. You could distribute the merit pay in percentages of base pay (perhaps in 0.5% increments up to 10% for the top performers), or you could allocate the merit awards in dollar amounts, such as $100 increments, ranging from a low of $100 to a high of perhaps $3,000.

Meanwhile, the union president appears in your office to urge you to distribute the merit pay as 2% across the board with the rest of the annual pay increase. His assessment is that all the guards are fully competent and deserve merit pay. Moreover, this approach would be noncontroversial. He notes that the senior members of the bargaining unit are particularly supportive of his proposal.

The following day, three junior officers schedule an appointment in your office. They state that, in their opinion, the highest performers are the recently hired guards. They offer the observation that the senior guards are by far the highest paid, whereas the less senior officers lag far behind in salary. A true "merit" award based on performance appraisals would be more valid and in accordance with the taxpayers' interests.

Questions

1. What is your view of the state legislature's merit award program? How could it have been better structured?
2. What issues are raised by the merit pay system that you must implement?
3. Develop a plan for distributing the merit pay funds in a manner that you can defend with reasonable comfort.

REFERENCES

AFSCME v. State of Washington. (1983). 578 F. Supp.

Ashenfelter, O. C. (1971, January). The effect of unionization on wages in the public sector: The case of fire fighters. *Industrial and Labor Relations Review*, *24*, 191–202.

Ashraf, J. (1997, Summer). The effects of unions on professors' salaries: The evidence over twenty years. *Journal of Labor Research*, *XXIII*, 339–449.

Ashraf, J. (1998). Collective bargaining and compensation at public junior colleges. *Journal of Collective Negotiations*, *27*(4), 393–399.

Ashraf, J., & Williams, M. F. (2008). The effect of faculty unions on salaries: Some recent evidence. *Journal of Collective Negotiations (Formerly Journal of Collective Negotiations in the Public Sector)*, *32*(2), 141–150.

Aubry, J. P., & Wandrei, K. (2020a, February). *Issue brief: An introduction to police and fire pensions*. Center for State and Local Government Excellence. https://research.missionsq.org/content/media/document/2020/02/policefirepensions2020.pdf

Aubry, J. P., & Wandrei, K. (2020b, April). *Issue brief: Have localities shifted away from traditional defined benefit plans?* Center for State and Local Government Excellence. https://research.missionsq.org/content/media/document/2020/04/local-dc-brief-april-2020.pdf

Aubry, J. P., & Yin, Y. (2023). *Public pension funded levels improve amidst rising interest rates issue in brief* (pp. 23–15). Center for Retirement Research at Boston College. https://crr.bc.edu/wp-content/uploads/2023/07/IB_23-15.pdf

Barbezat, D. A. (1989, April). The effects of collective bargaining on salaries in higher education. *Industrial and Labor Relations Review*, *42*, 443–455.

Belman, D., & Heywood, J. S. (1991, Spring). Direct and indirect effects of unionization and government employment on fringe benefit provision. *Journal of Labor Research*, *XII*, 111–122.

Belman, D., & Heywood, J. S. (1995, Spring). State and local government wage differentials: An intrastate analysis. *Journal of Labor Research*, *XVI*, 187–201.

Belman, D., & Heywood, J. S. (2004). The structure of compensation in the public sector. *Public Finance Review*, *32*(6), 568–587.

Belman, D., Heywood, J. S., & Lund, J. (1997, July). Public sector earnings and the extent of unionization. *Industrial and Labor Relations Review*, *50*, 610.

Bender, K. A., & Heywood, J. S. (2010). *Out of balance? Comparing public and private sector compensation over 20 years*. Center for State & Local Government Excellence. http://slge.org/wp0content/uploads/2011/12/Out-of-Balance_FINAL-REPORT_10-183.pdf

Benecki, S. (1978, May). Municipal expenditure levels and collective bargaining. *Industrial Relations*, *17*, 216–230.

Biasi, B. (2021). The labor market for teachers under different pay schemes. *American Economic Journal: Economic Policy*, *13*(3), 63–102.

Birnbaum, R. (1974, Winter). Unionization and faculty compensation. *Educational Record*, *55*, 29–33.

Blanchflower, D. G., & Bryson, A. (2004, Summer). What effect do unions have on wages now and would Freeman and Medoff be surprised? *Journal of Labor Research*, *25*, 1–31.

Bowman, J. S. (2010). The success of failure: The paradox of performance pay. In *Review of public personnel administration in the public sector (PERL no. 53)*. IPMA.

Brunner, E. J., & Ju, A. (2019). State collective bargaining laws and public-sector pay. *ILR Review*, *72*(2), 480–508.

Card, D., Lemieux, T., & Riddell, W. C. (2020). Unions and wage inequality: The roles of gender, skill and public sector employment. *Canadian Journal of Economics/Revue canadienne d'économique*, *53*(1), 140–173.

Chandler, T. D. (1995, Fall). Sanitation privatization and sanitation employees' wages. *Journal of Labor Research*, 137–153.

Chandler, T. D., & Gely, R. (1995). Protective service unions, political activities and bargaining outcomes. *Journal of Public Administration Research and Theory*, *5*(3), 295–318.

Choudhury, S. (1994, March). New evidence on public sector wage differentials. *Applied Economics*, 259.

Clark, T. N., & Ferguson, L. C. (1983). *City money*. Columbia University Press.

Congressional Budget Office. (2024, April). *Comparing the compensation of federal and private-sector employees in 2022*. https://www.cbo.gov/system/files/2024-04/59970-Compensation.pdf

County of Washington v. Gunther. (1981). http://supreme.justia.com/cases/federal/us/452/161/

Cox, W., & Brunelli, S. A. (1992, February). America's protected class: Why excess public employee compensation is bankrupting the state. *The State Facts*, 1–32.

Delaney, J. T. (1988, Fall). Teachers' collective bargaining outcomes and tradeoffs. *Journal of Labor Research*, *IX*, 363–377.

Doerner, W. M., & Doerner, W. G. (2010). Collective bargaining and job benefits: The case of Florida deputy sheriffs. *Police Quarterly*, *13*(4), 367–386.

Ehrenberg, R. G. (1972). *The demand for state and local government employees: An economic assessment*. Heath.

Ehrenberg, R. G., & Goldstein, G. S. (1975, July). A model of public sector wage determination. *Journal of Urban Economics*, 223–245.

Feldman, R., & Scheffler, R. (1982). The union impact on hospital wages and fringe benefits. *ILR Review*, *35*(2), 196–206.

Feuille, P., & Delaney, J. T. (1986, January). Collective bargaining, interest arbitration, and police salaries. *Industrial and Labor Relations Reviews*, *39*, 228–240.

Feuille, P., Delaney, J. T., & Hendricks, W. (1985, Winter). Police bargaining, arbitration, and fringe benefits. *Journal of Labor Research, VI*, 1–20.

Field, C., & Keller, R. L. (1976, November). How salaries of large cities compare with industry and federal pay. *Monthly Labor Review*, *99*, 23–28.

Fitzpatrick, M. D., & Goda, G. S. (2020, September). The prevalence of COLA adjustments in public sector retirement plans. In *Employer challenges in financing and managing pension plans, an NBER symposium*. https://www.nber.org/sites/default/files/2020-11/NB20-13%20Fitzpatrick%2C%20Goda.pdf

Flammang, J. A. (1986, May). Effective implementation: The case of comparable worth in San Jose. *Policy Studies Review, 5*, 815–837.

Frandsen, B. R. (2016). The effects of collective bargaining rights on public employee compensation: Evidence from teachers, firefighters, and police. *ILR Review*, *69*(1), 84–112.

Frandsen, B. R., & Webb, M. (2020). Public employee pensions and collective bargaining rights: Evidence from state and local government finances. *The Journal of Law, Economics & Policy*, *15*, 163.

Freeman, R. B. (1978). *Should we organize? The effects of faculty unions on academic compensation. Working paper no. 301*. National Bureau of Economic Research.

Freeman, R. B., & Medoff, J. L. (1984). *What do unions do?* Basic.

Freeman, R. B., & Valletta, R. G. (1988). The effects of public sector labor laws on labor market institutions and outcomes. In R. B. Freeman & C. Ichniowski (Eds.), *When public sector workers unionize* (pp. 81–106). University of Chicago Press.

Freund, J. L. (1974, April). Market and union influences on municipal employee wages. *Industrial and Labor Relations Review*, *27*, 391–404.

Friedman, D. (2024, December 23). The actual pay raises feds will see for 2025, based on locality pay. *Federal News Network*. https://federalnewsnetwork.com/pay/2024/12/the-actual-pay-raises-feds-will-see-for-2025-based-on-locality-pay/

Gerhart, P. F. (1976, April). Determinants of bargaining outcomes in local government labor relations. *Industrial and Labor Relations Review, 29*, 331–350.

Gill, C. (2009). Union impact on the effective adoption of high performance work practices. *Human Resource Management Review*, *19(1)*, 39–50.

Goldhaber, D., DeArmond, M., & DeBurgomaster, S. (2010). Teacher attitudes about compensation reform: Implications for reform implementation. *Industrial and Labor Relations Review*, *64*(3), 441–463.

Gomez-Mejia, L. R., & Balkin, D. B. (1984, Winter). Union impacts on secretarial earnings: A public sector case. *Industrial Relations, 23*, 95–102.

Guthrie-Morse, B., Leslie, L. L., & Hu, T.-W. (1981). Assessing the impact of faculty unions. *Journal of Higher Education*, *52*(3), 237–255.

Hall, W. C., & Vanderporten, D. (1977, February). Unionization, monopsony power, and police salaries. *Industrial Relations*, *16*, 94–100.

Hammer, T. H., & Wazeter, D. L. (1993). Dimensions of local union effectiveness. *Industrial and Labor Relations Review*, *46*(2), 302–319.

Hendrick, D. W., Henson, S. E., Krieg, J. M., & Wassell, C. S., Jr. (2010). Is there really a faculty union salary premium? *Industrial and Labor Relations*, *64*(3), 558–574.

Henson, S. E., Krieg, J. M., Wassell, C. S., Jr., & Hedrick, D. W. (2012). Collective bargaining and community college faculty: What is the wage impact? *Journal of Labor Research*, *33(1)*, 104–117.

Hirsch, B. T. (2004). Reconsidering union wage effects: Surveying new evidence on an old topic. *Journal of Labor Research*, *25*(2), 233–266.

Hirsch, B. T., & Schumacher, E. J. (2001). Private sector union density and the wage premium: Past, present, and future. *Journal of Labor Research*, *22*(3), 487–518.

Holzer, M. (1988, Spring). Productivity in, garbage out: Sanitation gains in New York. *Public Productivity Review, XI*, 37–50.

Hoover, G. A., & Peoples, J. (2003). Privatization of refuse removal and labor costs. *Journal of Labor Research, XXIV*(2), 293–305.

Hu, T.-W., & Leslie, L. (1982, June). The effects of collective bargaining on college faculty salaries and compensation. *Applied Economics*, *14*, 269–277.

Hunter, W. J., & Rankin, C. H. (1988). The composition of public sector compensation: The effect of unionization and bureaucratic size. *Journal of Labor Relations, IX*, 29–42.

Ichniowski, C., Freeman, R. B., & Laver, H. (1989). Collective bargaining laws, threat effects, and the determination of police compensation. *Journal of Labor Economics*, 7(2), 191–209.

Julius, D. J., & DiGiovanni, N., Jr. (2019). Academic collective bargaining: Status, process, and prospects. *Academic Labor: Research and Artistry*, *3*(1), 11.

Kalleberg, A. L., Marsden, P. V., Reynolds, J., & Knoke, D. (2006). Beyond profit? Sectoral differences in high-performance work practices. *Work and Occupations*, *33*(3), 271–302.

Karper, M. D., & Meckstroth, D. J. (1976, October). The impact of unionism on public wage rates. *Public Personnel Management*, *5*, 343–346.

Kearney, R. C. (1979). The impact of police unionization on municipal budgetary outcomes. *International Journal of Public Administration*, *1*(4), 361–379.

Kearney, R. C. (2003). Patterns of union decline and growth: An organizational ecology perspective. *Journal of Labor Research*, *24*(4), 561–578.

Kearney, R. C. (2005). Reinventing government and battling budget crises: Manager and municipal government actions in 2003. In International City Management Association (ICMA) (Ed.), *The municipal year book 2005*. ICMA.

Kearney, R. C., & Morgan, D. R. (1980a, Spring). The impact of unionization on the compensation of municipal police. *Journal of Collective Negotiations*, *9*, 361–379.

Kearney, R. C., & Morgan, D. R. (1980b, May). Unions and state employee compensation. *State and Local Government Review, 12*, 115–119.

Keefe, J. (2012). Are public employees overpaid? *Labor Studies Journal*, *37*(1), 104–126.

Kellough, J. E., & Selden, S. C. (1997). Pay-for-performance systems in state government perceptions of state agency personnel managers. *Review of Public Personnel Administration*, *17*(1), 5–21.

Kerrissey, J., & Meyers, N. (2022). Public-sector unions as equalizing institutions: Race, gender, and earnings. *ILR Review*, *75*(5), 1215–1239.

Kesselring, R. G. (1991, Winter). The economic effects of faculty unions. *Journal of Labor Research, XII*, 61–72.

Knies, E., & Leisink, P. (2018). People management in the public sector. In C. Brewster & J. Cerdin (Eds.), *HRM in mission driven organizations: Managing people in the not for profit sector* (pp. 15–46). Palgrave MacMillan.

Kochar, R. (2023, March 1). *The enduring grip of the gender pay gap*. Pew Research Center. https://www.pewresearch.org/social-trends/2023/03/01/the-enduring-grip-of-the-gender-pay-gap/

Krueger, A. B. (1988). Are public sector workers paid more than their alternative wage? Evidence from longitudinal data and job queues. In *When public sector workers unionize* (pp. 217–242). University of Chicago Press.

Labor Relations Information System. (2016, October 7). *St. Louis police union sues for freedom from firefighter parity*. Labor Relations Information System. https://lris.com/2016/10/st-louis-police-union-sues-for-freedom-from-firefighter-parity/

Legler, J. I. (1985, Spring). City, county and state government liability for sex-based wage discrimination after *County of Washington v. Gunther* and *AFSCME v. Washington*. *The Urban Lawyer, 17*, 229–275.

Leibig, M. T., & Kahn, W. L. (1987). *Public employee organizing and the law*. Bureau of National Affairs.

Lewis, G. B., & Stein, L. (1989, April). Unions and municipal decline. *American Politics Quarterly, 17*, 208–222.

Lewis, H. G. (1986). *Union relative wage effects: A survey*. University of Chicago Press.

Linneman, P. D., & Wachter, M. L. (1990, Winter). The economics of federal compensation. *Industrial Relations, 29*, 58–76.

Marshall, J. (1979, May–June). The effect of collective bargaining on faculty salaries in higher education. *Journal of Higher Education*, 310–322.

Matzer, J., Jr. (1988). A practical approach to productivity bargaining. In J. Matzer, Jr. (Ed.), *Pay and benefits: New ideas for local government*. International City Management Association.

Maynard, M. (2012, June 12). *Civil service reform passes in 3 states*. Governing the States and Localities. http://www.governing.com/blogs/view/civil-service-reform-passes.html

McGee, J. B., & Winters, M. A. (2017). How pensions contribute to the premium paid to experienced public school teachers. *Educational Researcher*, *46*(5), 250–258.

McGinnis, J. O., & Schanzenbach, M. (2010, August 1). The case against public sector unions. *Policy Review*, 1–22.

McGuinness, D. (2023, April 1). Firefighters lose pay parity lawsuit. *Houston Chronicle (TX)*, A001.

Merrifield, J. (1999). Monopsony power in the market for teachers: Why teachers should support market-based education reform. *Journal of Labor Research*, *XX*(3), 377–391.

Miller, M. L. (1996, May). The public/private pay debate: What do the data show? *Monthly Labor Review*, 18–29.

Moore, W. J., & Raisian, J. (1987). Union-nonunion wage differentials in the public administration, educational, and private sectors: 1970–1983. *The Review of Economics and Statistics, 69*, 608–616.

Morgan, D. R., & Kearney, R. C. (1977). Collective bargaining and faculty compensation: A comparative analysis. *Sociology of Education*, *50*, 28–39.

NASRA. (2024). *NASRA Issue brief: State and local government spending on public employee retirement systems.* https://www.nasra.org/files/Issue%20Briefs/NASRACostsBrief.pdf

National Women's Law Center. (2023, January). *Progress in the states for equal pay.* https://nwlc.org/wp-content/uploads/2023/01/Equal-Pay-Progress-in-the-States-1.12.23.pdf

NEA. (2024, March). *Stabilizing COVID + declining inflation: What does it mean for academe.* NEA Higher Education Faculty Salary Analysis: 2022–2023. https://www.nea.org/sites/default/files/2024-04/2024-higher-ed-salary-report_0.pdf

Newland, C. A. (1972, November–December). Personnel concerns in government productivity improvement. *Public Administration Review, 32*, 807–815.

O'Brien, K. M. (1994). The impact of union political activities on public-sector pay, employment and budget. *Industrial Relations, 33*(3), 265–278.

Orr, D. (1976). Public employee compensation levels. In *Public employee unions* (pp. 131–144). Institute for Contemporary Studies.

Park, S., & Berry, F. (2014). Successful diffusion of a failed policy: The case of pay-for-performance in the US federal government. *Public Management Review, 16*(6), 763–781.

Peng, J. (2004). Public pension funds and operating budgets: A tale of three states. *Public Budgeting and Finance, 24*(2), 59.

Perloff, J. M., & Wachter, M. L. (1984, October). Wage comparability in the U.S. postal service. *Industrial and Labor Relations Review, 38*, 26–35.

Perry, J. L., Engbers, T. A., & Jun, S. Y. (2009). Back to the future? Performance-related pay, empirical research, and the perils of persistence. *Public Administration Review, 69*(1), 39–51.

Pew. (2023, October). *Public retirement systems need sustainable policies to navigate volatile financial markets: State pension funding gap, 2021.* https://www.pewtrusts.org/-/media/assets/2023/11/public-retirement-systems-need-sustainable-policies_v5.pdf

Pew Center on the States. (2012, June). *The widening gap update.* http://www.pewstates.oprg/uploadedFiles/PCS_Assets/2012/Pew_Pensions_Update.pdf

Pham, L. D., Nguyen, T. D., & Springer, M. G. (2021). Teacher merit pay: A meta-analysis. *American Educational Research Journal, 58*(3), 527–566.

Podgursky, M. J., & Springer, M. G. (2007). Teacher performance pay: A review. *Journal of Policy Analysis and Management, 26*(4), 909–949.

President's Pay Agent. (1990). *Annual report.* President's Pay Agent.

President's Pay Agent. (2024). Report on locality-based comparability payments for the general schedule. In *Annual report of the president's pay agent for locality pay in 2024.* https://www.opm.gov/media/qyhbgbox/report-on-locality-based-comparability-payments-for-the-general-schedule.pdf

Reder, M. W. (1975). The theory of employment and wages in the public sector. In D. S. Hammermesh (Ed.), *Labor in the public and non-profit sector* (pp. 1–18). Princeton University Press.

Rose, N. (2024, April 4). City council supports FDNY EMS wage fight local 2507 president Oren Barzilay wants pay parity, not just words. *Queens Chronicle*. https://www.qchron.com/editions/queenswide/city-council-supports-fdny-ems-wage-fight/article_8d6b43fc-f2e3-5ce7-8c3a-e59ee07be666.html

Rubery, J. (2019). Joan Acker and doing comparable worth. *Gender, Work & Organization, 26*(12), 1786–1793.

Shapiro, D. (1978, January). Relative wage effects of unions in the public and private sectors. *Industrial and Labor Relations Review, 31*, 193–204.

Smith, R. L., & Lyons, W. (1980, November–December). The impact of fire fighter unionization on wages and working hours in American cities. *Public Administration Review, 40*, 568–574.

Smith, S. P. (1976, January). Pay differences between federal government and private sector workers. *Industrial and Labor Relations Review, 29*, 14–15.

Stein, R. M. (1990, May). The budgetary effects of municipal service contracting: A principal agent explanation. *American Journal of Political Science, 34*, 471–502.

Toulmin, L. M. (1988, March–April). The treasure hunt: Budget search behavior by public employee unions. *Public Administration Review, 48*, 620–680.

Trejo, S. J. (1991). Public sector unions and municipal employment. *Industrial Labor Relations Review, 45*, 166–180.

Urban Institute. (n.d.). *State and local backgrounders: State and local government pensions.* https://www.urban.org/policy-centers/cross-center-initiatives/state-and-local-finance-initiative/projects/state-and-local-backgrounders/state-and-local-government-pensions

U.S. Bureau of Labor Statistics (BLS). (2024, March 13). *Employer costs for employee compensation-December 2023.* https://www.bls.gov/news.release/archives/ecec_03132024.pdf

U.S. Census Bureau. (2023). *Census of governments, survey of public employment & payroll summary report: 2022.* https://www.census.gov/content/dam/Census/library/publications/2023/econ/2022_summary_brief.pdf

U.S. Government Accountability Office. (2024, March). *Human capital: Characteristics and administration of the federal wage system. GAO-24-106657.* https://www.gao.gov/assets/d24106657.pdf

U.S. Office of Personnel Management. (2022). *Release: OPM announces $15 minimum wage for U.S. federal civilian employees.* https://www.opm.gov/news/releases/2022/01/release-opm-announces-dollar15-minimum-wage-for-us-federal-civilian-employees/

U.S. Postal Service. (2024, February). *Postal history: Number of postal employees since 1926.* https://about.usps.com/who/profile/history/employees-since-1926.htm

Valletta, R. G. (1989, April). The impact of unionism on municipal expenditures and revenues. *Industrial and Labor Relations Review, 42*, 430–442.

Walters, J. (1999, January). The power of pay. *Government Executive*, 32–35.

Wellington, H. H., & Winter, R. K., Jr. (1971). *The unions and the cities.* Brookings.

Winters, J. V. (2011). Teacher salaries and teacher unions: A spatial econometric approach. *Industrial and Labor Relations Review, 64*(4), 747–764.

Zax, J. S. (1988, Fall). Wages, nonwage compensation, and municipal unions. *Industrial Relations, 27*, 301–317.

Zax, J. S. (1989, Winter). Employment and local public sector unions. *Industrial Relations, 28*, 21–31.

Zhang, L., Ehrenberg, R., & Liu, X. (2021). The increasing stratification of faculty employment at colleges and universities in the United States. In *Advances in industrial and labor relations* (pp. 73–97). Emerald Publishing Limited.

Zigarelli, M. A. (1996, Winter). Dispute resolution mechanisms and teacher bargaining outcomes. *Journal of Labor Research, XVII*, 135–148.

Chapter 7

Union Impacts

Personnel Processes and Policies

I. INTRODUCTION

The influence of public employee unions on wages, benefits, and budgets receives more than its fair share of media and scholarly attention. Impacts on personnel procedures and policies represent something of a hidden dimension of public sector unions. The average citizen has little interest in or understanding of public personnel administration or human resource management (HRM), particularly the shadowy realm of civil service systems. Yet, the nexus between unions and human resource processes and policies is very important in shaping the nature of government work and the quantity, quality, and cost of services rendered to citizens.

Personnel matters are salient on the union–management agenda for three reasons. First, union–management relations have matured in most state and local settings. Financial relationships and understandings between the two bargaining parties tend to stabilize over time. One result is a reduction in the real-dollar, upper range of compensation settlements. Unions, by their very nature, always want more. It is typical for them to gradually cast their bargaining nets farther and farther, expanding the scope of negotiations to include new areas. HRM rules and regulations are easily pulled into the union net.

Second, a seemingly permanent condition of government retrenchment has constrained the amount of resources that public employers can devote to the wages and benefits of employees. The driving philosophy behind the taxpayer rebellion of the 1970s and the recurrent antigovernment spending campaigns since then is that government spending is wasteful and should be cut back. Limitations have been imposed on state and local revenues and expenditures in most states. Discretionary funds have dramatically declined at all levels of government. One important result is that public employees rarely have an opportunity to enlarge their slice of the budgetary pie. When economic indicators turn downward in recessions, wage freezes, givebacks, layoffs, and related actions become commonplace. To maintain their membership in times of economic stress, and justify their existence, unions

DOI:10.4324/9781003403593-7

must be able to show positive results. Thus, they increasingly tend to turn their attention to the noneconomic personnel policy and process areas traditionally left to public sector management.

Finally, the composition of the American workforce has been rapidly changing. If unions are to remain a vital force in government, they must address the needs of an increasingly large proportion of women, minorities, and immigrants, as well as temporary, seasonal, and older workers. Full-time white males represent a declining proportion of the workforce. Extraordinary changes in personnel practices are under way, forcing employers and unions alike to consider training and development needs for new workers; day care, maternity leave, and elder care policies; and programs for accommodating older workers, among many other needs. In response, some unions in the public and nonprofit sectors have moved toward organizing and negotiating for social justice and the common good (Julius et al., 2023)

This chapter explores the impacts of unions and collective bargaining on HRM processes and policies. It begins with a discussion of merit systems in relation to collective bargaining. Next, four specific policies that threaten to undermine merit systems are examined: union security arrangements, the seniority criterion, affirmative action, and New Public Management (NPM) practices. Finally, the effects of unions on specific personnel processes—including promotions, retention, training, grievances, discipline, position classification, workload, and staffing as well as emerging policy areas—are addressed.

II. MERIT SYSTEMS

Merit systems are a product of the civil service reform movement that swept the United States during the late nineteenth and early twentieth centuries. The purpose of the reform movement was twofold: to ensure the political neutrality of civil servants by removing them from partisan political pressure and spoils politics, and to ensure that selection, promotion, and retention of public employees were carried out objectively in accordance with the principle of merit. The Pendleton Act of 1883 was intended to address both of these objectives at the national government level. A fundamental provision of the Pendleton Act was to create a bipartisan civil service commission charged with the duties of keeping political patronage out of public personnel administration and overseeing a merit system designed to implement the merit principle.

It is important that distinctions be made among the merit principle, the merit system, and the civil service system. The merit principle seeks to make employee competence the major criterion in decisions affecting the movement of employees into, within, and out of public organizations. Merit and fitness for a job are to replace spoils, patronage, favoritism, and other subjective criteria in all personnel decisions.

A merit system is a legally established set of rules and procedures created to implement the merit principle in the recruitment, selection, promotion, retention, and compensation of employees. The merit system is an administrative apparatus directed by a nonpartisan or bipartisan board or commission or a central personnel office with the purpose of implementing the principle of merit in government personnel decisions. In the federal sector, the U.S. Office of Personnel Management and the Merit Systems Protection Board implement personnel processes in accordance with the merit principle. In state and local governments, the responsibility is vested with an independent civil service commission or a central personnel agency in the executive branch.

Although state and local governments have their own merit systems, the Social Security Act of 1940 and subsequent federal laws require that state and local employees who are paid in full or in part by federal grant-in-aid funds to staff workers in welfare, employment security, health, vocational rehabilitation, homeland security, and other areas be hired under a merit system. Thus, the merit system is a standard feature of government personnel administration in the United States. It is so standard, in fact, that the terms "merit system" and "civil service system" are often used synonymously.

A civil service system is the personnel system for all nonmilitary employees of a government. The civil service system encompasses the merit system as well as all positions filled by patronage, policy making, and other appointments. A civil service system may or may not contain a merit system, but a merit system is always part of a civil service system.

The concept of the merit principle as the basis for government personnel decisions is nearly universally accepted. The problem lies in deciding what range of personnel functions is fundamental to maintaining the merit system and therefore should be exempt from collective bargaining. According to the federal Intergovernmental Personnel Act of 1970, the following elements are essential:

1 Recruitment, selection, and advancement of employees on the basis of relative ability, knowledge, and skills, including open consideration of qualified applicants for initial appointment
2 Equitable and adequate compensation
3 Training to ensure high-quality performance
4 Correction of inadequate performance or separation of those whose inadequate performance cannot be corrected
5 Fair treatment of all employees in all aspects of personnel administration irrespective of political affiliation, race, color, national origin, sex, or religion
6 Protection of employees against partisan political coercion

Public employee unions take issue with many of these "essential" merit system components, especially pay and benefit determination, grievance procedures, training, and position classification. They espouse the view that such matters should be subject to collective bargaining. Furthermore, unions have leveled attacks at the merit system concept itself as being defined and controlled by management. Merit systems are criticized because they are based on the unilateral decision-making process that unions have fought against from their earliest days. HRM directors, for example, are appointed by the chief executive. Although they may be "neutral" with respect to partisan politics, their actions are perceived to be pro-management.

Originally created to provide job security and protection against patronage, few civil service commissions remain today. The typical arrangement is for the head of a state or local personnel system to report directly to the chief executive rather than to a commission. The purpose of such a reporting relationship is to integrate the personnel function with the executive function, but there is nearly always some tendency for governors or mayors to politicize the system (Newland, 1987). Understandably, unions are concerned about unilateralism, favoritism, and other distasteful features of this arrangement.

Merit systems have come under increasing scrutiny by nonunion critics as well. The credibility of the federal merit system has been seriously eroded because of allegations and subsequent investigations finding widespread political patronage in federal recruitment and promotion policies. Abuse of the merit principle occurred during the Nixon administration in the Department of Housing and Urban Development; Office of Economic Opportunity; and Department of Health, Education, and Welfare. Explicit evidence of blatant patronage procedures were found in the Machiavellian "Malek Manual," written by a Nixon appointee, Fred Malek, to assist other political appointees in circumventing the merit principle in departmental personnel actions (Malek, 1980). Similar problems characterized the federal service during the Reagan years, when the merit system was undermined by converting positions from classified to appointive status, written tests for some positions were abandoned in favor of direct appointment, and career bureaucrats were seemingly debased at every opportunity by their political bosses (Stahl, 1990). The administration of George W. Bush was notorious for plugging unabashed (and sometimes incompetent) partisans into positions in the Departments of Defense, Justice, and Homeland Security and the Environmental Protection Agency and many other federal agencies (Moynihan, 2005; Brook & King, 2007; Thompson, 2007).

The administration of Donald J. Trump accelerated the practice of appointing inexperienced and unqualified friends and family members to positions in the oval office, federal agencies, and ambassadorships (King, & Riddlesperger, 2018; Lewis & Richardson, 2021; Muirhead & Rosenblum, 2022; Pfiffner, 2017). He also attempted, through Executive Order 13957, to convert a large swath of career civil servants with policy advisory roles to political appointees, thereby removing merit system protections. Although the Schedule F policy was not implemented, it remains a looming threat to merit system principles and the practice of public administration in the federal government (Moynihan, 2022). Biden revoked Schedule F during his first month in office (Wagner, 2021).

It is not only the federal merit system that has been condemned. State and local merit systems have also received equal criticism. Indeed, civil service and merit systems are under heavy and concerted attack globally (Kearney & Hays, 1998). The most commonly cited deficiencies are the following (Ingraham, 1996):

1 Excessive and constraining rules and regulations. Personnel systems continue to be plagued by stultifying, centralized control systems that hinder management authority and flexibility
2 Slow, unimaginative recruitment procedures that inhibit the hiring of qualified people
3 Restrictive selection systems, such as the notorious "rule of three"
4 Rigid classification systems that impede the efficient assignment and rewarding of work
5 Multiple levels of employee legal protections that hinder labor–management cooperation and protect incompetent workers
6 Isolation from citizens. Agency goals to serve clients have been displaced in some instances by internal rules, regulations, and processes

An early article by Savas and Ginsburg (1973, p. 600) pointed out problems with the New York City merit system. Unfortunately, these practices are still typical of certain other large cities:

> In trying to prevent itself from doing the wrong things—nepotism, patronage, prejudice, favoritism, corruption—the civil service system has been warped and distorted to the point where it can do hardly anything at all. In an attempt to protect against past abuses, the "merit system" has been perverted and transformed into a closed and meritless seniority system.

The merit system, then, is seemingly under attack from all directions. Unions want to undermine it by seizing more influence over HRM policies and procedures at the bargaining table. Many elected and appointed officials would like to abolish it in favor of a flexible, management-driven system. Georgia eliminated merit system coverage for all new employees in 1996; most now serve at will. Arizona enacted a similar law in 2012. Colorado and Tennessee also overhauled their state merit systems (Maynard, 2012a).

Clearly, the merit system is a downtrodden institution. Yet support for the merit principle remains even among most of the merit system's most adamant critics. If we throw out the merit system, what will replace it? New patronage? Short-term employment contracts? Is not incremental reform preferable? The union voice in this ongoing debate plays a critical role in determining which elements are truly essential to the merit system and which are not.

A. Interface Between Collective Bargaining and the Merit System

Several possible views on the interface between collective bargaining and merit systems exist. The first view holds that the two are irreconcilable and doomed to never-ending conflict. The second view maintains that one or the other ultimately prevails because the two systems cannot be mutually accommodated. The final perspective is that the merit system and collective bargaining can exist together peacefully if certain modifications are made with respect to the merit system. Most scholars, practitioners, and key stakeholders subscribe to the third point of view. As the late American Federation of State, County, and Municipal Employees (AFSCME) leader Jerry Wurf (1974, p. 433) once observed, "To pose an 'either–or' relationship between merit and collective bargaining is to ignore reality. Both have a legitimate place in government labor–management relationships. Both are here to stay."

The merit principle requires an administrative structure for its successful implementation; in other words, it requires a merit system. Abandonment of the merit system would result in alternatives that most HRM scholars and practitioners find unacceptable. As Spero and Capozzola (1973, p. 209) observed more than four decades ago, "The alternatives . . . are political patronage, large-scale corruption, and less merit, fitness, and personal initiative. The alternatives are systems which demean and degrade employees, leaving them bereft of security and at the mercy of shifting winds."

Few desire a return to the "spoils and boodle" days of public employment Instead, collective bargaining and the merit system can be made to coexist, even as they evolve. The adjustment process plays out in state legislative and court decisions addressing the difficult task of placing collective bargaining and the merit system in their respective and appropriate places. Mutual adjustment between the two systems is ongoing, with outcomes varying from place to place (Guiler & Shafritz, 2004). Though the professed desire of some political conservatives is to abolish both collective bargaining and the merit system in favor of at-will employment as they have done in Florida, Georgia, Missouri, Oklahoma, and Texas, one or both of these systems continue to be the operating reality in the vast majority of public jurisdictions.

B. Accommodating Collective Bargaining and the Merit System

In the absence of collective bargaining, merit systems remain largely unchallenged and unchanged. Personnel decisions are rendered unilaterally. Employee appeals or grievances may be dealt with individually by management or a grievance board. In the presence of bargaining, however, some tenets of the merit system are no longer absolute. Bargaining and compromise become the order of the day as many personnel issues are resolved at the negotiating table. Generally, the range of personnel matters affected by bargaining depends on the scope of negotiations as defined through labor agreements, the courts, and state legislation. Areas not subject to bargaining are governed by merit system rules and regulations. It is through scope of bargaining determinations that the conflict between collective bargaining and the merit system is engaged and resolved.

Most state collective bargaining laws limit negotiations to "wages, hours, and working conditions." Working conditions may be interpreted broadly or narrowly, depending on the terms and conditions of employment covered by existing state or local legislation, personnel rules and regulations, and areas excluded from the scope of bargaining by management rights clauses. Most efforts to accommodate collective bargaining and the merit system have been aimed at excluding certain key personnel matters from the scope of negotiations, thereby keeping them within the domain of management.

As bargaining laws developed, some state legislation mandated blanket exclusions, whereas other laws stipulated specific exclusions of merit-related items from negotiations. New Hampshire, Vermont, and Pennsylvania, for example, had blanket exclusions restricting collective bargaining to matters not covered under merit system rules and regulations. California, Massachusetts, Rhode Island, and Washington specifically excluded certain items from bargaining, such as recruitment, selection, or, more broadly, management rights. Other states, such as New York, Michigan, Minnesota, and Nebraska, did not attempt to accommodate collective bargaining and the merit system through statute, leaving decisions, essentially, to the courts.

In contrast, when Colorado enacted a law that provided collective bargaining rights for county employees in all counties of 75,000 or more people, it expanded the scope of bargaining over personnel matters. Traditionally, public sector bargaining laws have used vague language modeled on the National Labor Relations Act that allows for bargaining over bargaining over wages and other terms and conditions of employment. Colorado's law specifies various components of compensation including base wage or salary; any form of direct monetary payments; health, accident, life, and disability insurance; pension programs; paid time off; uniform and equipment allowances; and expense reimbursement (Colorado S.B. 22–230, 2022).

At the heart of the dispute are two related issues. First, which subjects should not be submitted to collective bargaining and thereby should be reserved as management rights? Second, which system should prevail when merit system provisions conflict with collective bargaining contract language?

Title VII of the Civil Service Reform Act (CSRA) established a three-tiered system in the federal government. Core management rights, including agency decisions on the mission, organization, budget, and number of employees, are prohibited or nonnegotiable. So are certain operational matters, including contracting out, hiring, firing, and reductions in force. The second tier incorporates mandatory negotiating topics, which generally involve implementing agency decisions. Examples include decisions on how to ease impacts on laid-off employees. The third tier incorporates nonmandatory, or permissive, issues. These issues, such as the use of new technology in performing work, are negotiable at the option of management (Ban, 1995, pp. 131–132). Conflicts over negotiability, which have been many because the boundaries between the three tiers are blurred, are resolved by the Federal Labor Relations Authority (FLRA) or the federal courts on a case-by-case basis. For example, unions successfully sued to block new "flexible" personnel rules promulgated by the Bush administration affecting 110,000 Department of Homeland Security employees and 650,000 employees in the Department of Defense (Thompson, 2007, p. 111).

The trend in the states and localities has been to place more and more items on the bargaining table, except for those that are directly concerned with the quantity and quality of government services and those that involve policy questions related to the mission of the government employer. Most states exclude from the scope of bargaining recruitment, selection, promotions, and other "management rights." The problem is that many such management rights are closely related to the "terms and conditions of employment" that are negotiable under collective bargaining statutes. For example, class size is both a teacher working condition and an element of education policy. Similarly, the issue of one- versus two-officer assignments to police cruisers contains elements of both working conditions and policy. Often, resolution resides with the courts, which typically apply a balancing test to determine what is negotiable. Would bargaining on the topic significantly abridge managerial prerogatives? Does the topic have a significant effect on the work of employees in the bargaining unit? Which effect is greater?

States differ as to how they respond when merit systems and collective bargaining provisions clash. Some states grant primacy to merit system provisions, but others (e.g., Connecticut, Massachusetts, Delaware, and Illinois) favor collective bargaining provisions in statute or contract. As an example, the Delaware statute (Labor–Management Services Administration, 1972, p. 34) provides,

> Where there is a conflict between any agreement . . . in matters appropriate to collective bargaining . . . and any charter, special act, ordinance, rules or regulations adopted by the municipal employer or its agents such as a personnel board or civil service commission . . . the terms of such agreement shall prevail.

To reiterate, if statutory law does not clearly assign priority to the merit system or bargaining provisions, the courts will make this determination on a case-by-case basis. Gradually, public employee unions have caused a shift in personnel decision making from the realm of management rights to the rhetoric of the bargaining table. Even in the federal sector, where neither the CSRA nor any other statute can legally be overridden through a collective bargaining agreement, certain personnel functions have been influenced by negotiated settlements.

Collective bargaining and the merit system are not incompatible, but their relationship has changed. Merit systems tend to be narrowest in coverage in the comprehensive bargaining states. Here they are reduced to their "essential" elements, depending on bargaining outcomes, legislation, court decisions, and political culture and values. This is not necessarily detrimental to efficiency, effectiveness, and equity in public employment, all of which are stated goals of unions as well as management.

However, merit systems continue to suffer a broad-based attack from individuals and organizations both inside and outside government for a variety of alleged (and actual) shortcomings. Collective bargaining has furnished fuel for merit system detractors by further complicating personnel rules and procedures and making "an already rule-bound field even more pervasively legalistic and litigious" (Newland, 1984, p. 39). Government is characterized by less flexible personnel systems and procedures and less management authority than the private sector. Collective bargaining generally compounds these tendencies (Coursey & Rainey, 1990).

Bargaining has also raised issues—union security and the seniority criterion—that threaten to undermine the merit principle itself. In states and localities with long experience with comprehensive bargaining systems dual personnel systems have developed, and efforts to integrate them are seldom witnessed. According to one experienced observer (Douglas, 1992), this may be inevitable because of a fundamental clash of values. Civil service systems are based on individualism, open competition, political neutrality, and other values that inherently conflict with the collective bargaining values of collectivism, equality, and uniform treatment.

C. Unions and Threats to the Merit Principle

There are at least four possible threats to consistent implementation of the merit principle in government. These include union security, seniority, affirmative action/diversity, and NPM.

1. Union Security

As discussed in detail in Chapter 3, there are four relevant variations of union security: union shop, agency shop/fair share, maintenance of membership, and dues checkoff. Union security provisions represent a threat to the merit principle. Prior to the *Janus v. American Federation of State, County, and Municipal Employees Council 31, et al.* (2018) decision, the argument was that competition for jobs may be restricted if those who do not wish to join or otherwise support a union do not apply for available positions; those with less "merit" possibly gain employment. Second, under agency/fair share, employees who refused to join a union or financially contribute to it could be fired whether they are competent or not.

Post-Janus, these arguments no longer hold much weight. All things considered, it is doubtful that the remaining union security clauses present a serious threat to the merit principle. Employees can no longer be required to join or contribute to a union as a condition of employment. However, other areas of union security provisions face growing political attacks. For example, West Virginia prohibits public employers from deducting union dues through the payroll system. Indiana and Michigan require public employees to re-authorize dues deductions every year. Michigan law also requires public employers to notify employees annually of their right not to join a union and allows public employees to revoke their membership at any time (Brannick & Holman, 2022). The predictable result is fewer dues-paying members of the bargaining unit, and a weakened union.

2. Seniority

Seniority involves granting preference in certain personnel actions based on an employee's length of service to the organization. In the private sector, the seniority criterion has long been applied through contract clauses to promotions, transfers, layoffs, vacation time, and other personnel matters without any measurable reduction in the efficiency and effectiveness of the workforce. In the public sector, the role of seniority in personnel decisions may be fixed in a collective bargaining contract or, more commonly, implemented through statute or civil service rules. In both business and government, seniority offers an advantage in personnel decisions because it is objective and quantifiable. Length of service with an organization or in a particular job or department is a matter of record and an indication of experience and, plausibly, achievement. In jurisdictions where promotional examinations are not validated (demonstrably job related), seniority may even be a superior indication of merit.

Seniority and merit do not inherently conflict in public employment. For example, application of the seniority criterion in determining vacation time, shift assignments, work locations, days off, and similar working conditions is widely accepted and presents little threat to the merit principle. In the case of promotions and layoffs, however, seniority and merit may be at odds. Public employee unions generally seek promotion of the senior qualified person. Unions regard seniority as a protection against favoritism in personnel decisions. Management, of course, believes that blindly applying this decision rule hampers flexibility and prefers to have the option of discounting seniority in selected promotion decisions.

When layoffs are based on last hired, first fired (as they normally are whether unions are key players or not), a perverse sort of self-seeking logic can arise in unionized settings in which more senior union members opt to exchange jobs of less senior members of the bargaining unit for their own security and well-being. Thus, the majority gives up nothing, whereas a small minority loses its livelihood. But in some settings, unions have chosen to protect jobs, foregoing pay raises. In negotiations with the governor during a severe budget shortfall in Connecticut, all but 1 of the 27 state bargaining units opted to defer pay increases to save jobs (only the state troopers chose wages, and they later reneged). Similarly, Tabernacle New Jersey teachers accepted the bare minimum in percentage increases on their salaries (between $200 and $500 for the year for those at the high end of the salary scale) to avoid layoffs for paraprofessional workers.

Ultimately, whether seniority detracts from merit considerations depends on how the criterion is applied. When seniority alone is the determining factor and other qualifications are ignored, merit suffers. For example, teacher unions have been criticized for negotiating seniority rules that leave principals little say in assigning teachers to classrooms. When jobs are at stake, seniority rules can result in veteran teachers being reassigned to instruct in subjects in which they have little or no knowledge or expertise while more junior, fully qualified teachers are laid off.

For promotions, strict application of seniority precludes management consideration of relevant factors such as examinations and performance evaluations. The most senior individual simply receives the promotion. Usually, however, promotions are based on some combination of factors, with years of service being treated as only one (or the tie-breaking) consideration. When seniority is used in this manner, its influence is moderated to a point where it coincides with merit. The length of service becomes the cutting point in promotion decisions in which more than one candidate meets the minimum job qualifications.

The use of seniority as a consideration in personnel decisions is long standing and it predates the growth of public employee unionism. It is a decision rule that management frequently applies voluntarily. It is much easier for personnel decisions to be grounded at least in part on an indisputably objective criterion that enhances employee morale and encourages worker loyalty than to rely entirely on relatively more esoteric considerations such as unstructured oral examinations, non-validated written examinations, or flawed performance evaluations.

Seniority may weaken management authority, but this is not always a bad thing. The seniority criterion's threat to the merit principle is overshadowed by more serious concerns, such as favoritism, non-validated examinations, and biased performance appraisals. Unions strongly adhere to the seniority criterion in personnel decisions because of demonstrated problems associated with unchecked management discretion.

3. Affirmative Action and Diversity

Merit, it has been argued, has two different components. The first is special consideration in hiring, promotion, and retention policies for competence. The second is special consideration in personnel decisions for being deserving. It is the latter aspect that throws collective bargaining and affirmative action into conflict.

Equal employment opportunity (EEO), as effectuated by the Equal Employment Opportunity Act of 1964, prohibits discrimination in employment procedures and practices on the basis of race, color, sex, religion, age, and other factors. EEO is a nearly universally accepted principle in the United States. However, achieving the EEO ideal is difficult, if not impossible, because of systematic discriminatory practices. Therefore, in an effort to eliminate barriers and alleviate imbalances in the workforce attributable to past discrimination, employers may take special "affirmative" actions, such as efforts to recruit, hire, and promote members of underrepresented and "protected" groups. The primary legal bases for affirmative action policies are Title VII of the 1964 Civil Rights Act, which prohibits private sector employment discrimination as a violation of the Fourteenth Amendment, and the Equal Employment Opportunity Act of 1972, which extends Title VII coverage to public employers.

Affirmative action and collective bargaining intersect in the use of the seniority criterion in personnel decisions. Problems arise when union-supported seniority rules inadvertently discriminate against women and other members of protected classes in promotions and layoffs because members of these groups may be the last hired. Affirmative action policies intended to overcome past or present discriminatory practices sometimes directly conflict with seniority clauses in collective bargaining contracts.

Public employee unions have a mixed record with respect to affirmative action and nondiscrimination. Organized labor has actively advocated legal rights and better working conditions for disadvantaged groups as part of its social and political agenda. EEO, affirmative action, and other diversity efforts are important items on this agenda, and they have been strongly promoted by some public employee unions, particularly AFSCME, Service Employees International Union, National Education Association (NEA), and American Federation of Teachers (AFT), all of which, of course, have sizable memberships of women and other protected classes.

On the other hand, craft-type unions in government have resisted EEO and affirmative action and management efforts to implement them (Riccucci, 1990). Police and firefighter unions have been especially staunch opponents of these principles, and their membership rolls remain overwhelmingly white and male. Many white male police and firefighters, and their unions, have fought to maintain discriminatory physical strength and agility tests and height requirements (the Americans with Disabilities Act [ADA] of 1990 has helped reduce this) and have ostracized and verbally abused women and minority employees (Riccucci, 1988, 1990; Sass & Troyer, 1999; Goode & Baldwin, 2005). Such practices were addressed in a 2010 court settlement involving a group of African American firefighters called the Club Valients and the largely white International Association of Firefighters Local 22 in Philadelphia. The Valients alleged that Local 22's city website posted racially harassing and discriminatory materials that created a hostile working environment (Shields, 2010). They have also regularly challenged local government affirmative action plans. Of course, not all police and firefighter organizations discriminate against women and minorities, and there is growing evidence that police unions are actively supporting hiring greater proportions of female and minority recruits (Sass & Troyer, 1999). Thus, occupational segregation in the protective services continues, but recent research indicates that the unions are not the primary culprits.

The empirical research presents mixed findings on unionization and minority and female employment. Kellough (1990) found that federal employee unions have not been an obstacle to African American, Latino, and female employment. Highly unionized federal agencies are likely to be more diverse in employee characteristics than those with weaker union presence. This may be due to the fact that federal unions have simply organized more effectively in agencies that are already integrated.

In an extensive panel study of union members over time, Artz (2012) found that whereas union membership reduces the job satisfaction of women in the private sector, those in government service report higher levels of job satisfaction, even more so than men. Artz (2012) attributes this to a greater proportion of women in public sector unions and in union leadership than in private employment, finding that male-dominated unions tend to disregard the interests of women members in issues such as flextime and family leave. Another extensive study (May, et al., 2010) determined that there is a higher percentage of women faculty at unionized universities and that they are tenured and promoted in greater proportions than at nonunionized higher education institutions.

The local government picture remains cloudy. Several studies found little or no relationship between municipal unionization and female and minority employment (Davis, 1984; Riccucci, 1986). However, Mladenka (1991) discovered that municipal unions have a strong and negative impact on African American job success, but only in cities with large black populations and nonreformed (i.e., mayor-council, district elections, and partisan elections) systems of government. Moreover, unions had little or no effect on black employees in administrative, professional, and protective service jobs. Mladenka (1991, p. 545) suggests that unions have less influence on hiring decisions made by professional city managers in reformed governments than they do in nonreformed governments, where "they operate to retard minority employment prospects severely." A variety of local conditions that are not related to unionization also influence minority and female employment. For instance, minorities generally fare better in cities with black or female mayors (Stein, 1986; Behr, 2000), high levels of diversity on city councils, and black personnel directors (Goode & Baldwin, 2005).

An issue that has received a great deal of attention in courts is the influence of seniority clauses on affirmative action during layoffs. In the private sector, the courts have found that seniority may be utilized as a decision rule for layoffs if (1) past hiring policies were not discriminatory, (2) individual workers who were laid off were not victims of prior employment discrimination, and (3) the criterion of seniority is applied in a neutral fashion with no intent to discriminate (*Waters v. Wisconsin Steelworks,* 1974; *Watkins v. Steelworkers Local 2369,* 1975). However, when seniority systems inhibit the promotion of women and minorities because of past discriminatory practices in hiring and transfers, they may be declared illegal (*Local 189, United Papermakers and Crown-Zellerback Corp. v. United States,* 1969).

Several U.S. Supreme Court decisions have directly addressed the seniority/affirmative action conflict in local governments. In *Memphis Firefighters Local Union No. 1784 v. Stotts* (1984), a federal district court had approved two affirmative action plans for improving the percentage of African American firefighters. A subsequent fiscal crisis forced the city to lay off 40 firefighters, most of whom were black, in compliance with a seniority clause in the collective bargaining contract. The black firefighters filed suit and won in the federal district and circuit courts. On review of an appeal by the firefighter union, however, the Supreme Court held that the lower courts should not have interfered with the seniority system to protect newly hired black employees. Thus, bona fide seniority systems take precedence over affirmative action when layoffs are required.

Importantly, the City of Memphis's affirmative action plan was in the form of a consent decree in which no finding or admission of intentional discrimination was made. Equally important, firefighter union was not a party to the decree (Seaver, 1984–85). Later Supreme Court decisions clarified *Stotts* and reduced its significance (*Wygant v. Jackson Board of Education*, 1986).

The lesson for local governments is that affected unions should be made formal parties to consent agreements concerning affirmative action or certain diversity enhancement procedures. Agreements can be incorporated into negotiated contracts. For example, minority and female employment gains may be protected through negotiated alternatives to layoffs, such as job sharing, voluntary layoffs, or buyouts.

The same lesson should be applied to measures taken to accommodate disabled employees under ADA. Under the duty of fair representation, unions must represent the interests of disabled members of the bargaining unit. Employers are advised to negotiate with the union on any job assignment, working hours, or other special dispensation for disabled employees. The U.S. Supreme Court decision in *U.S. Airways v. Barnett* (2002) indicates that courts will prioritize seniority provisions in collective bargaining contracts over the ADA. For instance, a management decision to accommodate a less senior maintenance worker with a disability by a transfer to a desk job that a more senior employee is qualified for would violate contractual seniority rights. Rather than bypassing the union, which invites a dispute, the employer should consult with the union to work out acceptable accommodations for all concerned.

A conservative U.S. Supreme Court has shown little sympathy for affirmative action in higher education admissions, contracting decisions, and hiring and promotion policies. Today, affirmative action programs are being dismantled at all levels of government, except in instances where a past history of illegal discrimination has been documented and the affirmative action program designed to redress past discrimination has been "narrowly tailored" (Riccucci, 1997; Goode & Baldwin, 2005, p. 4). The current emphasis is for employers to develop broadly construed diversity programs that embrace myriad workplace demographic concerns, such as gender, color, language, disability, and religion. In any case, affirmative action and diversity programs do redistribute jobs to women and minorities but with little or no loss of organizational efficiency (Holzer & Neumark, 2000).

4. New Public Management

NPM, formerly referred to in the United States as Reinventing Government, was initially based on a widely read book of the same name by Osborne and Gaebler (1992). It is a far-reaching approach to improving the performance, productivity, and responsiveness of government. Its key themes are de-bureaucratization, decentralization, downsizing, privatization, and managerialism (adopting business ideology and practices in government). In essence, NPM represents an attack on bureaucracy and "big government." Although NPM has chalked up many impressive achievements, as a broad strategy it remains riddled with inconsistencies and controversy (Ingrams et al., 2020; Funck & Karlsson, 2020; Kearney & Hays, 1998), from specious promises of empowering the very workers under assault to its simplistic theory of customer-driven government.

Unions, not unrealistically, tend to take NPM as a serious threat. At the federal level, Reinventing Government efforts were embodied in the National Performance Review (NPR) during the Clinton administration and spearheaded by Vice President Al Gore. The ambitious NPR initiatives included improvement of labor-management relations, which were widely recognized as being excessively adversarial and litigious. A presidential executive order (E.O. 12871) established the National Productivity Council (NPC) to coordinate agency-level labor–management partnerships for implementing a variety of NPR recommendations. E.O. 12871 also required agencies to negotiate with their unions on all subjects not expressly reserved to the president or Congress, thereby expanding the mandatory scope of bargaining and eliminating one of the three tiers of negotiability established by the CSRA.

Through the NPC, federal unions were significantly involved in developing labor–management partnerships. Sitting on the NPC were heads of the three largest federal unions (American Federation of Government Employees, National Treasury Employees Union [NTEU], and National Federation of Federal Employees). NPC recommendations included streamlining dispute resolution processes and providing training in alternative dispute resolution techniques. The NPC also encouraged collective bargaining for improving recruitment and selection, position classification, and performance management processes (U.S. National Partnership Council, 1994).

Despite serious efforts to construct an agreement on much-needed reform in federal HRM and labor relations practices, the signing of many agreements, and notable progress in the legislative and labor relations history in some agencies (e.g., Internal Revenue Service, Department of Labor, and Bureau of Engraving and Printing), the antiunion policies of the George W. Bush administration conspired to limit success (Doeringer et al., 1996; Moynihan, 2005). The restrictions of Title VII of the CSRA on union security, wage and benefit bargaining, and other areas effectively constrain the possibilities for union and management bilateral decision making. Decades of sometimes bitter adversarial relations have separated the parties into hostile camps in some agencies. Uncertainty over which topics should be addressed by partnerships and which should more appropriately be determined through collective bargaining creates confusion among labor and management officials. As one union leader reportedly described the ensuing role conflict, “It’s hard to represent someone who’s being screwed in the morning, and then flip the switch and be buddies with management in the afternoon, when we are still angry” (quoted in Ban, 1995, p. 134).

In agencies in which positive labor–management relations developed, the unions played a constructive role in government reform. In the IRS, for example, NTEU partnered with management to substantially reform an agency under extreme duress during congressional and public attacks in the late 1990s. However, in agencies unable to overcome their history of negative relationships, unions stifled reform attempts. For instance, unions in the Patent and Trademark Office were unable to agree with management on much of anything, even resisting plans to move into a new office building and efforts to progress toward a “paperless office” (Patent answers, 1999, p. 81). It “takes two to partner,” and the Bush administration’s rejection of the partnering process effectively derailed it for eight years.

President Barack Obama revived the partnership approach with a 2009 executive order creating labor–management forums “to improve delivery of government services.” The executive order narrowed President Clinton’s requirement to negotiate over permissive items to “several pilot projects” in selected agencies. A 2014 assessment of pilot projects identified barriers and successes of the partnership forums, Specifically, barriers included trust/relationship issues, scheduling, communication, and differing perspectives on the levels pre-decisional involvement between the parties. One key successful forum was the Naval Sea Systems Command project that used small teams to develop and implement ideas submitted by workers for improving current processes. Another was a Federal Aviation Administration project in which management and labor collaborated to implement a new computer system that replaced a 40-year-old system used at air traffic control centers nationwide. Third, the Federal Communications Commission substantially improved its ranking in the Best Places to Work in the Federal Government after enhancing labor-management relationships and employee engagement (U.S. Office of Personnel Management, 2014).

III. SPECIFIC IMPACTS OF UNIONS ON PERSONNEL FUNCTIONS AND POLICIES

A. Management Rights

1. Management Rights (Scope of Bargaining)

Union and management disagreements on which personnel functions and policies are essential to the merit principle and should therefore be reserved for management decision making only are closely linked to scope of bargaining disputes. Management rights are defined outside the scope of bargaining and are prohibited from collective negotiations. Whereas unions seek to define it very broadly, management tries to keep the scope of bargaining narrow.

A. Federal Employment

In the federal sector, the scope of bargaining is legally defined by Section 7106 of Title VII of the CSRA, which specifies management rights, and by management rights clauses incorporated into the contracts negotiated for the various federal agencies, departments, and other bodies (see Table 7.1).

Even though management rights and the scope of bargaining appear to be clearly specified, their practical application is somewhat nebulous, with results varying from agency to agency. The CSRA provides for negotiations over the procedures to be used by management in exercising its prerogatives. Federal unions do have a voice in how promotions, assignments, position classifications, transfers, layoffs, and other procedures are carried out. Most federal contracts also call for official union representation in establishing promotion, assignment, and other procedures. This is important because processes often determine outcomes.

President Clinton's E.O. 12871 opened the door to a more expansive scope of bargaining, but as repeatedly noted President George W. Bush rescinded it. Bush also launched attacks on bargaining rights and the scope of bargaining under the banner of "homeland security." The result, particularly in the Department of Homeland Security, was an expansion of management authority and the consequent narrowing of the scope of bargaining (Brook & King, 2007; Thompson, 2007). In contrast, President Biden's E.O. 13991 directed federal agencies bargain over permissible, non-mandatory subjects of bargaining when contracts are due to expire, and it instructed the Office of Personnel Management to develop

Table 7.1 Federal Management Rights Under Section 7106 of the CSRA

7106. Management rights

(a) Subject to subsection (b) of this section, nothing in this chapter shall affect the authority of any management official of any agency

- (1) to determine the mission, budget, organization, number of employees, and internal security practices of the agency; and
- (2) in accordance with applicable laws
  - (A) to hire, assign, direct, lay off, and retain employees in the agency, or to suspend, remove, reduce in grade or pay, or take other disciplinary action against such employees;
  - (B) to assign work, to make determinations with respect to contracting out, and to determine the personnel by which agency operations shall be conducted;
  - (C) with respect to filling positions, to make selections for appointments from
    - (i) among properly ranked and certified candidates for promotion; or
    - (ii) any other appropriate source;
  - (D) and to take whatever actions may be necessary to carry out the agency mission during emergencies.

(b) Nothing in this section shall preclude any agency and any labor organization from negotiating*

- (1) at the election of the agency, on the numbers, types, and grades of employees or positions assigned to any organizational subdivision, work project, or tour of duty, or on the technology, methods, and means of performing work;
- (2) procedures which management officials of the agency will observe in exercising any authority under this section; or
- (3) appropriate arrangements for employees adversely affected by the exercise of any authority under this section by such management officials.

recommendations to raise the base pay of federal employees and contractors to a minimum of $15 per hour.

Federal unions are prohibited from bargaining over matters that are governed through federal statute, such as hours of work, sick leave, annual leave, and holidays. However, because these and related matters require the implementation of procedures, unions often have an influential voice. For example, federal employee unions such as the American Federation of Government Employees (AFGE) have been particularly vocal about maintaining generous telework policies and opposing

* These are “permissive” topics under E.0.12871.

return to office plans in the wake of the COVID-19 pandemic. The Department of Housing and Urban Development has maintained a fairly gratuitous telework policy of up to four days per week (Weisner, 2024). In contrast, the Social Security Administration took steps to cut to telework for employees at agency headquarters (Musurlian, 2024)

Federal employee unions have made some inroads in these personnel areas and into the field of management rights. In the legal absence of wage and benefit bargaining and union security arrangements, they must justify their existence to current and potential members. Influence on personnel policies and procedures offers one promising track. However, the uniform, formal management rights as stipulated in the CSRA and union contracts have erected a barrier, albeit permeable, to expanding the scope of bargaining. As a consequence, federal management has generally retained its traditional rights more successfully than state and local managers who must operate within a union environment.

b. State and Local Governments

Although management rights clauses are common in state and local labor agreements, they tend to be less constrictive than the standard federal provisions. Most, however, are at least partly modeled on the federal management rights clause incorporated in Section 7106 of the CSRA.

Management rights clauses may be set out in state bargaining laws, local ordinances, and union contracts. Whatever the source, the effect is to place certain items outside the scope of bargaining. Unions ostensibly abide by legal restrictions on the subject matter of bargaining. As in the federal sector, however, decision-making procedures used to implement management policies may be negotiated. Additionally, state and local unions often insist on having a voice regarding the effects of management decisions in proscribed areas. As noted by Stanley (1972, p. 22), "The boundary is uncertain, the distinction fuzzy, because management really directs the work with the consent of employees." When management rights are not formally reserved through statute, ordinance, or contractual language, the presumption is that all working conditions and terms of employment are negotiable.

Even when management rights clauses exist, weak state and local managements have been known to bargain away some of their reserved rights. Municipal unions in New York City significantly eroded management rights more than four decades ago. Union gains were due in part to a muddied fiscal and political situation and certain decisions of the Board of Collective Bargaining interpreting management prerogatives. Horton (1973, p. 75) stated, "By 1970, the major unions for all practical purposes bargained with the City government on whatever managerial issues they wanted and refused to bargain on issues they wanted left alone." Once sacrificed, the loss of a management right becomes a permanent condition.

In general, the strength of management is directly related to the strength of the management rights clause in a labor agreement and how successfully it is enforced. Municipal management today is insistent on placing management rights clauses in labor contracts. More than 90% of American cities have such a clause in at least one union contract. Most frequently listed is the right to determine missions, policies, budget, and general operations.

Notwithstanding formal management rights verbiage, unions continue to encroach. Their effect on management depends on many factors, including bargaining history, political and organizational culture, union–management relationships, and leadership style, but one thing is certain: managing in a union environment is more difficult and complicated than managing in a union-free setting.

B. Management Structure

"Management structure" refers to the organization of managerial authority for personnel issues. Personnel policy making has become more centralized in the public sector in response to union activity. This is a union impact long observed in private employment as well. In a classic labor relations study, John F. Burton (1972) documented the centralization of management authority in public employment that resulted from collective bargaining in 40 local government units. Before the emergence of collective bargaining, management structure was characterized by a "bewildering fragmentation of authority for personnel issues among numerous management officials," including the chief executive officer, civil service commissioners, personnel director, department head, budget director, and city attorney (Burton, 1972, p. 127).

When collective bargaining first arises, the usual first response of local government management is to impose a bilateral system on the preexisting authority structure with little or no alteration. This is understandable because local governments use whatever labor relations expertise that exists to avoid disruption of authority relationships. However, the situation soon becomes unstable because (1) staff officials have little collective bargaining expertise, (2) labor relations are time consuming and demand full-time attention by officials, and (3) authority for labor relations remains fragmented in a jurisdiction with multiple centers of political power. The last problem is especially serious because it tends to promote end runs and whipsawing. After an initial experience with collective bargaining under these conditions, most cities have responded with efforts to centralize management structure and thereby stabilize labor–management relations.

Collective bargaining has had similar impacts on management structure in higher education institutions. There has been a marked (and much maligned by faculty) concentration of power in college and university central administrations at the expense of deans and department heads. Faculty bargaining further enhances administrative power and authority. Faculty power coalesces in unions in most cases, with union committees displacing the power and influence of traditional faculty senates.

The tendency in unionized government has been for the executive branch to acquire authority at the expense of the legislative body and independent civil service commissions. Then, as labor relations further develop centralization of management authority occurs within the executive branch, with bargaining authority being transferred from budget and human resource staff to full-time labor relations specialists. In many jurisdictions, selected aspects of collective bargaining and labor relations are contracted out to private specialists such as labor lawyers. These developments are both logical and advantageous to management because the executive branch is the best place to devise negotiating strategies and coordinate management's positions on issues. Labor relations specialists can master the vicissitudes of bargaining. Finally, there is an important advantage to having the executive branch negotiate the contracts that it ultimately will be required to administer.

From the union perspective, the centralization of management structure also may be considered a good thing. Unions, generally speaking, want to bargain with a party who can render binding decisions and deliver the goods. Fragmented management creates an unstable bargaining environment that can offer some short-run tactical advantages to a union, but in the long term, both parties benefit from positive mutual adjustment and the lessening of conflict within the context of a mature, defined collective bargaining relationship.

C. Personnel Processes

A wide spectrum of personnel processes are subject to negotiations. Many of them are included in Table 7.2.

1. Recruitment, Testing, and Selection

Recruitment, testing, and selection of employees are personnel functions that fall within the traditional purview of management. Generally speaking, they remain management prerogatives. Nonetheless, in some instances unions have penetrated these traditional areas of management rights.

Recruitment practices may be affected through union efforts to determine or at least influence job qualifications and position descriptions and any modifications to them. Experience suggests that resistance to changes in job qualifications is common. Unions are eager to assist in recruiting new workers to join the union family. Management's role is to guard against any sort of illegal or unethical bias in the recruitment process.

Some public employee unions oppose examination policies because of the absence of demonstrated validity of the testing instruments. AFSCME has

Table 7.2 **Nonmonetary Subjects Typically Included in Contracts**

Union rights	Discipline and discharge
Management rights	Holidays and vacations
Union security	Sick leave
Grievance procedures	Child care, elder care
Hours of work, work schedules	Leaves of absence
Alternative work arrangements (e.g., flextime and telecommuting)	Position classification
Health and safety	Training and education
Seniority	Past practices
Layoffs	Subcontracting
Bumping and recall procedures	Privatization
Labor-management committees	New technology
Inclement weather procedures	

frequently gone on record against written tests because they may discriminate against minorities and immigrants with low levels of education. AFSCME has suggested that performance tests should be used instead. Unions are also on guard against psychological and personality testing as well as the possibility of genetic screening of job applicants and even current employees. Might those current and prospective workers found to have genetic predispositions to disease be discriminated against? What about protection of privacy? In the absence of federal or state law on genetic screening, unions are certain to insist on addressing such questions at the bargaining table and in contracts (Barclay & Markel, 2007, 2008).

Employee selection also attracts union attention. Unions generally seek to limit management discretion in hiring. Conventionally, according to civil service rules, agency or department heads in a state or local government had to select a new employee from one of the top three scorers on an entrance examination—thus, the "rule of three." By permitting some degree of employer discretion, the rule of three implicitly recognizes the vagaries and imperfections of testing procedures. The trend today is to extend the selection pool to 5, 10, 20, or even more applicants. In some jurisdictions, however, the rule of one prevails despite recognized testing inadequacies. Here, agency or department heads are not allowed to exercise any discretion. They must offer the position to the individual who scores the highest on the examinations.

Teacher unions probably influence selection processes more than unions in any other occupational category. Analysis of a national sample of 80 collective bargaining contracts found that 84% of teacher agreements included policies governing teacher selection to fill existing vacancies. Typically, these provisions establish a hiring pool consisting of "teachers who have been laid off recently; requested voluntary transfer; been involuntarily transferred; returned from leave of absence; or served as substitutes" (Goldschmidt & Stuart, 1986, p. 354). Vacancies are filled by prioritizing these conditions and, usually, taking into account the seniority of pool members as well.

Unions also have an interest in shortening employee probationary periods as an additional means of restricting management hiring discretion. A major fault of public sector management is its failure to remove unsatisfactory workers during probationary periods, when termination usually cannot be appealed or grieved. The union position is that management should have to render a quicker determination of employee suitability than in the usual six months, giving probationary employees an even greater benefit of the doubt.

2. Promotions

Union interest aside, promotions safely remain a matter outside the sphere of union influence in most settings, with the exception of seniority preferences. What do the unions want with respect to promotions? They want non-entry-level jobs to be filled through the promotion of employees in the bargaining unit, taking into account seniority. This objective is not necessarily out of touch with management's basic preferences. Promotion from within is a decision rule for many government department heads, agency heads, and personnel directors because it is good for employee motivation and morale. It also minimizes recruitment and time costs. Seniority is often the primary criterion used in determining promotion for employees whose qualifications are relatively equal.

It should be mentioned, however, that exclusive promotion from within is not congruent with the merit principle because in this case highly qualified outsiders are not even considered for jobs. In fact, lateral entry that opens positions to persons outside the organization offers some distinct advantages. Public organizations, perhaps even more than private firms, need periodic infusions of new blood and fresh ideas. Moreover, individuals with private and nonprofit sector experience may contribute useful perspectives on how to do things differently in government.

3. Training and Development

Despite the pleas of training and development specialists, the formal training of public workers for improvement on the job or preparation for a higher ranking position has rarely been a high priority item in public sector HRM. The conventional perception is that training is desirable if extra funds can be found, but the training function should be the first to be cut during budget reductions. Thus, as a "stepchild" of public personnel administration, training has traditionally received minimal attention from management. Unions, too, were slow to recognize their potential role and responsibility in promoting the development of skills of their members.

However, unions today have gradually begun to value training programs for their membership. Some sponsor their own programs, such as assisting members to study for high school equivalency tests and promotional examinations. Career development for members of protected classes aids equal employment and diversity goals and can help crack the glass ceiling that blocks them from upper-level positions in many government organizations.

Unions have promoted three types of career development. The first type is helping workers in "dead-end" positions move into jobs with established career patterns (e.g., from data input clerk to office manager). The second type is creating new, permanent "bridge positions" and career ladders between existing jobs (e.g., various paraprofessional occupations). The third is upgrading workers' skills to qualify them for expected future vacancies (Figart, 1989). Unions also favor tuition reimbursement and paid leave for training and development-related activities.

Training and development have traditionally been neglected in public employment. However, training of government workers benefits the workers themselves, their unions, management, and the general public. Workers develop skills that can help them win promotions. Unions, management, and the citizenry gain from more effective, productive, and satisfied government workers.

Recent expansions of public sector labor management training partnerships hold promise for solving workforce development challenges. The collaborative approach to training and development can improve recruitment and retention of skilled workers, enhance productivity, and strengthen labor management relations (Walter, 2019). Training partnerships take a variety of forms including apprenticeships, pre-hire and new hire training, professional development workshops, and mentoring programs. For example, the state of Washington partnered with the nonprofit Imagine institute and SEIU local 925 to provide training and professional development opportunities for early learning/childcare workers in the state (Imagine Institute, n.d.). Similarly, the American federation of Teachers (AFT) and the National Education (NEA) frequently collaborate with local school districts to provide professional development opportunities for educators focused on helping new teachers gain skills in classroom management, creating career ladders that allow paraprofessionals to move into teaching, attaining micro-credentials. Likewise, the Public Works Department for the city of Phoenix partnered with the Laborers' International Union of North America (LIUNA) Local 777 on an apprenticeship program that aided in recruiting highly skilled employees and placing veterans and women in public sector jobs with good pay and benefits (Walter, 2019).

4. Position Classification and Staffing

In most public jurisdictions in the United States, jobs are organized into classes or groups on the basis of the responsibilities, duties, skills, and qualifications assigned to them. Positions are analyzed and evaluated on the job characteristics and the work performed and then grouped into classes according to their similarities and differences. Class standards establish the boundaries for each group of positions. Unions are interested in classification plans because they serve as the framework for the organization's compensation structure.

The product of position classification is an ordering of individual positions within job classes. For example, the HRM division within a state social services agency might contain the positions of personnel analyst I, II, and III; or a municipal finance office might be assigned a class for accountants, with the positions accountant I, II, and III and senior accountant. Usually, position classification is a management responsibility of the state central HRM agency and the local government personnel director, assisted as necessary by private consultants. In federal employment, position classification is a duty of the Office of Personnel Management.

Public management has typically viewed classification as a management prerogative and hence not a proper subject for bargaining. The basic argument is that the classification of positions is an objective, scientific enterprise that serves as the cornerstone of the merit system. Positions are placed into classes in accordance with empirically determined job descriptions. However, the union perspective is that position classification is inherently subjective and arbitrary, especially when positions are classified across occupational functions. For example, should a data entry person be compared to a maintenance worker or a senior secretary to a new assistant personnel officer? Such decisions, the unions claim, involve value judgments. Therefore, they should be subject to collective negotiations.

In federal employment, according to Title VII of the CSRA of 1978, agencies may negotiate "on the numbers, types, and grades of employees or positions assigned to any organizational subdivision, work project, or tour of duty." In most federal contracts, unions participate in position classification. In some, for instance, unions exercise influence through joint committees on position classification standards.

Position classification has also been pulled within the scope of bargaining in many state and local jurisdictions. Unions accept the need for a system of position classification, but they want to have a voice in it because it affects compensation so directly. They want to participate in decisions to assign new jobs to higher pay grades and to create new positions for promotional opportunities. They also seek higher pay and shorter time limits for employees working "out of class."

Reclassifying jobs to higher pay grades is a rather complex procedure involving a variety of personnel actors, including the department head, agency or department personnel staff, and the central personnel agency. Unions may directly negotiate for reclassification where it is permitted, or they may attempt to influence any or all of the personnel actors. The creation of new jobs is particularly sought for occupations in which employees have little opportunity for promotion after the first few years on the job. The police function serves as a good example. Police patrol officers can "top out" at maximum pay after about five years. Higher pay can be achieved only through cost-of-living adjustments, seniority pay, or promotion to a supervisory or investigative position (jobs for which a good patrol officer may not be suited). In some cases, unions have been instrumental in creating a new position, such as "master patrol officer," to reward senior officers on the beat with higher pay for their experience.

The matter of properly compensating employees for out-of-title work in higher rated jobs is also a concern. Unions submit that when an employee performs the duties of a higher paying job because of a vacation, illness, temporary vacancy, or some other reason, that employee should be fully compensated at the appropriate rate of pay. Moreover, the unions say, after a designated period of out-of-class work the "temporary" employee should be promoted into the job. Disagreements between unions and management on out-of-class work may be settled through grievance or merit system procedures, a partnership approach, or appropriate language in the contract. For example, a contract may stipulate that an employee will be paid at a higher rate if he or she works four or more hours at a higher rated position. Properly rewarding employees for the nature of the work they perform seems an equitable proposition for which unions often win support.

The trend is toward replacing stringent position classification systems with a more flexible approach known variously as broadbanding, pay banding, or flexible banding. Existing position classes are collapsed into a broader range of position descriptions, permitting greater management flexibility in both reassigning and rewarding employees. Managers like the enhanced flexibility; unions enjoy any pay advantage but do not like the extension of management authority in assigning jobs.

In some federal partnerships, unions and management have negotiated the terms of new broadbanding systems. A collaborative approach has proved to be productive in some state and local settings as well. But in others, where preemptory actions have abolished or significantly altered the traditional merit system and position classification in favor of nearly absolute management autonomy, unions have been vehemently opposed to broadbanding. Staffing levels are of inherent interest to unions, who link staffing to the quality of services. A larger, more fully staffed bargaining unit also translates into more members of that bargaining unit (see Chapter 6 for the tradeoffs between compensation levels and jobs).

5. Workload and Scheduling

These closely intertwined issues refer to the amount of work required of individuals or groups of employees, the decision as to how many workers are required to perform that work, and the manner and time in which the work is to be done. In federal employment, agencies may negotiate with unions over the numbers of employees or positions assigned to work projects as well as the means of performing work. They seldom bargain over total hours of employment, which are fixed, but alternative work arrangements (e.g., telecommuting) are negotiable. In state and local governments, maximum working hours may be set by law or by contract. In some locations, employee organizations have won major workload and scheduling concessions from management in overtime provisions, shift assignments, overtime compensation, weekend and holiday differentials, meal and rest periods, cleanup time, and transfers to other jobs or different locations.

Unions have campaigned and bargained for a shorter workweek for more than a century. The 40-hour week remains the standard, but reductions to 37.5 and 35 hours have been won in some jurisdictions. Police and firefighter unions have won reductions in total working hours as well as shift hours. Teachers bargain over the length of the school year and the school day, the number and size of classes, and the contours of year-round schooling. Teacher union efforts to shorten the length of the workday or school year face significant legal and practical limits from state laws mandating a standard school year and citizen and parental opposition to altering the public school timetable.

In an interesting departure from the norm aimed at improving a public education system in crisis, the Rochester New York School District and the Rochester Teachers' Association negotiated a longer school year. In exchange for a more than 40% increase in salaries, teachers agreed to work an extra five days a year, take personal responsibility for a group of students, and make home visits (Doherty & Lipsky, 1988, pp. 56–57). In 2024, schools in the following states: Colorado, New York, Connecticut, Massachusetts, and Tennessee agreed to add additional time in school as part of the "Time Collaborative," an initiative of the U.S. Department of Education, the Ford Foundation and the National Center for Time and Learning. The initiative expands the time in school by 300 hours per year. Individual schools will determine the how to achieve the increase through the daily classroom time and number of days on the school calendar (Chen, 2023).

Teachers have attained other gains in the general area of workload and scheduling and have managed to open the scope of bargaining wider than any other occupational function in the United States. Teachers have demanded and won relief from non-teaching chores, such as milk distribution; playground supervision; cafeteria, bus, and hall supervision; book distribution; and copying materials for classroom use. Duty-free lunch periods for teachers have also been established, as have limitations on work beyond the regular school day. Teachers have gained extra compensation for after-school administrative meetings, parent-teacher conferences, and other extracurricular activities. They have also won provisions limiting involuntary teacher transfers and requiring teacher assignments to be based on characteristics such as certification, seniority, and experience (Goldschmidt & Stuart, 1986, p. 354).

Teachers have staked a claim in the field of education policy making by demanding to include class size in the scope of bargaining (Stone, 2000, pp. 53–54). This appears to be an instance in which a workload factor links logically to the quality of education. More students mean more work for the teacher, less time for the teacher to spend with each student individually, and higher probability of disciplinary problems. Where class size falls within the scope of bargaining, student-teacher ratios tend to be smaller. When it is excluded from negotiations, teachers seek to win salary increases for large class sizes and workloads (Woodbury, 1985).

Other unions have been concerned with workload and scheduling, too. Nurses face enormous pressures in acute care departments and facilities under the best of circumstances, but when they have to work 12- to 16-hour shifts or double shifts because of staff shortages, patients are at greater risk from nursing error. Along with managed care and the infusion of profit-making considerations, the national nurse staffing shortage has exerted a significant negative effect on the nursing profession. Unions rightfully capitalize (and organize) in such a setting, fighting for a more favorable nurse-per-patient ratio, shorter hours, and improved working conditions (Clark & Clark, 2006). When health care workers at Kaiser Permanente went on strike twice within a period of 12 months, the eventual settlement terms included reduced caseloads for health care professionals, additional guaranteed time with patients, and a commitment from Kaiser to hire more therapists (Hwang, 2023)

Understaffing can create unacceptable and dangerous situations in other occupations as well. When the Federal Aviation Administration preemptively ended a negotiations impasse in 2006 by imposing a new contract with staffing cuts, new work rules, and a 30% pay cut air traffic controllers retired in droves. The long hours and staff shortages deeply concerned controllers, who feared that fatigue could lead to them making a deadly mistake in air traffic routing (Sniffen, 2007).

The existing staffing shortage was exacerbated by the COVID-19 pandemic and has yet to be resolved. In 2023, the U.S. Department of Transportation (DOT), Office of the Inspector General issued a report stating that the Federal Aviation Administration FAA made limited efforts address the staffing shortage of controllers at critical air traffic control facilities and recommended improvements (U.S. DOT, 2023). In 2024, the National Air Traffic Controllers Association (NATCA) warned the Federal Aviation Administration (FAA) of a looming crisis among the controllers. Specifically, controllers already working a regular six-day week, are routinely assigned mandatory overtime. This results in fatigue, burnout, and higher turnover. The union called on Congress to address the staffing shortage in its budget authorization (NATCA, 2024).

Police unions may interpret work assignments as a safety issue in situations involving one- or two-officer patrol cars. Some unions assert that two officers are necessary to maximize officer safety, but police management wants flexibility in assigning officers according to time of day and geographic area. Police unions have also struggled with management over the matter of using civilian employees for administrative, clerical, and dispatcher jobs, preferring to use sworn officers instead. Management typically prefers to keep more officers on the street by placing lower-paid civilians in support positions.

Unions have successfully engaged the issue of flexible work schedules. A growing percentage of the total public and private labor force is involved in flextime, job sharing, telecommuting, or permanent part-time work. Interest in such arrangements has developed with the changing demographics of the workforce, including semi-retired employees and working parents. Flextime and telework can help employees cope with difficult commutes and rush-hour traffic by permitting them to work at various times between 6:00 a.m. and 8:00 p.m.

In 2022, 87% of eligible federal employees participated in telework, as did a substantial number of state and local workers. Telework has been effective in reducing turnover intentions, enhancing work-life balance, increasing productivity, and improving management practices to ensure accountability and monitor employee performance (U.S. Office of Personnel Management, 2023). Telework policies vary at the state level. To illustrate, California requires state employees to be in the office at least two days per week (Ramos, 2024). In Oregon, state employees are encouraged to work remotely when: it is feasible, it benefits the state and the employees, and it does not conflict with a collective bargaining agreement (Department of Administrative Services, 2024). Maryland requires the state to negotiate the terms and conditions of telework when the employees affected by the policies are represented by a union (Mostris, 2021). It appears to be a win–win issue for unions and management. However, it causes financial problems in cities and towns where government offices are located over long-term commercial real estate vacancies and reduced foot traffic in restaurants and retail stores.

6. Grievances

Grievance procedures, which provide a formal avenue for employees to tell their side of the story in an objective setting about problems arising on the job, are second in union interest only to wages and benefits. As in the case of compensation, this is an element of HRM on which unions have had a significant effect. Virtually all bargaining jurisdictions have contracts with negotiated grievance procedures. Most provide for binding arbitration as a final step in cases in which grievances cannot be settled at the agency or department level. (Grievance procedures receive full treatment in Chapter 10.)

7. Employee Discipline

Closely related to grievance procedures is employee discipline. Disciplinary actions by management are frequently the triggering mechanism for grievance procedures. In general, unions have sought to protect employees from unfair disciplinary actions by formalizing the process and placing the burden of proof on management. They have also fought to negotiate procedures through collective bargaining instead of traditional civil service rules. Typically, unions represent the accused employee in any disciplinary proceeding.

It may well be that the most important union influence on disciplinary actions is tacit. Union influence is registered long before formal disciplinary actions are actually taken. This occurs because supervisors are fully aware that hasty or unfair adverse actions will be successfully contested.

8. Dismissals and Layoffs

It is not a simple matter to dismiss a government employee, even under abnormal circumstances, once the initial probationary period has expired. Due process is a powerful value in public personnel administration, and courts and arbitrators have consistently held that non-probationary public employees have property rights in their jobs. Public employers can rarely follow the employment-at-will doctrine and dismiss an employee for a good reason, a bad reason, or no reason at all (Muhl, 2001). Courts have become important policy makers in personnel matters. With respect to employee dismissals, the tendency is for the courts to establish procedural safeguards so elaborate that, for all practical purposes, public employees have become tenured, with "ownership" of their jobs. In combination with merit system protections, vigorous union appeals, and sympathetic arbitrators, this has made most public employees nearly immune from being fired (Hays, 1995).

Generally, workers covered by bargaining contracts enjoy comprehensive protections against arbitrary dismissal. Employers must prove "just cause" for a separation to stand. For their part, unions effectively fight anything that smacks of wrongful discharge. Indeed, such protective actions are a major selling point to potential union members. For example, Rushin's (2021) analysis of police arbitration cases over a 14-year period shows that arbitrators reduced or overturned discipline in 52% of cases. Where termination occurred, arbitrators required reinstatement in 49% of cases. Where suspensions occurred, arbitrators shortened the length by 49% on average.

An interesting issue concerns employee dismissal for off-duty misconduct. The principle that has evolved in courts and in arbitration hearings is that discharge is justified when the misconduct has a demonstrated adverse impact on the employer. Once the alleged misconduct is proved, it must be demonstrated that the misconduct damaged the agency's image or "product" through adverse publicity, through another employee's refusal to work with the offender, or by making the offender unable to perform his or her job. Generally, those in sensitive jobs such as law enforcement, fire protection, and teaching are held to higher standards than other government workers.

Teacher tenure became a hot-button issue in the late 2000s. First adopted in 1909, tenure policies were eventually enacted by nearly all states and school districts. Their purpose is to protect teachers from being fired on discriminatory or arbitrary grounds, such as gender, religion, nationality, cronyism, or political beliefs. Tenure, which is accompanied by strong job protection, is typically awarded after two or three years on the job. As the public spotlight was turned on ineffective teachers as a factor in poor student and school performance, tenure came under attack. To be sure, many teachers have been awarded tenure simply for showing up in the classroom for a sufficient length of time. Once awarded, tenure makes it extremely difficult for school administrators to dismiss poorly performing teachers. Until very recently, teacher unions staunchly defended tenure and fought any efforts to weaken it.

Beginning around 2010, governors, legislators, and school reformers took aim at tenure (Gabriel & Dillon, 2011). Idaho and Florida ended teacher tenure outright in 2011 (voters overturned the Idaho law in 2012), and eight states have made demonstrated effective performance a requirement for receiving tenure or stipulated that poor performance will result in the retraction of tenure (Bonner, 2012). In New York City, 97% of teachers eligible for tenure received it in 2007. But in 2012, tenure was awarded to only 55% of those eligible (Baker, 2012). The school board fired the entire teaching staff and administration in Central Falls, Rhode Island, in 2010 (Zezima, 2010). Confronted with a tsunami of criticism, the AFT and the NEA have grudgingly accepted certain limitations on tenure and recognized the need to make effective teacher performance a requisite for earning and keeping it. However, the teacher unions are adamant that teacher performance evaluation should involve much more than standardized test scores, including peer review of teaching.

9. Reductions in Force

Procedural protections for individual employees apply only marginally when agency- or government-wide reductions in force are implemented. Unions do exert influence on which workers are to be laid off and what the priority and procedures are for reemployment. Unions, of course, favor the criterion of seniority. "Bumping rights" is a common negotiation item that establishes the conditions under which a more senior qualified worker in one unit can displace a less senior worker in another unit during a reduction in force. The basic union position is that less-senior workers should be the first to be laid off and the last to be rehired. In general, this is not a point of contention with management, although seniority in retention and reemployment remains a common topic in formal contract negotiations.

Alternatives to layoffs are sometimes sought by unions, depending on member sentiment and management consent. Possibilities include job sharing (two full-time positions are collapsed into two half-time jobs), rotating layoffs, furloughs, voluntary days off without pay, and work sharing. Work sharing programs can be particularly helpful during downturns in the economy. Under these programs, employers temporarily reduce workers' hours rather than lay them off. This approach helps employers retain a skilled workforce and ramp up to a full-time schedule when the economy improves improve. Typically, employees are paid for the hours worked and they are able to collect pro-rated unemployment benefits to make up for lost working hours (Gilarsky et al., 2020). Rutgers University entered into such an arrangement with its unionized employees in response to the economic crisis created by the COVID-19 pandemic. Under this plan, covered employees were furloughed one day a week in June and July, 2020. Employees received supplementary unemployment benefits for each week that a furlough day was taken, under the benefit program authorized by the Coronavirus Aid, Relief, and Economic Security (CARES) Act.

10. Other Human Resource Management Policies

Unions have been influential in designing and establishing other human resource-related policies. Several are considered here: technological change; productivity; privatization; worker health and safety issues, such as smoking, disability, and drug use; workers' compensation; and miscellaneous terms and conditions of employment.

a. Technological Change

Private sector unions have long been interested in the consequences of technological change for their membership. Historically, unions have opposed labor-saving innovations that reduce the number of union jobs. Union success in this area has led to the practice of "featherbedding," in which idle employees are kept on a firm's payroll indefinitely.

There are limits to the application of labor-saving technology in the public sector because of the labor intensity of government services. Still, certain services are better candidates for technological innovations than others. Garbage collection is one such area, where changes have included trash compactors, standardized carts, automated collection systems, and one-person crews. Stanley (1972, p. 100) relates an amusing story involving early technological change in solid waste collection in Detroit:

> Management proposed increasing the productivity of garbage collection trips by using a rig known as a 'motherloader'—a garbage truck towing a trailer. The employees took one look at it, changed its name, and started for home. Management soon dropped the idea because the equipment had technical, as well as labor-relations, drawbacks.

Similarly, "bandit trucks" with one-person crews and nine-foot automatic arms have been opposed by sanitation unions, which claim that the massive vehicles are unable to navigate narrow streets or work on both sides of the road at the same time, leading to less efficient trash collection compared to traditional trucks.

The employment and work scheduling effects of information technology have received union scrutiny and become a frequent subject for bargaining. Automation can replace humans with technology, resulting in reduced demand for various support workers. Information technology also presents new opportunities for alternative work schedules and workplaces, as noted earlier. This was especially true during the pandemic, as software programs with the capacity to facilitate virtual meetings were adopted.

Most public employee unions claim that they are not opposed to technological changes, given the following conditions:

1 The changes can be shown to be beneficial to the particular service
2 Workers' jobs are adequately protected
3 Employees will share any monetary gains from productivity improvements
4 Changes in the place, rules, and hours of work are negotiated or, at a minimum, subject to consultation with the union
5 The union receives advance notice of planned technological change

The most important condition is that employees must be protected from job loss. Where this is not entirely possible severance pay, natural attrition, reassignments, early retirement, or other arrangements are utilized.

b. Productivity

Maximizing outputs while minimizing inputs—productivity—is a significant concern of public managers (Kearney & Berman, 1999). To improve levels of productivity, however, one must first be able to measure it. This presents problems in the public sector, where labor-intensive services, not goods or manufactured items, are the product. Government services do have identifiable output (process) and outcome (results) indicators, but in practice they are difficult to collect and interpret.

Empirical research on private sector unions has generated mixed findings. Freeman and Medoff (1984) concluded that unions enhance productivity. This occurs in unionized settings because management hires higher quality workers, purchases more capital-intensive technology, expands training opportunities, and benefits from lower employee turnover. Research also suggests that improvements in product quality and quantity are more likely to be achieved through programs jointly designed and administered by unions and management compared to settings with no union involvement (Kearney & Hays, 1994). However, unions can thwart productivity improvement efforts, and their wage-setting activities may cause research and development funds to be displaced by payroll costs. Also, although unionization may be associated with low turnover, it is related to higher absenteeism as well. To summarize, little reliable evidence exists regarding the productivity effects of private sector unions.

In government, the influence of unions on the quality and quantity of services is also uncertain or variable. With respect to productivity in specific functions, unions have cooperated in adopting productivity improvement technologies in some municipal sanitation departments but not others (Lewin, 1986). In a number of documented cases, work rules for police and firefighters have depressed productivity. Detroit offers an example, where highly trained, uniformed police officers mop floors and maintain patrol vehicles. Another productivity-sapping Detroit work rule prohibits drivers from joining parks and recreation crews in their tasks (Maynard, 2012b).

Sanitation unions have found themselves with a Hobson's choice in cities where privatization is a looming threat. Private contractors tend to be freely available and more productive and less expensive than municipal sanitation departments in collecting household and industrial waste, largely due to smaller crews, lower wages, inferior benefits, newer equipment, less absenteeism, and superior incentive systems (Lewin, 1986; Hoover & Peoples, 2003). If municipal unions fight technological change (such as new sanitation trucks with smaller crews), management may pursue privatization. Instead, if unions accept technological improvements workforce reductions eventually follow, diminishing the ranks of dues-paying members. Unions have adamantly—even violently—opposed technological change and privatization in some cities (e.g., Tampa, Florida; Salt Lake City, Utah; and Camden, New Jersey). In other cases, sanitation unions have addressed the issues through labor–management committees or productivity bargaining (Lewin, 1986).

For decades, a debate has raged over the issue of teacher productivity in public schools. The debate is really part of a larger dialogue over the role of teachers in education reform and in improving the quality of schools. Conservative scholars and pundits have laid much of the blame for the perceived deteriorating quality of public education (K–12) on teacher unions. Critics accuse unions of driving up costs, protecting incompetent teachers, ignoring the education needs of children, and opposing meaningful reform efforts, such as educational choice. Teacher unions and progressives view teachers as the key element in any serious effort to reform the schools. Unions argue that they boost productivity by giving teachers a meaningful voice in school and classroom decisions, thereby bolstering teacher morale and reducing turnover rates (Carini, 2008).

Several empirical studies have been conducted on the effects of teacher unions on public school productivity. Eberts and Stone (1987) found that for elementary schools unionized school districts were 7% more productive for average students than nonunion districts when productivity was measured in terms of student scores on standardized tests. However, union districts were about 7% less productive for students either significantly above or significantly below average, possibly because teacher unions support standardized educational practices more than specialized instruction techniques of greater benefit to very advanced and very delayed students. Across all students, the union productivity advantage was 3% (Eberts & Stone, 1987).

Kurth (1987) weighed in on the debate with an analysis of SAT scores. He determined that several factors were related to student test performance, including exposure to the written word, parental involvement, an urban environment, and education spending. Teachers' unions were found to have a highly negative impact on student performance. Kurth concluded that unions significantly impair teacher productivity and student educational achievement.

Kurth's findings were vigorously attacked by Nelson and Gould (1988), who argued that Kurth's mathematical model was mis-specified and his variables were poorly defined, leading to an erroneous conclusion. Reexamining the data, Nelson and Gould found that collective bargaining was associated with significantly higher SAT scores. Subsequent research supports Nelson and Gould' findings (Carini, 2008; Hoxby, 1996; Lovenheim, 2009; Nelson & Rosen, 1996/2000).

Zigarelli (1994) also found that unions are positively related to student performance. His model attributes the relationship between unions and student achievement to (1) teacher unions "shocking" school bureaucracies into more efficient practices that generate positive classroom outcomes and (2) union political activities that boost education funding. In a study of the effects of teacher unions on high school dropout rates, Zwerling and Thomason (1994) found that unions significantly reduce the likelihood of boys dropping out but only slightly decrease the female dropout rate. Han and Maloney (2022) examined the relationship between teachers' unions, socioeconomic status, and student performance. They found generally positive effects of teachers' unions on student performance on standardized tests. With respect to teacher quality, Han (2020) found that highly unionized districts dismiss more low-quality teachers and retain more high-quality teachers, thereby raising average teacher quality and educational outcomes. A reasonable conclusion is that teacher unions do not depress student achievement and, in fact, have a modest positive effect on it.

c. *Privatization*

The transfer of public goods and service provision responsibilities to the private sector has been a worldwide phenomenon since the rise of NPM in the 1980s. The movement has several impetuses, including ideological opposition to the size of the public sector, belief that the private sector can provide goods and services more efficiently (cheaply) than government, and the fiscal squeeze at all levels of government. In the United States, privatization has taken various forms: construction of a public facility by a private contractor (e.g., bridge or highway), services (e.g., information technology), government purchases of specialized services (e.g., legal assistance and engineering expertise) on a short-term basis, and contracting out public services to a private or nonprofit organization. Sanitation, transportation, and K–12 vouchers for education are the most common areas of outsourced services.

In most jurisdictions, privatization is considered a management right related to the efficient management of the workplace and therefore outside the scope of bargaining. In principle, unions do not object to constructing facilities, making specialized purchases, or contracting out professional services that their own members cannot perform, such as architecture, engineering, or creative services. It is when traditional government functions, such as sanitation or fire protection, are given over to the private sector that unions register vociferous opposition.

Unions contend that contracting out results in the termination of public employee jobs and the creation of new lower-paying jobs in the private sector. Therefore, it is a personnel matter that should fall within the scope of bargaining. In state and local governments, labor relations boards and the courts, with few exceptions, have supported the union position that the decision to contract out should be a mandatory subject of bargaining and that public employers are obligated to provide notice of the proposed work change to the unions and an opportunity to negotiate the issues.

For example, New Jersey passed a law in 2020 that places limits on the ability of public school districts and county colleges to enter into subcontracting agreements. Specifically, the law prohibits employers from imposing subcontracting during the term of an existing collective bargaining agreement. Employers may explore outsourcing during contract negotiations, provided that they notify the unions and the Public Employment Relations Commission 90 days before soliciting bids for outsourcing. Employers must also provide unions the opportunity to meet and consult with the employer over the decisions to outsource work and negotiate the impact of subcontracting on affected employees (New Jersey Legislature, 2020).

In the federal sector, agency management clearly controls contracting-out decisions despite union opposition. Federal management is fortified by (1) the Office of Management and Budget's circular A-76, a directive to federal agencies that requires work to be contracted out to a firm if it can conduct the work more economically; (2) Title VII of the CSRA, which grants management the authority to "make determinations with respect to contracting out"; and (3) actions during the George W. Bush administration that further narrowed the scope of bargaining on contracting activities.

Unions in state and local governments seek to discourage employers from contracting out, promising strident opposition if this path is taken. Any available political strings will be pulled and litigation filed. As suggested earlier, such opposition is entirely rational because the record shows that union membership declines where contracting out occurs. Moreover, there can be mutual benefits when unions force a careful, objective pace to privatization that diminishes the possibility of policy mistakes. Increasingly, unions seek to develop competitive bids to retain their public service production responsibilities, thereby eliminating the economic rationale for privatizing. They have done so successfully in several cities, including Phoenix, Philadelphia, and Indianapolis.

Nonetheless, privatization has registered substantial gains in functions such as sanitation; street construction; architectural and engineering services; legal counseling; vehicle towing; building repair, maintenance, and security; social services; and ambulance services. Chelsea, Massachusetts, even contracted out the entire public school system to Boston University for ten years. Massachusetts has privatized mental health care, prison health care, highway maintenance, and operation of highway rest stops, among many other activities. Interestingly, in cities where management–union relations are highly adversarial, the likelihood of privatization is greater than in cities with cooperative relations (Chandler & Feuille, 1991). Perhaps management is sorely tempted to try to rid itself of a perceived labor pest in such cities.

Contracting out does not eliminate unionization and the strike threat. On the contrary, private firms can be unionized, too, and often are, and their workers can legally strike. Furthermore, monetary savings may be illusory. Indiana's 2009 cancellation of a $1.34 billion contract with IBM to privatize the state's welfare services offers an instructive example of failed privatization (Schneider & Ruthhart, 2009). Similarly, New Jersey outsourced Hurricane Sandy relief efforts to a private contractor. The contractor billed the state over $51 million in the first eight months of the contract. However, company had agreed to a three-year service provision contract for a total of $67 million (Fine et al., 2016)

Quality and service levels sometimes decline, accountability may suffer, equity in service delivery may be sacrificed, and contracts may be awarded on the basis of political favoritism. Privatization has been particularly controversial in police and fire protection, prisons, and schools. For instance, the neglect of contract oversight in the New Jersey Department of Corrections Residential Community Release Program led to a halfway-house resident escaping and murdering a resident of Newark. It also called into question the quality of services the state was receiving in exchange for the over $60 million spent on the residential release program annually (Fine et al., 2016). Still, the outlook is for continued outsourcing ahead, with highways, bridges, mass transit, and water supply showing the strongest potential.

d. Health and Wellness

Myriad health- and safety-related issues have found their way to the bargaining table. This reflects new knowledge and information, changing technology, unions' traditional concern for the physical and psychological well-being of workers. The fact that public employees are not protected by the Occupational Safety and Health Act (OSHA) of 1970 (most states have OSHA-type legislation, however) has also played a role.

Four particular health issues have received increasing scrutiny from management and unions. These include: smoking in the workplace, HIV/AIDS, drug testing, and employee wellness programs. Unions want to formally register the perspectives of their membership on these important issues and to defend aggrieved individuals in the bargaining unit. With respect to smoking, The Centers for Disease Control and Prevention (CDC) have estimated that cigarette smoking cost over $600 billion in lost productivity and increased health-care expenditures in 2018. Cigarette smoking is believed to be responsible for more than 480,000 deaths per year from cancer, heart disease, pulmonary disease, and other ailments. In 2021, roughly 11.5% of U.S. adults smoked (CDC, 2023).

Employers are concerned with smoking (and secondhand smoke) because it affects them financially through increased absenteeism, higher insurance and medical care costs, and lost productivity. Moreover, most employers must enforce the expanding number of state and local laws that prohibit or restrict smoking in public places. Although the federal courts have not found a constitutional basis for a smoke-free workplace, some state courts have upheld a common-law right to a safe and healthy workplace, which includes protection from secondhand smoke. As of 2022, 27 states and the district of Columbia have passed laws to prohibit smoking in the workplace (CDC, 2024). An employer that fails to provide a safe and healthy place of work may be held responsible in court for negligence.

In response, employers have adopted policies not to hire active smokers and to prohibit employees from smoking on the job altogether. Some have prohibited off-the-job smoking as well, although the legal grounds for such actions are questionable, probably violating the right to privacy and due process (Wilson, 1989). An additional problem with employer actions against smokers is that it has discriminatory impacts—African Americans and Latinos are more likely to smoke than whites. Finally, employers in most states have a common-law duty to accommodate both smoking and nonsmoking employees, and 29 states prohibit employers from discriminating against smokers (Repa, 2005; Employee Benefit News, 2012).

Unions, of course, have a legal obligation to represent the interests of all members in the bargaining unit, regardless of smoking preference. Under collective bargaining laws and contracts, management may not unilaterally alter the terms and conditions of employment. Smoking restrictions and rules are terms and conditions of employment unless legislation, or a management rights clause clearly places such work rules and conditions within the realm of management authority. Thus, management and unions must usually negotiate or otherwise agree on smoking policy.

Even where state or local laws apply, the implementation of statutory restrictions through workplace rules should be negotiated with the unions. The alternative is for management to field any number of formal grievances and, possibly, litigation. Management's right to impose rules concerning smoking may be contested, usually through union representation of a grievant who has been disciplined or dismissed for rule breaking. Unions insist on consistent, nonbiased enforcement of smoking policies and sanctions where they exist.

With respect to disabilities, the Rehabilitation Act of 1973 and the ADA of 1990 protect persons with disabilities from discrimination in any HRM process. Disabled workers must be provided with "reasonable accommodation" by employers, subject to "business necessity" limitations. For example, workplaces must be made physically accessible to people using wheelchairs (reasonable accommodation) unless the workplace cannot be modified without extreme cost to the employer (business necessity). The ADA's definition of "disability" is expansive, covering an estimated 47.5 million Americans. Most of them are not in the workforce. Within the broad definitional umbrella of the ADA are orthopedic impairments, back problems, vision or hearing trouble, traumatic brain injury, alcoholism, drug abuse, mental illness, and HIV infection.

Employers, as well as unions charged with fair representation of all members of the bargaining unit, must walk a fine line between protecting the rights of the disabled worker and respecting the rights and preferences of their coworkers. For instance, a union must represent both an HIV-infected employee in terms of reasonable accommodation of his or her medical needs and treatments and the concerns of coworkers who (unreasonably) fear becoming infected with the virus. An employer should consult with the union before transferring a disabled worker or making accommodations that affect other employees.

Obesity presents a problem for both employers and unions. Obesity is not listed as a bona fide disability under the ADA definition of "impairment of a major life activity." Weight-based discrimination in the workplace stigmatizes the obese as undisciplined and lazy (Rudin & Pereles, 2012). Failing authoritative federal or state actions, this is a problem best settled on a case-by-case basis.

Alcohol abuse has always been a scourge of the American workplace. It is now joined by another serious addiction: illegal and prescription drugs. These "evil twins" cost the U.S. economy billions of dollars every year and account for a disproportionate percentage of discipline and dismissal cases. Substance abusers are less productive, more prone to turnover, tardiness, property damage, and dismissal. They are also more likely to get sick or be injured than other employees.

Unions seldom disagree with management rules prohibiting working under the influence of drugs or alcohol because the safety and productivity of all members are potentially at risk. However, unions do prefer to negotiate specific rules and procedures for addressing the problem. Unions will also aggressively defend employees accused of substance abuse. In the case of alcohol abuse, unions argue that discipline is unfair because alcoholism is a disease beyond one's own control. Most government employers accept this view and give alcoholic employees an opportunity for treatment and counseling through an employee assistance program (EAP) or on their own. If the worker is unable to conquer the addiction and his or her performance is judged unacceptable, discharge usually follows.

Although both alcoholics and drug addicts have some protection from adverse employment actions by the Rehabilitation Act and the ADA (they are considered to be disabled), drug abusers are more likely to be treated severely by management. Drug use is, after all, usually illegal, and a greater stigma is attached to it than to drinking. For example, off-duty drug use may directly result in discharge if a court conviction is made, whereas alcohol abuse rarely does, except indirectly through poor attendance and job performance. A worker guilty of using or selling drugs at the place of employment is also asking for discharge. Unions do not raise a significant barrier to such employer actions as long as members receive due process, and any policy alterations are submitted to the unions for consideration. The matter of testing employees for drug use is more contentious.

Few restraints exist on drug testing in the private and nonprofit sectors or on testing prospective employees in any setting. In government, constitutional issues are germane for ongoing employees, including the Fourth Amendment's right to privacy and freedom from unreasonable search and seizure, the equal protection clause of the Fourteenth Amendment, the Fifth Amendment's protection from self-incrimination, and various state constitutional protections. A nonunion jurisdiction may get away with unilaterally imposing a drug-testing policy on current employees. Where unions represent workers the policy is usually treated as a term or condition of employment, that is, a mandatory bargaining subject.

Under most circumstances, unions are adamantly opposed to drug testing, particularly if it is randomly imposed without a clear purpose. Drug testing is an invasive procedure that requires analyses of urine, blood, hair, saliva, or nail samples. It is not time specific, so it often "reveals more about the employee's off-duty lifestyle than about his ability to perform on the job" (Denenberg, 1987, p. 305). Laboratory testing procedures are notoriously unreliable.

Courts tend to side with the unions, unless the government employer can demonstrate a legitimate interest in testing (e.g., public safety) and a fair program that adequately guards employee rights. In *Skinner v. Railway Labor Executives' Association* (1989), the U.S. Supreme Court held that urine collection violates the reasonable right to privacy under certain conditions. In *NTEU v. Van Raab* (1989), the Supreme Court restricted the U.S. Customs Service's drug-testing program for candidates for promotion to those in "sensitive positions" involved in drug interdiction. Legitimate "reasonable" interest in testing for drug use is easier to prove for employees directly involved in protecting public health and safety, such as police, firefighters, train and mass transit drivers, air traffic controllers, and any worker who carries a firearm.

Some of the most interesting activity concerning the legality of drug testing has occurred in the federal government. Random drug testing in the military was ordered by President Nixon in 1971, and it continues today. In 1986, President Reagan punctuated his wife Nancy's "Just Say NO!" campaign by directing all executive agencies to randomly test all workers in sensitive positions. A fury of union litigation ensued, resulting in several court cases, rulings by the FLRA, and congressional involvement (Masters, 1988). The federal unions claimed that management must prove a link between a positive drug test and an individual's work performance before disciplinary actions can be taken. The federal agencies differed on this issue, asserting that drug testing is a nonnegotiable management right under Section 7106 of the CSRA. Drug-testing programs continue to be challenged in some federal agencies today and in several states.

When not fighting over drug testing in courts, arbitration venues, or across the bargaining table, unions and management can embark on cooperative ventures to address the drug abuse problem. Employee assistance plans provide aid and counseling to drug users that benefit both parties. So do drug prevention programs, sponsored or cosponsored by unions, which can marshal peer pressure against drug abuse and encourage users to seek help.

Wellness is a concern because high and rising employee health-care costs push employers to consider programs to help reduce them. Wellness programs encourage workers to lead healthy lifestyles by quitting smoking, eating better, exercising, and changing other negative behaviors. In theory, the employer saves money on lower health insurance claims, reduced absenteeism, higher worker morale, and improved productivity.

Unions generally support wellness programs. Rhode Island's "Rewards for Wellness" program has served a highly unionized labor force since 2008. Labor-management negotiations approved activities that enable employees to earn up to $500 a year in "co-share credit" toward their copays on health insurance by taking medical screening tests and health tutorials, ceasing tobacco use, and other such actions. Results indicate lower rates of hypertension, fewer health insurance claims, greater weight loss, and other positive outcomes (Rodriguez, 2012). Issues that a union might take special interest in include the possibility of a wellness program violating disability law, privacy rights, and mandatory (vs. elective) participation.

e. *Workers' Compensation*

Workers' compensation is a federal–state program that pays benefits to workers injured on the job, regardless of fault. Texas is the only state that does not require employers to purchase workers' compensation insurance (Texas Division of Insurance, n.d.). In 2020, the total annual employer costs for workers' compensation were approximately $93.0 billion (Murphy & Wolf, 2022). A study of workers' compensation claims (Hirsch et al., 1997) found that union members were significantly more likely to receive such benefits than similar nonunion workers. What are the reasons? Possibly because unions provide their members with more assistance and information about the program and, through contract and grievance procedures, protect filers from management-imposed penalties for filing claims. Moreover, union workers are more likely to hold dangerous jobs such as police and fire protection or corrections.

f. Miscellaneous Terms and Conditions

If a variable in the environment of work can even imaginatively be labeled a "working condition," then the odds are that some union, somewhere, has challenged management over it. In many instances, union interest in working conditions has led to improvements, especially within the area of employee safety. Safety, of course, is an important concern to both employees and management. Injuries or deaths at the workplace are anathema to both parties. Their prevention is normally recognized in labor agreements as the joint responsibility of management and labor. Unions, in particular, are vigilant concerning an employer's duty to provide a healthy and safe working environment, including the provision of protective equipment and clothing and expeditiously addressing potential health and safety threats. In some instances, unions have formed coalitions with environmental groups to protect worker safety and health in workplaces with toxic releases (Mayer, 2009).

For public school teachers, a safety-related issue is the need to protect teachers from violent students. Teachers feel that control over student disciplinary procedures is critical to their physical and emotional well-being. Discipline is an especially salient issue in big city school systems containing many students who are "difficult to teach." Generally, teachers want the right to expel from the classroom students who evidence intractable disciplinary problems and the right to be represented on student disciplinary committees. Courts have affirmed that negotiations over student disciplinary matters are within the scope of bargaining unless specifically excluded as a management right (*Sutherlin Education Association v. Sutherlin School District No. 130,* 1976).

Other work conditions subject to bargaining include meal and rest periods cleanup time, coffee breaks, locker rooms, clothing allowances, and mileage allowances. One early but exhaustive list of negotiated working conditions was attributed to the Social Service Employees Union in New York City (Stanley, 1972, pp. 110–111):

> The union's contract contains unusually detailed provisions on working time and free time, including travel time to get paychecks; grace periods for handicapped employees at the beginning and end of shifts; grace periods for delays

> due to inadequate elevator service; dismissal at 3 p.m. if the temperature reaches 92 degrees F; dismissal at noon if the temperature falls below 50 degrees outside and 68 degrees inside, or if it falls below those levels after 12 noon, dismissal within an hour . . . the contract assures the employee of a place to hang his coat, and—obviously essential in view of the preceding requirements—a thermometer.

You name it—it has been the subject of negotiations somewhere. The Minnesota Supreme Court ruled, on appeal, that facial hair and fingernail length are not mandatory subjects of bargaining for sheriffs' deputies. Ear studs? They are not banned in Boston, but officers are forbidden to wear them in Peotone, California and Vernon, Connecticut. Tattoos and body piercings arise as issues in negotiations and disciplinary proceedings if their presence (and visibility) is believed to negatively affect the workplace or be offensive to government's "customers." In some jurisdictions, tattoos and piercings are covered under a negotiated, comprehensive dress code (McKelvey & Ronalds, 2013).

As mentioned previously, teachers have had more success in broadening the scope of bargaining than any other occupational group, largely because there are significant elements of management and independent decision making in their daily duties. Among the working conditions negotiated in teacher contracts are the following:

- Class size provisions
- Number and functions of teacher aides
- School calendar
- Teacher representation on instructional policy committees
- Teacher evaluation procedures
- Special programs
- Curriculum
- Grading criteria
- Textbook selection
- Allocation of federal grant money
- Teaching methodologies
- Peer evaluation of teachers in lieu of principal's ratings
- Peer coaching and counseling
- School safety
- Teacher residency requirements
- Provisions for day care centers for teachers' children
- Teacher participation in school site selection

The cutting point in the scope of teacher negotiations seems to be how directly an issue affects the well-being of the individual teacher as opposed to its impact on the operation of the school system as a whole.

IV. CONCLUSION

As the purse strings of state and local governments have been cinched tight by fiscal constraints, a stingy yet mandate-heavy federal government, and a hypercritical citizenry, unions have turned from an almost exclusive concentration on wages and dollar-driven benefits to nonmonetary elements of human resource administration. Nonetheless, wages remain a visible and important issue for unions. Historically, public sector wage gains have been fairly modest. However, in 2022 and 2023 many unions fought to recoup losses resulting from cost-cutting measures during the pandemic. Unions representing state and local government workers were particularly vocal as they represent many front line service providers who had to assume risk and stay on the job during the pandemic. Pay raises in the public sector averaged 4.1% in 2022 and climbed to 5.5% in 2023 (Combs, 2024).

The clash between bargaining and merit systems is inherently a part of public sector labor relations, as unions seek to extend their sphere of influence and limit management authority. Unions want greater control of the workplace for their members. They work hard, and often successfully, to get it. Management today, however, is a more forceful and competent adversary in protecting its rights and prerogatives than it once was. In some ways, public management is made more effective and fairer by union involvement in workplace decisions. In other respects, the loss of flexibility in a union environment can impede management's response and adaptation to social, political, and economic changes.

A precarious balance exists between bureaucracy and democracy in the United States. Unions represent institutionalized bureaucratic power, whereas elected government officials and their appointees defend the principles and processes of representative government. As unions encroach on traditional areas of management rights, they sometimes penetrate the arena of public policy making. This is evident in public education, where teacher unions have fought and won a voice in determining a variety of education policies. It is also the case in nonprofit organizations, as health care workers have secured changes in staffing policies.

It is difficult to state with any assurance or finality whether union policy involvement is good or bad. In public education, it has clearly meant less flexibility for school management and some rigidity in school operations. However, teacher participation in determining how the learning process is structured may produce higher morale and, in the long run, positively affect the quality of program implementation. This is certainly the argument made by Rubinstein et al. (2024) in advocating for multi-stakeholder partnerships between school boards, teachers' unions, and administrators. In theory, this claim could be made by almost any occupational group in public employment, from corrections officers to sanitation engineers.

As a practical matter, there is a need for management–labor consultation over the role of public employees in policy determination. Final authority unquestionably should be retained by management and, ultimately, by elected officials. At the same time, the unions' voice is legitimate and can prove invaluable. The wise manager, the democratic manager, should not refuse to discuss policies raised by unions that are of direct concern to them and their members.

Ultimately, unions get only what management and arbitrators give to them. The protections of collective bargaining statutes, management rights clauses, ordinances, and merit systems shore up the defenses of management. So do political and economic factors in public employment that act as constraints on unions, not the least of which is public opinion. Public management is well served by using available resources and tools in establishing a firm, but not rigid, posture vis-à-vis the unions. Both parties in the relationship should strive to negotiate in an atmosphere of mutual respect and concern for public interest. However, as Chapter 8 points out, this is much easier said than done.

CASE STUDY 7.1 A BLOOMING LABOR DISPUTE

Nine-year-old Katie Corletta, a student at Horton Elementary, San Diego, California, was distressed about the condition of a public park across the street from her school. So, she organized a group of fellow third-graders to pick up the trash and plant a flower garden. They did a very nice job much to the delight of teachers and parents, who were impressed by the community spirit of the children.

Local 1029 of AFSCME was much less pleased. The municipal union, which represents Parks and Recreation Department employees, filed a prohibitive practices complaint, stating that it should have been informed and consulted about the student project because its members maintain the park by picking up broken glass and other trash, mowing the lawn, and repairing playground equipment.

Parents and the Parent Teacher Organization were shocked and outraged, and the children were confused: "we didn't think we were taking anything away from the union because they weren't planting flowers," Corletta said in a local newspaper report. "All we were doing is helping pick up trash. We're not mowing the lawn that the union people would do. We're just doing things they don't do."

Kenneth Boulware, president of Local 1029, said that the union had a serious problem with the city's lack of communication. Union members, he asserted, work nearly every day in the park. "Personally, I don't have a problem with third-graders," he said. "My problem is if they abandon the project, I'd have to have our people maintain it as they have in the past. And union workers should perform union work."

Questions

1 Why did the union react as it did when it discovered that the flower garden had been planted by the children? What were the possible justifications for the union action?

2 What contract language might apply to this situation?

3 If bargaining unit members had been laid off recently because of budget cuts, would this be important?

4 What are the implications for union–citizen relationships?

5 How would you have handled the issue if you were the union president?

CASE STUDY 7.2 A CHOCOLATE HIGH?

Jason, an employee of the State Department of Transportation with 18 years of experience, was passing by the coffee service area in the motor pool on a Wednesday when he spied a plate of brownies. Naturally, he ate one. Unfortunately, it was not an ordinary brownie. Even more unfortunately, he worked in a hazardous facility and was subject to random drug testing; the next day, his number was called.

Jason delivered his urine sample and thought no more of it until Thursday, when he was notified by his supervisor, Javier, that he had tested positive. When questioned about the results by his supervisor, Jason offered no explanation other than that he had been taking an over-the-counter cold medication and a wellness herb. Javier referred Jason to the Employee Assistance Program (EAP) for counseling. The EAP had no available appointments the next day, and neither the EAP nor Jason followed up Monday.

The following week, Jason was called into the HRM office and discharged for failing the drug test and refusing to seek EAP assistance. Shocked, Jason immediately proceeded to the union steward and filed a grievance seeking reinstatement to his position. In his statement, Jason said that he had not experienced any effects of marijuana and adamantly professed his innocence.

Shortly thereafter, Kenneth, one of Jason's coworkers, came forward to admit that he had baked some marijuana-laced brownies and placed them in the coffee area but that he did not intend them for Jason.

The case moved to a hearing officer.

Questions

1. If you were the hearing officer, what would you do after receiving Jason's grievance and Kenneth's admission?
2. Was Jason negligent and culpable for use of illegal drugs?
3. Should such situations be incorporated into a collective bargaining contract? Why or why not?

REFERENCES

Artz, B. (2012). Does the impact of union experience on job satisfaction differ by gender? *Industrial and Labor Relations Review*, *65*(2), 225–243.

Baker, A. (2012, August 17). Many New York City teachers denied tenure in policy shift. *New York Times*. www.nytimes.com

Ban, C. (1995). Unions, management and the NPR. In D. F. Kettl & J. J. DiIulio, Jr. (Eds.), *Inside the reinvention machine: Appraising governmental reform* (pp. 131–151). Brookings Institution.

Barclay, L. A., & Markel, K. S. (2007). Discrimination and stigmatization in work organizations: A multiple level framework for research on genetic testing. *Human Relations*, *60*(6), 953–980.

Barclay, L. A., & Markel, K. S. (2008). Genetic testing: Implications for the collective bargaining relationship. *Journal of Collective Negotiations (Formerly Journal of Collective Negotiations in the Public Sector)* *32*(3), 237–244.

Behr, J. G. (2000). Black and female municipal employment: A substantive benefit of minority political incorporation? *Journal of Urban Affairs*, *22*(3), 243–264.

Bonner, J. (2012, January 25). States weaken tenure rights for teachers. *USA Today*. www.usatoday.com

Brannick, P. M., & Holman, A. (2022, September). *The battle for worker freedom in the states: Grading state public sector labor laws*. The Commonwealth Foundation. https://www.commonwealthfoundation.org/wp-content/uploads/2022/09/Worker-Freedom-in-the-States-Sept-2022.pdf

Brook, D. A., & King, C. L. (2007, May–June). Civil service reform as national security: The Homeland Security Act of 2002. *Public Administration Review*, 399–407.

Burton, J. F. (1972, May). Local government bargaining and management structure. *Industrial Relations, 11*, 123–140.

Carini, R. M. (2008). Is collective bargaining detrimental to student achievement? Evidence from a national study. *Journal of Collective Negotiations (Formerly Journal of Collective Negotiations in the Public Sector)*, *32*(3), 215–235.

Centers for Disease Control and Prevention. (2023). *Burden of cigarette use in the U.S.* https://www.cdc.gov/tobacco/campaign/tips/resources/data/cigarette-smoking-in-united-states.html

Centers for Disease Control and Prevention. (2024). *Tobacco use in the workplace.* https://www.cdc.gov/niosh/substance-use/tobacco/index.html

Chandler, T., & Feuille, P. (1991, January–February). Municipal unions and privatization. *Public Administration Review, 51*, 15–22.

Chen, G. (2023, November 7). Longer school days coming for thousands of students next year. *Public School Review.* https://www.publicschoolreview.com/blog/longer-school-days-coming-for-thousands-of-students-next-year

Clark, P. F., & Clark, D. A. (2006). Union strategies for improving patient care: The key to nurse unionism. *Labor Studies Journal, 31*(1), 51–70.

Colorado Senate Bill 22-230, § 8-3.3-102 (4), 2022. https://leg.colorado.gov/sites/default/files/2022a_230_signed.pdf

Combs, R. (2024, March 19). *ANALYSIS: Unions won sky-high pay hikes in 2023 negotiations.* https://news.bloomberglaw.com/bloomberg-law-analysis/analysis-unions-won-sky-high-pay-hikes-in-2023-negotiations

Coursey, D., & Rainey, H. G. (1990, Spring). Perceptions of personnel system constraints in public, private, and hybrid organizations. *Review of Public Personnel Administration, 10*, 54–7 1.

Davis, C. (1984). Equity vs. fairness: The impact of collective bargaining policies on the implementation of affirmative action programs. *Journal of Collective Negotiations, 13*(3), 225–234.

Denenberg, T. S. (1987). Substance abuse: The challenge to industrial relations. In *40th annual proceedings of the industrial relations research association.* IRRA.

Department of Administrative Services. (2024, January 1). *State HR policy 50.050.01.* https://www.oregon.gov/das/Policies/50-050-01.pdf

Doeringer, P. B., Kaboolian, L., Watkins, M., & Watson, A. (1996). Beyond the merit model: New directions at the federal workplace? In D. Belman, M. Gunderson, & D. Hyatt (Eds.), *Public sector employment in a time of transition* (pp. 163–200). IRRA.

Doherty, R., & Lipsky, D. B. (1988). The education reform movement and the realities of collective bargaining. In B. D. Dennis (Ed.), *Proceedings of the 41st annual meeting of the IRRA* (pp. 51–59). IRRA.

Douglas, J. M. (1992, January–February). State civil service and collective bargaining: Systems in conflict. *Public Administration Review, 52*, 162–171.

Eberts, R. W., & Stone, J. A. (1987, April). Teacher unions and the productivity of public schools. *Industrial and Labor Relations Review, 40*, 354–363.

Employee Benefit News. (2012, December 20). http://ebn.benefitnews.com/news/

Figart, D. M. (1989). Collective bargaining and career development for women in the public sector. *Journal of Collective Negotiations, 18*(4), 301–313.

Fine, J., Mareschal, P. M., Hersh, D., & Leach, K. (2016). Contracting, performance management, and accountability: Political symbolism versus good governance. *Journal of Strategic Contracting and Negotiation*, *2*(4), 294–312.

Freeman, R. B., & Medoff, J. L. (1984). *What do unions do?* Basic.

Funck, E. K., & Karlsson, T. S. (2020). Twenty-five years of studying new public management in public administration: Accomplishments and limitations. *Financial Accountability & Management*, *36*(4), 347–375.

Gabriel, T., & Dillon, S. (2011, January 31). GOP governors take aim at teacher tenure. *New York Times*. www.nytimes.com

Gilarsky, M., Nunn, R., & Parsons, J. (2020, April 16) *What is work sharing and how can it help the labor market?* Brookings Institute. https://www.brookings.edu/articles/what-is-work-sharing-and-how-can-it-help-the-labor-market/

Goldschmidt, S. M., & Stuart, L. E. (1986, April). The extent and impact of educational policy bargaining. *Industrial and Labor Relations Review, 39*, 350–360.

Goode, S. J., & Baldwin, N. J. (2005). Predictions of African American representation in municipal government. *Review of Public Personnel Administration*, *25*(29), 29–55.

Guiler, J. K., & Shafritz, J. M. (2004). Dual personnel systems—organized labor and civil service: Side by side in the public sector. *Journal of Labor Relations*, *25*(2), 199–209.

Han, E. S. (2020). The myth of unions' overprotection of bad teachers: Evidence from the district–teacher matched data on teacher turnover. *Industrial Relations: A Journal of Economy and Society*, *59*(2), 316–352.

Han, E. S., & Maloney, T. N. (2022). Teachers' unionization, socioeconomic status, and student performance in the United States. *American Journal of Education*, *128*(2), 281–325.

Hays, S. W. (1995). Employee discipline and removal: Coping with job security. In S. B. Hays & R. C. Kearney (Eds.), *Public personnel administration: Problems and prospects* (pp. 145–161). Prentice-Hall.

Hirsch, B. T., McPherson, D. A., & Dumond, M. A. (1997). Recipiency in union and nonunion workplaces. *Industrial and Labor Relations Review*, *50*(2), 213–236.

Holzer, H., & Neumark, D. (2000, September). Assessing affirmative action. *Journal of Economic Literature, 38*, 485–568.

Hoover, G. A., & Peoples, J. (2003). Privatization of refuse removal and labor costs. *Journal of Labor Research, XXIV*(2), 293–305.

Horton, R. D. (1973). *Municipal labor relations in New York City*. Praeger.

Hoxby, C. M. (1996). How teachers' unions affect education production. *Quarterly Journal of Economics*, *111*(3), 671–718.

Hwang, K. (2023, October 17). *Kaiser unions went on strike twice in 12 months. The latest walkout led to a 'historic' deal.* https://www.pressdemocrat.com/article/news/kaiser-permanente-unions-went-on-strike-twice-in-12-months-the-latest-walk/

Imagine Institute. (n.d.). *Who we are*. https://imaginewa.org/who-we-are/

Ingraham, P. (1996). Evolving public service systems. In J. L. Perry (Ed.), *Handbook of public administration* (2nd ed., pp. 375–391). Jossey-Bass.

Ingrams, A., Piotrowski, S., & Berliner, D. (2020). Learning from our mistakes: Public management reform and the hope of open government. *Perspectives on Public Management and Governance*, *3*(4), 257–272.

Janus v. American Federation of State, County, and Municipal Employees, Council 31 et al. (2018). https://www.supremecourt.gov/opinions/17pdf/16-1466_2b3j.pdf

Julius, D. J., Abrams, J., & Baron, J. N. (2023). *Labor management relations in the post pandemic museum environment.* https://smlr.rutgers.edu/sites/default/files/Documents/Centers/CGWE/CGWE_WorkingPaper2023-1_JuliusAbramsBaron.pdf

Kearney, R. C., & Berman, E. M. (1999). *Public sector performance: Management, motivation and measurement.* Westview.

Kearney, R. C., & Hays, S. (1994). Labor management relations and participative decision making toward a new paradigm. *Public Administration Review*, *54*(1), 44–51.

Kearney, R. C., & Hays, S. (1998, Fall). Reinventing government: The new public management and civil service systems in international perspective. *Review of Public Personnel Administration*, *18*, 38–54.

Kellough, J. E. (1990, September–October). Integration in the public workplace: Determinants of minority and female employment in federal agencies. *Public Administration Review*, *50*, 557–566.

King, J. D., & Riddlesperger, J. W., Jr. (2018). The Trump transition: Beginning a distinctive presidency. *Social Science Quarterly*, *99*(5), 1821–1836.

Kurth, M. M. (1987, Fall). Teachers' unions and excellence in education: An analysis of the decline in SAT scores. *Journal of Labor Research, VII*, 351–367.

Labor—Management Services Administration. (1972). *Collective bargaining in public employment and the merit system.* Government Printing Office.

Lewin, D. (1986). Public employee unionism and labor relations in the 1990s: An analysis of transformation. In S. M. Lipset (Ed.), *Unions in transition* (pp. 241–264). Institute for Contemporary Studies.

Lewis, D. E., & Richardson, M. D. (2021). The very best people: President Trump and the management of executive personnel. *Presidential Studies Quarterly*, *51*(1), 51–70.

Local 189, United Papermakers and Crown-Zellerback Corp. v. United States. (1969). 416 F. 2d. 980.

Lovenheim, M. F. (2009). The effect of teachers' unions on education production: Evidence from union election certifications in three midwestern states. *Journal of Labor Economics*, *27*(4), 525–587.

Malek Manual. (1980). *Classics of public personnel policy* (2nd ed., pp. 58–81, F. J. Thompson, Ed.). Brooks/Cole.

Masters, M. F. (1988). The negotiability of drug testing in the federal sector: A political perspective. *Journal of Collective Negotiations*, *17*(4), 309–325.

May, A. M., Moorhouse, E. A., & Bossard, J. A. (2010). Representation of women faculty at public research universities: Do unions matter? *Industrial and Labor Relations Review*, *63*(4), 699–718.

Mayer, B. (2009). *Blue-Green coalitions: Fighting for safe workplaces and healthy communities.* ILR Press.

Maynard, M. (2012a, June 12). *Civil service reform passes in 3 states.* Governing the States and Localities. http://www.governing.com/blogs/view/civil-service-reform-passes.html

Maynard, M. (2012b, July 6). Detroit and its unions fight over work rules. *Stateline.* http://www.pewstates.org/projects/stateline/headlines/detroit-and-its-unions-fight-over-work-rules-85899403238

McKelvey, S., & Ronalds, J. (2013, February 19). *Dress codes: Tattoos, facial piercings and Bermuda shorts—the new professional norm?* https://www.lexology.com/library/detail.aspx?g=f338a456-28e9-4789-923c-a2d42bebaa6f

Memphis Firefighters Local Union No. 1784 v. Stotts. (1984). 34 EPD 34,415, 467 U.S. 561 S. Ct.

Mladenka, K. R. (1991, June). Public employee unions, reformism, and black employment in 1200 American cities. *Urban Affairs Quarterly, 26*, 532–548.

Mostris, K. (2021, August 6). *New telework legislation became law this year: How does it impact state employees?* AFSCME Maryland Council 3. https://www.afscmemd.org/council-3-updates-1/new-telework-legislation-became-law-year-how-does-it

Moynihan, D. P. (2005). Homeland security and the US public management policy agenda. *Governance*, *18*(2), 171–196.

Moynihan, D. P. (2022). Public management for populists: Trump's schedule F executive order and the future of the civil service. *Public Administration Review*, *82*(1), 174–178.

Muhl, C. J. (2001). The employment-at-will doctrine: Three major exceptions. *Monthly Labor Review*, *124*(1).

Muirhead, R., & Rosenblum, N. L. (2022). The path from conspiracy to ungoverning. *Social Research: An International Quarterly*, *89*(3), 501–524.

Murphy, G., & Wolf, J. (2022). *Workers' compensation: Benefits, costs, and coverage (2020 data).* National Academy of Social Insurance. https://www.nasi.org/wp-content/uploads/2022/11/2022-Workers-Compensation-Report-2020-Data.pdf

Musurlian, P. (2024, February 2). AFGE expresses fears about future telework cuts for social security employees. *Federal News Network.* https://federalnewsnetwork.com/federal-newscast/2024/02/afge-expresses-fears-about-future-telework-cuts-for-social-security-employees/

NATCA. (2024, April 19). *NATCA calls on FAA to collaborate on air traffic controller fatigue.* https://www.natca.org/2024/04/19/natca-calls-on-faa-to-collaborate-on-air-traffic-controller-fatigue/

Nelson, F. H., & Gould, J. C. (1988). Teachers' unions and excellence in education: Comment. *Journal of Labor Research*, *9*(4), 379–387.

Nelson, F. H., & Rosen, M. (2000). Are teachers' unions hurting American education? A state-by-state analysis of the impact of collective bargaining among teachers on student performance. In T. Loveless (Ed.), *Conflicting missions? Teachers unions and educational reform* (pp. 47–68). Brookings Institution Press. (Original work published 1996)

New Jersey Legislature. (2020). Bill S2303 Aca (1R), Session 2020–2021. https://pub.njleg.state.nj.us/Bills/2020/PL20/79_.PDF

Newland, C. A. (1984, Spring). Crucial issues for public personnel professionals. *Public Personnel Management, 13*, 15–46.

Newland, C. A. (1987, January/February). Public executives: Imperium, sacerdatrum, collegium? *Public Administration Review, 47*, 45–56.

NTEU v. Van Raab. (1989). 109 S. Ct. 1384.

Osborne, D., & Gaebler, T. (1992). *Reinventing government: How the entrepreneurial spirit is transforming the public sector*. Addison-Wesley.

Patent Answers. (1999, February). *Government executive*. https://www.govexec.com/magazine/1999/02/patent-answers/6292/

Pfiffner, J. P. (2017). The unusual presidency of Donald Trump. *Political Insight, 8*(2), 9–11.

Ramos, R. (2024, April 11). California issues new hybrid work model policy for state employees. Here's what we know. *CBS Sacramento*. https://www.cbsnews.com/sacramento/news/california-new-hybrid-work-model-policy/

Repa, B. K. (2005). *Your rights in the workplace*. Nolo.

Riccucci, N. M. (1986). Female and minority employment in city government: The role of unions. *Policy Studies Journal, 15*(1), 3–15.

Riccucci, N. M. (1988). A typology for union discrimination: A public sector perspective. *Public Personnel Management, 17*(1), 41.

Riccucci, N. M. (1990). *Women, minorities, and unions in the public sector*. Greenwood.

Riccucci, N. M. (1997). Will affirmative action survive into the 21st century? In *Public personnel management: Current concerns, future challenges*. Pearson.

Rodriguez, S. K. (2012, March 23). Rewards for wellness: State of Rhode Island employee health plan. *State of Rhode Island Document*. http://www.wellness.ri.gov

Rubinstein, S., Heckscher, C., & McCarthy, J. (2024). *Democracy and reform in public schools: The case for collaborative partnerships*. Harvard Education Press.

Rudin, J., & Pereles, K. (2012). Notes on the ADA: Overweight and overdue: Weight-based discrimination and the ADA amendments act. *Labor Law Journal, 63*(2), 137–142.

Rushin, S. (2021). Police arbitration. *Vanderbilt Law Review, 74*, 1023.

Sass, D. R., & Troyer, J. L. (1999, Fall). Affirmative action, political representation, unions and female public employment. *Journal of Labor Research, 20*, 571–587.

Savas, E. S., & Ginsburg, S. G. (1973, Summer). The civil service: A meritless system? *The Public Interest, 32*, 70–85.

Schneider, M. B., & Ruthhart, B. (2009, October 16). Indiana axes welfare contract with IBM. *The Indianapolis Star*. www.indystar.com

Seaver, D. F. (1984–85, Winter). The Stotts decision: Is it the death knell for seniority systems? *Employee Relations Law Journal, 3*, 497–504.

Shields, J. (2010, June 17). Black firefighters settle lawsuit against Philadelphia. *The Philadelphia Inquirer*. www.philly.com

Skinner v. Railway Labor Executives' Association. (1989). 109 S. Ct. 1402.

Sniffen, M. J. (2007). Air traffic controllers exit in droves. *The News and Observer*, 3A.

Spero, S. D., & Capozzola, J. M. (1973). *The urban community and its unionized bureaucracies*. Dunellen.

Stahl, O. G. (1990). A retrospective and prospective: The moral dimension. In S. W. Hays & R. C. Kearney (Eds.), *Public personnel administration: Problems and prospects* (pp. 308–321). Prentice-Hall.

Stanley, D. T. (1972). *Managing local government under union pressure*. Brookings.

Stein, L. (1986, May). Representative local government: Minorities in the municipal workforce. *Journal of Politics, 48*, 694–713.

Stone, J. A. (2000). Collective bargaining in public schools. In T. Loveless (Ed.), *Conflicting missions? Teachers unions and educational reform* (pp. 47–68). Brookings Institution Press.

Sutherlin Education Association v. Sutherlin School District No. 130. (1976). 548 P. 2d. 208.

Texas Division of Insurance. (n.d.). *Workers compensation insurance guide*. https://www.tdi.texas.gov/pubs/consumer/cb030.html

Thompson, J. R. (2007). Federal labor-management relations reforms under Bush: Enlightened management or quest for control? *Review of Public Personnel Administration, 27*(2), 105–124.

U.S. Airways v. Barnett. (2002). 535 U.S. 391.

U.S. DOT. (2023, June 21). *FAA faces controller staffing challenges as air traffic operations return to pre-pandemic levels at critical facilities*. Office of the Inspector General. https://www.oig.dot.gov/sites/default/files/FAA%20Controller%20Staffing%20and%20Training%20at%20Critical%20Facilities%20Final%20Report-06-21-23.pdf

U.S. National Partnership Council. (1994). *A new vision for labor management relations*. Government Printing Office.

U.S. Office of Personnel Management. (2014). *Labor-management relations in the executive branch*. https://www.opm.gov/policy-data-oversight/labor-relations/reports/labor-management-relations-in-the-executive-branch-2014.pdf

U.S. Office of Personnel Management. (2023, December). *Status of telework in the federal government report to congress fiscal year 2022*. https://www.opm.gov/telework/documents-for-telework/2023-report-to-congress.pdf

Wagner, E. (2021, January 22). Biden signs executive order killing schedule F, restoring collective bargaining rights. *Government Executive*. https://www.govexec.com/management/2021/01/biden-sign-executive-order-killing-schedule-f-restoring-collective-bargaining-rights/171569/

Walter, K. (2019). *Public sector training partnerships build power*. Center for American Progress. https://www.americanprogress.org/article/public-sector-training-partnerships-build-power/

Waters v. Wisconsin Steelworks. (1974). 502 F. 2d. 1309 CA-7.

Watkins v. Steelworkers Local 2369. (1975). 516 F. 2d. 41 CA-5.

Weisner, M. (2024, January 29). Telework, pay incentives vary as HUD struggles with attrition. *Federal Times*. https://www.federaltimes.com/federal-oversight/watchdogs/2024/01/29/telework-pay-incentives-vary-as-hud-struggles-with-rising-attrition/

Wilson, T. M. (1989, Summer). Smoking in the workplace: Dimensions of policy. *Review of Public Personnel, 9*, 32–45.

Woodbury, S. A. (1985, January). The scope of bargaining and bargaining outcomes in the public schools. *Industrial and Labor Relations Review, 38*, 195–209.

Wurf, J. (1974, September–October). Merit: A union view. *Public Administration Review, 34*, 431–434.

Wygant v. Jackson Board of Education. (1986). 476 U.S. 267.

Zezima, K. (2010, February 23). A vote to fire all teachers at a failing high school. *New York Times*. www.nytimes.com.

Zigarelli, M. A. (1994). The linkages between teacher unions and student achievement. *Journal of Collective Negotiations, 23*(4), 299–319.

Zwerling, H. L., & Thomason, T. (1994). The effects of teacher unions on the probability of dropping out of high school. *Journal of Collective Negotiations, 23*(3), 239–250.

Chapter 8

Strike!

I. INTRODUCTION

As observed in Chapter 1, there is nothing new or entirely surprising about workers withholding their labor. Work stoppages were fairly common in American mines, factories, and transportation industries in the period preceding passage of the National Labor Relations Act (NLRA). Many of these strikes were met with violence. Shogan (2004) relates the story of the country's largest mine strike in *The Battle of Blair Mountain*. In the fall of 1921, more than 10,000 armed members of the United Mine Workers of America's "Red Bandana Army" marched through the mountains and valleys of West Virginia to fight for the freedom of their jailed brothers. Troops from West Virginia and the federal government, along with thugs from the Felt-Dobbs Detective Agency, attacked the miners with clubs and guns in a bloody battle. For the first—and so far only—time, government aircraft dropped bombs on U.S. citizens on domestic soil.

Public strikes have not been so violent, but they have been plentiful. Ziskind (1940) chronicled multiple public employee strikes that occurred very early in the history of the Republic, including an 1835 strike of civilian yard workers in the Navy Department and an 1880 walkout by Pennsylvania teachers. Early federal employee work stoppages also occurred in the Government Printing Office (1863) and in federal arsenals (1890s).

However, the first strong wave of government employee strikes did not take place until the early 1900s. The causes of these early work stoppages were as diverse as their participants. For example, Connecticut legislators walked out in 1911, demanding the elimination of "paid agents" who were acting as lobbyists on the floor of the state senate. Workers at the Watertown (New York) Arsenal struck during the same year over the introduction of Tayloristic time study techniques. Moth workers, whose jobs entailed the extermination of biting moths, struck at least four times in Massachusetts between 1907 and 1917 for higher

DOI:10.4324/9781003403593-8

wages. Even gravediggers in Milford, Massachusetts hung up their shovels over the issue of Sunday work in 1913 (Ziskind, 1940, p. 96).

The most controversial strikes during the early 1900s involved firefighters and police. Firefighters incensed over egregiously poor working conditions (low pay, 24-hour duty with time home only for meals, and 1 day off out of every 8 days) struck in locations all over the country during the years 1903–1921. Police refused the call to duty in a number of large cities, including Cincinnati and Boston (see Case Study 8.1). They, too, demanded improved working conditions, shorter hours, and wage increases.

Today, some of the place names and worker demands have changed, but public employee work stoppages continue to occur. This chapter examines the anatomy of public employee strikes in the United States. First, data on their frequency are presented. Next, arguments for and against the strike are discussed. The relevant legislation on work stoppages in both the public and private sectors is summarized, along with research findings on why public workers go out on strike. Strike tactics and strategies of employers and unions are examined next, including the role of the injunction and penalties for work stoppages. Finally, some speculation is offered on public employee job actions in the future. Throughout the discussion, case studies are used to help capture the flavor of the strike as the ultimate weapon in labor's arsenal, beginning with the infamous 1919 Boston police strike.

CASE STUDY 8.1 THE BOSTON POLICE STRIKE OF 1919

A period of rapid monetary inflation usually characterizes the economy of a nation winding down from a large war effort. This has been the case after all major wars involving the United States. Following World War I, prices of goods and services began climbing rapidly. However, police wages in Boston ranged from only $900 to $1400 per year, with an average annual salary of $1000. Out of his salary, each officer was required to pay about $200 per year for uniforms and equipment. Inflation hit these and other low-wage public workers very hard indeed.

Compounding the unhappiness of Boston police were exceptionally long working hours: day workers were on duty 73–78 hours per week; the night shift 83–91 hours; and "wagon men" were required to be on the job up to 98 hours per week. Each officer had to sleep in the station house one night per week, where conditions were filthy and decrepit. The beds were infested with cockroaches and bedbugs. Other relatively minor job irritants included the necessity to secure special permission to travel out of Boston city limits and the requirement to run personal errands for superiors. Police spokesmen had taken various grievances to the commissioner on several occasions, but no actions were forthcoming.

In 1919, "Boston's finest" applied for and received a municipal police charter from the American Federation of Labor (AFL). The Boston police commissioner declared that union membership was grounds for dismissal from the force, firing several officers as an example to others. In protest, almost the entire force (1,140 out of 1,540) walked off the job. The commissioner responded by firing all striking police officers.

Without adequate police personnel, law and order broke down. Rioting, looting, violence, and general mayhem spread throughout the city, causing the mayor to declare a state of "tumult and riot" and to call in the Massachusetts State Guard. Governor Calvin Coolidge readily complied with the mayor's request, issuing his famous statement that "there is no right to strike against the public safety by anybody, anywhere, any time." Although Coolidge's actual role in ending the strike was limited and the positive publicity he received undeserved (Spero, 1970, pp. 252–281), the episode did help him considerably in his later quest for the presidency of the United States.

The Guard established and maintained law and order until new police officers could be recruited. The striking policemen were not rehired, yet they did win something of a pyrrhic victory: new officers were granted virtually all of the demands made by the strikers, including an entrance salary of $1,400, free uniforms, a pension system, and positive changes in working conditions. The strike had the added benefit of encouraging similar improvements in the lot of policemen in numerous other cities around the region.

From the perspective of public sector unionization, however, the strike had to be considered a resounding defeat. Fear resulting from the Boston violence, combined with the more generalized "red scare" of Communists, forced all 37 AFL—chartered police locals—and more than 50 International Association of Fire Fighters—chartered firefighter locals—to relinquish their charters following the strike. Unionization among municipal protective services employees was set back a good 40 years.

Questions

1 Could a strike of this intensity, followed by widespread violence, happen in a major U.S. city today? What circumstances might provoke such an event?

2 What factors would have to be present for a contemporary strike to generate a similar amount of public attention and fear?

II. A STRIKE BY ANY OTHER NAME

The term "strike" is believed to be derived from the act of sailors hauling down or "striking" their sails in response to violent winds. Today, however, expressions characterizing a work stoppage are limited in number only by the fertile imaginations of their participants. Across the country, firefighters have called in sick with the "red rash," police with the virulent "blue flu," and teachers with "chalk-dust fever." For example, in 2014, 44 firefighters (red rash) and 142 police officers (blue flu) in Memphis protested a plan to increase health insurance premiums and decrease retirees benefits with a sick out (Fretland, 2014). In 2020 teachers in New York City staged a wildcat sick out (chalk dust fever) to call attention to the need for workplace protections with the advent of the COVID-19 pandemic (Worthington et al., 2024). Teachers in Haverhill, Massachusetts engaged in "work-to-rule" in September 2022 to call attention to the lack of progress on contract negotiations and eventually went on strike for four days in October the same year (State House News Service, 2022; Pinkham, 2022).

These and other activities, such as mass resignations, continuous "professional meetings," "professional holidays," work slowdowns, "work-to-the-rule," picketing, and protest marches, all fall into the category of "job actions." Not all job actions, however, are properly labeled "strikes" or "work stoppages." Generally, the courts and other interested parties have interpreted "strike" in accordance with the Taft–Hartley Act (Section 501) definition, which is "any concerted stoppage of work by employees . . . and any concerted slow-down or other concerted interruption of operations by employees." Thus, a strike entails the interruption of normal job operations through a walkout, slowdown, sick-out, or any other tactic that disrupts work.

Most of the job actions mentioned in the preceding discussion probably would be interpreted as work stoppages by the courts (which have been fairly strict in these determinations). Exceptions might include picketing and protest marches by off-duty workers that do not interfere with the job performance of on-duty employees. The NLRA grants all private sector employees the right to withhold their labor through a strike, whether or not they belong to a union. Most public employees do not enjoy a legal right to strike, although 12 states permit work stoppages for specified groups of workers, subject to certain conditions.

The majority of public employee strikes are authorized either formally (through a strike vote) or informally by the employee organization. Those work stoppages that are not formally authorized are referred to as wildcat strikes. A strike that occurs simultaneously among different government services in the same jurisdiction is called a general strike.

Employers can institute a strike of their own, known as a lockout. In a lockout, the employer refuses to permit employees to work, literally or symbolically locking the doors to keep them out. The objective is to apply pressure for a contract settlement to encourage employees to reject, or decertify, the union. Lockouts occasionally occur in the private sector and in professional sports (for instance, the 2012 National Hockey League lockout and the 2021–2022 Major League Baseball lockout), but they are extremely rare in the public sector.

III. PUBLIC SECTOR STRIKE ACTIVITY

Although comparisons with private sector strike activity vary by year, the evidence is clear that a smaller percentage of public workers go out on strike and that they strike for much shorter periods of time than do workers in the private sector. Overall, strike activity increased in 2023. Roughly 458,900 workers were involved in "major work stoppages" in 2023, an increase of 280% over the previous year in which 120,600 workers took part in major work stoppages. (Poydock & Sherer, 2024). The Bureau of Labor Statistics (BLS) defines major work stoppages as those involving more than 1000 workers and lasting for more than one shift (U.S. BLS, 2024a).

Approximately 75% of major work stoppages in 2023 occurred in the private sector. Of these, more than half took place in the health care field. There were five major work stoppages at the state government level. Most of these stoppages occurred in public colleges and universities. At the local government level there were three major work stoppages, involving public elementary schools (Poydock & Sherer, 2024).

However, the BLS definition of major work stoppages does not capture all strike activity. The Cornell Labor Action Tracker identified 470 work stoppages (466 strikes and 4 lockouts) encompassing approximately 539,000 workers in 2023. By this count, there were roughly 24,874,522 strike days in 2023. The Coalition of Kaiser Permanente Unions strike and the Los Angeles Unified School District strike were among the highest profile strikes in 2023. Strike activity increased every year across the period 2021–2023 (Ritchie et al., 2024).

Nonetheless, government strikes account for a relatively small proportion of all work stoppages in the United States. That strikes in public employment are briefer (averaging about 12 days compared to 21 days in the private sector) is explained by several factors, including the "essential" nature of some government services, the illegality of some public sector work stoppages, the lack of union "strike funds" to help support strikers (who are not paid during a strike), more frequent use of court injunctions to halt stoppages, greater publicity and political pressure for settlement, and the negative political consequences when quick settlements are not attained. In addition, private firms can build up product inventories to help ride out a strike; public employers rarely enjoy that option.

The peak year for public employee turmoil was 1979. Since then, indications point toward a steep drop in work stoppages. However, caution must be used in interpreting federal data. Strike data for 1960–1980 include all known work stoppages. In 1981, the Bureau of Labor Statistics stopped collecting information on job actions involving fewer than 1,000 workers. Most strikes in the public sector engage fewer than 1,000 individuals (U.S. Bureau of Labor Statistics, 2019). The other immediate cause of the decline in job actions was the virulent antiunion posture of the Reagan administration, which became painfully palpable during the Professional Air Traffic Controllers strike of 1981 (see Case Study 8.3).

Strikes also declined dramatically in the private sector. During the 1970s, nearly 300 major work stoppages occurred per year, compared with fewer than 100 annually during the 1980s, 33 in the 1990s, and only 19 in the early 2000s (U.S. Bureau of Labor Statistics, 2024b). Here, likely causal factors include weak economic conditions and job displacement in union-intensive manufacturing industries; the willingness of employers to hire permanent replacements for striking workers; the attraction of moving operations to cheaper labor markets in the United States or overseas; and, again, the aggressive actions by the Reagan administration in firing the federal air traffic controllers.

Hiring nonunion replacement workers has been particularly effective in repressing strikes in business. Historically, even if such workers ("scabs," to the union members) were hired temporarily, they were terminated when the strike ended, and union members were reemployed. A 1989 U.S. Supreme Court ruling (*TWA v. Independent Federation of Flight Attendants*, 1989) upheld the Mackay Doctrine of 1935, which established the right of private sector employers to hire permanent replacements for strikers (*National Labor Relations Board v. Mackay Radio and Telegraph,* 1938).

Permanent replacements were rarely employed until the 1980s. By then, public opinion had slowly turned against the unions on this key issue and competitive pressures increased the inclination of firms to play hardball. A final impetus was President Reagan's firing of striking air traffic controllers in 1981 and replacing them with new employees. The Mackay Doctrine made the strike a double-edged sword that can either win the union concessions from a firm or result in dismissal of strikers and, essentially, the demise of the union. As such, it has seriously undermined the power of the strike and even reformulated it into a management weapon (Victor, 1992; Kosterlitz, 1997). Further depleting the power of the strike has been companies' increased willingness to impose lockouts to win union concessions when negotiations deadlock (Greenhouse, 2012).

The majority of government strikes take place at the local government level, and most have involved teachers, who have accounted for about three out of every four work stoppages since 1982. Five states have recorded the majority of major work stoppages since 1993: California, Illinois, Washington, New York, and Pennsylvania (U.S. Bureau of Labor Statistics, 2024c). The data on strike duration vary by issue, function, and region. Work stoppages in the South tend to be larger and more intense, perhaps because of the general absence of legal machinery to guide the parties in resolving disputes and the fierce employer resistance to unions. What may be the longest recorded strike by public workers took place in 1970 in Maryland, a border state (neither north nor south), when Garrett County road workers walked out for 207 days in an effort to gain recognition of their union. The strike was finally ended when three county commissioners lost their re-election campaigns. The newly elected commissioners were more amenable to negotiating a settlement (Levine & Caloia, 2020).

There is a tendency for local government work stoppages to spill over into two or more functions. Police often have been joined on the picket line by firefighters, and vice versa. Similarly, sanitation, streets and highways, parks, and sewage workers sometimes join ranks. Teachers, hospital employees, and social service workers typically walk out alone.

Something approaching a general strike has occurred in several cities. In Toledo, Ohio, 3,700 city workers went out on strike July 1, 1979, including police, firefighters, and sanitation workers (Henry, 2009). During a July 1986 strike in Philadelphia, sanitation employees were joined by nearly 10,000 other strikers who shut down libraries, museums, and swimming pools (Stevens, 1986). In April 1991, 5,000 Montana state employees, representing almost every state agency, struck for several days, requiring National Guard troops to staff prisons and the Montana Center for the Aged (AP, 1991). And in October 2001, about 28,000 Minnesota state employees left their workplaces for two weeks. Among the ranks of striking workers were correctional officers, janitors, computer specialists, highway maintenance workers, zoo employees, and workers in nursing and psychiatric facilities (Greenhouse, 2001).

In 2018–2019, a wave of teachers strikes spread across the country. A series of rolling strikes among educational workers spread from West Virginia (35,000) to Oklahoma (45,000) and Kentucky (26,000). Over a period of a few months, 267,000 more teachers in Arizona, Colorado, and North Carolina walked off the job (Van Dam, 2019). These were followed by strikes in 2019 in large cities such as Los Angeles and Chicago, and smaller municipalities such as Montclair, New Jersey (Bradford, 2021).

Although public employee work stoppages attenuated in most areas in the early 2000s, they saw an upsurge beginning in 2018. For some public agencies, such as the Philadelphia transit system known as SEPTA, work stoppages occur with a variety of workers (including SEPTA police) on a regular basis. In fact, SEPTA is known as the most strike-prone transit agency in the nation with strikes that occurred in 1971, 1975, 1977, twice in 1981, 1982, 1983, twice in 1986, 1995, 1998, 2005, 2009, 2012, 2016, 2019, and 2023. SEPTA narrowly averted a strike with the Transport Workers Union (TWU) in 2023, but the SEPTA police walked off the job in that year as contract negotiations broke down (Hendrickson & Smith, 2023; Perez-Castells, 2023; Rinde, 2023). Against this backdrop, arguments for and against the strike continue to be debated among government officials, union leaders, academics, the media, and others. Section IV reviews the philosophical and practical points in the debate over the legitimacy of strikes by public servants.

IV. THE RIGHT TO STRIKE IN PUBLIC EMPLOYMENT

The strike issue has been called "the most controversial, urgent, and misunderstood problem of labor relations in public employment" (Spero & Capozzola, 1973, p. 239). The central dilemma to be addressed is as follows: is it equitable and realistic to deny public employees the right to strike while guaranteeing the same right to private workers in vital sectors of the American economy?

A. The Sovereignty Argument

Those who would deny the right to strike to all public employees have trotted out the now-stale argument of sovereignty. In his adamant refusal to concede the right of Boston police officers to strike against the city, Massachusetts Governor Calvin Coolidge charged the officers with "desertion of duty." The mayor of Cincinnati called the 1918 strike by that city's police "the most dastardly crime ever committed in the City of Cincinnati" (Ziskind, 1940, pp. 3, 37). These men, along with other presidents, governors, mayors, and judges, were staunch believers in the notion that a sovereign government has the inherent and unique right to weigh the merits of disputes in which that government is a party, "in order to head off insurrection, rebellion, and eventual anarchy" (Capozzola, 1979, p. 178). Most scholars date the origins of the sovereignty doctrine to Englishman Thomas Hobbes, who laid out the arguments for a sovereign state in a book, *Leviathan.* Assertions that "the King can do no wrong" were transposed into the American experience through the body of common law by early English settlers.

With respect to public employee strikes, the sovereignty doctrine asserts that because sovereignty is constitutionally vested in the people of a democratic nation-state, permitting government workers to strike surrenders government authority to determine public policy to a special interest. In theory, a strike constitutes a direct challenge to the people's will. In practice, it creates a climate of disrespect for government and the law. In theory and in principle, these are legitimate concerns.

However, events have made the practical applicability of the sovereignty argument suspect. The "sovereign" power of the state has long been waived, delegated to, and shared with interest groups, firms, and various other entities (Lowi, 1979). Public employee unions legitimately view the concept as a legal ruse to clothe government with the absolute right to act not only unilaterally and paternalistically but also arbitrarily and capriciously in determining all facets of the employment relationship. Perpetuation of the myth shields inept administrators, blinds the vision of competent ones, and enables irresponsible managers to escape their obligations by retreating behind a curtain of sovereignty (Capozzola, 1979, p. 179).

Finally, the sovereignty argument has been laid to rest in those states that have, through democratic processes, permitted strikes by public employees without political, economic, or social collapse. Sovereignty does not, in fact, preclude government from entering into collective bargaining arrangements or legally establishing the right of public employees to strike. The recognition of this fact means that the sovereignty argument rarely carries much weight in the public employee strike controversy today.

B. Distortion of the Political Process

Early critics Harry H. Wellington and Ralph K. Winter (1971, p. 25) argued that public employee strikes threaten the survival of the "normal" political process by giving public sector unions political and policy advantages over other interest groups. This excessive power, they claim, is augmented by union lobbying and voting activities. It distorts the political process and diminishes democratic decision making.

Like sovereignty, this is an ill-defined and ambiguous argument. For example, what is the "normal" political process? Where is the evidence of "distortion"? Wellington and Winter's overstatement of the problem is probably a product of the time in which they wrote *The Unions and the Cities* (the late 1960s), a period of strong emergent unionism in governments administered by unprepared and weak public managers.

C. Lack of Market Constraints

In the private sector, high labor costs tend to be held down by competition and consumer product demand. Pay hikes must be accounted for by raising product prices or improving productivity. If labor costs rise excessively, consumers will purchase their goods and services from another producer, substitute for them, or do without. It is argued that in the public sector no such market constraints exist because public services are monopolies. There is little or no opportunity for comparison shopping by citizens. Thus, unions can make extravagant demands and win them by threatening to strike.

This line of argument has been rebutted on numerous occasions (Fowler, 1974; Burton & Krider, 1975; Capozzola, 1979). More so today than perhaps ever before, market constraints do operate during public sector strikes. Employees sacrifice wages while tax revenues continue to accrue to the government employer. The workers often come out net financial losers. Although no profit motive can be said to exist in the public sector, there are strong political pressures brought to bear on public sector unions to forgo the strike or to settle quickly in the event one transpires. Public officials are also under great pressure not to raise taxes or fees, especially to fund employee compensation increases. Pushed too far, city councils and state legislatures may seek to subcontract government services to private and nonprofit providers, thereby laying off workers and creating competition in the market for public goods.

D. Essential Services

According to opponents of the right to strike, public employees are engaged in providing services essential to the community. A strike poses unacceptable threats to the public health, safety, and well-being. It also prompts public officials to cave in to citizen pressure to settle with the union. One critic compared a public employee strike to a siege, in which an "indispensable element of the public welfare . . . is made hostage by a numerically superior force and held, in effect, for ransom" (Saso, 1970, p. 37).

However, it is clear that not all government services are essential to the public's immediate health, safety, and well-being. Teacher strikes, for example, have lasted for months, disrupting the school year and the lives of pupils and parents. But there is no evidence that any long-term damage to the students or the parents has resulted or that student performance has been adversely affected (Thornicroft, 1994; Zwerling, 2007). Strikes by police, firefighters, and, in some instances, sanitation workers are much more serious and may indeed pose a threat to the well-being of citizens.

It must be recognized, however, that state law enforcement personnel have successfully assisted non-striking police officers in maintaining law and order. Similarly, volunteer fire departments effectively protect a much larger geographical area of the United States than municipal firefighters. Additionally, most people are not incapable of delivering their own garbage and recyclables to landfills or central collection stations. It should further be recognized that many government services are contracted out to private and nonprofit organizations, including private schools, sanitation companies, private security firms, human resource management (HRM) companies, and various health-care organizations. Such functions are not so essential that they cannot be handled adequately in the private sector.

It is also important to understand that some services traditionally provided by private and nonprofit concerns are as crucial—if not more so—than many public services. This fact has been demonstrated by the serious impact of strikes by railroad workers, coal miners, utility employees, truckers, dock workers, and nursing home and hospital workers. The Taft–Hartley law recognizes the essential nature of these and other functions in the private sector by providing for presidential and congressional actions to help contain and settle a strike that poses a threat to the well-being of the nation.

Unfortunately, there is no bright line solution to determine which public and private sector services are "essential" and which are not. If there were, then logic would dictate that all strikes by workers in critical functions—regardless of sector of the economy—be prohibited. But it is very difficult to separate essential from nonessential services, especially when matters of strike location and duration are considered along with various extenuating circumstances (such as season of the year during sanitation strikes).

There have been some efforts to categorize work stoppages in accordance with their essentiality. For example, Burton and Krider (1975) suggested identifying government services as essential (police and fire protection), intermediate (sanitation, health care, transit, water, and sewer), and nonessential (education, streets, parks, recreation, welfare, and general administration). Strikes would be prohibited for essential services and permitted for intermediate services unless they presented a demonstrated threat to citizens' health or safety. Workers in nonessential functions would be granted the right to strike. Some state laws permitting a limited right to strike have taken this approach (e.g., in Alaska).

To many public workers and their unions, the claim that public servants should be saddled with special responsibilities and constraints on their labor activities does not hold water. Since the social turmoil of the 1960s, government workers have insisted on having the same rights of citizenship as their private sector counterparts, including the right to walk off the job. As Spero and Capozzola (1973, pp. 269–270) put it,

> The legalistic public–private dichotomy has little relevance to the municipal employee. He has the same dreams, desires, fears, frustrations, problems and hopes as his counterpart in private industry. Excessive theorizing falls on deaf ears, as the municipal worker pays the same taxes, buys the same food and shelter, and has no more immunity from disease than a private employee.

Should they not enjoy equal protection under the law, as long as a strike does not present a clear and immediate danger to the community?

Strike bans are not particularly effective and are sometimes ignored. Strikes will continue to occur whether or not they are legally forbidden. As a study commission noted in Pennsylvania in recommending the right to strike, "Twenty years of experience [under a no-strike law] has taught us that such a policy is unreasonable and unenforceable, particularly when coupled with ineffective or nonexistent collective bargaining" (Schneider, 1988, p. 199).

Moreover, public management has gained experience contending with strikes, and when it receives greater public support than the union, it can win a strike. Striking public workers do not get paid, and public sector unions do not normally maintain strike funds. Yet government revenues continue to come in, improving the employer's financial position (unless the strike ultimately accomplishes the financial objectives of the union, including retroactive payment of strikers' wages). In addition, a public management skilled in media relations can channel almost unbearable public pressure on a striking union and help force concessions on its leaders and rank and file.

E. The Postal Strike of 1970

Strikes by federal employees have never been legal. However, on March 18, 1970, movement of the U.S. mail slowed to a trickle as postal employees in New York City, then across the nation, walked off their jobs in wildcat strikes over low wage levels, dissatisfaction with their treatment by Congress, and the inability of their unions to "deliver." It was the largest strike of federal employees in American history.

After a back-to-work order was ignored, government and union leaders reached an accord: strikers would go back to work in return for a formal discussion with administration officials over pay, postal reform, and other issues. However, the union rank and file refused to accept the agreement. The strike continued to spread across the country. By March 20, close to 200,000 postal workers failed to report to work and much of the nation was without mail service. The strike threatened to disrupt the economy as the flow of financial documents and other important materials was squeezed to a trickle (FedEx, UPS, and Internet transfers were not available in 1970).

President Richard Nixon declared a state of national emergency and ordered federal troops into New York City to move the mail. He also called out 15,000 Army reserves and 12,000 members of the National Guard. The president informed the striking postal workers that negotiations would not begin until they returned to work. Through unofficial channels, however, the postal employees were told that if they returned to their jobs Congress would directly address their grievances. By March 25, most of the striking workers were back on the job.

Postal employees soon settled for a retroactive pay increase. Congress approved the pay provisions with great haste and the president signed them into law. Shortly thereafter, with the strong support of the postal unions, the Postal Reorganization Act established the mail service as a government corporation, removing postal workers from labor relations coverage under Executive Order 11491, and granted full private sector collective bargaining privileges (except for the right to strike). Thus, through the strike, postal workers won preferential treatment, including the critical right to negotiate pay and benefits.

The financial benefits of the settlement were soon evident. Whereas other federal white-collar workers received a 47% salary increase from 1970 through 1977, the postal employees' salaries were hiked by 94%. Generous pay settlements have been exacerbated by retiree health-care accounting requirements. Specifically, the United States Postal Service has been hobbled by the burden of pre-funding its retiree health care benefits 75 years into the future, as mandated by the Postal Accountability and Enhancement Act (PAEA) of 2006. No other government agencies or private sector business face similar requirements (Anderson et al., 2020). This has resulted in chronic budget deficits for the U.S. Postal Service, and the proposed termination of Saturday mail deliveries.

V. LEGISLATION PERTAINING TO STRIKES

In private employment, the rights of workers to strike and employers to lock them out are viewed as essential components of the free process of collective bargaining, as legally embodied in the NLRA. In public employment, the right to strike traditionally has been denied by various federal and state laws. Federal workers are forbidden to strike by Public Law 330 (1955) and the 1978 Civil Service Reform Act. Members of the Armed Forces are prohibited from striking by Department of Defense Directive 1354.1.

Following the Boston police strike of 1919, a series of antistrike ordinances were adopted by numerous cities, including Salt Lake City, Philadelphia, San Antonio, Chicago, and Detroit. The U.S. Congress passed a law outlawing strikes in the District of Columbia. A second wave of strike prohibitions came just after World War II, when nine states enacted laws banning strikes, with language similar to Taft–Hartley's original prohibition against federal employee work stoppages. The constitutionality of these various strike prohibitions has been consistently upheld by the courts. In addition, most state courts (with few exceptions) have held that state employees have no right to engage in work stoppages in the absence of legislative authorization.

Some or all public employee strikes are outlawed in 38 states through statute, court decision, or attorney general opinion. Furthermore, the vast majority of collective bargaining contracts contain no-strike clauses intended to prevent stoppages during the life of the contract. A typical clause reads, "The union and its employees expressly agree that there will be no strikes, slowdowns, picketing during working hours, work stoppages, mass absenteeism, mass feigned illness, or other forms of interference with the operations of the police department." Nonetheless, public employees have struck repeatedly. From 1958 to 1968, no state authorized a strike for any of its workers, but the number of public employee strikes increased 17-fold from the previous decade. Penalties were infrequently invoked against striking union members or their organizations.

In recognition of the failure of strike prohibitions to prevent government work stoppages, nine states have now legislatively granted at least some of their employees a limited right to strike. Vermont was the first: Act No. 198 of 1967 provided that local government work stoppages are prohibited only if the strike is found to endanger the public health, safety, or welfare. Pennsylvania followed with permissive legislation of its own in 1970; Hawaii, Alaska, Montana, Oregon, Minnesota, Wisconsin,

Ohio, and Illinois complete the list. In addition, state supreme courts in California, Colorado, Idaho, and Louisiana have upheld the right of public employees to strike.

Table 8.1 summarizes the policies of those states that have legalized the strike through legislation or court decisions. Most of these statutes specifically exclude designated "essential employees" from the strike right, particularly police, firefighters, correctional officers, and hospital workers. Most also require compliance with specific prestrike provisions, such as mediation, fact-finding, and prior

Table 8.1 Permissive Strike States, 2023

State	*Covered Employees*	*Policy*
Alaska	All public employees	Right to strike for semi-essential and non-essential workers. Police, firefighters, correctional workers, and hospital employees may not strike. Limited strike right for public utilities, sanitation, snow removal, and schools, after exhaustion of mediation. Other workers may strike upon majority vote
California	Some municipal employees	California Supreme Court held that strikes by nonessential employees were legal except in cases where the strike posed an imminent threat to public health and safety.
Colorado	All public employees	Colorado Supreme Court held that public employee strikes were legal.
Hawaii	All public employees	Strike permitted after exhaustion of impasse resolution procedures and 60 days after issue of fact-finding report. Ten days' notice by the union is required. Strikes endangering public health and safety are illegal, as are strikes by firefighters and other essential employees.
Illinois	All public employees	Mediation and five days' notice required before the strike. Prohibited if a strike constitutes a clear and present danger to public health and safety. Firefighters, law enforcement, and security employees may not strike.
Louisiana	All public employees	Louisiana Supreme Court held that all public employee strikes are legal.
Minnesota	All public employees	Strikes prohibited except where employer refuses request for binding arbitration or refuses to submit to arbitration award. Teachers have the right to strike following expiration of contract, 60 days of mediation, and 10-day notice. Nonteaching local employees and state employees may strike after expiration of contract, 45 days mediation, and 10-day notice. No strikes by essential employees.

(Continued)

Table 8.1 (Continued)

State	Covered Employees	Policy
Montana	Public health nurses	Strikes permitted. Nurses must give 30 days' notice; no other nurses' strike may occur within 150 miles.
Ohio	All public employees	Mediation, fact-finding, and 10-day notice required before the strike. No strikes by public safety personnel.
Oregon	All public employees	Strikes permitted after completion of mediation and fact-finding, elapse of 10-day strike notice, and 30-day cooling-off period. No strikes by police, firefighters, or hospital guards.
Pennsylvania	All public employees except prison guards, court employees, police, and fire	Strike permitted after exhaustion of impasse resolution procedures, unless strike presents clear and present danger to public health, safety, or welfare.
Vermont	Municipal employees	Strikes permitted 30 days after fact-finding report where parties have not agreed to arbitration and there is no danger to public health, safety, or welfare. Teacher strikes may be prohibited by courts if it endangers a sound program of education. No strikes by state employees.

Source: the author, taken from various state websites.

notice. All of them have triggers that prohibit strikes in cases involving a threat to the public health and safety.

In Louisiana, Colorado, Idaho, and Montana, state supreme courts applied the private sector right-to-strike principle to public employment. A judicial action with the greatest potential influence in other states occurred in 1985 in California, where the state supreme court ruled that in the absence of express statutory language forbidding the strike, local government employees could legally walk off the job (*County Sanitation District 2 v. Los Angeles County Employees Association, Local 660*, 1985). The California Supreme Court has a reputation as a trendsetter among the state high courts, and its opinions are widely disseminated. In this particular case, the court systematically examined, then dismissed, traditional arguments against public sector strikes. It concluded that the conventional common-law prohibition against strikes was outdated and without merit and that the right to strike was constitutionally protected as a necessary corollary of the right to join a union (Hogler, 1986).

A spate of criticism of the court's reasoning ensued, accompanied by concern that the decision preempted legislative authority and would prompt similar findings in other states not expressly prohibiting strikes. So far, however, no other courts have reached a California-type conclusion.

VI. PUBLIC POLICY AND THE INCIDENCE OF STRIKES

The relationship between state policies on strikes and the incidence of public employee work stoppages presents an interesting and important question for empirical analysis. Unfortunately, research has been hampered by methodological problems and the lack of comprehensive, reliable, comparative data on public employee work stoppages. Since 1981, the federal government has collected and published strike data only on job actions involving 1,000 or more workers.

As noted in Section III, most government work stoppages involve much smaller numbers. The difficulty of assessing the results of permissive and restrictive strike laws is compounded by the effects of various political, economic, and labor force factors on strike incidence. However, published research does permit us to draw several conclusions.

First, a statutory prohibition against strikes may discourage them, but it clearly does not prevent them. This general finding holds both in states that mandate or permit collective bargaining and in those states that do not provide for bargaining. Studies do indicate that the nature of sanctions imposed on striking workers and their unions are related to strike activity. Specifically, consistently enforced penalties tend to reduce the incidence of work stoppages. Second, compulsory interest arbitration tends to reduce strike activity. Strikes are least likely to occur in states that provide for the finality of compulsory arbitration (Olson, 1988; Partridge, 1996; Hebdon & Stern, 2003). Alternatives to strikes are addressed in Chapter 9. Third, the effects of permissive strike policies vary from state to state and by employee function. For example, teacher strikes have occurred more frequently in Pennsylvania than in any other state.

Other states legally permitting strikes have experienced no greater incidence of work stoppages than those that prohibit it. One examination of strikes four years before and four years after the adoption of permissive strike laws revealed in most states a brief jump in the number of work stoppages, then a decline to earlier levels (Sterret & Aboud, 1982, pp. 41–46). Vermont, the first state to enact a permissive law, did not experience its first strike until eight years later. Studies of strikes in Ohio, Illinois, and Minnesota, following passage of collective bargaining statutes legalizing work stoppages for certain categories of employees, found a decrease in strike activity in all three states (GERR, 1990; Ley & Wines, 1993).

A comprehensive examination of public sector strike bans and consequent strike activity concluded that job actions are more frequent in states with no-strike laws (Hebdon & Stern, 2003). The inference is that strike bans are ineffective in reducing work stoppages. Clearly, most public employee unions do not look upon permissive strike policies as an open door to walk out. Teacher exceptionalism in

Pennsylvania and several other states is more a result of state or school district policies that reschedule missed school days than of strike policies. Jurisdictions mandating a fixed number of workdays during the school year typically reschedule days missed due to teacher strikes by extending the school year or canceling holidays, much as in the event of snow or hurricane days. Thus, the financial costs of striking are low for the teachers, who are paid later for the days they missed while on strike (Olson, 1988).

VII. WHY PUBLIC EMPLOYEES STRIKE

With the exception of periodic localized outbursts, public workers until about 1965 were generally perceived to be meek and humble servants of the people. "Public employees were so docile a group that they scarcely seemed part of the American labor movement. Public work was regarded as a short step above the dole, the refuge of lazy, dimwitted people willing to exchange a decent wage and the respect of their fellow men for security and an undemanding job. Public employee uprisings were few, and they met severe censure" (Williams, 1977, p. 16).

Federal employees, in particular

> had been relatively passive for two decades, they were thought to have been professionalized into objective, politically neutral competence, cleansed of radicalism by three decades of loyalty oaths and security investigations, and made both happy and prosperous by very generous salary increases. The outbreak of protest in the federal service obviously jarred these conceptions.
>
> (Hershey, 1973, p. xi)

Why the sudden militancy of public workers in the 1960s? Why do they continue to engage in disruptive job actions today, albeit at a much slower pace?

Until the early 1980s, the Bureau of Labor Statistics recorded the major reason given for each work stoppage in industry and government. Most private sector strikes were attributed to wage and benefit disputes. The figures were similar for the public sector, with economic disputes also fostering the most strikes. That economic issues have provoked a large percentage of strikes in industry and government reflects the fact that wage and benefit issues usually top a union's list of demands in a new bargaining relationship. Of course, the official reason given for a work stoppage reveals little about either the broader macro-level factors related to a strike or the more immediate process-related variables that contribute to a complete breakdown in negotiations.

A. Macro-level Factors

In the private sector, until fairly recently, there was a strong association between unions' propensity to strike and prevailing business conditions (known as the business cycle). Work stoppages tended to increase during periods of rising prices and falling unemployment and decrease during economic recessions. For example, postwar boom periods following World War II and the wars in Korea and Vietnam saw a substantial rise in the number of work stoppages (Ashenfelter & Johnson, 1969).

Economic expansion usually means plentiful job opportunities. A striker who is permanently dismissed should be able to find another position. Conversely, during periods of economic decline, unemployment levels rise, and jobs are hard to locate. Workers are less likely to risk being fired for a job action. The relationship between strike activity and the business cycle has been similar in public employment (Partridge, 1991).

What has changed recently is the nature of job opportunities. Private sector manufacturing workers permanently replaced during a strike find it very difficult to locate a similarly paying job today, regardless of the business cycle. This is due in large part to the enormous shift in employment to information technology, services, and other sectors as manufacturing has declined.

In the private sector, strikes also are related to the nature of the industry and the work involved. Strikes are most common among homogeneous groups of workers who have little opportunity for economic advancement (e.g., coal miners and dock workers). Physical labor (unskilled or semiskilled), unpleasant or dangerous work surroundings, and seasonal casual jobs have been positively associated with strike behavior as well (Burton & Krider, 1975).

Similar patterns are evident in the public sector. The largest number of strikes were by homogeneous unions of teachers, transportation workers, health-care workers, sanitation workers, and, in the early days, police and firefighters. Working conditions are highly variable in these occupational categories, but dangerous situations are not uncommon in any of them (e.g., teachers in inner-city schools; sanitation workers loading, compacting, and unloading solid waste). One can imagine few jobs more unpleasant than working all day in close proximity to garbage.

B. Micro-level Factors

Three types of micro-level variables are related to strike activity: demographic and attitudinal factors, bargaining power and costs of disagreement, and faulty negotiations.

1. Demographic and Attitudinal Factors

For job actions, gender seems to be insignificant; age is more important. Older employees, who have the most to lose and the least to gain from a strike, tend to be more conservative about a job action (Maki & Strand, 1984), but younger workers are more willing to walk out. Education level may also be related to strike behavior. Earlier research found the higher the level of schooling, the lower the propensity to strike (Maki & Strand, 1984; Shutt, 1982). Newer evidence suggests that workers with higher levels of education and a social justice orientation, such as those working for museums, policy think tanks, and social service organizations are more likely to strike (Julius et al., 2023; Rendon, 2023; Satow, 2023).

Research further suggests that job satisfaction, favorable attitudes toward the employer, worker autonomy in the workplace, and progressive HRM practices are negatively related to strike activity (Godard, 1992; Ng, 1991) and that those most strongly committed to the union are more likely to vote for a strike than less committed members (Martin & Sinclair, 2001; Wheeler, 1985). Finally, workers consider the potential costs and benefits of going on strike from an individual perspective, including their current level of pay and benefits versus the perceived costs of striking (financial as well as family related) and the availability of job alternatives should the strike fail (Martin & Sinclair, 2001).

2. Bargaining Power and Disagreement Costs

The bargaining power of the respective parties influences strike behavior. Burton and Krider (1975) measure bargaining power as the union's ability to obtain wages greater than the employer would have voluntarily paid on the basis of market conditions. They assert that strong private sector unions are less likely to strike than weak unions because they tend to accept less than what they could actually get through a full display of power (which would harm the competitive market position of the employer). The employer also tends to give them "more" to avoid a costly and painful confrontation.

Relative bargaining power for any union fluctuates with economic and employment conditions, union membership strength and commitment, the union's ability to control the labor market, effectiveness and leadership skills of management and union negotiators, public opinion, and an almost limitless number of other factors that vary, in government, by service function and employer. Despite impressive attempts, no single, simple equation has been derived to represent all the vicissitudes of public sector bargaining, and neither is it likely to be. Furthermore, the relationship of the strike to bargaining power is nebulous: "strikes may be a manifestation of weakness, as well as a demonstration of power" (Spero & Capozzola, 1973, pp. 250–251).

Notwithstanding the extreme complexity and turbidity of the bargaining power concept, some useful insights into a bargaining relationship and potential work stoppages can be derived. For instance, the union and management costs of disagreeing may be calculated in the context of the threat of a strike to help discern "true" attitudes and beliefs or where the parties are "coming from." Cartter

(1959) was one of the earliest scholars to view strikes from this perspective, as represented by the following equation:

$$\frac{\textit{Cost of disagreeing with Y}}{\textit{Cost of agreeing on Y's terms}} = \textit{Bargaining attitude of X}$$

For example, teachers' costs of attempting to settle a bargaining dispute through a walkout are lower in jurisdictions that mandate a fixed number of days in the school year and thus require strikers to make up lost days on holidays or during the early summer. Where strikes result in a reduction in school days or where school districts fill in for striking teachers with substitutes, the costs of disagreement can be considerably higher because pay may be deducted. Similarly, as discussed Section VIII.E, the costs of striking are higher in jurisdictions that enforce severe sanctions as a matter of course and lower where strike penalties are rarely applied, often forgiven, or nonexistent.

3. Faulty Negotiations

Strikes may erupt from what Hicks (1932) referred to as faulty negotiations. This occurs when one or both parties err in assessing the other's true bargaining position, willingness to engage in a strike, or understanding of what a "reasonable" settlement would look like. Faulty negotiations may be as elusive an explanation for work stoppages as bargaining power, but there are many instances in which the bargaining process clearly collapses because of inept—or inexperienced—negotiators, personality conflicts, unrealistic demands, communications breakdowns, or the lack of good faith bargaining.

To illustrate, faulty negotiations because of severe personality conflicts characterized the Bay Area Rapid Transit strike of 1997. While union and management representatives deadlocked over minor issues and denounced one another in dueling press conferences, the strike of 2,600 Service Employees International Union–affiliated workers inconvenienced some 275,000 mass transit riders for several days (Fagan et al., 1997). In other situations, one party, perceiving a benefit, appears reluctant to negotiate in good faith. The 2004 3-day walkout by New York City daycare workers serving poor families followed more than 4 years without a contract and 3.5 years without a raise (Kaufman, 2004). Trash collectors, garbage sorters, and truck drivers called a 48-hour strike in San Mateo County, California, in 2010 in support of 12 county landfill workers whose contract had expired 8 months earlier (Fimrite, 2010). In each of these cases, one or both parties perceived some benefit in dragging out negotiations. Another example of faulty negotiations is documented in Case Study 8.2.

In a perfect world, negotiators for both sides would have complete information and full knowledge of all important variables, including the other party's true position. A Pareto-optimal solution would be devised at the bargaining table and both parties would "win." Unfortunately, this perfect world is inhabited by divergent interests and perceptions of reality, schisms within the ranks of both management and labor, unequal bargaining power, the Hydra of public opinion, intense personality conflicts, diabolical political machinations, and uncountable related factors. Even an offhand comment on the gender of chief negotiators can matter (Montgomery & Benedict, 1989). Case Study 8.2 describes the 2012 Chicago teachers' strike, whose precipitators included faulty negotiations between new Mayor Rahm Emanuel and Chicago Teachers Union (CTU) President Karen Lewis.

Faulty negotiations may be minimized by experience and maturity. Over time, bargaining parties develop protocols to reveal indirectly where each truly stands on the issues (Reder & Neumann, 1980). As the parties become familiar with one another, the likelihood of a strike occurring because of faulty negotiations is reduced. This view is supported by the higher incidence of strikes in new bargaining relationships and research findings that experienced negotiators make fewer mistakes in assessing their opponents' actual position (Montgomery & Benedict, 1989). The greater the bargaining experience, the less the likelihood of a strike. Carried to the extreme, secret agreements between union and management negotiators have been known to make bargaining a charade, with the most important outcomes predetermined.

CASE STUDY 8.2 FAULTY NEGOTIATIONS IN CHICAGO

Twenty-six thousand public school teachers in the nation's third largest school system stayed out of the classrooms as the 2012 school year began, inconveniencing 350,000 students, their parents, and many others. As a mayoral candidate in 2011, Rahm Emanuel had criticized the teachers and the CTU on many occasions and proposed a state law limiting strike rights. Once in office, he rescinded a 4% raise that had been agreed to in a collective bargaining contract. New bargaining broke down over pay, teacher evaluation, priority for rehiring laid-off teachers for new openings, the length of the school day, and, in the eyes of the union membership, basic respect for teachers.

Calling the job action a "strike of choice," Emanuel remonstrated, "Don't take it out on the kids of the City of Chicago if you have a problem with me," and "I will not stand by while the children of Chicago are played as pawns in an internal dispute with a union" (Davey, 2012;

Rossi et al., 2012). Calling the strike "illegal," the mayor filed a lawsuit seeking a return-to-work injunction to send teachers into the classroom. He traded insults in the media with CTU President Lewis (who was no shrinking violet herself) (Webber, 2012).

After seven days of vitriol and hard bargaining, a deal was reached that both sides proclaimed to be a win.

Questions

1 When negotiations, such as those in Chicago, unravel and accusations are tossed about like confetti, is one party or the other usually at fault? Is that the case here?

2 Based on the brief preceding description and your own Internet research, was faulty negotiations the "cause" of the strike or were fundamental differences the principal reasons?

3 Do you think the national debate over education reform and teacher unions played a role in provoking the strike? Why or why not? (Again, Internet research will yield further background on the strike.)

VIII. STRIKE TACTICS

A. The Union

Work stoppages usually come after rejection of the employer's last offer and a majority vote of the union membership to strike. Worker solidarity is important. The strike meeting itself is run enthusiastically, with great grandstanding, emotional avowals, and thunderous applause. The union leader's goal is to win a unanimous vote for a walkout.

The union must move quickly to build up maximum pressure on the employer and elected officials. Timing the strike and its announcement to have the fullest impact is important to the union also. For example, maximum media coverage normally is available Monday through Thursday. A strike announcement made on Friday afternoon or over the weekend can go relatively unheralded. Similarly, little immediate impact is registered if transit workers walk off the job on a Saturday.

Transport Workers Union Local 234 at SEPTA went on strike for six days in November 2016. Pension improvements and working conditions were the largest areas of contention. Candidates running for office worried about voter turnout in the general election. On November 4, SEPTA filed a lawsuit requesting a preliminary injunction and an end the ongoing strike. The court denied this request. On November 6, the City of Philadelphia sought an injunction to temporarily halt the SEPTA strike for Election Day, Tuesday, November 8. On Monday, November, 7 SEPTA and the Transport Workers Union Local 234 reached an agreement ending the strike.

Pressure tactics are quickly applied: news conferences, mass meetings, media advertisements, e-mail blasts, lobbying, and picket lines all help apprise the public and elected officials of the union's point of view. Picket lines have high visibility and, if other union members refuse to cross them, they create powerful new pressures on public officials and management. Strikes can even disperse geographically. Striking Houston janitors set up picket lines in Chicago, Washington, D.C., New York City, and other cities in late 2006 to bring national pressure on employers. Pension sympathizers may also honor picket lines, as the University of Minnesota learned during an American Federation of State, County, and Municipal Employees strike by 3,500 clerical, technical, and health-care workers in September 2007. Offices had to be closed or services reduced all across campus for nearly three weeks. Elsewhere, picket lines have shut down classrooms, transit systems, and garbage collection.

Ill-timed strikes, however, may produce lingering hard feelings on the part of an inconvenienced or angry public. A 2001 Minnesota state employee strike came on the heels of the September 11 terrorist attacks on New York City and Washington, D.C. Residents of the Gopher State have still not forgiven the strikers. The strategic timing significance of a work stoppage is perhaps no better illustrated than in the 1979 walkout by New Orleans police. The Teamsters-affiliated union announced its strike on the Friday night before Mardi Gras weekend. In more than 120 years, the internationally famed festival had been canceled only seven times—five times during war and twice for epidemics. The walkout, officially over bargaining rights for management-level police officers, benefits, and working conditions, also entailed rivalries between two police unions and racial overtones (the mayor was black, the police force largely white).

The strike threatened to wreak economic havoc on the City of New Orleans, which expected to realize $250 million from Mardi Gras that year. Before the strike was settled 15 days later, 18 parades were canceled or moved to the suburbs and thousands of tourists left the city early or avoided the festival altogether. The union gained a number of concessions from city officials but lost something perhaps of greater value—its public support. Before the strike ended, antiunion rhetoric became strident and widespread. Vitriol and "base, vile behavior" on both sides tainted labor–management relations for many years. In retrospect, the union's timing strategy may have been ill advised (Salerno, 1981).

Union leaders do not usually call a strike without carefully considering the possible ramifications and the odds of winning it. A strike committee composed of various stewards and unit representatives is typically formed to analyze the costs and benefits. If a work stoppage is indeed the decision, the strike committee operates out of a control center to direct picketing actions and media relations, handle members' questions, maintain solidarity, and coordinate with other unions (Gagala, 1983, pp. 230–241). Strike websites, chat rooms, and e-mail groups are set up to communicate rapidly with strike leaders and supporters. Photos and video clips are posted for media use.

Sometimes job actions other than a full work stoppage are employed. By "working to the rule," employees refuse to perform activities not in their job descriptions, turn down overtime work, and otherwise legally interfere with the operations of the employer. For example, Delaware correctional officers refused overtime in 2004 to protest low pay and a record high number of unfilled vacancies (Parra, 2004). As another illustration, employees may protest what they consider to be unsafe conditions by assembling en masse in the supervisor's office or filing reams of grievance paperwork. Where strikes are prohibited by law and alternatives such as arbitration are not available, absenteeism, negligence, reduced effort, rudeness in dealing with customers, and even sabotage may occur (Hebdon & Stern, 1998).

Events proceed at a rapid pace during most public employee strikes. In private employment, management usually has accumulated inventories and otherwise prepared itself for a possible work stoppage. Public services are provided directly by people; tangible material products seldom exist. Nationally affiliated unions typically maintain strike funds to help out-of-work members get by financially until paychecks begin to flow again, an option not generally available to striking public employees. But public sector services are not conducive to inventory accumulation. There is strong pressure to restore services as soon as possible. Thus, workers are motivated to seek a speedy settlement—an outcome also appreciated by the inconvenienced general citizenry.

When a quick resolution is not in the cards, a determined union elevates the level and scope of conflict. In a study of social movement unionism, Johnston (1994) suggested that any collective action by public employees is likely to experience greater success if the union is able to (1) frame its demands in terms of the "public interest" and (2) form coalitions with program clients, other unions and groups of employees, elected officials, agency or departmental management, or other entities. For instance, a strike over pay inequities for female employees might be presented as a fight for the interests of all women. Similarly, a teachers' strike might be articulated as being for the "good of the children." A walkout by health-care workers might be framed as being about "patient safety." Likewise, a strike by school bus drivers might be about "children's safety." Finally, a strike by predominantly African American or Latino workers might be portrayed as a "struggle for civil rights."

B. Management

In legalized strike jurisdictions, employers must ask themselves how far they will go before taking a strike, how long a strike they can withstand, and what the likely results of it will be. Early in the public sector experience, most employers would go the extra mile to avoid a strike. Alternatively, in the event one did occur, employers would try to settle it as expeditiously as possible with only passing regard for the long-term results.

The tendency of public managers to cave in to avoid the turmoil and confusion of a strike has lessened. Management recognizes that certain factors favor them during work stoppages. As already noted, government tax revenues continue to be collected whereas employee wages stop. Without a substantial strike fund, public employees can be seriously inconvenienced both by their loss of wages and benefits and by the curtailment of government services upon which they and their families, like all other citizens, depend. Furthermore, striking public workers face citizen hostility that often tilts public opinion in favor of management. In addition, there is always the disturbing possibility that striking government workers won't be badly missed, thus calling into question the need for the services they have provided in the past or raising the specter of privatization.

Even work stoppages in police and fire services, arguably the most "essential" of all local government functions, do not always have adverse impacts. Although the Boston police strike was accompanied by shocking episodes of crime and general breakdowns in law and order, such was not the outcome in other incidents, including police strikes in New York City, Albuquerque, and San Francisco. In these and many other jurisdictions, public managers utilized long-range planning to cope with strikes by providing temporary substitute labor. For example, local police supervisors, county law enforcement personnel, and state highway patrol officers can augment non-striking police personnel. With respect to firefighters, adjacent districts or volunteer fire departments can assist during strikes. Through contingency planning, essential services can be maintained during a work stoppage. Planning may have the added benefit of reducing the likelihood of a strike occurring in the first place.

C. Contingency Planning for the Strike

Despite the fact that work stoppages in government are rare today, strike planning is a sound and necessary management practice to maintain critical services and ensure a strong management bargaining position. Although contingency planning is more common today than in the past, many employers continue to ignore the need for it.

Comparing municipal strike preparation to disaster and other emergency preparedness requirements is instructive (Levesque, 1980). Certain groups of personnel should be identified. These include: (1) a strike task force composed of the city manager, assistant city manager, city attorney, director of public works, chiefs of police and fire, and the HRM director and (2) strike operations personnel consisting of department heads and other management employees.

The principal duties of the task force are to maintain essential services by assessing problems on a day-to-day basis and to create alternative approaches for dealing with them. Strike operations personnel oversee and perform critical services in their functional domains. In the event of a general strike, the task force can implement a strike plan to continue operating designated essential services and as many other services as possible while shutting down government functions not posing a threat to the public health and safety. A strike headquarters may be designated in advance. As in any emergency, reliable communication channels must be established to link the task force with the union leaders, strike operations personnel, the media, the legislative body, the mayor, and the general public.

The strike contingency plan should identify in detail which personnel can be utilized to maintain essential services. An inventory of supervisory skills and job experiences aids in assigning managers to essential line operations. Private contractors can be enlisted to provide services on a temporary basis. Intergovernmental cooperation through formal mutual aid pacts is also advised. Such agreements serve to augment supervisory personnel or to replace them in the unlikely event that they, too, walk out. Importantly, the contingency plan should provide for the protection of non-striking workers through arrangements such as carpools, escorts, patrolled parking lots, and telework.

During the work stoppage, the public employer attempts to garner public support for the management position to apply maximum pressure on wavering union members to return to work. A number of strategies may be used, most of them involving manipulation of electronic and print media. For example, management might consider publishing salaries of striking workers or showing how increased taxes and/or expenditures would result from bowing to union demands.

Pawtucket, Rhode Island, is a city that once held the dubious honor of experiencing the most teacher strikes in the United States. Its superintendent, Robert J. Gerardi (1986), offered the following suggestions. Be aware of election-year pressures on elected officials for a quick settlement. Designate a single spokesperson to deal with the media, so that conflicting information will be minimal. Be prepared for teacher unions to use pressure tactics on the school board and administrators, such as daily picket lines and unfair labor practice charges. He advised management negotiators to avoid giving away the store and noted that the union team will be counting on management fatigue.

D. The Injunction

An injunction is a request by the public employer (as plaintiff) to a state or local court to halt a strike or other job action. First, however, a temporary (or ex parte) restraining order, intended to stop a job action until a final determination as to its legality can be made by the court. To obtain the order, the employer must show prima facie evidence of jeopardy to public health or safety, or of the intentional interruption of a legally mandated government function. In practice, the temporary restraining order is often used simply to serve notice on the public employee union of government concern and to set the stage for imposing sanctions, such as fines or dismissals. If the work stoppage continues, the court may hold a hearing and issue a preliminary injunction aimed at stopping the job action until a final decision can be reached on whether to issue a permanent injunction. Permanent injunctions are normally not required in public employment because of the short duration of most strikes.

Until passage of the Norris-LaGuardia Act in 1932, the courts tended to be very quick—even to the point of abuse—to issue injunctions against almost any type of job action, from strikes to picketing. The injunctions immediately placed unions in the unpalatable position of having to either order their members back to work or keep them off the job in violation of the law. The Norris-LaGuardia Act forbids federal courts from issuing injunctions in labor disputes unless they threaten public health or safety or are accompanied by fraud or violence. However, the act does not cover public employees, who can be enjoined from job actions by state or local courts.

Before 1968, most courts held that injunctions against illegal work stoppages did not require the public employer to demonstrate irreparable harm to the operations of government or to public health and safety. Injunctions were routinely granted upon request. In that year, however, in *School District for the City of Holland et al. v. Holland Education Association* (1968), the Michigan Supreme Court refused to issue an injunction against teachers who failed to report for work because the school districts did not demonstrate irreparable injury or breach of the peace. Taking a strict approach to issuing an injunction, the court stated,

> We must concede that the mere failure of a public school system to begin its school year on the appointed day cannot be classified as a catastrophic event. We are also aware that there has been no public furor when schools are closed down for inclement weather, or on the day a presidential candidate comes to town, or when the basketball team wins the championship.

The *Holland* case set an important precedent for other states by implying that the employer should approach the court with "clean hands" after having bargained in good faith. The mere injunctive request was not, in and of itself, enough to merit court action. Interestingly, Michigan law expressly forbids public employee strikes.

Today, the courts require the public employer to demonstrate that some harm results from a job action before it will enjoin that action. When faculty unions at

Rutgers University went on strike in 2023 after bargaining for over a year without a contract, the university president, Jonathan Holloway, threatened to seek a court injunction to break the strike and force faculty back to work. Holloway eventually walked back the threat of injunction after Governor Murphy invited both parties to his office to engage in a dialogue about the dispute (Roberts-Grmela, 2023).

Use of the injunction simply to avoid inconvenience or escape confronting the causes of labor conflict head on has been an increasingly untenable behavior for government employers. Even when injunctions are won, enforcement of contempt of court penalties may be counterproductive, intensifying employer–employee conflict and making martyrs out of jailed leaders. If penalties are not enforced, the credibility of management is damaged. Either way, management may not emerge in a stronger position.

This is not to say that there is no legitimate role for the injunction. To the contrary, serious threats to the health and safety of citizens resulting from a strike are appropriately met with an injunction. A work stoppage in violation of an ongoing contract may properly be enjoined. What is called for is flexibility, with employer and court decision making appropriate to the circumstances surrounding each case.

E. Strike Penalties

If a strike is illegal or if a court injunction and back-to-work order are secured, yet strikers defy them, should public workers be punished? If so, how severely, and what penalties should be invoked? Excessively harsh strike penalties imposed by the courts or by the employer may be counterproductive by encouraging strikers to extend their job action with the belief that they have nothing to lose. Alternatively, strikers may take a calculated risk that the employer will not actually follow through with strong sanctions, such as dismissal.

Illegal walkouts by schoolteachers present a particularly delicate situation because of the special relationship between teachers and their students. When 700 Monmouth, New Jersey, teachers walked out over an increase in their health insurance premiums in 2001, a state judge ordered them back to duty. The teachers defied the order, so the judge, beginning with names starting with the letter A, jailed the teachers (alphabetically) until the union called off the strike nine days later. Arrests can result in serious and lasting damage to a public school system, including a loss of student respect for a "convicted criminal."

When, however, an illegal walkout extends for a prolonged period of time or causes great hardship, the public employer wants to apply new pressures for settlement, and management believes that sanctions must be leveled, a number of options are available. Union members and/or officials may be imprisoned, fined, fired, demoted, or suspended. The union may be decertified. Alternatively, the dues checkoff may be suspended or revoked.

Most states provide statutory strike penalties. In Georgia, striking state employees can receive five years' probation and no pay increase for three years. Nevada law establishes a $50,000 fine per day against a striking union, with a $1,000 daily fine plus imprisonment for the union officials. Michigan levies a fine of one day's pay for each day's strike on school employees and daily monetary penalties against the union as well. Striking teachers in Maryland may have their union decertified as exclusive representative in the school district.

New York's Taylor Law sets out substantial penalties for striking workers including loss of two days' pay for each strike day and suspension of the dues checkoff. Generally, the Taylor Law sanctions (as amended in 1968) have been regularly enforced and strike incidence has been minimized, indicating the value of flexibility and consistency in enforcing strike penalties. For instance, New York City transit workers went on strike in December 2005 over pensions, health insurance, and worker safety issues, despite being warned of "dire consequences" by Governor Pataki and Mayor Bloomberg. A state supreme court judge slapped them with one injunction and then a second. The noncomplying Transport Workers Union was held in contempt of court and fined $1 million a day. The union leader, Roger Toussaint, was jailed. When the workers finally returned to their subways, trains, and buses, the fine had run to $2.5 million, and Toussaint had sat in jail for four days (Greenhouse & Chan, 2006; Lueck, 2006).

In sum, New York's tough Taylor Law does force striking unions and their members back to the job. In many instances, however, severe punishments, such as dismissals, jail time, and heavy fines, are not carried out. In some cases, penalties imposed on illegal strikers are forgiven after the strike is settled. Yet mild penalties might be ignored by the union. The middle ground of moderate sanctions consistently enforced may be the best course of action to reduce the probability of strikes, particularly where binding arbitration is available to resolve disputes (Currie & McConnell, 1994; Partridge, 1996).

Although striking employees are often threatened with dismissal and sometimes fired outright, as in the case of the epic Professional Air Traffic Controllers Organization (PATCO) strike (see Case Study 8.3), management usually opposes such actions as a practical matter because they do not want to lose good employees for whom they have made an investment in time and training. Often, there is dissension within the ranks of management over such decisions. Disagreements over the proper course of action create an interesting political rivalry between those who want to dismiss striking workers and those who do not. Elected officials may find themselves deeply divided in such disputes as well.

CASE STUDY 8.3 THE PATCO STRIKE

PATCO was established in 1968 as a "professional society" of federal air traffic controllers. Relations with the controllers' "employer," the Federal Aviation Administration (FAA), were stormy from the beginning. Within two years, PATCO had staged a sick-out, and the FAA had responded by canceling the organization's dues checkoff system. A report commissioned by the U.S. Department of Transportation (DOT) categorized PATCO–FAA labor–management relations as "the worst in the federal sector."

On March 25, 1970, PATCO called its first nationwide job action—a sick-out that lasted 3 weeks—over FAA transfer of four PATCO members who were engaged in organizing efforts in Baton Rouge, Louisiana. It was a serious mistake, resulting in a union membership decline from more than 7,500 to less than 3,000 and near bankruptcy from a $100 million damage suit brought by the airlines. As part of the settlement, PATCO agreed to a permanent no-strike injunction. PATCO spent the next three years seeking reinstatement of hundreds of controllers who were fired and suspended from duty by the FAA. Meanwhile, the FAA unsuccessfully fought PATCO's petition for certification as exclusive representative of the controllers. In 1973, the first contract negotiations were held. Throughout the remainder of the 1970s, PATCO and the FAA negotiated a series of one-year contracts, almost always in an atmosphere of crisis and work slowdowns.

Accumulating bitterness from hostile contract negotiations and waves of grievances filed under the various written agreements came to a head as the last contract expired in March 1981 and negotiations over a new contract reached an impasse. The dispute involved PATCO's demands concerning salaries, work hours, retirement programs, and other benefits that, to be granted, would require special treatment of the controllers somewhat similar to that accorded postal workers. PATCO President Robert Poli polled his membership on whether to go out on strike. Seventy-five percent voted for a walkout, and when Poli submitted the FAA's last best offer to the rank and file, they rejected the package by a 20-to-1 margin.

After two subsequent months of negotiation and federal mediation, the two sides were, in mediator Kenneth Moffett's words, "still miles apart." PATCO was asking for $575 million in new salaries and benefits, while the FAA said it would agree to $40 million and no more. On August 3, 1981,

12,000 controllers refused to report to their control towers at airports throughout the United States.

If the controllers thought President Ronald Reagan, a former head of the Screen Actors' Guild (and whom PATCO had endorsed for president), would be sympathetic to their cause, they were sadly and fatally mistaken. Reagan labeled them "lawbreakers," sought the imprisonment of strike leaders, and summarily dismissed from federal service all the strikers who refused to return to work within 48 hours. A federal judge supported the president by imposing accelerating fines on the union that would total $1 million per day.

If PATCO leaders were counting on public sympathy for the controllers to help encourage the FAA and the Reagan administration to compromise or back down, they were wrong again. The average citizen—even the typical union member—found it difficult to identify with the relatively well-paid controllers who were demanding a maximum salary of $59,000 (about $203,919 in 2024 dollars), almost unequaled retirement benefits, and a 32-hour workweek. Moreover, the strikers were clearly in violation of several federal laws and their oath of office. When Reagan and DOT Secretary Drew Lewis declared the strike over (because all strikers had been fired) and the DOT began hiring new controllers, there was little public outcry. There was, however, concern by air travelers that the nation's air traffic control system would be unable to function safely, amid predictions by the airline industry of massive layoffs and flight cancellations.

Meanwhile, as new recruits began fast-track training to become air traffic controllers, some 2,500 supervisors were joined in directing aircraft by about 800 military controllers, the 5,000 civilian controllers who had stayed on the job or returned within the amnesty period, and hundreds of recently retired controllers. Despite PATCO predictions of terrible air disasters and a crippled industry, neither happened. Commercial flights continued, although at reduced levels, and accidents occurred at or below normal levels. The airlines lost a great deal of money, but they never wavered in supporting the president.

Three months later, PATCO was officially decertified as a bargaining representative by the Federal Labor Relations Authority. Subsequent court appeals by the union were fruitless. The once proud and aggressive organization of professional air traffic controllers had been destroyed by its own strategic mistakes and a hostile administration.

In hindsight, the strategic errors of PATCO are obvious. First, the union badly misread public reaction to the strike and to its demands. Little sympathy was offered to the highly paid white-collar workers during a period of citizen resistance to government taxation and spending. Second, the union failed to publicize legitimate grievances, including congested airways, tremendous mental strain on overworked controllers, and the need for improvements in technology. Third, PATCO did not anticipate the strong Reagan administration reaction to the strike and the government's determination to "stick to its guns." Finally, PATCO did not make the time or effort to garner the support of other federal and private sector unions before the strike. Although controllers in Canada and Portugal did refuse to route U.S. flights over their air space for several days, the actions were short lived and not very troublesome. Organized labor in the United States abandoned the striking controllers and refused to respect their picket lines. Had domestic union support been stronger, the airline industry could have been brought to the brink of financial disaster, which would have tremendously increased settlement pressure on the administration.

Years later, in 1987, air traffic controllers voted in a new union: the National Air Traffic Controllers Association (NATCA), organized by John Thornton, one of the controllers sacked by Mr. Reagan. The new union adopted a no-strike pledge and disavowed illegal job actions, while renewing many of its earlier complaints concerning heavy workloads and an autocratic FAA. In 1989, NATCA successfully (and peacefully) negotiated its first contract. In 1993, President Clinton lifted the ban on rehiring the controllers fired by Reagan. Sadly, most were past retirement age or had moved on to other careers.

Questions

1 Were "faulty negotiations" in play in the events leading up to the PATCO strike? If so, how?

2 How did public opinion play a role?

3 If he had been able to exercise hindsight, how might Poli have played his cards differently?

4 Why do you think President Reagan reacted so strongly to the air traffic controller strike? How might subsequent presidents have handled the events differently?

IX. CONCLUSIONS AND A LOOK AHEAD

Even in the event of initial management determination to dismiss striking workers, it frequently proves difficult to carry out the final action. Firing striking public employees can provoke more problems than officials want. The real politics of public sector strike policy often diverge substantially from formal provisions in the statutes. Nonetheless, many employee discharges have been announced and permanently carried out. For the public employer, the paramount tasks are to avoid strikes when possible; always protect the public's health, safety, and well-being; and promote solutions through good faith bargaining.

Work stoppages and related job actions by public workers have been recorded since the 1830s. The incidence and intensity of government work stoppage increased dramatically from 1965 to the late 1970s, especially at the local level. Since then, the number of strikes has declined significantly, both in government and in the private sector.

The vast majority of public employee work stoppages have occurred in the face of philosophical and legal prohibitions by governments. The sovereignty doctrine, although essentially irrelevant in those jurisdictions engaging in collective bargaining with their workers, remains pertinent where negotiations are prohibited. Nonetheless, government employee work stoppages have taken place in all states. Early on in the public sector experience, strikes did seem to bias the political process in favor of the unions. This was followed by a long period in which work stoppages generated strong political and economic counter-pressures on striking employees and their unions.

As the "ultimate weapon in labor's arsenal," the public employee work stoppage appears to have lost much of its firepower. Employer recognition of the apparent inevitability of strikes has resulted in a more mature, calculated approach by management. Negotiating skills, training, experience, and planning have improved greatly during the past decade, especially at the local government level. As Bornstein (1980) remarked,

> Public management came of age in the 1970s. Public sector negotiators have learned well from the private sector that there are 10,000 ways to say 'no' to a union's demands without bargaining in bad faith. And they have learned the ultimate lesson from private sector management: Never blink an eye at a union's strike threats; talk softly and carry a big strike contingency plan.

Several signs would seem to portend heightened public sector strike activity. Government employment has become less desirable because of cost-saving layoffs and hiring freezes, limited wage gains, reductions in pension and health-care benefits, outsourcing and contracting out, and bureaucrat bashing by citizens and elected officials. Working conditions have deteriorated for many public workers: classroom teachers face unruly and violence-prone students; police officers endure life-threatening encounters with violent offenders; and social workers must attempt to intervene in the affairs of dysfunctional families. Attacks on the very existence of unions and collective bargaining are being launched by antiunion forces in several states.

The PATCO debacle was a seminal event in American labor history that continues to influence public sector unions today, especially at the federal level. That a highly skilled group of professionals in what is clearly an essential service could be relatively easily replaced, and their union absolutely crushed, made all organized labor enormously insecure. The PATCO strike marked a major change in political climate, with very negative implications for the unions.

Another factor discouraging government work stoppages is management is more experienced at the bargaining game. When a strike is called, it is much better prepared to cope effectively. Where strikes continue to be illegal, sanctions, when consistently enforced, can be very painful for the union and for individual members, who face the loss of their livelihood. Concern for job security may override a desire for wage and benefit increases.

Public perceptions play a strong role in the efficacy of strikes and can either suppress or elevate workers' demands. The RedforEd teachers strikes in 2018–2019 were an important turning point in the trend of work stoppages by public employees. These strikes garnered strong support from the general public.

Political and economic realities also influence the character of public and nonprofit sector strikes. In the wake of the post-pandemic worker burnout among frontline service providers, the great resignation, and low unemployment, government and nonprofit agencies faced challenges recruiting and retaining employees. The post-COVID-19 "hot labor summers" in 2022 and 2023 changed the national mood, along with government and nonprofit employers' reactions to strikes.

Overall, bargaining relationships have matured and stabilized. Many union leaders have reached a comfortable accommodation with management. Moreover, alternatives to the strike, as intended, have proven successful in deterring them. Mediation, fact-finding, and especially binding interest arbitration provide more peaceful venues for settling contract disputes. They are discussed in Chapter 9.

REFERENCES

Anderson, S., Klinger, S., & Wakamo, B. (2020). *How congress manufactured a postal crisis—and how to fix it*. Institute for Policy Studies. https://ips-dc.org/how-congress-manufactured-a-postal-crisis-and-how-to-fix-it/

AP. (1991, April 27). Montana state worker strike spreads as more guard troops are sent in. *The New York Times*. https://www.nytimes.com/1991/04/27/us/montana-state-worker-strike-spreads-as-more-guard-troops-are-sent-in.html

Ashenfelter, O. C., & Johnson, G. E. (1969, March). Bargaining theory, trade unions, and industrial strike activity. *American Economic Review*, 35–49.

Bornstein, T. (1980). Legacies of local government collective bargaining in the 1970s. *Labor Law Journal*, *31*(3), 165–173.

Bradford, D. (2021, February 11). A rolling national teacher strike is why schools are closed. *Education Next*. https://www.educationnext.org/rolling-national-teacher-strike-is-why-schools-are-closed/

Burton, J. F., & Krider, C. E. (1975). The incidence of strikes in public employment. In D. Hammermesh (Ed.), *Labor in the public and nonprofit sectors* (pp. 135–177). Princeton University Press.

Capozzola, J. M. (1979, April). Public employee strikes: Myths and realities. *National Civil Review*, *68*, 178–188.

Cartter, A. M. (1959). *Theory of wages and employment*. Irwin.

County Sanitation Dist. v. Los Angeles County Employees Association, Local 660. (1985). 699 P. 2d 835, 38 Cal. 3d 564, 214 Cal. Rptr. 424 (1985).

Currie, J., & McConnell, S. (1994, September). Collective bargaining in the public sector: The effect of legal structures on dispute costs and wages. *The American Economic Review, 81*, 693–718.

Davey, M. (2012, September 10). Teachers' strike in Chicago tests mayor and union. *New York Times*. www.nytimes.com

Fagan, K., Cabanatuan, M., & DelVecchio, R. (1997, September 13). Acrimonious BART talks go nowhere. *San Francisco Chronicle*.

Fimrite, P. (2010, August 26). Two-day trash strike hits San Mateo County. *San Francisco Chronicle*. www.sfgate.com

Fowler, R. B. (1974, March–April). Normative aspects of public employee strikes. *Public Personnel Management*, 129–137.

Fretland, K. (2014, July 9). *44 firefighters out sick Saturday; 142 police*. https://archive.commercialappeal.com/news/44-firefighters-out-sick-saturday-142-police-ep-507589864-324365621.html/

Gagala, K. (1983). *Union organizing and staying organized*. Reston Publishing.

Gerardi, R. J. (1986). Recommendations for handling a strike. *Journal of Collective Negotiations, 15*(4), 367–372.

GERR. (1990, August 6). Government employee relations report, 991–992. *Bureau of National Affairs*.

Godard, J. (1992, October). Strikes as collective voice: A behavioral analysis of strike activity. *Industrial and Labor Relations Review, 46*, 161–175.

Greenhouse, S. (2001, October 2). 28,000 state workers strike in Minnesota, drawing fire. *The New York Times*. https://www.nytimes.com/2001/10/02/us/28000-state-workers-strike-in-minnesota-drawing-fire.html

Greenhouse, S. (2012, January 22) More lockouts as companies battle unions. *New York Times*. www.nytimes.com

Greenhouse, S., & Chan, S. (2006, January 22). In transit dispute, navigating without a map. *New York Times*.

Hebdon, R. P., & Stern, R. N. (1998, January). Tradeoffs among expressions of industrial conflict: Public sector strike bans and grievance arbitration. *Industrial and Labor Relations Review, 51*, 204–221.

Hebdon, R. P., & Stern, R. N. (2003). Do public-sector strike bans really prevent conflict? *Industrial Relations, 42*(3), 493–512.

Hendrickson, B., & Smith, B. (2023, October 28). *SEPTA reaches tentative deal with transport workers union to avert strike*. https://6abc.com/septa-strike-2023-transport-workers-union-local-234-philadelphia-pa-twu-update/13981749/

Henry, T. (2009, May 10). The Toledo municipal strike of 1979: When chaos reigned. *The Blade*. https://www.toledoblade.com/local/2009/05/10/The-Toledo-Municipal-Strike-of-1979-When-chaos-reigned/stories/200905100043

Hershey, C. (1973). *Protest in the public service*. Lexington Books.

Hicks, J. R. (1932). *The theory of wages*. Macmillan.

Hogler, R. L. (1986, February). The common law of public employee strikes: A new rule in California. *Labor Law Journal, 37*, 94–103.

Johnston, P. (1994). *Success while others fail: Social movement unionism and the public workplace*. Cornell University Press.

Julius, J., Abrams, J., & Baron, J. (2023). *Labor management relations in the post pandemic museum environment*. https://smlr.rutgers.edu/sites/default/files/Documents/Centers/CGWE/CGWE_WorkingPaper2023-1_JuliusAbramsBaron.pdf

Kaufman, L. (2004, December 18). Abuse victims and the city settle lawsuit. *New York Times*. https://www.nytimes.com/2004/12/18/nyregion/abuse-victims-and-the-city-settle-lawsuit.html

Kosterlitz, J. (1997, December 20). Busted unions. *National Journal, 29*, 2522–2555.

Levesque, J. D. (1980, March–April). Municipal strike planning: The logistics of allocating resources. *Public Personnel Management, 9*, 61–67.

Levine, P., & Caloia, S. (2020, April 7). *Garrett county road workers strike: 50 years later*. AFSCME. https://www.afscme.org/blog/garrett-county-road-workers-strike-50-years-later

Ley, R. D., & Wines, W. A. (1993). Teacher bargaining in Minnesota: Retrospect on the 1980's and prospect of fewer bargaining units. *Journal of Collective Negotiations, 22*(3), 233–244.

Lowi, T. (1979). *The end of liberalism* (2nd ed.). LRP.

Lueck, T. J. (2006, April 18). Transit union is fined $2.5 million over December strike. *New York Times*.

Maki, D., & Strand, K. (1984, Winter). The determinants of strike activity. *Relations Industrielles, 39*, 77–91.

Martin, J. E., & Sinclair, R. R. (2001). A multiple motive perspective on strike propensities. *Journal of Organizational Behavior, 22*, 387–407.

Montgomery, E., & Benedict, M. E. (1989, April). The impact of bargainer experience on teacher strikes. *Industrial and Labor Relations Review, 42*, 380–392.

National Labor Relations Board v. Mackay Radio & Telegraph Co., 304 U.S. 333. (1938).

Ng, I. (1991, Spring). Predictors of strike voting behavior: The case of university faculty. *Journal of Labor Research, XII*, 123–134.

Olson, C. A. (1988). Dispute resolution in the public sector. In B. Aaron, J. M. Najita, & J. L. Stern (Eds.), *Public-sector bargaining* (2nd ed., pp. 160–188). Bureau of National Affairs.

Parra, E. (2004, September). *Support grows for prison OT protest.* www.delawareonline.com

Partridge, D. M. (1991). A time series analysis of public sector strike activity. *Journal of Collective Negotiations, 20*(1), 3–21.

Partridge, D. M. (1996). Teacher strikes and public policy—does the law matter? *Journal of Collective Negotiations, 25*(1), 3–21.

Perez-Castells, A. (2023, November 20). SEPTA police are on strike. Here's what you need to know for your commute. *The Philadelphia Inquirer.* https://www.inquirer.com/jobs/labor/septa-transit-police-strike-salary-contract-union-20231120.html

Pinkham, A. (2022, October 18). Haverhill teachers strike concludes with a full tentative agreement reached. *The Beacon.* https://merrimacknewspaper.com/haverhill-teachers-strike-concludes-with-a-full-tentative-agreement-reached/

Poydock, M., & Sherer, J. (2024). *Major strike activity increased by 280% in 2023: Many workers still need policies that protect their right to strike.* Economic Policy Institute. https://files.epi.org/uploads/279299.pdf

Reder, M., & Neumann, G. (1980). Conflict and contract: The case of strikes. *Journal of Political Economy, 88*(5), 867–886.

Rendon, J. (2023, January 10) Here come the nonprofit unions. *The Chronicle of Philanthropy.* https://www.philanthropy.com/article/here-come-the-nonprofit-unions

Rinde, M. (2023, December 15). Here's why SEPTA police are on strike and what it might take to end it. *Billy Penn at WHYY.* https://billypenn.com/2023/12/15/septa-police-strike-better-wages/

Ritchie, K., Kallas, J., & Iyer, D. K. (2024). *Labor action tracker: Annual report 2023.* ILR School, Cornell University & LER School, University of Illinois. https://www.ilr.cornell.edu/faculty-and-research/labor-action-tracker-2023

Roberts-Grmela, J. (2023, April 10). Rutgers' president threatened to take striking instructors to court. Then he walked it back. *The Chronicle of Higher Education.* https://www.chronicle.com/article/rutgers-president-threatened-to-take-striking-instructors-to-court-then-he-walked-it-back

Rossi, R., Guy, S., & Dudek, M. (2012, September 17). Mayor Emanuel to ask judge to end Chicago teachers union strike. *Chicago Sun-Times.*

Salerno, C. A. (1981). *Police at the bargaining table.* Charles C. Thomas.

Saso, C. D. (1970). *Coping with public employee strikes.* Public Personnel Association.

Satow, J. (2023, April 28). They want to change the world. They would also like a raise. *The New York Times.* https://www.nytimes.com/2023/04/28/nyregion/nonprofits-unions.html

Schneider, B. V. H. (1988). Public sector labor legislation—An evolutionary analysis. In B. J. Aaron, J. R. Grodin, & J. L. Stern (Eds.), *Public sector bargaining* (pp. 191–223). Bureau of National Affairs.

School District for the City of Holland et al. v. Holland Education Association. (1968). 380 Mich. 312, 157 NW 2d. 206.

Shogan, R. (2004). *The battle of blair mountain: The story of America's largest labor uprising.* Westview Press.

Shutt, R. K. (1982, April). Models of militancy: Support for strikes and work actions among public employees. *Industrial and Labor Relations Review, 35*, 406–422.

Spero, S. D. (1970). *Government as employer.* Southern Illinois University Press.

Spero, S. D., & Capozzola, J. M. (1973). *The urban community and its unionized bureaucracies.* Dunellen.

State House News Service. (2022, September 20). Students for teachers plan walk-out today in support of fair contracts for haverhill teachers. *Wavelengths.* https://whav.net/2022/09/20/students-for-teachers-plan-walk-out-today-in-support-of-fair-contracts-for-haverhill-teachers/

Sterret, G., & Aboud, A. (1982). *The right to strike in public employment.* ILR.

Stevens, W. K. (1986, July 21). Philadelphia workers vote to end 20-day strike. *The New York Times.* https://www.nytimes.com/1986/07/21/us/philadelphia-workers-vote-to-end-20-day-strike.html

Thornicroft, K. W. (1994). Teacher strikes and student achievement: Evidence from Ohio. *Journal of Collective Negotiations, 23*(1), 27–39.

TWA, Inc. v. Independent Federation of Flight Attendants. (1989). 489 U.S. 426, 109 S. Ct. 1225, 103 L. Ed. 2d 456.

U.S. Bureau of Labor Statistics. (2019, January 23). Work stoppages: History. In *Handbook of methods.* https://www.bls.gov/opub/hom/wsp/history.htm

U.S. Bureau of Labor Statistics. (2024a, February 21). *Major work stoppages in 2023.* https://www.bls.gov/news.release/archives/wkstp_02212024.pdf

U.S. Bureau of Labor Statistics. (2024b, February 21). Annual work stoppages involving 1,000 or more workers, 1947–Present. *Work Stoppages.* https://www.bls.gov/web/wkstp/annual-listing.htm

U.S. Bureau of Labor Statistics. (2024c, February 21). Detailed monthly listing, 1993–Present. *Work Stoppages*. https://www.bls.gov/web/wkstp/annual-listing.htm

Van Dam, A. (2019, February 14). Teacher strikes made 2018 the biggest year for worker protest in a generation. *The Washington Post*. https://www.washingtonpost.com/us-policy/2019/02/14/with-teachers-lead-more-workers-went-strike-than-any-year-since/

Victor, K. (1992, June 6). Labor's sawed-off stick. *National Journal*, 1353–1356.

Webber, T. (2012, September 19). After teachers strike, doubts about implications. *USA Today*.

Wellington, H. H., & Winter, R. K., Jr. (1971). *The unions and the cities*. Brookings.

Wheeler, H. N. (1985). *Industrial conflict: An integrative theory*. University of South Carolina Press.

Williams, R. M. (1977, March 5). The clamor over municipal unions. *Saturday Review*, 5–7.

Worthington, A., Jallot, A., & Madi, M. (2024, March 19). The 2020 wildcat teacher sick-out that shut down NYC schools. *Jacobin*. https://jacobin.com/2024/03/new-york-public-schools-covid-strike-uft-sick-out

Ziskind, D. (1940). *One thousand strikes of government employees*. Columbia University Press.

Zwerling, H. L. (2007). Pennsylvania teachers' strikes and academic performance. In *Pennsylvania state education association briefing paper*. http://sersanea.org/Pennsylvania%20Teachers'%20Strikes%20and%20Academic%20Performance%20Final%20.pdf

Chapter 9

Resolving Impasses

Alternatives to the Strike

I. INTRODUCTION

Collective bargaining involves people at the table and their constituent advisors. Together, these parties choose what the nature of the dialogue will be in negotiations and whether settlements will be achieved. Some parties want to walk away or to drag out the talks for reasons that are personal or political. They do not want a deal, or at least they do not want a deal quickly. In other cases, the desired outcome of bargaining—attaining a workable solution that maintains the relationship—gets displaced as the parties get entangled in the processes or become bogged down in personality conflicts. Process issues and party conduct can become so contentious that mediators or other third parties have to remind everyone that the goal is a contract settlement, not landing punches on the other side.

Experienced negotiators know that "all cases settle eventually." However, they do not settle in the same way. No two contract negotiations are the same. Patterns certainly exist, but even subtle differences can matter a great deal in determining bargaining outcomes. As public administrators have learned in many contexts, there is no one best way. Sometimes, despite the best efforts of the parties, a negotiated settlement is not obtained. In the private sector, this usually means a strike. In government, it may produce a strike in some cases, but much more often an impasse is addressed through third-party dispute resolution mechanisms.

Despite the modest trend during recent years for public employers to accept the strike as a legitimate component of labor relations and collective bargaining, the majority of state and local governments continue to prohibit strikes. If strikes are prohibited, labor unions are at a distinct disadvantage in collective negotiations unless alternative impasse resolution procedures are available. In virtually all government jurisdictions in which collective bargaining takes place, some form of impasse device is provided to help balance the power of unions and management. The dispute resolution mechanisms developed in U.S. labor relations are

DOI:10.4324/9781003403593-9

increasingly being adapted to settle conflicts in other venues, from environmental disputes to divorces (Mareschal, 2002a; Mareschal & Rudin, 2009).

This chapter examines the three principal measures used in public sector impasse resolution: mediation, fact-finding, and arbitration (including final offer arbitration). We consider their various permutations, advantages and disadvantages, and relative effectiveness. The chapter concludes with a look at several new techniques that have been suggested or experimented with in various jurisdictions. The focus in this chapter is on disputes over interests that occur during contract negotiations. In Chapter 10, impasses over rights—or grievances—under the terms of an existing contract are addressed.

II. PRIVATE SECTOR EXPERIENCE

The right to strike for unions in the private sector is guaranteed by the National Labor Relations Act (NLRA). It is generally perceived to be a legitimate and fundamental part of private sector labor relations. Third-party procedures for resolving contract disputes short of strikes are used much less frequently in the private sector than in public employment. Nevertheless, mediation, fact-finding, and arbitration all have a long history in the private sector that predates their utilization in government.

The conventional procedure for private sector parties seeking to avoid a strike is to call in a mediator if no agreement has been attained within 30–60 days of contract expiration. Typically, a mediator is assigned by the Federal Mediation and Conciliation Service (FMCS), an independent federal agency established under 1947 amendments to the NLRA. The FMCS is also empowered under the NLRA to offer its services, even if not requested. If the mediator sent by this neutral peacemaker fails to steer the parties into an agreement through the powers of persuasion, fact-finding or arbitration may begin.

Fact-finding is a quasi-judicial process in which a neutral third party (individual or panel) examines the "facts" of the impasse, hears the arguments of the parties, and issues findings and recommendations. Fact-finding's history dates back to 1902, when President Theodore Roosevelt appointed through an executive order the first fact-finding board (the Anthracite Coal Commission). Similar fact-finding entities were established by executive orders of Presidents Woodrow Wilson, Franklin Roosevelt, and Harry Truman. In addition, ad hoc fact-finding boards have been used on many occasions in critical industries such as steel, autos, and railroads.

Binding arbitration by a neutral third party to settle unresolved disputes over the terms and conditions of a new contract, known as interest arbitration, has a long history (it was first recorded in Connecticut copper mines in the eighteenth century). However, it is seldom used in industry. Generally, the strike is the final impasse resolution procedure in the private sector, although mediation and fact-finding are often given an opportunity to work first.

III. IMPASSE RESOLUTION IN FEDERAL EMPLOYMENT

Before Executive Order 10988 (E.O. 10988) of 1962, impasses between federal agencies and unions representing their employees were resolved on an agency-by-agency basis without the benefit of legal or statutory guidance. E.O. 10988 only partially filled the legal–structural void because it provided no binding interest arbitration procedures except for advisory arbitration in cases involving unit determination and representation disputes. The arbitrator's sphere of decision making was highly constrained. This lack of adequate impasse resolution procedures was a major source of criticism of the executive order and a prime reason for issuance of Executive Order 11491 (E.O. 11491) by President Nixon. E.O. 11491 authorized the FMCS to aid in resolving federal impasses upon the request of one or both parties. Depending on the situation, the FMCS could recommend mediation, fact-finding, or arbitration and assign trained personnel to help settle the dispute.

Under the Civil Service Reform Act of 1978 (CSRA), the FMCS continues to play a leading role in assisting federal agencies to resolve negotiation impasses. FMCS is a major provider of technical assistance in conflict resolution and labor relations across all sectors in the United States and abroad. Under Section 7119 of the CSRA, if FMCS assistance or other voluntary arrangements fail to settle a dispute, either party may request the intervention of the Federal Service Impasses Panel (FSIP) or mutually agree to a binding arbitration procedure, which must win FSIP approval.

The FSIP is composed of a chairperson and six members appointed by the president for overlapping five-year terms. When asked to intervene in a federal labor dispute, the FSIP can make one of several possible determinations: (1) that it cannot exercise jurisdiction, (2) that negotiations should resume, (3) that negotiations should resume with mediation, (4) that fact-finding should be implemented, or (5) that other procedures, such as arbitration, should be used. The parties have the option of using FSIP mediators, fact finders, or arbitrators and, with FSIP permission, an outside arbitrator.

In cases where voluntary settlement proves elusive, the FSIP is authorized to hold hearings, take sworn testimony or depositions, issue subpoenas, and take "whatever action is necessary" within its authority to resolve the impasse, including final offer arbitration. Final offer arbitration differs from conventional arbitration in that the arbitrator must accept the "most reasonable" last offer of one party or the other, without modification or "splitting the difference." FSIP impasse decisions are enforced by the Federal Labor Relations Authority, which can impose unfair labor practice (ULP) penalties against a noncomplying party (Smith, 2006).

Issues heard by the FSIP concern disputes over facilities (e.g., parking and office space), hours of work, ground rules for negotiations, and various human resource management issues.

Disputes involving postal workers are covered under the 1970 Postal Reorganization Act. If the parties fail to reach a contract agreement or mutually adopt a binding impasse resolution procedure, the FMCS is authorized to establish a fact-finding panel consisting of three persons (two selected by the parties, a third chosen by the two selectees). The panel must issue a report of its findings within 45 days; settlement recommendations are optional. If an agreement is not forthcoming within 90 days, the FMCS creates a three-member arbitration board through the same procedures. The board holds hearings, takes evidence, and makes a binding decision within 45 days. Costs of the fact-finding panel and arbitration board are shared equally by the two parties.

Postal Service negotiations went to arbitration for the first time in a 1984 dispute involving 500,000 employees, the most ever participating in an arbitration settlement in the United States. The parties were $13 billion apart in their final demands, with the major point of disagreement being the most appropriate way to measure wage and job comparability. The arbitration panel found that postal workers were making more money than comparable private sector employees. They issued a salary decision of "moderate restraint," adding about $4 billion to postal costs (Loewenberg, 1985). In 2007, an arbitration panel was called upon to impose a settlement after bargaining with the National Rural Letter Carriers Association collapsed.

IV. STATE AND LOCAL GOVERNMENT IMPASSE PROCEDURES

State law governs collective bargaining for public sector employees. Since support for public sector collective bargaining rights changes with shifts in the political environment, state laws on collective bargaining are frequently amended following transformations in the political landscape of a particular state. Currently, at least 39 states have legislation providing for some sort of impasse resolution procedure for one or more categories of employees (see Table 9.1). Mediation is the most common statutory dispute resolution procedure, followed by fact-finding and arbitration. More specifically, at least 37 states provide for mediation, at least 28 states provide for fact-finding, and at least 27 states provide for arbitration in their statutes.

Some additional approaches to impasse resolution include advisory arbitration in Alaska, med-arb in Maine, and settlement by a citizens' conciliation council in Ohio. Several states allow the parties to agree upon their own impasse resolution procedure. The wide variety of state approaches to resolving contract impasses provides a rich ground for experimentation and research. Not surprisingly, a great deal has been written on the use—and the impacts—of impasse procedures.

Table 9.1 State Legislation on Dispute Resolution Procedures for State and Local Employees, 2023

State	*Mediation*	*Fact Finding*	*Arbitration (Conventional)*	*Arbitration (Final Offer)*
Alabama				
Alaska	X		X	
Arizona				
Arkansas				
California	X	X		X
Colorado	X	X		
Connecticut	X			X
Delaware	X			X
Florida	X	X		
Georgia	X			
Hawaii	X			
Idaho	X	X		
Illinois	X	X	X	X
Indiana	X	X		
Iowa	X			X
Kansas	X	X		
Kentucky	X	X		
Louisiana				
Maine	X	X	X	
Maryland	X	X		X
Massachusetts	X	X	X	X
Michigan	X	X	X	X
Minnesota	X		X	X
Mississippi				
Missouri				
Montana	X	X	X	X
Nebraska	X	X		
Nevada	X	X		X
New Hampshire	X	X		
New Jersey	X	X	X	
New Mexico	X			X
New York	X	X	X	

(*Continued*)

Table 9.1 (Continued)

State	*Mediation*	*Fact Finding*	*Arbitration (Conventional)*	*Arbitration (Final Offer)*
North Carolina				
North Dakota	X	X		
Ohio	X	X	X	X
Oklahoma		X		X
Oregon	X	X		X
Pennsylvania	X	X	X	X
Rhode Island	X	X	X	
South Carolina				
South Dakota	X	X		
Tennessee				
Texas	X		X	
Utah	X	X		
Vermont	X	X	X	X
Virginia				
Washington	X	X	X	
West Virginia				
Wisconsin	X	X	X	X
Wyoming			X	

Neutral third parties for state and local labor impasses may be obtained from a number of sources, including the state Public Employment Relations Board (PERB), state or local impasse agencies, the FMCS, or lists of private third parties provided by organizations such as the American Arbitration Association, the National Academy of Arbitrators, or the National Center for Dispute Settlement. Some states and localities employ part-time, ad-hoc neutrals. The FMCS offers its services to help state and local jurisdictions develop their own dispute resolution capabilities. Where such capabilities are not available, the FMCS will assist in resolving disputes when requested to do so by one or both parties. It will also provide technical assistance for training programs.

The FMCS has been particularly active in providing services to public school districts. For example, the FMCS has provided mediation services, training support, and a grant to create a labor–management council to a partnership of the Charlotte County School Board, Charlotte Florida Education Association, and Charlotte County Support Personnel Association. Similarly, the FMCS facilitated meetings between the American Federation of Teachers and the American

Association of School Administrators. As a result of these meetings, the working groups reached agreement on a general framework for education reform (Cohen, 2012).

A. Mediation

An impasse in contract negotiations may be declared when a deadline has been reached, an important bargaining issue appears insurmountable, or the relationship between the parties has degenerated to name calling and accusations. In mediation, an impartial third party helps the others to achieve a voluntary agreement on substantive issues in dispute. He or she also may try to help the parties maintain or improve the quality of their relationship. Mediation may be requested by either or both parties in a state or local dispute. In some states, such as North Dakota, both parties must make the request. In contrast, other states such as New York permit the state PERB to intervene at its own initiative.

As noted in Section IV, the mediator may be provided by the FMCS, state or local agencies, or private sources. The federal service is furnished only where no state or local mediation assistance is available. In 2023, the FMCS (2023) was involved in over 2,460 collective bargaining mediation cases across the public and private sectors. Where state legislation governs the impasse resolution process, mediators may be selected by the parties from certified lists, or, as in Vermont, the state PERB may assign a neutral party on request. As a general rule, because the success of a mediator is premised upon the degree of confidence and trust in which he or she is held, mediators are sought out who are fully acceptable to both parties.

FMCS-provided mediators generally have achieved an excellent record and reputation. They are experienced, well-trained, full-time professionals (Dilts & Haber, 1989; Mareschal, 2002b). State-assigned and ad hoc mediators vary in skill and experience. The quality of state-appointed neutrals is improving with continued seasoning in public sector impasses. Meanwhile, the parties at impasse usually do well to avoid allowing local community figures or elected officials to serve as mediators. Although the intentions of local notables may be quite honorable, their lack of experience and expertise in resolving labor disputes can lead to unintended and undesirable outcomes.

Mediation is very informal, quite private, and highly individualistic. Records are not kept, so one is forced to rely mostly on anecdotes or personal experience to gain an understanding of what transpires. The process is intriguing. As Zack (1985, p. 180) observed,

> It brings together two opposing parties, frequently antagonistic and hostile in their relationship; interposes a third party between them, often of their mutual selection; and creates thereby the expectation that the three forces will be able

> to achieve an agreement when the two parties could not. . . . Even the participants in the process often are astonished that it actually works.

The mediator typically begins by calling a joint session to review the most recent proposals on unresolved bargaining issues along with an already agreed-upon list of items. At the mediator's discretion, separate meetings may be held. Mediation ground rules must be decided, including no speaking out of turn, no personal attacks, and the need for confidentiality. Formal statements may then be obtained from each party regarding its positions on remaining questions. Next, after considering the respective bargaining postures of the two parties, the mediator is likely to meet with each of them privately to gain their confidence and to explore negotiating room on the issues.

The mediator strives immediately to gain the confidence of the parties by listening closely to what they have to say and making sure to appear evenhanded in everything that is done. It is important that any contact with one party be reported to the other and that all relevant information be shared. Through the mediation process, all participants are continually made aware of their obligation to reach a settlement. Communication channels must remain open. Indeed, a major function of mediation is to keep the parties at the bargaining table to avoid a lengthy period of stasis or stalemate.

Some mediators believe in doing an extensive analysis of the issues and parties in dispute and designing contingent and noncontingent strategies for dealing with the parties. Other mediators, recognizing that many complications and complexities will work themselves out, focus on the people involved. They know that the parties are more familiar with the jurisdiction and its problems than the mediator can ever be. They also understand that the parties can resolve their difficulties if they can be helped to talk productively and persevere in moving toward settlement.

Two basic strategies are available to mediators. The nondirective—or broad strategy—is aimed at producing a climate conducive to settlement and assisting the parties to become more adept at the bargaining table. The mediator may press the parties to focus first on issues relatively easy to resolve, while suppressing negative or hostile outbursts. Even the nondirective mediator must also "orchestrate" (Kolb, 1983) various administrative details (time and place of meetings), structure and order the issues that must be considered, ensure that negotiations move at an orderly pace, and keep the substance of the negotiations private.

A major objective of the nondirective mediator is to help the parties to explore potential avenues for accommodation. Trial balloons may be launched by the mediator and pondered without risk to the parties. The mediator can assist the parties in properly presenting offers and proposals at the bargaining table. Seemingly innocuous factors such as the language used or the way an offer is communicated can be a bar to settlement. Often, toning down the language while still preserving the substance of the proposal is effective. Attention by the mediator to such relatively minor problems may mean the difference between settlement and continued impasse.

"Directive strategies" are intended to help the parties generate options, discern points of compromise, make them face the consequences of their respective situations, offer suggestions for settlement, and, in some cases, apply pressure for settlement. The directive mediator, in other words, attempts to take control of negotiations and bring things to closure. In extreme instances, the mediator may even provoke a crisis by, for example, publicly labeling a party as intransigent or obstructive or stalking out of a nonproductive caucus in apparent disgust.

The bifocal model of mediation is an alternative to the directive and nondirective strategies. Mediators that adopt the bifocal model combine elements of the directive and nondirective strategies by pursuing an agreement on the immediate issues in dispute while attempting to improve the overall relationship between the parties (Mareschal, 2003). In employing the bifocal model, mediators can give more weight to either directive or nondirective strategies depending on the phase of the mediation process. A nondirective posture is good for facilitating an agreement when the parties are comfortable with one another and well intentioned. As negotiations move close to an agreement but remain snagged over one or more issues, the mediator may become more directive in his or her approach.

A mismatch between the nature of the dispute and mediation tactics may push the parties into greater intransigence in their positions and doom the process to failure (Posthuma et al., 2002). Whatever tactics are brought into play, the successful mediator must maintain the trust of the parties, master the intricacies of the situation, and be persuasive in motivating union and management negotiators to steer toward a conclusion. Mediators must understand that mediation is a lengthy process and should be prepared to take small steps to achieve agreement between the parties (Mareschal, 2003). Mediators must also understand that uncontrollable external factors (e.g., economic problems and political variables) may ultimately be more important than the mediator's strategies in determining whether settlement is attained (Kolb & Rubin, 1989).

To help the parties work together, the mediator typically calls for joint sessions. In these meetings, he or she employs various techniques. One is "idea charting," which is a form of brainstorming. Here, the mediator goes around the room asking each individual to identify the issues that are most important to resolve. Each issue that is mentioned is written on a flip chart or displayed on a screen. The parties discuss and clarify the issues, and the underlying interests represented by the issues. Idea charting helps each party focus on the mediator and the written ideas, rather than on their peers and personal notebooks.

For example, suppose a management representative says, "We want to change the way care is provided to certain patients and relocate them to another building." "Why?" someone asks. "Because these patients are dangerous and our visiting psychiatric support people would be better used if we could relocate the patients. We could also use better psychiatric aides, which would benefit our vocational program. And we need to keep costs down, and this might help." The issue here is to move patients into a common facility for the reasons given.

The union may agree that this is a legitimate interest of managers and be willing to talk about it. And management's interest may prompt the union to identify its own related issues. The union could observe that "members fear new facilities, current wards are already understaffed, and the proposed changes might put persons in danger by consolidating potentially violent patients. Union members might have to work out of class or have their caseloads increased. Moreover, the building in question is a firetrap." Throughout, the mediator tries to help the parties identify key interests and drop unimportant ones, develop criteria for addressing them, generate alternative proposals, and decide on the most pragmatic path to settlement.

At any time, a team may request a caucus to discuss what concessions or compromises might be offered and under what conditions. Mediators usually attend the caucuses and provide assistance if needed. Mediators can also call a private caucus to remind an obstreperous party about the ground rules, such as no threats and accusations. Eventually, there may come a breakthrough where at least one significant issue is resolved. Once the dam breaks, the chances are improved for more accommodations. However, particularly sticky issues may simply be deal breakers. The agreement can stand or fall on how the parties treat one another and react when the going gets tough.

The principal goal of mediation is to reach a "good settlement." That is, a settlement that can win widespread acceptance among the constituencies of the parties and can be lived with. For the purposes of the mediator, the public interest or the fairness of the outcome is of secondary importance.

1. Traits of an Effective Mediator

Effective mediators need to have both substantive and process knowledge (Mareschal, 2005a, 2005b). Examples of substantive knowledge include labor relations skills and experience. Process knowledge refers to facilitation and problem-solving skills. Specific traits ascribed to effective mediators read like the Scout code: experienced, skilled, unbiased, open, creative, inventive, patient, and persevering. This person should also be intelligent, tenacious, humorous, persuasive, empathetic, and full of stamina. Mediators should have the "patience of Job," "the guile of Machiavelli," and "the wisdom of Solomon" (Simkin, 1971, p. 53). They should evince optimism tempered with realism. They should seek to build trust by being genuine and straightforward.

The relationship between the parties is essential to the successful outcome of the mediation process. A collaborative orientation of parties in a dispute facilitates agreement (Mareschal, 2005b). Therefore, to be effective, mediators need to engage in relationship-building efforts, accepting the need for emotionalism and venting by the parties but preventing it from shattering the process. Everyone knows that there are games going on at the table, under the table, in the room, and out of the room, and that potential troublemakers hover everywhere.

The mediator must try to keep fully abreast of goings on by joining meetings in the halls, parking lot, or local bar. It is often at such "side meetings" that breakthroughs occur. The mediator also needs diplomatic skills in dealing with the media. For instance, there is the classic television shot of a mediator coming out of negotiations to meet the press. "What is going on?" the reporter asks. The response, "They are talking." "How would you characterize the talks?" The mediator observes, "They are frank and candid."

Although these qualities "are not the stuff of which professional curricula are made" (Kressel, 1977, p. 270), formal training in labor relations, labor law, conflict resolution techniques, and facilitation are important for the novice mediator. A task force of the FMCS (1996) identified several competencies that mediators for the agency should achieve, including expertise in collective bargaining and other labor management processes, facilitation, and problem-solving skills; knowledge of tools to improve organizational effectiveness; and conflict resolution skills. There remains a certain lack of standards concerning who is qualified to practice mediation (Bellman, 1998; Mareschal, 1998). Certificate programs abound, but some of them fall well short of being rigorous. Even if a set of universal standards were agreed to and taught, mediation would remain an art, not a science. Effective mediators are adaptive, flexible, and resilient, using their best judgment under the circumstances and making things up when necessary. The road to settlement always has many twists and turns.

2. Advantages and Disadvantages of Mediation as a Technique for Resolving Impasses

Mediation's utility as a dispute settlement technique is evidenced by its frequent application to public sector impasses. A major advantage of mediation over other impasse procedures is its flexibility. It is an inexpensive informal process that permits the parties and the neutral great latitude in devising a settlement, in large part because no written record of the proceedings is required. Thus, alternative settlement packages can be explored through the mediator without placing formal proposals on the table.

The informal nature of mediation also helps break down communication barriers that may have developed as negotiations atrophied. Mediation can help "educate" inexperienced negotiators on the vicissitudes of the bargaining process and on the specific viewpoints and positions of the opposing parties. Another advantage is that agreements attained through mediation are reached by the parties voluntarily. Since the terms of settlement are not imposed, they are more likely to be fully accepted by the parties and their constituencies. Finally, mediation moderates labor conflicts by opening points of disagreement to different meanings, interpretations, and possibilities (Kolb & Rubin, 1989, p. 4).

Despite the considerable advantages of mediation as a dispute resolution procedure, there are unfavorable aspects as well. Two major criticisms may be offered. First and foremost, there is no element of finality to mediation. The mediator cannot force a settlement. There is no final report, only a voluntary settlement or a declaration of failure and prompt consideration of other impasse resolution alternatives. Second, good mediators are hard to come by. The special talents and personality traits exhibited by successful mediators are problematic to teach and difficult to emulate.

On balance, mediation is an effective means of resolving an impasse early and relatively amicably. When it succeeds, the impasse is broken and an agreement that both parties can live with is attained. In this way, the future relationship between labor and management is protected.

Mediation is more successful under some conditions than others. The technique appears to be most effective when the mediator is experienced, highly skilled, and tenacious and the parties are less sophisticated and experienced (Kochan & Jick, 1978; Karim & Pegnetter, 1983). Here, the strategies and personal qualities of the directive neutral have maximum impact (Downie, 1992). Experience and tenacity are particularly important traits of an effective mediator. As one commented, "Mediation doesn't start until both of the parties have told the mediator there's no more room for compromise" (Briggs & Koys, 1989, p. 519). In situations in which the two parties have lengthy experience with collective bargaining, the mediator's role may be a less directive one, with attention focused on possible terms of agreement.

Mediation is most effective under the following three conditions. First, overcommitment to a position stifles negotiations between the parties. Second, the dispute is of limited difficulty or intensity, and the parties communicate openly and share information willingly. Third, the parties are motivated to attain a settlement. The probability of reaching a settlement increases when mediation is followed by compulsory binding arbitration rather than by fact-finding (Kochan, 1979, p. 179; Payne et al., 2000).

Mediation appears to be less fruitful under certain conditions. These include when mediation takes place in large jurisdictions, and when the parties have a poor relationship, have gone to impasse frequently, and engage in disruptive communication behaviors and dirty tricks. The effectiveness of mediation is also weaker where the basic dispute involves the ability of the employer to pay. Finally, mediation tends to be less successful where the parties face strong political and/or constituent pressures that encourage them to use the full range of impasse resolution procedures (Kochan et al., 1979; Payne et al., 2000; Mareschal, 2005b).

B. Fact-finding

As is the case with mediation, fact-finding normally may be initiated by either party, although in some states it can be invoked by the PERB. An individual fact finder or a panel (usually composed of three members) is appointed from the same sources used for mediators. Often, the same names appear because many mediators also act as fact finders. In legal contexts providing for both mediation and fact-finding, the latter is usually used only after mediation fails to resolve the dispute. In comparison to mediation, fact-finding is a formal proceeding consisting of a quasi-judicial hearing by the neutral of both parties' positions and evidence, a written record of the facts and events, and, in most cases, written recommendations for settlement. The recommendations are not binding. Nevertheless, an Indiana law from 2011 that outlines the alternative dispute resolution process for resolving collective bargaining impasses between teachers' unions and school employers departed from the traditional nonbinding outcome for fact-finding. Unlike the old law that provided for advisory fact-finding decisions, under the 2011 law, the purpose of fact-finding is to provide a final solution to the dispute (Carrell & Bales, 2013).

It has been widely noted in the literature of public sector impasse procedures that "fact-finding" is a misnomer. As Simkin (1979, p. 337) pointed out, "The words fact finding conjure up notions of preciseness, of objectivity, of virtue. They even have a godlike quality. Who can disagree with facts?" Yet, as McKelvey (1969, pp. 528–529) explained, "Although the 'name of the game' is fact-finding . . . the sport itself has little to do with fact-finding in the literal sense of determining objective facts through the judicial processes of trial and proof to provide evidentiary answers" In other words, rarely is there a single set of "facts" underlying any collective bargaining impasse. On the contrary, there are at least two different "objective" interpretations of the circumstances surrounding all components of any dispute. The principal task of the fact finder is to determine which set or mix of "facts" is most convincing in any given labor relations context.

It should come as no surprise to the student of public administration and politics that two sets of actors portray varying interpretations of reality. If the facts of a situation were apparent to all, the neutral's job would be much simpler. However, public sector employment issues tend to be complex, and "the plethora of facts produced may well overwhelm the fact finders" (Spero & Capozzola, 1973, p. 283). Moreover, each party naturally seeks to put a favorable spin on the facts.

1. The Fact-finding Process

The formal role of the fact finder is to enter an interest dispute, hear both sides of the story, collect relevant data, and issue recommendations for a settlement. Although the factfinder's recommendations are not binding, they have the potential to impact the outcome of the dispute. For example, if the impasse goes beyond fact-finding to the next stage of the resolution process, the fact-finder's commentary may be used in an arbitration hearing.

The process is more formal than mediation because it takes place in a quasi-judicial, adversarial atmosphere. This does not mean that the two processes are clearly separable. Mediators, too, deal with "facts," and fact finders frequently mediate between the two parties, particularly when fact-finding is the last impasse procedure offered before a strike or unilateral imposition of terms by management.

The mediative role of fact-finding is evident in a study of the first seven years of fact-finding in Michigan, where it was found that 20% of the disputes going to fact-finding were settled before a final report and recommendations were issued, even though fact finders in that state are not given formal authority to mediate disputes (Stieber & Wolkinson, 1977). The impasse procedure in New Jersey involves a combination of mediation and fact-finding. First, a mediator works with the parties to reach voluntary agreement. If this stage of impasse resolution fails, the Public Employment Relations Commission (PERC) Director of Conciliation may invoke fact-finding. The fact finder collects information and recommends a settlement. If the parties refuse to accept the fact finder's recommendation, the Director of Conciliation may take whatever steps are necessary to negotiate a voluntary settlement, including appointing a super conciliator. At this point, if the parties fail to reach agreement, the employer can impose their "last best offer" (LBO). However, public school employees are exempted from the LBO provision.

Usually, for fact-finding to be successful, recommendations must be acceptable to both parties. Thus, the fact finder often probes the range of the parties' expectations through off-the-record meetings and reveals each side's expectations to the other. Sometimes, voluntary agreement results. This practical reality is formally recognized in Ohio, where the collective bargaining law officially encourages fact-finding panels to mediate at any time.

The hearings generally take one or two days. Transcripts of the proceedings are required in some jurisdictions. After a period of time in which the fact finders examine and analyze the data and testimony presented to them, they normally issue recommendations on all unresolved issues. At this point, the formal duties of the fact finder are complete. Informally, the fact finder may act as a mediator by trying to convince the parties to accept the recommendations and settle.

The role of the fact finder varies with the circumstances of the individual dispute. In some cases, fact-finding is undertaken in a climate of cooperation, as when the parties unite to promote a common goal, such as legislative enactment of a statute that would benefit them both. Here, the legislative body may be the adversary as the parties look to the fact finder as an important ally in pressing their case. In other situations, fact-finding may be used by one or both parties to give credibility to an agreement they would have reached anyway so that the chances of rank-and-file and/or legislative ratification are heightened. Also, fact-finding, if followed by public recommendations, can bring public opinion into play to encourage compromise by an obstreperous party.

In arriving at their conclusions, fact finders often concentrate their investigations on data allowing a comparison of the local circumstances with other, similar jurisdictions. Fact finders are concerned that their recommendations are fair. Thus, wages, benefits, and working conditions in other agencies or jurisdiction are important considerations. Hence, the fact finder can focus on variables such as ability to pay, cost of living, and the nature of the local labor market. In some states, like Florida, fact-finding criteria are delineated in statute. Generally, fact finders strongly desire to convince the parties to accept their recommendations as the best option available for settling the dispute.

The issue of recommendations—whether they should be offered and, if so, to what audience—has been the subject of some controversy. Fact-finding without recommendations differs little from mediation, and, as one expert has argued (Simkin, 1979, p. 340), it "is likely to be an exercise in futility." With respect to fact-finding with recommendations, however, the question arises as to whom they should be issued: to the parties alone or to the parties and the general public? The recommendations, of course, may be rejected by one or both parties.

In some states, however, it is quite challenging for the parties to reject the fact-finder's assessment. For example, in Ohio, the fact-finder's report can be rejected by either party, with the stipulation that it must be rejected by a three-fifth's vote. For the union, this is defined as three-fifths of the bargaining unit, not simply three-fifths of the votes cast. If neither management nor the union reject the fact-finder's recommendations, the recommendations become the terms of the collective bargaining agreement (Ohio Revised Code §4117.14, 2023; Slater, 2019).

The potential advantage of public notice of recommendations, as indicated earlier in this section, is that it can mobilize public pressure for a settlement, especially in the case of an extreme position by one of the parties. Cynics, however, point out the extremely low level of public interest in most labor disputes and, indeed, politics in general and note the overall lack of citizen understanding of the collective bargaining process. If the local media are also uninformed, indifferent, or otherwise incapable of explaining the complexities of the labor dispute to their reading and viewing audiences, then making public recommendations may seem to be an empty gesture. Furthermore, once recommendations are disclosed, the negotiation process may shut down and the parties become more polarized than ever.

2. Advantages and Disadvantages of Fact-finding

Several benefits are claimed for fact-finding as an impasse resolution procedure. It provides an opportunity for the parties to cool off and analyze their positions after temper and patience wear thin. It is a time-consuming process that permits them to collect both their thoughts and data supporting their respective interests. The fact finder's report can lower the expectations of one or both parties (Karper, 1994), thereby decreasing the level of uncertainty and the outward ranges for contract settlement (Dickinson & Hunnicutt, 2005). It can also serve as a new basis for continued negotiations toward a voluntary settlement, or it can represent a helpful scapegoat to justify a painful settlement (Marmo, 1995). Furthermore, fact-finding does permit the public to enter the bargaining arena by revealing unresolved issues and how the parties stand on them (Elkouri & Elkouri, 2003). In the case of extreme posturing, the taxpaying public has an opportunity to chastise the more immoderate party.

The major criticism of fact-finding is that, like mediation, it lacks finality. Even if the parties agree on the basic facts, their interpretations of them may vary wildly. Fact-finding is also faulted in many settings for a relatively low rate of success in settling impasses and for drawing out impasses unnecessarily instead of proceeding directly to arbitration or a strike.

Other problems with fact-finding have been recognized, some of them of sufficient magnitude to support arguments for elimination of the technique, especially where utilized as an intermediate step between mediation and arbitration. The mere availability of fact-finding may lead to excessive use by some parties and thus "chill" the bargaining process. Public opinion appears to exert little influence on the parties' positions. It is further argued that the parties tend to revert to more extreme positions after fact-finding fails and that fact-finding seldom reduces the number of issues going to arbitration, even though arbitration awards may deviate little from recommendations of the fact finder. In New York, Kochan et al. (1979) determined that they were identical in 70% of the cases examined.

However, the single most salient criticism of the effectiveness of this method of resolving interest disputes is its lack of finality. That is, either the union or management may reject the fact finder's recommendations. The 2011 Indiana law addresses the lack of finality concern by establishing that the purpose of fact-finding is to provide a final solution to a dispute when the parties fail to resolve the dispute by themselves, and mediation is unsuccessful (Carrell & Bales, 2013). Although the new law uses the term "fact-finding," the process that it describes is similar to arbitration.

It is difficult to render an accurate assessment of fact-finding's effectiveness. Some fact finders act primarily as mediators. Others are more like a judge and jury. Fact-finding procedures vary from state to state. Generally, only the most difficult disputes—those that cannot be settled with mediation—go to fact-finding, which of course depresses the success rate.

Although several collective bargaining states have dropped fact-finding, a majority continue to use it as a technique for resolving labor impasses. The process appears to work rather well in Ohio. In 2023 and 2024, for example, the State Employee Relations Board appointed fact finders in 240 disputes. The parties voluntarily settled prior to issuance of the fact finder's report 56% of the cases. The parties accepted the fact finder's recommendations in 66% of the disputes (Ohio State Employment Relations Board, 2023, 2024).

Florida's experience with fact-finding under a special magistrate is more ambivalent. A survey of fact-finding participants in 28 cases found that only about 50% of labor and management respondents felt fact-finding was effective in creating movement toward settlement, exposing the truth, or clarifying issues (Jennings et al., 1988). However, a substantial majority of participants said they would use the process again for a variety of face-saving and political benefits. Another study (Magnusen & Renovitch, 1989) was also moderately supportive of the special magistrate procedure, observing that although very few findings are accepted in their entirety, many of the special magistrate's specific recommendations do end up in the labor contract. Florida represents a unique case: if the special magistrate hearing fails to produce an agreement, the dispute is settled directly by the appropriate legislative body (e.g., city council, state legislature, or school board).

C. Arbitration

Arbitration, in any of its various permutations, is the most controversial impasse resolution procedure short of the strike. Like fact-finding, arbitration involves a formal quasi-judicial setting in which each party presents evidence supporting its position to a single neutral or a multimember board. The major difference is that the arbitrator's report, in most cases, is final and binding on the parties. Thus, arbitration is intended to serve as a direct alternative to the strike and to unilateral employer decision making. Ideally, it results in a fair settlement for the parties while protecting the public interest.

In this chapter, our focus is on interest arbitration, which is concerned with formulating a new contract. In Chapter 10, grievance arbitration is discussed. The purpose of grievance arbitration is to determine the rights and claims of the respective parties under an existing contract.

Although the practice of arbitration has ancient historical roots, arbitration in public employment is of fairly recent vintage. It was first established in federal employment with binding arbitration provisions for postal workers under the Postal Reorganization Act of 1970. State governments began enacting public sector arbitration provisions in 1965, starting with Wyoming and Maine.

The arbitrator's decision under some impasse situations is advisory. That is, the parties do not have to accept it as final. For example, in the event of an impasse in collective bargaining negotiations between a municipal school district, a regional educational attendance area, or a state boarding school and its employees, the law in Alaska requires the parties to submit their dispute to advisory arbitration before engaging in a strike. This strategy, however, is rare in the public sector and generally out of favor because it is a distinction without a difference from fact-finding with recommendations. In most jurisdictions, arbitration (usually following mediation, fact-finding, or both) is binding and final.

Arbitration may be voluntary or compulsory. In the former, the parties jointly agree to settle an impasse through arbitration (often before an impasse even occurs). In the latter, binding arbitration is mandated by statute or by an administrative agency, usually after mediation and/or fact-finding have been exhausted. Generally speaking, both management and labor prefer voluntary arbitration, although police and firefighter organizations have been supportive of the compulsory form.

Finally, arbitration may be conventional or final offer. Conventional arbitration is the traditional approach in which the decision-making authority of the neutral is unfettered. He or she may accept one party's last offer or, as is often the case, "split the difference" between the final positions. Final offer requires the arbitrator to select the LBO of one of the parties as the final terms for settlement; no compromising is permitted. Final offer arbitration may be by package, in which the neutral must select the LBO of one party or the other in its entirety—or by issue—where the items under impasse are decided on separately by the arbitrator.

Several states provide for compulsory tripartite arbitration, with each party designating a neutral and the third neutral chosen by the parties' designees or by an administrative agency. Most states, however, make single or tripartite arbitration optional to the parties. In many cases, they select a single arbitrator because it is less expensive and time consuming.

The first arbitration statutes were enacted for public safety personnel on the grounds that strikes by police and firefighters could not be tolerated. Thus, some alternative to the strike should be offered. Many states continue to restrict arbitration to public safety services. Others have extended the technique to nonprotective service personnel in state and local governments.

1. The Arbitration Process

Arbitration involves the following steps: selection of one or more arbitrators, formal hearings with the presentation of evidence (but arbitrators are not bound by the formal rules of evidence that prevail in the courtroom), and a final written decision by the arbitrator.

a. Arbitrator Selection

When a single arbitrator is to rule in a given case, they may be selected by the parties or appointed by a state agency, state court, or independent arbitration agency. Careful screening of candidates is necessary to ensure that the selected neutral (1) will evidence no bias toward either party, (2) is cognizant of procedural due process requirements, (3) is experienced, (4) is timely in making decisions, (5) will write clear, unambiguous awards, and (6) will be knowledgeable of any special circumstances surrounding the impasse or its governmental context (Ver Ploeg, 1988).

If a tripartite arbitration structure is used, a different situation prevails. Arbitrators are selected by the individual parties to take two of the three panel seats typically act as unabashed advocates for their appointing party (Kochan et al., 1979). Therefore, bargaining carries over into tripartite arbitration, with the independent neutral attempting to develop an award acceptable to the other two arbitrators. Evidence of this process is presented by Kochan et al. (1979), who found that about 60% of the arbitration awards they examined in New York were unanimous rulings, indicating a compromise settlement was fashioned by the independent neutral.

Labor and management negotiators usually do their homework before arbitrator selection takes place. Names and arbitration history are checked out with colleagues in other jurisdictions. Prior decisions may be read, and tallies done on employer–union win/loss records under various arbitrators. Union and industry research departments may be asked for information, online searches are run, and law firms may be retained to assess credentials. Some private firms "keep score" and sell their opinions on prospective arbitrators to interested parties. The "overriding goal is (to) select an arbitrator who will maximize [the party's] chance of winning" (Nelson, 1986, pp. 703–704).

Interestingly, the disputants do not normally consider fact finders to be acceptable as arbitrators, although arbitrators are usually accepted as fact finders (Dilts, 1984; Elsea et al., 1990). Perhaps this is attributable to the superior training and experience of most arbitrators. Also, some "rights" or grievance arbitrators refuse to work as interest arbitrators. The reasons for this vary: the pressure cooker and fishbowl environment of interest arbitration; the greater risk to an arbitrator's professional reputation (and monetary income) from a highly visible, interest impasse decision; or a dislike of final offer arbitration (Helburn & Rodgers, 1985; Vest et al., 1990).

b. Decision-making Criteria

Most arbitration statutes specify certain criteria that the arbitrators must consider in rendering their decisions. The criteria in some states are rather broad, such a requiring that "equity" and the "public interest" be considered. Other states are more specific. In Massachusetts, for example, the panel must consider ability to pay; hazards of employment; physical, educational, and mental qualifications; job training and skills involved; comparable wages, hours, and working conditions; cost of living; long- and short-term debt; average property tax burden; and other specific factors. Similarly, the New Jersey statute specifies that arbitrators take into account wages, salaries, hours, conditions of employment, history of negotiations, and pattern of salary and benefit changes.

The use of comparative data such as salary and benefit information from similar categories of workers in neighboring jurisdictions or in the private sector plays a very important role in some arbitrators' decision making (Turpin, 1998). Inflation and cost-of-living factors are also salient, along with the employer's ability to pay (Bazerman, 1985; Bazerman & Farber, 1985; Feuille & Schwochau, 1988). There is a great deal of variation across states in the level of detail and specificity of criteria for comparators. Some states provide guidance on which types of employees are comparable. Often this includes identifying acceptable cost-of-living indicators and directing arbitrators on assigning weight to various factors (Slater, 2019).

In New Jersey, arbitrators are instructed to consider comparability factors such as geography, characteristics of the population, and tax revenues and expenditures. In Ohio, arbitrators are directed to make comparisons to both public and private sector workers performing comparable work (Ohio Revised Code §§ 4117.14). The Oregon statute is even more specific. Here arbitrators may take into account comparable employees working outside of the state, but only for impasses with state employees or impasses that occur in cities with over 32,500 residents or counties with over 40,000 residents (Oregon Revised Statutes, §243.746, 2023; Slater, 2019).

Typically, however, arbitrators focus narrowly on the immediate bargaining context and "anchor" their judgments to the terms of the previous contract to maintain stability in the relationships between the parties. Often, this means splitting the difference between final positions, in the case of conventional arbitration or selecting the most "moderate" last offer when final offer arbitration is used. One specific result is that existing salary structures and relationships are maintained with incremental, percentage-based adjustments (Dell'Omo, 1989). This is yet another illustration of the power of incremental decision making. The predictability of arbitration outcomes led Bloom (1988, p. 123) to suggest that this process "could probably be accomplished more inexpensively by averaging the parties' final offers and adding on some noise using a computer's random number generator."

Nonetheless, arbitrators vary greatly in the weight they place on various decision criteria (Dell'Omo, 1990). The ability to pay offers a good case in point. It is up to the employer to marshal the strongest possible arguments for inability to pay what the union is asking, using revenue and expenditure projections, accounting data, debt levels, and other relevant information, such as a credible listing of potential service and program cutbacks or cancellations. The employer's case may be persuasive to some arbitrators. However, assessing the employer's arguments about the ability to pay is not a precise science. Arbitrators may look for evidence on a variety of economic indicators noted earlier, as well as the potential impact on other units of government at the state and municipal levels in addition to the agency involved in the impasse (Slater, 2019).

Others, however, translate inability to pay into unwillingness to pay. If the city or state must hike taxes or fees to comply with the arbitrator's compensation decision, then so be it (Dell'Omo, 1989, p. 11). In all fairness, arbitrator vacillation and uncertainty in applying the ability-to-pay principle is encouraged by ambiguity and the lack of statutory specificity as to which factors should be considered and how they should be weighted. For example, does inability to pay mean that statutory or constitutional spending limitations would have to be breached? That no additional funds could possibly be transferred into salaries? That service could not be maintained at current levels without hiking taxes or fees to meet union demands?

Generally speaking, arbitrators, like fact finders, must be concerned with the fairness of their award and its acceptability to each party. The importance of acceptability is illustrated by the continuation of negotiations and, in some cases, mediation during the arbitration process (see Section IV.E.1). For example, Gerhart and Drotning (1980) showed that in Michigan, the majority of arbitration cases are settled before the arbitrator issues an award. The neutrals frequently "caucus with the parties privately and give them clues, sometimes subtle and sometimes not so subtle, concerning what the arbitrators are likely to consider the 'more reasonable' position." The arbitrator's concern for fairness means that in states where arbitration is preceded by fact-finding, the process often amounts to a "show cause" hearing as to why the fact finder's recommendations should not be imposed by the arbitrator (Holden, 1976).

What happens when a final binding award is rendered and one or both parties refuse to accept it? Several states provide appellate rights through the courts to ensure due process and a reasonable award. As a general principle, arbitration appeals are strongly discouraged so that they do not become a normal part of impasse resolution. They can be costly, time consuming, and anathema to free collective bargaining (Kochan et al., 1979, p. 133). Yet, an appellate path must be provided to correct instances of injustice or illegality.

Typically, arbitration decisions may be appealed if obtained by fraud, legal error, or collusion. In Michigan, for example, orders of the arbitration panel are reviewable by the court for reasons that the arbitration panel was without or exceeded its jurisdiction; the order was unsupported by competent, material, and substantial evidence; or the order was procured by fraud, collusion, or other unlawful means. In Ohio, all final offer settlement awards are subject to review by the court in any of the following cases: the award was procured by corruption, fraud, or undue means; arbitrators demonstrated evident partiality or corruption; arbitrators exceeded their powers; and arbitrators were guilty of misconduct. Other states provide for appeals through an administrative body or the legislature. For example, in New Jersey, the parties may file an appeal to the arbitrators' decision with PERC.

An unusual statute that served as a compelling example of the need for finality in arbitration was the 1971 Oklahoma Firefighters' and Policemen's Arbitration Act, which provided that rulings by an arbitration panel were binding on the union (if the municipality also accepted the decision) but that the city was not bound to abide by the arbitrators' award. When, in 1975, the Oklahoma City Police Department and Oklahoma City went to arbitration over the size of a wage increase, the city refused to accept the decision of the panel, which had supported the union's position. The police instituted a work slowdown, to no effect, and then marched into the city manager's office en masse to turn in their badges. The strike ended three days later when the city made a compromise wage offer (Greer, 1978). The law was amended in 2005 to require final offer arbitration. But in another awkward Oklahoma two-step, if a city's offer is not selected by the arbitration board, the city may submit both final offers to the voters in a special election.

Clearly, for arbitration to serve successfully as an alternative to the strike, the arbitrators' decisions must be final and binding on both parties and each must fully accept the process as a legitimate means for resolving interest disputes. For arbitration to function in a meaningful fashion, only the legislative body or, in extraordinary circumstances, the courts or the voters should be able to alter arbitrators' awards. Although arbitration issues are frequently brought into the judicial process, the courts have almost universally adopted the assumption of arbitrability prevalent in the private sector, which recognizes the superiority of the arbitrator's expertise over that of the judge (Jascourt, 1979, pp. 159–165).

2. Advantages and Disadvantages of Arbitration

The major advantage of arbitration as compared to mediation and fact-finding is that it supplies a balanced measure of finality to impasses. In mediation and fact-finding, the employer enjoys more discretion and bargaining power than the union, as long as the strike is illegal or infeasible. With arbitration, the interests of the parties are balanced while an end to the impasse is finalized, avoiding a strike and its accompanying service disruptions.

Research indicates that arbitration has, indeed, been more successful in preventing strikes than statutory strike prohibitions alone (Ichniowski, 1982; Gunderson et al., 1996; Lipsky & Katz, 2006), although it has not completely eliminated them. Of course, as long as there are public employers and workers, the strike threat can never be totally exterminated no matter what strategy is used. Nonetheless, the tendency of arbitration to settle most public sector impasses short of the strike contributes to rational budget making, the continuous provision of public services, and, in a broader sense, social and political stability.

To say that the use of arbitration in public sector labor disputes is controversial is to understate the case greatly. There are three major complaints against arbitration. First, it constitutes an illegal delegation of authority to persons not held responsible through democratic processes. Second, it tends to distort settlements and redistribute resources in favor of the unions. Third, it destroys or chills free collective bargaining. Each criticism is discussed in Sections IV.2.a–d.

a. Illegal Delegation of Authority

It has been asserted that arbitration constitutes an illegal delegation of authority to persons who are not responsive or accountable to the electorate. Yet, they are charged with making decisions on the expenditure of public monies and other important issues related to the provision of public services. Thus, it is claimed that arbitration is inimical to the operation of representative government and democracy because the accountability of elected executive and legislative officials is sacrificed to an arbitration decision on public issues.

Clearly, there is no direct link between an arbitrator and the electorate. He or she is at least four levels removed from the electorate if appointed by an administrative agency, such as a state PERB. When an arbitrator is provided by a nongovernmental entity, such as the American Arbitration Association, there is scarcely even an indirect link to the citizenry. Such fractures in governmental accountability through the delegation of decision-making authority to private sector entities have been the subject of extensive debate in the literature of political science for many years (Lowi, 1979).

Malin (2013) examined the frequency by which public sector unions in Illinois and Ohio engage in strikes and arbitration under both right-to-strike and interest arbitration regimes. He concluded that arbitration allows union leaders and public officials to avoid accountability for difficult decisions that could be otherwise reached through collective bargaining. The data show that in Illinois and Ohio, the number of strikes among unions operating under a right-to-strike regime declined substantially following the financial crisis of 2007–2009 and subsequent recession. In contrast, in Illinois, once stimulus funds were exhausted, the use of arbitration increased among unions operating under an interest arbitration regime.

It appears that under the right-to-strike regime, the parties attempted to avoid strikes, which are unlikely to garner popular support during economic recessions. Instead, the parties in these states took responsibility for difficult decisions by engaging in collective bargaining. Under the interest arbitration regime, the parties transferred the responsibility for difficult decisions to arbitrators. These findings led Malin (2013) to conclude that during hard economic times, parties bargaining under a right-to-strike regime are more accountable to constituents compared to parties bargaining under an interest arbitration regime.

Nevertheless, in the specific case of public sector arbitration and the delegation of authority, the state courts are the final arbiters on questions of law and arbitrability. Early judicial decisions were nearly unanimous in declaring arbitration illegal. Arbitration was rejected as early as 1873 by the Illinois Supreme Court and thereafter by attorneys general and courts in Maryland, Ohio, Indiana, Florida, and Minnesota (Spero & Capozzola, 1973, pp. 289–290). Along with the allegation of illegal delegation of legislative authority, the principal grounds for court challenges are as follows. First, arbitration statutes do not sufficiently limit an arbitrator's discretion. Second, the statutes unconstitutionally delegate taxation authority. Third, the selection of arbitrators violates the principle of "one person, one vote" (Grodin, 1979, p. 242).

Arbitration has been ruled unconstitutional or illegal by courts in five states: South Dakota, Colorado, Utah, Nebraska, and Maryland. The constitutional issue of illegal delegation of authority was the basis for rejection of arbitration in Colorado and Utah. In South Dakota and Maryland, arbitration was prohibited because of the presence of "ripper clauses" in the state constitution that forbid legislative delegation of the municipal fiscal and service provision functions to a private entity (Grodin, 1979, pp. 242–243). Depending on the grounds used by courts to find public sector interest arbitration provisions unconstitutional, a state legislature can amend the state statutes to address the concerns of the court. For example, if the court finds that interest arbitration provisions constitute an unlawful delegation of power because the statute failed to include standards to guide arbitrators, the legislature may choose to amend the statute to include such standards.

Rulings that find interest arbitration unconstitutional or illegal, however, are in the minority. At least 16 state courts have upheld statutes providing for compulsory arbitration. One of the most frequently cited rulings is the Michigan case of *Dearborn Firefighters Local 412 v. City of Dearborn* (1975), in which a divided state supreme court held that a compulsory arbitration statute did not divest home-rule cities of constitutionally granted powers. Nor, despite the presence of a ripper clause, did it cause an illegal delegation of power to private persons or a surrender of the power of the city to impose taxes. As a general rule, the state courts have upheld compulsory arbitration when they have

> found that there is a public interest in preventing strikes, that illegal delegation does not occur when there are statutory provisions of explicit standards and guidelines for arbitrators and procedural safeguards in the form of court review, and that the power to tax has not been transferred in that an arbitration act is regulatory, and does not in itself impose a burden or charge.
>
> (Schneider, 1988, p. 206)

Among the actions that legislative bodies can take to make arbitration more amenable in a democracy are to specify in the arbitration statute restrictions on the scope of the arbitrator's authority, limitations on the statute's coverage, and strict decision-making criteria (Feuille, 1979, p. 72). Interest arbitration is compulsory in disputes involving police and firefighters in New Jersey. Yet, the state caps the amount by which arbitrators may increase base salary items at 2% per year. In addition, arbitrators can be compelled to set forth the basis of their findings publicly. Moreover, in the final analysis, the legislature retains the power to override arbitration decisions or to terminate arbitration or any other delegation of legislative power (*Carofano v. City of Bridgeport,* 1985).

Still, the legal issues surrounding arbitration can be murky. The Ohio Supreme Court struck down the binding arbitration provision in 1988, only to reconsider and uphold it a year later. Although most courts have upheld statutes providing for compulsory arbitration and states have developed legal innovations to restrict the scope of the arbitrator's authority, the transfer of power to set labor costs in the public sector to a third-party arbitrator remains controversial as a matter of political theory. It is also a decision difficult to explain to the general public (Bellman, 2013).

b. Arbitration Favors Unions

Ideally, arbitrators should balance the interests of both parties in arriving at the terms of a settlement. Although this certainly is what the arbitrator intends, he or she must contend with competing contradictory values in reaching a decision. This is especially true when balancing the tradeoffs involved with assuring comparable wages, benefits, and working conditions against those of protecting the taxpayer from excessive government personnel costs. If such a balance can be attained, then, over time, neither party should benefit from arbitration more than the other.

However, public sector managers widely believe that the interest arbitration deck is stacked against them and in favor of the unions. During state legislative debates in the 1970s and 1980s on proposed arbitration laws, the fervor of union support for the process as a substitute for strikes was exceeded only by that of public managers' opposition. Management resentment and dissatisfaction with arbitration and, in truth, all other third-party procedures except, perhaps, mediation linger. When an unfavorable arbitration award is rendered, employers complain loudly that the decision gives short shrift to the impacts of the decision on taxpayers and the financial health of the jurisdiction.

Has compulsory interest arbitration been a windfall for unions, as management and many public officials believe? The empirical evidence indicates that it has not. Although some studies have found that wage rates are slightly higher in jurisdictions permitting arbitration, the effects are not statistically significant. However, it does appear that the "availability" of arbitration has a significant positive impact on salaries and benefits. This relationship has been associated with police, firefighter and teacher arbitration (Feuille & Delaney, 1986; Zigarelli, 1996).

Several factors are at play here. First, the unions have an equal opportunity to submit supporting data to a true neutral whom they have helped select. From a practical standpoint, the arbitrator must be very careful to render a "fair" compensation decision if he or she wants to work in the same capacity again in another jurisdiction. Word gets around quickly when an arbitration settlement is perceived to be inequitable. Management is aware of these tendencies and consequently may be more likely to settle a contract on terms more favorable to the union than if arbitration were not the next step. The union, of course, will not hesitate to opt for arbitration when management takes a hard position viewed by the union to be against the interests of its membership. Hence, using arbitration is less important to gains in union pay and benefits than having the legal authority and potential to use it.

A related impact of arbitration is on the distribution of salaries. Generally, arbitration tends to exert a leveling effect by enhancing the economic status of bargaining units that have lagged in pay gains for their members (Feuille et al., 1985a). The availability, and at least occasional use, of compulsory arbitration helps units at the low end of the pay scale catch up with similar units through arbitrators' emphasis on the comparability criterion (Bazerman, 1985; Feuille & Schwochau, 1988).

It must be noted that arbitration procedures established through state legislation can be amended to tilt the scales in the direction of management. For example, Pennsylvania has restricted terms of settlements and interest arbitration decisions by imposing fiscal considerations, subject to legislative review. Connecticut's arbitration laws for state agencies and municipalities assumed a high profile during the early 1990s, as employers lodged complaints that arbitration rulings were financially crippling them. The state senate responded by rejecting more than 12 contracts that had been decided by arbitrators. The legislature also amended the municipal arbitration law to permit local governments to appeal arbitrator decisions to a second arbitration panel, which may revoke the decision of the first panel (Keating, 1994).

c. *Arbitration Chills Collective Bargaining*

The argument that arbitration destroys free collective bargaining is grounded in certain related assumptions. First, it is claimed that the presence of a credible strike threat forces the parties into a compromise. Where arbitration substitutes for the strike, there is less incentive for timely settlement; the bargaining process is chilled. Second, it is said that availability of arbitration leads to its use as a crutch, particularly by the weaker party in a bargaining relationship. Since arbitrators try to accommodate both sides in a dispute, weak labor organizations may achieve a better outcome through arbitration than through collective bargaining (Craver, 2013).

Even when arbitrators are required to choose from the final offers of the parties, the worst outcome for weak labor organizations is having to accept the final offer of the employer. The worst outcome is likely to be similar to the collective bargaining outcome. Arbitration, therefore, provides weak parties in a bargaining relationship with an opportunity to achieve a better outcome than they could hope to obtain through collective bargaining. Hence, arbitration may exercise a "narcotic effect" by making the parties addicted to its use rather than settling disputes.

The chilling-effect argument goes as follows: if one party thinks that it will get a better deal from the arbitrator than from a negotiated agreement, that party thus has an incentive to go to arbitration. Evidence of the chilling effect is found in several studies. In the early Pennsylvania bargaining experience, some 30% of police and firefighter disputes went to arbitration, whereas in Wisconsin, the incidence of usage was about 15% (Rehmus, 1975). Other indications of the chilling effect are found in Minnesota from 1973 to 1980. In negotiations involving essential services, which are denied the right to strike, 30% of those going to mediation ended in arbitration versus only 9% for nonessential services (which are permitted to strike) (Champlin & Bognanno, 1985). Avgar et al. (2023) find that interest arbitration is more effective at reducing the probability of strikes than fact-finding is.

The narcotic effect has also been verified by researchers (Bolton & Katok, 1998). For example, Kochan et al. (1979) and Lipsky and Drotning (1977) reported evidence of a narcotic effect in New York. Further evidence of the parties becoming habituated to third-party impasse procedures was found for municipal workers in Pennsylvania (Loewenberg & Klinetop, 1992) and Ohio (Graham & Perry, 1993). Apparently, the "new toy" of arbitration is tried out by the parties to see what transpires and as sometimes happens in the case of hard drugs, the users eventually become addicted.

Stronger indications of the narcotic effect were reported by Kochan and Baderschneider (1978, 1981) for police and firefighters in New York State between 1968 and 1976. During this period, 85% of the firefighter bargaining units and more than 90% of the police units went to impasse at least once, with the total percentage of units going to impasse increasing steadily from 41% in the early part of the period to 65% by the latter part. Moreover, 80% of those units reaching an impasse in the first and second rounds of contract negotiations during this period also went to impasse in the third (Kochan & Baderschneider, 1981, p. 438).

However, different methods of analysis and quantitative techniques have yielded disparate results, indicating that positive narcotic effects characterize the early experience with impasse procedures, followed by stabilization and even negative effects ("rejection") as the parties become dissatisfied with third-party intervention (Butler & Ehrenberg, 1981; Chelius & Extejt, 1985; Lewin, 1985). In a subsequent study on the effects of mandatory interest arbitration on police and firefighters in New York, Kochan et al. (2010) found little support for the earlier reports of a narcotic effect exercised by arbitration on collective bargaining. In comparing the experience with interest arbitration by police and firefighters in New York over time, they observed that strikes have been avoided in the 30 years of mandatory interest arbitration and the initial reliance on arbitration considerably declined. Similarly, Avgar et al. (2023) find that there is scant evidence of excessive use of arbitration.

Even if, as seems likely, arbitration exerts a modest chilling effect on negotiations, it stretches the point to argue that this constitutes the demise of free collective bargaining. A large majority of settlements continue to be negotiated without arbitration. Even when arbitration is invoked, it frequently serves as a forum for continuing negotiations. In addition, as is discussed in Section IV.D, final offer arbitration reduces the chilling and narcotic effects, helping collective bargaining remain a viable process.

d. Other Criticisms

Interest arbitration has several other drawbacks. First, interest arbitration is conservative in nature (Kochan et al., 2010: Malin, 2013). Arbitrators are generally reluctant to take innovative approaches in their practice and usually impose decisions that accommodate both parties in the dispute. Therefore, arbitration may help the parties overcome an impasse in the collective bargaining process but result in an outcome that may not be superior to what parties could achieve by continuing the negotiations.

Second, interest arbitration tends to suppress and redirect conflict between parties rather than resolve conflict (Malin, 2013, p. 156). The arbitrator may in fact impose a solution to the conflict that could leave both parties unsatisfied (Carrell & Bales, 2013, p. 15). Hence, arbitration decisions may aggravate conflict and contribute toward an unfavorable environment for future negotiations.

Third, Bellman (2013) argues that the enactment of mandatory arbitration provisions has the effect of redistributing power within the union structure, providing statewide labor organizations with an elevated status. Several factors contribute to the redistribution of power among unions. Large labor organizations have greater capacity to influence the content of legal provisions on arbitration. Moreover, under arbitration regimes, to achieve improvements in the workplace, unions have to refocus their efforts from organizing and fostering solidarity among employees to data management and analysis functions. Since unions have to rely on experts for data management and presentation skills, the larger professionalized labor organizations hold an advantage over smaller organizations. The reliance on experts, nevertheless, conflicts "with orthodox concepts of strength based on local concerted efforts and shared risk taking that have characterized American unionism" (Bellman, 2013, p. 41).

D. Final Offer Arbitration

Final offer arbitration, like conventional arbitration, does not escape the criticism of delegating authority to private individuals who are not responsible to the electorate. Nevertheless, final offer arbitration represents an improvement over conventional arbitration because it limits the options of the arbitrator to the final offers of the parties. In this way it removes the ability to draft an entirely new public sector contract from the hands of an unelected third party (Carrell & Bales, 2013, p. 31).

Final offer arbitration is also intended to allay concern that arbitration exerts chilling and narcotic effects on free collective bargaining. Presently in use in 18 states and several local governments in some form for one or more employee groups (but most often for police and firefighters), final offer arbitration was first tried by Eugene, Oregon, in 1971. Wisconsin and Michigan adopted it as an impasse strategy in 1972. The final offer may be decided by package, as in Nevada or by issue, as in Ohio.

Under final offer arbitration by package, the arbitrator, after examining the proposed terms for each issue in dispute, is required to choose the offer that appears most reasonable overall. Since both parties may provide unreasonable offers, this approach to arbitration may result in the imposition of unreasonable terms on one party to a dispute. Issue-by-issue arbitration helps preclude a Hobson's choice involving two unreasonable final offer packages by allowing the arbitrator to reject the unreasonable terms from each proposal and combine in a final contract, issue by issue, the most reasonable terms.

Regardless of the specific form, final offer requires the arbitrator or panel to choose the final proposal of either management or the union. In some "tri-offer" jurisdictions, the fact-finder's conclusions may be substituted for the parties' last offers. The major objectives of final offer are to increase the risks of not settling and to encourage a narrowing of the differences between the parties. Conventional arbitration has been faulted for chilling the bargaining relationship by tacitly encouraging the parties to assume extreme positions in the hope that the neutral will "split the difference." Under final offer, the most reasonable position normally prevails—no compromise by the arbitrator is permitted.

States that provide package final offer operate under the assumption that the parties will have an incentive to settle out of a fear that even one issue position perceived to be extreme by the arbitrator will result in rejection of the entire last offer and "sudden death." Under final offer arbitration, the fear of having an entire proposal rejected by the arbitrator may exacerbate the inhibition of innovation characteristic to conventional arbitration (Malin, 2013, p. 156). Under final offer by issue, the arbitrator has greater flexibility in settling the impasse and the parties have more flexibility in designing their offers.

The two strategies do appear to have divergent effects. Although the evidence is somewhat mixed, there are indications that final offer by package creates a greater level of uncertainty than final offer by issue, thereby providing greater encouragement for the parties to settle (Farber, 1980). Using an experimental design under laboratory conditions, Subbarao (1978) found that package selection maximizes pressure on the parties and leads to genuine bargaining. On the other hand, issue selection interferes with free negotiations and may produce the same narcotic effect found in conventional arbitration.

The evidence with regard to the narcotic effect is not entirely clear in comparing final offer arbitration of either the package or issue variety with conventional arbitration. After examining a number of empirical studies, Feuille (1975) concluded that final-offer arbitration procedures produce somewhat better negotiated agreements than conventional arbitration procedures do. In some instances, this may be attributable to differences in bargaining climate and bargaining histories in the respective conventional and final offer states rather than to differences in impasse law and procedures (Kochan et al., 1979).

Meaningful comparison is further complicated because the actual practice of final offer arbitration often diverges from what is stipulated in legislation. For instance, during the final offer hearing, "final" offers may be changed between the hearing's opening and closing by one or both parties. Sometimes a whole series of "final" offers are proffered. Such practices are often encouraged by arbitrators who, in effect, are acting as mediators to promote voluntary settlement. In some jurisdictions, this process is institutionalized in the form of "med-arb," which is discussed in Section IV.E.1.

In addition to using final offer by issue, some states, like Michigan, distinguish between economic and nonmonetary issues. Such states use final offer on the former and conventional arbitration on the latter. Vermont and Ohio permit final offers to be selected from either the last offers of the parties or the fact finder's recommendations. For arbitrations involving police, firefighters, and prison guards in Ohio, the standard approach is final offer arbitration with issue-by-issue decisions. However, if both parties agree, they are able to use other modalities including conventional arbitration and total package arbitration (Slater, 2019).

Several exotic arbitration processes have developed in the private sector that may find use in government. In "high–low arbitration" (aka "bracketed arbitration"), the parties agree in advance to the high and low parameters for the award. If the arbitrator, who is kept in the dark on these parameters or brackets, makes an award in between the high and low figures, that award stands. If the award is lower than the low bracket, the agreed-upon low figure is paid, and vice versa for a high award.

"Night baseball arbitration" features an exchange of offers by the parties. The arbitrator, operating behind a veil of ignorance concerning the offers, enters the proceedings and makes an award and the parties must accept the last offer closest to the arbitrator's decision. In a variant of the process, final offers are sealed and compared to a nonbinding arbitration decision. The arbitrator then selects the final offer that is closest to his or her opinion.

Another variation on the issue-by-issue arbitration has been proposed in the literature. If implemented in practice, it would require arbitrators to subtract the entire difference (or one-half or one-quarter of the difference) between the final issue-by-issue offers from the more reasonable offers (Craver, 2013). The model aims to address the potential chilling effect of interest arbitration. Assuming that weak labor organizations are likely to obtain excessive gains through arbitration, the model penalizes labor unions in the arbitration process. Theoretically, the model would negate the assumed advantage of labor organizations in arbitration and encourage parties to a dispute to make rational final offers (Craver, 2013).

E. Other Impasse Resolution Procedures

1. Med-arb

Med-arb combines the mediation and arbitration functions in a single third party. It is a hybrid process in which meditation takes place first. If mediation fails to produce a settlement, the same neutral has the authority to render a binding decision through arbitration. This technique, "mediation with a club," is intended to provide a strong incentive for voluntary settlement by the parties during the mediation stage by keeping the demands of the parties reasonable. If extreme positions are taken by a party, the med-arbitrator is likely to view them as uncompromising and rule against that party during arbitration (Campolieti & Riddell, 2020). As an alternative to the strike or conventional arbitration, med-arb has the added advantage of the arbitrator's intimate familiarity with the issues gained during the mediation stage. The arbitration award, if it becomes necessary, is likely to be firmly grounded in the facts and circumstances surrounding the dispute and thus acceptable to the parties.

Med-arb has not been widely adopted throughout the United States, which perhaps is explained by the fact that neutrals well trained and experienced in both mediation and arbitration are hard to find. However, the U.S. Postal Service utilized med-arb successfully in resolving an impasse involving 600,000 postal employees in 1978. The procedure was suggested by the FMCS and accepted by both parties in a dispute involving layoffs and the size of future wage increases. The issues finally were resolved through an arbitration award issued by the med-arbitrator.

At the state level, Wisconsin has used the technique in the past for municipal and school district employees. Ohio and New Jersey have bargaining laws that authorize mediation during arbitration. Another example of med-arb is the case of judicial employees in Maine. Judicial employees and their employers may agree in advance to a med-arb procedure in the event of a dispute. The med-arbitrator' role is to encourage a voluntary agreement between parties and settle the dispute through arbitration if the parties fail to reach an agreement after a reasonable period of mediation. The med-arbitrator's recommendations and findings related to controversies over salaries, pensions, and insurance are advisory. Decisions on all other issues are final and binding on the parties.

Lester's (1984) results indicate that med-arb has experienced some success in settling impasses before arbitration and in discouraging strikes. If a dispute does move to arbitration, the mediator should have good information on the nature of the dispute and might be able to quickly broker a voluntary agreement. A problem is that the specter of arbitration—and the fear of disclosures—may hinder discussions with the mediator. Other research indicates that that med-arb results in more cases going to arbitration because the parties are more inclined to pass the buck to the arbitrator (Campolieti & Riddell, 2020).

2. Arb-med

Arb-med may be thought of as the reverse of med-arb. The neutral first makes a final arbitration decision on the dispute but does not communicate it to the parties. Mediation then commences with the goal of a voluntary settlement. If one is not produced, then the arbitration decision is announced. The greatest strength of this approach is that it motivates disputants to settle by themselves (Ross & Conlon, 2000). Research indicates that arb-med enjoys a higher success rate than straight mediation, chiefly due to lower expectations that encourage cooperation (Ross & Conlon, 2000). Moreover, arb-med tends to move along more expeditiously than med-arb (Conlon et al., 2002).

3. Labor–management Committees

A labor–management committee is a group of management and labor appointees within an agency or workplace who have agreed to work cooperatively to discuss and resolve workplace issues of concern. The committee may be authorized by law or collective bargaining contract. The committee may address any matter of mutual concern, but it cannot overturn or contradict any term or provision in the existing contract.

Massachusetts was the first state to experiment with labor–management committees as an impasse resolution strategy in 1978. A breakdown in good faith bargaining in municipal government had occurred, primarily over the issue of how to settle impasses. Former Secretary of Labor John Dunlop, a professor at Harvard University who had experience with establishing labor–management committees in industry, suggested that Massachusetts create its own committee for the resolution of labor disputes (Midwest Center for Public Sector Labor Relations, 1979). Shortly thereafter, the Massachusetts Labor–Management Committee for Municipal Police and Fire was incorporated into legislation.

The Massachusetts Joint Committee has statutory authority to invoke jurisdiction over any police or firefighter negotiations either before or during impasse. The committee enters disputes upon the request of one or both parties. Its job is to confer with the parties and encourage voluntary settlement. If these mediative efforts fail, the committee may invoke binding arbitration in any form it desires. Reports of the Massachusetts experience indicate that it has been a success, with only a small proportion of cases going to arbitration (Mass.gov, 2008). Alaska, Indiana, Pennsylvania, New York, New Jersey, Oregon, and other collective bargaining states have also reported success with labor–management committees, particularly in improving occupational health and safety conditions.

Rubinstein et al. (2024) examine a more intense form of labor-management committees in the public education system known as collaborative partnerships. The partnerships have shown success in addressing issues related to improving work life that are commonly relegated to the last minutes of bargaining sessions. Although the partnerships do not directly address wages, benefits, and job security, participants have reported instances in which the school administrators supported teachers' concerns over these issues in bargaining sessions. They attribute this shared perspective to the partnership process. Further discussion of labor–management committees is found in Chapter 11.

4. Letting the Taxpayers Decide

Strong strains of direct democracy have played on the political heartstrings of many Americans since the earliest European coastal settlements developed independently along the Atlantic. The concept of direct democracy has even been applied to dispute settlement in public employment. When in doubt, some argue, it is best to let the people decide through a vote.

One of the first to interject this line of thought into labor–management conflicts was Zagoria (1973), who suggested granting either party the right to take a contested issue to the public through placing the fact finder's recommendations on a ballot and making the terms of the voters' choice retroactive. Until the people made their decision, issues mutually resolved between the parties could be implemented immediately (Zagoria, 1973) or the parties could remain under the terms of the old contract (Foegen, 1974). Thus, a strike would be skirted and those who ultimately have to foot the bill for labor settlements, tax-paying citizens, would render a final judgment. Further advantage would accrue, at least in theory, from democratically involving the public in determining what is in its own "interest."

Public referenda have been used to settle limited collective bargaining issues since at least 1947 in Texas, when police and firefighter organizations tried to win increased wages, shorter working hours, pay parity, and changes in civil service laws (Helburn & Matthews, 1980). Antiunion charter referenda have been held in a number of California cities. For example, a 1985 San Francisco referendum rescinded comparable-worth-based pay increases that had been won in collective bargaining. Oklahoma police and firefighters must take an impasse to randomly selected city council members, who select from the parties' final offers. If one or both parties still refuse to accept the outcome, the dispute goes to the whole council.

Several cities in Colorado are among the few jurisdictions that legislatively provide for impasse resolution through public referendum. An ordinance in Lakewood, for example, requires that interest disputes proceeding without settlement through mediation and fact-finding be submitted to the voters if the fact finder's recommendations are rejected by either party. It is the rejecting party's position that is placed in the ballot. In Denver, the positions of both parties may be considered by the voting public if each rejects the fact finder's recommendations. The costs of the election (which are substantial) are paid by the rejecting party or shared by both if neither accepts the recommendations.

On the face of it, resolving bargaining impasses through referendum may sound like an excellent idea. The uncertainty, or outright fear, of public involvement at the ballot box should provide a strong incentive for voluntary settlement. It imposes political accountability on a process often criticized for lacking it. Paying for the referendum represents a measure of economic hardship to the parties, who must also lay out money for campaign expenses (Hogler & Thompson, 1985).

There are some important disadvantages, however. First of all, as any person with survey research experience will attest, it is very difficult to reduce complex issues to simple terms. The problem is patently evident when a referendum is held on any issue. Second, the process assumes that voters will educate themselves on the relevant issues and make an intelligent choice—a risky assumption at best. Third, excessive delays ensue while the election machinery is programmed, ballots prepared, polling places organized, and so on, complicating the budgetary process. Fourth, excessive politicization of collective bargaining issues can lead to rigid, uncompromising postures by the major parties and harmful outcomes. Fifth, voters are highly unlikely to approve of any wage or fringe benefit increase that can lead to higher taxes. This potentially biases the process against the union position. It is little wonder that public employee unions have fought hard to keep off the ballot proposed referenda that could adversely affect them.

Settlement by a citizens' conciliation council is another alternative impasse resolution procedure that allows for citizen participation. This alternative is available to public employers and exclusive representatives in Ohio. According to the law in Ohio, citizens' conciliation councils are composed of three residents within the jurisdiction of the public employer. The employer and the exclusive representative each select one council member. Within five days after their appointment, the two selected council members should designate the third member of the council. If the two selected council members fail to agree on a third member, the State Employment Relations Board appoints the third member. The settlements issued by citizens' conciliation councils are final. Although in many aspects similar to arbitration, this procedure mitigates the illegal delegation of authority concern by allowing residents to decide the outcomes of labor impasses.

5. Unfair Labor Practice

Another impasse resolution alternative is the ULP. The ULP process can be used to resolve issues such as scope of bargaining and complaints concerning the failure to bargain in good faith. States commonly define the refusal to bargain collectively by either the public employer or exclusive representative of employees as a ULP.

Depending on the state, the PERB, state boards of labor relations (SBLR), state employment relations boards, or equivalent entities are empowered to prevent and remedy ULPs. For example, in New York State, the PERB rules on ULPs unless it can assist the parties to agree voluntarily.

In a usual investigation of a ULP, the entity empowered to rule on the prohibited practice holds hearings and examines evidence to determine if a party is engaging or has been engaged in a ULP. Upon examining all evidence, the entity empowered to investigate ULPs states its finding of fact. Then it issues an order to either dismiss the complaint or require the party that engages in a ULP to cease and desist from the prohibited practice. Some states expressly prohibit or allow the entity investigating ULPs to order arbitration if the public employer or employee representative refuses to bargain collectively in good faith.

In Connecticut, the SBLR can order arbitration and direct the party that refused to bargain in good faith to pay the full cost of arbitration. In Delaware, the Police Officers' and Firefighters' Employment Relations Act allows the PERB to take a reasonable affirmative action to remedy ULPs by the public employer or exclusive representative of police and firefighters. However, the Act expressly prohibits the PERB from issuing any order providing for binding interest arbitration on issues arising in collective bargaining between the parties involved. Most of the ULP cases never reach a formal hearing, being resolved successfully beforehand (Riccucci & Ban, 1989).

V. SEARCH FOR FLEXIBILITY

The choice of alternative dispute resolution procedures has important implications for employment systems (Budd & Colvin, 2008). To develop approaches to impasse resolution that are appropriate for a particular set of circumstances, states need to evaluate the advantages and disadvantages of each procedure. An effective comparison of the different dispute resolution procedures requires the use of consistent criteria for evaluation. Research has used speed and satisfaction as the primary criteria for evaluation (Budd & Colvin, 2008). Nevertheless, these criteria fail to capture some important aspects of the employment relationship that go beyond the efficiency dimension.

Budd and Colvin (2008) argue for a more comprehensive framework for evaluation that concurrently considers the dimensions of efficiency, equity, and voice. Within this framework, the efficiency dimension measures how well the dispute resolution system conserves scarce resources. The equity dimension measures how well the dispute resolution system meets the standard of fairness and impartiality in decision making. The voice dimension measures the ability of individuals to meaningfully participate in the dispute resolution process. In addition to serving as a tool for evaluation, this framework can be used to design dispute resolution procedures that maximize one or more of the efficiency, equity, and voice dimensions (Budd & Colvin, 2008).

Each interest dispute is different. Given any particular set of circumstances, one or a variety of settlement approaches may be appropriate. As with most everything else, there is no “one best way.” When public policy deems the strike unacceptable as a means of settling labor disputes, alternatives to the strike are necessary. Generally, the states have developed approaches that permit more than one impasse resolution procedure. The norm is mediation and/or fact-finding followed by compulsory binding arbitration, either conventional or final offer. The exact dispute resolution package varies for different occupational groups, with arbitration often available only to public safety personnel.

One of the most flexible approaches to impasse resolution is found in the Ohio statute. At any time before 45 days prior to the expiration date of the collective bargaining agreement, the statute allows the parties to submit the issues in dispute to any mutually agreed-upon dispute resolution procedure. According to the statute, mutually agreed-upon procedures may include conventional arbitration; final offer arbitration by package or by issue; arbitration that would include among the choices for the arbitrator the recommendations of the fact finder, if such recommendations exist; settlement by a citizens’ conciliation council; or any other procedure mutually agreed to by the parties.

If the parties do not agree to a dispute resolution procedure, the statutory provisions apply. The statutory procedures include mediation and fact-finding for all public sector employees. Mediation may continue during fact-finding. If the parties fail to reach an agreement within seven days after the publication of recommendations provided by the fact-finding panel, most public employees have the right to strike. The Ohio statute provides for a final offer settlement procedure for police, firefighters, and other employees that are prohibited from engaging in strikes.

Another flexible approach to impasse resolution is found in the Iowa statute. Even before collective bargaining begins, the two parties themselves are required to reach agreement on which dispute resolution procedure will be used in the event of an impasse (a strategy borrowed from the Canadian labor relations experience). If the parties are unable to arrive at a procedural agreement, then statutory impasse procedures will be invoked. The statutory procedures include the appointment by the PERB, upon the request of either party, of an impartial and disinterested person to act as a mediator. If the dispute persists ten days after the appointment of a mediator, the PERB has the power, upon request of either party, to arrange for final offer arbitration.

Clearly, the state and local governments are serving well in their traditional roles as political laboratories. In developing procedures to resolve interest disputes, the states and localities provide strong evidence of the need to adapt procedures to circumstances. In this sense, public sector impasse resolution strategies illustrate the ends (an acceptable bargaining settlement) justifying the means (mediation/fact-finding/arbitration, etc.).

No one is more aware of the ends justifying the means than the neutrals themselves. It is not unusual for neutrals to exceed their statutory authority in the quest for a voluntary settlement. As noted in Section IV.D, arbitrators frequently serve a mediative function even in the absence of a med-arb or arb-med provision. In fact, mediation may continue throughout fact-finding and arbitration, culminating in a voluntary settlement just before the arbitrator's award. Gradually, distinctions among the various dispute resolution processes have become blurred, as mediation often goes on during—and occasionally even after—fact-finding and arbitration.

This supports arguments for combining mediation and fact-finding in a single neutral and suggests some potential benefits from conducting fact-finding before mediation. If the parties know that fact-finding can be followed by mediation through the same person, they should be less apt to hold back information from the neutral; voluntary settlement is encouraged once most of the relevant data have been placed on the table.

Moreover, a tripartite arbitration or fact-finding panel composed of a neutral and representatives from each party should be recognized for what it is in reality—mediation at a higher level. In sum, those who argue against permitting mediation during other impasse resolution processes are missing the point. The ultimate goal is a final acceptable settlement that avoids the strike. The means to resolution of the dispute are not as important as the voluntary settlement itself. The more dispute resolution procedures, in general, and interest arbitration, in particular, divert from rigid adjudication-like processes and are developed as integral parts of the collective bargaining process, the more likely parties will be to resolve their dispute by agreement (Malin, 2013). Therefore, flexibility, not ill-founded rigidity, is the key.

VI. UNCERTAINTY: BENEFIT OR BANE?

The conventional wisdom in impasse resolution holds that there is a direct relationship between uncertainty and the likelihood of voluntary settlement. Thus, impasse procedures should create an ocean of insecurity and misgivings so that the parties will be forced to swim to an island of compromise. Arbitration supposedly fulfills this intent because the parties can never be certain which side will be disadvantaged by the neutral's decision. As noted, however, there is a marked tendency for arbitrators to split the difference between the opposing offers, thus establishing some boundaries within which it normally can be assumed the award will fall. Final offer arbitration, its supporters claim, creates much greater levels of uncertainty through the mandate of an all-or-nothing choice; better for the risk-averse party to compromise than face losing everything.

However, some doubt can be cast upon the conventional assumption regarding uncertainty and propensity to settle (Gerhart & Drotning, 1980). Certainly, there are some significant costs to both unions and management when an impasse drags on. Union members may sacrifice wages and benefits and the union itself must pay certain monetary costs, including attorney fees and at least part of the fees and expenses for neutrals. Management absorbs costs of attorneys and neutrals also, along with certain political debits as the result of citizen unhappiness if services are disrupted. However, it should not be forgotten that in the event of a work stoppage, management may benefit financially from foregoing wage and benefit payments and politically from "hanging tough" with the union.

Gerhart and Drotning (1980) claimed that when each party feels reasonably certain in its predictions of the costs and benefits of impasse for itself and for the other party, a settlement is highly likely. Uncertainty over the relative costs and benefits of impasse encourages the parties to delay settlement. This hypothesis received support from Farber (1980), whose model of the final offer arbitration process indicates that final offers tend to diverge greatly when uncertainty is high. Knowledge—or at least apparent knowledge—of the respective costs and benefits helps bring the parties to a compromise.

This perspective is intuitive if one considers the nature of the collective bargaining process itself. For example, if both parties are cognizant of the other's bottom line on a disputed issue, then the basis for compromise is readily apparent. To take the example a step further, a city may truly have an inability to pay a wage increase greater than 6%, that is, the bottom line. The union's bottom line may be a 4% wage increase. Grounds for settlement are readily apparent to both parties if knowledge exists of the respective "unyielding" positions. Of course, the real world of labor relations is not so simple, and knowledge of true bargaining positions is not so easy to gain.

VII. CONCLUSION: THE BENEFITS OF IMPASSE PROCEDURES

As indicated in Chapter 8, 12 states now permit strikes through statute, state supreme court decision, or de facto procedures for one or more groups of employees. This would not be so if third-party procedures were always successful in practice and presented no problems for accountability and representative democracy. A number of troublesome aspects that accompany the use of various impasse procedures have been discussed, including the lack of finality, the chilling and narcotic effects of the delegation of public decision-making authority to parties not accountable to the electorate, and claims by public managers that arbitration awards tend to favor the union's point of view. In addition, third-party procedures can be time consuming and expensive. Although a requirement that the parties share expenses or that the losing party pay all costs of the neutral helps overcome this objection.

It is usually in the interests of the parties to settle as soon as possible, so that union members can begin receiving any new pay and benefits and the government employer can finalize the budget and prepare for new compensation arrangements. Time delays as a result of impasse procedures can be enervating. The period from impasse declaration to award may be several months or even a year. In New York, "In many cases, an agreement that the arbitrators were still deciding had (itself) expired, and it was time to renegotiate another contract" (Kochan et al., 1979, p. 154).

Third-party procedures (particularly arbitration) have clearly been abused in some jurisdictions by the unions. Unions that are small in membership, lacking in political resources, or laboring under other limitations vis-à-vis management may look upon impasse procedures as a means of gaining something not available at the bargaining table. Based on her research in New York City, McCormick (1979) concluded that interest arbitration did not function as a strike substitute for small, less powerful, "nonessential" unions.

Rather, arbitration was invoked more than 90% of the time by bargaining units that were too weak to mount a meaningful strike. McCormick attributes three different roles to arbitration. These include: (1) providing a forum for less powerful groups to plead for parity arrangements with stronger unions; (2) facilitating intraorganizational bargaining within the union and management ranks, so that a lack of consensus on bargaining positions can be overcome by an arbitrator's ruling (in other words, to promote face-saving for top officials in both parties); and (3) helping union leaders "to go all the way" for their membership, thereby asserting a leadership role and strengthening their positions within the organization.

One would assume that the chilling and narcotic effects of third-party procedures would lessen in jurisdictions that have bargained collectively for many years and developed negotiating expertise. Arbitration is a "learning experience" for the parties, who adjust their expectations about arbitrators' beliefs in each subsequent contract that goes to arbitration (Olson & Rau, 1997). A narrowing gap between the parties' expectations (the settlement zone) should be conducive to a negotiated agreement. Future research should be able to tell us if this is indeed the case.

It must be noted that in the majority of bargaining relationships, third-party procedures work satisfactorily. Mediation continues to be highly valued as a flexible and informal method of resolving disputes. Fact-finding has proved useful in many jurisdictions. As a dispute resolution device that includes a distinct measure of finality, arbitration in its various forms has been shown to be a reliable alternative to the strike.

In further defense of the various third-party procedures, it must be recognized that they fulfill important functions not directly related to avoiding the strike. Impasse resolution procedures act as safety valves to help contain labor–management conflict and solve labor-related problems (Lester, 1986; Babcock & Olson, 1992). For instance, impasse procedures help one or both parties save face when settlements are painful. When a voluntary compromise is unlikely to win acceptance by rank-and-file union members or management, reliance on a third party to dictate the necessary settlement tends to deflect criticism and blame from the negotiating team to the neutral. Thus, union and management leaders can retain their positions of authority by using the neutral as a buffer or scapegoat, and constructive labor–management relations are maintained. These "arbitrated" agreements have been commonplace in many jurisdictions, including New York City, Michigan, New Jersey, and Wisconsin (Lester, 1986).

Dispute resolution procedures also act to reduce conflict and build consensus between the two parties on labor relations issues that have been subjects of contention. Actually, the most useful long-term function of impasse procedures, particularly arbitration, "may be the manner in which it quietly absorbs and accommodates conflicting interest group claims over scarce public resources" (Feuille, 1979, p. 75). In this sense, dispute resolution procedures contribute to social and political stability by providing an alternative to overt conflict and strikes.

Are third-party procedures ethically superior to the strike in public employment? In responding to this question, we must defer to Burton (1978), who concluded that "the relevant standard is the jurisdiction's law. Public sector strikes that are legal are ethical, and vice versa." Public employee unions are interest groups that have a strong voice in state and local government legislative bodies. Their preferences, as likely as not, are for third-party dispute resolution procedures. Although public employers have demonstrated an increasing propensity to take a strike, they, too, usually prefer settlement through less conflictual means. Like unions, public employers also make their desires known to legislators.

CASE STUDY 9.1 TOUGH TIMES IN GARDEN JUNCTION

New federal mandates, a failed sewer system, the loss of a major employer, and a national economic recession have slammed the finances of Garden Junction. The city council and City Manager Donald Lilly cannot be blamed for worrying about the financial viability of the small (pop. 50,000) town. Few opportunities for growing municipal revenues appear to exist. Hence, the council and Manager Lilly have been engaged in serious discussions about tough long-term changes.

The municipal work force numbers 175 employees. Collective bargaining contracts govern pay, benefits, and working conditions. All six major contracts are presently in negotiations. There has already been a flood of retirements, with the recent retirees joining the ranks of nearly 1,200 earlier pensioners. The retirement plan is defined benefit, with participants enjoying generous payouts that are pegged to cost-of-living increases.

Pension expenses are consuming a growing portion of the operating budget, as the system has been funded from the annual budget. Switching to a defined contribution plan in which the city would dedicate a percentage of employee salary to a fund presents an attractive option. Present contributions would fund future payouts, with participants determining the distribution of their pension investments and the level of their monthly pension check dependent on individual investment choices.

Labor relations in Garden Junction have been fairly constructive, but the shift in retirement plan funding is likely to provoke strident union opposition. Union president Vinny Calabria has already voiced the union's position and suffice it to say that it is not positive. Calabria asserts that the city pension system is based on past understandings, and benefits cannot be reduced without union agreement. However, a consultants' study has recommended that the city establish a mandatory defined contribution plan for all present and newly hired employees. Significant savings are anticipated once the plan is implemented. The consultant's proposal is brought before the council and, following the views of the consultant and the city manager, it is approved. The issue moves to the bargaining table.

Union and management negotiators work out agreements on pay and some minor changes in conditions of work. The pension issue ties them up in a serious impasse. Under state law, the issue moves to conventional, binding arbitration under a single neutral appointed by the state PERB. Each party presents its arguments: the union for continuation of the defined benefit plan, but with a small (2% of salary) copayment into the pension fund from the salary of current employees; management for adoption of a defined contribution plan, with the city transferring 6% of employee salary matched by 4% of city funds into individual retirement accounts.

You are sent by the PERB to Garden Junction to settle the impasse:

1 How would you begin to carry out your assignment?

2 What information would you examine in determining the viability of the benefit change and the nature of your decision?

3 Are there reasonable alternatives to a mandatory defined contribution plan for all employees?

4 Explain and defend your decision

REFERENCES

Avgar, A. C., Colvin, A. J., Katz, H. C., & Nobles, K. G. (2023). A fragmented and heavily privatized dispute resolution system: *The United States. Industrial Relations Journal, 54*(4–5), 304–320.

Babcock, L. C., & Olson, C. A. (1992). The causes of impasses in labor disputes. *Industrial Relations, 31*(2).

Bazerman, M. H. (1985, July). Norms of distributive justice in interest arbitration. *Industrial and Labor Relations Review, 38*, 558–570.

Bazerman, M. H., & Farber, H. (1985, October). Arbitrator decision making: When are final offers important? *Industrial and Labor Relations Review, 39*, 76–89.

Bellman, H. S. (1998). Some reflections on the practice of mediation. *Negotiation Journal, 14*, 205–210.

Bellman, H. S. (2013). The importance of impasse resolution procedures to recent revisions of Wisconsin public sector labor law. *Ohio State Journal on Dispute Resolution, 28*(1), 37–44.

Bloom, D. E. (1988). Arbitrator behavior in public sector wage disputes. In R. B. Freeman & C. Ichniowski (Eds.), *When public sector workers unionize* (pp. 107–128). University of Chicago Press.

Bolton, G. E., & Katok, E. (1998). Reinterpreting arbitration's narcotic effect: An experimental study of learning in repeated bargaining. *Games and Economic Behavior, 25*(1), 1–33.

Briggs, S., & Koys, D. J. (1989, August). What makes labor mediators effective? *Labor Law Journal*, 517–520.

Budd, J. W., & Colvin, A. J. S. (2008). Improved metrics for workplace dispute resolution procedures: Efficiency, equity, and voice. *Industrial Relations, 47*(3), 460–480.

Burton, J. F., Jr. (1978). *Public sector strikes: Legal, ethical, and practical considerations.* Cornell University, New York State School of Industrial and Labor Relations. Reprint Series No. 448.

Butler, R. J., & Ehrenberg, R. G. (1981, October). Estimating the narcotic effect of public sector impasse procedures. *Industrial and Labor Relations Review, 35*, 3–20.

Campolieti, M., & Riddell, C. (2020). Does mediation-arbitration reduce arbitration rates? Evidence from a natural experiment. *ILR Review, 73*(1), 211–235.

Carofano v. City of Bridgeport. (1985). 196 Conn. 623, 495 A. 2d 1016.

Carrell, M., & Bales, R. (2013). Considering final offer arbitration to resolve public sector impasses in times of concession bargaining. *Ohio State Journal on Dispute Resolution, 28*(1), 1–36.

Champlin, F. C., & Bognanno, M. F. (1985, Fall). "Chilling" under arbitration and mixed strike-arbitration regimes. *Journal of Labor Research, VI*, 375–387.

Chelius, J. R., & Extejt, M. M. (1985, July). The narcotic effect of impasse resolution procedures. *Industrial and Labor Relations Review, 38*, 629–637.

Cohen, G. H. (2012). Advancing student achievement in the United States public schools through labor-management collaboration: The FMCS'S evolving role in education reform. *St. John's Law Review, 86*(2), 465–484.

Conlon, D. E., Moon, H., & Ng, K. Y. (2002). Putting the cart before the horse: The benefits of arbitrating before mediating. *Journal of Applied Psychology, 87*(5), 978–984.

Craver, C. B. (2013). The use of alternative dispute resolution techniques to resolve public sector bargaining disputes. *Ohio State Journal on Dispute Resolution, 28*(1), 45–62.

Dearborn Firefighters Local 412 v. City of Dearborn. (1975). 394 Mich. 229, 231 N.W. 2d 226.

Dell'Omo, G. G. (1989, June). Wage disputes in interest arbitration: Arbitrators weigh the criteria. *Arbitration Journal, 44*, 4–13.

Dell'Omo, G. G. (1990, Spring). Capturing arbitrator decision policies under a public sector interest arbitration statute. *Review of Public Personnel Administration, 10*, 19–38.

Dickinson, D. L., & Hunnicutt, L. (2005). Does fact-finding promote settlement? Theory and a test. *Economic Inquiry, 43*(2), 401–416.

Dilts, D. A. (1984). An examination of fact finding as a method of dispute settlement and training grounds for arbitrators. *Journal of Collective Negotiations, 13*(1), 251–258.

Dilts, D. A., & Haber, L. J. (1989). The mediation of contract disputes in the Iowa public sector. *Journal of Collective Negotiations, 18*(2), 145–151.

Downie, B. M. (1992). *Strikes, disputes and policy making: Resolving disputes in Ontario education* (pp. 233–249). IRC Press.

Elkouri, F., & Elkouri, E. A. (2003). *How arbitration works* (6th ed., p. 1266). Bureau of National Affairs Books.

Elsea, S. W., Dilts, D. A., & Haber, L. J. (1990). Factfinders and arbitrators in Iowa: Are they the same neutrals? *Journal of Collective Negotiations, 19*(1), 61–67.

Farber, H. S. (1980, December). An analysis of final-offer arbitration. *Journal of Conflict Resolution, 24*, 683–705.

Feuille, P. (1975). Final-offer arbitration and the chilling effect. *Industrial Relations, 14*(3), 302–310.

Feuille, P. (1979). Selected benefits and costs of compulsory arbitration. *Industrial and Labor Relations Review, 33*(1), 64–76.

Feuille, P., & Delaney, J. T. (1986, January). Collective bargaining, interest arbitration, and police salaries. *Industrial and Labor Relations Review,* 39, 228–240.

Feuille, P., Delaney, J. T., & Hendricks, W. (1985a, Spring). The impact of interest arbitration on police contracts. *Industrial Relations, 24*, 161–181.

Feuille, P., & Schwochau, S. (1988, March). The decision of interest arbitrators. *Arbitration Journal, 43*, 28–35.

FMCS. (1996). *Forces of change: Report of the mediator task force on the future of FMCS* (2nd ed.). U.S. General Printing Office.

FMCS. (2023). *Federal mediation and conciliation service fiscal year 2023: Performance and accountability report (PAR)*. https://www.fmcs.gov/wp-content/uploads/2023/11/FMCS-PAR-FY2023.pdf

Foegen, J. H. (1974). Public sector strike prevention: Let the taxpayer decide. *Journal of Collective Negotiations, 3*(3), 221–225.

Gerhart, P. F., & Drotning, J. E. (1980). Do uncertain cost/benefit estimates prolong public-sector disputes? *Monthly Labor Review, 103*(9), 26–30.

Graham, H., & Perry, J. (1993). Interest arbitration in Ohio: The narcotic effect revisited. *Journal of Collective Negotiations, 22*(4), 323–366.

Greer, C. R. (1978, April). Public sector bargaining legislation and strike: A case study. *Labor Law Journal*, 241–247.

Grodin, J. R. (1979). Judicial response to public-sector arbitration. In B. Aaron, J. R. Grodin, & J. L. Stern (Eds.), *Public sector bargaining* (pp. 224–253). Bureau of National Affairs.

Gunderson, M., Hebdon, R., & Hyatt, D. (1996). Collective bargaining in the public sector: A comment. *American Economic Review, 86*(3), 315–326.

Helburn, I. B., & Matthews, J. L. (1980). The referendum as an alternative to bargaining. *Journal of Collective Negotiations, 9*(2), 93–105.

Helburn, I. B., & Rodgers, R. C. (1985, May–June). Hesitancy of arbitrators to accept interest arbitration cases: A test of conventional wisdom. *Public Administration Review, 45*, 398–402.

Hogler, R. L., & Thompson, M. J. (1985, July). Collective negotiations in education and the public interest: A proposed method of impasse resolution. *Journal of Law and Education, 14*, 443–469.

Holden, L. T., Jr. (1976, March). Final-offer arbitration in Massachusetts: One year later. *Arbitration Journal*, 26–35.

Ichniowski, C. (1982). Arbitration and police bargaining: Prescription for the blue flu. *Industrial Relations, 21*(2), 149–166.

Jascourt, H. D. (1979). Recent trends and developments. In H. D. Jascourt (Ed.), *Government labor relations: Trends and information for the future* (pp. 3–31). Moore.

Jennings, K. M., Paulson, S. K., & Williamson, S. A. (1988). Assessing the effectiveness of Florida's impasse resolution procedures: A survey of public sector practitioners. *Public Personnel Management, 17*(3), 253–260.

Karim, A., & Pegnetter, R. (1983, Winter). Mediator strategies and qualities and mediation effectiveness. *Industrial Relations, 22*, 105–114.

Karper, M. D. (1994). Fact finding in public employment: Promise or illusion revisited. *Journal of Collective Negotiations in the Public Sector, 23*(4), 287–297.

Keating, C. (1994, February 17). Arbitrator withdraws teachers' raises. *Hartford (CT) Courant*, A1, B9.

Kochan, T. A. (1979). Dynamics of dispute resolution in the public sector. In B. Aaron, J. R. Grodin, & J. L. Stern (Eds.), *Public-sector bargaining* (pp. 150–190). Bureau of National Affairs (IRRA Series).

Kochan, T. A., & Baderschneider, J. (1978, July). Dependence on impasse procedures: Police and firefighters in New York State. *Industrial and Labor Relations Review, 31*, 431–449.

Kochan, T. A., & Baderschneider, J. (1981, October). Estimating the narcotic effect: Choosing techniques that fit the problem. *Industrial and Labor Relations Review, 35*(1), 3–20.

Kochan, T. A., & Jick, T. (1978, June). The public sector mediation process. *Journal of Conflict Resolution, 22*, 209–238.

Kochan, T. A., Lipsky, D. B., Newhart, M., & Benson, A. (2010). The long haul effects of interest arbitration: The case of New York State's Taylor law. *Industrial and Labor Relations Review, 63*(4), 565–585.

Kochan, T. A., Mironi, M., Ehrenberg, R. G., Baderschneider, J., & Jick, T. (1979). *Dispute resolution under fact-finding and arbitration: An empirical evaluation*. American Arbitration Association.

Kolb, D. M. (1983). *The mediators*. MIT Press.

Kolb, D. M., & Rubin, J. Z. (1989). *Research into mediation*. Dispute Resolution Forum, National Institute for Dispute Resolution.

Kressel, K. (1977). Labor mediation: An exploratory survey. In D. Lewin, P. Feuille, & T. A. Kochan (Eds.), *Public sector labor relations: Analysis and readings* (pp. 252–272). Horton.

Lester, R. A. (1984). *Labor arbitration in state and local government: An examination of experience in eight states and New York City*. Princeton University Industrial Relations Section.

Lester, R. A. (1986, June). Lessons from experience with interest arbitration in nine jurisdictions. *Arbitration Journal, 41*, 34–37.

Lewin, D. (1985, Winter). The effects of regulation on public sector labor relations: Theory and evidence. *Journal of Labor Research, VI*, 77–95.

Lipsky, D. B., & Drotning, J. E. (1977). The relation between teacher salaries and the use of impasse procedures under New York's Taylor Law: 1968–1972. *Journal of Collective Negotiations, 6*(3), 229–244.

Lipsky, D. B., & Katz, H. C. (2006, December). Alternative approaches to interest arbitration: Lessons from New York City. *Public Personnel Management, 35*, 265–282.

Loewenberg, J. J. (1985). What's $13 billion among friends? The 1984 postal arbitration. In *38th annual proceedings of the IRRA*. IRRA.

Loewenberg, J. J., & Klinetop, W. A. (1992). The second decade of interest arbitration in Pennsylvania. *Journal of Collective Negotiations, 21*(4), 353–367.

Lowi, T. (1979). *The end of liberalism* (2nd ed.). LRP.

Magnusen, K. O., & Renovitch, P. A. (1989). Dispute resolution in Florida's public sector: Insight into impasse. *Journal of Collective Negotiations, 18*(3), 241–252.

Malin, M. H. (2013). Two models of interest arbitration. *Ohio State Journal on Dispute Resolution, 28*(1), 145–170.

Mareschal, P. M. (1998, Fall). Providing high quality mediation. *Review of Public Personnel Administration*, 55–67.

Mareschal, P. M. (2002a). New frontiers in alternative dispute resolution. *International Journal of Public Administration, 25*(11), 1255–1266.

Mareschal, P. M. (2002b). Mastering the art of dispute resolution: Best practices from the FMCS. *International Journal of Public Administration, 25*(11), 1351–1377.

Mareschal, P. M. (2003). Solving problems and transforming relationships: The bifocal approach to mediation. *The American Review of Public Administration, 33*(4), 423–448.

Mareschal, P. M. (2005a). Building a better future through mediation: Insights from a survey of FMCS mediators. *Journal of Collective Negotiations, 30*(4), 307–324.

Mareschal, P. M. (2005b). What makes mediation work? Mediators' perspectives on resolving disputes. *Industrial Relations, 44*(3), 509–517.

Mareschal, P. M., & Rudin, J. P. (2009). Regulation of child custody mediation: A patchwork quilt. *Journal of Public Management & Social Policy, 15*(1).

Marmo, M. (1995). The role of fact finding and interest arbitration in selling a settlement. *Journal of Collective Negotiations, 24*(1), 77–96.

Mass.gov. (2008). *Joint labor management committee.* Retrieved January 2, 2008, from www.mass.gov/jlmc/arbitration.htm

McCormick, M. (1979). A functional analysis of interest arbitration in New York City municipal government, 1968–1975. In M. J. Levine & E. C. Hagburg (Eds.), *Labor relations in the public sector.* Brighton.

McKelvey, J. T. (1969). Fact-finding in public employment disputes: Promise or illusion? *Industrial and Labor Relations Review, 22*(4), 528–543.

Midwest Center for Public Sector Labor Relations. (1979). *Labor legislation in the public sector.* Indiana University School of Public and Environmental Affairs.

Nelson, N. E. (1986, October). The selection of arbitrators. *Labor Law Journal*, 703–711.

Ohio Revised Code § 4117.14. (2023). https://codes.ohio.gov/ohio-revised-code/section-4117.14

Ohio State Employment Relations Board. (2023). *Annual report.* https://dam.assets.ohio.gov/image/upload/serb.ohio.gov/PDF/Annual_Report/Annual_Report_2023.pdf

Ohio State Employment Relations Board. (2024). *Annual report.* https://dam.assets.ohio.gov/image/upload/serb.ohio.gov/PDF/Annual_Report/Annual_Report_2024.pdf

Olson, C. A., & Rau, B. L (1997). Learning from interest arbitration: The next round. *Industrial and Labor Relations Review, 50*(2), 237–251.

Oregon Revised Statutes § 243.746. (2023). https://www.oregonlegislature.gov/bills_laws/ors/ors243.html

Payne, K., Kohler, P., Cangemi, J. P., & Fuqua, H., Jr. (2000). Communication and strategies in the mediation of disputes. *Journal of Collective Negotiations, 29*(1), 29–47.

Posthuma, R. A., Dworkin, J. B., & Swift, M. S. (2002). Mediator tactics and sources of conflict: Facilitating and inhibiting effects. *Industrial Relations, 41*(1), 94–109.

Rehmus, C. M. (1975). Binding arbitration in the public sector. In P. M. Voos (Ed.), *Proceedings of the twenty-seventh annual winter meeting* (pp. 307–314). The University of Michigan, IRRA Series.

Riccucci, N., & Ban, C. (1989, Spring). The unfair labor practice process as a dispute-resolution technique in the public sector: The case of New York State. *Review of Public Personnel Administration, 9*, 51–67.

Ross, W. H., & Conlon, D. E. (2000). Hybrid forms of third-party dispute resolution: Theoretical implications of combining mediation and arbitration. *The Academy of Management Review, 25*(2), 416–427.

Rubinstein, S., Heckscher, C., & McCarthy, J. (2024). *Democracy and reform in public schools: The case for collaborative partnerships*. Harvard Education Press.

Schneider, B. V. H. (1988). Public sector labor legislation—an evolutionary analysis. In B. J. Aaron, J. R. Grodin, & J. L. Stern (Eds.), *Public sector bargaining* (pp. 191–223). Bureau of National Affairs.

Simkin, W. E. (1971). *Mediation and the dynamics of collective bargaining*. BNA.

Simkin, W. E. (1979). Fact-finding: Its values and limitations. In M. J. Levine & E. C. Hagburg (Eds.), *Labor relations in the public sector: Readings, cases, and experiential exercises*. Brighton.

Slater, J. E. (2019). Strike rights of essential employees in the USA. In M. M. Mironi & M. Schlachter (Eds.), *Regulating strikes in essential services: A comparative 'law in action' perspective*. Kluwer Law International BV.

Smith, C. G. (2006). Interest arbitration in the federal service. *International Journal of Public Administration, 29*(9), 639–660.

Spero, S. D., & Capozzola, J. M. (1973). *The urban community and its unionized bureaucracies*. Dunellen.

Stieber, J., & Wolkinson, B. W. (1977, February). Fact-finding views by fact-finders: The Michigan experience. *Labor Law Journal, 28*, 89–101.

Subbarao, A. V. (1978, March). The impact of binding interest arbitration on negotiation and process outcome. *Journal of Conflict Resolution, 22*, 79–103.

Turpin, R. (1998). An analysis of public sector interest: Arbitrators assessment of wage comparability. *Journal of Collective Negotiations, 27*(1), 45–51.

Ver Ploeg, C. D. (1988, March). Labor arbitration: The participants' perspectives. *Arbitration Journal, 43*, 36–43.

Vest, M. J., O'Brien, F. P., & Vest, J. M. (1990, Fall). Explaining rights arbitrator willingness to accept public sector interest arbitration cases. *Public Personnel Management, 19*, 331–343.

Zack, A. M. (1985). *Public sector mediation*. Bureau of National Affairs.

Zagoria, S. (1973, May). Resolving impasses by public referendum. *Monthly Labor Review*, 36–38.

Zigarelli, M. A. (1996, Winter). Dispute resolution mechanisms and teacher bargaining outcomes. *Journal of Labor Research, XVII*, 135–148.

Chapter 10

Living with the Contract

I. INTRODUCTION

After the chairs are pushed back from the table, the written agreement signed, hands shaken all around, and photo opportunities provided for the media, the two parties to the agreement must begin the difficult task of applying and interpreting the broad terms of the contract on a day-to-day basis. Although contract negotiations steal the limelight of labor relations, the true test of the soundness and maturity of the relationship between union and management comes with implementation of the agreement. It is through living with the contract that collective bargaining exerts its greatest effects on the behavior and attitudes of individual public workers (Kochan, 1980).

A collective bargaining agreement may be effectively administered by each party, or it may be poorly administered. The union, like an unruly child, may test management by attempting to tilt interpretation of the contract to its advantage by picketing, walkouts, or job slowdowns. An immature management team may ignore the collective bargaining agreement and attempt to implement terms and conditions of employment unilaterally. Just as in a marriage, conflicts and disputes are inherent in any labor–management relationship. The key to a healthy and stable employment relationship is to manage conflict and controversy over implementation of the contract in a constructive manner, with due consideration of the rights and responsibilities of each party. Both parties must strive to resolve their differences amicably in the short term to maintain a positive long-term relationship.

In this chapter, after a brief examination of collective bargaining agreements and their administration in the public sector, our attention focuses on the primary means for living peacefully with the contract. This generally involves having a responsive and effective grievance procedure culminating in binding grievance arbitration.

DOI:10.4324/9781003403593-10

II. COLLECTIVE BARGAINING AGREEMENT

The negotiated contract serves as the legal foundation, or "law of the workplace." It replaces the unilateral determination of employment decisions by management with a shared decision-making process between equals. The collective bargaining agreement is traditionally referred to as a "contract" much in the sense of a commercial contract. Like the commercial contract, the collective bargaining agreement is enforceable in the courts. At the same time, a labor agreement is more than a business contract in that it attempts to construct a democratic system for governance of the workplace. Also, when a commercial contract expires, the rights and duties of the parties are terminated. Labor agreements have a life beyond contract expiration, particularly with regard to employer obligations to contribute to health insurance and pension plans and to honor procedures established during the term of the contract.

In private sector labor management relationships, the basis for legal recourse involving contracts is found in Section 301(a) of the Labor–Management Relations Act (LMRA). The LMRA stipulates that union or management violations of contract terms may be challenged by a lawsuit in federal district court. In the public sector, litigation to enforce contracts is usually taken before a state court or the Federal Labor Relations Authority (FLRA). Other potential remedies are available in both private industry and government, including unfair labor practice (ULP) charges before the National Labor Relations Board or the state labor board or agency. As a general rule, however, contractual disputes are settled within the parameters of the agreement itself, without resort to external appeal.

A. Contents of the Agreement

The typical collective bargaining contract runs anywhere from 10 to 100 pages. The document may be very basic and limited in scope or exceedingly detailed and complex. All labor relations contracts, however, are intended to provide rules for governing the parties' relationships on a day-to-day basis and to delineate the duties, rights, and responsibilities of the respective parties.

Generally speaking, contract provisions may be classified as (1) fixed, (2) contingent, or (3) dispute resolution procedures. Fixed provisions usually remain unchanged over the life of the agreement. Contingent provisions govern union or management actions in a changing labor relations environment. Dispute resolution procedures outline the process for resolving conflicts arising from contract interpretation and application (Table 10.1 provides examples for each category of contract provisions).

Contract provisions may be also classified into (1) employee rights and obligations, (2) union rights and obligations, (3) management rights and obligations, and

Table 10.1 Types of Contract Provisions

Types of Provisions	*Description*	Examples	
Fixed	Fixed provisions usually remain unchanged over the life of the agreement	• Contract duration • Boundaries of the bargaining unit • Management rights • Wages • Hours of Work • Benefits • Holidays, vacation, and sick leave	• Union recognition and rights • Union security • Antidiscrimination clauses • Residency requirements • Union political activities • Official time • Reopening clause
Contingent	Contingent provisions are intended to govern union or management actions in a changing labor relations environment	• Discharges • Layoffs • Reductions in force/ recall of laid-off workers • Promotions	• Work scheduling • Work assignments • Transfers • Discipline • Outsourcing
Dispute resolution procedures	Dispute resolution procedures are designed to resolve conflicts arising from contract interpretation and application, particularly of the contingent provisions	• Grievance procedure (steps) • Mediation • Arbitration/ expedited arbitration	• Powers of the arbitrator • Selection of arbitrators • Expenses of arbitration • No-strike clause

(4) grievance and arbitration procedure (Budd, 2021). Typical provisions related to employee rights specify salary schedules for different types of employees, overtime compensation requirements, leave entitlements, and job benefits. Under collective bargaining agreements, public employees may be entitled to annual leave, sick leave, personal leave, childcare leave, other types of leave, and a range of holidays. Common benefits include life, health, dental, vision, and disability insurance as well as pension benefits. Primary employee obligations involve conducting assigned duties and following work rules.

Most collective bargaining agreements in the public sector contain seniority provisions. Seniority refers to an employee's length of service to the organization. In accordance with length of service, employees gain preference in work events such as layoffs, transfers, and promotions. Layoff provisions usually require the reduction in the number of employees in reverse order of seniority. Provisions related to voluntary transfers and promotions may require employers to give preference to employees in the order of greatest seniority when filling vacancies and making transfer decisions. In some cases, employers may be required to consider seniority as the sole criteria for making layoff, transfer, and promotion decisions. In others they may have to evaluate seniority along with other factors such as employee skills, knowledge, and abilities. Seniority, nevertheless, may be designated as the determining decision factor when employees considered for layoff, transfer, or promotion are substantially equal on all other factors.

Under collective bargaining agreements, unions may recognize the authority of the employer to take disciplinary action against employees. Nevertheless, unions may also negotiate limits to such authority, requiring that disciplinary action be timely, reasonable, and taken for just cause. Disciplinary action is usually considered reasonable if it is appropriate to the seriousness of the incident. Progressive disciplinary action may be required. Contracts may further specify the time within which the employer may take disciplinary action and enumerate reasons that constitute just cause. Examples of just cause include failure to conduct assigned duties; violation of work rules, policies, and regulations; unsatisfactory service; and inappropriate conduct, among others.

Collective bargaining agreements typically specify several union rights and obligations. Most contracts contain a union recognition clause in which the employer recognizes a particular union as the exclusive representative of the employees in a bargaining unit. In addition to union recognition, more specific union protection provisions may be negotiated into the contract. Employers may be expressly prohibited from supporting, financially or otherwise, any other labor organization with the purpose of undermining the union recognized as the exclusive representative of employees. Furthermore, employers may be expressly prohibited from eroding or reducing the bargaining unit by assigning tasks that are commonly performed by union members to nonunion employees.

Several union rights included in collective bargaining agreements are designed to facilitate union activity and continuity. For example, unions may have the right to have union dues deducted by the employer directly from employee paychecks where such practice does not conflict with state law. Unions may also have the right to maintain bulletin boards on the premises of the employer, have the opportunity to give a presentation to new employees during orientation, provide new employees with information packets, and have office space assigned to them at locations that are easily accessible to employees. Union leaders may have the right to take time off from work for union business purposes. Examples of union obligations include the duty of fair representation and refraining from engaging in strikes.

Union and employee rights correspond to employer obligations. Therefore, collective bargaining agreements may require employers to refrain from aiding other unions. In addition, employers may be obliged to provide the union with an office space, deduct union dues from employee paychecks, furnish union information packets to new employees, allow unions to represent workers in disciplinary investigations, provide a healthy and safe work environment, and discipline workers only for just cause, among others.

To maintain control over traditional management functions, employers usually negotiate into collective bargaining agreements management rights clauses. Management rights may include the right to determine the mission, budget, and organizational structure of the agency; select, promote, and discipline employees for just cause; adopt work rules that regulate performance and conduct of employees; and manage affairs efficiently. Other management rights include ensuring that management may exercise its regular and customary functions without limits.

Dispute resolution procedures are designed to resolve conflicts arising from contract interpretation and application, particularly of the contingent provisions. The majority of labor agreements contain a no-strike provision for the life of the contract and a multistep grievance procedure culminating in binding arbitration of contract disputes (Avgar et al., 2023). As noted previously, another common procedure for resolving disputes is to file a ULP complaint with the appropriate state or federal organization.

In living with the contract, dispute resolution provisions are particularly important. Every clause in the contract may be subject to differing interpretations. Like other written instruments, the labor contract simply describes the terms agreed upon by the parties. Like any document, it may suffer from vague wording. The pressure and time constraints of negotiations, along with the fatigue they often precipitate, are not conducive to precise writing.

During negotiations, various tones and intonations, facial expressions, body language, and contexts enrich and expand upon formal language. What may appear to be perfectly clear to the negotiating teams may later seem to be riddled with ambiguities to those who have only the written words before them. Furthermore, interpretation of contract provisions can be complicated by deliberately ambiguous language that helps to avoid a negotiations impasse. Poor drafting and "legalese" compound uncertainties.

To minimize contract ambiguity, the drafters of the agreement should use short, declarative sentences; avoid excessive legalisms; be precise with terms such as "agency," "union," and "employee;" carefully outline procedures in a step-by-step format; and use examples to clarify abstract clauses. In addition, they should have a draft of the agreement proofread by individuals who were not present at the bargaining table. The drafters should also strive to avoid polysyllabic words and nebulous terms such as "reasonable," "equitable," and "normally."

Scott and Suchan (1987) assessed the readability of a sample of public sector collective bargaining contracts using three readability formulas, including the Fog Index. They found that virtually all of the contracts were difficult to read and understand, requiring at a minimum the reading comprehension skills of a college graduate. Obviously, many stewards, frontline supervisors, and union rank and file may be expected to have difficulty applying the provisions of such contracts. Scott and Suchan (1987) recommend that technical writers be used to draft contracts in plain, clear language. Nonetheless, as long as humans are fallible, vagueness and contradictions will be found in their written agreements.

B. Disseminating the Agreement

Just as management is the initiator of most personnel-related actions, management also has the primary responsibility for implementing the collective bargaining contract. As the action agent, management initiates policy under the agreement and the union reacts, through either compliance or challenge. It is commonly observed that management administers the contract and the union enforces it. But management may also be accused of errors of omission or inaction (Meyer, 2002).

Assuming legislative ratification of a negotiated collective bargaining agreement, management's first task is to disseminate the contract throughout the organization and to educate the respective constituencies on specific provisions and grievance procedures. The contract is typically reproduced in its entirety. Often, the most important provisions are summarized and explained. A fundamental principle of contract administration is that all managers and members of the bargaining unit should receive a copy of the contract as soon as possible. Supervisors should be allocated a sufficient number of copies to distribute to each of their subordinates, including those who are not members of the union (they are parties to the contract nonetheless). Usually, the public employer assumes responsibility for the costs of printing and distributing the agreement and collateral materials, or for making them available online.

The key individuals in contract dissemination are management supervisor and union stewards. If these people become intimately familiar with the contract terms early in the life of the agreement, there should be fewer misunderstandings and, as a consequence, fewer unnecessary grievances. In fact, it is not a bad idea for supervisors to begin familiarizing themselves with a new contract while it is still being negotiated. Such early involvement enhances understanding of contract provisions as they are finalized. It also enables supervisors to serve as valuable channels of communication between employees and management during negotiations. Moreover, it provides an early assessment of the potential impact of various union and management proposals. Once a new contract is signed, supervisors should quickly be given a written analysis of each provision. Special training sessions should be held to explain the management perspective on each clause and its intent.

The union should also train its stewards in the provisions of the new contract. As rank-and-file leaders, stewards play a crucial role in union management relations. They are a combination of agents of socialization, communicators, and problem solvers. Through their contract enforcement responsibilities, they resolve workers' conflicts with supervisors and with other bargaining unit members (Keefe, 2003). The bargaining agreement is "the most tangible product the union has to sell," and it can be used to elevate member commitment to the union (Clark & Gallagher, 1988, p. 16). New members may be familiarized with contract provisions during both union- and management-sponsored orientation programs. Benefits could accrue to both labor and management from joint training and orientation sessions, but such programs are relatively uncommon. For example, in a recent study of a large, national public sector union, Clark (2021) found that only slightly more than one third of newly hired bargaining unit members attended a formal orientation session.

C. Administering the Agreement

Management organization for administering the contract varies with the size of the employer. In smaller school districts or municipalities, communication usually flows freely within the ranks of management, and authoritative interpretation of contract clauses is readily forthcoming. In governmental units of greater size, multiple levels of supervision can hinder prompt and effective contract administration. Informal communication channels that function very well in smaller jurisdictions tend to be supplanted by formal integrative structures, such as a central labor relations office, which coordinates labor relations policies between agencies or departments. Interorganizational politics frequently makes the job of the central office difficult at best. For example, a district director of a state social service agency who is well connected with the agency head or influential political figures may decide to run personnel operations in her own way, ignoring the contract.

For successful administration of the bargaining agreement, two important objectives must be met. First, the contract must be implemented in a uniform and consistent manner by both parties. Management should almost compulsively enforce all contract provisions to avoid undermining the agreement. The supervisor who, in an effort to be a "nice guy," violates the contract by, for example, permitting employees to leave work a couple of hours before quitting time to get an early start on vacation or holiday leave, is inadvertently sacrificing a management right and setting the table for future grievances. The same is true of the supervisor who overlooks an employee violation of agency rules to "give him/her/them a break."

In sum, administrators must be extremely cautious in making ad hoc exceptions and modifications to contractual procedures. The union steward, for his or her part, should police the agreement vigorously and represent all members of the bargaining unit, whether union member or not, in an impartial manner. Although stringent adherence to the formal contract by the parties may seem to be impersonal, inflexible, and overly rigid at times, labor relations experts insist that a commitment to make no exception to the rules is much preferred to inconsistent contract administration and the inevitable perceptions of unfairness that result.

Stringent adherence to the formal contract by the parties, nevertheless, does not hinder flexibility in contract administration. During negotiations, the parties often integrate intentionally flexible provisions into the agreement. Flexibility in contract language allows the parties to defer conflict during negotiations and navigate the dynamic labor relations environment during contract implementation. Taking advantage of flexibility in contract provisions, while maintaining uniformity in contract implementation, requires the cooperation of the union and management. Inadequate cooperation of union and management, however, results in contracts that are often more flexible as written than as practiced (Price, 2009).

The second essential objective for successful contract administration is to maintain open communication channels between the union and management representatives. The adversarial approach that typically characterizes the contract negotiations process should be replaced by a more cooperative relationship once the agreement is signed. It has been estimated that managers spend up to 50% of their time resolving conflicts.

Conflict between the parties is certain to continue during contract implementation. But conflict is not necessarily an undesirable thing. Constructive confrontation can be conducted in a healthy and positive atmosphere through negotiated grievance procedures. Careful monitoring of the labor–management relationship through, for example, grievance analysis can provide appropriate feedback for identifying problems at an early stage. Effective grievance procedures are a necessary prerequisite of successful contract administration and, indeed, an important extension of the collective bargaining process. Grievances effectively addressed today help prevent new grievances tomorrow.

Availability of grievance procedures has advantages for unions, employees, and management. The union benefits both tangibly and intangibly from representing members of the bargaining unit. Union support allows employees to voice their positions more freely, avoid potential repercussions, and ensure an equitable dispute resolution process (Avgar, 2021; Daugherty, 2011). Management gains from improved workforce morale and early problem identification. Conflict within the contract permits members of the organization to confront important issues constructively and cooperatively while advancing the organization's mission (Rahim, 1992).

To illustrate, in a study of teachers' unions in New York Choi and Chung (2016) found that the voice mechanism provided by collectively negotiated grievance procedures is associated with lower rates of teacher turnover. Moreover, when the voice mechanism includes binding arbitration, as opposed advisory arbitration, the relationship between voice and lowered turnover is even stronger. Lower turnover helps management save on the costs of recruitment, selection, and training.

Similarly, Coggburn et al. (2020) find that grievance procedures improve the perceptions organizational justice for both grievants and management.

III. GRIEVANCE PROCEDURES

A grievance is an employee or union complaint (or, albeit infrequently, a management complaint) arising out of dissatisfaction with some aspect of the contract or the work environment. The primary purpose of a grievance is to overturn a management action. Usually, the grievance involves an alleged violation of a clause in the negotiated contract. The nature of a grievance is limited only by circumstance. The most common grievance subjects are disciplinary actions, such as reprimands, suspensions, or discharges; absenteeism; health and safety issues; vacation assignments; job assignments; promotions; discrimination; overtime; layoffs; and reductions in force.

Employee grievances over the terms, conditions, or continuation of employment may be resolved in several ways in the public sector. This includes unilateral determination by management, civil service procedures, ULPs, and contractual grievance procedures. The primary objective of a grievance procedure is to provide a means for a worker to register a formal complaint about working conditions, arbitrary management actions, or other matters and receive a fair hearing.

In the absence of unions and contractual grievance procedures, employees usually must either represent themselves or privately secure the services of an attorney. It is common in nonunion jurisdictions for official grievance processes to seriously disadvantage the employee and favor management. Where unions are present, negotiated grievance procedures and union representation level the playing field or even tilt it in favor of the employee.

Although nearly all negotiated agreements contain grievance procedures (the estimate is 95%), their scope varies. Some contracts stipulate grievance procedures but never directly address the issue of what constitutes a grievance. Most contracts, however, either define grievances very broadly as any disagreement or dispute between management and the employee or union or define them narrowly by specifying the types of grievances that may be raised under the terms of the agreement. Some contracts specifically exclude certain matters from the negotiated grievance procedure, such as designated management rights (e.g., selection, promotion, and performance appraisal).

Even for noncontract-related grievances, some means of resolution should be provided. If a grievance is raised, it means a problem exists whether or not it is grievable under the contract. By addressing noncontract grievances through, for example, alternative dispute resolution (ADR) procedures, management gains an opportunity to resolve potential problems in an early stage of development, before the acorn of a problem grows into a hulking oak.

Negotiated grievance procedures have supplanted traditional civil service appeals systems in virtually all jurisdictions in which unions engage in collective bargaining. There are important distinctions between the two legal settings. Civil service grievance procedures are established in statute or by the employer. In contrast, negotiated procedures are established bilaterally through union and management negotiations and embodied in the contract.

A grieving worker under a civil service system is essentially appealing a management decision to higher authority. A negotiated grievance procedure represents a continuation of the collective bargaining process through which the parties' rights and responsibilities are clarified continually. Final decision-making authority in a civil service system typically resides in a commission of elected or appointed officials who must attempt to balance dual, and sometimes conflicting, responsibilities as both the executive personnel arm of management and the protector of classified employees and the merit system. Whereas nearly all negotiated grievance procedures provide for final decision making by a "disinterested" third-party arbitrator (Avgar et al., 2023). Finally, the scope of civil service grievance procedures is typically restricted by state law, municipal ordinance, or commission rules and regulations. Negotiated procedures are usually much less limited in scope.

The functions of negotiated grievance procedures go beyond merely furnishing a basic forum for employee complaints. Grievance procedures help avoid strikes and other labor actions in two important ways. First, in the absence of grievance procedures, unions would be more likely to resort to labor actions rather than litigation to resolve disputes over contract application (Malin, 2010). Second, negotiating grievance and arbitration provisions into the contract allows the parties to defer potential disputes over specific issues to case-by-case negotiation (Malin, 2010). In the absence of a process to defer conflict, the parties would be more likely to reach an impasse in collective bargaining, which may increase the likelihood of unions to resort to labor actions.

Grievance procedures also help resolve differences in interpreting the written agreement, protect the rights of the union, identify new issues for negotiations, and, in general, promote labor–management harmony in living together with the contract. Other important functions of the negotiated grievance procedure include detecting underlying problems in the agreement and in the basic functions of human resource management. To illustrate, Choi and Chung (2016) contend that grievance mechanisms in public school districts serve as a voice mechanism that allows teachers to speak up about problems, rather than seek a job elsewhere. Specifically, they find that districts with strong grievances procedures have lower turnover rates at the individual level. Choi and Chung (2016) suggest that the lower turnover rates may have a positive effect on organizational performance. In this sense, the grievance procedure represents an extension of the bargaining process.

Although negotiated and civil service grievance procedures differ conceptually, in practice they sometimes overlap, providing multiple points of access to the grievant. For example, an adverse action such as dismissal may be appealed to a civil service commission or taken to arbitration through the negotiated contract in some jurisdictions. Additional appellate venues exist if the dismissal results in charges of sexual, racial, or other forms of discrimination.

Federal sector grievance procedures represent the best (or worst) example of multiple dispute resolution venues. A single dispute between a union-represented grievant and an agency "may be litigated before four separate agencies and with as many as ten different procedures" (Feder, 1989, p. 269). At any given time, a grievance may be pending before the FLRA (contract dispute), Merit Systems Protection Board (MSPB) (disciplinary action), the Office of Special Counsel (whistleblower reprimand), and the Equal Employment Opportunity Commission (EEOC) (discrimination complaint).

Within the FLRA alone, there are several ADR paths. Not surprisingly, confusion and lengthy delays plague the process. "Mixed cases" involving allegations of discrimination, and one or more related matters often take 4 years or longer for settlement, especially if findings of the various grievance-deciding bodies diverge. Such costly, convoluted, and bewildering procedures negatively affect the quality of federal labor–management relations. This has led to suggestions to replace this multiplicity of grievance-hearing bodies with a single federal dispute resolution board (Feder, 1989).

Similar levels of redundancy and complexity are also found in some states. For example, Zirkel (2016), notes that there is a "multi-level panoply of laws" that impacts the outcome of teacher-school board grievances in New York. These include laws that impact all employers such as the Age Discrimination in Employment Act (ADEA), laws that impact public sector employers, and laws specifically focused on K-12 education, such as teacher certification laws. Other states (e.g., New Jersey and Maine) have attempted to end the confusion by amending their collective bargaining laws so that the negotiated contractual procedure takes precedence over all other channels of appeal. Florida requires the grievant to choose either the negotiated procedure or a civil service procedure.

A. Causes of Grievances

As noted in Section II.A, grievances spring from diverse sources in the workplace. The three major causes of grievances are misunderstandings, intentional violations, and symptomatic grievances. These sources are discussed in more detail later.

"Misunderstandings" probably represent the most frequent source of grievances in most employment relationships. Such cases can result from deliberate or unintentional ambiguities in a negotiated contract, misinterpretation or misunderstanding of contract language by one or both parties, or ignorance or ineptitude in contract administration on the part of the union steward or the supervisor. For example, a manager who demonstrates incompetence in applying the terms of the contract is likely to find his or her decisions increasingly challenged by a leery steward. As a result, the number of grievances will rise.

"Intentional violations" typically involve management's circumvention of a contract provision because of "special circumstances" that have developed. For example, management may change the hours of work to meet client demands or reduce working hours because of a budget shortfall. To foreclose a waiver of future contract rights, the union grieves.

"Symptomatic grievances" are indicative of some underlying problem in the workplace that is causing employee frustration. For example, an underqualified or overqualified worker may file a petty grievance out of personal frustration. Stewards may raise grievances to harass management just before or during contract negotiations. In some cases, a "hard ass" supervisor may arbitrarily crack down on coffee breaks and casual conversation. Conflictual relations during contract negotiations often carry over into the administration of the agreement. Any particularly contentious issues that remain unresolved in the contract are apt to generate grievances.

Environmental factors that induce complaints may be included within the category of symptomatic grievances. These factors, which characterize the broad organizational context of union–management relationships, are found in the work environment, task organization and technology, and socioeconomic conditions. In an early study of the U.S. steel industry, Peach and Livernash (1974) found that grievance rates were higher in work units with low-skilled employees, repetitious work, jobs requiring constant attention, and other unfavorable working conditions. Muchinsky and Maasarani (1980) tested the applicability to two large state agencies in Iowa and had similar findings. In Iowa, the work environments at the Department of Social Services (DSS) and the Department of Transportation (DOT) were closely related to the frequency and subject matter of grievances. For instance, state hospital and prison employees in DSS filed a great many grievances over matters of discipline, health, safety, and transfers. The authors concluded that these grievances were related to the stress-ridden nature of their work. At DOT, the majority of grievances were concerned with hours of work, wages, and benefits.

Grievances have also been associated with characteristics of the individual worker. Grievants tend to be younger, have more formal education, exhibit greater absenteeism, and earn lower wages. They are also likely to be more active in their union than non-grievants. Furthermore, grievants tend to have a weak commitment to the job (especially students or part-time workers) and to their supervisors. Some studies have found that minorities are more likely to file grievances than whites (Labig & Greer, 1988).

An organization characterized by a comparatively high number of grievances is not necessarily an "unhealthy organization." However, grievances are costly in terms of their demands on management time, energy, and resources. The emergence of many grievances may simply reflect the lack of an effective union screening process to shut off frivolous complaints or combative union stewards (Bemmels, 1994).

A relatively small number of grievances may signal trouble in terms of a lack of employee faith in the grievance procedure or their union. Low grievance rates may also be related to the availability of a more frequently used alternative such as a civil service system appellate route. Alternate grievance procedures, in conjunction with a narrower scope of bargaining, have been cited as major reasons for the lower incidence of grievances in government as compared to industry (Stewart & Davy, 1992, p. 323).

The number of grievances in an organization may also depend on the approach that management takes to contract interpretation. Management may take the liberal approach to contract interpretation and test how much the union is willing to overlook before taking action. On the other hand, management may adhere to a strict interpretation of the contract and avoid conflict with the union (Price, 2009). A restrictive approach to contract interpretation by management may lead to a smaller number of grievances compared to a liberal approach.

Organizations in which managers experience limited discretionary power may also have a lower-than-expected incidence of grievances. Daugherty (2011, p. 81) explains that "over involvement of union oversight can lead to negative outcomes of grievance settlements and unnecessary suppression of management control." More specifically, an outcome of a grievance settlement that is unfavorable to management may have negative consequences, on a professional level, for managers involved in the dispute. Managers who understand the potential negative implications of unfavorable grievance settlements may choose to avoid intervening in failed agreements and practice passive management.

There is probably some "ideal" range of grievances per employee in a healthy organization, However, no mathematical equation or metric has been derived that accurately reflects the total ambience of the workplace. Therefore, it is important to keep grievance channels open and functional to serve as a safety valve, clear up ambiguous contract language, and otherwise ensure an adequate flow of employee feedback.

B. The Grievance Process

Although there is a great deal of variance in written, negotiated grievance procedures among public employers, almost every plan consists of step-by-step techniques for grievance resolution. Nearly all public sector grievance procedures culminate in binding arbitration. Two overriding concerns for any grievance procedure are that they (1) encourage the rapid and fair settlement of complaints and (2) promote resolution of the grievance at the lowest possible level. The

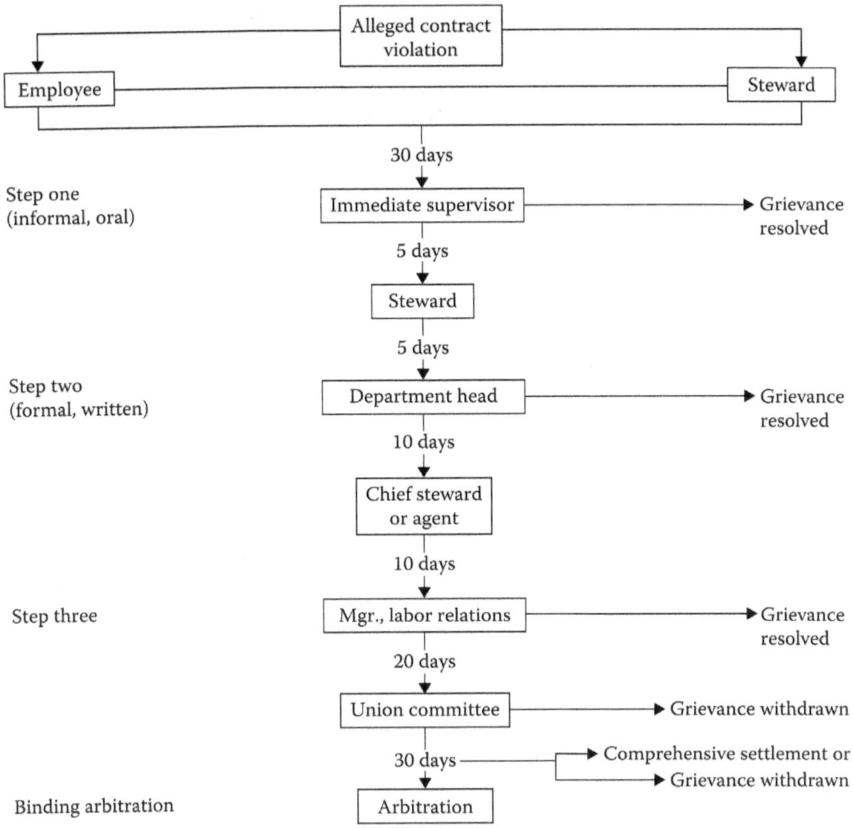

Figure 10.1 Grievance process.

Source: adapted from McPherson, D.S., *Resolving Grievances: A Practical Approach*, Reston Publishing, Reston, VA, 1983.

number of steps in the procedure usually corresponds with clear lines of management authority.

Most grievance plans include three basic steps, followed by arbitration (see Figure 10.1). First, the complaint is raised and responded to at the supervisory level. During this initial phase, a strong effort should be made to settle the grievance informally. Often the grievance is handled orally, which permits more flexibility than can exist once the complaint is reduced to a written form. The duty of the supervisor during this phase is to get the full story from the grieving employee. The supervisor should also consult with the union steward if necessary and investigate the complaint by collecting data and/or interviewing other workers to determine if there are adequate factual grounds for the complaint. After gathering this information, the supervisor should render a decision. Then, he/she/they should record the basis of the decision and document any corroborating information in anticipation of an employee appeal.

The usual second step in the grievance procedure involves union intervention and marks the commencement of a "formal" grievance. If the union grievance committee determines that further action should be taken on appeal, the complaint is summarized in writing, signed by the grievant, and forwarded to the next management level (see Figure 10.1). At this point, both parties are well served by carefully collecting and retaining complete and accurate records of the case. The responsibility of management at this juncture is to review the complaint in view of relevant contract language and other significant information and try to find a means for resolving the dispute. Fairness and promptness should be of major concern to both the union and management. It is important to demonstrate to all interested parties, especially the rank and file, that the grievance system works as intended.

If the complaint remains unresolved, higher levels of management become involved. In municipalities, the department head may make the final pre-arbitration determination or, especially in middle-sized and smaller localities, the mayor or city manager may function as penultimate arbiter of the grievance. In school districts, the local school board or superintendent often makes the final management decision before third-party intervention. Policy in state governments varies, with state grievance committees, agency and department heads, or labor relations divisions making final pre-arbitration judgment. Even when grievances are settled during the early procedural stages, top management often plays an important role by consulting informally with supervisors.

The final venue in more than 90% of negotiated public sector grievance procedures is binding grievance arbitration by a neutral third party. For contracts that do not call for third-party intervention, management makes the final determination unilaterally. In some cases, alternatives such as grievance mediation are employed.

Most contracts specify time limits to encourage prompt processing of unresolved grievances through the system. Normally, a grievance must be initiated within a certain period of time, or it will not be permitted to go forward through the appellate route. Such time constraints benefit labor by precluding management from using delay tactics. They also help alleviate employee frustration over untreated complaints. Time limits benefit management by preventing work disruptions and avoiding retroactive pay awards. Both parties gain from the timely use of evidence concerning the grievance. Although the exact time limits vary among contracts, a common requirement is that management representatives render a decision at each step and forward it to the grievant within five or ten working days of receiving the complaint. The employee, if still dissatisfied, has the same period of time to take the case to the next level of appeal.

The time required for grievance resolution is "largely a function of the complexity of the issue and its importance to [the] basic interests" of the parties involved (McPherson, 1983, p. 31). If the parties mutually seek to resolve the dispute quickly and satisfactorily, that is likely to happen. If one or both parties choose to "stand on principle" or fight it out to the end, binding arbitration is the result.

Occasionally, management's interests may be served by foot dragging. For example, where management intentionally violates a work rule in the legitimate interests of efficiency or serving the public, there is little incentive to handle the resulting grievance in a timely fashion. This is because the conventional rule is for employees to "work now, grieve later" to avoid insubordination charges. Thus, management can get away with a contract violation or unfair labor practice while the grievance is pending. However, time limits place a ceiling on such delaying tactics.

C. Representation of the Grievant

1. The Steward

An employee registering a grievance under the contract is entitled to representation by the union steward and, in a growing number of instances, a union or personal attorney. In most public jurisdictions, the employee also has the right to have union representation during disciplinary hearings, investigations of alleged employee misconduct, and arbitration proceedings. The steward plays a key part in representing the employee and ensuring that management implements the provisions of the contract evenhandedly.

The steward fills an elected or appointed position within the union for a term that runs one year or more. The steward typically is obliged to deal with employee problems during working hours. Management recognizes the importance of the steward function by releasing the steward for union work with pay at the regularly assigned rate.

In 2019, bargaining unit employees at the federal level spent about 2.6 million hours performing representation duties on official time. This represents a decrease of 28% compared to fiscal year 2016. The estimated payroll costs (salaries and benefits) for official time in 2019 was $135 million (U.S. Office of Personnel Management, 2020). Representation duties included: participation in term negotiations, mid-term negotiations, dispute resolution, and general labor–management activities. Out of the total number of hours spent on all types of representation duties, bargaining unit employees spent about 390,000 hours processing grievances (U.S. Office of Personnel Management, 2020).

In addition to receiving pay for union work at the regularly assigned rate stewards generally are granted "superseniority" to protect them from layoffs or other management actions that could adversely affect the performance of their duties. Another major function of the steward is to enlist new union members.

A bargaining unit may have several stewards consistent with different levels of management authority. If so, a chief steward exercises some authority over the various shop stewards.

The steward's role can be quite complicated when supervisors belong to the bargaining unit. A steward can be tasked with representing his/her own supervisor before higher management. In other situations, a steward who also happens to be a supervisor may have to represent a subordinate. Even more confounding, the steward's supervisor may have taken the action that gave rise to the grievance. Thus, the steward can represent a grievant who has a grievance against the steward's immediate supervisor, who is also in the bargaining unit and presumably has the right to union representation. Such role confusion stands as compelling testimony for the need to exclude supervisors from rank-and-file bargaining units.

Grievance handling can be a sensitive area for the steward and the union. It is clearly of fundamental importance to both the union and the overall quality of labor–management relations. The steward is in a key role to influence the behavior and attitudes of bargaining unit members. Stewards handle members' grievances and resolve conflicts with management and other bargaining unit employees. Effective stewards can nurture strong commitment to the union and maximize dues-paying membership (Clark & Gallagher, 1988; Keefe, 2003). The quality of labor–management relations is enhanced by stewards who can collaborate effectively with supervisors while fully discharging their representation duties. Stewards rarely receive extra monetary compensation for their efforts to carry out union–management relations within a high-pressure, stressful environment. In many ways, it is a labor of the heart.

2. Union Duty of Fair Representation

The union's duty of fair representation results from its designation as exclusive bargaining agent for all employees in the bargaining unit. In exchange for this designation, the union agrees to represent fairly, honestly, and in good faith all employees even if they are not members of the union. The union's legal duty to represent all members of the bargaining unit is provided for in the contract or in state labor legislation. The standards for determining fair representation were developed in the federal courts for the private sector and applied to public employment, with little consideration given to public/private sector differences. Several key court cases delineate the duty of fair representation.

The most frequently cited case is *Vaca v. Sipes* (1967), in which the Supreme Court held that the only instance in which a union violates its duty of fair representation in deciding not to arbitrate a grievance is when it acts in an arbitrary or discriminatory fashion or in bad faith. The burden of proof, therefore, would rest with the grievant. However, a later decision, *Hines v. Anchor Motor Freight* (1976), held that the "perfunctory" processing of a grievance may also violate the duty of fair representation, particularly where the union does not investigate the potential merits of a grievance before dropping it. Given that unions have limited funds for grievance processing, they cannot take every complaint all the way to arbitration. Under most public sector contracts and statutes, the union—not the grievant—decides which cases it will take to arbitration. Unions typically avoid those that have questionable merit or reflect narrow interests or settling before arbitration.

Although "mere negligence" in grievance handling does not necessarily breach the duty of fair representation, the union does have the legal responsibility to exercise a minimum level of care in meeting time limits and pursuing the evidence submitted by the grievant. The best route for the union is usually to file the grievance, then conduct as thorough an investigation as feasible, dropping the grievance only if it clearly has no merit. Otherwise, the union may be subjected to an unfair labor practice charge or a civil suit for breach of contract. As a result, the duty of fair representation may induce unions to initiate more grievance procedures to avoid potential liability (Bingham et al., 2010).

The union that neglects the duty of fair representation may be courting financial catastrophe. In *Bowen v. U.S. Postal Service* (1983), the U.S. Supreme Court ruled that a union failing to properly represent an employee fired illegally from the job is liable for a portion of the employee's lost wages. Charles V. Bowen, a member of the American Postal Workers Union (APWU), was dismissed by the U.S. Postal Service (USPS) because of an alleged altercation with a fellow worker. He requested the union to initiate arbitration proceedings, but the APWU refused. Bowen then sued the USPS for illegally firing him and sued the union for failing to discharge its duty of fair representation under Section 301(a) of the Labor–Management Relations Act of 1947.

A 5:4 majority held that Bowen was entitled to recover financial damages from both the employer and the union, apportioned according to degree of fault. The Court reasoned that the union's liability begins at the time when final resolution of the dispute would have been obtained through the grievance procedure, had the union fully represented the employee. Thus, the employer's liability is limited, but the union could be held responsible for back wages for years, as a case slowly makes its way through the courts. One outcome could be union bankruptcy. Another result of *Bowen* is that unions, to the consternation of management, now tend to err on the side of caution by carrying even meritless grievances all the way to arbitration. This causes inevitable congestion and delays in the grievance process.

Bowen sounded a warning bell for unions at all levels of government, but it applied specifically only to postal workers covered by the Labor–Management Relations Act. A 1989 U.S. Supreme Court decision held that other federal employees cannot sue their union for breach of the duty of fair representation because an administrative remedy (the FLRA) is provided for by the Civil Service Reform Act (CSRA) of 1978 (*Karahalios v. NFFE,* 1989). At the state and local levels, state courts and public employee relations boards make determinations concerning the duty of fair representation.

IV. GRIEVANCE ARBITRATION

Any grievance procedure is intended to provide strong incentives for the parties to settle quickly. Both generally want to avoid the trouble and expense of a prolonged grievance and to maintain a healthy, cooperative labor relations environment. Inevitably, however, some grievances are not easily resolved. For these troublesome cases, grievance arbitration (also known as rights arbitration) is used as the final step in meeting the complaint. As with other dispute resolution procedures, grievance arbitration has the role of preventing strikes and other labor actions. In addition, grievance arbitration has developed a role as a substitute for litigation of public law claims (Malin, 2010).

In grievance arbitration, an outside neutral is brought in by the parties to review the facts and hear the evidence and testimony favoring each position. The union attempts to show that the contract, language, precedent, or past practice covers the facts of the grievance and that the action taken by management was inappropriate in light of these considerations. Management presents similar evidence to justify the implemented measures. The role of the arbitrator, then, is to render a final binding judgment based on presentations of the evidence and the language of the contract.

Grievance arbitration was first used in the United States in 1871 in the coal industry. It gained widespread acceptance throughout the private sector during World War II as a technique strongly advocated by the War Labor Board to avoid the time and monetary costs of taking contract disputes to the courts. Grievance arbitration was granted formal legal status in Section 203(d) of the Taft–Hartley Act and received further protection through a series of Supreme Court cases known as the "Steelworkers trilogy" (see discussion in Section IV.B). These cases established the doctrine that arbitration awards are not subject to review in the courts unless due process has been denied or the arbitrator has exceeded his or her authority. Today, grievance arbitration has achieved almost universal acceptance in unionized settings in the private sector and is used in many government settings as well. Arbitration of grievances is required in the federal sector as a final step in the negotiated grievance procedure.

Although widely used, grievance arbitration, like interest arbitration, has been condemned by critics as an illegal delegation of government authority to an outside party who is not responsible to the citizenry or to elected officials. There are alternative public sector forums for the binding settlement of grievances, including civil service commissions, state or local government grievance committees, state labor agencies, federal or state equal employment opportunity commissions, and the courts. The courts generally have held that public sector grievance arbitration is not legal unless specifically provided for in appropriate enabling legislation (Bowers, 1976, p. 35). Where enabling legislation exists and the parties involved consent to binding arbitration of grievances, the courts generally view grievance arbitration as legal and desirable, as long as the arbitrator does not exceed his/her/their legal authority in making the decision.

A. Arbitrability

Before a grievance can be taken to binding arbitration and the merits of the case considered, the dispute must be found to be arbitrable. In other words, the disputants must have agreed to place the case before the arbitrator and the arbitrator must have the requisite authority to rule. Claims of non-arbitrability are most often made by management, whose previous decision or action is upheld when arbitration is denied. Claims of non-arbitrability may be raised on procedural or substantive grounds. A determination of procedural arbitrability depends on the extent to which there has been compliance with the requirements set forth in the contract for filing and processing grievances. Substantive arbitrability refers to whether the agreement and the law include or specifically exclude the issue(s) in question from arbitration (Bowers, 1976, p. 65).

Examples of procedural arguments against arbitrability include failure to sign the grievance or submit it in a timely manner, failure to cite the provision of the contract purportedly violated, or other such irregularities. The claim that a dispute should not be arbitrated because the contract has expired has not been supported by the courts as long as it can be demonstrated that the grievance definitely occurred during the life of the contract. Even when grievances are filed after contract expiration, grievance arbitration is usually extended as part of the continuing duty to bargain (Decker, 1994, pp. 160–162).

Substantive grounds for challenging arbitrability include the scope of the definition of "grievance" in the contract, management rights, and conflicts with state or administrative rules. For example, management may claim that an employee's copayment of a physician's bills is to be settled by the employer and the insurance company, not by an arbitrator. Most questions of arbitrability are decided by the arbitrator, although the courts sometimes must make the determination (Decker, 1994, p. 151). Often, an arbitrator will take arbitrability arguments under advisement and hear the merits of the case the same day. This way if the arbitrator decides the case is arbitrable he/she/they can then render a judgment. This increases the risk for both parties and may encourage them to settle voluntarily.

B. Court Review of Arbitrators' Decisions

The presumption of the federal courts in private sector cases has been that issue taken to arbitration should be settled by the arbitrator—not by the courts—based on the terms of the contract. Judges should not substitute their opinions for those of the arbitrator unless the arbitrator is guilty of fraud, misconduct, or gross unfairness, or the award violates established public policy. This basic principle was established in the Steelworkers trilogy, three Supreme Court cases in 1960 involving the United Steelworkers of America. The Court's decisions established arbitration as final and binding and essentially exempt from court review (Edwards et al., 1979, pp. 73–77; Coleman & Vasquez, 1997).

However, deference to the Steelworkers trilogy was relaxed somewhat in *Alexander v. Gardner-Denver* (1975). In this case the U.S. Supreme Court ruled that, contrary to the trilogy, an arbitrator's decision is not final and binding if a violation of Title VII of the Civil Rights Act of 1964 has occurred. Thus, a grievant can pursue a Title VII case through grievance arbitration under the contract or independently in the courts. In other words, statutory rights may outweigh contractual rights. This principle was applied in *Barrentine v. Arkansas Best Freight Systems* (1981). Here the Supreme Court ruled that a grievant's claim arising from statutory rights (the Fair Labor Standards Act, in this case) may be subject to judicial review, even if it was submitted to arbitration earlier.

Some state courts (e.g., Wisconsin and Minnesota) have adopted the trilogy standards wholesale, deciding that arbitrators, not judges, should resolve labor disputes. Other state courts, however, have ignored or given short shrift to the trilogy principles. Some courts have substituted a scope of bargaining test to determine the breadth of the arbitrator's authority. This approach juxtaposes the legal scope of bargaining and the subject of the grievance to decide whether the grievance should have been submitted to arbitration. In other states, courts have overturned arbitrators' rulings because they violated public policy as embodied in statutes, previous court decisions, or common practice (Nicolau, 1997; Bodah, 1999). Other grounds for setting aside an arbitrator's decision are fraud or misconduct by the arbitrator. Errors of fact, law, or interpretation by the arbitrator are not sufficient to invalidate an award (Decker, 1994).

Thus, public sector grievance arbitration may lack a strong presumption of finality depending on the government jurisdiction. The use of grievance arbitration could be significantly altered through court actions involving federal and state regulations, such as equal employment opportunity (EEO), disability, and occupational health and safety standards, if the courts determine that certain individual rights go beyond contract stipulations (Levine, 1985). In public employment, the problem is accentuated by various federal, state, and local laws that precede collective bargaining and provide employees with rights and remedies beyond those established in the bargaining contract.

Perhaps nowhere is this problem better illustrated than in equal employment opportunity issues, where multiple forums exist. As noted in Section III, a discrimination complaint may be taken to grievance arbitration, the FLRA, the EEOC or a state or local counterpart, the federal district court, a state court, or other venues.

A grievance arbitration decision is not necessarily final and binding in discrimination cases, which may be carried from forum to forum with de novo consideration in a continuing search for a finding that satisfies the grievant.

Nevertheless, a U.S. Supreme Court case resolved some of the controversy surrounding binding arbitration provisions for statutory discrimination claims. In *14 Penn Plaza LLC v. Pyett* (2009), the Court concluded that "a collective bargaining agreement that clearly and unmistakably requires union members to arbitrate ADEA (Age Discrimination in Employment Act, 1967) claims is enforceable as a matter of federal law." The decision in *14 Penn Plaza LLC v. Pyett* effectively allows unions and employers to waive the right of employees to a judicial forum for statutory discrimination claims in favor of arbitration (Twomey, 2010).

C. Selection of the Arbitrator

Like interest arbitration, grievance arbitration may be conducted by a single neutral or by a tribunal. Three- or five-member arbitration panels usually are composed of each party's appointees and one or more mutually agreed-upon third-party neutrals. Tribunals offer the opportunity for a full accounting of relevant information and arguments by the parties. The advocate-members can clarify their parties' positions, identify possible problems with a proposed award, and even negotiate a settlement. The single arbitrator is less expensive and more expeditious in issuing a decision—an important advantage that helps account for its substantially greater use (Veglahn, 1987).

Grievance arbitrators, like interest arbitrators, are usually selected from rosters provided by the American Arbitration Association (AAA), the National Academy of Arbitrators, the Federal Mediation and Conciliation Service (FMCS), the relevant state agency, or a local bar association. The organizations furnish management and the union with biographical information on prospective arbitrators. AAA biographical sketches include such pertinent background information as experience, qualifications, and fees. FMCS's Arbitration Information Tracking system provides a computerized biographical data retrieval system, updated after each case decided by an arbitrator, and rotates FMCS arbitrator designees for panel referrals to encourage balanced use of qualified neutrals. These services are provided free by FMCS.

Generally, both the union and management are very interested in the arbitrator's track record, years of experience, and demographic traits. However, such data are of limited utility in predicting an arbitrator's decision (Kauffman et al., 1994). Ordinarily, if the parties are unable to agree on a selection, they will strike names from the FMCS or AAA list until only one remains. Lists typically contain five to seven names.

All arbitrators, regardless of the list on which their name is found, must be paid for their time. Compensation usually varies from $1,000 to $3,000 per day, depending on the reputation, experience, and demand for individual arbitrators and the nature of the case. Additional costs of arbitration include the filing fee; arbitrator's meals, lodging, and travel; and payment for researching and writing the opinion.

Arbitrators vary in their academic training, but most hold graduate or professional degrees and are associated with universities in some manner. Many are based in law schools. The heavy involvement of law school faculty and attorneys has been vigorously criticized by those who claim that lawyer-arbitrators tend to be too technical in procedure, overly aggressive with witnesses and the opposing counsel, overly reliant on precedent, and excessively concerned with winning instead of problem solving. Pro-legalists recognize lawyers' skills in analyzing facts and presenting them in an orderly fashion in the courtroom. They defend the use of attorneys as arbitrators. Still, it is generally recognized that one does not require legal training to perform well as an arbitrator.

Notwithstanding their excellent qualifications and pedigrees, new rights arbitrators have a difficult time gaining acceptance. The number of cases going to arbitration has increased steadily, much faster than the number of arbitrators deemed widely acceptable by labor and management representatives. The qualified but inexperienced arbitrator faces a catch-22 situation familiar to many university graduates. That is, one needs experience to be hired, but one cannot obtain experience without a job. Arbitrator selection consistently favors a relatively small pool of experienced neutrals. These arbitrators have large caseloads and, as a consequence, are slower in deciding awards.

D. Problems in Grievance Arbitration

Two major grievance arbitration problems have already been alluded to: monetary costs and lengthy delays. Other concerns include lack of diversity among arbitrators and barriers to entry in the profession. More serious concerns include lack of transparency and perceived lack of social justice in arbitration cases involving police misconduct. We turn to the concerns over costs and delays first.

1. Monetary Costs and Delays

Given a reasonably healthy labor–management relationship, perhaps the price of arbitration is not completely undesirable. It may inspire the parties to settle at an early stage in the process. Further economic incentive to settle a grievance before arbitration can be achieved through "loser-pays arbitration," in which the party with the weakest case must pay the arbitrator's fees and expenses in their entirety.

When the union and its members, out of frustration or for other reasons, constantly file grievances, petty or otherwise, the work environment becomes toxic. The union can quickly deplete its financial reserves. Sometimes, good faith and common sense are more important to the long-term relationship between the union and management than is resolute attention to contract details.

For example, municipal unions in Hartford, Connecticut, spawned widespread criticism by filing grievances over work done by volunteers. When students from local colleges painted some rooms in a public school, the janitors' union forced the city to pay the janitors hundreds of dollars on the grounds that the union should have done the painting. Similarly, the American Federation of State, County, and Municipal Employees (AFSCME) local filed a grievance over volunteers painting and repairing park benches. Of course, the shoe can fit the other foot as well. A recalcitrant management may constantly violate the contract, forcing the frustrated union to go broke from the expense of appeals or to go on strike in violation of the agreement.

Excessive time delay is the most maligned aspect of grievance arbitration. It may take months from the day a grievance is filed before it reaches arbitration. After that, it may take a year or more before a final judgment is rendered by the arbitrators. Such delays, sometimes exceeding a total of two or three years, can lower employee morale and destroy faith in the collective bargaining agreement. As Coulson (1980, p. 496) explained, "Union members expect arbitration to be a swift and rational avenue of justice. Members become frustrated, alienated, and bitter when they are faced with unexplained delays, when legal mumbo jumbo."

The grievance arbitration process, like any legal or quasi-legal proceeding, is fraught with opportunity for delay and procrastination. As Coulson (1980) notes, the numerous stages of the grievance process provide multiple opportunities for delay. The steps involved are similar to those in a civil or criminal court case and include the following:

1. Preparation for the arbitration hearing (assembling facts and records, obtaining depositions, scheduling witnesses and testimony, and other preliminary matters)
2. Setting the hearing date and format
3. Opening statements to the arbitrator
4. Presentation of the case by the initiating party (documentary evidence, witness testimony, cross-examination, etc.; transcripts may be made)
5. Presentation of the case by the responding party
6. Closing arguments
7. Preparation of the post-hearing briefs (written arguments) and transmittal to the arbitrator
8. Making the award (may consist of a single statement of findings or a summary of the hearing and the arbitrator's reasoning in making the award)

In addition to the complexity of the process, Steel et al. (2022), found that much of the delay in labor arbitration cases can be attributed to procrastination on the part of arbitrators. The arbitrators in the study were highly qualified members of the National Academy of Arbitrators (NAA) with decades of experience. Within this group, procrastination should have been limited and rare. However, Steel et al. (2022) found that procrastination among labor arbitrators was related to dispositional traits such as self-efficacy and sensitivity to time, as well as self-regulatory skills such as organization, multitasking, and pacing style. Arbitrators who scored above the mean for decision time took on average 86 days to prepare their decisions, while those below the mean took roughly 26 days. These delays in writing decisions have negative consequences for the parties to the dispute.

Monetary costs and delays in grievance arbitration are considered to be more serious problems by unions than by management. Management has deeper pockets to pay arbitration costs. As observed in Section III.B, delays often result in management getting its way at least until the arbitration award is rendered. Management's principal concern, according to a survey of users of FMCS arbitration services, is the poor quality of arbitrators' decisions (Berkeley, 1989).

2. Repercussions for the Parties Involved in Arbitration

Another problem with grievance arbitration has to do with what happens to the grievant and his or her supervisor once voluntary or arbitrated settlement occurs. A disturbing analysis of outcomes of grievance activity in four unionized organizations over two- and three-year periods indicates that grievants and their supervisors suffer retribution from their employers. Lewin and Peterson (1999) examined grievance activity and post-settlement outcomes in a steel manufacturing firm, a retail department store, a nonprofit hospital, and a local public school district. Results indicated that grievants' performance ratings, work attendance rates, and promotion rates declined post-settlement. At the same time, turnover rates for grievants increased in comparison to non-grievants. Similarly, supervisors of grievance filers received lower performance ratings and promotion rates and "were significantly more likely to be terminated from their jobs than supervisors of non-filers" (Lewin & Peterson, 1999, p. 572).

These chilling findings were not attributable to grievance filers and their supervisors being less competent performers than non-grievants and their supervisors. No significant differences were detectable in job performance evaluations between the two groups in the years before and during the filing and settling of grievances. The conclusion is that personnel involved in grievances tend to be punished, much like whistle-blowers experience retribution after they expose their employer's wrongdoing. The unfortunate implication for employees who feel they have been treated unfairly on the job is that they should suffer silently or face retribution (Boroff & Lewin, 1997). The message to supervisors is to overlook minor offenses by subordinates.

3. Lack of Diversity and Barriers to Entry to the Profession

Various researchers have called attention to the lack of demographic diversity in the arbitration profession and barriers to entry (Avgar et al., 2023; Gough & Colvin, 2020; Gould, 2006; Green, 2017; Tudy-Jackson, 2011). Avgar et al. (2023) note that approximately 2,000 professional neutrals provide labor/employment dispute resolution services in the U.S. However, most labor arbitration cases are handled by roughly 600 members of the NAA.

To gain entry to the NAA practitioners must meet two conditions. First, they need to have handled at least 50 cases over a 5-year period. Second, they must be nominated by other arbitrators and labor relations advocates. Unsurprisingly, a recent survey (Katz et al., 2023) indicates that 93% of NAA members are white and 79% are male. Only 21% of NAA members are female and less than 7% are Black, Hispanic, or Asian. In a separate survey Gough & Colvin (2020) report that most labor arbitrators are practicing attorneys. Moreover, they are more likely to represent employers (61%) than employees (30%) in their law practices. Arbitrators who have work experience as a management-side defense counsel are less likely to rule in favor of employees in arbitration cases.

The lack of diversity among arbitrators raises multiple concerns. For example, Gould (2006) notes that Black employees bringing charges of racial discrimination on the job are highly unlikely to face an arbitrator who looks like them or has any direct experience with racial discrimination at work. The lack of clear entry points and career ladders for Black, Hispanic, and Asian practitioners makes it difficult to gain a foothold in the profession. The lack of mentors and role models for underrepresented groups pose additional obstacles (Tudy-Jackson, 2011).

4. Perceptions of Social Justice in Cases Involving Police Discipline

Finally, there have been growing concerns about the use of arbitration in cases involving police misconduct. Increasingly, interactions between police and the non-white communities they serve are characterized by apprehension and hostility. Recent cases of excessive force in communities of color have created a sense of urgency around police reforms (Headley & Wright, 2019).

Disciplinary procedures are one tool to hold agencies and officers accountable to the public. The right to appeal disciplinary decisions is a key component of due process and not necessarily a threat to accountability. However, police contracts often include clauses that impede discipline and accountability, such as expungement of records of misconduct and statutes of limitations on imposing discipline (Harris & Sweeney, 2021; Rad et al., 2023).

At the same time, police disciplinary procedures have been criticized as uneven and arbitrary. Rushin's (2021) analysis of arbitration cases over a 14-year period shows that arbitrators reduced or overturned discipline in 52% of cases. Where termination occurred, arbitrators required reinstatement in 46% of cases. Where suspensions occurred, arbitrators shortened the length by 49% on average. The most common reason for overturning or reducing punishment was the arbitrators' perceptions that the punishment was too harsh for the given offense.

Rushin (2021) finds that the disciplinary appeal process for police officers serves as an opportunity to completely re-adjudicate cases before an arbitrator. The original sanction imposed serves as merely the ceiling for disciplinary measures. In the most egregious cases, arbitration may obscure previously alarming offenses and lead officers to be rehired at the same or different departments (Archbold, 2021). As currently structured, police arbitration can usurp disciplinary decisions made by chiefs, city leaders, and civilian review boards. This poses the danger of undermining perceptions of trust, fairness, and police legitimacy in communities.

E. Standards for Arbitrator Decision Making

The degree of arbitrator emphasis on legal principles and procedures reflects the approach taken to grievance arbitration. Those assuming a strict constructionist posture believe the contract should be the primary instrument governing the relationship between the parties and the decision of the arbitrator. Such an approach is likely to require procedural rules as extensive as those used in the courtroom and to mandate written transcripts, court reporters, and post-hearing briefs. "Problem-solving" arbitrators, on the other hand, view the contract as a document providing general guidelines for the parties and the arbitrator, with the arbitrator's function being primarily mediative in promoting mutual accommodation between the parties. Problem-solving neutrals tend to take a more expansive and innovative approach than strict constructionists with their narrow judicial perspective.

Of course, any arbitrator's principal interpretive duty is to make an award in accordance with the express terms and conditions of the contract and the key testimony, evidence, and other elements of the case at hand. The legal doctrine of stare decisis used to establish case precedent in the courtroom does not usually apply to grievance arbitration. Rather, each decision is arrived at de novo, with the existing agreement serving as the primary benchmark for the arbitration award. Arbitrators take a number of specific case-related factors into account in arriving at a decision. These include management's conduct and consistency in applying the language of the contract; the grievant's work history, job performance, and seniority; procedural errors by either party; and various mitigating circumstances (Bohlander, 1994; Haber & Karim, 1995; Simpson & Martocchio, 1997).

In attempting to interpret the contract, arbitrators sometimes find that the language is unclear or ambiguous. For instance, a contract may state that leave time around Christmas should be applied for "as soon as possible." In such cases, certain "rules of contract construction" are adopted by arbitrators, including the following:

1 The common or popular meaning of language takes precedence over a special meaning
2 Technical words are ascribed technical meaning unless local usage clearly indicates a different intention by the parties
3 Conflicts between general provisions and specific provisions are settled in favor of the latter
4 The express inclusion of certain items or guarantees in the contract means that those not listed were intentionally excluded
5 The intent of the parties when the language was written is considered; witnesses, notes, rough drafts, and other sources may be examined to help determine what the parties intended by certain words

When the language of the agreement is exceedingly ambiguous or incomplete with regard to the grievance, the arbitrator must step beyond the contract to determine the parties' intent. Several standards may be used to discern the parties' intent when they signed the agreement. These include past practice, prior bargaining record, previous arbitration awards, and various other conditions.

1. Past Practice

Past practice is the standard most frequently used to clear up hazy language or to guide the arbitrator when the contract is silent. A widely accepted definition of past practice is "a reasonably uniform response to a recurring situation over a substantial period of time which has been recognized by the parties implicitly or explicitly as the proper response" (Miller, 1979, p. 203). As "the objective manifestation of the meanings the parties assumed at the time the agreement was signed" (Ferris, 1975, p. 226), past practices carry great weight in contract interpretation. For example, if municipal trash collectors have been provided with cleanup time at the end of their shift for several years and the director of sanitation suddenly revokes this practice even though job conditions have not changed, an arbitrator (barring contract language to the contrary) would have strong reason for siding with the grieving sanitation workers.

2. Prior Bargaining Record

The second standard used by arbitrators to clarify contract language is the prior bargaining record of the parties, particularly when the new language is confusing. Here, the neutral may examine minutes or other records of bargaining sessions, contract supplements, or, on occasion, oral testimony. A common practice is for the arbitrator to find against the party who drafted new contract language when an ambiguity forces the loss of a benefit by the other party. The logic here is that the drafting party had the opportunity to avoid any potential doubt of the intended meaning of the language. Only when the drafting party can show that the other party had not been confused or misled as to the intent of the language is the drafting party freed of this responsibility.

3. Previous Arbitration Awards

As noted in Section IV.E, stare decisis does not have formal application in grievance arbitration. Each case is treated as unique. Nonetheless, prior decisions can and do exert an impact on subsequent rulings when circumstances are similar. Many awards are published and read by other arbitrators. Although not legally binding, such decisions are likely at least to have an indirect instructive influence on some neutrals.

A study by Dilts and Moore (2009) confirms that labor arbitrators have developed a "common law" of disciplinary arbitration. This may imply that arbitrators look for guidance in the existing body of arbitration decisions. After analyzing 256 discharge and disciplinary arbitration cases, Dilts and Moore (2009) found that arbitrators consistently apply several criteria to decide such cases. These criteria include whether the employer conducted its investigation in a fair and objective manner; whether the employer has applied rules, orders, and penalties to all employees without discrimination; whether the employer gave notice of prohibited conduct to the employee; and whether the penalty was proportional to the seriousness of the offense (Dilts & Moore, 2009).

4. Other Considerations

After listening to the arguments and examining the evidence and elements of the grievance case, the arbitrator must determine which party should prevail. The parties need to construct their arguments carefully to obtain a favorable award. Research shows that arbitrators consider factors in combination rather than in isolation when reaching arbitration decisions (Gely & Chandler, 2008). For example, arguments focused on the events leading to the disciplinary action are more successful for unions when used in combination with arguments related to the work history of the grievant (Gely & Chandler, 2008). Therefore, the parties may need to provide a combination of arguments to be successful.

In cases involving sexual harassment grievances, Abraham and Voos (2021) show that arbitrators take organizational justice into account. From the 1990s through the late 2010s, management became more stringent in punishing sexual harassment. Along with this trend, procedural justice (due process) has played a more prominent role in arbitrators' decisions to overturn or modify management's disciplinary actions. In cases where arbitrators determined that an employee had engaged in sexual harassment, distributive justice (equity) also took on greater importance. That is, the arbitrators determined that the discipline imposed by management was too harsh considering the employee's previous work performance and length of service (Abraham & Voos, 2021).

In most grievance arbitration hearings, the burden of proof rests with the party that brings the action. Management has the burden of proof in disciplinary and discharge cases. The union normally shoulders the burden in contract interpretation issues. Studies have shown that the party bearing the burden of proof loses more often than it wins, no doubt because "it is more difficult to prove a claim than to refute it" (Dilts & Leonard, 1989, p. 340). Interestingly, an early study showed that public sector grievants tend to fare better than private sector grievants in winning cases (Mesch, 1995). Other research has shown that the origin of disciplinary cases, public or private sector, is not significantly related to case outcomes (Dilts & Moore, 2009).

In addition to legal factors, nonlegal factors may have an effect on arbitration outcomes. Like decision makers in all settings, arbitrators often unconsciously filter case information through their sets of personal values. If they permit their personal values to influence their decisions, arbitrators can be guilty of bias. For example, alcohol abusers are often treated more sympathetically in substance abuse discharge cases than are abusers of illegal drugs. The alcoholic tends to be viewed as a person suffering from an illness, but the illegal drug user is held personally responsible for misbehavior. Yet, most contracts do not distinguish between the use of alcohol or other "intoxicants" on the job (Thornicroft, 1989).

Does the grievant's gender matter? The evidence is inconclusive. Early studies found that women were more likely than men to win their grievances (Bemmels, 1988). The implication was that arbitrators, who are predominantly male, tend to give women preferential treatment (as do judges in criminal cases). Subsequent research found either no gender-associated differences in arbitration outcomes (Steen et al., 1994; Dilts & Moore, 2009) or, that women lose more cases than men do (Mesch, 1995). If male arbitrators once acted paternalistically toward female grievants, perhaps they are now sensitized to avoid gender bias. In general, the arbitrator's gender, experience, training, and occupation are not important determinants of case outcomes (Zirkel & Breslin, 1995).

V. GRIEVANCE PROCEDURES IN FEDERAL EMPLOYMENT

No uniform system for handling federal employee grievances was established until President Kennedy issued Executive Order (E.O) 10988 in 1962. E.O. 10988 directed all federal agencies to develop grievance and appellate procedures, including, if desired, advisory arbitration as a final step. Final decision-making authority on grievance systems continued to reside with agency heads, as they were free to reject the advisory opinion of an arbitrator. Meanwhile, grievants could process their complaints through regular, preexisting agency procedures if they so desired. This bifurcated system was roundly criticized by both unions and management. The absence of a final and binding step short of unilateral management action was a source of particular discontent for the unions.

The inadequacies of the federal grievance procedures were addressed in President Richard Nixon's E.O. 11491 of 1969. Specifically, E.O. 11491 permitted negotiated procedures, including binding arbitration, to serve as the exclusive method for resolving grievances over the life of the contract. A subsequent amendment to E.O. 11491 (E.O. 11616) mandated negotiated grievance procedures in all federal labor–management contracts. Under these executive orders, federal agencies and their unions established step-by-step procedures similar to those in the private sector and state and local governments, with many of them culminating in binding arbitration.

Federal grievance procedures today are provided for in Title VII of the CSRA of 1978. The CSRA incorporated many of the executive order provisions. Under the CSRA, federal employees and their unions are guaranteed the right to present and process grievances for cases involving demotions, dismissals, and other adverse actions. They may do so under either the negotiated system or regular agency statutory procedures but not both.

The negotiated grievance procedure is the only channel available to bargaining unit employees for matters covered solely by the contract. Complaints involving discrimination, occupational health and safety, and other matters addressed in federal laws may be processed through the contractual procedure without prejudice to subsequent review of the case by the EEOC, the MSPB, or the federal courts. A federal arbitration award may be appealed by either party to the FLRA on multiple grounds. These include: the terms of the award conflict with existing statutes or agency regulations, the arbitrator exceeded his or her authority, the award was not taken from the written contract, the arbitrator was biased or refused to hear pertinent information, or the award was based on incomplete information (Edwards et al., 1979).

The award must be appealed within 30 days, or it becomes final. All federal labor agreements today must provide for some form of final binding arbitration. A majority stipulate that a single arbitrator is to be chosen from lists provided by the AAA or FMCS and that arbitration costs be shared by the parties. The grounds for contesting arbitration awards are fairly narrow. Appeals pertaining to adverse actions by management may be taken directly to the federal courts. Despite this alternative, a relatively high percentage of federal awards are appealed to the FLRA (Frazier, 1986), causing case backlogs. The FLRA usually upholds the arbitrator's decision.

Generally, the federal grievance process has not received great acclaim. Frivolous and frequent complaints clog up a system that becomes plagued by high costs and cumbersome, lengthy procedures. The options for informal resolution of problems at an early stage are scarce (Roberts, 1994; Sulzner, 1997). In recent years, understaffing at the FLRA has exacerbated the backlogs. As noted in Chapter 3, on average the FLRA took 395 days in 2021, 405 days in 2022, and 299 days in 2023 to decide/resolve arbitration case appeals. This timeline is not expected to improve substantially in coming years due to ongoing vacancies in key Presidential positions (U.S. Federal Labor Relations Authority, 2023).

VI. NEW DIRECTIONS IN GRIEVANCE HANDLING

Criticisms leveled at conventional grievance procedures have led to a search for reforms and alternatives that would be faster, simpler, and less expensive. One reform, known as expedited arbitration, essentially speeds up existing arbitration processes. Other new directions in handling grievances are characterized by the term "alternative dispute resolution."

A. Expedited Arbitration

Expedited grievance arbitration (also known as "instant arbitration") is designed to reduce the time and monetary costs of resolving grievances. It was first used in the private sector in a 1971 contract between ten steel producers and the United Steelworkers of America to reduce a large backlog of unsettled grievance cases. In public employment, expedited arbitration was initiated in a 1973 contract between postal workers and the USPS.

Expedited arbitration systems vary from place to place, but most are characterized by the following:

1 Cases are screened to identify routine, nonprecedential grievances; such cases are then sent on to expedited arbitration
2 An informal atmosphere is maintained, with no transcripts or written briefs
3 The arbitrator must issue the award within a very short period of time (often following a brief recess or 24 hours)
4 The award is written in one page or less
5 The arbitrator may hear more than one case in a single day
6 Costs are low and are shared by the parties

Expedited arbitration differs from conventional grievance arbitration in its informal, nonjudicial atmosphere and the timelier nature of the proceedings. Expedited arbitration is not intended to replace regular arbitration. Rather it is intended to be used in conjunction with traditional arbitration to quickly resolve less important or minor grievances.

A large accumulation of minor disciplinary cases persuaded the USPS and four major unions to implement expedited arbitration on an experimental basis in

1973. Within two years, the backlog had been reduced substantially (Frost, 1978, p. 468). Today, expedited arbitration in the USPS begins with a national screening committee that assigns grievances to expedited or regular arbitration. Cases to be expedited are listed with the FMCS or AAA for assignment by those organizations to individual arbitrators. Decisions may be issued either orally or in a one-page written form required within 48 hours of the completion of the hearing. Awards may not be used as precedent for subsequent cases.

Although expedited arbitration in the USPS has recorded time and cost savings, some difficulties have arisen. Initially, there was a high rate of resignations by arbitrators who felt overburdened by the pressure of hearing up to three cases per day. The dropout rate decreased considerably as arbitrators became more accustomed to the procedure. In addition, like other grievance procedures, expedited arbitration suffers from a shortage of trained personnel. However, the USPS instituted a training program in conjunction with the AAA that has helped alleviate this problem.

Critics have charged that expedited arbitration discourages joint problem solving between the parties and that the lack of precedent and written decisions discourages uniformity in arbitration awards. At the same time, the process offers important advantages. When routine, relatively uncomplicated complaints are processed, there should be little or no loss of decision quality. Grievances concerning job reinstatement or back pay are especially suited for expedited arbitration because the rapid decision diminishes the financial liability of the employer while ensuring that a wronged employee receives what is coming without delay. Expedited arbitration reduces both costs and delays in settling grievances. A popular adage holds that "justice delayed is justice denied." As long as its limitations and proper applications are understood, expedited arbitration can help public employees receive a fair and timely hearing of their grievances.

B. Alternative Dispute Resolution

Labor–management conflict tends to escalate. Conflict may grow directly, such as through increasingly vitriolic confrontations or indirectly, through ignoring the conflict until the problem inflates into significant proportions. As noted in Section IV.D, the conventional grievance processes, court actions, and regulatory procedures are likely to be time consuming, expensive, and frustrating. In these adversarial processes, for every winner there is a loser. The basic premise of ADR is that labor and management representatives can constructively confront issues and mutually explore their fair resolution. Conflict is viewed not as warfare, but as an opportunity to develop positive outcomes that reasonably satisfy both parties (Faerman, 1996).

ADR includes a variety of processes and mechanisms that involve joint decision making in which the parties, with the assistance of a facilitator or mediator, work through their problems until they find a settlement with which they can live. Hence, grievances are resolved before they move to arbitration. The relationship between the parties does not suffer from adversarial engagement; ideally, it even improves.

C. Grievance Mediation

Grievance mediation involves intervention by a neutral mediator into a potential or actual impasse over the application or interpretation of contract terms. The goal of grievance mediation, like mediation of interest disputes, is for the neutral to help the parties resolve their differences voluntarily. The mediators act much as they would in an interest dispute, meeting individually and jointly with the parties to try to devise a mutually acceptable settlement. Grievance mediators may use their knowledge of the facts to convince the party with the weaker position to settle instead of going to arbitration (Caraway, 1989, p. 496). Like mediators of interest disputes, grievance mediators may use directive, nondirective, or a combination of both strategies to facilitate a settlement between the parties.

Grievance mediation offers cost savings because it avoids arbitrator fees, attorneys' fees, travel, and related legal costs. Cost advantages also accrue because grievance mediation is a much faster process than arbitration. For example, Goldberg (2004) found that in a private-sector context that grievance mediation took on average 43.5 days to complete compared to 473 days for arbitration. The mediator operates in a relatively informal and highly flexible atmosphere free from the procedural constraints placed on an arbitrator. The mediator's proposed solution, for instance, normally does not have to be reduced to writing, and case preparation is much less thorough. Monetary savings are particularly significant for federal sector grievance mediation, where the FMCS will furnish a mediator to the parties without charge, and in state and local jurisdictions that avail themselves of FMCS services or free mediation aid from the state labor relations agency. Even when mediators must be paid, savings over arbitration may easily run into thousands of dollars.

An additional advantage of grievance mediation is that it sets no precedents for future contract interpretation. If, for example, a grievance arises over an issue that has not fully ripened, such as discrimination against a domestic partner, it may be more advisable to mediate a settlement than arbitrate it because the binding feature of arbitration may cause future problems. Thus, grievance mediation allows a new issue or problem to develop more fully before a precedent-setting ruling addresses it.

Users of grievance mediation (both grievants and management) report greater satisfaction with the final resolution of the dispute than do those who go to arbitration. For example, Coggburn et al. (2020) find that satisfaction with the mediation process and perceptions are high for both grievants and respondents. The process is much less adversarial and combative than arbitration. It relies on joint problem solving by the parties, who may explore a variety of options without risking anything even if arbitration must ultimately be employed. The mediator helps the parties sort out the key issues from the less important ones and to discover where their true interests reside. Then, the mediator helps develop a solution that satisfies the interests of both parties (Kriesky, 1994). Favorable results have been reported from California (Caraway, 1989), Massachusetts (Bonner, 1992), Michigan (Gregory & Rooney, 1980), Ohio (Nelson & Uddin, 1995), Washington (Skratek, 1987), the USPS, and several federal agencies. Coggburn et al. (2020) conclude that mediation provides a sensible middle ground between the complex steps involved in traditional grievance handling and attempts to strip public employees of workplace protections.

The USPS has been a leader in grievance mediation, implementing a number of pilot projects during the 1990s. For example, under the REDRESS program (Resolve Employment Disputes Reach Equitable Solutions Swiftly), members of bargaining units are offered an alternative to the conventional EEO complaint process (USPS, 2024). Within two weeks of receiving a request, the USPS schedules mediation. The EEO Alternative Dispute Resolution specialist selects and sends an experienced neutral to the USPS facility. The employee may choose to be represented by a private attorney, a union representative, or a coworker. The mediator applies interest-based techniques to help resolve the dispute. If mediation fails, the employee may return to the conventional EEO process.

A 72.3% case closure rate was recorded for the REDRESS program (Bingham et al., 2009). Rather than achieving a maximum number of settlements, the primary aim of the REDRESS program is to have a positive, transformative effect on the relationship between management and employees. Therefore, the case closure rate, in addition to cases in which the parties settled their disputes through mediation, includes cases in which the parties reached an agreement within 30 days thereafter and cases in which the complaining party dropped, withdrew, or failed to pursue the case further (Bingham, et al., 2009). REDRESS users reported satisfaction with mediators, outcomes, speed of outcomes, as well as with their ability "to control the process, present one's views and participate in the process, and receive respect and fair treatment from the mediator" (Bingham, 1997, p. 29; Bingham et al., 2009). A study that compared the REDRESS mediation model to the EEO complaint process and grievance arbitration found that employees were more satisfied with the mediation process than with the other two dispute resolution procedures (Bingham et al., 2010). Reports on grievance mediation experiences in state and local governments also indicate substantial savings in time and money, remarkably high rates of settlement, and overall satisfaction with the process on the part of both unions and management (Kriesky, 1994).

Are the much-touted benefits of grievance mediation as great as reported? Feuille (1992) has raised questions about the accuracy of reported time and monetary savings. He suggested that a large proportion of the grievances sent to mediation would not have been arbitrated anyway because of being dropped or settled before arbitration. Moreover, he has proposed that the existence of mediation might keep grievances active longer and thereby increase total costs. Thus, the purported benefits of grievance mediation could be illusory (Feuille, 1992).

The race and gender of mediator may create expectations of symbolic and active representation for those workers choosing to use grievance meditation. In a study of the USPS REDRESS program, Hibbard et al. (2022) raise concerns about the impact that mediators' race and gender can have on the grievants' satisfaction with the outcome of their cases. Specifically, for sex discrimination and race discrimination cases, the grievants were less satisfied with the outcome when the mediator's gender or race matched that of the grievant. Hibbard et al. (2022) conclude that the requirement for mediators to conduct their cases impartially restricts the ability of female and African American mediators to represent the grievants' interests.

There are other disadvantages to grievance mediation. There is the predictable shortage of trained neutrals. Arbitrators appear to be unsuitable for grievance mediation chores because of a basic professional conflict of interest. That is, if grievances can be settled at a low cost through mediation, fewer cases will pass on to arbitration. As a consequence, the income of arbitrators will atrophy. Also, the lack of a written record and formal procedures makes grievance mediation inappropriate for seminal, precedent-setting cases or complex EEO-type cases that can be litigated beyond the contractual procedures.

Other ADR methods include the ombuds and peer review. The ombuds is a neutral third party designated by an organization to assist a grievant in resolving a conflict. The ombuds may provide counseling, help develop factual information, and attempt to reconcile the disputing parties through the power of persuasion. Usually, the ombuds is hired by the organization to work full time at resolving conflicts.

Peer review uses a panel of employees (or employees and managers). Prior to review, the panel receives training in handling sensitive issues. The panel then listens to the parties' arguments, reviews the evidence, and makes a decision on the issue in dispute. The decision of panel members may or may not be binding on the parties (U.S. General Accounting Office, 1997).

VII. CONCLUSION

Labor and management alike share important responsibilities to ensure that they and their constituencies live with the contract in a reasonably efficacious fashion. In a healthy cooperative relationship, they avoid the "brinkmanship" of constantly pushing grievance procedures to the final step in an effort to make the other side blink. Both parties strive to ensure that their representatives in labor–management relations, especially supervisors and union stewards, are well trained in grievance handling and intimately familiar with the terms and conditions of the agreement. Both sides explicitly seek to keep communication channels open and clear and resolve grievances at the lowest level possible. Finally, both strive to keep time and monetary costs low.

Each party has its own special responsibilities in effectively administering the agreement and handling grievances. For its part, management should monitor the behavior of supervisors in administering the contract to ensure negotiated grievance procedures are functioning properly and grievants receive a fair hearing. Management also should be willing to admit when it is wrong.

Union representatives should carefully screen employee complaints and drop those that are petty. At the same time, they take great care to ensure that valid grievances receive a fair hearing. The union must also take caution to represent each member of the bargaining unit with the same energy and dedication, whether the employee is a member of the union or not. Conflict on the terms and conditions of the contract is both inevitable and healthy. The goal is to manage that conflict productively and avoid damaging the long-term relationship between the parties.

CASE STUDY 10.1 CHAIN OF CUSTODY

On March 1, the city of Garden Way hired Thelma Woodall, age 23, as an administrative assistant in the office of the mayor. Thelma was the top candidate among those interviewed for the job, and she appeared to be a bright, energetic, and personable employee.

Garden Way had recently begun a mandatory drug-testing program in which all essential and confidential employees are randomly screened for illegal drug use. Thelma was tested on March 3, and her urine sample was positive for marijuana. At first, Thelma denied using marijuana, but finally she admitted taking two puffs on a reefer at a party on February 10. She said it was the only occasion she had ever used any prohibited substance.

Thelma was discharged both for the positive drug test results and for initially lying about her drug use. She appealed through the grievance procedure and was represented by her local AFSCME unit. In arbitration, management introduced as evidence the two reasons for Thelma's discharge along with the fact that she was still a probationary employee. The union introduced evidence that a significant chain-of-custody problem existed with the urine sample and asserted that the sample could not be traced conclusively to Thelma. Additionally, the union stated that Thelma's drug use occurred before she was hired, that it took place off the job, and that her performance on the job to date had been excellent.

Questions

1 If you were the arbitrator hearing this case, explain what your ruling would be and the reasons you would give for your decision

2 Explain what additional evidence, facts, or testimony you would seek

3 Is it fair and reasonable to discharge Thelma, given the circumstances of the case?

CASE STUDY 10.2 THE ARBITRATION CASE OF KEYSHAUN KING

Keyshaun King, a motor pool mechanic, had been a good employee for more than seven years. But he was fed up with Billy Barnhill, another mechanic. Barnhill was a bumbler, always dropping tools, nicking hoses, and banging bumpers. However, he tended to do okay when closely supervised. He had occasionally made comments to King and other African American workers that could be interpreted as racist, but they tried to overlook his insensitivity in the interest of positive workplace relations.

King had tried his best to be tolerant, but on August 2, when Barnhill's wrench slipped from an alternator and smacked into King's cheek, leaving a 2-inch gash and a certain bruise, King's patience evaporated. In pain, King grabbed the wrench from Barnhill and pushed him away. Two other employees heard King yell in pain and saw him grab the wrench and shove Barnhill.

Barnhill took exception to King's reaction, muttered "You people are all alike!" and marched into the shift supervisor's office to report the incident, asserting that King had attacked, assaulted, and threatened him. The supervisor, Jimmy Jackson, dismissed Barnhill and called King into his office. "What happened, Keyshaun?" he asked. King admitted seizing the wrench with one hand and bracing against Barnhill's shoulder with the other. He also related what he heard Barnhill say. Jackson sent both employees home for the day.

Jackson was aware that Barnhill was borderline incompetent, but he had had no cause to take disciplinary action against him until now. He liked Barnhill's loyalty and dependability along with his willingness to pitch in and work overtime when needed, but this incident troubled him. Was there just cause to fire one or both of them? Or would a lesser disciplinary action be more appropriate?

Jackson went to the employee manual, where he read the following passage:

> Just cause shall serve as the basis for disciplinary action and includes, but is not limited to: dishonesty, inefficiency, unprofessional conduct, falsification of records, fighting, racial or sexual taunting, violation of city policy, destruction of property, or possession or being under the influence of alcohol or narcotics.

He would have to take the issue to higher management authority, the chief motor pool supervisor.

The chief supervisor, Hank Hawkings, was known as a hard ass. He had recently dealt with another physical altercation on a different shift, for which he fired both combatants without a hearing. This case did not appear to be terribly distinct; so, in the interest of consistency, Hawkings called each worker into his office the next morning when they reported to work and sacked them both.

King and Barnhill both appealed the action. You are the grievance arbitrator.

Questions

1 Which arguments should be given greatest weight: those based on the employee manual, those based on the collective bargaining agreement, or mitigating factors given by the grievant and his witnesses? Explain

2 How might "unprofessional conduct," "taunting," and "fighting" be defined? Explain

3 How would you rule in this case? Explain the reasons for your decision

REFERENCES

14 Penn Plaza LLC v. Pyett. (2009). 556 U.S. 247.

Abraham, S. E., & Voos, P. B. (2021). Procedural and distributive justice in sexual harassment arbitrations: Evolution of decisions in the union context. In *Advances in industrial and labor relations* (pp. 99–123). Emerald Publishing Limited.

Age Discrimination in Employment Act of 1967 (ADEA; 29 U.S.C. § 621 to 29 U.S.C. §634).https://www.eeoc.gov/statutes/age-discrimination-employment-act-1967

Alexander v. Gardner-Denver. (1975). 415 U.S. S. Ct. 36, 7 EPD.

Archbold, C. A. (2021). Police accountability in the USA: Gaining traction or spinning wheels? *Policing: A Journal of Policy and Practice*, *15*(3), 1665–1683.

Avgar, A. C. (2021). Relational exchange in non-union firms: A configurational framework for workplace dispute resolution and voice. *ILR Review*, *74*(3), 607–636.

Avgar, A. C., Colvin, A. J., Katz, H. C., & Nobles, K. G. (2023). A fragmented and heavily privatized dispute resolution system: The United States. *Industrial Relations Journal*, *54*(4–5), 304–320.

Barrentine v. Arkansas Best Freight Systems. (1981). 450 U.S. 728, 90 LC.

Bemmels, B. (1988, January). The effect of grievants' gender on arbitrators' decisions. *Industrial and Labor Relations Review, 41*, 251–262.

Bemmels, B. (1994, January). The determinants of grievance initiation. *Industrial and Labor Relations Review, 47*, 285–301.

Berkeley, A. E. (1989, November). The most serious faults in labor-management arbitration today and what can be done to remedy them. *Labor Law Journal*, 728–733.

Bingham, L. B. (1997). Mediating employment disputes: Perceptions of REDRESS at the United States postal service. *Review of Public Personnel Administration*, *17*(2), 20–30.

Bingham, L. B., Hallberlin, C. J., Walker, D. A., & Chung, W. T. (2009). Dispute system design and justice in employment dispute resolution: Mediation at the workplace. *Harvard Negotiation Law Review*, *14*(1), 1–50.

Bingham, L. B., Raines, S. S., Hedeen, T., & Napoli, L. M. (2010). Mediation in employment and creeping legalism: Implications for dispute systems design. *Journal of Dispute Resolution, 2010*(1), 129–150.

Bodah, M. (1999). Rethinking the Rhode Island trilogy: An erosion of the judiciary support for arbitration. *Journal of Collective Negotiations*, *20*(1), 53–67.

Bohlander, G. W. (1994). Why arbitrators overturn managers in employee suspension and discharge cases. *Journal of Collective Negotiations*, *23*(1), 73–89.

Bonner, R. (1992). *Grievance mediation in state and local government.* State and Local Government Labor Management Committee.

Boroff, K., & Lewin, D. (1997, October). Loyalty, voice and intent to exit a union firm: A conceptual and empirical analysis. *Industrial and Labor Relations Review, 51*, 50–63.

Bowen v. U.S. Postal Service. (1983). 103 S. Ct. 588.

Bowers, M. H. (1976). *Contract administration in the public sector (PERL no. 53)*. IPMA.

Budd, J. W. (2021). *Labor relations: Striking a balance* (6th ed.). McGraw Hill.

Caraway, J. M. (1989, Fall). Grievance mediation: Is it worth using? *Journal of Law and Education, 18*, 495–502.

Choi, Y., & Chung, I. H. (2016). Voice effects of public sector unions on turnover: Evidence from teacher contracts. *Public Personnel Management*, *45*(2), 213–233.

Clark, P. F. (2021). The impact of new member orientation programs on union member commitment: Evidence from a national study in a post-Janus setting. *Labor Studies Journal*, *46*(2), 158–181.

Clark, P. F., & Gallagher, D. G. (1988, Fall). The role of the steward in shaping member attitudes toward the grievance procedure. *Labor Studies Journal, 13*, 3–17.

Coggburn, J. D., Daley, D. M., Jameson, J. K., & Berry-James, R. M. (2020). Assessing the six-factor model of organizational justice in the context of workplace mediation. *Review of Public Personnel Administration*, *40*(3), 355–383.

Coleman, C., & Vasquez, J. (1997). Mandatory arbitration of statutory issues under collective bargaining: Austin and its progeny. *Labor Law Journal*, *48*(12), 703–726.

Coulson, R. (1980). New views of arbitration: Satisfying the demands of the employee. In *Proceedings of the 1980 spring meeting* (pp. 495–497). IRRA.

Daugherty, D. (2011). Union initiated obstacles that limit discretionary power of mid-level managers of the social security administration. *Hilltop Review*, *5*(1), 78–85.

Decker, K. H. (1994). Public sector grievance arbitration procedures. In J. Rabin, T. Vocino, W. B. Hildreth, & G. J. Miller (Eds.), *Handbook of public sector labor relations* (pp. 135–182). Dekker.

Dilts, D. A., & Leonard, E. C., Jr. (1989). Win-loss rates in public sector grievance arbitration cases: Implications for the selection of arbitrators. *Journal of Collective Negotiations, 18*(4), 337–344.

Dilts, D. A., & Moore, J. S. (2009). Do arbitrators use just cause standards in deciding discharge and discipline cases? A test. *Journal of Labor Research*, *30*(3), 245–261.

Edwards, H. T., Clark, R. T., Jr., & Graver, C. B. (1979). *Labor relations law in the Public Sector* (2nd ed.). Bobbs-Merrill.

Faerman, S. R. (1996). Managing conflicts creatively. In J. L. Perry (Ed.), *Handbook of public administration* (pp. 632–646). Jossey-Bass.

Feder, D. L. (1989, May). Pick a forum—any forum: A proposal for a federal dispute resolution board. *Labor Law Journal, 40*, 268–280.

Ferris, F. D. (1975, July–August). Contract interpretation—a bread-and-butter talent. *Public Personnel Management, 4*, 223–230.

Feuille, P. (1992). Why does grievance mediation resolve grievances? *Negotiation Journal*, *8*(2), 131–145.

Frazier, H. B., III. (1986, March). Arbitration in the federal sector. *The Arbitration Journal, 41*, 70–76.

Frost, F. W. (1978, August). New developments in labor arbitration: Expedited arbitration experience in the U.S. postal service. *Labor Law Journal*, 465–469.

Gely, R., & Chandler, T. D. (2008). Exploring the "lumpiness" of grievance arbitration decision making. *Journal of Collective Negotiations, 32*(4), 287–305.

Goldberg, S. B. (2004). How interest-based, grievance mediation performs over the long term. *Dispute Resolution Journal, 59*(4), 8–16.

Gough, M. D., & Colvin, A. J. (2020). Decision-maker and context effects in employment arbitration. *ILR Review, 73*(2), 479–497.

Gould, W. B., IV. (2006). Kissing cousins: The federal arbitration act and modern labor arbitration. *Emory Law Journal, 55*, 609.

Green, M. Z. (2017). Reconsidering prejudice in alternative dispute resolution for Black work matters. *SMUL Reviews, 70*, 639.

Gregory, G. A., & Rooney, R. E., Jr. (1980, August). Grievance mediation: A trend in the cost-conscious eighties. *Labor Law Journal*, 502–508.

Haber, L. J., & Karim, A. R. (1995). Arbitral standards in public sector and private sector substance abuse discharge cases: A comparison. *Journal of Collective Negotiations, 24*(1), 55–61.

Harris, C., & Sweeney, M. M. (2021). Police union contracts: An analysis of large cities. *Policing: A Journal of Policy and Practice, 15*(1), 622–634.

Headley, A. M., & Wright, J. E. (2019). National police reform commissions: Evidence-based practices or unfulfilled promises? *The Review of Black Political Economy, 46*(4), 277–305.

Hibbard, P. F., Blomgren Amsler, L., & Jackman, M. S. (2022). Representative bureaucracy and organizational justice in mediation. *Journal of Public Administration Research and Theory, 32*(4), 717–735.

Hines v. Anchor Motor Freight. (1976). 424 U.S. 554, 96 S. Ct. 1048.

Karahalios v. NFFE. (1989). 57 Law Week 43 11.

Katz, H., Colvin, A., Avgar, A., Nobles, K., & Gough, M. (2023). *2022 NAA member survey: Diversity, practice characteristics and remote technologies*. https://ecommons.cornell.edu/server/api/core/bitstreams/6677c345-a097-4e81-8449-01471a009f41/content

Kauffman, N., Vanlwaarden, D., & Floyd, C. (1994). Values and arbitrator selection. *Labor Law Journal, 45*(1), 49–54.

Keefe, J. H. (2003). Can unions be transformational agents in public sector workplace redesign? In J. Brock & D. B. Lipsky (Eds.), *Going public: The role of labor management relations in delivering quality government services* (pp. 211–234). Industrial Relations Research Association.

Kochan, T. A. (1980). *Collective bargaining and industrial relations*. Irwin.

Kriesky, J. (1994). Workers' rights and contract grievance dispute resolution. In J. Rabin, T. Vocino, W. B. Hildreth, & G. J. Miller (Eds.), *Handbook of public sector labor relations* (pp. 233–252). Dekker.

Labig, C. E., Jr., & Greer, C. R. (1988, Winter). Grievance initiation: A literature survey and suggestions for future research. *Journal of Labor Research, IX*, 1–27.

Levine, M. J. (1985, Spring). Judicial review of arbitration awards: Criticisms and remedies. *Employee Relations Law Journal, 10*, 669–683.

Lewin, D., & Peterson, R. (1999). Behavioral outcomes of grievance activity. *Journal of Industrial Relations, 38*(4), 554–575.

Malin, M. H. (2010). The evolving schizophrenic nature of labor arbitration. *Journal of Dispute Resolution, 2010*(1), 57–87.

McPherson, D. S. (1983). *Resolving grievances: A practical approach*. Reston Publishing.

Mesch, D. (1995). Arbitration and gender: Analysis of cases taken to arbitration in the public sector. *Journal of Collective Negotiations, 24*(3), 207–218.

Meyer, D. (2002). Problem creation and resolution in unionized workplaces: A review of the grievance procedure. *Labor Studies Journal, 27*(3), 81–99.

Miller, R. L. (1979). An arbitrator looks at contract interpretation. *Journal of Collective Negotiations, 8*(3), 197–208.

Muchinsky, P. M., & Maasarani, M. A. (1980). Work environment effects on public sector grievances. *Personnel Psychology, 33*, 403–414.

Nelson, N. E., & Uddin, M. (1995, April). Arbitrators as mediators. *Labor Law Journal*, 205–213.

Nicolau, C. (1997). Whatever happened to arbitral finality? Is it their fault or ours? *Labor Law Journal, 40*(5), 151–160.

Peach, D., & Livernash, R. (1974). *Grievance initiation and resolution*. Harvard University Press.

Price, M. (2009). *Teacher union contracts and high school reform*. Center on Reinventing Public Education, University of Washington.

Rad, A. N., Kirk, D. S., & Jones, W. P. (2023). Police unionism, accountability, and misconduct. *Annual Review of Criminology, 6*, 181–203.

Rahim, M. A. (1992). *Managing conflict in organizations* (2nd ed.). Praeger.

Roberts, H. C., Jr. (1994). Contemporary perspectives and the future of American unions. In J. Rabin (Ed.), *Handbook of public sector labor relations* (pp. 393–417). Dekker.

Rushin, S. (2021). Police arbitration. *Vanderbilt Law Review, 74*, 1023.

Scott, C., & Suchan, J. (1987, Spring). Public sector collective bargaining agreements: How readable are they? *Public Personnel Management, 16*, 15–22.

Simpson, P. A., & Martocchio, J. J. (1997). Factors on arbitration outcomes. *Industrial and Labor Relations Review, 50*(2), 252–267.

Skratek, S. P. (1987, June). Grievance mediation of contractual disputes in Washington State public education. *Labor Law Journal, 38*, 370–376.

Steel, P., Taras, D., Ponak, A., & Kammeyer-Mueller, J. (2022). Self-regulation of slippery deadlines: The role of procrastination in work performance. *Frontiers in Psychology, 12*, 783789.

Steen, J., Perrewe, P., & Hochwater, W. (1994). A reexamination of gender bias in arbitration decisions. *Labor Law Journal*, *45*(5), 298–305.

Stewart, G., & Davy, J. (1992). An empirical examination of grievance resolution and filing rates in the public and private sectors. *Journal of Collective Negotiations*, *21*(4), 323–335.

Sulzner, G. T. (1997). New roles, new strategies: Reinventing the public union. In C. Ban & N. M. Riccuci (Eds.), *Public personnel management: Current concerns, future challenges* (2nd ed., pp. 157–172). Longman.

Thornicroft, K. W. (1989, September). Arbitrators, social values, and the burden of proof in substance abuse discharge cases. *Labor Law Journal*, 582–593.

Tudy-Jackson, J. (2011). Non-traditional approaches to ADR processes that engage African-American communities and Africa-American ADR professionals. *Capital University Law Review*, *39*, 921.

Twomey, D. P. (2010). The Supreme Court's 14 Penn Plaza, LLC v. Pyett decision: Impact and fairness considerations for collective bargaining. *Labor Law Journal*, *61*(2), 55–66.

U.S. Federal Labor Relations Authority (FLRA). (2023). *Performance and accountability report 2023*. https://www.flra.gov/system/files/webfm/FLRA%20Agency-wide/Public%20Affairs/PAR/FLRA%20FY2023%20PAR.pdf

U.S. General Accounting Office (GAO). (1997). *Alternate dispute resolution. Employers experience with ADR in the workplace*. GAO.

U.S. Office of Personnel Management. (2020). *Taxpayer-funded union time usage in the federal government fiscal year 2019*. https://www.opm.gov/about-us/reports-publications/agency-reports/taxpayer-funded-union-time-fy-2019.pdf

U.S. Postal Service (USPS). (2024). *How REDRESS works*. http://about.usps.com/what-we-are-doing/redress/about.htm

Vaca v. Sipes. (1967). 386 U.S. 171, 87 S. Ct. 903.

Veglahn, P. A. (1987, June). Grievance arbitration by arbitration boards: A survey of the parties. *Arbitration Journal, 42*, 47–54.

Zirkel, P. A. (2016). Teacher-school board grievance arbitration awards in the courts: Facts and figures. *Dispute Resolution Journal*, *71*(1), 87.

Zirkel, P. A., & Breslin, P. H. (1995). Correlates of grievance arbitration awards. *Journal of Collective Negotiations*, *24*(1), 45–54.

Chapter 11

Public Employee Unions in the Future

I. INTRODUCTION

Like a prizefighter on the ropes trying to survive and recover, unions in the United States are in danger of a technical knockout. Private sector labor organizations have been buffeted by many forces during the past 75 years and as noted in Chapter 1, they seem to be headed down for the count. Public employee unions have been rocked by blows as well but will survive to finish the fight. Following a brief discussion of the steady decline of private sector unions, this concluding chapter examines the growing challenges and seemingly shrinking opportunities for unions in government.

II. DECLINE OF PRIVATE SECTOR UNIONS

Labor union membership in the private sector workplace has been falling since 1954. At the apex of union density, one-third of the nation's nonagricultural workers were members of unions. The proportion had fallen to about 12% by 1990 and dropped to a meager 6.0% in 2023. Despite occasional excitement and expressions of hope in the labor community, and the promises of more vigorous national leadership, the labor movement is in a much-weakened position today.

The fading fortunes of private sector unions have generated an abundance of discussion, debate, and scholarly research. Membership decline is attributed to far-reaching economic changes in the United States and abroad. These include structural changes in the economy, a shift away from manufacturing and toward the service sector, globalization, increasing use of technology, and the changing composition of the workforce.

International competition and offshoring played key roles in the decline of manufacturing in the U.S. The manufacturing jobs that remained were shifted from high-wage, union-friendly locations in the rust belt to low-wage, union-hostile places in the southern states (Nunn et al., 2019; Visser, 2019). Moreover,

DOI:10.4324/9781003403593-11

service sector workers proved difficult to organize because the workplaces are much smaller than manufacturing settings and the transaction costs of union organizing are higher. In addition, high turnover in the service sector weakens employees' commitment to unions (Naidu, 2022).

The rise in non-standard work arrangements also contributed to the decline in unionization. In essence, employers decentralized human resource management, created customized working schedules, and separated work tasks into smaller components. These arrangements facilitated the subcontracting of employment and greater use of part-time employees and temporary workers (Visser, 2019). Advancements in technology facilitated the rise of the gig economy. Many gig workers in large technology companies such as Uber, Lyft, and DoorDash are classified as independent contractors. Therefore, they are not protected under existing labor laws.

Finally, politics played a role in the decline of unionization. Organized labor has successfully advocated for policies that protect all workers, such as health and safety standards, unemployment benefits, and retirement benefits. In the service sector, organized labor has pushed for increases in the minimum wage through campaigns such as "The Fight for $15" and pressured large corporations like Walmart and Amazon to increase workers' pay. While the campaigns have had some success in raising wages, these policies do not directly build union power (Naidu, 2022). Despite these policy gains, unions lack a unified political base. Over the past decade, Republican candidates have gained support from blue collar workers. In recent elections, blue collar workers have been driven more by economic concerns like high rates of inflation and difficulty buying homes than they have been by the social elements of the Democratic platform (Katz, 2023).

In the United States, changes in social and political values have elevated individualism and the pursuit of wealth over the values of social equity and collective action that nurtured unionization. Public policy under the National Labor Relations Act (NLRA) is only marginally conducive to unionization and collective bargaining (Bazelon, 2020; Kochan et al., 2023). The effectiveness of the law varies with presidential administrations. Under Bush administration appointees (2001–2009), the NLRB was consistently hostile toward unions and collective bargaining. For example, its rulings extending collective bargaining exemptions by expanding the definition of "supervisor" undermined collective bargaining rights for a large number of union members. Even a Democratic Congress and president proved unable to level the playing field for unions during the Obama years (2009–2017). Unions hung their hopes on the proposed Employee Free Choice Act, which would have established the right of employees to gain union representation through majority sign-up rather than by secret ballot elections. However, the Employee Free Choice Act failed to pass Congress on at least five occasions.

Under Donald Trump's first presidential term (2017–2021) the NLRB scaled back private sector workers' rights to form unions and engage in collective bargaining. The changes were made through a series of NLRB decisions, rulemaking, and general counsel initiatives. Some of the changes enacted include placing limits on where and how workers can organize and protest, fragmenting bargaining units, weakening the test for independent contractor status, and narrowing the range of actions considered to be protected concerted activities. In addition, the NLRB was underfunded and understaffed during Trump's first term (Bazelon, 2020, McNicholas et al., 2019).

During the Biden presidency, the pendulum swung back toward protecting workers' rights. To begin with the Biden administration initiated and Congress approved a $25 million increase in funding for the NLRB. This funding allowed the Board to avert cutbacks in staffing and services. In addition, under Biden the NLRB restored a broader definition of protected concerted activity and a more protective test of independent contractor status. The General Counsel initiated an awareness campaign to inform workers of their rights under the law. The NLRB also established partnerships with other federal agencies such as the Department of Labor, Department of Justice, Federal Trade Commission, and the Consumer Financial Protection Bureau to promote coordination, information sharing, and enforcement (Meyerson, 2023; Rhinehart et al., 2024). Despite these changes, the Board still lacks sufficient funding and staffing to address the needs of the growing number of private sector workers and the increased number of claims being filed. To illustrate, the total case intake at NLRB field offices increased 23% in Fiscal Year 2022 (NLRB, 2024).

The revitalization of the AFL–CIO under the leadership of John Sweeney (1995–2000) raised hopes of boosting the fortunes of unions. As noted in Chapter 1, those hopes were dashed in 2005 when several unions including the Service Employees International Union (SEIU), Teamsters, Carpenters, Laborers, United Farm Workers, Food and Commercial Workers (UFCW), and UNITE-HERE established their own umbrella organization called Change to Win (CTW). In 2009, Sweeney stepped down from his position and Richard L. Trumka was elected president of the AFL-CIO.

Although CTW promised to build power for workers, it soon lost momentum. Internal conflicts due to the SEIU's radical restructuring of health-care locals and overreach in the internal affairs of UNITE-HERE weakened CTW. In 2009, the UFCW, UNITE-HERE, and the Laborers left CTW. These unions rejoined the AFL-CIO in 2010. The Carpenters also left CTW in 2009 and the Teamsters left CTW in 2022. Neither rejoined the AFL-CIO (Early, 2023).

Also, in 2022 the remaining members of CTW, the SEIU and United Farm Workers, joined together with the Communication Workers of America (CWA) to launch a mission driven organization known as the Strategic Organizing Center (SOC). SOC has supported organizing campaigns at Starbucks and among service industry workers in the South. It has also supported efforts to identify and improve health and safety issues at Amazon warehouses (Strategic Organizing Center, 2024).

In an effort to strengthen organizing and collective bargaining rights, labor unions invested their energy on the Richard L. Trumka Protecting the Right to Organize Act (The Pro Act). The act, named after the late AFL-CIO leader, is designed to hold employers accountable for violations of workers' rights, expand the range of employees covered under labor law, protect worker voice, and modernize union elections and enforcement processes (AFL-CIO, 2024). The act is opposed by business and industry groups as well as most Republican legislators. It was introduced in Congress in May 2019, February 2021, and February 2023. Each time the act has failed to gain traction.

High profile union organizing campaigns at Starbucks, Amazon, and Volkswagen have garnered media attention. In 2023, 191,000 workers gained union representation. Areas of union growth in the private sector include manufacturing, transportation and warehousing, private educational services, and private health care and social assistance. Despite these gains, the overall percentage of workers represented by unions declined from 11.3% to 11.2% (Shierholz et al., 2024). Even when they do organize, unions face strong opposition from employers. For example, union organizers at Starbucks have often been fired after successful campaigns. Starbucks workers and Starbucks Workers United have filed hundreds of unfair labor practice claims with the NLRB (Jamieson, 2023).

In general, employers spend over $400 million per year on union avoidance consultants (McNicholas et al., 2023). As of 2022, Starbucks had retained had at least 110 attorneys from the largest union avoidance firm in the U.S., Littler Mendelson. Under Littler Mendelson's guidance Starbucks deployed an array of tactics including holding multiple captive audience meetings, spamming employees with anti-union text messages, hiring new employees just ahead of union elections, and providing raises to employees at non-union stores, while denying them to employees at unionized locations (Facundo, 2023).

Although the organizing victory at the Amazon warehouse in Staten Island in 2022 raised hopes, by mid-2024 they had not organized other locations or secured a first contract. Amazon management filed challenges to the election and refused to meet at the bargaining table with the union. Amazon also implemented a new policy that prohibits off-duty employees from entering facilities or outdoor workspaces. Amazon then charged a union organizer with violating the policy and terminated his employment. These policies are likely to discourage further organizing (Chapman & Hadero, 2024; Hsu, 2023).

The UAW fared slightly better in its efforts to secure gains for workers. In November 2023, the UAW secured historic gains for autoworkers at General Motors, Ford, and Stellantis. Specifically, the contract provided for wage gains of at least 25% over the next four years, improvements in the 401k plan, and cost of living increases tied to inflation. As with any negotiation, the UAW did not get everything on their list of demands (e.g., retiree health care and pensions). It did end years of concession bargaining and the gains were sufficient to win ratification by the membership (Domonoske, 2023). With this victory, the UAW turned to organizing production plants in the South. The UAW successfully organized a Volkswagen plant in Chattanooga, Tennessee. From there the UAW planned to organize a Mercedes-Benz plant in Vance, Alabama, and a Hyundai plant in Montgomery, Alabama. However, the workers at the Mercedes-Benz plant voted against unionization in May 2024 and the campaign at Hyundai was put on hold (Bisaha, 2024).

Subsequently, UAW President Shawn Fain came under investigation by a court-appointed monitor amid allegations that he retaliated against a vice president for failing to comply with actions that would have benefitted Fain's domestic partner and her sister. The UAW has been under federal monitorship since 2021 as a result of corruption charges against former union leaders. Eleven of the previous leaders were convicted of felonies (Scheiber, 2024). Although the monitor noted that the UAW had improved its structures for audits and compliance, concerns remain over personnel compliance, and perceptions of favoritism (Campbell, 2024)

In 2009, on the heels of the Great Recession, union approval dropped to an all-time low of 48% (Saad, 2023). However, for the past several years, favorability ratings have hovered between 67% and 71%, among the highest levels of approval since the 1960s (Gallup, 2024). At the same time, levels of support differ across political affiliations and demographic characteristics. Roughly 94% of Democrats, 67% of Independents, and 49% of Republicans support unions (Brenan, 2024). By gender, approval levels were marginally higher for women (70%) than men (67%). Similarly, 75% of non-white respondents approved of unions compared to 68% of white respondents. The union approval rate for younger workers (age 18–34) stands at 77%, while that of older workers (55+) is 66% (McIntosh, 2024). Moreover, multiple recent polls show that workers today are substantially less likely to oppose unionization than they were in the past. There has also been an increase in the number of workers who are unsure if they would support unionization in their workplace. Ahlquist et al. (2024) label this group the "union curious."

Although the downward spiral of private sector unions is slowing, the barriers to reversing the trend in a meaningful way are high. To begin with, U.S. employers use a wide array of legal and illegal tactics to discourage employees form joining unions. A recent study indicates that private sector employers were charged with violating federal law in 41.5% of union representation cases before the NLRB (McNicholas et al., 2019). As noted earlier, the union avoidance industry is rapidly expanding. The four largest union avoidance firms regularly appear on lists of the top 50 law firms in the U.S. Two of the top firms, Littler Mendelson and Ogletree Deakins, both had revenues exceeding half a billion dollars in 2018 (Logan, 2019).

Attorneys from these firms have been appointed to various government positions with labor agencies. For example, William Emanuel, a former senior union avoidance consultant with Littler Mendelson was appointed to the NLRB and served from 2017–2021. Similarly, Katherine Templeton, a former union avoidance consultant with Ogletree Deakins, served as the North Carolina Director of Labor, Licensing, and Industry under Governor Nikki Haley and was considered for a cabinet position as Secretary of Labor under the first Trump administration (Logan, 2019).

In some cases, local politicians have sided with private sector employers in persuading employees not to join unions. To illustrate, during the 2014 campaign to organize workers at the Volkswagen plant in Chattanooga, Tennessee, State Senator Bo Watson threatened workers with the loss of state subsidies if they voted in favor of the union. He emphasized that the state was "pro-business" and "Right to Work." House Majority Leader Gerald McCormick also advised workers to reject the union (Webb, 2014). In a subsequent organizing campaign in 2019, Tennessee Governor Bill Lee led a captive audience speech at the plant in which he promoted non-union workplaces and encouraged employees to communicate directly with the employer instead of the union (Evanoff, 2019). Pressure from elected officials adds one more obstacle for private sector unions.

III. CHALLENGES FOR PUBLIC EMPLOYEE UNIONS

Like their counterparts in the world of business, unions in government also confront challenges. Although they have not yet experienced the downward spiral suffered by private sector organizations, public employee unions reached a membership plateau during the early 1980s. For the past three decades, they have been weathering an uncomfortably high level of public and legislative attacks. These have manifested through calls for outsourcing and privatization of public services, citizen resistance to paying taxes and fees, negative public opinion about government and its workers, and legislative rollbacks of longstanding collective bargaining rights. For purposes of discussion, the principal challenges confronting public employee unions may be categorized as fiscal, structural, public policy, and strategic.

A. Fiscal Squeeze

Even during periods of strong national economic prosperity, government growth has been moderate. However, following the Great Recession (2007–2009), governments at all levels experienced lengthy periods of retrenchment. The federal budget soared to record deficits in 2012. The downturn created strong pressures for tax cuts, exposed the financial weakness of Social Security and Medicare, and elevated the persistent policy problems of Medicaid funding, public education, environmental protection, and criminal justice, among other priorities. Federal, state, and local budget cuts resulted in hundreds of thousands of public employee layoffs. The flow of federal dollars normally passed through to the states and localities was turned down in volume. State and local governments encountered structurally induced budget weakness for several years.

Democratic and Republican legislators and chief executives were forced to deal with the fiscal squeeze in ways unfavorable to unions and their membership. For example, cost-of-living-adjustments (COLAs) in most state and local government pension plans were adjusted downward. States and localities raised copays for health care, raised the retirement age and time-in-service for pensions, and shifted toward defined contribution or hybrid pension plans to lower employers' costs.

During the immediate aftermath of the Great Recession, compensation increases were absent or modest in most jurisdictions. State and local employment dropped sharply even in growing jurisdictions, depressing union membership figures. Contracting out government services to private and nonprofit providers displaced public employees' jobs across the country. The federal government's response to the recession, the Troubled Asset Relief Program (TARP), prevented an even sharper downturn, but it was insufficient to foster a rapid recovery and job growth.

Both wages and employment were stagnant over the next decade. Employment in the federal, state, and local government sectors was slow to rebound to prerecession levels. In many areas of the country, public sector employment remained below 2007 levels at the start of the COVID-19 pandemic. Employment in state governments did not return to pre-recession levels until 2016. Local governments returned to prerecession levels in 2019 (Hinkley, 2020).

The COVID-19 pandemic brought about a rapid decline in economic activity and steep job losses at the beginning of 2020. By the end of April 2020, approximately 20 million jobs were lost. At the federal level, policy makers enacted extensive recovery and relief programs though the Coronavirus Aid, Relief, and Economic Security (CARES) Act in 2020 and the American Rescue Plan in 2021 to strengthen the economy and alleviate hardship (Center on Budget and Policy Priorities, 2024). Overall, the federal government transferred $900 billion to state and local governments during and after the COVID-19 pandemic. Of these funds, The American Rescue Plan provided $350 billion in direct support to state and local governments. As a result, employment in state and local governments recovered much faster than it did following the Great Recession (Van Nostrand et al., 2024).

As of 2021, most states were contributing sufficient resources to their retirement systems to keep pension debt stable. Even the states that were deficient in 2014—Kentucky, Michigan, New Jersey, and Rhode Island—were above the threshold for potential insolvency in 2021 (Pew, 2023). As noted in earlier chapters, public sector wage gains have historically been fairly modest. However, in 2022 and 2023 many unions fought to recoup losses resulting from cost-cutting measures during the pandemic. Unions representing state and local government workers were particularly vocal as they represent many front-line service providers who had to assume risk and stay on the job during the pandemic. Pay raises in the public sector averaged 4.1% in 2022 and climbed to 5.5% in 2023 (Combs, 2024).

The implications for public employee unions are mixed. Public sector employment fell during both the Great Recession and the COVID-19 Pandemic. The recovery was smoother for the COVID-19 Pandemic, due in large part to the substantial provision of federal funding. Wage gains in some areas were outweighed by rising inflation. For example, salaries for higher education faculty increased by an average of 4% from 2021 to 2023. However, inflation was nearly 6% over this period and the end result was a loss in purchasing power. Stress and burnout among frontline service providers has led to increased turnover. Public schools are facing a severe teacher shortage, with 406,964 teaching positions either unfilled or staffed by teachers not fully certified for their assignments (Tan et al., 2024). Law enforcement is also facing staffing shortages. The shortage of police officers is not new, but it was exacerbated the COVID-19 and social protests over police use of force (Hutton, 2024). Social services are another area facing severe shortages. The U.S. Bureau of Labor Statistics has identified a shortage of 74,000 social workers each year for the next decade, with rural areas facing the biggest gaps. As with other frontline workers, caregiver fatigue is having a negative impact on morale and contributing to burnout (Castronuovo, 2024). The implications are negative for government and citizens alike, as agencies lose critical employees and their reservoirs of institutional memory.

For the unions, these trends have important implications. First, membership rolls have declined in many jurisdictions, with a corresponding weakening in union financial resources and bargaining power. Second, fiscal constraints mean that unions are able to do less for the members of their bargaining units in terms of wages and benefits, no matter how fiercely they engage in the political arena and at the bargaining table. Ironically, public employees may perceive the need for collective representation most strongly during times of government fiscal stress, but they may also see unions as less able to deliver improvements for them.

B. Structural Challenges

Like the business sector, the public sector is experiencing new global economic, political, and social forces. Among the most critical of these forces for public employees and their unions are technological change, the attractions of a market economy that has produced a resource shift from government to the private sector, and the changing demographics of the workforce. Public employee unions enjoyed some of their greatest early success in organizing blue-collar and office workers who performed job tasks that essentially replicated those in the private sector. Gradually, however, technological innovations have made it increasingly feasible to replace such employees with machines, software, and artificial intelligence.

The character of much government work (e.g., police and fire protection, classroom teaching, and social service casework) makes technological substitution for labor problematic. Nonetheless, new technology and software have supplanted some public employees, in areas such as printing and production, HR and finance, data entry, and sanitation collection. There are many other examples of technologically driven attrition, and additional ones will emerge. For unions to maintain their levels of membership and financial resources, members displaced by technology must in turn be replaced by signing up new members or establishing new bargaining units for previously non-represented workers.

A second structural threat to unions is a shift in ownership, management, financing, or control of public services from government to the private economy. Multiple forces, including tax resistance, negative public opinion toward government, and public worship of the private marketplace, are conspiring to transfer government functions and activities to the private and nonprofit sectors. These powerful forces are augmented by the common perspective that, at least in theory, private and nonprofit service providers could accomplish nearly all of the work of government. This line of reasoning represents a serious threat to public employee unions.

The negative effects of privatization and outsourcing on public employee unions are obvious. Privatization depresses public employment and union membership. Many of the jobs being outsourced are those of direct service providers such as counselors, caseworkers, laborers, and corrections officers. Other common examples of contracting out are water services and sanitation. As a result, the relative proportion of predominantly nonunion professional and administrative positions is growing.

Privatization's effects are registered with every public job lost to a private or nonprofit provider. For example, several states have turned over various components of welfare program administration to private contractors, placing an estimated quarter of a million government social service jobs at risk. In the embattled public education community, thousands of teaching jobs have been lost to private schools as voucher plans are adopted. Despite such general affection for privatization, there is little evidence of genuine cost savings. For instance, a meta-analysis of 38 studies on water provision and solid waste collection services "does not reveal a systematic relationship between cost savings and private production" (Bel et al., 2010).

The third structural problem is a human capital challenge. It is common knowledge that the U.S. labor force is becoming increasingly female, older, Latino, African American, Asian, and foreign-born. These trends are projected to extend into the near future. Some of these new workers require special accommodation by employers and unions. The culture of work is undergoing dramatic change with important implications for interpersonal, interorganizational, and supervisor-subordinate relations.

The organizational health and well-being of public sector unions depends greatly on how effectively they respond to employment issues associated with demographic and sociocultural changes in the labor force. To remain viable organizations, unions must convince the new workforce that they can effectively represent the interests and concerns and job-related needs of these workers. As demonstrated by largely unsuccessful efforts to organize Southern workers and recruit new members from the expanding information technology sector, the unions' record is mixed.

In general, out of necessity, public sector unions have chalked up a much better record of incorporating women and minorities into union affairs and leadership positions than private sector unions. The American Federation of Government Employees (AFGE); American Federation of State, County, and Municipal Employees (AFSCME); the National Education Association (NEA); the American Federation of Teachers (AFT); and SEIU report substantial numbers of women and people of color in their ranks, including top leadership positions. AFSCME has aggressively pursued discrimination complaints. Public employee unions have also promoted and bargained for more flexible and family-friendly benefits.

As if these other structural challenges were not daunting enough, the baby-boom retirement bulge presents another. With an increasing proportion of today's baby boomers eligible for retirement with each passing year, unions are facing a significant loss of staunch union advocates and leaders. Given these changes, unions need to turn their unwavering attention to young labor force entrants.

C. Public Policy Challenges

Whether one subscribes to the theory that comprehensive bargaining laws generate high levels of union membership or to the competing theory that high levels of unionization impel such laws, there is a strong positive relationship between the two variables. Public employees in comprehensive bargaining states are in a highly favorable policy environment, as reflected by strong membership figures. As is true of distributive and redistributive policies everywhere, what is once granted is difficult to take away. Until very recently, public managers and most elected officials had little incentive to take on public employee unions in jurisdictions in which bargaining rights are strong and widely applied. Managers did not want to sacrifice valuable time and human resources to a losing assault on unions. For their part, politicians must consider public employee votes and union campaign contributions.

Nonetheless, the Great Recession ushered in a sea change in public sector labor relations. The retrenchment of public sector collective bargaining rights was driven by well-funded corporate conservative activists and Republican gains in state legislatures and gubernatorial offices in what Peck (2016, p. 6) terms a "fast-policy project." The primary internal and external actors were governors, legislators, and state political parties. The go-betweens in the diffusion of restrictive labor policies included organizations such as American Legislative Exchange Council (ALEC), the State Policy Network (SPN), and Americans for Prosperity (AFP). These organizations collaborate with large corporations and legislators to promote business-friendly legislation. Some of the most prominent corporate associates include Koch Industries, Altria/Phillip Morris, Corrections Corporation of America, and Connections Academy (an online education corporation) (Hertel-Fernandez, 2018; Lafer, 2017).

In the wake of the 2007–2009 economic crisis, anti-union policies spread quickly through what is known as copy-and-paste lawmaking (Jansa et al., 2019) and aggravated policy experimentation (Peck, 2016). Public officials aggressively sought to revoke state bargaining laws in states such as Wisconsin, Ohio, Indiana, Michigan, Idaho, and Tennessee. Attacks on union security provisions through right-to-work legislation—and legislative restrictions on the political use of union dues—occurred in several states. As has been noted, such actions severely damaged union strength in affected jurisdictions.

In addition to legislative restrictions, three U.S. Supreme Court eroded the precedent set in *Abood v. Detroit Board of Education* (1977) that allowed public sector unions to collect agency fees from employees who choose not to become members of their unions. In the first of these cases, *Harris v. Quinn* (2014), the U.S. Supreme Court ruled that the collection of agency fees from home care workers who do not wish to join the union was unconstitutional. In the second case, *Friedrichs v. California Teachers Association* (2016), the court deadlocked in June 2016. In the third case *Janus v. American Federation of State, County and Municipal Employees* (2018) the court overturned agency fee provision the grounds that it interfered with public employees' free speech rights. Since unions have a legal duty to represent all workers in the bargaining unit, the ruling on this case poses an enormous free-rider problem for public sector unions.

Outcomes following the *Janus v. AFSCME* decision have been mixed. Some states acted to further weaken public sector collective bargaining rights. Arkansas prohibited collective bargaining for all public employees except police, firefighters, other public safety officers, and federal transit workers. With respect to union security, state level legislation made it easier for employee to opt out of the union (Indiana and Florida), required employers to inform employees of their right to opt-out (Indiana, Florida, Oklahoma, Michigan, and Texas), and prohibited public employers from using payroll dues deduction (Arkansas–teachers only, West Virginia, Florida). Arizona banned release time for public sector employees to conduct union business. Oklahoma did not officially ban release time, but it prohibited employees from receiving salary and benefits and accruing seniority while on release time. The state of Florida took restrictions a step further by requiring public sector unions to maintain a level of 60% of bargaining unit employees as dues paying members. Unions that fail to maintain this level are required to hold annual recertification elections.

Other states expanded public sector collective bargaining rights. For example, Virginia granted collective bargaining rights to local government employees and Colorado granted bargaining rights to state and county employees. Several states made payroll dues deductions easier (California, Hawaii, Illinois, Massachusetts, and Washington). Ten states enacted legislation making it easier for unions access to existing and new employees by providing unions with contact details and/or unions access to new employee orientations. California, Massachusetts, New Jersey, New York, and Rhode Island have allowed unions to provide members-only services and in some cases to charge non-members for grievance handling and arbitration. Other states have enacted provisions to prohibit public sector employers from discouraging employees from joining the union or encouraging them to resign from the union and to revoke their dues authorization (California, Connecticut, Illinois, New Jersey, and Washington).

Without membership expansion, unions in government risk the same stagnation and subsequent membership losses that have decimated their counterparts in the corporate world. Although the greater danger comes from existential assaults on unions through revoking collective bargaining rights, privatization remains an imminent threat. Whether it is NPM, reengineering, right sizing, or whatever the next management fad is called, further privatization could significantly deplete union membership and resources and keep public sector unions in a reactive and defensive posture. At the federal level, President-elect Donald Trump's plan to create a Department of Government Efficiency heightens concerns over downsizing and privatization. The losses for federal, state, and local unions could rise substantially due to persistent pressures to contain labor costs and reduce the size of government.

D. Strategic Challenges

The strategic choices to be made by public employee unions are equally daunting. Like their private sector counterparts, they are caught in a web of global and domestic forces that threaten to deplete their political and economic resources and reduce membership levels. The redistribution of service-provision activities and jobs to the private and nonprofit sectors represents a serious challenge for public sector unions, as does the weak support for public service on the part of citizens and elected officials. However, in comparison to private sector unions, those representing government employees generally function in a less hostile political environment. In general, their strategic choices and actions have been more astute and their national leadership more adept at coping with emerging challenges and issues than has been the case with unions in the private sector.

Their political proclivities mean that public employee unions are pulled toward the Democratic Party. However, especially at the local level, union leaders have learned how to work on all sides of the table. Symbiotic relationships between unions and elected and appointed officials of all political persuasions are common. The mutuality of interests ranges from fighting for better health care to seeking jurisdiction-wide improvements in pay and benefits for all public servants. The opportunity for multilateral bargaining with elected officials provides public employee unions with multiple paths to political influence during contract negotiations.

Police unions, in particular, wield a substantial amount of power because they bargain directly with the state or local entity that employs them. Most elected officials do not want to appear unsupportive of the police force. In addition, elected officials often seek the endorsement of police unions as well as contributions from their political action committees (Clark, 2024).

Although favorability of unions in general is trending upward (Gallup, 2024), support for public sector unions is not universal. Advocacy organizations such as ALEC and SPN, as well as think tanks such as the Commonwealth Foundation view public sector unions as a drain on taxpayers' resources. For example, Anzia and Moe (2015) contend that public sector unions drive up the costs of government through both collective bargaining and political action. Similarly, they conclude that labor laws produce effects that benefit Democrats and harm Republicans (Anzia & Moe, 2016). Teacher unions receive more than their fair share of blame for the perceived shortcomings of public education (Donn & Kirby, 2024). Teachers' unions adamantly oppose threatening education reform proposals, such as abolishing teacher tenure or establishing voucher plans. In most cases, the unions have been successful in these endeavors and have, as a consequence, come to be perceived as a major obstacle to change (Hartney & Flavin, 2011; Mishak, 2012).

In the years after the Great Recession state legislative attempts to restrict collected bargaining rights often targeted teachers, while shielding police and firefighters (Wade, 2018). Attacks on teacher unions through films such as *Won't Back Down* and *Waiting for Superman*, accompanied by orchestrated criticism campaigns sponsored by conservative groups, pushed the NEA and AFT into a corner (Greenblatt, 2012). Even traditional Democratic allies of teacher unions have wavered, criticizing union intransigence over education reform proposals. The criticism reached a new low when the former secretary of state and C.I.A. director Mike Pompeo called Randi Weingarten "the most dangerous person in the world" in 2022 (Mahler, 2023). She remained a topic of discussion at the 2024 Republican national convention.

Within a difficult and ever-changing economic and political environment, public sector unions have demonstrated a degree of adaptability. They have achieved consistently better results from their organizing activities than private sector unions. Since the beginning of the modern era of public sector collective bargaining, nearly all unions in government have, perhaps as much out of necessity as by choice, made special efforts to organize women and minorities and to elevate them into leadership positions. Exceptions are police and firefighter organizations, which, until recently, resisted members who were not white males.

Successful unions have sought out dissatisfied workers of all demographic characteristics in any setting. SEIU and AFSCME, in particular, have demonstrated that they have learned this key principle about leveraging public employee work dissatisfaction into membership gains. Pay inequity is an example of an issue causing dissatisfaction among female workers that unions have successfully exploited. Another is poor treatment of immigrant workers. Low pay, minimal benefits, and poor working conditions for custodial, nursing home, daycare, and health-care workers have presented organizing opportunities as well.

On the whole, national public employee union leadership has been superior to and much more statesmanlike than that of private sector organizations. Union leaders have helped their respective organizations strategically adapt and respond to enormous changes in their environments, finding ways to float with the social, economic, and political currents rather than trying to swim upstream. Such adaptive behavior will continue to be critical to public employee unions as they marshal their resources to confront the challenges facing them today.

Astute national leadership is critically important to the future success of unions in the public sector. So is the quality of leadership in the thousands of locals throughout the federal, state, and local governments. However, in more instances than the unions would care to admit, some locals have acted selfishly, irresponsibly, and stupidly in assiduously protecting their perceived rights and contract provisions. Featherbedding, working to the rule, insisting that volunteers be forbidden to perform needed union-related work, calling ill-advised work stoppages, and aggressively defending felonious or incompetent members are some examples.

Strategic errors and public relations miscues at the lowest levels can rebound into issues of national media visibility, confirming the beliefs of those who dislike unions and causing a negative bias in the opinions of previously neutral observers. It is impossible to know with any degree of empirical precision just how adept local leadership is. It is known that a large proportion of local union presidents are part-time representatives who have risen through the ranks with little or no specialized training or preparation other than on-the-job experience (Sulzner, 1997, pp. 168–169). The potential benefits of training and education for these individuals should be obvious to national organizations.

IV. OPPORTUNITIES

The profound structural, political, technological, economic, and related changes that are affecting public employee unions pose various known and unknown dangers. At the same time, they also present opportunities. To survive, public employee organizations must adapt to these critical changes in their environment through innovative strategies and actions designed to roll back the tide of anti-unionism fervor and recapture public and political support.

Although there is extraordinarily little if anything that unions can do about the fiscal conditions, they can help management search for productivity and efficiency improvements that enhance organizational performance. Recognizing that employee financial gains are seldom going to exceed the annual rise in the cost-of-living index, and that exceedingly generous health-care and retirement benefits are likely to be contained, or rolled back, unions can focus their attention at the bargaining table on other issues. These include working conditions, various human resource policies, and productivity enhancements. Many potential bargaining issues do not have significant financial impacts. Examples include flexible working hours, telecommuting, and flexible benefits packages.

The structural changes confronting unions present certain opportunities. NPM poses a number of challenges to unions, but it is simply not going to succeed in organized jurisdictions without union cooperation. Management recognizes that employee organizations must be integrally involved in reengineering, job redesign, privatization, and other initiatives if they are to get off the ground, let alone succeed. To defuse the typical automatic union opposition to contracting out work, for example, public officials can provide unions with opportunities to demonstrate how they can help cut costs and enhance efficiencies through participation and collaboration in work design (Gerhart, 1994, pp. 125–129).

Unions in Cleveland, Indianapolis, Phoenix, and other cities have insisted on submitting their own bids to win back contracted work, and in many instances, they have been successful. Research indicates that when unions respond constructively to privatization discussions and proposals, mutually acceptable solutions short of privatization can often be found (Jalette & Hebdon, 2012). When public officials are determined to fully shift a service to a private or nonprofit provider, unions can turn their effort to ensuring that no current union members will lose their jobs. They can also commit resources to organize those nongovernment workers who are performing the contract work.

The rapidly expanding ranks of public employee telecommuters and contract workers offer an interesting opportunity to unions. Technology adoption during the COVID-19 pandemic catapulted the "virtual office" from concept to reality. A growing number of jobs can be performed almost anywhere and do not require fixed office space and standard work hours. Federal and state government employees are increasingly working from home part time or full time. Some "digital nomads" operate from a portable office as they travel from location to location. A recent report by the U.S. Office of Personnel Management (2022) noted that telework in federal agencies improved attainment of goals in employee recruitment, attitudes, and retention. Moreover, agencies that were able to track costs reported substantial savings in commuting costs and reduced employee absences.

Telework is recognized as being good for the environment (fewer cars on the road), good for employees' stress levels (no long morning and afternoon commutes), and good for the organizational budget (reduced need for physical office space). Although federal, state, and local government unions have advocated for strong remote work policies following the COVID-19 pandemic, the question remains, is telecommuting good for unions? The virtual office removes employees from much daily interaction with their coworkers and effectively makes them free agents, working on their own with minimal daily supervision. The tendency is toward worker autonomy, not collective action through an employee organization. Telecommuting lends itself to contract workers rather than to permanent employees, as work is transformed from a communal enterprise to an autonomous individual activity. On the other hand, even stay-at-home employees may perceive a need for representation on such issues as the type of equipment needed and who should provide and service it, ergonomic and health-and-safety considerations, and the need for an organization to look out for employees' interests when they are not physically on the job site every day.

Despite a slight decline in public employee union membership during 2021–2024, several potentially rich organizing opportunities remain. One of them is rather conventional in that it involves low-wage workers in tough working environments, the traditional mother lode for union organizing in private employment. Sometimes neglected in the scholarly and media attention paid to globalization, information technology, and outsourcing are the working conditions of the low-paid but particularly important public and nonprofit workers who clean office buildings, empty bedpans, and deal with young children and senior adults who cannot help themselves.

Paul Johnston (1994) has described the organizing possibilities presented by "social movement unionism," in which the interests of custodial workers, nurses, and others converge with social causes involving women, minority, and immigrant workers in low-wage public jobs. According to Johnston, when unions frame their demands for these workers in such a manner as to make them congruent with public policy in the public interest, they have the potential for success. Examples include framing improved pay and benefits and favorable work rule changes in the context of union demands for racial, social, gender, and economic justice (Engeman, 2015; Lyon, 2023; Mareschal & Ciorici, 2021)

An early success was the Justice for Janitors movement, which tied together demands for improving the compensation and working conditions of custodial workers with a call for an end to economic and social bias against predominantly Black and Latino workers. SEIU 1199 in Florida represents low-wage workers in nursing homes and other facilities. Florida 1199 partnered with local chapters of the National Association for the Advancement of Colored People (NAACP), Haitian organizations, immigrant rights organizations, and others to create progressive alliances in advocating for workers' rights (Devinatz, 2008; Nissen, 2003). In

Baltimore, AFSCME partnered with religious groups and other organizations in support of a living wage for impoverished workers (Devinatz, 2008). Teachers' unions have also taken up common good bargaining and broadened their demands to encompass issues such as access to health care, housing, immigration, and racial justice (McCartin et al., 2020).

An important target today is the burgeoning health-care industry, which lies at the nexus of the public, nonprofit, and private sectors in hospitals, clinics, nursing homes, and related entities. The health-care sector is expected to account for roughly 45% of employment growth from 2022 through 2032 (U.S. Bureau of Labor Statistics, 2023). Moreover, union density in the sector stands at 8.2% (U.S. Bureau of Labor Statistics, 2024). Health-care unions have traditionally linked their demands to broader public interest issues. For example, these unions contend that addressing issues such as understaffing and mandatory overtime will lead to improved patient care (Avgar et al., 2024).

In recent years there has been a surge of organizing in the nonprofit sector, including hospitals and other health-care related organizations, social service and social justice organizations, museums, and policy think tanks (see earlier chapters). Unions and nonprofits are often aligned on issues of economic justice, such as immigration, the living wage, and health care. Currently, unions are organizing these nonprofits' employees. Nonprofit boards and managers typically have pro-union sympathies, but when their own workers organize, managers may be conflicted in their feelings. For example, the Southern Poverty Law Center (SLPC) an organization devoted to confronting racism and promoting economic justice and children's rights, opposed a unionization drive in 2022. Early in the campaign SLPC hired a union avoidance lawyer who represented Amazon in its union opposition battle. Although this attorney was eventually replaced, SLPC followed up by laying off 81 staff members, including several union activists in mid-2024.

In large nonprofits it is natural for there to be a growing division between management and workers that drives a perceived need for a greater employee voice. Employees may become dissatisfied with a nonprofit's bottom-line fixation, particularly when there is a perception that clients, such as patients, are put at risk. As observed in Chapter 3, new structural arrangements may be needed to organize some nonprofit workers such as those who work in the client's home, with the operative question being, "Who is the employer?" (Delp & Quan, 2002; Mareschal & Ciorici, 2021).

Public and nonprofit sector unions have political opportunities and try hard to exploit them. They have ramped up their electoral activities in efforts to influence the views of candidates and the outcomes of elections. Union members are more likely to vote than nonmembers, and they are most likely to vote for candidates endorsed by unions. During the last several general elections, unions have shown increased sophistication in mobilizing their members and their families. As the 2020 election approached, with significant implications for the presidency,

Congress, and redistricting of congressional and state election districts, national labor organizations committed substantial human and financial resources to campaign-related activities. However, a similar approach in 2024 was unsuccessful.

Clearly, unions need to do a better job of promoting a more positive public perception. AFSCME, NEA, AFT, SEIU, and other public employee unions periodically run local, regional, and national publicity campaigns to influence opinion on specific issues (e.g., environmental protection and public education) as well as to engender warmer feelings toward the organization and its membership. The AFL-CIO also runs candidate training programs in several states to prepare union members to engage in politics and run for elected office (Sojourner, 2013). This is a long-range strategy that is worth greater attention from the unions, for whom public support has risen but as noted Chapter 5, are facing the erosion of collective bargaining rights through executive orders, legislative changes, and court decisions.

V. LABOR–MANAGEMENT COOPERATION AND PARTICIPATIVE DECISION MAKING

The movement from an adversarial to an interest-based approach to collective bargaining was discussed at length in Chapter 5. This and other forms of labor-management cooperation represent a potentially significant transformation in how decisions are made, and conflicts are resolved in a union setting. Various mechanisms exist for labor–management cooperation, including "quality improvement" approaches, labor–management committees (LMCs), labor-management partnerships (LMPs), and employee involvement programs. Each involves regularly scheduled meetings of labor and management representatives to discuss, analyze, and resolve problems either arising under the interpretation and application of the contract or appearing in the workplace but outside the purview of the contract.

Ideally, the core feature of each of them is participative decision making (PDM), defined as a formal process for exercising employee voice in organizational decision making and ensuring that employee views and decisions are given serious consideration by management representatives (Kearney & Hays, 1994). The model envisions bottom-up authority structures and meaningful employee participation in organizational decisions. In collective bargaining environments, it means labor–management cooperation outside the strictures of formal bargaining.

A. Advantages of Cooperation

Extensive literature on private sector PDM indicates positive impacts on individual worker productivity, job satisfaction, personal growth and development, and willingness to change (Kearney & Hays, 1994). PDM's benefits to the individual employee are believed to contribute directly and indirectly to desired organizational outcomes. For example, when participation increases worker satisfaction and commitment to the job, it may also produce less turnover, fewer absences and sick days, lower accident rates (Schwochau et al., 1997, p. 381), stronger commitment to the organization (Verma & McKersie, 1987), and improvements in communication patterns (Ospina & Yaroni, 2003). PDM's organizational benefits include improving employees' ability to perform technical tasks (Mohrman & Lawler, 1988), respond effectively to a rapidly changing work environment, and accommodate changes in the nature of work. There may also be fewer grievances unfair labor practices, and other conflictual activities.

Research findings are less conclusive concerning the effects of PDM on organizational efficiency and productivity (Wagner, 1994), but there is evidence that organizational performance is enhanced through the early identification of emerging workplace problems (Levine, 1995). From a broader perspective, participation has civic and social value as well. It "can stimulate the development of civil society because it encourages individuals to develop and practice habits that are critical to self-sufficiency, self-rule, and . . . individual responsibility" (Delaney, 1996, p. 46). In other words, PDM helps encourage responsible self-government and adds value to employees, the workplace, and the employing organization (Nissen, 2003).

Despite the many advantages associated with PDM, its application to private employment is restricted by the language of the NLRA. Before legalization of full collective bargaining rights for private sector unions by the NLRA of 1935, it was common for employers to resist unions through "representation plans" that established committees of workers and managers that were supposed to meet on workplace concerns. These plans were forced on workers by management, which strictly reserved its power to make all important decisions. Unions viewed such plans as subterfuges for corporate opposition to unions and collective bargaining (Kelly, 1998). A related tactic was the "company union," created and essentially directed by the employer under the pretense of being a legitimate labor organization.

To preclude such evasions by businesses, the NLRA stipulated that it is an unfair labor practice for an employer to "dominate or interfere with the formation or administration of any labor organization or contribute financial or other support to it" [NLRA, Section 8(a)(2)]. Federal case law and NLRB hearings determined that LMCs and similar mechanisms are illegal under the NLRA if they are created and dominated by the employer. To be legal, employee participation programs in the private sector must be established and operated with a substantial degree of employee independence from management. The implication is that the only legal PDM program is either one with strong employee decision-making authority or one created and implemented with union participation (Delaney, 1996).

In the public sector, little systematic empirical research has been published on the PDM experience. In theory, government could be the playing field where the future of PDM action will transpire. However, a strong adversarial spirit still prevails in most unionized jurisdictions. Moreover, NLRA language, principles, and procedures are embedded in many state bargaining statutes.

Nonetheless, experimental participative approaches have gradually gained support at all levels of government. LMCs have been used to develop day care and employee assistance programs in New York State, with outcomes of lower health-care costs and higher employee morale and attendance rates. In Massachusetts, LMCs were established throughout state government to address health and safety, career ladders, childcare, performance appraisal, and other issues. In Ohio, LMCs have dealt with staffing patterns, employee security, and dress codes.

Similarly, LMPs have been used in a variety of public and quasi-public sector workplaces. For example, in California the Joint Workforce Investment (JWI) is a partnership between the Santa Clara Valley Transportation Authority (VTA) and the Amalgamated Transit Union, Local 265 (ATU) to promote long-term professional development and health and wellness of employees. In Washington, the Imagine Institute provides training and builds career pathways for childcare workers. The state of Oregon established a partnership with SEIU Local 503 and AFSCME Council 75. The Uplift Oregon LMP delivers training programs to help employees understand and make the best use of state retirement and health benefit plans.

In federal employment, "partnering" initiatives between unions and management to solve workplace problems were required of all federal agencies by President Clinton's Executive Order 12871. By 1996, it was reported that almost 90% of federal agencies were actively partnering (Lane, 1996, p. 41). Many of these partnerships reported significant improvements in various federal organizational maladies, including communications and collaborative decision making (Albright, 2004; Masters et al., 2005). The changes registered were not earth shattering, but most participants reported improvements in overall labor–management relationships (Masters et al., 2005; Tobias, 2004).

However, the partnerships rapidly deteriorated when President Bush revoked Clinton's executive order and soon thereafter peppered agency leadership with antiunion appointees, (Masters et al., 2005). President Obama reestablished labor–management partnerships with a 2010 executive order, but "their record of accomplishment [was] thin" (Losey, 2011). Pilot projects in 12 federal agencies to evaluate permitting unions to bargain over "permissive subjects" also registered only modest gains, although some agencies reported faster issue resolution, more open dialogue, and more collaborative problem solving (National Council on Federal Labor-Management Relations, 2012). With E.O. 13812, (2017), President Trump revoked Obama's order creating labor management forums and prevented federal agencies from using public funds for labor management cooperation in the future (Masters et al., 2020). In 2024, President Biden restored labor management forums with EO 14119. Subsequently, the U.S. Office of Personnel Management

(OPM) issued guidelines directing agencies to work with unions to recreate labor forums based on a shared vision.

Public and nonprofit managers are generally receptive to the principle of labor-management cooperation. Labor relations in some jurisdictions may be replete with adversarial encounters, but, in general, relationships between the parties are more peaceful than those in the private sector. The fierce battles that characterized many public jurisdictions during the early years of unionization and bargaining gradually moderated in most cases, as union and management roles and expectations stabilized and matured. With the almost shocking exception of President Reagan's mass firing of 12,000 striking air traffic controllers in 1981, very few government workers have lost their jobs during the past four decades because of union organizing or work stoppages.

Of course, public managers and those who work for them share important characteristics and interests. Most of them consider themselves to be public service professionals who work for the public interest in critical fields such as health care, education, and law enforcement. They do not pursue profits or the short-term interests of owners or shareholders. Program success and gains in productivity can produce compensation gains for all public employees and special recognition for managers. Labor and management also share key enemies: namely, bureaucrat bashers, budget pinchers, hostile politicians, and negative public opinion. This assortment of characteristics and interests shared by public managers and workers makes cooperation and PDM more feasible than in most private sector settings.

B. Conditions Necessary for Successful Labor–management Cooperation

To succeed, PDM, LMCs, and other cooperative approaches and techniques cannot simply be imposed by a reform-minded elected official or an agency head. Certain facilitative conditions are necessary to create a receptive environment. The most critical facilitative conditions are a foundation of trust and mutual respect among managers and workers, a strong level of commitment by all key parties to make the program work over the long haul, win–win expectations, and an appropriate technique for bringing PDM to fruition.

Constructing a foundation of trust and mutual respect requires overcoming suspicions of union leaders. One primary union concern is that PDM is a new way to manipulate employees and their unions. Another is that PDM is likely to weaken collective bargaining, grievance systems, and employee commitment to the union. Suspicions and doubt may also infect the ranks of mid-level managers, who feel threatened by a potential loss of authority, or even their jobs, when PDM programs are implemented (Lawler & Mohrman, 1985).

In negative adversarial settings, trust and respect must be constructed from the ground up. This is a tough task, and failures have been recorded. The U.S.

Postal Service's history of confrontational labor relations within a context of an autocratic management style, rigid work rules, and difficult working conditions created a setting predisposed against meaningful PDM (U.S. General Accounting Office, 1994). Labor–management partnerships in Miami, Florida, struggled in the face of high levels of workplace conflict, low employee morale, and a chaotic labor relations climate that included serious internal divisions in the ranks of both labor and city management (Bryson, 1999).

However, other jurisdictions have reported success in converting hostile relationships into a productive cooperative situation. For example, the San Francisco Bay Area Union Sanitation District, long burdened by adversarial relations and low levels of trust and morale, engaged in a far-reaching change strategy that opened direct communication lines between management and union representatives. The program resulted in less contentious contract negotiations and attained impressive improvements in operations.

The second precondition for successful PDM is a strong level of commitment by top officials, managers, and employees. Significant levels of time, attention, and resources must be invested in the program if it is to work over the long haul. The heaviest burden rests with mid-level managers and union leaders. However, virtually all employees must shoulder some responsibility by committing themselves to working cooperatively with former adversaries. Top officials must exercise leadership and make available sufficient financial and personnel resources for training, oversight, and related activities. Sincere sustained commitment from top-level officials is especially important. This is difficult to secure when newly elected officials or their appointees fail to continue the collaborative policies adopted by their predecessors. Financial problems leading to workforce cutbacks or reorganizations can also undermine PDM.

The third condition for successful PDM is that the parties must be committed to discovering interest-based, win–win solutions to organizational problems and conflicts. Examples of successful win–win expectations and outcomes may be found at all levels of government. Under the National Performance Council, federal agencies developed partnerships premised on interest-based processes that effectively addressed contract and workplace disputes and myriad other problems. Federal partnerships dealt with equal employment opportunity concerns, grievance prevention and resolution, unfair labor practices, incentive pay systems, and a gain-sharing program (Ferris & Cooper, 1994).

Numerous examples of interest-based programs have been reported in state and local jurisdictions, including Wisconsin state government; Ramsey County, Missouri (Brainerd, 1998); and Portland, Maine (Peightal et al., 1998). Successful collaborative programs have been operational in school districts as well. For example, sustained collaborative partnerships between public school administrators and local teachers' unions have been operated for over ten years in California, Florida, Virginia, New York, Minnesota, and Ohio (Rubinstein et al., 2024).

Finally, PDM requires an appropriate technique for effective implementation. Many different but related tools are available to structure participative interactions, from health-and-safety committees and quality of work life programs to quality circles (small groups of workers that meet regularly to develop suggestions for improving work procedures, product or service quality, or other concerns) and employee engagement programs. Through such techniques, employees are involved and empowered to engage as partners in decision making. For instance, OPM encourages federal agencies to implement policies and practices to maximize employee engagement. Toward this end, OPM offers training programs and resources to agencies to foster engagement. OPM also monitors progress by conducting an annual Federal Employee Viewpoint Survey (FEVS). In 2024, FEVs results showed that the governmentwide Employee Engagement Index reached a new high of 73 (out of 100). This was the highest EEI score since the index was incorporated in the FEVS in 2010. Officials attributed the rise in the EEI to the president's efforts to reinforce civil service protections, enhance the voice of frontline workers by establishing a more balanced labor relations climate, and implement the Task Force on Worker Organizing and Empowerment (U.S. Office of Personnel Management, 2024).

The most widely adopted participation strategies today are labor-management committees (LMCs) and labor-management partnerships (LMPs). LMCs focus on resolving issues outside the formal contract and are found at all levels of government. LMCs apply win–win principles and push decision making to as low a level of the organization as possible. LMPs are often focused on workforce development and training programs. In sum, numerous techniques are available for structuring and implementing meaningful employee participation in making organizational decisions. The specific technique is not nearly as critical to program success as are the needs for mutual trust and respect, strong commitment, and win–win expectations.

C. Future of Labor–management Cooperation

Despite the advantages of labor–management cooperation, substantial obstacles remain. The NLRA's premise of adversarialism as the answer to all labor–management conflicts is firmly embedded in the legal framework and mentality of most unionized public jurisdictions. The lengthy and emotional history of early organizing campaigns and bargaining encounters is tough to overcome. Mutual distrust and suspicion prevail among union and management representatives in many bargaining settings. Management's innate discomfort with unions is amplified by a nagging fear of losing authority and control over employees in the bargaining unit. Likewise, union leaders, many of whom made their reputations by aggressively fighting management, are fearful that consultative and participative management proposals are Trojan horses that will unleash demands to eliminate jobs, dilute union power, impose givebacks and concessions, and ultimately displace the union as the collective voice of workers.

To be successful, PDM requires sustained commitment of resources. Maintaining sufficient resources is always problematic in a political system characterized by frequent turnover of elected and appointed officials and personal, partisan, and special interest groups' political agendas. A comfortable and functional relationship between collective bargaining and PDM is the key to expansion. Collective bargaining continues to serve a vital purpose by jointly setting wages, benefits, and terms and conditions of employment. Union representation in grievance procedures remains important as well. PDM opens a new window of joint problem-solving possibilities.

PDM is not a quick cure for all problems that arise labor–management relations. Role conflicts are endemic, as management and union representatives must make the transition back and forth from adversarial to cooperative interactions. Perhaps unions should designate "partnership stewards" for PDM activities and "grievance stewards" for more traditional encounters with management. In the current environment, changes in work practices are rapidly evolving to require more group-oriented work and fewer supervisory levels. Whether embodied in statute or common practice, the conventional distinctions between supervisors and workers are blurring in practice. This poses significant challenges for unions and collective bargaining. With ongoing retrenchment of collective bargaining rights, labor–management collaboration may be a viable path to joint problem-solving moving forward.

VI. PUBLIC EMPLOYEE UNIONS IN THE 2020S: CONCLUSION

Despite persistent hopes for rejuvenation, unions in the private sector of the United States have been resolutely marching toward oblivion for the past 75 years. Only about 6% of private sector workers belong to unions today. This appears to be a global phenomenon; unions are in decline in virtually all economically advanced nations. Numerous factors have contributed to union decline, the most important of which are probably the shift from manufacturing to service and knowledge-based economies and the globalization of labor and production. The extent of union decline is much greater in the United States than it is elsewhere. Union density in the European Union averages 23% across the member states but is substantially higher—70%—in the Nordic countries (Dazelle, 2024). In Canada union density is roughly 30% (Statistics Canada, 2024). In these countries, workforces and unions remain more powerful political and economic forces.

Public sector union membership in the U.S. leveled off in the late 1970s and has since recorded a slight decline. The public-sector union membership rate was fairly steady from 1983 (36.7 %) to 2011 (37.0 %). However, it began declining in the years following the Great Recession and dropped to 32.5 % in 2023 (U.S. Bureau of Labor Statistics, 2024). A more dramatic drop in membership in government will come if legal protections are repealed in the federal, state, and local sectors. Looking ahead, public employee unions face both obstacles and prospects on the path to renewal in the 2020s.

A. Obstacles

Public employee unions face a number of challenges. At the federal level a key challenge is the proposed committee on government efficiency. While improved efficiency and reduction of waste should be lauded for the benefits such measures could generate for citizens, the proposed committee is focused on privatizing essential government services, laying off federal employees, and consolidating power to the executive branch. The trickle-down effects of reduced federal support could create government financial stress at the state and local levels as well as citizen hostility and negative actions by state legislatures.

At the state and local levels, public sector unions continue to face obstacles related to the *Janus v. American Federation of State, County and Municipal Employees* (2018) decision. As mentioned earlier, organizations such as ALEC, AFP, and SPN play central roles in the diffusion of anti-union public policies. These organizations continue to push model legislation to state governments to weaken collective bargaining rights and undermine union security. This model legislation includes policies that prohibit paid release time for union activities, affirm workers' *Janus* rights, and require periodic re-certification of unions (Slabinski, 2019).

The recent restrictions on collective bargaining rights limit state and local government's ability to set higher standards for protecting workers and are often written in ways that make the laws difficult to repeal. These reforms silence the voice of both public sector unions and the clientele that public employees serve. The end result is an erosion of the ability to participate in democratic processes for public sector union members and for beneficiaries of public programs.

Over two decades ago, Morehouse and Jewell (2004) expressed concern that corporations dominated the process of interest group representation. In the ensuing years, the role of corporate interests in public policy has multiplied. As a counterbalance, labor unions remain the most prominent non-market institution promoting voice at work and economic justice. Although there were glimmers of hope in some states that expanded the classes of employees eligible for collective bargaining rights and the subjects of bargaining, unions face an uphill battle.

Given the current environment of intense political partisanship and polarization, the destabilization is likely to continue. Public sector unions will need to engage in continuous soul searching and reinvention if they are to move beyond mere rhetoric on key issues and maintain relevance for the increasingly diverse public and nonprofit workforce. Somehow they must reverse the antiunion, public-workers-as-the-problem narrative to recapture favorable perceptions on the part of public officials and the general public.

B. Prospects

Despite the rhetoric, collective bargaining in the public sector has never been solely about protecting public employees' self-interest. In fact, most people join the public sector with a sense of mission and a desire to serve the community. Continued erosion in collective bargaining rights and the subsequent decline of public sector unions is cause for concern on a number of fronts. First, it will impact the cost of government, the types of workers attracted to employment in the public sector, and the quality of public services. Second, it has broader implications for income distribution, social equity, civil society, democracy, and basic human rights.

What will it take to turn the tide? Visser (2024) contends that union revitalization requires an outward-looking approach to form new coalitions, draw on new resources, and innovate. At the same time, unions must develop new ways of communicating with both members and non-members, building consensus, and making decisions. Since membership size largely determines the power of labor organizations, unions will have to increase worker mobilization and engagement in union activities.

Internally, public sector unions must focus on persuading bargaining unit members to become union members. Clark (2021) demonstrates that high quality new employee orientation sessions have a positive impact on overall union commitment. Beyond the new employee orientation unions, Hodges (2021) emphasizes the need to strengthen engagement with existing employees through conversations at work, home visits, newsletters, text messages, and mobile apps. In addition, unions must devote adequate resources to contract enforcement as a means to promoting employee voice and improving perceptions of workplace fairness (Avgar et al., 2018).

Rising inequality, the growth of precarious employment, and declining living standards for the middle class all provide incentives for collective action. Public and nonprofit sector unions may do well to focus on specific groups of workers. For example, a recent Gallup poll shows that 77% of respondents ages 18–34 approve of labor unions. This cohort includes members of Gen Z over the age of 18 and some Millennials (Glass, 2024). Workers in this cohort of the labor market face dismal job prospects. The jobs that are available typically pay low wages, offer little or no opportunity for advancement, do not provide fringe benefits such as health care and pensions, and lack security.

Women are another potentially lucrative group for organizing. Women's approval of unions has been trending upward since 2006, and in 2018 women's approval of unions was 8.5 percentage points higher than men's approval

(Torre, 2023). Union coverage generally results in higher wages and better employer-provided benefits for women, especially for women of color (Sun et al., 2020). Since women are typically employed in subordinate positions, unionization could serve as a ladder to gender equity (Torre, 2023).

Black men have higher union membership rates other demographic groups. The union wage premium for Black workers is 20%. At the same time recent negative economic trends have fallen heavily on black men. To illustrate, a 2020 study on intergenerational mobility showed that black men fared worse than white men and women and Black women (U.S. Department of the Treasury, 2023). Black men stand to benefit from unionization and policies designed to strengthen unions.

Externally, promising strategies for unions to regain lost ground include political action, the formation of coalitions and social movement unionism. Moving forward, labor will have to develop new approaches to advance its agenda. To survive, unions will have to continue building broad alliances with other institutions and with the communities within which they are embedded. Retrenchment of public social services negatively affects both communities and public sector workers. Thus, it offers incentives and opportunities for unions to build and sustain labor–community coalitions. This was demonstrated in both the Bargaining for the Common Good (BCG) and the #RedforEd uprisings in 2018–2019. Both the BCG campaigns and the #RedforEd uprisings used similar messages, emphasized building community alliances, and used strikes as tactical weapons to make demands that go beyond traditional bargaining subjects (McCartin et al., 2020).

Expanding the union discourse to include human rights, social equity, and democracy may help attract new coalition members and improve the public perception of unions. Previous research shows that union membership not only reduces racial resentment but also results in White unionized workers becoming more likely to support affirmative action and government efforts to improve the social and economic standing of the Black community (Frymer & Grumbach, 2021). Unions will have to make the argument that a democratic society needs unions, both because workers should have the right to associate to promote their shared interests and because a democratic society requires that its members have a voice. This approach may help replace the current politics of resentment, which portrays public sector employees as enemies of the community, with the politics of solidarity, in which unions can bring public sector employees and community members together to work toward common goals.

The new upsurge in union activity provides opportunities for unions to establish their relevancy to a larger range of workers. Unions seeking to expand organizing and mobilization would do well to focus on the groups of workers and themes described earlier. A good starting point would be the areas that have recently expanded collective bargaining rights for public and quasi-public sector employees. In these states, the government has signaled that it sees unions as providing some benefits to society and has taken action to facilitate collective bargaining.

From there it is up to unions, as Visser (2024, p. 647) notes, to provide the "blueprint" that communicates the shared purpose and to build alliances that generate positive externalities.

REFERENCES

Abood v. Detroit Board of Education. (1977). 430 U.S. 209, 975 Ct. 1782.

AFL-CIO. (2024). *What is the PRO act?* https://aflcio.org/pro-act

Ahlquist, J. S., Grumbach, J., & Kochan, T. (2024, July 16). *The rise of the 'union curious.' Support for unionization among America's frontline workers*. Economic Policy Institute. https://www.epi.org/publication/rise-of-the-union-curious/#full-report

Albright, R. R. (2004). The U.S. department of transportation's partnership experience: Implications for the future. *Journal of Labor Research*, *25*(1), 43–54.

Anzia, S. F., & Moe, T. M. (2015). Public sector unions and the costs of government. *The Journal of Politics*, *77*(1), 114–127.

Anzia, S. F., & Moe, T. M. (2016). Do politicians use policy to make politics? The case of public-sector labor laws. *American Political Science Review*, *110*(4), 763–777.

Avgar, A., Boris, M. B., Bruno, R., & Chung, W. (2018). Worker voice and union revitalization: The role of contract enforcement at SEIU. *Labor Studies Journal*, *43*(3), 209–233.

Avgar, A., Eaton, A. E., Givan, R. K., & Litwin, A. S. (2024). Labor relations in the healthcare industry: A portrait of contradictions. In H. R. Stanger, P. F. Clark, & J. T. Delaney (Eds.), *Union organizing and collective bargaining at a critical moment: Opportunities for renewal or continued decline* (pp. 185–209). Labor Employment Relations Association.

Bazelon, E. (2020, February 19). Why are workers struggling? Because labor law is broken. *The New York Times*.

Bel, G., Fageda, X., & Warner, M. E. (2010). Is private production of public services cheaper than public production? A meta-regression analysis of solid waste and water services. *Journal of Policy Analysis and Management*, *29*(3), 553–577.

Bisaha, S. (2024, July 22). The UAW's union dreams seemed unstoppable. Then came the realities of the South. *WWNO—New Orleans Public Radio*. https://www.wwno.org/economy/2024-07-22/the-uaws-union-dreams-seemed-unstoppable-then-came-the-realities-of-the-south

Brainerd, R. (1998, Spring). Interest-based bargaining: Labor and management working together in Ramsey County, Minnesota. *Public Personnel Management*, *27*, 51–68.

Brenan, M. (2024, September 9). Democratic party still seen as better for union members. *Gallup*. https://news.gallup.com/poll/650147/democratic-party-seen-better-union-members.aspx

Bryson, W. (1999). *The Miami story: The pros and cons of the collaborative process*. National Academy of Public Administration. www.alliance.napawash.org.

Campbell, J. (2024, July 16). Federal monitor reports pervasive culture of fear and slow reforms at UAW. *CBT News*. https://www.cbtnews.com/federal-monitor-reports-pervasive-culture-of-fear-and-slow-reforms-at-uaw/

Castronuovo, C. (2024, January 25). States push single social work license to boost labor supply (1). *Bloomberg Law*. https://news.bloomberglaw.com/health-law-and-business/states-pursue-single-social-work-license-to-boost-labor-supply

Center on Budget and Policy Priorities. (2024, April 3). *Chart book: Tracking the recovery from the pandemic recession*. https://www.cbpp.org/research/economy/tracking-the-recovery-from-the-pandemic-recession

Chapman, M., & Hadero, H. (2024, June 18). Amazon labor union members vote overwhelmingly in favor of an affiliation with the teamsters. *AP News*. https://apnews.com/article/amazon-union-teamsters-labor-warehouse-0d0d751d6800495ed0296e33b4f5835e

Clark, P. F. (2021). The impact of new member orientation programs on union member commitment: Evidence from a national study in a post-Janus setting. *Labor Studies Journal*, *46*(2), 158–181.

Clark, P. F. (2024). Police collective bargaining: An integral part of U.S. law enforcement. In H. R. Stanger, P. F. Clark, & J. T. Delaney (Eds.), *Union organizing and collective bargaining at a critical moment: Opportunities for renewal or continued decline* (pp. 229–254). Labor and Employment Relations Association Series.

Combs, R. (2024, March 19). ANALYSIS: Unions won sky-high pay hikes in 2023 negotiations. *Bloomberg Law*. https://news.bloomberglaw.com/bloomberg-law-analysis/analysis-unions-won-sky-high-pay-hikes-in-2023-negotiations

Dazelle, E. (2024, May 2). A closer look: Labor-management cooperation in Europe. *U.S. Department of Labor Blog*. https://blog.dol.gov/2024/05/02/a-closer-look-labor-management-cooperation-in-europe

Delaney, J. T. (1996, Winter). Workplace cooperation: Current problems, new techniques. *Journal of Labor Research, XVII*, 45–61.

Delp, L., & Quan, K. (2002). Homecare worker organizing in California: An analysis of a successful strategy. *Labor Studies Journal*, *27*(1), 1–23.

Devinatz, V. G. (2008). Social-movement unionism and U.S. labor's uncertain future. *Journal of Collective Negotiations (Formerly Journal of Collective Negotiations in the Public Sector), 32*(3), 203–213.

Domonoske, C. (2023, November 17). *Big 3 autoworkers vote 'yes' to historic UAW contracts*. https://www.npr.org/2023/11/16/1212381342/gm-autoworkers-vote-yes-approve-uaw-contract-ford-stellantis

Donn, C. B., & Kirby, B. J. (2024). Teachers and unions: Collective bargaining in the schools and the politics of public education. In H. R. Stanger, P. F. Clark, & J. T. Delaney (Eds.), *Union organizing and collective bargaining at a critical moment: Opportunities for renewal or continued decline* (pp. 211–227). Labor and Employment Relations Association Series.

Early, S. (2023, August 21). SEIU & the carpenters: Still "changing to win" or changing the wrong way? *BeyondChron*. https://beyondchron.org/seiu-the-carpenters-still-changing-to-win-or-changing-the-wrong-way/

Engeman, C. (2015). Social movement unionism in practice: Organizational dimensions of union mobilization in the Los Angeles immigrant rights marches. *Work, Employment and Society*, *29*(3), 444–461.

Evanoff, T. (2019, May 1). *Ahead of UAW vote, Gov. Bill Lee touts non-union workplace in speech at Volkswagen plant*. https://www.commercialappeal.com/story/money/cars/2019/05/01/tennessee-governor-bill-lee-touts-non-union-vw-chattanooga-prior-uaw-vote/3638585002/

Exec. Order No. 13812, 3 C.F.R. (2017). https://www.federalregister.gov/documents/2017/10/04/2017–21559/revocation-of-executive-order-creating-labor-management-forums

Facundo, J. (2023, October 5). Lawyers, not Persuaders: The anti-labor law firm Littler Mendelson's reputation is a premier example of the limitations in existing labor law. *The American Prospect*. https://prospect.org/justice/2023-10-05-lawyers-not-persuaders-littler-mendelson/

Ferris, F., & Cooper, R. (1994). Two views of one agency: The IRS and NTEU. *The Public Manager*, *23*(2), 27–31.

Friedrichs v. California Teachers Association. (2016). 578 U.S. ____.

Frymer, P., & Grumbach, J. M. (2021). Labor unions and white racial politics. *American Journal of Political Science*, *65*(1), 225–240.

Gallup. (2024). *Labor unions*. https://news.gallup.com/poll/12751/labor-unions.aspx

Gerhart, P. F. (1994). Maintenance of the union-management relationship. In J. Rabin, T. Vocino, W. B. Hildreth, & G. J. Miller (Eds.), *Handbook of public sector labor relations* (pp. 97–132). Dekker.

Glass, A. (2024). *Explaining young workers' support for unions*. Center for American Progress. https://www.americanprogress.org/article/explaining-young-workers-support-for-unions/

Greenblatt, A. (2012, September 10). *Chicago strike emblematic of union struggle*. NPR. http://www.npr.org/2012/09/10/160891750/chicago-strike-emblematic-of-union-struggle.

Harris v. Quinn. (2014). 573 U.S. 616.

Hartney, M., & Flavin, P. (2011). From the schoolhouse to the statehouse: Teacher union political activism and US state education reform policy. *State Politics & Policy Quarterly*, *11*(3), 251–268.

Hertel-Fernandez, A. (2018). Policy feedback as political weapon: Conservative advocacy and the demobilization of the public sector labor movement. *Perspectives on Politics*, *16*(2), 364–379.

Hinkley, S. (2020, October 21). *Public sector impacts of the great recession and COVID-19.* UC Berkeley Labor Center. https://laborcenter.berkeley.edu/public-sector-impacts-great-recession-and-covid-19/

Hodges, A. C. (2021). The U.S. labor relations system after Janus v. AFSCME: An early assessment. *Employee Responsibilities and Rights Journal*, *33*, 49–60. https://doi.org/10.1007/s10672-020-09362-y

Hsu, A. (2023, March 31). *Labor's labors lost? A year after stunning victory at Amazon, unions are stalled.* NPR. https://www.npr.org/2023/03/28/1165294695/labor-union-starbucks-amazon-howard-schultz-workers

Hutton, Z. (2024, August 12). Why it's so hard to recruit police officers. *Governing.* https://www.governing.com/workforce/why-its-so-hard-to-recruit-police-officers

Jalette, P., & Hebdon, R. (2012). Unions and privatization: Opening the "black box". *Industrial and Labor Relations Review*, *65*(1), 2.

Jamieson, D. (2023, November 14). Starbucks insists it isn't union-busting. A growing list of rulings say otherwise. *HuffPost.* https://www.huffpost.com/entry/starbucks-labor-board-rulings_n_65528978e4b09c9500ab5b69

Jansa, J. M., Hansen, E. R., & Gray, V. H. (2019). Copy and paste lawmaking: Legislative professionalism and policy reinvention in the states. *American Politics Research*, *47*(4), 739–767. https://doi.org/10.1177/1532673X18776628

Janus v. American Federation of State, County, and Municipal Employees, Council 31. (2018). 585 U.S. ___.

Johnston, P. (1994). *Success while others fail: Social movement unionism and the public workplace.* Cornell University Press.

Katz, D. (2023). *The decline of the American labor union.* https://www.gisreportsonline.com/r/decline-american-union/

Kearney, R. C., & Hays, S. (1994). Labor management relations and participative decision making toward a new paradigm. *Public Administration Review*, *54*(1), 44–51.

Kelly, E. P. (1998). Historical perspectives on ideological and legal challenges to labor management participation efforts. *International Journal of Organizational Theory and Behavior, 4*, 459–479.

Kochan, T. A., Fine, J. R., Bronfenbrenner, K., Naidu, S., Barnes, J., Diaz-Linhart, Y., Kallas, J., Kim, J., Minster, A., Tong, D., Townsend, P., & Twiss, D. (2023). An overview of US workers' current organizing efforts and collective actions. *Work and Occupations*, *50*(3), 335–350.

Lafer, G. (2017). *The one percent solution: How corporations are remaking America one state at a time.* Cornell University Press.

Lane, C. M. (1996, February). Bittersweet partnerships. *Government Executive,* 41–44.

Lawler, E. E., III., & Mohrman, S. A. (1985, January–February). Quality circles after the Fed. *Harvard Business Review, 85*, 65–71.

Levine, D. I. (1995). *Reinventing the workplace: How business and employees can both win*. The Brookings Institution.

Logan, J. (2019). The new union avoidance internationalism. *Work Organisation, Labour & Globalisation*, *13*(2), 57–77. https://doi.org/10.13169/workorgalaboglob.13.2.0057

Losey, S. (2011, October 30). Labor partnerships: Talk, but few results. *Federal Times*. www.federaltimes.com

Lyon, M. A. (2023). Current perspectives on teacher unionization, and what they're missing. *Educational Policy*, *37*(5), 1420–1443.

Mahler, J. (2023, April 28). The most dangerous person in the world is Randi Weingarten. *New York Times Magazine*. https://www.nytimes.com/2023/04/28/magazine/randi-weingarten-teachers-unions.html

Mareschal, P. M., & Ciorici, P. (2021). Against all odds: Achieving collective action among home care workers in Oregon. *Labor History*, *62*(3), 334–352.

Masters, M. F., Albright, R. R., & Eplion, D. (2005). What did partnership do? Evidence from the federal sector. *Industrial and Labor Relations Review*, *59*(3), 367–385.

Masters, M. F., Albright, R. R., & Gibney, R. F. (2020). The Ebb and flow of federal sector labor-management relations policies under four successive presidents. *Employee Responsibilities and Rights Journal*, *32*, 139–166.

McCartin, J. A., Sneiderman, M., & BP-weeks, M. (2020). Combustible convergence: Bargaining for the common good and the #RedforEd uprisings of 2018. *Labor Studies Journal*, *45*(1), 97–113.

McIntosh, D. (2024, September 20). Gallup: 70% approve of unions. *Northwest Labor Press*. https://nwlaborpress.org/2024/09/gallup-70-approve-of-unions/

McNicholas, C., Poydock, M., Sanders, S., & Zipperer, B. (2023). *Employers spend more than $400 million per year on 'union-avoidance' consultants to bolster their union-busting efforts*. Economic Policy Institute. https://www.epi.org/publication/union-avoidance/

McNicholas, C., Poydock, M., Wolfe, J., Zipperer, B., Lafer, G., & Loustaunau, L. (2019). *Unlawful: US employers are charged with violating federal law in 41.5% of all union election campaigns*. Economic Policy Institute. https://www.epi.org/publication/unlawful-employer-opposition-to-union-election-campaigns/

Meyerson, H. (2023, August 28). Biden's NLRB brings workers' rights back from the dead. *The American Prospect*. https://prospect.org/labor/2023-08-28-bidens-nlrb-brings-workers-rights-back/

Mishak, M. J. (2012, August 18). California teachers association a powerful force in Sacramento. *Los Angeles Times*. www.latimes.com

Mohrman, S. A., & Lawler, E. E. (1988). Participative management behavior and organizational change. *Journal of Organizational Change Management*, *1*, 45–59.

Morehouse, S. M., & Jewell, M. E. (2004). States as laboratories: A reprise. *Annual Review of Political Science*, 7(1), 177–203.

Naidu, S. (2022). Is there any future for a US labor movement? *Journal of Economic Perspectives*, *36*(4), 3–28.

National Council on Federal Labor-Management Relations. (2012, May). *Report to the president on negotiation over permissive subjects of bargaining: Pilot projects*. National Council on Federal Labor-Management Relations.

Nissen, B. (2003). Alternative strategic directions for the U.S. labor movement: Recent scholarship. *Labor Studies Journal*, *28*(1), 133–155.

NLRB. (2024, October 14). *Union petitions filed with NLRB double since FY 2021, Up 27% since FY 2023*. National Labor Relations Board. https://www.nlrb.gov/news-outreach/news-story/union-petitions-filed-with-nlrb-double-since-fy-2021-up-27-since-fy-2023

Nunn, R., O'Donnell, J., & Shambaugh, J. (2019). *The shift in private sector union participation: Explanation and effects*. The Hamilton Project.

Ospina, S., & Yaroni, A. (2003, July–August). Understanding cooperative behavior in labor management cooperation: A theory-building exercise. *Public Administration Review, 63*, 455–471.

Peck, J. (2016). The right to work, and the right at work. *Economic Geography*, *92*(1), 4–30.

Peightal, P., Souza, D., Bray, B., Rague, J., Pritchard, J., & Thomas, J. (1998, Spring). Labor management cooperation: City of Portland, Maine. *Public Personnel Management, 27*, 85–92.

Pew. (2023, October). *Public retirement systems need sustainable policies to navigate volatile financial markets: State pension funding gap, 2021*. https://www.pewtrusts.org/-/media/assets/2023/11/public-retirement-systems-need-sustainable-policies_v5.pdf

Rhinehart, L., McNicholas, C., & Poydock, M. (2024). *The Biden board: How President Biden's NLRB appointees are restoring and supporting workers' rights*. Economic Policy Institute. https://www.epi.org/publication/bidens-nlrb-restoring-rights/

Rubinstein, S., Heckscher, C., & McCarthy, J. (2024). *Democracy and reform in public schools: The case for collaborative partnerships*. Harvard Education Press.

Saad, L. (2023). More in U.S. see unions strengthening and want it that way. *Gallup.com*. https://news.gallup.com/poll/510281/unions-strengthening.aspx

Scheiber, N. (2024, July 9). U.A.W. monitor reveals details about investigation into union leader. *The New York Times*. https://www.nytimes.com/2024/07/09/business/uaw-monitorinvestigation-shawn-fain.html

Schwochau, S., Delaney, J., Jarley, P., & Fiorito, J. (1997, Summer). Employee participation and assessment of support for organizational policy change. *Journal of Labor Research, XVIII*, 379–401.

Shierholz, H., McNicholas, C., Poydock, M., & Sherer, J. (2024). *Workers want unions, but the latest data point to obstacles in their path: Private-sector unionization rose by more than a quarter million in 2023, while unionization in state and local governments fell*. https://www.epi.org/publication/union-membership-data/

Slabinski, M. (2019, March 29). A current glimpse of public sector union policy in the states. *ALEC*. https://www.alec.org/article/a-current-glimpse-of-public-sector-union-policy-in-the-states/

Sojourner, A. J. (2013). Do unions promote members' electoral office holding? Evidence from correlates of state legislatures' occupational shares. *ILR Review*, *66*(2), 467–486.

Statistics Canada. (2024, October 14). *Quality of employment in Canada: Collective bargaining coverage rate, 2023. Catalogue no. 14-28-0001-x*. https://www150.statcan.gc.ca/n1/pub/14-28-0001/2024001/article/00010-eng.pdf

Strategic Organizing Center. (2024). *About*. https://thesoc.org/about/

Sulzner, G. T. (1997). New roles, new strategies: Reinventing the public union. In C. Ban & N. M. Riccucci (Eds.), *Public personnel management: Current concerns, future challenges* (2nd ed., pp. 157–172). Longman.

Sun, C., Hall, A., & Shaw, E. (2020, September 1). *Stronger together: Union membership boosts women's earnings and economic security*. Institute for Women's Policy Research. https://iwpr.org/wp-content/uploads/2021/08/Stronger-Together-Union-Membership-Boosts-Womens-Earnings-and-Economic-Security_FINAL.pdf

Tan, T. S., Arellano, I., & Patrick, S. K. (2024, August). *State teacher shortages 2024 update*. Learning Policy Institute. https://learningpolicyinstitute.org/product/state-teacher-shortages-vacancy-resource-tool-2024

Tobias, R. M. (2004). The future of federal government labor relations and the mutual interests of Congress, the administration, and unions. *Journal of Labor Research*, *25*(1), 19–41.

Torre, M. (2023). Women in the new labor activism: Gender trends in attitudes toward unions. *Work and Occupations*, *50*(3), 412–419. https://doi.org/10.1177/07308884231162950

U.S. Bureau of Labor Statistics. (2023, October). *Industry and occupational employment projections overview and highlights, 2022–32*. https://www.bls.gov/opub/mlr/2023/article/industry-and-occupational-employment-projections-overview-and-highlights-2022–32.htm

U.S. Bureau of Labor Statistics. (2024, January 23). *Union members—2023*. https://www.bls.gov/news.release/pdf/union2.pdf

U.S. Department of the Treasury. (2023, August). *Labor unions and the middle class*. https://home.treasury.gov/system/files/136/Labor-Unions-And-The-Middle-Class.pdf

U.S. General Accounting Office. (1994). *U.S. postal service: Labor management problems persist on the workroom floor*. Government Printing Office, GAOIGGO 94-201 A.

U.S. Office of Personnel Management. (2022, December). *Status of telework in the federal government report to congress, fiscal year 2021*. https://www.opm.gov/telework/documents-for-telework/2022-report-to-congress.pdf

U.S. Office of Personnel Management. (2024, October 17). *OPM releases 2024 federal employee viewpoint survey results: Results show increasingly engaged workforce, highest-ever employee engagement index score*. https://www.opm.gov/news/releases/2024/10/opm-releases-2024-federal-employee-viewpoint-survey-results/

Van Nostrand, E., Feiveson, L., & Sinclair, T. (2024, March 11). *State and local governments in the post-COVID recovery*. U.S. Department of the Treasury. https://home.treasury.gov/news/featured-stories/state-and-local-governments-in-the-post-covid-recovery

Verma, A., & McKersie, R. B. (1987, July). Employee involvement: The implication of noninvolvement by unions. *Industrial and Labor Relations Review, 40*, 556–568.

Visser, J. (2019). Trade unions in the balance. In *ILO ACTRAV working paper*. https://etufegypt.com/wp-content/uploads/2019/10/wcms_722482.pdf

Visser, J. (2024). Will they rise again? Four scenarios for the future of trade unions. *Economic and Industrial Democracy*, *45*(3), 629–652. https://doi.org/10.1177/0143831X231178850

Wade, M. M. (2018). Targeting teachers while shielding cops? The politics of punishing enemies and rewarding friends in American state collective bargaining reform agendas. *Journal of Labor and Society*, *21*(2), 137–157.

Wagner, J. (1994, April). Participation effects on performance and satisfaction: A reconsideration of research evidence. *Academy of Management Review, 19*, 312–330.

Webb, H. (2014, February 10). *Bo Watson says VW May lose state help if the UAW is voted in at Chattanooga plant; McCormick urges workers to reject union; Corker to hold press conference; democrats respond*. https://www.chattanoogan.com/2014/2/10/269310/Bo-Watson-Says-VW-May-Lose-State-Help.aspx

Index

Note: Page numbers in *italics* indicate figures, **bold** indicate tables in the text, and references following "n" refer notes.

Abood v. Detroit Board of Education (1977) 37, 100, 102, 436
Abraham, S. E. 410
ADA *see* Americans with Disabilities Act
administrative agency 95–97, 103, 118, 120, 139, 351, 356
ADR *see* Alternative dispute resolution
affirmative action plan 251–255
AFGE *see* American Federation of Government Employees
AFGE, et al. v. Donald H. Rumsfeld 73
AFL *see* American Federation of Labor
AFL–CIO *see* American Federation of Labor–Congress of Industrial Organizations
AFSCME *see* American Federation of State, County, and Municipal Employees
AFSCME v. State of Washington (1983) 204
AFSCME Local 201 v. City of Muskegon (1963) 64
AFT *see* American Federation of Teachers
Age Discrimination in Employment Act (1967) **80**, 392, 403
agency operations, efficiency of 96, 120, 121
agreement: collective bargaining (*see* collective bargaining agreement); federal labor 72, 412
Ahlquist, J. S. 230
Alexander v. Gardner-Denver (1975) 402
alternate grievance procedures 394
alternative dispute resolution (ADR) 390, 414–415
Amalgamated Transit Union, Local 265 (ATU) 445
Amazon 15, 35, 42–43, 428–429, 442
American Arbitration Association (AAA) 403
American Association of University Professors (AAUP) 51
American Federation of Government Employees (AFGE) 16, 17, 32–34, 71, 258, 435
American Federation of Labor (AFL) 6–7, 297
American Federation of Labor–Congress of Industrial Organizations (AFL–CIO) 7, 13–14, 71, 92, 428, 443
American Federation of State, County, and Municipal Employees (AFSCME) 17, 37, 44–47, 54, 92, 105, 120, 246, 252, 262, 285, 405, 435, 439, 443;

congressional elections 166; public opinion of unions 168–169
American Federation of Teachers (AFT) 16, 48–51, 55, 65, 252, 264, 435, 443
American Legislative Exchange Council (ALEC) 37, 106–107, 436, 438
American Medical Association 55
American Nurses Association 55
American Postal Workers Union (APWU) 35, 399
American Rescue Plan (2021) 432
Americans for Prosperity (AFP) 436
Americans with Disabilities Act (ADA) **80**, 252, 279, 280
American unionism: business unionism 5–10; description 2–4; ideological battles in 4–5
American workers to join unions 23–26
Anzia, S. F. 82, 116, 438
APWU *see* American Postal Workers Union
arbitration 350–351, 419–420; advantages and disadvantages 355–361; awards 410; collective bargaining and 359–361; criticisms 361; decision-making criteria 352–355; favorable to unions 358–359; final offer 351, 361–364, 370–371; illegal delegation of authority 356–358; process 351–355; roles of 372
arbitration, grievance 400–411
Arbitration Information Tracking system 403
arbitrator: decisions, court review of 401–402; selection of 351–352, 403–404; standards for decision making 408–411
arb-med procedure 365
armed forces, organization of 34
Artz, B. 253
Atkins v. City of Charlotte (1969) 65
attitudinal factors related to strike 312–313
Avgar, A. C. 360, 407
Baderschneider, J. 360
Baker v. Carr [1962] 22
bargaining: agenda 154; agreement (*see* collective bargaining agreement); certification of representative 126–127; collective (*see* collective bargaining); contrasting approaches **180**; federal government, responsibility in 135; hard approach to 172, 179, **180**; history 121; homilies **160**; informal 85; laws 81, 84; local government, responsibility in 137–140; management authority 134; multilateral 133; outcome 334; power 2, 313–314; rights 437, 450; scope of 97, 257; soft approach to 173, 179, **180**; specification and centralization of management bargaining authority 134; standards in good faith **157**; state government, responsibility in 135–137; status **39–40**; traditional 172–175; zone 180
bargaining unit determination 96; agency operations efficiency 121; fragmentation 121–122; majority support 124–126; steps 119–120, *120*; supervisors and confidential employees 122–124
Barrentine v. Arkansas Best Freight Systems (1981) 402
The Battle of Blair Mountain (Shogan) 295
Bay Area Rapid Transit strike of 1997 314
Bayh, E. 91
BCG campaigns 452
Beil, M. 174–175
Bellman, H. S. 361
Belman, D. 208–209
Bender, K. A. 211
Berry, W. D. 42
Biasi, B. 216
Biden, J. 74–76, 245, 257, 428, 445
bifocal model of mediation 342

binding arbitration 335–336, 345, 350–351
Blaylock, K. 33
Bloom, D. E. 353
Bloomberg, M. 174
blue-skying 158
blurred management responsibility 117
bona fide supervisors 123
Bornstein, T. 327
Boston Police Strike of 1919 17, 296–297, 307
Boulwarism 173
boundaries of bargaining units 122
Bowen, Charles V. 399
Bowen v. U.S. Postal Service (1983) 127, 399
Brotherhood of Railway Clerks v. Allen (1963) 100
Brunelli, S. A. 208
Brunner, E. J. 215, 217–218
Bryant-Anderson, R. 131
Budd, J. W. 368
budget: authority 132; crisis in state government 143–145; outcomes 195–197; process 193–195
bumping rights 271
Bureau of Labor Statistics 208, 227, 299–300, 311
Burton, J. F. 260, 305, 313, 373
Bush, George W. 72–73, 228, 244, 248, 256–257, 427, 445
business: cycle 311–312; unionism 5–10

California State Employees Association 45, 104
California Supreme Court 182, 309
California Teachers Association 48, 104
Capozzola, J. M. 128, 246, 305
cardholders 130
Carofano v. City of Bridgeport (1985) 357
Carter, J. 71
Cartter, A. M. 313–314
Centers for Disease Control and Prevention (CDC) 278
Central Intelligence Agency (CIA) 68
certification of bargaining representative 126–127
chain of custody 418–419
Chamberlain, N. W. 181
Change to Win (CTW) 14, 46, 428
Chicago, faulty negotiations in 315–316
Chicago Teachers Union (CTU) 139, 315
Chicago Teachers Union v. Hudson (1986) 101
chief negotiator 138–139
Child, J. 130
chilling effect 360
Choi, Y. 389, 391
Christie, C. 136
Chung, I. H. 389, 391
CIA *see* Central Intelligence Agency
Citizens United v. FEC decision 165
Civil Rights Act of 1964 **80**, 252, 402
Civil Rights Act of 1991 **80**
civil service grievance procedures 391–392
Civil Service Reform Act (CSRA) 32, 63, 135, 257, 265, 336, 399; drop in bargaining units 122; established three-tiered system 247; exceptions from 72–75; federal grievance procedures 412; FLRA 77; labor relations in federal employment 71–72; legislation pertaining to strikes 307
civil service systems 22, 241, 242–243
civil society, implications for 444
Clark, P. F. 388, 451
Cleveland Board of Education v. Loudermill (1985) 65
Club Valients 252
Coggburn, J. D. 390, 415–416
collective bargaining 63, 67, 104, 182, 334, 449; accommodating 246–249; arbitration, chilling effect of 359–361; certification of representative 126–127; contract negotiations (*see* contract negotiations); environment 114–116; excessive politicization issues

367; lack of policies 85–90; laws and contracts 278; parties 116–118; policy *86*; in private sector 152; process 118; public sector (*see* Public sector collective bargaining); representation election 124–126; states prohibiting 85–90; states with comprehensive 93–103; system 229–231; wage and benefit allotment 193–194
collective bargaining agreement 382; administration of 388–390; contents of 383–387; dissemination 387–388
Collective Bargaining and Member Advocacy (CBMA) 49
Colvin, A. J. S. 368, 407
common law of disciplinary arbitration 410
Commonwealth v. Hunt (1842) 2
Commonwealth Foundation 438
Communications Workers of America v. Beck (1998) 100
Communication Workers of America (CWA) 428
communist unions 5
community-of-interest principle 120, 122
comparable worth 203–204
comparative data 353
compensation decision process, politics and decision rules in 200–206
compulsory binding arbitration 345, 350–351
compulsory tripartite arbitration 351
concession bargaining 159–163
conditions of employment 71
confidential employees 122–124
conflict: avoiding 173; labor–management 366, 412, 414; management 133; unresolved prior 179
Congress of Industrial Organizations (CIO) 6–7
Connecticut State Police Union 162
constitutional rights 64, 65
contingency planning for strike 319–320
contingent provisions 383
contract: administration 388–390; ratification of 181–182; workers 440–441
contract negotiations 127–128, 382; bargaining management authority 135–136; conflict management 133; diffused management authority 132–133; federal government, bargaining responsibility in 135; local government, bargaining responsibility in 137–140; management, tips and tricks for **161**; multilateral bargaining 133; public participation in 140–142; sanitation workers 183–186; state government, bargaining responsibility in 135–137; union 128–132
contract provisions: interpretation of 386; types 383–384, **384**
conventional arbitration 351, 353, 361–362, 413
conventional collective bargaining 139
Coolidge, C. 17, 297
copy-and-paste lawmaking 436
Cornell Labor Action Tracker 299
Coronavirus Aid, Relief, and Economic Security (CARES) Act (2020) 272, 432
cost of living 198, 203
cost-of-living adjustments (COLAs) 210, 432
Coulson, R. 405
council member 139
County of Washington v. Gunther (1981) 204
County Sanitation District 2 v. Los Angeles County Employees Association, Local 660 (1985) 309
COVID-19 pandemic 14, 21, 42, 211, 258–259, 272, 328, 441; Chicago Teachers Union and 139; job losses 432; public education's response to 165; public sector employment 432–433; staffing shortage due to 48, 268; technology adoption during 440;

on working conditions and collective bargaining 4, 56; workplace protections with advent of 298
cowboy mentality 131
Cox, W. 208
craft unions 2
criminal conspiracy doctrine 1, 2, 4
CSRA *see* Civil Service Reform Act
Culver, J. 182
Cuomo, A. 136
cyberunions 155

Dade County Classroom Teachers Association v. Ryan (1968) 93
Dahl, R. 181
Daniels, M. 91
Daugherty, D. 394
Davenport v. Washington Education Association (2007) 100
Davis, R. S. 157
Dayton, M. 136
Dearborn Firefighters Local 412 v. City of Dearborn (1975) 357
decision-making authority 132, 411
Defense Health Agency (DHA) 33
defined benefit plans 210
defined contribution plans 210
DeJoy, L. 35
demographic factors, strikes 312–313
Department of Defense (DoD) HRM system 73
Department of Homeland Security (DHS) 73
Department of Social Services (DSS) 393
Department of Transportation (DOT) 268, 393
DeSantis, R. 93
Dickerson, N. T. 131
diffused management authority 132–133
digital nomads 440
Dilts, D. A. 410
direct democracy 366
directive strategy of mediator 342
direct public access to collective bargaining 140
disagreement costs 313–314
disciplinary action 385
dispute resolution procedures: alternative 368; contract provisions 383, 386; mutually agreed-upon 369; state legislation on **338–339**; third-party 334, 358, 371–373
distributive bargaining *see* traditional bargaining
doctrine of privilege 65
DoD *see* Department of Defense
Doerner, W. G. 217
Doerner, W. M. 217
Donahoe, Patrick R. 35
Drotning, J. E. 354, 360, 371
drug testing 280–281
Dunlop, J. 365

EAP *see* employee assistance program
Eberts, R. W. 274
econometric models 38
economic expansion 312
economic models 38
EEO *see* equal employment opportunity
EFCA *see* Employee Free Choice Act
Elazar, D. J. 42
election, representation 124–126
electoral activities, collective bargaining 165–168
Ellis v. Railway Clerks (1984) 100, 101
Emanuel, R. 139, 175, 315
Emanuel, W. 430–431
empirical research on private sector unions 273–274
employee assistance program (EAP) 280, 286
employee compensation: cross-sectional research designs 213; effect of union 212–214; measurement error and unexplained variance 212; neglect of benefits 213; operationalization of

union 212; political factors 199–200; threat effects 213; unit of analysis 212–213; values and political ideology of researchers 214
Employee Free Choice Act (EFCA) 67, 427–428
employee organizations, membership of state and local 44–56
Employee Retirement Income Security Act (1974) **80**
employees: assistance plans 281; confidential 122–124; desires of 120; disciplinary actions 269–270; dismissals and layoffs 270–271; government 18–19; involvement programs 443; nonprofit organization 442; rights 95; role in budgetary process 193; union (*see* unions); wages and benefits 198
employment: federal (*see* federal employment); government (*see* government employment)
environment of collective bargaining: financial setting and incentives 114; nature of work 115; role of politics 115–116
equal employment opportunity (EEO) 252, 402
Equal Employment Opportunity Act of 1964 252
Equal Employment Opportunity Act of 1972 **80**
Equal Employment Opportunity Commission (EEOC) 392
exclusive recognition 127
Executive Order 10988 16, 22, 34, 68–69, 336, 411
Executive Order 11491 69–70, 306, 336, 412
Executive Order 11616 of 1971 70
Executive Order 11838 70
Executive Order 12871 257
Executive Order 13991 257
expedited grievance arbitration 413–414
FAA *see* Federal Aviation Administration
fact-finding impasse resolution 335; advantages and disadvantages 348–350; process 346–348
factions 64
faculty governance 124
Fain, S. 430
Fair Labor Standards Act **80**
Fair Share 32, 98
Family and Medical Leave Act (1993) **80**
Farber, H. S. 371
fast-policy project 435
faulty negotiations 314–316
FBI *see* Federal Bureau of Investigation
featherbedding 272, 439
federal arbitration award 412
Federal Aviation Administration (FAA) 230, 268, 324
federal budget 431
Federal Bureau of Investigation (FBI) 68
Federal Employees Pay Comparability Act (FEPCA) 228
federal employee unions 32–33, 225–226; classified civil service 228–229; collective bargaining system 229–231; wage system 226–228
federal employment 67–68; Civil Service Reform Act 71–72; executive orders 68–70; Federal Labor Relations Authority 75–77; grievance procedures in 411–413; impasse resolution in 336–337; partnering 445
federal government: bargaining responsibility in 135; public employee unions 31–36; supervisors in 123
federal grievance procedures 412
federal labor–management contracts 412
Federal Labor Relations Authority (FLRA) 71, 248, 325, 336, 383, 392, 412; labor relations in federal employment 75–77; unit determination 119
Federal Labor Relations Council (FLRC) 70

federal labor relations policy 32
federal laws 78–81, 412
federal management 276
Federal Mediation and Conciliation Service (FMCS) 70, 335–337, 403; mediators 340; services offered 339; task force of 344
Federal Pay Agent 208
Federal Pay Comparability Act 226
federal sector grievance procedures 392
Federal Service Impasses Panel (FSIP) 70, 336, 337
federal wage system (FWS) 226–228
Feldman, S. 50
Felt-Dobbs Detective Agency 295
FEPCA *see* Federal Employees Pay Comparability Act
Feuille, P. 363, 416
The Fight for $15 campaign 427
final-average-salary defined benefit pensions (FASDB) 215
final offer arbitration 261–264, 351, 370–371
financial setting of collective bargaining 114
fiscal capacity 199
fiscal challenges, public employee unions 431–439
Fisher, R. 172, 173
Fitzpatrick, M. D. 210
fixed provisions 383
FLRA *see* Federal Labor Relations Authority
FLRC *see* Federal Labor Relations Council
FMCS *see* Federal Mediation and Conciliation Service
Fog Index 386
FOP *see* Fraternal Order of Police
14 Penn Plaza LLC v. Pyett (2009) 403
fragmentation of bargaining units 121–122
Frandsen, B. R. 215, 217, 219
Fraternal Order of Police (FOP) 44, 54, 92
Freeman, R. B. 273
free riders 32, 98
Friedrichs v. California Teachers Association (2016) 37, 102, 436
frustrated unions 162, 168
FSIP *see* Federal Service Impasses Panel
functionally specific organizations: education 48–51; health care 55–56; higher education 51–54
FWS *see* Federal wage system

Gaebler, T. 255
Gainsharing *see* productivity bargaining
garbage collection, human resource management policy in 272
Garcetti v. Ceballos (2006) 66
Garcia v. San Antonio Metropolitan Transit Authority (1985) 80
Garden Junction case 373–374
general-purpose unions 46–48
General Schedule (GS) wage system 71, 228–229
general strike 298
Gerardi, Robert J. 320
Gerhart, P. F. 354, 371
Ginsburg, S. G. 245
Giuliani, R. 174
Givhan v. Western Line Consolidated School District (1979) 66
Goda, G. S. 210
Goldberg, S. B. 415
Gompers, S. 5, 6
good faith bargaining 156, **157**
Gough, M. D. 407
Gould, J. C. 6, 275
Gould, W. B. 407
Governmental Accountability Office, U.S. 208
Governmental Accounting Standards Board 210
government employment: growth of 19–21; nature of 18–19
government fiscal constraints 284

government substitution 11
Great Depression 6
Great Recession 4, 20, 41, 90, 114, 139, 209, 430; concession bargaining 159; economic crisis 431; public sector employment during 433; sea change in public sector 435
grievance arbitration 400–401; arbitrability 401; arbitrator decision making, standards for 408–411; barriers to entry 407; in cases involving police misconduct 407–408; court review of arbitrators' decisions 401–402; demographic diversity, lack of 407; grievant's gender 411; hearings 411; monetary costs and delays in 404–406; problems in 404–408; repercussions for parties in arbitration 406; selection 403–404
grievance handling 398, 399, 413–417
grievance mediation 415–417
grievance procedures 269, 389–392; causes of 392–394; in federal employment 411–413; negotiated *vs.* civil service 391–392; process 394–397; representation of grievant 397–400; steward 397–398
GS wage system *see* General Schedule (GS) wage system

Han, E. S. 275
hard bargaining 172, 179, **180**
Harpoon, The 15–16
Harris v. Quinn (2014) 37, 102, 436
Hatch Act 171
Hawaii Public Employee Relations Act of 1970 93
health-care 210, 220, 442; benefits of sanitation workers 184–185; functionally specific organizations 55–56
Helsby, R. D. 137
Henry, M. K. 48
Heywood, J. S. 208–209, 211
Hibbard, P. F. 417
Hicks, J. R. 314
higher education, functionally specific organizations 51–54
high–low arbitration 363
Hill, J. 4
Hines v. Anchor Motor Freight (1976) 398
Hirschman, A. 23
Hobbes, T. 302
Hodges, A. C. 451
Hoffa, J. 89
Horton, R. D. 259
HR 980: Public Safety Employer–Employee Cooperation Act of 2007 79
HRM policies *see* human resource management (HRM) policies
Hudson notice 101
human capital challenge, public employee unions 434
human resource management (HRM) policies: health and wellness 277–281; miscellaneous terms and conditions 282–283; privatization 275–277; productivity 273–275; technological change 272–273; workers' compensation 281–282
human rights 451, 452
Hutcheson, William L. 7

IAFF *see* International Association of Firefighters
IBB *see* interest-based bargaining
IBT *see* International Brotherhood of Teamsters
idea charting 342
Illinois State Employees Association 45
ILO *see* International Labor Organization
ILWU *see* International Longshore and Warehouse Union
immature management 382
impasse resolution procedures 97; arbitration (*see* arbitration); arb-med

365; benefits 371–373; fact-finding (*see* fact-finding impasse resolution); in federal employment 336–337; labor–management committee 365–366; letting taxpayers decision 366–367; med-arb 364–365; mediation (*see* mediation); search for flexibility 368–370; state and local government 337, 339–340; ULP 367–368; uncertainty 370–371
inability to pay 205
incentives 114
independent judgment 124
Indianapolis Education Association v. Lewallen (1969) 66
indirect public access to collective bargaining 140
Industrial Workers of the World (IWW) 4
informal bargaining 85
informal communication 388
instant arbitration *see* expedited grievance arbitration
integrative bargaining *see* interest-based bargaining
intentional violations 393
interest arbitration 335, 356, 357, 361
interest-based bargaining (IBB): comparison of traditional and 175; contrasting bargaining approaches **180**; intraorganizational conflict 178; potential 182; prevalence of integrative strategy 180; principles 175
Intergovernmental Personnel Act 243
internal bargaining processes 171–181; IBB (*see* interest-based bargaining); traditional negotiations 172–175
Internal Revenue Service (1938) 34
International Association of Firefighters (IAFF) 17, 45, 120
International Association of Machinists v. Street (1961) 100
International Association of Machinists and Aerospace Workers 34
International Brotherhood of Police Officers 54
International Brotherhood of Teamsters (IBT) 44, 48
international competition 426
International Convention 47
International Labor Organization (ILO) 89
International Longshore and Warehouse Union (ILWU) 5
International Union of Police Associations (IUPA) 54
internecine union warfare 46
interorganizational politics 388
intraorganizational conflict 178
iron law of oligarchy 129–130
Iseki, H. 88
issue-by-issue arbitration 362, 363
IUPA *see* International Union of Police Associations
IWW *see* Industrial Workers of the World

Jackson, A. 15
Janus v. AFSCME (2018) 99, 102, 436
Janus v. American Federation of State, County, and Municipal Employees Council 31, et al. (2018) 37, 98, 249, 436, 450
Jewell, M. E. 450
Johnson, L. 69
Johnston, P. 318, 441
Joint Workforce Investment (JWI) 445
Ju, A. 215, 217–218
justice for janitors movement 25, 441

Kalleberg, A. L. 225
Karahalios v. NFFE (1989) 399
Keefe, J. 209
Kellough, J. E., 253
Kennedy, John F. 22, 68
Keyeshian v. Board of Regents (1967) 65
Keyshaun King case 419–420
Knies, E. 225
Knights of Labor 6, 15
knowledge of effective mediator 343

Knox v. SEIU Local 1000 101
Kochan, T. A. 133–134, 349, 352, 360
Krider, C. E. 305, 313
Krueger, A. B. 208
Kuhn, J. W. 181
Kurth, M. M. 275

labor: agreements 383; dispute 285–286; and management 446; organizations 2, 3, 5, 361; roles 186; unions, approval level of *169*, 170, *170*
Laborers' International Union of North America (LIUNA) Local 777 264
labor–management committees (LMCs) 365–366, 443–446, 448
labor–management conflict 366, 412, 414
labor–management cooperation: advantages of 443–446; conditions necessary for successful 446–448; future of 448–449
labor-management partnerships (LMPs) 443, 445, 448
labor–management relations: administrative agency 95–96; bargaining scope and impasse resolution procedures 97; employee rights and employer rights 95; initiative and referendum 103–104; in nonprofit organizations 104–105; quality of 398; recognition procedures 96–97; unfair labor practices 102–103; union security 97–102; unit determination 96
Labor–Management Relations Act (LMRA) 383, 399
Labor Management Relations Act of 1947 *see* Taft–Hartley Act
Labor Management Reporting and Disclosure Act of 1959 *see* Landrum–Griffin Act
Landrum–Griffin Act 66, 70
Lane v. Franks (2014) 66
last best offer (LBO) provision 347, 351
late-night bargaining 179
layoff provisions 384
legal environment: changes in 22; public employee compensation 199–200; unfavorable 11–12
legislative committee 181
legislative contract ratification 182
legislative plagiarism 106
Lehnert v. Ferris Faculty Association (1991) 101
Leisink, P. 225
Lester, R. A. 364
Letter Carriers v. Blount (1969) 65
Lewin, D. 406
Lewis, H. G. 211
Lewis, John L. 7
Lewis, K. 175
Lightfoot, L. 139
Lipsky, D. B. 360
Littler Mendelson 429–430
Livernash, R. 393
living wage 442
Lloyd–LaFollette Act (1912) 16, 68–69
LMCs *see* labor–management committees
lobbying 164–165
Local 189, United Papermakers and Crown-Zellerback Corp. v. United States (1969) 254
local government: bargaining responsibility in 137–140; comprehensive model of unionization 38, *41*; employee organizations in (*see* employee organizations); federal legislation for 78–81; legal basis of labor relations in 77–78; policies 81–85; unionization 37–44
lockout, strike 298
loser-pays arbitration 404
Lowell Female Labor Reform Association (LFLRA) 3
Luce, S. 163

Maasarani, M.A. 393
MacKay Doctrine 12, 300
macro-level factors of strike 311–312
Madison, James 64
Malin, M. H. 356
Malloy, D. 136, 161–162
Maloney, T. N. 275
management: authority 116, 117; conflict 133; immature 382; opposition 12; structure 260–261
management rights 248, 386; federal employment 257–259, **258**; scope of bargaining 257; state and local governments 259–260
mandatory interest arbitration, effects of 360
market constraints, lack of 303–304
Massachusetts Joint Committee 365
Massachusetts State Employees Association 45
mayors, in bargaining process 138, 139
McAuliffe v. City of New Bedford (1892) 63–64
McCormick, G. 431
McCormick, M. 372
McElroy, Edward J. 50
McEntee, G. 47, 204
McGee, J. B. 215
McKelvey, J. T. 346
McKersie, R. B. 172
McLaughlin v. Tilendis (1967) 65
Meany, G. 7
med-arb procedure 364–365
mediation 335, 337; advantages and disadvantages 344–345; bifocal model 342; state and local government impasse procedures 340; strategies to 341; traits of effective mediator 343–344
Medoff, J. L. 273
meet-and-confer policies 91
Memphis Firefighters Local Union No. 1784 v. Stotts (1984) 254
Memphis formula 88
mere negligence 399
merit pay 201, 231–232
merit principle: affirmative action and diversity 251–255; NPM 255–257; seniority 250–251; union security 249–250
merit systems 242; collective bargaining and 246–249; interface *vs.* bargaining 246; Intergovernmental Personnel Act 243; merit principle (*see* merit principle)
Merit Systems Protection Board (MSPB) 73, 208, 243, 392
Michels, R. 129
micro-level factors of strike 312–314; bargaining power and disagreement costs 313–314; demographic and attitudinal factors 312–313; faulty negotiations 314–316
Milkman, R. 163
Miller, M. L. 208
Miranda v. Arizona (1966) 23
misunderstanding 392
Mladenka, K. R. 253
Moe, T. M. 82, 116, 438
Molly Maguires 4
monopsony 199
Moore, J. S. 410
Morehouse, S. M. 450
MSPB *see* Merit Systems Protection Board
Muchinsky, P. M. 393
multidimensional bargaining 113
multilateral bargaining 133
Murphy, P. 136

Napolitano, J. 86
NAPO *see* National Association of Police Organizations
narcotic effect 359–3560
NATCA *see* National Air Traffic Controllers Association

National Academy of Arbitrators (NAA) 403, 406
National Air Traffic Controllers Association (NATCA) 34, 230, 268, 326
National Association for the Advancement of Colored People (NAACP) 441
National Association of Government Employees 16, 45
National Association of Letter Carriers 15, 35, 166
National Association of Police Organizations (NAPO) 54
National Center on Educational Statistics 48
National Defense Authorization Act 73
National Education Association (NEA) 16, 48–51, 90, 94, 206, 252, 264, 435, 443
National Federation of Federal Employees (NFFE) 16, 33, 34, 71
National Labor Relations Act (NLRA) 11, 52, 55, 66–68, 94, 295, 444; bargaining agent for local government under 88; collective bargaining agreements under 87; deny bargaining rights 123; duty to bargain defined by 156; FMCS under 335; labor rights granted to private sector workers in 16; model 229; nonprofit organizations 104–105; principles 94, 96; private sector legal environment under 44; public policy under 427; recognition procedures 96; scope of bargaining 97
National Labor Relations Board (NLRB) 11, 56, 66, 67, 78, 119, 123, 383, 427–428, 444
National Labor Relations Board v. Mackay Radio and Telegraph (1938) 300
National Labor Relations Board v. Yeshiva University (1980) 124
National Nurses United 37
National Performance Council 447
National Performance Review (NPR) 255
National Postal Mail Handlers Union 35
National Productivity Council (NPC) 255
National Rural Letter Carriers Association 35
National Security Personnel System (NSPS) 73
National Teachers Association (NTA) 16
National Trades Union 2
National Treasury Employees Union (NTEU) 33, 34, 71
National Wage Policy Committee 227
NEA *see* National Education Association
negotiated grievance procedure 390–391
Nelson, F. H. 275
New Public Management (NPM) 255–257, 437, 440
New York Letter Carriers 15
NFFE *see* National Federation of Federal Employees
night baseball arbitration 363
Nixon, R. 69–70, 306, 336, 412
NLRA *see* National Labor Relations Act
NLRB *see* National Labor Relations Board
NLRB v. Yeshiva (1980) 52
nonarbitrability, claims of 401
noncomprehensive policies, states with 90–93
noncontract-related grievances 390
nondirective strategy of mediator 341, 342
nonprofit organizations 36–37, 104–105, 442
Nonprofit Professional Employees Union (NPEU-IFPTE) 37
nonunion replacement workers, hiring 300
Norris-LaGuardia Act (1932) 321
NPM *see* New Public Management
NPR *see* National Performance Review
NSPS *see* National Security Personnel System
NTA *see* National Teachers Association
NTEU *see* National Treasury Employees Union
NTEU v. Michael Chertoff (2005) 73
NTEU v. Van Raab (1989) 280

Obama, B. 74, 79, 256, 427, 445
O'Brien, Sean M. 48
Occupational Safety and Health Act (OSHA) **80**, 278
Office and Professional Employees Association 105
Office and Professional Employees International Union (OPEIU) 37
Office of Collective Bargaining (OCB) 140
Office of Labor–management relations 71
Office of Personnel Management (OPM) 71, 227, 243, 257, 265, 440, 445–446
Office of Special Counsel 392
offshoring 426
Ogletree Deakins 430–431
Oklahoma Firefighters' and Policemen's Arbitration Act 354–355
ombuds 417
open communication 389
open conflicts 133–134
OPM *see* Office of Personnel Management
opportunity wage 198–199
organized labor 13, 427
Osborne, D. 255
OSHA *see* Occupational Safety and Health Act
outsourcing on public employee unions, negative effects of 434

PACs *see* political action committees
participative decision making (PDM) 443–449; *see also* labor–management cooperation
partnering, federal employment 445
past practice 409
PATCO *see* Professional Air Traffic Controllers Organization
paycheck protection 104
pay inequity 439
PDM *see* participative decision making
Peach, D. 393
Peck, J. 435
peer review 417
penalties, strike 322–323
Pendleton Act of 1883 67, 171, 242
PEOPLE *see* Public Employees Organized to Promote Legislative Equality
PERB *see* Public Employment Relations Board
Perloff, J. M. 208
permanent replacements 300
permissive strike states (2023) **308–309**
personnel functions: dismissals and layoffs 270–271; grievances and employee discipline 269; human resource management policies (*see* human resource management (HRM) policies); nonmonetary subjects in contracts **262**; position classification and staffing 265–266; promotions 263; recruitment, testing, and selection 261–263; reductions in force 271–272; training and development 263–264; workload and scheduling 266–269
Peterson, R. 406
petition 120
Pham, L. D. 216
Pickering v. Board of Education (1968) 65
point factor analysis 204–205
police: arbitration 270, 408; discipline 407–408; misconduct 407–408; strikes 296–297
Police Officers' and Firefighters' Employment Relations Act 368
Police officers *see* Boston Police Strike of 1919; Fraternal Order of Police
policy environment, unfavorable 11–12
Poli, R. 324
political action committees (PACs) 165–166
political activity, public employee 170–171
political culture, unionization 42, 87
political factors, impact on government compensation 199–200
political ideology **39–40**

political laboratory, of labor relations policies 105
political process, distortion of 303
politics role in unions 115–116
positive employee relations 12
positive human resource management 43
Postal Accountability and Enhancement Act (2006) 307
postal employees 35
Postal Employee Unions **35**
Postal Reform Act of 2022 35
Postal Reorganization Act of 1970 77, 230, 306, 337, 350
Postal Service negotiations 337
postal strike of 1970 306–307
postal workers 14
Powderly, Terence V. 6
power authority 132
prevailing rate 201–202, 227, 230
principled bargaining 179
prior bargaining record of parties 409–410
private sector: organizations 115–116; public and 113–118, 207–211
private sector unions: decline of 10–15, 426–431; membership in **8–10**; right to strike for 335–336; spillover of 21–22
privatization 275–277, 434
The Pro Act *see* Right to Organize Act
problem-solving arbitrators 408
procedural arbitrability, determination of 401
process knowledge 343
productivity bargaining (gainsharing) 223–225
Professional Air Traffic Controllers Organization (PATCO) 34; strike 324–326
Protecting the Right to Organize Act 429
protective services, functionally specific organizations 54
psychological contract 131
public education 48–51
public employee labor relations policy 38
public employee political activity, restrictions on 170–171
Public Employee Relations Act of 1974 93
public employee relations board 94, 95, 96, 118, 140, 349
Public Employees Organized to Promote Legislative Equality (PEOPLE) 47
public employees strike 311–315; macro-level factors 311–312; micro-level factors (*see* Micro-level factors of strike)
public employee unions 367, 373; in 2020s 449–453; benefits 218–220; challenges 431–439, 450–451; decline 426–431; description 426; effect on wages and benefits 220–221; federal government 31–36; labor–management cooperation and participative decision making 443–449; methodological problems 214–221; opportunities 439–443; rise of 19–23; salary and wages 214–218; women's approval of 451–452; *see also* federal employee unions
Public Employment Relations Board (PERB) 339, 340, 346, 368, 374
Public Employment Relations Commission (PERC) 347
public employment, right to strike in 302; essential services 304–306; market constraints, lack of 303–304; political process, distortion of 303; postal strike of 1970 306–307; sovereignty argument 302–303
public opinion, collective bargaining 168–170
public participation in contract negotiations 140–142
public policy: challenges, public employee unions 435–437; labor organizations 2; of strikes 310–311
public referendum 103, 366

Public Safety Employer–Employee Cooperation Act (2007) 79
public sector: grievance arbitration 402; impasse resolution, measures in 336; strike activity 299–302; unionism, legal environment for 19
public sector collective bargaining: concession 159–163; duty of parties to 156; electoral activities 165–168; external politics 163–171; identifying proposals 152–154; internal bargaining processes (*see* internal bargaining processes); lobbying 164–165; preparation for 154–156; private sector and 113–118, 152; public employee political activity, restrictions on 170–171; public opinion 168–170; script 156–159
public sector workers: compensation, responding to increase 221–223; financial impacts of 191–192; pay gap with private sector workers 207–211

Quill, M. 129, 158

Railway Employee Department, IAM v. Hanson (1956) 100
Railway Labor Act (RLA) 66, 68
rank-and-file union members 130
ratification of contract 181–182
Reagan, R. 12, 34, 228, 325, 446
recognition procedures 96–97
#RedforEd uprisings 452
referendum: initiative and 103–104; resolving bargaining impasses through 366
Rehabilitation Act of 1973 279–280
representation election 124–126
research assistants (RAs) 53
Resolve Employment Disputes Reach Equitable Solutions Swiftly (REDRESS) program 416–417
Rewards for Wellness program 281
Reynolds v. Simms [1964] 22
Rhoades, G. 53
Rights arbitration *see* grievance arbitration
right-to-work laws 38, 99, *99*
RLA *see* Railway Labor Act
Roby, P.A. 131
Rooks, D. 131
Roosevelt, Theodore 15
Rubinstein, S. 284, 366
rules of contract construction 408–409
rumors 174
Rushin, S. 270, 407–408

salary 214–218
Salary Reform Act 226
sanitation unions 274
Saunders, L. 47
Savas, E. S. 245
Schedule F policy 244–245
scheduling, personnel 266–269
Schneider, B.V. H. 81
School District for the City of Holland et al. v. Holland Education Association (1968) 321
Schultz, George P. 70
Scott, C. 386–387
script in bargaining 156–159
secret ballot 125
Service Employees International Union (SEIU) 13, 37, 44–48, 54, 55, 89, 105, 162, 252, 443, 435, 439
sexual harassment grievances 410
Shanker, A. 49–50
Shogan, R. 295
Shostak, A. B. 155
Shuler, L. 14
sick leave 185
significant wage premium 208
Simkin, W. E. 341
Skinner v. Railway Labor Executives' Association (1989) 280
Sloane, A. A. 6–7

Smith v. Arkansas State Highway Commission Employees Local 1315 (1979) 66
Snyder, R. 136
social change, era of 23
social equity 169, 427, 451, 452
social movement unionism 441
Social Security Act **80**
Social Service Employees Union 282
socioeconomic factors, influence government wage and benefit 197–199
soft bargaining 173, 179, **180**
Sojourner, A. J. 167
Southern Poverty Law Center (SLPC) 442
sovereign government 64
sovereignty argument 302–303
specification and centralization of management bargaining authority 134
Spero, S. D. 3, 128, 246, 305
Spitzer, E. 105
Stanley, D. T. 259, 272
Starbucks 15, 42, 428–429
state bargaining status **82–84**
state boards of labor relations (SBLR) 368
State Employee Relations Board 349
State Employees Association of North Carolina (SEANC) 45, 89
state government: bargaining responsibility in 135–137; budget crisis in 143–145; comprehensive model of unionization 38, *41*; employee organizations in (*see* employee organizations); federal legislation for 78–81; legal basis of labor relations in 77–78; policies 81–85; unionization 37–44
state legislation 81
State Policy Network (SPN) 436, 438
state political system 43
statutory agency criteria for unit determination 120
Staudohar, P. D. 93
Steel, P. 405–406
Steelworkers trilogy 400, 402
steward 397–398
Stieber, J. 18, 115
Stone, J. A. 274
strategic challenges for public employee unions 437–439
strategic factors, private sector union decline 13–15
Strategic Organizing Center (SOC) 428
strike 295–296, 298–299, 334; attitudinal factors toward 312–313; Boston Police Strike of 1919 296–297; defined 298; legislation pertaining to 307–310; PATCO 324–326; public employee (*see* public employees strike); in public employment (*see* public employment, right to strike in); public policy and incidence of 310–311; public sector activity 299–302; SEPTA 301, 316–317; tactics of (*see* tactics of strike)
strike funds 299
Striketober 56
structural challenges for public employee unions 433–435
structural elements, of private sector union decline 10–11
Subbarao, A. V. 362
subordinates' bargaining units 123
substantive arbitrability 401
substantive knowledge 343
Suchan, J. 386–387
sunbelt states, unionization in 42–43
sunshine bargaining 141
supervisors, exclusion of 122–124
Sutherlin Education Association v. Sutherlin School District No. 130 (1976) 282
Sweeney, John J. 13–14, 428
symptomatic grievances 393

tactics of strike: contingency planning 319–320; injunction 320–322; management 319; penalties 322–323; union 316–318

Taft–Hartley Act 11, 122, 298, 304; Section 2(2) 67; Section 14(b) of 99; Section 203(d) of 400
Taylor, Frederick W. 6
Tayloristic time study techniques 295
Taylor Law 323
teacher contracts, working conditions negotiated in 283
teaching assistants (TA) 53
telecommuting 441
telework 269, 441
Templeton, Katherine 431
Tener, J. B. 137
Tennessee Valley Authority (TVA) 226, 229–230
third-party dispute resolution procedures 334, 358, 371–373
Thomason, T. 275
traditional bargaining 172–175, 179, 452
Transportation Security Administration 73
Transport Workers Union (TWU) 129, 158, 301, 323
tripartite arbitration 351, 370
Troubled Asset Relief Program (TARP) 432
troublemakers 130
Trumka, Richard L. 14, 429
Trump, Donald J. 244, 427–428
turmoil, era of 23
TWA v. Independent Federation of Flight Attendants (1989) 300

UAW 429–430
ULP *see* unfair labor practice
unemployment: effect on wages 199; unionization 41
unfair labor practice (ULP) 66, 69, 70, 94, 102–103, 336, 367–368, 383
union-advocated public policies 11
union-avoidance tactics 43
union-busting 4, 43
union commitment 131
union impacts: merit systems (*see* merit systems); personnel functions (*see* personnel functions)
union instrumentality 131
unionization 297; higher education 52; museums 15, 36, 56, 301, 313, 442; state and local government 37–44
union leaders 57–58, 385, 439
union membership 56; in men and women 25, 451–452; by public and private sectors *24*
Union Relative Wage Effects: A Survey (Lewis) 211
unions 145–147; arbitration favorable to 358–359; budget making and 192–197; for college/university faculty 216–217; in contract negotiations 128–132; contracts 196; density **39–40**; duty of fair representation 398–400; effects in public and private sectors 211–212; effects on public employee compensation 214–221; electoral activities 165–168; firefighters 217–218; general-purpose 46–48; government workers 23–26; history of 15–18; lobbying 164–165; monetary impacts of 206–207; municipal employees 218; operationalization of 212; police 217, 268; postal, wages and benefits 230; public approval ratings of 169; public employee unions, rise of 19–23; right to form and join 63–67; security policies 97–102; in state and local governments 278–279; state employees 218; strength 56; survey 144; teachers 216–217, 268, 274; wages and benefits 198; *see also* private sector unions: public employee unions
unit determination 96, 118–126
United Farm Workers 428
United Mine Workers of America 295

United States Civil Service Commission v. Letter Carriers (1973) 171
United University Professions (UUP) 129
unresolved prior conflict 179
Urban Mass Transportation Act of 1964 **80**, 87, 88
Ury, W. 172, 173
U.S. Airways v. Barnett (2002) 254
U.S. Bureau of Labor Statistics 38, 208, 433
U.S. Civil Service Commission 16
U.S. Congress 307
U.S. Department of Transportation (DOT) 324
U.S. Governmental Accountability Office 208
U.S. Postal Service (USPS) 35, 399, 416

Vaca v. Sipes (1967) 127, 398
Virginia Governmental Employees Association (VGEA) 46, 86
Virginia legislature 86
Virginia v. Arlington County Board of Education (1977) 90
virtual office 440–441
Visser, J. 451, 453
Volkswagen 429–431
Voos, P. B. 410

Wachter, M. L. 208
Wade, M. M. 90
wages 185, 198–199; in federal employee unions 226–228; public employee unions on compensation 214–218; unemployment effect on 199
Wagner Act *see* National Labor Relations Act (NLRA)
Walton, R. E. 172
Wanamaker, D. K. 92
War Labor Board 400
Waters v. Wisconsin Steelworks (1974) 254
Watkins v. Steelworkers Local 2369 (1975) 254
Watson, B. 431
Webb, M. 219
Weil, D. 114
Weingarten, R. 50, 57–58, 438
Wellington, H. H. 79, 207, 303
wellness programs 281
Wells, D. D. 159
Wilson, William L. 15
win–lose outcome 174
Winter, Ralph K. 79, 207, 303
Winters, M. A. 215
win–win bargaining *see* interest-based bargaining
Witney, F. 6–7
Wobblies 4
Won't Back Down and *Waiting for Superman* (film) 438
workers' compensation 281–282
workload, personnel 266–269
work product speech 66
work stoppages 295, 298–301, 316, 321
Wurf, J. 17, 246
Wygant v. Jackson Board of Education (1986) 254

Zack, A. M. 340
Zander, Arnold 17
zero-sum bargaining 172, 174–175, 183
Zigarelli, M. A. 275
Zirkel, P. A. 392
Ziskind, D. 295
Zwerling, H. L. 275

Kolibri 360 GmbH
Ferdinand-Jühlke-Straße 7
99095 Erfurt, Deutschland
produktsicherheit@kolibri360.de